MEN BEHAVING BADLY

THE BEST OF MEN BEHAVING BADLY

Written by
Simon Nye

Edited by
Elaine Cameron

HEADLINE

First published in 2000
by **HEADLINE BOOK PUBLISHING**

10 9 8 7 6 5 4 3 2 1

Series 1 and 2 of *Men Behaving Badly* were first broadcast on ITV. The remaining programmes were broadcast on the BBC.

British Library Cataloguing in Publication Data

Nye, Simon, 1958-
Best of men behaving badly
1. Men behaving badly (Television program)
2.Television scripts
I. Title
791.4'572

ISBN 0 7472 7038 4 (hardback)
ISBN 0 7472 7039 2 (trade paperback)

Typeset by
Letterpart Limited, Reigate, Surrey

Designed by
designsection, Frome, Somerset

Printed and bound in Great Britain by
Mackays of Chatham plc, Chatham, Kent

Picture Credits:
All pictures ©**designsection** and ©**THEM** except, (p.10, p.105, p.106, p.140, p.149, p.201) ©**Syndication International**; (p.20) ©**Times Media Pte Ltd**; (p.54) ©**Images Colour Library**; (p.101) ©**Penny Gentieu/Stone**; (p.193) ©**Photex/CORBIS**; (p.308) ©**The Purcell Team/CORBIS**; (p.309) ©**Eric and David Hosking/CORBIS**; (p.333) ©**Stone Imaging**; (p.370) ©**Robert Dowling/CORBIS**

HEADLINE BOOK PUBLISHING
A division of Hodder Headline
338 Euston Road
London NW1 3BH

www.headline.co.uk
www.hodderheadline.com

Contents

Introd

Men Behaving Badly started life as a novel which I wrote in 1984 and have managed to spin out for a wonderfully long time. It has spawned a 42-episode sitcom, an American version and a coffee-table lifestyle manual, a party CD, half a dozen Comic Relief-style sketches, a lager-heavy shampoo and an advent calendar. There have been chips called, mystifyingly, Chips Behaving Badly, for which my royalties cheque went strangely missing. My only regret is that we never came up with a satisfying range of *MBB* pants.

The show was commissioned by ITV in 1991 because it has a fantastically persuasive and determined producer, Beryl Vertue, and because Harry Enfield agreed to star in it. We went on to make seven series, more or less one a year. We had our arguments, but in a business famous for 'hissy-fits' (bitching) and 'tanties' (tantrums), not to mention 'minty' behaviour (moodiness), *Men Behaving Badly* was as fun to make as, hopefully, it looks.

uction

A typical episode was produced like this. On Tuesday morning we gathered in the rehearsal room to read through the script. On American sitcoms the writers manically 'laugh up' all the jokes, as if to suggest that each gag reinvents the very idea of comedy. Over here we tend to shuffle through the episode ruefully. Some of us were usually working from the wrong draft. Neil Morrissey, though delightful and professional, often was not at his best before midday. We all drank lots of tea and, if we were feeling confident, ate a bun. Caroline Quentin's dog was usually running around somewhere. I would get depressed because nobody was laughing, or because they were laughing too much so we had clearly peaked too soon.

By the second day the jokes stopped being funny. Leslie Ash would creep under the duvet in her comedy bedroom and nod off. The producer, director or actors might suggest improvements ranging from 'Why doesn't he/she come in with his/her hat on back to front?' to 'Do I really have to say this?' I hate arguments so usually panicked and offered to cut everything that did not work, until it was pointed out that this would leave the episode thirteen minutes short.

Rehearsals went on all week until Sunday, when after a gruelling day sorting out camera shots and stumbling through a dress rehearsal ('I'm sorry, she's not really going to wear that is she?'), the audience were let in. They usually laughed, and everyone relaxed, although I would remain paranoid throughout that the warm-up man, Ted Robbins, was getting bigger laughs than the script.

Men Behaving Badly has been linked to and even blamed for Lad culture. Several MPs accused us of dumbing down Britain, to which we could only answer: Well, you started it. Flattering though it is to be considered part of the *Zeitgeist* and to have helped dismantle some of the absurdities of political correctness, I have always considered *Men* to be clearly the work of bleeding-heart liberals. The women are smarter and more intelligent than the men. The dangers of excessive alcohol (searing hangover, tendency to talk gibberish) are made plain in almost every episode. And the characters all despise violence, although they do occasionally fall over and hurt themselves. So this is the book of the scripts. For reasons of space we have had to miss out some episodes. It is probably just as well – each series throws up at least one runt, and the first two series are particularly thick with them. These scripts are the ones we took into rehearsals. As you will see, scenes were often trimmed to make the length, and we altered lots of the endings, but generally little was changed.

A chance to thank some people: the brilliant actors, without whom a script of *Men Behaving Badly* would be thirty pointless pieces of paper, script-editor Elaine Cameron, who diplomatically told me when I should try harder, Martin Dennis, who directed all the episodes, and taught me a lot about how to write a situation comedy, Beryl Vertue, who thought *Men Behaving Badly* might make a good TV show and rescued me from a career as a translator. And Claudia, whose only criticism of the show has been my fondness for jokes about nuns.

SERIES ONE

SERIES ONE: EPISODE ONE

INTRUDERS

This was the first script I wrote for TV. I tried at first to use dialogue from my novel *Men Behaving Badly*, on the grounds that only thirteen people had bought the book and it's a shame to waste anything. Needless to say, that was like trying to make an omelette out of an apple pie, and not a very good apple pie at that. (Although a novel can evolve into a good sitcom – the first Reggie Perrin novel is terrific.)

The first time an audience laughs at something you've written is an odd feeling. It really is like having sex the first time – you feel elated but surprised, as though there's been some kind of delightful mistake. I was in any case already overexcited at working with Leslie Ash, the prettiest woman in Britain, and was not able to talk to her without stuttering and dribbling.

We filmed a pilot episode, and I thought it went very well until I noticed that afterwards the actors looked like they'd just been involved in a car crash rather than a comedy show. Harry Enfield was so distressed he went through his contract with a microscope, looking for a get-out clause.

The show was in better shape by the time we recorded this script, but it's still a bit of a mess. There are only seven scenes; nowadays I usually have about twenty on the basis that if you don't keep a plate spinning, it will crash to the ground. At the time I believed that funny dialogue was all you really needed.

The ending, as always, was a bit of a bugger. Starting and finishing an episode are the hardest things about sitcom writing. The opening is tricky because there's no momentum, and the audience are in go-on-then-make-me-laugh-you-overpaid-bastard mode. The last scene is hard because you want it to be satisfying but surprising. When in doubt, end a show by having a character throw something in the air and freeze frame on it.

1. GARY'S FLAT: KITCHEN

Morning. Gary is standing up, drying dishes. Dermot is sitting down with his eyes half closed. Gary is dressed in a tacky shirt and tie; Dermot is still in his dressing gown. Dermot takes a long swallow from his mug of tea, emptying it. As he puts it down we see that he has a teabag in his mouth. He spits it out disgustedly.

GARY
Oh, yeah, I left your teabag in.

DERMOT
I thought for a minute my tongue had fallen off.

GARY
Well, you won't need it now Lisa's ditched you.

DERMOT
We were supposed to be going on holiday together. I've already bought my flip-flops.

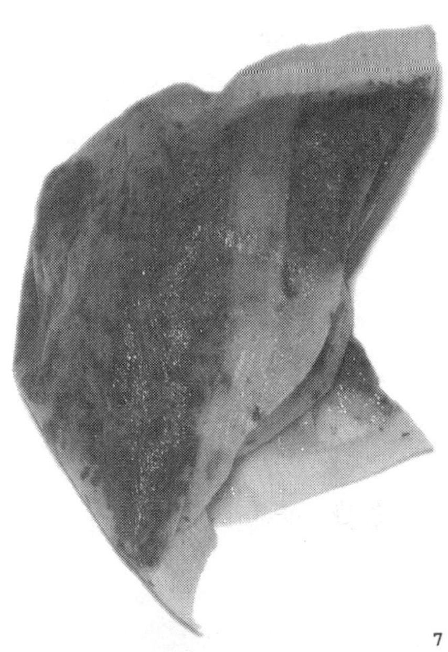

GARY
You can't afford a holiday.
Dermot picks up a manila envelope and waves it at Gary.

DERMOT
Tax rebate.

GARY
(*Looking in the envelope, holding up the cheque*) You've never stayed in a job long enough to pay tax.

DERMOT
Maybe there's, like, money back if you collect fifty P45s.
Gary grunts. Dermot takes the cheque back, smiling to himself.

DERMOT
I'll buy Lisa an expensive present. (*Lewd growling*) Something with a lot of straps.

GARY
You're forgetting something.

DERMOT
(*Holding up the cheque*) Do I owe you some of this?

GARY
No, Dermot, all of it. And if you buy so much as a newspaper with it I'll nail your head to the fridge. How'm I going to keep this mortgage up if you don't pay your rent?

DERMOT
You could sell one of your kidneys.
Dermot closes his eyes, depressed. He sighs. Gary softens.

GARY
You're really upset about that girl, aren't you?

DERMOT
(*Really upset*) Kind of.

GARY
(*With quiet concern*) Do you want to-to talk about it?

DERMOT
Yeah.

GARY
(*Sitting down*) It's bound to be sad when you split up – you remember all those little things you did together . . . (*Pausing*) What was she like in bed? Was she a squealer or a moaner?

DERMOT
Oh, leave it out, will you?

GARY
Well, if you don't want to talk about it.
Gary gets up briskly.

GARY
I'm cooking tonight. What do you fancy?

DERMOT
Anything that takes my mind off sex.

GARY
Toad in the Hole? A couple of dumplings? (*Dermot is still not reacting*) Something wobbly in an oyster sauce—

DERMOT
Bugger off, will you?

GARY
Oh, snap out of it, you've got a new job to look forward to today.

DERMOT
Great.

GARY
Selling is a challenging occupation.

DERMOT
I'm no good at it. Buying – I'm okay at that.

GARY
Look, drop in at my office at lunchtime, give me the cash you owe me, and I'll teach you how to handle the public.

DERMOT
I thought I'd just let them sort of . . . mill about.

GARY
Mill about? And then what's supposed to happen?

DERMOT
Well, then I hoped they'd . . . go home.

GARY
I can't decide, Dermot – you're either very stupid or . . . very, very stupid.

DERMOT
Is Dorothy coming round tonight?

GARY
I don't know, she just seems to turn up nowadays. I came back from work the other day and found her trying to rearrange the kitchen.

DERMOT
(*Looking around at the chaotic interior*) What's wrong with it?

GARY
(*Also baffled*) I don't know. I'm going to dump her.

DERMOT
Why?

GARY
We've been together for two years. She's . . . worn out.

DERMOT
Oh, right.

GARY
She used to be really enthusiastic in bed.

DERMOT
What, and then she met you?

GARY
(*Ignoring him*) And now, I know what she likes, she knows what I like . . . After a while you want it the way you like it but—

DERMOT
With someone else?

GARY
Exactly.

DERMOT
So how are you going to tell her?

GARY
I'll have to make it look like it's her decision.

DERMOT
Moody silence.

GARY
Yeah, give her an hour or so of moody silence.

DERMOT
Loll your head a bit . . .

GARY
Yeah – (*Counting on his fingers*) moody silence, loll my head, maybe do some sighing.

DERMOT
But not too loud, or that'll interfere with your moody silence.

GARY
Good point. (*Speeding up*) Then I'll ask for my keys back, say I need some time to get in touch with myself, and she'll say, 'That's it, our relationship's going backwards. We're finished, Gary.' I'll look shattered, call a cab before she changes her mind and stand at the window with my lip all kind of . . . quivery. Then you and me can go and get a pizza.

DERMOT
Yeah, that's the trouble – twenty years ago men could just come straight out with it. Nowadays, you've just got to handle these things sensitively.

2. GARY'S OFFICE

Lunchtime. Evidence of food having been eaten: empty Tupperware on George's desk, sandwich wrappings on Gary's. Gary is sitting at the main desk in his shirtsleeves. George is working at the other desk. Gary has started to slit open a box with a Swiss Army knife.

GEORGE
Trusty old Swiss Army knife, eh? I know someone who crossed the Sahara Desert with one.

GARY
What did he get?

GEORGE
Eh?

GARY
Sorry, I thought it was a joke.

GEORGE
He said the stubby blade was useful for scraping the flies off his teeth.

GARY
Oh, please.
Gary lifts a yellow object out of the box. They look at it speculatively.

GARY
(*Grandly*) George, you've heard of the wheel clamp?

GEORGE
Yes.

GARY
You're already familiar with the door knob?

GEORGE
Yes.

GARY
(*Triumphantly holding it*) This is a—

GEORGE
Knob wheel?

GARY
Door clamp.
They stare at it for a good moment.

GARY
What a crap idea. Who sent it?
There is a knock on the office door, and Anthea puts her head round it. She is a smiling, pathologically nervous woman in her fifties.

GARY
Come on in, Anthea, I won't hurt you. Probably.
She edges into the room, carrying some papers. She approaches Gary.

ANTHEA
Hello, er, I couldn't understand some of your last tape – letter to Burridge Security Products. (*She points to a passage she has typed*) So, I've tentatively typed in 'disappointing standard of design'.

GARY
(*Studying her typing, then looking at her sternly*) I've warned you about this before, Anthea. Go away and put back what I actually said.
Anthea winces, looking back at Gary even more nervously.

GARY
'Conceived by a moron and engineered by a git' is how I believe I phrased it.

ANTHEA
You don't think that's a bit undiplomatic?

GARY
Anthea, we're trying to sell reliable security equipment, and these people offer us a safe with a lock you could pick with a banana sandwich.

ANTHEA
Maybe we could settle for adding the word 'utterly' to my suggestion.

GARY
I'm sorry, Anthea. My 'git' is not negotiable.

ANTHEA
Oh.
She edges to the door.

GARY
I let you take my 'bollocks' out last week, and it left a nasty taste in my mouth.
Anthea looks at him in alarm, then leaves.

GEORGE
You really take security seriously, don't you?

GARY
I'm just trying to create a crime-free society where children can grow up without being corrupted. (*Pause*) I don't know why, I can't stand the little bastards.

GEORGE
Perhaps you should move out to the country like me. We don't get much crime. A bit of pilfering from bird tables but otherwise . . .

GARY
You're lucky, George. The bloke in the flat upstairs from me moved out yesterday, and I reckon we'll have squatters in before you can say 'government housing policy'.
George has got up from his desk, ambled over to the pencil-sharpener attached to the other desk and is now turning the handle.

GARY
That's a biro you're trying to sharpen.

GEORGE
(*Stopping*) I could never be a squatter. You know, having to share the bathroom with people you haven't been properly introduced to.
The door opens, and Dermot comes in, wearing a raincoat over his suit.

DERMOT
Hi, George.

GEORGE
Hello, Dermot, how are you?

DERMOT
Mustn't complain. (*After considering*) Depressed, poor, totally shagged-out . . .

GEORGE
Gary tells me you're embarking on a career in retailing.

DERMOT
He means I'm working in a shop.

GEORGE
What happened to the dog-walking?

DERMOT
I had a few losses in traffic . . . Anyway I always planned to try out one or two jobs before deciding what to do.

GEORGE
How many have you had?

DERMOT
Sixty-three.

GARY
So how'd it go this morning?

DERMOT
Hell. I had to spend half an hour crouching inside a kitchen unit until it all calmed down.

GARY
You didn't!

DERMOT
Yeah. The workmanship inside those units is terrific, you know. You'd expect the odd screwhead to show, wouldn't you?

GARY
You should be out there selling, pushing yourself. Shouldn't he, George?

GEORGE
(*Meeker than ever*) Oh, yes, it's very important to be aggressive.

GARY
Look, it's simple. (*Bringing the clamp over and putting it in front of Dermot*) I'll turn you into a salesman.

DERMOT
Make sure you turn me back into a human being afterwards.

GARY
Show me what you can do. Sell that to George.

DERMOT
(*Staring at the clamp*) George, do you want to buy this?

GEORGE
Not really.

DERMOT
He doesn't want to buy it, Gary.

GARY
All right, let's recreate market conditions. (*To Dermot*) You're trying to sell this security device to George, who's a little old lady.

GEORGE
Can I be Welsh?

GARY
Eh?

GEORGE
I'd like to be a little old Welsh lady.

GARY
If you must.

DERMOT
(*To Gary*) Have I got to be Welsh, too? It always comes out Pakistani.

GARY
It doesn't bloody matter. Just do it, this is for your benefit.

DERMOT
Madam (*Reading from the accompanying literature*) 'The Impregnatron Door Clamp provides a second line of defence against unwelcome guests.'

GEORGE
(*In a Welsh voice*) Woll, that's a mercy.

DERMOT
I'll just get my assistant to show you how it works.
Gary scowls and takes it over to the door. Consulting the instructions, he starts to attach it to the doorknob.

DERMOT
(*Reading again, woodenly*) 'This mobile marvel fits easily over handles, rendering the door unopenable—'

GEORGE
(*Still in character*) Yes, I'll buy one of those, then, thank you.
Gary tuts and snorts in disgust.

DERMOT
So, when did you leave Wales and come to London?

GEORGE
(*Still Welsh*) Well, there's a funny story attached to that, actually.

DERMOT
Really?

GEORGE
Yes, we'd been out gathering slate and so on, when—

GARY
(*Still attaching the clamp*) Oh, shut up, you two.

GEORGE
(*In his normal voice*) No, I enjoyed that. Could I play it with a stutter now?

GARY
No. (*To Dermot*) Have you brought me that money?

DERMOT
Tonight, okay?

GARY
Huh. (*Standing up, looking at the clamp proudly*) British ingenuity, eh? It would've taken four hundred Japanese working round the clock to come up with this. (*Reading*) 'Even the most determined intruder will have trouble—'
The door opens suddenly, and the clamp falls noisily to the floor at Gary's feet. He looks at it, then glances up to find Anthea standing meekly in the doorway.

GARY
You're like a bull in a china shop, aren't you, Anthea?
He closes the door again forcefully.

3. GARY'S FLAT: KITCHEN

Same day, early evening. Gary is sitting at a table, reading a recipe book. Bags and ingredients are laid out before him. Dermot – dressed as before in his raincoat and carrying one large, glossy plastic bag and one smaller one – passes through the hall behind Gary without disturbing him. He exits towards his bedroom.

GARY
(*Reading*) 'Ask the butcher to cut the liver into the thinnest slices possible.' (*He reaches into a bag and holds up a huge piece of uncut liver, stares at it blankly, puts it down and reads on*) 'Crush the peppercorns in a pestle and mortar, if you have one.' I haven't. 'If you haven't, use the back of a tablespoon.'
Gary finds a spoon on the table, takes a black pepper out of the jar and tries to crush it with the spoon. The pepper shoots off the table. He goes off looking for it in a corner of the kitchen.
A tired-looking Dermot enters the kitchen. He sees Gary crouching on the floor.

DERMOT
Don't say that speck of dust has got back into the house.
Dermot sits down heavily. Gary straightens up and returns to the table.

DERMOT
God, I'm wiped out. I fell asleep against this woman on the bus. She was all right until I started dribbling on her shoulder at Oxford Circus.
Gary takes the liver out of the bag and puts it on a plate in front of Dermot.

GARY
Slice this.
Gary goes about the cooking. Dermot forces himself to his feet and goes to wash his hands.

GARY
So your new employers didn't offer you a cigar and a seat on the board, then?

DERMOT
They didn't offer me any kind of seat. I was standing up all afternoon, fantasising about sofas.

GARY
Makes a change from your usual fantasies about semi-naked women in bits of white underwear.

DERMOT
Not really, these sofas had semi-naked women in them. They'd just squeezed up to let me sit down.
Gary lays the knife in one of Dermot's clean hands and a large piece of liver in the other palm.

GARY
That's your trouble – you're obsessed with sex.

DERMOT
(*Gently squeezing the liver*) It's your fault – you keep giving me suggestive food.
Dermot notices he is getting blood on the sleeves of his raincoat. He looks at his hands then, still holding the liver in one hand and the knife in the other, takes off his raincoat, dragging the liver and the knife up through the sleeves. He drapes the coat over the back of a chair. Unperturbed, he starts to slice. Gary watches him do all this.

DERMOT
What are you cooking, anyway?

GARY
It's basically an adaptation of a Persian dish in a rather subtle juniper sauce. (*Pause*) Followed by jelly and ice cream.

DERMOT
With hundreds and thousands?

GARY
Yeah.

DERMOT
Good, I need something to take my mind off Lisa. I taught her all my beer-mat tricks, you know.

GARY
(*Not listening*) Great.

DERMOT
(*With anguish*) Why did she leave me?

GARY
Maybe you shouldn't have slept with her best friend.

DERMOT
Yeah, women don't like that, do they? Her teeth went all kind of . . . clenched. Like in *Dallas*.
Dermot clenches his teeth. Gary grunts.

DERMOT
Is this mine? (*Picking up mug of tea and coat, and leaving the room*) I'm going to change.

GARY
(*Calling after him*) Well, change into something useful (*Looking unenthusiastically at the plate of half-cut liver*) . . . like a curry.
A few seconds later Dermot returns with a teabag in his mouth and spits it into the bin.

4. DERMOT'S BEDROOM

Night-time. Dermot's room reflects his personality – stylish in a neglected sort of way. It contains a king-size bed. Dermot is trying on his sharp new suit in front of the mirror. As he does so he carries on a conversation with Gary, who is still in the kitchen.

GARY
(*Offscreen*) Hey, it looks like someone called Deborah's about to move in upstairs. A letter's arrived for her.

DERMOT
Great. What does it say?

GARY
(*Offscreen*) How should I know? It's private.
Dermot strikes a sharp Italian pose.

DERMOT
Hey! Deb? What's hot (*Thrusting groin*), lives downstairs (*Thrusting again*), and knows how to— (*On the verge of thrusting again a sharp twinge has him clutching his back*) Christ, that hurts . . .

GARY
(*Offscreen*) Well, I had a bit of a look, obviously. Her mother enjoyed her holiday in France, but the weather was disappointing.
Dermot dangles his sunglasses and adopts a Gallic drawl.

DERMOT
'Allo, Debbie, pleeze to meet you. Je m'appelle 'Dermo'.

GARY
(*Offscreen*) We must have her round.

DERMOT
Yeah. (*Putting his shades back on and strutting like a black dude*) Yo, Debsie! Come on down, man.

GARY
(*Offscreen*) Here, have you got that sharp knife in there with you?

DERMOT
(*Still posing*) Yeah, it's in here on the mantelpiece, I'll bring it out.

GARY
(*Offscreen, coming closer*) It's all right, I need it now. I'll come and get it.
Dermot looks at his suit in alarm, grabs his dressing gown and puts it on. The trouser legs can still be seen; he hastily rolls them up, so that the suit is completely hidden. Gary appears in the door. He sees one empty and one full bag on the bed. For a moment he stares at Dermot, who is still wearing his sunglasses.

GARY
Have you been spending the money you owe me?

DERMOT
No!
One of his trouser legs unrolls, emerging from under his dressing gown. Gary goes up to Dermot and pulls the lapels of his dressing gown apart to reveal the suit.

DERMOT
I'm looking after it for a friend!

GARY
You piece of scum.

DERMOT
It's an investment.

GARY
It's a bloody new bloody suit.

DERMOT
When I see a cheque I go out of control. I'm the same with tight black skirts actually.
Gary grabs Dermot by the lapels.

GARY
Listen, this is my money. What would you say if I emptied your wallet and went on a spending spree?

DERMOT
I'd say, what can you buy nowadays with a library ticket and a photo of Lisa bending down on Brighton beach?

GARY
What else have you bought for yourself?

DERMOT
Nothing.

GARY
What's in this bag?
Gary picks it up off the bed and is about to open it.

DERMOT
It's a . . . cookery book.

GARY
You expect me to believe that, do you?
Dermot gently takes back the bag.

DERMOT
I know you're tired of me cooking the same thing all the time.

GARY
(*Relenting*) All right.

DERMOT
Not that there's anything wrong with fish fingers on toast . . .

GARY
(*Walking out*) And take off those stupid sunglasses.

5. LIVING ROOM

Later that evening. Gary and Dermot are sitting at the table, starting to serve themselves.

GARY
That's one thing women find hard to believe, isn't it? That two men can have a quiet evening in on their own, enjoying a civilised and thoughtful conversation.

DERMOT
Yeah, what was that one we didn't finish this morning?

GARY
About Patsy Kensit's bicycle.
They sit back and think about that.

DERMOT
No – about Dorothy. You sure you know what you're doing?

GARY
(*Arrogantly*) Oh, yeah.

DERMOT
You realise she taught you everything you know.

GARY
Like what?

DERMOT
Well, sex. The way I heard it, you'd been pressing the wrong buttons down there for years.

GARY
Yes, she put me right on a few technical details—

DERMOT
She said it was like sleeping with a badly informed Labrador.

GARY
(*Looking hurt*) A Labrador?

DERMOT
It's a nice dog!

GARY
You see, men need more time to themselves. I mean, our ancestors were all hunters, weren't they?

DERMOT
I thought you said your granddad was a French polisher.

GARY
Further back. The men would leave the cave and go off to be on their own for days.

DERMOT
So you wanted Dorothy to wait in a cave until you called, did you?

GARY
No, of course not. It didn't have to be a cave, she could have waited at her mother's.

DERMOT
Fair enough.
They are ready to eat. Gary tucks his serviette into the neck of his shirt.

GARY
Let's be frank, Dermot. One of the reasons I let you live here is that otherwise Dorothy'd be round on the next bus with her family-size shampoo and her pot plants.

DERMOT
If you're going to treat me like a security guard I want a salary and one of those peaked hats.

GARY
I'm feeding you, aren't I?
Dermot grunts. He takes a mouthful and stares at his plate doubtfully.

DERMOT
This is the subtle juniper sauce, is it?

GARY
No, I couldn't get junipers. I used a tin of rhubarb I found in a cupboard.

DERMOT
(*Happily eating*) Oh, right.
The front door slams. After a moment Dorothy bustles into the room.

DOROTHY
Honestly, the potholes in your road, I almost fell off my bike twice. A twelve-hour shift and not so much as a Mars Bar between bedpans. Then the lift goes on the blink, and we've got a hysterectomy stuck between two floors.
She pulls up a spare chair and sits at the table, quickly kissing Gary.

GARY
Evening, Dorothy.

DOROTHY
You didn't tell me you were cooking, Gary.

GARY
(*To Dermot*) You'll have to give half your food to Dorothy.

DOROTHY
Hello, Dermot.

DERMOT
Hello, Dorothy, you're looking well.

DOROTHY
Hear that, Gary – a compliment. Remember compliments?

GARY
They embarrass me. Anyway, you know you're looking well – you're a nurse. *Gary takes Dermot's plate away from him as he sits with his cutlery poised in his hands, and puts half on to a spare vegetable dish that he gives back to Dermot. He gives Dermot's old plate to Dorothy. Dermot looks at his vegetable dish, resigned. He has to eat his food with the serving spoon.*

DOROTHY
I thought I'd pay a spontaneous visit. (*Starting to eat vigorously but wincing on tasting the rhubarb*) So, what have you two been up to?

GARY
(*Evasive, moody*) Discussing life, women . . .
Dorothy runs her hand down Gary's cheek with mock sensuality.

DOROTHY
That's what turns me on about you – you're not just a burglar-alarm salesman, you're also a philosopher.
She takes Gary's plate away from him, scrapes some of his food into Dermot's bowl and gives it back.

GARY
Dorothy, do you have to flaunt our relationship at Dermot like this while he's sitting there, destroyed for the love of a woman.

DERMOT
(*Eating cheerfully*) It's okay, I'm starting to pick up the pieces.

GARY
And I'd prefer it if you didn't arrive unannounced like this and interrupt our conv—

DOROTHY
(*Getting up*) Interrupt your brain-dead ideas about women. Yes, well, I think you're ready to re-enter the real world now.
Dorothy ruffles Gary's hair.

DOROTHY
(*Leaving the room*) I'm just going to run a bath.

GARY
See, look at the way she just comes in!

DERMOT
You gave her the keys.

GARY
Only so she could let herself out!

DERMOT
What's the problem? At least we'll have a clean bath when she's finished.

GARY
No, I tell you, it's over. I'm going to start on the moody silences.

DERMOT
(*After a pause*) Have you started or are you going to wait for her to come back—

GARY
Shut up.
Gary goes moody and silent. With no one to talk to, Dermot does the same.

DERMOT
(*Eventually*) God, it's boring, isn't it?

GARY
Yeah, I hope I don't have to keep this up for long.

DERMOT
Maybe you should just leave your clothes on a beach somewhere and get a completely new identity.

GARY
No, Dorothy's going to be an emotional wreck afterwards – I don't want to put ideas about suicide into her head.
Dermot gives Gary a discreet you-cannot-be-serious glance. Gary is. Dorothy returns and sits down. Gary lolls his head and tries to look drained and upset. Pause.

DOROTHY
What's wrong with your neck?
Gary maintains his moody silence. Dorothy tuts and eats. Gary intensifies his refusal to speak.

DOROTHY
Funny thing happened at the hospital today—

GARY
Can you pay a bit of attention, I'm in a mood here.

DOROTHY
(*Eating*) Is that what it is.

GARY
Dorothy, I'd like my keys back.

DOROTHY
You want to finish with me, is that it?

DERMOT
That didn't take long.

GARY
(*Patently bullshitting*) No! I just think it's important for two people to retain their

privacy. Believe me, I wouldn't dream of giving my door keys to anyone else but you. And I'm not against you making the occasional unexpected visit. As long as we pencil it in a few days in advance.

DOROTHY
I can see through you, Gary.

GARY
Are you sure?
Gary looks awkward. Dermot stands up.

DERMOT
I think I'll leave you to it.

DOROTHY
No, finish your liver, Dermot. It's full of iron.
Dermot sits down again. Under Gary's sharp stare, Dermot eats – at first nibbling, then wolfing it down and making a quick exit.

GARY
So you think splitting up's a good idea?

DOROTHY
I do if you're going to make things difficult the whole time.

GARY
You can cope with the idea of being on your own?

DOROTHY
Well, let's face it, we haven't been getting on that well.

GARY
Haven't we?

DOROTHY
I sometimes think the only thing that's keeping us together is sex.

GARY
Even with a badly informed Labrador, Dermot tells me.
Dorothy looks slightly embarrassed.

DERMOT
(*Offscreen, from the kitchen*) Sorry, Dorothy.

GARY
Dermot! Go to your room.
We see Dermot by the cooker. He picks up a newspaper and rustles it.

DERMOT
It's okay. I'm reading the paper now.
He carries on snooping. Cut back to Dorothy and Gary.

DOROTHY
Here are your keys.
She puts them on the table.

GARY
So this is it, then?

DOROTHY
Seems to be.

GARY
(*Getting impatient*) So, you're okay, then?

DOROTHY
Well, you don't go out with someone for two years without—

GARY
I know . . . I'm upset too.

DOROTHY
I was going to say: without wanting to try out a few other people.

GARY
There's no need to be callous.

DOROTHY
If you want to end it, fine. I've got to carry on with my life. (*Dropping voice*) See how things work out with Trevor . . .

GARY
(*Suddenly alert*) Who?

DERMOT
(*Offscreen, calling out*) Trevor.
Cut to Dermot, eavesdropping. The doorbell rings; Dermot gets up to answer it.

GARY
Who's Trevor?

DOROTHY
He's just a . . . friend.

GARY
What kind of friend?

DOROTHY
A friend. You know, a friend.

GARY
The talking-to kind of friend or the getting-naked kind of friend?

DOROTHY
I'm not going into—

GARY
That's great, isn't it – you're honest with a person, you make a commitment to them, and then you find out they've got a bloody friend.
Dorothy remains inscrutable.

GARY
What's he got that I haven't?

DOROTHY
He doesn't sit there adjusting his underwear. He talks to me.

GARY
All right, I'll talk to you.

DOROTHY
He's sensitive.

GARY
I'm sensitive.

DOROTHY
He's a doctor . . .

GARY
(*Pause*) I'm sensitive . . .
Further pause while they look at each other. They allow themselves to become almost tender and serious.

GARY
Dorothy, I don't like the idea of . . . not sleeping with you again.

DOROTHY
Now you're just being romantic.
He takes her hand. She considers him.

GARY
I suppose I'm a bit confused.
He runs his finger up her wrist. They smile sexily.

DOROTHY
That doesn't feel confused.

GARY
What does it feel like?

DOROTHY
Foreplay.
Dermot has entered quietly with Deborah. Gary and Dorothy have bedroom eyes and have not noticed.

GARY
Love me, noodle?

DOROTHY
Love you, donkey.
They look up and see Dermot and Deborah. Dorothy takes it in her stride; Gary quickly releases her hand.

DOROTHY
Dermot, you didn't tell me you had a new friend.

DERMOT
We haven't known each other long.

DEBORAH
Hello, I'm Deborah. I've bought the flat upstairs.
Gary gets to his feet instantly.

GARY
Pleased to meet you, my name's Gary. This is Dorothy, she's my . . . she's a nurse.
Dorothy glares at Gary.

DEBORAH
Does anyone know what this is?
She produces the clamp, which Gary takes from her.

GARY
I took the precaution of immobilising your door. Total security, you see.

DEBORAH
I just touched it, and it fell off.

GARY
The concept still needs some fine tuning.

DEBORAH
It fell on to the bridge of my foot.
In unison Gary and Dermot immediately move forward towards her feet.

GARY/DERMOT
That's awful . . ./Let me look at that.

DOROTHY
I'm a nurse – if anyone needs any treatment, I'll be giving it.
Deborah steps back clutching her handbag, alarmed at the attention.

DEBORAH
I'm fine.

DERMOT
Let me put your foot in a sling for you.

DEBORAH
Thank you, but I have to go and measure up. I'm moving in tomorrow.

DERMOT
You don't want to go measuring up straight after a serious foot injury like that. (*Quickly handing Deborah Gary's glass of wine*) Have some wine.
She takes it slightly reluctantly.

GARY
Will you be living . . . in a . . . sharing situation?

DEBORAH
No. Do you all live in this flat?

GARY
No, Dorothy lives with her mother. (*Pause*) Miles away.

Dorothy smiles facetiously.

DERMOT
(*To Deborah*) So, it's just you on your own then?'

DEBORAH
Yes, at the moment.

DERMOT
Just the one person?

DOROTHY
I know – let's run through the numbers again, shall we?

GARY
So you bought the flat upstairs. (*Nodding*) Or the 'upstairs flat' as we call it. Barry used to live there.

DEBORAH
Yes, what was he like?

GARY
Well, he never really talked to us after we sold his tortoise.

DEBORAH
Oh. And are the neighbours all right?

DERMOT
Not as all right as you.

GARY
This is a really friendly house. We've always seen ourselves as a community.

DOROTHY
Except when you were setting fire to Barry's moped.

DERMOT
Oh, we were just playing around. He loved a joke, old Barry.

GARY
Have you got someone to help move you in?

DEBORAH
Yeah, a friend of mine's got a van, and he'll be giving me a hand. I'm afraid there'll be a lot of humping upstairs.
Gary and Dermot look at her sharply. Seeing this, Dorothy tuts and looks away.

DERMOT
Well, I'm completely here if you want me.

DEBORAH
Thanks.

DERMOT
In fact, your bathroom's just above my bedroom so I can hear you in the shower.
Deborah gives a polite but sceptical smile.

DEBORAH
Anyway, tell me about yourselves.

DOROTHY
Well, Gary and I have been going out together for a couple of years now.

DEBORAH
You must get on all right together, then.

DOROTHY
Yes, in fact we were just off to bed, weren't we, donkey?
Gary laughs awkwardly.

DEBORAH
(*Getting ready to go*) Anyway, we can get to know each other properly later on.

GARY
Yes, drop in any time.

DERMOT
Night or day.
Dorothy is looking at Gary accusingly. He looks at her and then back to Deborah.

GARY
As long as we pencil it in a few days in advance.

DEBORAH
(*Seeing the keys*) Actually, can I ask you a favour? I don't have a spare set of front-door keys, and I was hoping I could borrow some from you.
They all look at the keys.

GARY
Oh, look, here are some.

DERMOT
Oh, yes.

DOROTHY
(*Quietly to herself*) I can't believe this . . .
Dermot picks up the keys and shows them to Deborah.

DERMOT
These three open the door to our flat, in case your facilities haven't been connected up, and you want to . . . borrow some electricity or something.

DEBORAH
Thanks, that's kind. Wait, I've brought a little moving-in present.
She rummages in her bag and holds out a small box. Gary and Dermot both move towards her, but Gary gets there first and holds up the gift.

GARY
Thanks.

DEBORAH
Chocolates, they're Belgian.

GARY
Never mind. That's great.

DERMOT
(*Taking the chocolates*) Now that is brilliant. Brilliant. That's really brilliant.

GARY
Hey, wait, I've got a present for you. I'll go and get it.
Gary leaves the room. Dermot is momentarily confused by this but then smiles winningly at Deborah.

DOROTHY
(*To Deborah*) Unfortunately chocolate irritates Gary's bowel.

DEBORAH
Oh, dear. It's difficult to know what to buy, especially for men.

DOROTHY
I find Gary always responds well to anything from a toyshop.
Dorothy and Deborah look at each other conspiratorially. Gary reappears with Dermot's bag from the bookshop.

GARY
I bought this to give to whoever moved in upstairs.
Dermot recognises it and smirks.

DERMOT
(*To Gary*) It's appropriate, is it, this present?

GARY
Oh, yeah, perfect. (*Giving the bag to Deborah*) I thought you might read this and try out some of the ideas on us.

DEBORAH
(*Opening the bag*) You really didn't have to.
They watch as Deborah gets out a large hardback with a naked couple on it.

A Pocket Guide to SENSATIONAL SEX
Talking & intimacy
Good communication, as well as sexy talk, is a sure way for you both to increase your sexual pleasure.
to reading aloud from erotic literature. Honeyed words make you feel loved and desirable, and therefore more aroused.
Your pleasure can also be expressed in sounds, such as moans and sighs, which will inflame you both. And don't forget that the ear is an erogenous zone in its own right.
Sexy talk is like verbal foreplay, some call it aural sex. The human voice is a powerful aphrodisiac. It can vary from whispering softly to your partner just what and how you feel during lovemaking.
14
CHAPTER TWO
BEFORE YOU ENJOY FULL INTERCOURSE, THERE ARE MANY TECHNIQUES FOR LOVEMAKING THAT CAN AROUSE INTENSE EROTIC FEELINGS – SAVOUR THEM TO THE FULL.
FABULOUS FOREPLAY

DEBORAH
(*Reading*) *Let's Make Love: Your Guide to Improbable Sex*. Well, you don't beat about the bush, do you?
Dorothy grabs her coat and marches out of the room. Gary rushes after her.

6. HALL

A moment later. Dorothy turns to face Gary, hitting him with her bag.

DOROTHY
(*Turning*) You're pathetic.

GARY
It's meant to be a cookery book!

7. LIVING ROOM

The front door is heard to slam soon afterwards. Deborah is still examining the book dubiously.

DERMOT
Well, it's educational . . .

DEBORAH
(*Handing it back to him*) I prefer a book with a good story. (*Moving to the door*) I ought to be going.

DERMOT
(*Going with her*) We must get together some time, for a meal . . .
Deborah exits, smiling sceptically. The front door shuts. Dermot stands there, holding the book. Gary appears, staring icily at Dermot.

DERMOT
I think everyone enjoyed themselves, didn't they?

LAGER BEER
ANNO 1366
STELLA ARTOIS
LEUVEN
BELGIUM'S ORIGINAL BEER
Strong Continental Lager
440 ml
Alc. 5.2% Vol.

SERIES TWO

SERIES TWO: EPISODE ONE

gary and tony

I can't say that this episode still makes me laugh, but writers are a notoriously joyless bunch. Not only do we believe the glass is half empty, rather than half full, we also worry that it has a crack in it. I still hadn't really hit my stride, and the series is a disaster hair-wise. Martin's vaguely Nazi crop would not be too bad if it didn't contrast so wildly with Neil and Leslie's hairstyles, which are, simply, a terrible, terrible mistake. In his defence, at the time Neil was receiving hundreds of letters a week from fans asking him how he got his hair so long and nice.

Harry Enfield's leaving meant that the episode had to be about Gary finding a new flatmate and Tony moving in. Montages of duff applicants are hard to resist for a writer – see *The Commitments* for a particularly fine example. I make an appearance in this episode as 'Catatonic student', the perfect writer's part because I only have to sit there looking stupid.

It took me a while to write properly for Neil Morrissey, who is a much subtler actor than he is given credit for. And, crucially, he is charming. That charm was missing in Tony's equivalent in the American version of *Men*, with the result that you just wanted to slap him and tell him to get a job.

I like to think I no longer write lines like 'You did say Dermot was about as much fun to live with as nose hair', a formulation that was taken as far as it could go in *Blackadder*. The main problem with this and similar joke set-ups is that nobody actually uses them in real life. Although as a comedy writer it is obviously unwise to go overboard on this real-life thing.

1. THE CROWN

After work. Gary is sitting at the bar with a pint, looking depressed. He is writing in a notebook. Les, the pub's super-uncouth landlord, is noisily eating a packet of crisps. Gary looks up, pointedly. Les crunches another crisp. In sudden irritation, Gary grabs the bag, crushes it very small and hands it back to Les. Gary goes back to his notebook. Dorothy comes in and joins Gary. She looks around at the shabby interior and at Les, who is scratching himself.

DOROTHY
That's why I like going out with you, Gary, it's an endless orgy of glamour and entertainment.
They give each other a peck on the cheek.

GARY
Dorothy's usual, please, Les.

LES
(*Hesitating*) Refresh my memory.

DOROTHY
Vodka in a chipped glass with a dribble of flat tonic and an aftertaste of cigarette ash.

LES
Oh, yeah, I remember now.
He turns away to get the drink.

GARY
I've had some bad news.

DOROTHY
Don't tell me Norma Major's still refusing to have your love child.

GARY
No, Dermot's sent me a postcard. He's not coming back.
Dorothy's face clouds. Gary hands her a postcard.

DOROTHY
(*Reading*) 'Have fallen in love with a croupier called Letizia. We are going round the world on her Yamaha.' Isn't that an organ?

GARY
No, a motorbike.

DOROTHY
'Send my Polynesian Love-Balls and other important items to my mum. Sell everything else, my saucepan etcetera to cover what I owe you.' Oh, isn't that generous of him?

GARY
It would have been, if his possessions weren't worth (*consulting notebook*) sixteen pounds thirty pence, by my calculations.

DOROTHY
How much does he owe you?

GARY
Eight hundred and twenty-seven quid.
Dorothy takes her drink and her change from Les. She is still reading.

DOROTHY
'Weather lovely. Rimini has a Body Shop.'
She turns over the postcard.

DOROTHY
Oh, look, a donkey. Having sex with another donkey.
She and Gary move over to a table.

GARY
Why doesn't anyone offer to take me round the world?

DOROTHY
Because they know they'd have a crap time.
Gary does a yes-that-must-be-it expression. They sit down.

DOROTHY
I'll miss Dermot.
Gary grunts.

GARY
I won't.

DOROTHY
You will. (*Smiling ironically*) He was your mate.

GARY
What's that supposed to mean?

DOROTHY
Why are some men too embarrassed to admit they like other men?
Gary makes a squeamish expression. Dorothy rolls her eyes.

GARY
He was there to help with the mortgage. I'll have to get somebody else to move in . . .
They find themselves looking at each other.

DOROTHY/GARY
Don't even think of asking./I'm sorry, Dorothy, it wouldn't work . . .
An awkward pause. Gary picks up the notebook.

GARY
I was just writing an ad for the paper.

DOROTHY
Let's have a look.

GARY
No, you'll only use it as an excuse for a cheap laugh.

DOROTHY
I won't.

GARY
You always do.

DOROTHY
I won't. (*Taking the notebook and then reading it*) No, that looks fine.
She puts it back on the table. Gary looks grateful. They sip their drinks.

DOROTHY
You don't think 'Jacuzzi' is pushing it a bit?

GARY
Why?

DOROTHY
You haven't got one.

GARY
No, but if you whooj the shower attachment around under the water when you're in the bath, it's just like it. Honestly.

DOROTHY
You don't think you should put 'bath with shower attachment that can be whoojed around'?

GARY
Too many words.
Les has been hovering, wiping tables.

LES
I'll tell you how to make a Jacuzzi when you're sitting in the bath.

GARY
Les, are you going to say what I think you're going to say?

LES
Yes.
He wanders off. Dorothy glances back at the advertisement.

DOROTHY
'Share with immensely likeable, high-flying executive.' That's . . . you, is it?

GARY
Yes.
Dorothy manages to smother a smile. Gary just looks at her. Dorothy peers again at what Gary has written.

DOROTHY
'Large summerhouse'?
Gary ponders grudgingly, pen in hand.

GARY/DOROTHY
Small shed.

2. GARY'S OFFICE

Gary's security firm, one morning a few days later. Gary is sitting at his desk, chewing a pencil. George is at his own desk, working on some figures.

GARY
You see, I don't want to encourage the wrong kind of person.

GEORGE
No. Marjorie and I once talked about taking in lodgers, but she was scared there'd be congestion on the stairs.

GARY
God, yes, scary.

GEORGE
So then we thought about letting the room downstairs next to our living room.

GARY
Isn't that your kitchen?

GEORGE
Yes. I think that's why we decided against it in the end.

GARY
Well, these questions should weed out any unsuitable applicants.

GEORGE
Ask me one.

GARY
Okay. (*Consulting list*) 'What does your father do?' (*Looking hurriedly up at George*) No, we'll skip that one. 'Are you very likely to bring a lot of young women into my home, quite likely, or frankly not very likely?' (*George struggling to decide*) No, we'll skip that one too. (*Consulting list again*) 'What is the capital of Tanzania?'

GEORGE
Dar es Salaam.

GARY
(*Writing it in notebook*) Oh, is it?

GEORGE
Is that relevant?

GARY
Of course it is. We're going to be having stimulating chats, I don't want Mr Stupid cluttering up my sofa.

Anthea enters from her office. She is not only as nervy as ever but also clearly put out. She places a pile of typed documents on the far edge of Gary's desk and turns to leave.

GARY
Anthea, I hope this display of petulance isn't going to last.

ANTHEA
I'm just asking for a decent pay rise.

GARY
It's the same for me.

ANTHEA
But I earn a pittance.

GARY
I think you'll find it's the industry-standard pittance.

ANTHEA
Well, it isn't fair.
Gary starts to leaf through the documents.

GARY
The world isn't fair. If it was, I'd be shacked up with my seventeen-year-old niece.

ANTHEA
Well, I'm sorry, but I've started working to rule.
Gary is staring at a typed letter.

GARY
Have you let this go out, Anthea?

ANTHEA
I simply put down what was on the dictaphone.

GARY
So you sent out a letter to a major client ending: 'Give the slimy half-wit the usual fob-off. Er. Yours with the deepest contempt blah blah. George, do you have to poke around in your ears while I'm dictating?'

Gary seethes. Anthea twitches wildly in trepidation.

GARY
Anthea, go to your room.

3. GARY'S FLAT: LIVING ROOM

Morning. Gary is sitting on the edge of an armchair. Slumped on the sofa opposite him is a fat slob in a dirty denim jacket. Gary is trying to be polite. He is marking off answers on a clipboard.

GARY
So . . . are you working at the moment?

SLOB
Yeah, bit of this, bit of that.

GARY
(*Writing it down*) Bit of this . . . bit of that.

SLOB
Bit of the other.
Gary laughs hysterically, to be sociable. The slob surveys the room.

SLOB
Well, looks all right to me. Where's your toilet?

GARY
There isn't one.

4. HALL

Midday. Cut sharply to an unstoppably chatty woman, standing in the hall with Gary, who has his mouth open.

CHATTERBOX
. . . and then the phone bill came in, and I said, '*No way* am I paying any of this, I don't even know anyone in Canada.' I probably ring my homeopath once a week, that's all, and I knew they were drinking my milk because I put a biro-mark on the inside of the carton. And it was always me who ended up buying the toilet rolls, even though I used less than everyone else because, well, I'll tell you about that when I move in, okay! So I grind my teeth, I mean, so what?
Gary has casually thrown his clipboard on to the floor.

CHATTERBOX
What was I saying . . . ?

5. KITCHEN

Dusk. Gary is sitting at the table with a catatonic mature student, who is fidgeting with his scarf. Long pause.

GARY
Never mind. Let's try another one. What's the capital of Tanzania?
Another lengthy pause.

GARY
Nod once if you can hear me.

6. HALL

The following day. Gary has just opened the front door, to a likeable, young Geordie with a strong but not impenetrable accent.

GEORDIE
Ah was passin' an wor reckoned this street'll dee, an'awll, an I'll gan give it a visit, like. Alreet?
A pause while Gary stares at him.

GARY
I'm sorry, I'm looking for someone with English as their first language.

7. KITCHEN

That night. Gary, now in the other chair, is opposite a normal-looking man in his mid-twenties. Gary is weary by now but seems encouraged by this candidate.

MR NORMAL
No, I can't think of any irritating habits off hand.

GARY
You don't . . . clean between your toes with the sofa cushion or anything?

MR NORMAL
God, no, who'd do a thing like that?

GARY
Hah, yeah. (*Pause*) Well, Dermot did actually, my last flatmate.

MR NORMAL
I shared with somebody who used to dry his underwear out in the microwave.

GARY
Dermot waited till he had enough stains then brushed them off.
Pause while they weigh each other up.

GARY
Well, we seem to get on all right, so, um . . .

MR NORMAL
Do you have a girlfriend?

GARY
Er, yes . . .

MR NORMAL
I don't have one at the moment, so I wondered if you'd let her watch while I stroke my nipples?
Gary looks at him evenly.

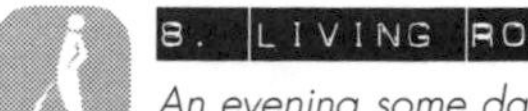

8. LIVING ROOM

An evening some days later. Deborah and Dorothy are sitting on the sofa. Gary is in the armchair, morosely eating peanuts. They sit in silence for a while. Gary sighs heavily.

DEBORAH
So how many people have you seen?

GARY
Three social inadequates, three psychopaths, a man with a big dog and my mother.

DOROTHY
And the eight people who turned you down.

GARY
They must have lost my phone number.

DEBORAH
I don't want a psychopath living downstairs.

GARY
I quite liked the psychopaths. It was my mother who scared me.

DOROTHY
If you really want to find someone, try to be more charming.

GARY
I've been charming. I've shown off everything in the flat—

DEBORAH
Yes, don't ever knock on my door again at midnight with a man in a tank top and refer to me as a feature.
The doorbell rings.

9. COMMUNAL HALLWAY

Later that evening. Gary opens the door to a long-haired young man in a T-shirt and a leather jacket. This is Tony – personable, relaxed, slightly vacant.

TONY
Is this the place with the room to let?

GARY
Yes. Who are you?

TONY
Tony?
He consults a dog-eared list.

GARY
You should have come last week.

TONY
I lost the piece of paper with your address on it.
Gary leads Tony into his flat.

TONY
Yeah, I don't know what happened, but . . .

A moment later, still explaining, Tony follows Gary in.

TONY
So then I realised it must have slipped down the lining of my jacket 'cos I could kind of feel a bit of paper, you know. (*To Deborah and Dorothy, in passing*) Hi – and I tried to ease it round and out of an armhole but that didn't work, so I had to undo a lot of the stitching with these blunt scissors I found, which took, like, ages.
A pause. Deborah, Dorothy and Gary are looking at Tony.

TONY
And, um, there it was.

DEBORAH
What?

TONY
An old bus ticket. I found the address down the back of the sofa.
Another awkward pause.

TONY
Shall I come in again?

GARY
This is Tony.

TONY
Hi.

GARY
(*Introducing*) Deborah lives upstairs. But I'm working on it. (*Laughing gauchely, alone*) No, no, that's me being funny. And Dorothy, my sort of girlfriend.

DOROTHY
Thanks, Gary.

DEBORAH
What do you do, Tony?

TONY
Oh, I'm in the music business.

GARY
(*With boyish enthusiasm*) Do you know Barry White?

TONY
No.

GARY
(*Smiling dreamily, then suddenly businesslike*) Okay, this is the procedure we'll be following: I'll start by introducing you to the key features and facilities, then I'll be offering you the beverage of your choice and asking you a series of simple questions.

DEBORAH
Oh, get on with it, Gary.

GARY
Right. This is the living room with its U-shape seating amenity. Up here (*Indicating a wall-mounted cupboard*) are the glassware facilities, bit of an heirloom so I'd rather you didn't touch.

TONY
Yeah, magic . . .
He wanders into the kitchen.

GARY
These are handy units, look.
Gary helpfully demonstrates by opening a drawer. He looks around and finds Tony gone. Deborah and Dorothy smile sardonically.

11. KITCHEN

Seconds later. The kitchen is a mess. Tony is looking around airily. Gary comes in. The sink is piled high with pots and pans.

TONY
Nice pots.
Embarrassed, Gary tidies up as he goes.

GARY
Yes, plenty of potware, for cooking and so on. Cutlery here in the drawer for the cutlery. Mantelpiece – useful for . . . resting things on.

TONY
(*Looking at the dirty dishes in the sink*) Yeah, I think I could be at home here.
Tony drifts off into the corridor. Gary follows him stiffly.

GARY
(*Offscreen, echoey*) And this is the bathroom.

TONY
(*Offscreen*) Nice wallpaper.

GARY
(*Offscreen*) No, that's fungus.

12. LIVING ROOM

A little later. The door is heard slamming. Gary returns, rejoining Dorothy and Deborah.

DEBORAH
Well, he seems very nice.

GARY
I don't know – he's not as ideal as Dermot, is he?

DOROTHY
You did say Dermot was about as much fun to live with as nose hair.
Gary ponders morosely.

DEBORAH
People aren't exactly pleading to move in, are they?
The doorbell goes. Gary is lost in his thoughts. Deborah sighs and goes to answer it.

GARY
Maybe I should readvertise in *The Times*?

DOROTHY
So that's it – you think he's not professional enough for you.

GARY
I'm just concerned that we should be able to communicate at a sophisticated level—

DOROTHY
Like your conversations with Dermot, I suppose. Two hours on whether small, pointy breasts are more interesting than large, round ones.

GARY
Exactly.

DOROTHY
It's pure snobbery. Just because he sells records.

GARY
It isn't. I'd have just as many doubts if he . . . owned his own record company.

DOROTHY
(*Picking up a business card*) Maybe he does, he's left a card: 'Tony Smart Records Ltd'.
Gary takes the card and reads. He brightens immediately.

GARY
Oh, well, I'm sure he'll fit in.
Deborah reappears with Tony.

TONY
I left my bag here, sorry.

GARY
No, I'm glad you came back, because, um . . . (*Grandly offering his hand*) welcome aboard.

TONY
(*Casually*) Oh, cheers. I'll turn up tomorrow morning, shall I – eight-ish?

GARY
Don't you have to . . . give some notice?

TONY
You're right. Better make that nearer nine. (*Turning to Deborah and Dorothy*) Well, see you soon.

GARY
I hope you didn't mind all the questions.

TONY
Nah – you've got to check out I'm not weird or anything.
Deborah hands Tony his plastic bag.

DEBORAH
This is heavy, what've you got in there?

TONY
Oh, friend of mine runs a butcher's, and he had this pig's head left over . . .
He pulls out the pig's head by the ears.

TONY
He says the eyes explode if you do it in the microwave.

13. TONY'S BEDROOM

The next morning. Gary is clearing the last of Dermot's possessions away into boxes. He is on his knees looking under the bed. He pulls out a pair of dubious-looking underpants, which he hastily throws into a box. Then his hand comes out caught in a pile of spaghetti so old it is green with mould and welded to its plate.

GARY
Oh, there it is . . .
He reaches under the bed again and brings out a Star Wars plastic sword.

GARY
Oh, grow up, Dermot.
He turns it on, and it flashes. In spite of himself, Gary gets up and starts to fence with it playfully, really getting into it.

GARY
Nice action . . .
He throws it in the box and goes over to the wardrobe. He puts a trendy shirt and jacket in another box, then reaches in and brings out a Bullworker, which he gives a pitying glance. He tries it out, to no avail. Then throws it away. Finally he retrieves the last item – an absurd Pluto hat with large floppy ears. Gary puts it on. The doorbell rings. Gary goes to answer it, still wearing the ears.

14. KITCHEN

Moments later Gary leads Tony through the kitchen. Tony is carrying a couple of bags.

GARY
I'd stay to show you how everything works, but I'm late for work.
Gary turns to face Tony who, typically British, does not ask Gary why he is wearing a hat with large floppy ears.

TONY
No problem. I'll find my own way around.

GARY
I've been clearing out Dermot's room.
Gary turns and makes for the bedroom.

15. TONY'S ROOM

As they walk in to the room, Gary picks up a box.

GARY
Have a look through, you might find something you like. I know he'd want his Condom Gift Set to go to a good home.

TONY
Thanks. What was he like?

GARY
We got on pretty well. I mean, at times it was a bit difficult to take him seriously, to be honest.
Gary scratches his neck. His Pluto ears flop about.

TONY
Right . . .

GARY
Anyway, see you tonight.
Gary leaves with his box. Tony puts down his bags and looks around speculatively. The front door slams as Gary leaves. From his bag Tony empties some books and an alarm clock, which he places next to the bed. He idly presses a button, and an electronic voice emerges from it: 'Get up, you lazy bastard.' Next he brings out some clothes and a Bullworker, which he puts in the wardrobe. Then a Star Wars sword, which he briefly tries out. He walks around some more and then wanders out.

16. KITCHEN/ LIVING ROOM

Tony mooches around. He opens the fridge door; it contains an awful lot of lager and a lump of cheese, which he takes out and begins to eat. He goes over to the mantelpiece and picks up a postcard.

TONY
(*Reading*) 'Having a great time in spite of riding the Yamaha into a sobbing bitch.' (*Holding up card to read it better*) 'Sodding ditch. Istanbul has a WH Smiths. Love, Dermot and Letizia. PS I left some spaghetti in my room. You might as well throw it away.'
Tony puts the card back and strolls around again. He takes in the room.

TONY
(*Pointing vaguely*) U-shape seating amenity.
He goes over to the wall-mounted cupboard, pulls the door open, and the cupboard plummets to the floor. Sound of many glasses smashing into small pieces. Tony remains immobile, his hands still raised to where the cupboard was. Eventually he looks down; broken glass has fallen out of the cupboard and gone everywhere. He looks around for something to clear it up with. A knock on the door. Tony tries to shove the glass back in with his feet.

17. COMMUNAL HALLWAY

Moments later Tony opens the door to Deborah. Her manner with him is subtly flirtatious.

DEBORAH
You've arrived, then?

TONY
Yeah. Come in.
Tony shuts the door behind her.

DEBORAH
Am I interrupting anything?

TONY
No, I was just . . . smashing up a load of glasses.
Deborah smiles uneasily.

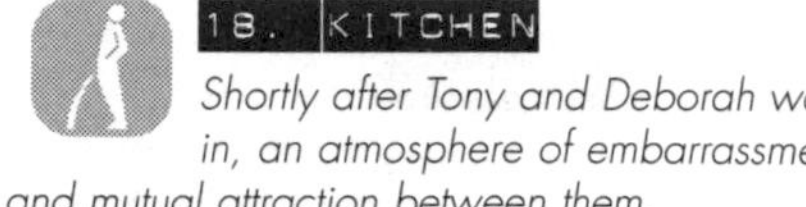

18. KITCHEN

Shortly after Tony and Deborah walk in, an atmosphere of embarrassment and mutual attraction between them.

TONY
Coffee?

DEBORAH
Thanks.

TONY
(*Looking lost*) Where's the kettle?

DEBORAH
Um, they usually just used the hot tap . . . No, here you are.
Deborah unearths a kettle under a pile of kitchen mess. Tony goes about making the coffee.

TONY
So, how long have you known Gary?

DEBORAH
Since I moved in a few months ago. He's been very kind.

TONY
Yeah, he seems quite—

DEBORAH
Well, not exactly kind. (*Pause*) Irritating. He did help me out when my boyfriend was getting violent.

TONY
(*Surprised*) What, Gary kicked your boyfriend out?

DEBORAH
No, he was head-butted and fell over.
Tony nods earnestly.

TONY
What happened to your bloke?

DEBORAH
I think he got a bit of a bruise up here, on his forehead.

TONY
No, I mean, are you still together?

DEBORAH
No.
A meaningful pause.

DEBORAH
What about you?

TONY
No. I'm hopeless – you know, I see a girl and . . . we seem to be getting on and then . . . it all goes wrong.

DEBORAH
Do you know why?

TONY
I think I'm just shy. I suppose I need a woman to, like, take me and show me the ropes.
He seems genuinely vulnerable. Deborah is clearly sympathetic.

DEBORAH
I shouldn't worry – women are supposed to be attracted to vulnerable men.

TONY
(*Vulnerable look*) Do you really think so?

19. GARY'S OFFICE

Later that morning. The office is more chaotic than before. Gary, apparently alone, has a typewriter on his desk and is struggling to type a letter.

GARY
K-k-k-k. George, where's the K?

GEORGE
(*Offscreen, muffled voice*) I don't know. Have you tried looking in the manual?

GARY
There's got to be a K here somewhere – I've seen Anthea using it. (*He carries on looking*) C – that'll do.
He types the letter C. George now emerges from behind a filing cabinet. He is wearing Dermot's clothes, those that Gary was sorting out earlier: a particularly flamboyant shirt with a string tie, skintight jeans and a trendy jacket.

GEORGE
Are you sure Dermot shouldn't have these back?

GARY
Those . . . possibly.

GEORGE
Modern clothes are very snug around the groin, aren't they?

GARY
(*Concentrating on his typing again*) Mm.

GEORGE
When I was a young man I could get a side of beef down my trousers. Not that I tried, of course. Well, only the once.

GARY
Maybe a jumper would be more you.

GEORGE
No, no, I'm starting to get the hang of these.
George goes back to his desk and sits down, stiffly.

GEORGE
You seem to be taking a while over that letter.

GARY
Just being thorough. It's a pretty pathetic boss who can't do a bit of simple typing once in a while.
Gary looks at the word he has just typed. He pulls the paper out of the typewriter, crumples it up and throws it into the bin.

GEORGE
Isn't it time you patched up this dispute with Anthea?

GARY
Not until she starts to work properly.
He puts another piece of paper into the typewriter.

GARY
The sooner she stops acting childishly, the sooner I put the wheels back on her typing chair.

GEORGE
But we've always worked so well together.

GARY
I've offered her a modest but fair pay rise, and what does she do? She deliberately spends three hours typing a short memo.

GEORGE
It's quicker than y—

GARY
I know it's quicker than me, that's besides the point.
Gary has typed two words and is trying to apply some Tipp-Ex. He carefully removes the paper from the typewriter so he can get to the word better.

GEORGE
I think you made things worse by taking the bulb out of her Anglepoise and confiscating her biscuits.

GARY
Merely sticking to CBI guidelines, George.
Gary lifts up the Tipp-Ex brush. It is now firmly stuck to the sheet of paper. He looks at it in despair, sighs heavily.

GARY
All right, let's get this over with.
He goes over to the door to Anthea's office and opens it. She is in near darkness, trying to read by the light of a torch.

GARY
(*Apparently conciliatory*) Are you free for a moment, Anthea? We need to sort this out.
Anthea's defiant expression softens. She gets up and follows Gary in.

GARY
There comes a time in industrial relations when a little compromise is needed.

ANTHEA
Yes.
They look at each other with understanding and mutual respect.

GARY
Well, Anthea, I've tried to compromise, but you haven't, so I'm afraid I'm going to have to lock you in the stationery cupboard.
Anthea's mouth drops open: a gesture of helplessness. Gary approaches her and takes her gently by the arm.

GEORGE
Isn't that a bit cruel?

GARY
I wouldn't normally do this, as you know, but there's a recession on.

ANTHEA
But I haven't done anything wrong.

GARY
(*Leading her over*) Ah, that's what Goebbels said, of course. Only in German.
She stops.

ANTHEA
All right, all right.

GARY
You'll go back to working normally?

ANTHEA
Yes.

GARY
(*Bright and friendly*) Excellent. I always say – you can't go wrong if you treat your staff like human beings.
Anthea stands there looking crestfallen.

20. GARY'S FLAT: LIVING ROOM

That evening Gary and Tony are sitting together on the sofa, low-key, each holding a can of lager, half-watching the television. They have already established a rapport.

GARY
So, what do you think of Deborah?
Tony makes an appreciative lads-together expression. Gary does the same. Tony does another, adding an appreciative snort. So does Gary.

TONY
That's not being sexist or anything.

GARY
No, no. I straightened things out between her and her last boyfriend, you know.

TONY
I heard, yeah.

GARY
I think that whole business hurt her a bit. (*Gently rubbing his forehead*) Well, me too, as it happens.

TONY
Mind you, we've all been hurt that way, haven't we?

GARY
God, absolutely, me too, terribly hurt.

TONY
Women don't always understand, do they, that men suffer too, and—

GARY
And that that affects our, um, ability to, um . . . thing.
He trails off completely, distracted by the TV.

TONY
I've just had to dump a girlfriend.

GARY
It's never easy, is it?

TONY
No. I rang her up today and told her I'd moved in with Deborah.

GARY
Yeah, that way she knows she was ditched for a good reason.

TONY
Yep. I told her I'd agonised for ages but in the end . . . Deborah's got a sports car.

GARY
Uh-huh. How did she take it?

TONY
I don't know. My ten pence ran out.
They watch the TV solemnly and both snigger inanely at something on screen, then go instantly deadpan again.

TONY
What about you and Dorothy?

GARY
We've been together for a couple of years now.

TONY
That's not bad, is it? I mean, that's commitment.

GARY
Yeah, women always complain that men are frightened of committing themselves. I mean, where do they get that idea from?

TONY
We tell them.

GARY
(*Considering*) Yeah, that's probably it.

TONY
Where is Dorothy?

GARY
In the bath. (*Laddish innuendo*) She normally asks me to hop in with her. Gives a terrific soaping, does Dorothy.
Dorothy comes in from her bath, drying her hair with a towel.

DOROTHY
So, Tony, has Gary sapped your life spirit, alienated your friends and made you want to strangle him with an electric flex yet?

TONY
No.

DOROTHY
Oh, of course – you haven't been going out with him for three years, have you?
Gary laughs nervously. Tony joins in, out of solidarity.

GARY
(*To Tony*) Bit of the old banter, ha.

DOROTHY
I've left the water in the bath for you, Gary – you know you always get back from work smelling like a llama.
She sits down next to Gary on the sofa, kissing him on the cheek. He sighs, gets to his feet and leaves. Dorothy and Tony smile at each other.

DOROTHY
So, why did you leave your old place?

TONY
Trouble with the landlord. I think he wanted us all out.
Dorothy nods sympathetically.

DOROTHY
Tenants really get a rough deal sometimes, don't they?

TONY
I'm not surprised really. We hadn't paid any rent for three years.

DOROTHY
Were you squatting?

TONY
No, we just hadn't got round to it.
Dorothy gives Tony a slightly alarmed smile. Gary enters with Deborah, who is carrying a book and an envelope.

GARY
Drink, Deborah?

DEBORAH
No, I won't stay. I've got a lot to do.

TONY
Go on.

DEBORAH
(*Instantly*) Okay.
Tony gives her a can of lager. She sits down.

DOROTHY
What's the book?
Deborah reluctantly hands it to Dorothy.

DOROTHY
'How to Overcome Shyness and Form New Relationships'.

DEBORAH
My mum gave it to me. She thinks women who aren't married by the age of twenty-five are psychologically disturbed.
Dorothy hands it to Tony, who takes it, uneasily.

TONY
Thanks.

GARY
(*Looking over at the book*) Oh, God, let's all be sensitive and complicated, shall we?
Deborah and Dorothy glare at Gary.

DOROTHY
Just because you're insensitive, it doesn't mean Tony is.
Deborah produces a small white envelope. She looks perplexed.

DEBORAH
I've just found this on the mat. I don't understand – it's addressed to Tony and Deborah.
Tony quickly tries to snatch the envelope back from Deborah. Alerted by this reaction, Deborah holds on to it. She opens it and takes out a note.

DEBORAH
(*Reading*) 'Deborah: the next time you seduce someone's boyfriend don't pick a lying moron who pretends to be shy then tries to pull your sister, who borrows your money to get you a present then buys himself a tortoise with it—'
We are slowly panning across the four faces: Deborah is increasingly tight-lipped, Tony guilty looking and Dorothy cynical. Gary is grinning.

DEBORAH
—'and who dumps you because he's found a girlfriend with a sports car. You deserve each other. Tony: I have left your guitar outside, together with a surprise for you both.'
Deborah folds the note, visibly furious with Tony, who is trying to look innocent.

DEBORAH
How disappointing.
Dorothy is already at the window. She pulls back the curtain and looks out.

DOROTHY
Um, Deborah . . .
The four of them gather in front of the window, looking out at the road, their mouths are all open.

21. NIGHT STREET

Deborah's open-top sports car is parked outside. It has been filled with a large amount of manure, which is steaming eerily in the streetlights. Sticking out of it, neck first, like a satanic totem pole, is an electric guitar.

22. LIVING ROOM

Moments later. Deborah turns to Tony, speechless. Tony is still trying to look innocent.

TONY
You want to wash that off before it stains your upholstery.

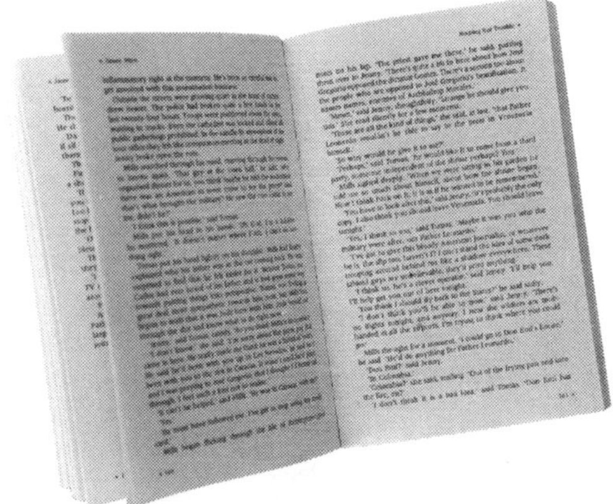

SERIES TWO: EPISODE THREE

HOW TO DUMP YOUR *girlfriend*

Men Behaving Badly generally works best when it's *about* something, in this case men's inability to end a relationship properly. I always struggle to come up with a convincing answer when people ask me, 'Where do you get your ideas from?' The fact is that the ideas are normally rather banal; it's what you do with them that counts.

This episode helped explain why Dorothy hung out with a slob like Gary: she was a bit of a slob herself. Caroline Quentin was always understandably anxious that Dorothy should be more than a finger-wagging girlfriend in a nurse's uniform. On the other hand if she were one of the lads, the sitcom's delicate ecosystem would break down. Oh, it's all so bloody complicated.

Given her comedy credentials, Caroline has been heroically reticent about asking me to change lines. If she didn't like a joke the most she would do was show a vague sadness around the eyes. In the first series we had a couple of major rows about sexual politics. She accused me of wish-fulfilment when I wrote an attractive woman who met Dermot and instantly asked him to bed. My defence – of course it's wish-fulfilment, why else do you think writers write? – was admittedly shoddy. We eventually found a compromise, and since then no woman has ever asked a man out in any of my shows, so that showed her.

Martin Clunes is on fine, pompous form here. Gary needs this earnest side to his character, the side that enables him to work in a drab office by day then be a lord of drunken misrule in the evenings.

The episode features the first of the few girlfriends Neil was allowed: Pat. We discovered too late that Pat's bra strap was visible when she was in bed with Tony. The sitcom is a very chaste genre, with none of that sordid 'Shut up and take your top off, love' mentality you get in TV drama. Having said that, I blame the director Martin Dennis for not insisting that all actresses involved in bed scenes have their bras confiscated when entering Teddington Studios.

1. GARY'S FLAT: TONY'S BEDROOM

Night-time. Pat, an attractive young woman, is sitting up in bed, relaxed but alert. Tony is dozing next to her. She gazes round at the room, which is horribly untidy and dirty. The bedside table has several used mugs on it. Pat casually goes to move one – a novelty mug, shaped like a woman's torso – which looks like falling off. It is stuck so hard, the handles come away instead. She tosses it away in disgust. She looks at Tony, frustrated that he is not awake. She nudges him, but he doesn't respond. So she pushes him brutally. He stirs, looking aggrieved.

PAT
(*Suddenly sweet*) All right.

TONY
Um.
He remains only half awake.

PAT
Why do men fall asleep after making love?

TONY
(*Without thinking*) So that we don't have to talk.

PAT
Oh, thanks.

TONY
No, I mean – to regain our strength so we can perform again in twenty minutes.

PAT
(*Snuggling up*) It shouldn't be a performance – it's a celebration of our love.
Tony squeezes her hand romantically.

PAT
You even fell asleep after we had sex in that aeroplane toilet.

TONY
It was just a quick snooze.

PAT
It wasn't that quick – you missed two meals and a movie.

TONY
(*Smiling*) Good holiday, though, wasn't it?

PAT
Mm. Where shall we go this year?
Tony looks slightly shifty. He puts his arm round Pat.

TONY
Let's not think about it yet. You've just been away a couple of months.

PAT
And I come back to find you've moved in here. I thought we were going to live together.
Tony lights up a cigarette.

TONY
Why? This way I stay fresh and interesting.
He coughs chestily.

PAT
What's Gary like?

TONY
Ears like the FA Cup, enjoys a drink. Nice guy.

PAT
Where is he tonight?

TONY
Taking his girlfriend out to the Ritz.

PAT
(*Impressed*) Well, hey.

TONY
No, Rits Kebabs, on the corner. They do a terrific blancmange apparently.
Pat is surveying the room.

PAT
Doesn't this mess depress you?

TONY
Gary's drawing up a cleaning rota. Mind you, the way I see it, the more stuff you leave on the floor, the less there is to hoover.
There is a flex next to the bed. Pat pulls it and brings out a video camera. She frowns at Tony.

PAT
What are you doing with a video camera by the bed, Tony?

TONY
Neville lent it to me. I was doing this short experimental film about my feet.

PAT
Have you been sleeping with anyone while I was away?

TONY
No!

PAT
Who's Deborah?

TONY
(*Worried*) W-why?

PAT
You just said her name in your sleep.

TONY
Come on, you know people say weird things in their sleep. You once ordered a pizza.

PAT
Have I ever said: 'Come here, Deborah, I'm enormous.'?
A pause, as Tony struggles to remember.

TONY
No . . . I don't remember you saying that. But I may have been asleep.
Pat bites her lip. She is genuinely upset.

TONY
She lives upstairs. She's really ugly.
Pat looks away, unconvinced. Tony leans across her playfully and picks up the video camera. He pretends to film her.

TONY
Come on. I'll make you a movie star – which film do you want to be in?
Pat softens into a grudging smile.

PAT
Get stuffed, Tony.

TONY
I don't know that one. I'm afraid it'll have to be *Danish Dentist on the Job.*
She gives him a facetious smile.

2. LIVING ROOM
The following evening. Dorothy is sharing the sofa with Tony. Deborah is in an armchair. The three of them are sitting dutifully, looking bored. The room is desperately untidy. Gary is colouring in a box with green felt pen on a large year planner chart with movable plastic blobs stuck on it.

GARY
So, any questions?
A pause. Nobody can be bothered to ask a question.

DEBORAH
(*Slightly croaky*) What are the grey blobs?

GARY
Hoovering.

DEBORAH
What's red?

GARY
(*Interested*) Ah, now . . .
Dorothy rolls her eyes. Gary points to the chart with a pointer.

GARY
Orangey-red is when I dust the top of the fridge, purply-red is when Tony has to scrape the phlegmy gunk off the floor behind the fridge.

TONY
What are all those black lines?

GARY
That's, er, you, Tony.

TONY
So a grey blob with a black line through it means that on that day I hoover the flat.
Gary looks at the chart.

GARY
(*Patronisingly*) You're being a tiny bit simplistic there, Tony, aren't you?

TONY
Am I?

GARY
A grey blob with a line through it on the second file here means that you hoover the flat to a basic standard. If it's on the first file here (*Indicating with pointer*) it means you have to go right to the edges and move the furniture. Okay?
Dorothy puts her hand up.

DOROTHY
Can I ask a question?

GARY
Of course.

DOROTHY
May I strangle you?

GARY
Any questions of a more . . . technical nature?

DOROTHY
What are all the big Ds?

GARY
That's D for Dorothy.

DOROTHY
I don't live here.
Gary consults a notebook.

GARY
Yes, but I've been totting up the number of times you've spent the night here over the last two months—
Dorothy smoulders with annoyance. Tony goes to the kitchen to get a drink.

GARY
—and it comes out at two point six nights a week, which, extrapolated over the year, means you should do nineteen per cent of the cleaning.
He smiles with self-satisfaction.

DOROTHY
I only stay because you beg me to.

GARY
That's not true.

DOROTHY
(*Wheedling imitation*) 'Harvey needs his pink anorak.'
Gary now looks embarrassed. Tony has returned with a can of lager.

DEBORAH
(*Smirking*) Who's Harvey, Gary?

GARY
Can we get on?

DOROTHY
If I only do three per cent of the cleaning will you let me off with some light foreplay?
The three of them snigger. Gary remains impassive.

GARY
(*Businesslike*) So, Deborah, communal areas in green, rule 6b operates every third Tuesday, as discussed—

DEBORAH
I don't feel very well, I'm going upstairs.
Deborah gets up to leave. So does Tony. Dorothy pulls a pillow over her head and curls up on the sofa. Gary holds his hands up, like a teacher whose pupils are hurrying away.

GARY
Um, before you all go, will you take your schedules with you. First starred cleaning day is tomorrow, remember. Thank you.
Tony follows Deborah out into the hall.

TONY
Are you okay?

DEBORAH
My head feels like it's got a dog running around inside it.

TONY
What kind of dog?

DEBORAH
(*Tetchy*) Any dog, Tony.

TONY
You need someone to look after you. Boyfriend, or something.
He leans against the wall, head on one side in a model-like pose.

DEBORAH
I'm saving myself for someone normal.
Deborah is too groggy to pay Tony much attention. He 'sensually' opens his shirt, ripping off the top two buttons.

TONY
So, you're going to be all right up there on your own?

DEBORAH
I've got someone coming round to look after me, actually.
She opens the door wearily and leaves.

TONY
Bang on the floor if you need help . . . (*Calling after her*) putting your legs in your pyjamas.
He shuts the door thoughtfully.

3. KITCHEN

Moments later. The kitchen is as squalid as the rest of the flat. Gary is cutting a large chunk of bread off a loaf. Tony saunters in from the hall.

GARY
(*Mouth full*) It's funny, isn't it? Women don't understand that when we do something, we like to do it properly.

TONY
Maybe we should clean a room a year. But, like, really well, you know?

GARY
No, I mean, that rota. That's not the kind of thing Germaine Greer could come up with, is it?
Tony grunts.

GARY
And I'm a bit of a feminist, as you know.
Tony sits down at the kitchen table.

GARY
Hey, who was your nice-looking friend last night?

TONY
Pat – yeah, we've been seeing each other about six months. She's lots of fun, bright.

GARY
Great.

TONY
Doesn't go barmy if I wear the same pants for five days.

GARY
That's important.

TONY
I'm giving her the elbow.

GARY
Oh. Why?

TONY
Well, when I'm, you know, doing it, I keep pretending I'm with Deborah.

GARY
So do I. What's the problem?

TONY
No, I mean all the time.

GARY
It'll pass. (*Lowering his voice*) In bed I used to pretend Dorothy was two synchronised swimmers.
Dorothy walks through the kitchen, sleepily.

DOROTHY
(*Yawning*) Must have been pretty crowded – I already had the Chippendales in there with me.
She goes through to the bedroom. Gary cranes his head after her, perturbed.

TONY
No, Deborah won't take me seriously if I don't get rid of Pat.

GARY
Who says she'll take you seriously then?

TONY
Well, the way I see it, I'm on site, and I've got great hair.

GARY
My old flatmate offered to pay her poll tax if she'd spend a weekend with him in Bournemouth.

TONY
No, Pat's got to go.

GARY
Oh, well, fair enough.

TONY
And I owe it to her to, you know, handle it tactfully.

GARY
What, get her drunk and tell her?

TONY
Yeah. No, I can't tell her to her face.

GARY
Painful, isn't it?

TONY
Yeah, I broke up with a girl in a restaurant once. You should have seen the way she stubbed out her cigarette.

GARY
How?

TONY
Here, on my eye. Hurt like buggery.

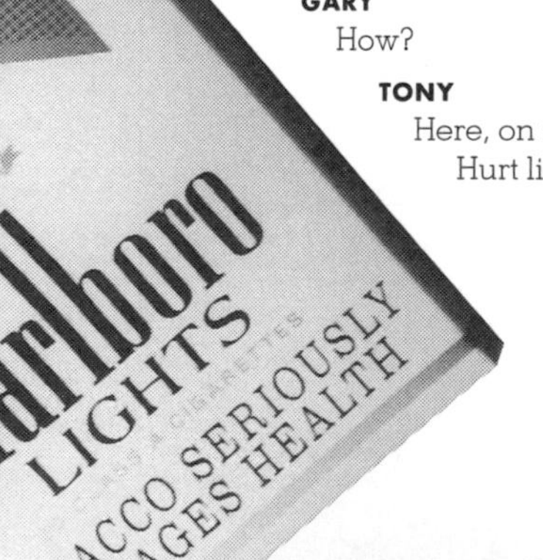

GARY
I sent a letter to this girl once. Got the envelopes muddled up – I asked her if she'd fix it for me to go bungy jumping, and I told Jimmy Savile we'd never click in bed.
Tony winces supportively.

GARY
(*Wistfully*) Still, he took it very well . . .

4. DIY SUPERSTORE

Gary is pushing a trolley full of cleaning materials down an aisle. He stops to examine a long-handled, flip-top dustpan. Gary plays with it, childishly fascinated. He looks around for some litter, but he can not find any. So he searches in a pocket and drops the contents – an old tissue, keys, a tube of sweets – on to the floor. He now tries to pick them up using the telescopic lever. Gary eventually succeeds, smiling hugely. Cut to the in-store café, which looks down on the shop floor. Dorothy and Tony are morosely drinking coffee.

DOROTHY
I'm sure this cleaning thing is just Gary getting his own back.

TONY
Why would he do that?

DOROTHY
Last week I told him it wasn't hygienic to leave his finger-nail clippings embedded in the soap.

TONY
Why's that?
Dorothy looks at Tony pityingly. They gaze wearily over in Gary's direction. Cut back to Gary, who is still playing with the dustpan. He has taken off one of his shoes and is trying to pick that up. Two children are now watching him.

DOROTHY'S VOICE-OVER
Sad, isn't it? How anyone can be enthralled by—

TONY'S VOICE-OVER
(*Enthralled*) Yes! He's done it!
Gary has finally managed to get his shoe inside the dustpan. He gives a modest shrug of triumph and walks towards the check-out. Cut to a little later: Tony and Dorothy, staring into their coffee cups.

TONY
(*Sympathetic*) Deborah's ill in bed.

DOROTHY
Oh, dear.

TONY
That means I'll have to clean the hall.

DOROTHY
You seemed keen on Deborah the other day.

TONY
Yeah, she's brilliant . . .

DOROTHY
Poor Deborah, living upstairs from Europe's biggest libido lake.

TONY
No, it's kind of like a fairytale: princess in the tower—

DOROTHY
Hideous trogs on the ground floor.
Dorothy looks bored and irritable.

DOROTHY
I suppose it won't be long before you're banging on her door with a smile on your face and a jar of Vick.

TONY
I'm not like that. Are you jealous of Deborah?

DOROTHY
(*Protesting too much*) No!

TONY
Sorry. I suppose Gary's all you want.

DOROTHY
Yes . . .
An uneasy pause.

DOROTHY
Well, of course, he's not all I want. What do you think I am, simple?

TONY
So why are you going out with him?
Dorothy's eye has been drawn to Gary, who is on the far side of the café, making his way towards them. He is laden with bags. As he catches sight of Dorothy and Tony, Gary smiles. He lifts up the bags, enthusiastic about his purchases.

DOROTHY'S VOICE-OVER
(*Tenderly*) Oh, I know, I forget how thoughtful and gentle he is sometimes . . .
As he comes nearer, still smiling, Gary – thoughtless and ungentle – knocks the coffee cup out of a customer's hand with the handle of a broom that is sticking out of a bag.

5. GARY'S FLAT: KITCHEN

That night Tony is on his own in the still chaotic kitchen. Heavy rock is coming out of a cassette player. He is hastily throwing together a meal. Onions are frying in the pan. The toaster pops up, revealing two undercooked beefburgers. Tony examines one, decides they are not quite done and presses the toaster again. He opens a large packet of hamburger buns and gets one out. It is encrusted with mould. Tony reluctantly throws it away and wonders what to do. He gets out a packet of thick-cut white bread, finds a pair of kitchen scissors and cuts two slices into two ragged circles. He puts it on a plate on an orange plastic tray. He adds a can of low-calorie Coke and a smeary milk bottle. Looking around for a flower to put in it, Tony makes do with pieces of tired lettuce. The telephone can just be heard above the music. Tony turns off the cassette and goes to answer the phone in the hall.

TONY
Hello? Pat.
He is instantly uneasy but adopts an upbeat voice. The phone is on a long lead so he can maintain his conversation while cooking.

TONY
Yeah, sorry, I've been . . . ill.
Receiver wedged at his ear, Tony skewers a beefburger with a fork and carries it over to the tray. He arranges it on the circular bread.

TONY
(*Cheerfully*) Depression. Yeah, I feel like I just want to . . . (*Scooping up the other beefburger*) sit in a dark room and . . . cry.
While listening to the phone, Tony is busily adding the onion and the other beefburger and slapping the bread on top.

TONY
No, I'll call you when I feel better.
He opens the oven and brings out an obscenely large baked potato, which he squeezes on to the plate. Then ketchup in a café-style plastic tomato. As a final flourish he folds up an old copy of the Sunday Sport and arranges it artistically on the tray. He picks up the tray and carries it out of the kitchen, still talking into the phone.

TONY
No, everything's fine. Bye.

6. DEBORAH'S FLAT

Deborah is lying on the sofa, asleep under a blanket. Sound of the door being kicked gently.

TONY
(*Muffled, through the door*) Deborah?
She remains fast asleep.

TONY
(*Again, from outside*) I've brought you a nutritious snack.
He comes in, managing to open the door with one hand. He carries the tray over and stands in front of Deborah.

TONY
Mm.
She does not stir. He points at the various items on the tray.

TONY
Beefburgers for protein, potato for energy, low-calorie drink for . . . (*Scrutinising the can*) E211 and phosphoric acid.
Another man – Stewart – appears unexpectedly from the kitchen. He is good looking and is also carrying a tray for Deborah. Baffled, he comes in and stands opposite Tony in front of the sofa. Tony's pitiful tray compares disastrously with Stewart's, which has on it a healthy, succulent meal plus orange juice, strawberries, stunning flowers and a folded copy of Private Eye. *They look at each other for a moment.*

TONY
Who are you?

STEWART
Stewart.

TONY
What do you think you're doing, Stewart?

STEWART
Deborah's not well, I've prepared her a meal—

TONY
I've prepared her a meal.

STEWART
(*Looking at Tony's tray*) She'll die if she eats that!

TONY
This is her favourite food, actually—
Deborah stirs, interrupting them, then goes quiet again.

STEWART
Oh, I've only known her a couple of days.

TONY
She's allergic to strawberries. Face comes up like an elephant seal.

STEWART
Sorry.

TONY
(*Innocently*) Where did you meet her – was it the drug-rehab centre?
Stewart's face clouds.

STEWART
No. She was queuing behind me in a shop.

TONY
She shouldn't have been out shopping on her own!
Deborah wakes up, opening her eyes. She is feverish and out-of-it. The men have both put their trays down where she can see them.

DEBORAH
This can't be me, my legs aren't tartan.

TONY
It's okay, Debs, it's a blanket.
She sees the two trays.

DEBORAH
I can't eat anything. (*Looking at Tony's tray*) Maybe just something from here.
Tony smiles at Stewart. Deborah picks up the large plastic tomato and tries to eat it. Tony gently takes it from Deborah and puts it on the tray. Deborah dozes off again.

TONY
(*Mock angry*) What have you done to her?

STEWART
No – it must be the fever.

TONY
Well, it's okay now, I can look after my own girlfriend.

STEWART
Oh, I didn't realise . . . How long have you been going out together?

TONY
Eight years.

STEWART
She didn't say.
Tony puts his arm on Stewart's shoulder and escorts him towards the door.

TONY
Look, she was the same last time she was doing cold turkey – slipped out to the supermarket in her dressing gown and came back with a fourteen-year-old shelf filler.

STEWART
Oh, my God.

TONY
I think it would be best if you just left, don't you?
He bundles a confused Stewart out of the door

and shuts it. He turns round, an innocent expression on his face.

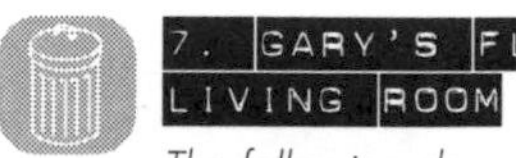

7. GARY'S FLAT: LIVING ROOM

The following day – Saturday afternoon. Gary's cleaning charts are still up. The room is only slightly cleaner. Dorothy is sitting in an armchair, flicking through a magazine, wearing a comedy-cleaner's scarf in her hair. She is surrounded by cleaning equipment.

GARY
(*Offscreen, calling through*) Dorothy is the stain under the sofa coming off?

DOROTHY
(*Not looking up*) Yes.

GARY
(*Offscreen*) Which is the most effective, do you reckon, Jif or Liquid Ajax?

DOROTHY
(*Idly, reading*) Well, I find that for really stubborn stains . . .

GARY
Yes?

DOROTHY
. . . you can't beat sitting down in an armchair reading a magazine.
Gary laughs as though she is joking. Dorothy chuckles to humour him.

8. KITCHEN

Moments later. Gary is scrubbing the mantelpiece. The kitchen has been transformed – immaculately clean, everything put away.

GARY
I don't know why housewives complain about cleaning, do you?

DOROTHY
(*Offscreen, subdued*) You really are an irritating man, aren't you.

GARY
Sorry?

DOROTHY
(*Offscreen*) I said 'No. It's so satisfying!'
Gary considers this for a moment, then resumes his scrubbing.

GARY
I hope our amusing banter isn't distracting you from what you're doing.
Dorothy turns a page audibly.

DOROTHY
(*Offscreen*) No.
Tony comes in from his bedroom. Gary stops him.

GARY
You'll have to take your shoes off.

TONY
I've just been in my bedroom.

GARY
Precisely.
Leaning on the fridge, Tony unlaces his trainers. He is looking around.

TONY
Where is everything?

GARY
I've reorganised storage arrangements.
Tony opens the fridge door. The fridge is now packed full of objects that had been on the mantelpiece: postcards, a candlestick, tin pans etc.

GARY
That's temporary.

TONY
No, that's a good idea, that – cold postcards.
Tony now has his shoes off, revealing dirty bare feet. Gary looks at them.

GARY
Okay, put your shoes back on.
Gary goes through into the living room.

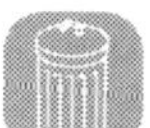

9. LIVING ROOM

As he walks into the room Gary finds Dorothy still reading the magazine.

GARY
What are you playing at?

DOROTHY
Well, I checked the plan, and I'm not down for anything for another six weeks.
Gary goes over and looks at the chart. He looks back at her seriously.

GARY
You've been tampering with my Sasko, haven't you?

DOROTHY
(*Wide-eyed*) No.

GARY
Where are they, Dorothy?

DOROTHY
You haven't cleaned for three years, and now you expect someone who doesn't even live here to scrub underneath your sofa.

GARY
Where are the letter Ds? Open out your pockets.

DOROTHY
I've eaten them.

GARY
(*Angrily looking at the chart*) Dorothy, I'm going to shut my eyes, and when I open them again, I want it back the way it was, okay?
Dorothy appears to look guilty. Gary shuts his eyes. Dorothy gets to her feet slowly, finds a table lighter and quietly sets fire to Gary's chart. Within seconds, the chart is alight. Gary still has his eyes shut.

GARY
Can I open them now?

10. HALL

Meanwhile, Tony is in the hall, sitting on a chair. He is half-heartedly dusting the bits of the chair he can reach without moving. He hears something in the communal hallway outside, gets to his feet.

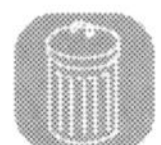

11. COMMUNAL HALLWAY

Deborah is bent over the stairs, trying to focus on the floor as she wipes it with a mop. She is less out-of-it than before but obviously still pathetically feverish.

TONY
Are you okay?

DEBORAH
Gary just came up and said I had to do the floor.

TONY
Didn't you tell him you weren't feeling too good?

DEBORAH
Yes, he said if my temperature goes above a hundred and two I could sit on the stairs for a bit.
Gary comes through, carrying in a metal waste-paper bin the still burning remains of his chart.

TONY
Something on fire, Gary?

GARY
(*Tight-lipped*) Bit of a disagreement with Dorothy, that's all.
Gary goes out of the front door. Tony looks into Deborah's strained face. He puts his arm round her 'caringly'.

TONY
You don't look well.

DEBORAH
No . . .

TONY
Why don't you come and lie down in my bedroom?

12. LIVING ROOM

Later that evening. Dorothy, Gary and Tony are sitting up at the table, eating their beefburgers in silence. The mood is chilly.

TONY
I think I should go and check on Deborah.

DOROTHY
Hasn't she suffered enough?

TONY
She needs looking after.

DOROTHY
You mean you want to shag her while she's drugged.
Tony looks hurt.

TONY
No, I'm serious about her.
Dorothy realises she has gone too far.

DOROTHY
Sorry.

GARY
(*Eating, perky again*) He must be serious to drop Pat. I wouldn't go after Deborah if I had a nice girlfriend.
Dorothy casually throws her glass of wine in Gary's face.

GARY
What did I say?!
As Gary mops himself down, Deborah comes through the door. She looks a little better but is still huddled in a blanket. Tony goes over quickly to help her into her seat.

DOROTHY
Wouldn't you rather be in bed, Deborah?

DEBORAH
No, I've been getting these nightmares – weird people bringing me trays of food.
Tony sits her down in a chair, propping her up like an invalid and sitting down close to her.

TONY
Yeah, you want to be down here where I can look at you—after you—we can.
Deborah is now completely swaddled in her blanket. The others carry on eating. Gary and Tony

smile at Deborah encouragingly. The front doorbell rings. Tony gets up to answer it.

13. COMMUNAL HALLWAY

Tony opens the door to Pat. She is angrily holding a piece of paper in her hand.

PAT
How could you do this?!
She comes into the hall. Tony looks towards the living room, anxiously.

PAT
Everyone at work read it.

TONY
What is it?

PAT
You should bloody know, you sent it.
She thrusts it at Tony, who takes the paper and scans it quickly.

TONY
Won't keep you a moment.
He abruptly goes back into his flat and shuts the door, leaving Pat standing there.

14. LIVING ROOM

Tony comes back in, poker-faced.

TONY
Can I have a quick word, Gary?
Gary gets to his feet.

DEBORAH
Who is it?

TONY
(*Quickly inventing*) It's the people next door. They want us to . . . push-start their car.

DOROTHY
They haven't got a car.
Tony hesitates painfully.

TONY
They've . . . stolen one.
Tony and Gary leave, suspiciously, shutting the door.

15. COMMUNAL HALLWAY

In the hallway together seconds later.

TONY
Did you send this?

GARY
You told me where she worked. I thought you wanted to chuck her.
Tony picks up the piece of paper.

TONY
Yeah, but not by fax.

GARY
Why? It's instant, modern, tactful—

TONY
(*Reading the fax*) 'For the attention of: Pat. I cannot go out with you any more. Sorry for any inconvenience. Fond regards, Tony.'
Tony looks up at Gary accusingly.

GARY
Which bit don't you like?

TONY
(*Ignoring him*) 'PS We have not been clicking in bed.' Even I'm not that insensitive.

GARY
I think you're overreacting—
There is banging on the door that interrupts him.

PAT
(*Shouting through angrily*) Can we talk, please, Tony?

TONY
Deborah mustn't see Pat. Get her to go upstairs.
Sighing, Gary turns and goes back into the living room. Tony opens the door and lets Pat in.

TONY
Look, I can explain about this.
Pat sighs, calming down. She follows Tony towards the bedroom.

16. LIVING ROOM

A moment later Gary is standing awkwardly in front of Deborah and Dorothy. He does not know what to say.

DEBORAH
Did you get the car going?

GARY
Yes. (*Pause*) Brrm brrm.
He laughs nervously. Then bends down to look at Deborah closely.

GARY
Deborah, you look *awful.*

DEBORAH
Thanks.

GARY
I think you should be in bed.
He attempts to move her.

DEBORAH
I've just got out of bed.

GARY
Yes, but I heard your phone ringing upstairs.

DEBORAH
I won't get to it in time.

GARY
You will if you run.
Deborah and Dorothy look at Gary oddly.

GARY
Okay, the truth is I'd like you to go because I have something important to tell Dorothy.
Deborah looks confused but gets up. Gary bundles her out of the room.

17. TONY'S BEDROOM

Shortly afterwards Tony and Pat are sitting on the bed, having a heart to heart. Tony is earnestly explaining.

TONY
So, what I said to Gary was, 'If only someone would get rid of that Cat.' Next door's cat. Cat, you see, it sounds like Pat . . .
Pat is looking at him sceptically.

TONY
Pat, cat. Pat, cat. Pat, cat – see, they sound similar . . .

PAT
Yes, you've made the point, Tony.
She softens, relenting.

PAT
You would tell me to my face if you wanted to split up?

TONY
Pat, I swear, it's the last thing I want to do.

18. LIVING ROOM

Meanwhile Gary is on the sofa with Dorothy, trying to win her over. Dorothy looks fed up with him and is fiddling with the remote control of the television.

GARY
So Tony sent her this fax saying he wanted to split up, and for some reason she thought it was insensitive—

DOROTHY
Funny, that.

GARY
Yes. (*Moving closer to her*) Sorry about earlier, you know.
He playfully jiggles Dorothy's lips with his finger. She is not amused.

DOROTHY
Gary, it's been a bad day. Can we do something that doesn't involve me listening to you?

GARY
Yeah, tell you what (*Leaning forward and picking up a video*) you'll like this.
He puts the video into the machine. They settle down to watch.

DOROTHY
(*Cheering up*) What is it?

GARY
Tony's made this video about his feet.
Dorothy's face falls. Gary activates the remote control.

19. HALL

Back in the hall Tony watches as Pat puts on her coat. There is an awkwardness between them.

PAT
Right. Well. See you soon.

TONY
Yup. Definitely.
They kiss uneasily.

PAT
I'll just say goodbye to the others . . .

TONY
(*Frowning*) Er . . .
He is too late to stop Pat going through the living-room door.

20. LIVING ROOM

Gary and Dorothy are watching the video intently. They look round as Pat enters.

GARY
(*Uneasily*) Hi.

PAT
I won't interrupt, I just came to . . .
She breaks off, distracted by what is on the TV screen. Tony has also entered the room and is looking apprehensive.

PAT
What's this?

TONY
You don't want to watch this—

GARY
No, it's good.

We switch point of view so that we are now watching the video on the TV screen. It is a shaky shot of Tony's foot, which he has painted to look like a face. He is wriggling his foot 'amusingly'.

GARY
See, that's funny that is.
The video cuts sharply. We now see Tony talking into a tripod-mounted camera, which is on a slight tilt. He is solemn but obviously hopelessly insincere.

TONY'S VOICE-OVER
(*On tape, to camera*) Pat, I've decided that it's better for us both if we, um, call it a day. I think it was Byron who said: (*Reading from a piece of paper, confused, stiffly*) 'There's not a joy the world can give like that it takes away.' I think that sums it up very well, don't you?
He accidentally knocks the camera, so it tilts more. He leans forward to straighten it.

TONY'S VOICE-OVER
(*On tape*) So . . . I'm biking you over this tape, Pat. (*Pause*) Hope you're well and everything.
He stares fixedly into the camera for a moment, then puts his thumb up to Pat, holding it there until he leans forward and turns off the camera. The screen cuts back to Tony's amusing foot. Everyone is looking at Tony for explanation. He hesitates, then turns to Pat.

TONY
Oh, no. This isn't you. This is *another* Pat.

SERIES THREE

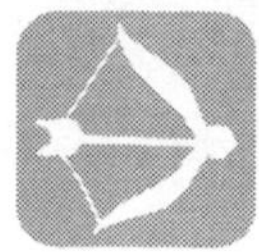

Lovers

ITV axed *MBB* after the second series. You could see why: viewing figures had fallen slightly, and the show desperately needed to be on after nine o'clock, which was when ITV preferred to play one of its three-dozen dramas about the police or hospitals.

The BBC is a good place for a sitcom, for several reasons. You get five minutes more than on commercial TV, minutes in which you can luxuriate a little more in the characters and get to know them. The BBC repeats most of its comedies, so you have two chances to be seen (or about eight, by now, in the case of most episodes of *Men Behaving Badly*). And the powers that be rarely interfere with the writing process, especially if you have a strong producer like Beryl. I have never had an amusing BBC memo telling me to reduce my use of the word 'bush', for example.

If the BBC had been in the business of sending memos they might have queried the seedy tone of the two scenes here in which Tony ogles Deborah while she is exercising. Of course, I like to think I was satirising leery behaviour, but so did Benny Hill. In this episode special praise must go to Neil Morrissey for jumping around in his pants incurring a massive loss of dignity. In fact, now I think about it, *Men Behaving Badly* has been one long exercise in humiliating Neil. Ah, well.

By now I was getting the hang of how to structure an episode: one Gary/Dorothy plot and one Tony/Deborah plot; one story primarily visual, the other a 'relationship' problem. End on Gary and Tony chatting on the sofa. But I never cracked catch-phrases. *'Allo 'Allo*, for example, had so many catch phrases it only left room for about ten minutes of new dialogue. After seven series the best we came up with was Tony's 'Sod you, then', which comes a very poor second to 'Stupid boy' or 'I do not believe it'.

1. THE CROWN

Early evening. The pub is as tatty as ever. Gary and Tony are sitting at the bar, idly drinking. Les is wiping tables.

TONY
What d'you reckon on troilism?

GARY
What, the little puppet chap?

TONY
No, that's Troy Tempest.

GARY
Oh, yeah.

TONY
No, three-in-a-bed sex, threesomes, you know.

GARY
(*Bluffing, laddish*) Oh, yeah. It's good that. I turned down an eightsome once.
Tony gives him a querying look.

GARY
It's like a threesome . . . plus a fivesome. Minivan full of birds, pulled up at the lights, one of them wound down the window and shouted out, 'Jump in and give us all a baby.'

TONY/GARY
He-heh!
They calm down.

TONY
(*Suddenly po-faced*) That's a bit forward.

GARY
Yeah. They were nuns, actually. I think they'd had one carafe too many at the Happy Eater.

TONY
Have you ever, like, done that role-playing in bed?

GARY
Yeah. I once asked Dorothy to dress up, pretend she was a nurse.

TONY
She is a nurse.

GARY
Yeah, it didn't really work. Then she asked me to dress up as a farmer and come and rescue her.

TONY
Are you sure she didn't say fireman?

GARY
Yeah, yeah, turns out she did. Little bit embarrassing. I've still got the smock, actually.
They take their pints and go over to sit down. There are magazines on the table and a hand-written sign, Reading Area.

GARY
How's your hunt for a job going?

TONY
Oh, I don't want to rush into anything.

GARY
It wouldn't hurt to pay me a bit of rent, though, mate.

TONY
(*Getting out wallet*) Oh, am I a couple of quid behind? I'll settle up now, what's the damage?

GARY
Um, six hundred and fifty-seven quid.
Tony peers into his nearly empty wallet, pretends to calculate if he has enough. He quietly puts it away.

TONY
Actually, I wouldn't mind hanging around the house for a bit. Deborah's been put on part-time working (*Leery*) so all day she's, like, upstairs, and I'm downstairs. It's like that programme . . .

GARY
Sad Horny Neighbour?

TONY
No, *Upstairs Downstairs*. And she's just split up with Denzil. I reckon if I make my move now I'll be in there.

GARY
Tony, face it, the only way you'll 'be in there' is if you're both marooned on a desert island, and she eats a poisonous berry, or a nut, which makes her deaf, blind, forgetful and desperate for sex.

TONY
So, sort of, fifty-fifty chance, then?

LES
(*Coming over*) What d'you think of my Reading Area? I'm moving up-market.

TONY
(*Looking around*) Why?
Tony has picked up a dog-eared women's magazine and is flicking through it. Les is wearing a disgusting 'smart' tie with his disgusting shirt.

LES
The brewery says I'm attracting too many old men with saliva hanging out of the sides of their mouths. I found the mags in a bin.
Tony is disgustedly holding open his magazine.

TONY
Yeah, there's an old fried egg squashed inside this one.

LES
Oh. I'll take that away then.
Les peels off the fried egg, puts the magazine back on the table and wanders back to the bar with the egg in his hand. Tony gingerly picks up the magazine he was reading.

TONY
It says in this survey that twelve per cent of all men have paid for sex.

GARY
Yeah, I have.

TONY
Did you tell Dorothy?

GARY
No, it was Dorothy.

TONY
What, role-playing?

GARY
No, she just . . . knew I was desperate.

TONY
(*Reading*) How many women have you slept with?
Gary immediately looks nervous.

GARY
Um. Oh. I couldn't say.

TONY
I think it's important that you get experience, isn't it, so you don't feel you've missed out.

GARY
(*Edgily*) How many have you had then?
Tony does a laddish laugh. Gary joins in. Then is serious again.

GARY
No, how many?

TONY
I don't know about you but I stopped counting when I reached fifty.

GARY
Fifty, yeah, nothing, kids' stuff.

TONY
I guess I'm a bit of a feminist: I worship women, each one of them.

GARY
But . . . not for very long, obviously.

TONY
No, well, there's two billion women out there. I mean, it's a race against time, isn't it?

2. GARY'S FLAT: HIS BEDROOM

Later that night. Gary is sitting up in bed, slightly drunk, brooding. Dorothy is lying next to him, reading a book. Gary is toying with her hair.

GARY
Dorothy?

DOROTHY
Yes.

GARY
You know sex?

DOROTHY
(*Reading*) Um, is that the one where two people bounce up and down together with everything flapping about?

GARY
Yes. Yes it is. You know how some people have lots of partners, and others possibly don't have quite so many?

DOROTHY
Mm. I love it when you tease me to breaking-point with your probing questions.

GARY
How many have you had?
Dorothy looks over at Gary.

DOROTHY
You should never ask a woman that, Gary.

GARY
Why?

DOROTHY
Because if she says a lot she's a slut, if she says not very many she's a frigid old witch.

GARY
So . . . which are you?
Dorothy puts her book down.

DOROTHY
Well, if I had to pigeonhole myself I'd say I was in the 'woman-with-disappointing-boyfriend' category.
Gary stares at Dorothy impassively.

DOROTHY
Gary, what's brought this on?

GARY
Oh, nothing, nothing.
Dorothy picks up her book again and starts to read. Still pensive, Gary picks up his book. He turns a page. It is a pop-up book. A model of the Eiffel Tower pops up. Gary tries to interest himself in it but is too preoccupied.

GARY
What would you say was average, though, for a woman?

DOROTHY
(*Reading*) Two hundred and thirty?

GARY
Don't be disgusting—

DOROTHY
(*Losing patience*) Gary, I think it's reasonable for people our age to have had perhaps a dozen partners, all right? Safe, loving encounters for discovery and pleasure.

GARY
Twelve? For a girl? (*Shuddering once, then again*) You've . . . what . . . twelve men have . . .

DOROTHY
I'm sorry if you're worried that you're sleeping with a trollop.

GARY
Doesn't worry me. I've been a bit of a trollop myself. No shortage of frantic humping in my life, I can tell you. If you laid all my lovers end to end they'd probably stretch to . . . (*Pointing vaguely*) the corner of Manor Road, no, further, probably to that tricky little roundabout next to the Texaco garage. I've broadcast my seed pretty thickly, I can tell you.

DOROTHY
Thank you for that traffic and farming update.

GARY
There've been times when I've fallen out of one bed and climbed straight into the next without even . . . stopping to retie my pyjama cord—

DOROTHY
Gary, do you want me to get in a taxi and go home, or are you just accidentally very annoying?

GARY
Sorry.

DOROTHY
What's the matter with you?
He puts his arm round Dorothy's shoulders. She frowns at him then snuggles up.

GARY
Sorry.

DOROTHY
If you've got some problem you want to share with me, you only have to say, you know that.

GARY
And you'll understand.

DOROTHY
Of course.
Gary still looks worried.

3. LIVING ROOM

The next day, mid-morning. Tony comes in from the kitchen, holding a bowl of cereal and mug of tea. He is slobbing around, enjoying the freedom of home life. He stops as he hears footsteps in Deborah's flat upstairs, listens, then relaxes when they stop. He carefully sits down in the armchair, putting the cereal bowl on one arm of the chair and his tea on the other. He looks for the remote control, which is just out of reach. He gets out of the chair, almost knocking over the tea, gets the zapper, sits down and turns on the TV, settling down to enjoy himself. He flicks between the channels, looking increasingly desperate.

VOICE-OVER
(Kilroy-*type presentation*) Anybody else think tall people have more fun? You at the end there—

VOICE-OVER
(*Geography programme, earnest foreign narration, haunting music*) The snake pounces and eats the toad whole. The toad escapes momentarily, leaving a leg inside its predator's mouth, but a maimed toad is no match for a hungry snake—

VOICE-OVER
(Pebble Mill-*type programme*) And now, music from Kenny Ball and His Jazz Band—

VOICE-OVER
(Sesame Street-*type programme, American voice*) D is for dopey. And donkey. And dry cleaning. And . . . hey, you do one. What's this?
Tony settles down to watch. He looks around for his cereal spoon but can not find it. He looks up at the TV.

TONY
Shop.

VOICE-OVER
(Sesame Street-*style*) Delicatessen.
He puts his hands down the sides of the armchair, under the cushions. This pulls the fabric on the arms, and the cereal and tea fall into his lap. He jumps up, yelping, brushing himself down. Tony hears a distant door slamming upstairs. He rushes around looking for something to tidy himself up with. Not finding anything, he rushes out into the hall anyway.

4. COMMUNAL HALLWAY

Tony emerges, looking anxiously at Deborah's door. He pretends to be interested in a pot plant. Deborah comes out of her flat, in a hurry. Tony turns round, trying to look casual yet sexy.

DEBORAH
Hi, Tony.

TONY
Deb!
She smiles fondly at him then notices the hideous, steaming stains down the front of his trousers: Readybrek and tea. Tony follows her eyes. He makes a noise and gesture of a small explosion at crotch level and laughs awkwardly. Deborah heads for the front door. She is carrying a sports bag.

TONY
I was sorry to hear that you've split up with Denzil.
He tuts insincerely.

DEBORAH
(*Sad*) Oh, it hadn't been going well, you know. It was just a question of who said it first.

TONY
So, who finally, you know—

DEBORAH
(*Snapping*) He did.

TONY
Do you want to come in and talk about it? I could help you piece together your shattered self-respect—

DEBORAH
No, I'm fine.

TONY
– make you feel less like some bloke's miserable plaything, something to be used and then discarded. Like a toy a child gets at Christmas and then quickly loses interest in.

DEBORAH
I feel better already.

TONY
No problem. Coffee?

DEBORAH
Thanks, but I've got my step class in a few minutes.

TONY
Oh, can I come?
Deborah thinks about it. She looks him over.

DEBORAH
All right. If you hurry.
They smile at each other. Tony dashes off.

5. GARY'S OFFICE

Later that morning. Gary is sitting at his desk, brooding. George, wearing a cardigan, is fiddling with a large old camera, polishing it.

GEORGE
It used to be my father's, actually. He once took pictures of us on the beach in Newquay. They came back with the horizon sort of on a slope, so after that we always called the place Wonquay.
George smiles hopefully in Gary's direction.

GARY
(*Preoccupied*) Mm, comical.

GEORGE
Then the same thing happened the following year in Weston-super-Mare. But we couldn't think of an amusing alternative.

GARY
(*Dully*) What about Weston-Sloping-Mare?

GEORGE
Oh, very good. It was a shame you weren't on holiday with us.

GARY
Yes, it's one of those tragedies.

GEORGE
The year after that we went to Cardigan.
Gary sighs, losing patience. George, still polishing his camera, persists.

GEORGE
But we forgot to take the camera. Funnily enough we also forgot to take our cardigans—

GARY
George, don't make me sit on your head until you're no longer able to speak.
George looks at Gary queryingly.

GEORGE
Are you all right? You've been very out of sorts.

GARY
Can I ask you a very personal question?

GEORGE
(*In a world of his own*) Can I have you up against a wall, Gary?
Gary just looks at George.

GEORGE
I need to take your picture for the security pass.

GARY
Oh, yes. (*Getting up*) The thing is – George, are you completely happy with the number of women you've been intimate with?

Gary goes and stands against a wall. Looking into his viewfinder, George positions himself.

GEORGE
Oh, yes. Marjorie's the only woman I've ever needed. We're as much in love today as we were when we first met in that fire-damaged Co-op.
Gary flashes a confused glance at George, who is lining up the shot.

GEORGE
Lovely. I'm a bit worried about getting your ears in.
Gary holds his ears flat against his head. George's comment has cheered him up.

GARY
George, can I say it's nice to meet a man who isn't ashamed to admit that his sexual experience is limited.

GEORGE
Oh, I wouldn't say limited. In my bachelor days I was like a rat up a drainpipe.
Gary looks depressed again.

GEORGE
Huge smile!
Gary, still holding his ears, continues to look depressed.

6. SPORTS CENTRE

Tony and Deborah are walking down a corridor. She is wearing smart aerobics gear, he is dressed in mud-encrusted shorts and a comedy rubber bleeding-heart T-shirt.

TONY
Isn't it kind of dumb, though, having to jump on and off a step?

DEBORAH
No dumber than football. At least in step classes we don't try to kick each other over.

TONY
We should try it, that might make it more interesting. Sorry about the gear. We've been barred from the launderette.

DEBORAH
Why?

TONY
They just . . . don't like us.

DEBORAH
I'd let you use my washing machine only I've had some upsetting experiences with men's pants in the past.
They have stopped outside the gym doors.

TONY
(*Tenderly*) Deborah, I hope doing sport together like this will, you know, bring us closer, allow us to spend some time together.

DEBORAH
(*Tenderly*) Yeah, you never know, do you.

TONY
I don't want you to think this is just a tacky excuse to see you sweating and bending over.

7. SPORTS CENTRE: GYM

Tony and Deborah enter. A few people are already chatting and warming up, others are coming in all the time. Tony will be one of only three men in the class. The steps are all laid out.

TONY
(*To Deborah, looking around*) Why don't I stand behind you so I can watch and learn?
He looks up to find that Deborah has gone over to talk to a friend. Tony stands on a step, trying it out. He looks up to find a pretty woman grinning flirtatiously at him. He playfully pretends to be surfing on his step. She is still smiling. He grins back. Showing off even more, Tony adopts a ridiculous Charles Atlas pose. He looks up to find that she was grinning at the hunky instructor standing behind him. The instructor has now gone over to talk to her. Tony tries to pass off his antics as genuine stretching exercises.
He 'casually' positions himself behind a young woman in a particularly high-cut leotard. He stands smugly behind her, but the woman sees a friend and goes over to say hello. Her place is taken by a fat bloke with a bad case of workman's bum. He spots Deborah standing next to another attractive woman in a skimpy leotard. He goes over to stand behind them, but a woman takes the place he wants.

TONY
Excuse me, I have to go there.

WOMAN
Why?

TONY
Um. I'm blind so I have to be near my friend (*Indicating Deborah*), in case I fall off my step.
The woman smiles uneasily and walks away. The instructor now claps his hands for attention and addresses the class. Tony looks happy with where he is standing.

INSTRUCTOR
Hello, everyone. Let's do it facing the other way for a change.
Everyone turns 180 degrees. Tony's face falls. He is now at the front, exposed to every gaze. The instructor turns on the throbbing music.

8. GARY'S OFFICE

George is photographing Anthea, who is posing, as nervously tremulous as ever. Gary is doing some paperwork, still fretting.

ANTHEA
Could I try one with me looking a little quizzical, you know?
Anthea puts her finger to her chin and adopts a quizzical expression. George snaps away.

GEORGE
Lovely.

ANTHEA
Perhaps something this way? (*Turning her face*) You probably noticed, this is my happy-go-lucky side.

GARY
Anthea, this is for a security pass. You're not going on the cover of Italian *Vogue*.

ANTHEA
I'm sorry it's just that it's not often I get photographed.

GEORGE
I thought you said you were in a picture in your local paper recently.

ANTHEA
Yes, but it was one of those satellite pictures, you know. You could see the whole of Dorking. And most of Guildford.

GARY
Can I ask you a very personal question, Anthea?

ANTHEA
(*Terrified*) Yes.

GARY
How many men have you been intimate with?

ANTHEA
Will this affect my Christmas bonus?
Gary sees Anthea's scared expression.

GARY
Oh, never mind, Anthea.
Anthea picks up her shorthand notebook and leaves. George drifts back to his desk, winding back the film in his camera.

GEORGE
You're letting this sex business get to you, aren't you?

GARY
Well, it's my generation. We're supposed to be at it night and day. Somebody my age should have got through enough condoms to . . . rubberise Ipswich.

GEORGE
Did you want to?

GARY
It's not a question of wanting to. It's my duty as a single guy living in the swinging city. I should have two hundred notches in my bed post. It's supposed to look like . . . a notchy thing. Tony's is incredibly notchy.

GEORGE
So how many notches have you got in yours?
Gary is quiet. A solemn moment.

GARY
Four.

GEORGE
Yes, it's not very many is it.

GARY
Oh, thanks a lot.

GEORGE
No, no, it doesn't matter.

GARY
It does! Women don't respect a man who's only had three partners.

GEORGE
You said four.

GARY
Well, three and a half.

GEORGE
What was the half?

GARY
Well, we were poised, you know, and she changed her mind.

GEORGE
Why?

GARY
She remembered she'd left her moped in a disabled-parking zone.
Gary puts his head in his hands. George looks sympathetic.

GEORGE
I think you should be proud. You've resisted trivial involvements, you've been faithful. That's rather beautiful.

GARY
No, I've just been turned down a lot.

GEORGE
Oh. Still, think of the time you've saved.

GARY
Saved for what?! Oh yes, that's always happening. 'Gary – Linda Evangelista and Winona Ryder are here to make love to you.' No, I'm sorry I'd rather save the time!

GEORGE
Shall I make us a nice cup of tea?

GARY
You don't understand, George. I've spent my life boasting about my conquests and the truth is I've probably slept with fewer people than Anthea!
They look at each other.

GARY
And, George, if you ever tell anyone, I'll make sure you're the first person to be strangled with his own cardigan.

9. THE CROWN

That night. The pub is slightly more crowded than usual. Les has been making an effort: each table has a plastic flower on it, stuck in a half-pint glass. Dorothy and Deborah are sitting at Les's Reading Area table, chatting and eating Twiglets. Gary and Tony are away at the bar, ordering more drinks. Deborah is flicking through the women's magazine containing the sex survey.

DEBORAH
I love these sex surveys.

DOROTHY
Except there's always something scary, like one man in eight has had sex with a fence.

DEBORAH
It's not something you want to boast about it, is it?

DOROTHY
Gary would. The way he tells it, before he met me he spent his life going from one pulsating super-model to the next. He doesn't go into much detail, he just uses phrases like: 'Well, I didn't have my trousers on much that week, as you can imagine,' then makes his lip go up on one side.
She mimics a moronic smirk.

DEBORAH
He's okay, though, isn't he?

DOROTHY
(*Eating a Twiglet*) Yeah, he's perfect. If you're going to have a boyfriend, you might as well have one you can mock mercilessly. What's happening between you and Tony?

DEBORAH
Oh, I'm getting over Denzil really. I'm just letting Tony entertain me.

DOROTHY
Wouldn't it be less painful to hire Cannon and Ball?

DEBORAH
Oh, I quite like him. He's a bit like a puppy. He sort of runs around me, yapping and sniffing at everything with a bottom.

DOROTHY
So are you going to give it a go?

DEBORAH
I don't know. Maybe I'll just wait and see if he manages to be a bit more . . . sensitive.
Tony and Gary return from the bar. They hand round the drinks.

TONY
(*To Deborah*) There you go, toots, get that down you.

GARY
Hello, ladies. What's got an attractive blonde head and comes in pints?

DOROTHY
Mm, we were just talking about sensitivity.

GARY
Tony's sensitive, aren't you, mate? You cried in *Driving Miss Daisy*.

DEBORAH
So what? Just because in here you qualify as sensitive if you can go for ten minutes without spitting or dribbling.

TONY
No, it's going up-market – cultural quiz, lovely new flowers, Beaujolais Nouveau tasting.

DOROTHY
(*Picking up handbill*) Mm, although I see Les is calling it a 'Frog Booze Bash'.

GARY
He's making an effort. The poor bloke's spent three weeks getting this quiz together, ploughing through reference books. I mean, it's not much fun being Les, you know.

DOROTHY
It can't be. Sorry.
Les has stepped on to an improvised stage. He is holding a microphone.

LES
(*Best MC's voice*) Good evening, ladies and gentlemen, welcome to the Crown on a typically festive session for our inaugural Quiz Night. You're in your teams already I trust—
Deborah and Tony exchange a coy smile. Gary and Dorothy (the other team) exchange a blank stare.

LES
—so let's have a clean, civilised contest with no use of encyclopaedias, pre-arranged signals or mobile phones. Pens and paper at the ready. (*Clearing throat*) In which film did Scandinavian beauty Britt Ekland first get her kit off?
Gary and Tony instantly write down their answers. The other teams in the pub also consult and scribble something down. Dorothy and Deborah can not believe it.

LES
Number two. You buy eight pints of Skol and half a dozen Pernod chasers out of a twenty-quid note. With your change, how many johnnies can you get out of the machine in the bog?
The boys frown earnestly as they work it out, then jot down an answer. Dorothy and Deborah look blank.

DOROTHY
Er, Gary?

GARY
What?

DOROTHY
(*Getting up*) I'm off home.

GARY
No, stay, please, it'll get easier.

LES
Number three. Mozart's famous concerto for flute and harp is in which key?
The contestants look confused. Dorothy looks pleasantly surprised. She sits down.

LES
Only joking. In which film did feisty American actress Demi Moore first get her kit off?
Heads go down again. Dorothy sits in her chair, looking irritable. Tony and Gary finish answering their question.

LES
Number four. Getting a little bit serious here: what is the average number of sexual partners a man aged thirty will have? No peeking in the magazine over there in the Reading Area.
Dorothy notices Gary's uneasy expression.

DOROTHY
What d'you reckon, Gary?

GARY
Oh, goodness. Fifty?

DOROTHY
Isn't that rather a lot?

GARY
Ooh, no. I should imagine that's about right.

DOROTHY
Not for you, it isn't.
Tony has heard this, seen Gary's tense expression. He intervenes, as though to stop a fight.

TONY
Leave it, mate. It's not worth it.

GARY
(*To Dorothy*) Sorry?

LES
Some serious conferring going on over there! First prize, remember, is all the pork scratchings you can eat in five minutes, so it's worth thinking hard.

DOROTHY
You haven't slept with fifty women.

GARY
(*Pausing, edgy*) Yes, I have.
Dorothy and Gary face each other off.

GARY
I can prove it.

DOROTHY
Okay.
Gary swallows hard.

10. GARY'S FLAT: LIVING ROOM

One morning later that week. Tony is rushing around the flat, glancing at his watch. He is wearing a new tracksuit. He touches a radiator: it is very hot. He checks that everything is set up correctly. He has pushed the living-room furniture back and laid down two gym mats. He looks at them, then moves them closer. The doorbell goes.

TONY
(*Calling out*) It's open!
He kicks the gym mats even closer and quickly adjusts his hair. Deborah comes in, wearing a sensible tracksuit. They smile, nervously flirtatious.

DEBORAH
Hi.

TONY
Hi.

DEBORAH
It's hot in here.

TONY
Yeah, the heating's stuck on. (*Rolling his eyes theatrically*) We'll both be down to our skimpy little underthings if we're not careful.
Tony tut-tuts. Deborah smiles at him indulgently.

DEBORAH
We could always open the windows.

TONY
No, we sealed them up. Wasps. (*Clapping hands*) Right, shall we start?

DEBORAH
It feels a bit peculiar, doing this here.

TONY
No, it's like getting drunk and mooning from the back of taxis. After a couple of times it seems like the most natural thing in the world.
Deborah nods, humouring him. Tony goes over to a pile of videos, flicking through them.

TONY
Who do you want: Cindy Crawford, Victoria Principal, Jaclyn Smith, Marie Helvin or Jerry Hall?

DEBORAH
I don't really m—

TONY
Linda Lusardi, Felicity Kendal, Angela Lansbury . . . (*Pausing and tossing it aside*) that was a mistake – Latoya Jackson or Cher?

DEBORAH
(*Lost for words*) You've . . . got the lot.

TONY
No, we're missing an early Raquel Welch, but Gary's got his feelers out.

DEBORAH
Who does the best exercises?

TONY
Oh, we don't exercise to them.

DEBORAH
I'll let you choose. It's a bit . . . sad, but you're obviously an expert.

TONY
Okay.
He puts a video in. It comes on, exercises already under way. Tony slips off his tracksuit, revealing laughably tiny shorts and a singlet. Deborah smiles wryly. They stand on their mats and gyrate in accordance with the video. We watch them for a moment going through their routine, po-facedly obeying the TV screen.

INSTRUCTOR'S VOICE-OVER
(*American woman*) Okay, reach up, really pump. Let's be careful not to hyper-extend. Hands on your thighs and: circle. Let's travel – we're on a journey . . .
After going through a run of particularly absurd, jiggly exercises, Tony looks visibly tired and bored. He starts sneaking looks across at Deborah, who is carrying on untroubled. She has turned away from Tony slightly so doesn't notice him going to the back of the room for a rest. He takes a swig of beer and thinks about lighting up a cigarette. Then his eyes fall on a camera. He thinks for a while then picks it up, preparing to photograph Deborah as she exercises.

INSTRUCTOR'S VOICE-OVER
That feels good, doesn't it? Tuck the thighs in. Release the ribs. Goo-ood. We're gonna pulse with the knees now . . .
To get a better angle, he leans against the radiator. It takes him several seconds to realise that his bare legs have been touching the scorching radiator. He leaps aside, trying to suppress a scream, jumping up and down with the pain. He finds himself jumping up and down again next to Deborah. She looks over at him and smiles. Tony manages to smile back.

11. GARY'S OFFICE

That morning. Gary, wearing the same look of anguish, is standing between Anthea and George. They are posing in front of George's tripod-mounted camera. Anthea and George are wearing elaborately smart clothes. George has Brylcreemed his hair. They hold fixed smiles for several seconds. The flash goes off.

GEORGE
There.

ANTHEA
Lovely.

GEORGE
I could get quite interested in photography, you know.

ANTHEA
Yes, it's a rather good hobby.

GEORGE
Mm, I had some very pleasant hours in the darkroom enlarging the pictures I took the other day.

ANTHEA
Oh, super.

GARY
Excuse me, does this office have to sound like an episode of *The Little House on the Prairie*?

ANTHEA
Well, we're a bit like them really. The little office on the prairie.

GARY
Don't be twee, Anthea.
Gary sits down at his desk. Behind him is a large blow-up of the picture of him pinning back his ears, looking amusingly glum. Behind George's desk is a picture taken of him looking simple. George rummages in a plastic bag and brings out a large, card-mounted blow-up.

GEORGE
I thought we could send this up to Head Office for them to put in the staff magazine.
George holds up the eccentric group photo: Anthea and Gary standing, holding George, who is lying horizontally, a 'Today'-like pose.

GARY
Yes, I can see the caption now: 'The London Office shortly before its staff were released into the community.' No more photography, please, George.

GEORGE
It's all work-related.

GARY
No, I've seen this before, you're entering that twilight world where you don't know if you're a clerk in a security company or Lord Lichfield.
Anthea approaches Gary's desk.

ANTHEA
I've made you a little case for your security pass.
She produces a small cloth pouch with GARY embroidered on it in bright lettering.

GARY
(*Genuine*) Thank you, Anthea.

ANTHEA
And I had lots of material left over so I've made us all Tupperware pouches.
She produces a much larger cloth pouch, also with GARY embroidered on it.

GARY
Thanks.

ANTHEA
Well, you've seemed a little down in the mouth recently.

GARY
(*Holding up his pouch, managing to smile*) Not any more.
Anthea leaves, satisfied. Gary's face slowly falls.

GARY
I'm depressed, George. I have to prove to Dorothy that I've had fifty lovers when I've only had three, and now I own a hand-embroidered Tupperware pouch.

GEORGE
I meant to ask, who were your three ladyfriends?
Gary looks dreamily nostalgic.

GARY
Ah. Pat, she was the first. It wasn't her real name, people just called her that because you only had to pat her, and she'd sleep with you.
George reacts.

GARY
No, she was nice. She had this little dimple in her chin. She used to keep a Trebor Mint in it – you know, like some people leave a cigarette behind their ear, to have later.
George nods, understanding.

GARY
Then there was Lesley. I suppose I took her for granted. She left me in the end, one Christmas. She'd bought me a cashmere coat and a gold tie-pin.

GEORGE
What did you buy her?

GARY
Tissues.

GEORGE
A box of tissues?

GARY
Of course a box. I'm not going to give her loose tissues, am I? I'm not peculiar. (*Sighing*) And Dorothy, obviously.

GEORGE
She's a lovely lady.

GARY
Yes. Yes she is.
Gary smiles fondly. George smiles fondly too, then.

GEORGE
Of course, she's quite scary—

GARY
(*Joining in*) Scary, yes. Exactly. So how am I going to prove to her that I'd need to hire the National Exhibition Centre to accommodate my ex-lovers, when in fact they'd all fit in one large cardboard box.

12. SWIMMING BATHS

That afternoon. A view of a swimming pool, people playing about. In the distance some lads are showing off their diving skills.

DEBORAH
(*Offscreen*) How did you get those marks?

TONY
(*Also offscreen*) What marks?

DEBORAH
(*Offscreen*) Those marks.

TONY
(*Offscreen*) Oh, they come and go.
Tony and Deborah walk into shot, wandering beside the pool in their swimming gear. Tony has livid red welts on the backs of his legs, the ribs of the radiator clearly visible.

TONY
I . . . rescued this cat from a burning warehouse when I was about seventeen. While I was doing it this radiator fell on the backs on my legs.

DEBORAH
Nasty . . .
Cut to a little later. Deborah is sitting at the edge of the pool, her feet in the water. She is happily watching people splashing about. The lads by the diving boards are showing off to her, doing impressive dives from a springboard. The hunkiest of them smiles at Deborah, who smiles back. Someone calls across to gain Deborah's attention. She looks. It is Tony, triumphantly pointing to some kids' water wings that he is slipping on his arms. He takes one wing off and stretches an arm over his head.
Deborah smiles back wanly, to encourage him. Tony notices her look away and watch admiringly as the hunky swimmer executes a perfect swallow dive from the top board. He emerges from the water, glistening, and smiles at Deborah. Cut to a minute later. Deborah, now in the pool, glances up at the top board. Switching point of view, we are on the top board, looking through Tony's eyes. We can see his pale hand, desperately gripping the rail.

TONY'S VOICE-OVER
(*Nervy*) Just don't do anything hasty.
From Tony's perspective we see Deborah miles below, waving.

TONY'S VOICE-OVER
Yeah, right, I'm supposed to wave back, am I?
The camera shakes and sways wildly as Tony obviously tries to wave back, before grabbing the bar again.

TONY'S VOICE-OVER
Maybe if I just stand here for long enough she'll get cold and have to go in to change. (*The hunky diver is swimming alongside Deborah, flirting*) Oh, well, here goes.
We pull back gradually from Tony's face. He looks increasingly ill with fright, his skin greener and his expression more forlorn. We cut back to Deborah, watching Tony. Her look of concern grows. She shuts her eyes, suddenly appalled . . .

13. GARY'S FLAT: KITCHEN

The following evening. Gary is washing up, not very well. Dorothy is doing something complicated to her hair, which is wrapped in silver foil.

GARY
Did I tell you? Tony vomited from the top diving board at the pool yesterday afternoon.

DOROTHY
Very Tony.

GARY
Apparently the filter mechanism exploded.

DOROTHY
I can imagine. What was he doing on the top board?

GARY
I think he was just . . . standing there and vomiting.

DOROTHY
Trying to impress Deborah presumably.

GARY
Yeah, he's tried everything. He even got all his hair cut off for her. Did he show you the little hair man he made out of his clippings?

DOROTHY
No. She quite likes him though, so he might as well keep trying. It can't get much worse

after humiliation, second-degree burns and high-altitude barfing.

GARY
He's giving sport one last go. They're playing squash together. Maybe then he'll give up trying to add her to his list of conquests.

DOROTHY
(*Teasing*) Oh, yes, weren't you supposed to be showing me evidence of your exhausting sexual career?

GARY
Okay.
He gets up and goes out, into the living room. Dorothy frowns, surprised.

DOROTHY
(*Calling after him*) I didn't mean it, Gary. I'm not sure I really want—

GARY
No, no, I don't want us to have any secrets from each other. Let's get it all out into the open.
He comes back in, carrying a large envelope. He gets out a pile of loose photos and some letters.

GARY
Right. Here are some snaps of various girlfriends of mine whose existence you seem to doubt. Here's one, look.
Gary hands Dorothy a photo. She sighs and looks at it.

GARY
That's Nicola, just after we met. I didn't have my trousers on much that week, as you can imagine.
He does his smirk. Dorothy hands the photo back. She looks subdued.

GARY
And this is me with . . . Tiffany. We're kind of horsing around there, you know how it is. She was (*Blowing out his cheeks in amazement, smug smile*) incredible, just don't get me on to Tiffany.

DOROTHY
What are you trying to prove?

GARY
Nothing. (*Rummaging in the bag*) Ah yes. This is a letter from someone called . . . Caroline—

DOROTHY
(*Glancing at it*) Carolyn.

GARY
Whatever. She was . . . part Cherokee. Interesting.

DOROTHY
Her spelling's as bad as yours.

GARY
Really? I think she spells (*Glancing over*) 'You are the most considerate and physically astonishing lover I've ever had' all right, doesn't she?
Dorothy lays the letter aside, upset.

DOROTHY
Gary. You never said anything about . . . This is really hurtful.

GARY
Well, fair's fair, Dorothy. You made out I was a liar and a pathetic guy!
He sees her sad face, goes and embraces her. They stand there, arms round each other. A tender moment. Gary looks pleased to have got away with it.

GARY
It's okay, it's all over.
There is the distant sound of the front door slamming. Gary's eyes snap open in sudden alarm. He glances anxiously towards the door and tries gently to free himself from Dorothy's arms. She hangs on to him. He stretches out towards the photos on the kitchen table but can not quite reach. The door into the flat shuts audibly. Panicking, still in Dorothy's embrace, Gary picks up a towel from the back of a chair and tries to throw it over the photos. It misses.

GARY
Dorothy, can I just—

DOROTHY
(*Strictly*) Hug me properly, Gary.
Tony comes in.

TONY
Hi, guys. Am I disturbing anything?

DOROTHY
No, we were just making up. (*Sniffing*) We've had a row.
Tony sees the photographs on the table. Gary is panicking.

TONY
What are you doing with my photographs?

GARY
No, no. My photographs.

TONY
You've been through my drawers. (*Leafing through photos*) Look, that's Mandy Sturgess. And Sarah.

GARY
(*Pause*) What, you went out with Mandy and Sarah too?
Tony and Dorothy stare at Gary.

GARY
No, no, look, they're mine. I'm in those two, with that gorgeous brunette, with her back to the camera.
Dorothy doesn't need to look.

DOROTHY
Gary, that's Anthea.
We glimpse the black-and-white photographs of Anthea (face obscured) and Gary together, fooling around.

DOROTHY
You made Anthea go out to the car park behind your office, and you used her for your own personal gain.

GARY
(*Losing confidence*) But, the letters—

DOROTHY
Yes, I think it was seeing the phrase 'Yours faithfully, George' crossed out to read, 'All my love, Moist Thighs' that set alarm bells ringing.

GARY
So, you knew.

DOROTHY
Gary. I always know.

14. LIVING ROOM

Later. Tony and Gary are sitting slumped on the sofa, boozing. Cans of lager litter the coffee table in front of them. They are vaguely watching the TV screen.

GARY
Turn it up, it's good this bit.

TONY
Won't it wake up Dorothy?

GARY
No, I recognise her breathing. On nights like this we could strap her to the front of the Gatwick Express, and she wouldn't wake up.
Tony turns up the volume. We can now hear that it is a fitness video: to background music, a young American woman is calling out instructions.

TONY/GARY
(*Simultaneously reciting, well-practised*) Mm-mm. We're raising our pelvises and tilting them, tilt that pelvis. You want to feel good now, don't you?
Tony turns down the volume. They watch on.

TONY
I tell you what's funny about sex. When I'm going out with someone, I always get the hots for my last-but-one girlfriend, do you know what I mean?

Gary looks impassive.

TONY
No, I don't suppose you do, do you?

GARY
Look, mate, in this day and age you've got to be pretty stupid to measure success by how many women you've slept with.

TONY
You're right. All credit to you. (*After a pause*) Mind you, that's how you were still measuring it earlier tonight, wasn't it?

GARY
Mm. How's Debs?

TONY
Brilliant.

GARY
Brilliant.

TONY
Yeah, things are hotting up nicely.

GARY
Squash all right, was it?

TONY
Yeah, great. We had to finish early, though. She broke her racket across the back of my neck.

GARY
Accidentally?

TONY
Yeah, must have been.

GARY
Yeah. It's good this bit.
Tony turns up the volume again. They both smile. They join in with the fitness instructor again.

GARY/TONY
Okay, then and stretch those thighs. /Yup, I know, it's hurting. Okay now, up on your haunches.

TONY/GARY
Let's make every day a buttock-firming day . . .
They watch on, sipping lager.

TONY/GARY
Classic.

SERIES THREE: EPISODE FIVE

Cleaning Lady

I hesitated before introducing a foreign character, in this case a pretty Portuguese cleaner, because there are about eighteen traps you can fall into including racism, accentism, cliché and failing to be amusing. But in the end, what the hell. I played it safe by making Elena perfectly intelligent. The real challenge is to create a character like Apu in *The Simpsons*, an earnest and not especially bright Asian shopkeeper, who works because he is funny. The least helpful thing a writer can do is make the 'minority' character the dull, sensible one, surrounded by the interesting, flawed ones who might be silly but make you laugh.

I knew Martin Clunes would be fantastic at wheedling desperation when he is begging Elena to be his friend. In fact the episode moves along nicely until for some reason I allowed it to drift into farce, which is not my favourite genre. In a long-running series it is tempting to try out all the forms – pastiche, flashback, the 'weekend-away' plot, the 'real-time' episode – if only to keep the viewers guessing.

This was another episode for which I could not find a proper ending. The show as broadcast ends on a fart gag, which I was not very happy about. In rehearsals Martin and Neil regularly offered fart gags, which I always turned down, worried they would alienate our more sensitive viewers, by which I suppose I mean my mother.

1. THE CROWN

Sunday lunchtime. Tony is 'working' behind the bar, Gary is sitting at a bar stool, drinking.

TONY
You know what I hate about this job?
Gary glances over at Les, who has come in, looking particularly unappetising.

GARY
Having to give Les a full body massage before you come on shift?

TONY
No.

GARY
All the hanging around in international airports? Ha.

TONY
No. The low status. Bar staff aren't respected in society.

GARY
Maybe that's because the work requires all the intelligence of . . . a biscuit.

TONY
No, that's why Deborah prefers Ray to me, because he's got a flashier job. She loves me, so subconsciously she, like, wants me to prove I'm worthy of her by bettering myself.

GARY
(*Nodding 'understandingly'*) That's bollocks, isn't it, Tony?
Les comes over.

LES
Ere, lads, did I tell you? My brother Les is coming back from Poland tomorrow.

TONY
Um, Les . . . your name's Les.

LES
Yeah, you know how when you're young you want everything your brother's got. Well, I wanted his name.

TONY
So what's your real name Les?

LES
Des.
Gary and Tony stare at him, taking this in.

LES
Yeah, Les went to watch Watford play Sparta Prague in 1983 and missed the coach home. It's a bit of a bugger to get back so he decided to stay in Czechoslovakia. He married this Czech girl, but she went off.

TONY
What, with a Czech bloke?

LES
No, she went off, you know, stopped looking after herself. It's sad to see a woman let herself go, isn't it?
They watch Les scratching himself, looking horribly gone to seed. He goes off to serve a customer.

TONY
I've got to get out of this place.

GARY
Yeah, you need a new career, mate.

TONY
I could be an escort.

GARY
What, one of those little cars?

TONY
No, those guys that get paid to take women out and sleep with them.

GARY
'Hello, Deborah, will you go out with me now, by the way I'm a prostitute.'

TONY
Yeah, maybe not.

GARY
What are you good at?

TONY
I can make my tongue into a tube, like that. Most men can't do that.
Tony stands there with his tongue stuck out, in a tube shape. Gary watches.

GARY
It's not really a career though, is it . . .?

2. GARY'S FLAT: LIVING ROOM

Later that day. The room is a mess: unwashed mugs on the coffee table and old socks lying around. Gary and Dorothy are slobbing around on the sofa, watching Italian soccer on Channel 4. Neither is paying much attention to Tony.

TONY
I could be an actor.

DOROTHY
Mm.

TONY
I've watched loads of telly, it's got to rub off. I could have a stall in *EastEnders*. (*Acting*) 'All right, me old china? D'you want to buy something from me stall?' Like that.

DOROTHY
I don't know why I come here. It's like being dead, except you have to watch football.

GARY
(*Drowsy, snuggling up*) It's nice. One day you'll look back on these lazy Sunday afternoons and—

DOROTHY
And burst into tears, yeah.

TONY
Or I could be a bull fighter. You get that nice costume that makes your shoulders go all wide.

GARY
Shut up, Tony.

DOROTHY
Why do Italian footballers look like male models whereas English footballers look like they've just come out of prison?

TONY
I could be a model.

DOROTHY
Shut up, Tony.

GARY
Pass the paper, Dorothy.
Dorothy leans over the side of the sofa. Her eyes glued to the TV, she runs her hand only cursorily across the carpet.

DOROTHY
I can't find it.
She looks down at her hand. The palm is now black with dirt. She holds it up to Gary.

DOROTHY
Look at that?!

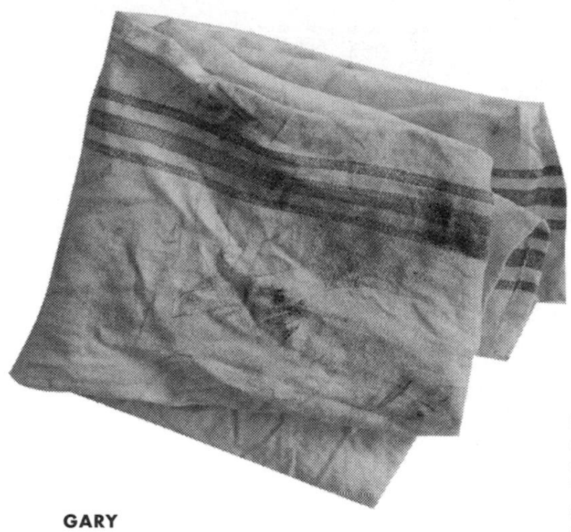

GARY
I hope you didn't get that on our carpet.

DOROTHY
It's from your carpet.

TONY
I could be an expert on . . . chickens.

DOROTHY/GARY
Tony, shut up./Shut up, Tony.

TONY
Sorry.
Dorothy goes into the kitchen to wash her hands.

GARY
(*Calling to her*) Tony was supposed to be cleaning the flat in lieu of rent.

TONY
I had to stop, the hoover exploded.

GARY
Only because you made it suck up half a pint of lager.

TONY
Well, I wanted to see if it would explode.
Dorothy comes back in. She holds up a spectacularly cruddy towel and tea cloth.

DOROTHY
Look at that.

GARY
I'm sorry, what's your point?

DOROTHY
I know you two have a reputation to maintain as the dirty men of Europe, but if you don't get a cleaner I'm not coming back here.
She sits down on the sofa.

GARY
I'm not exploiting some poor, dribbly, bent-over cleaner just to satisfy your bourgeois standards.

DOROTHY
I just don't want to be the first State Registered Nurse to catch plague from her boyfriend's carpet.

GARY
If you have a cleaner you have to feed them biscuits and listen to them droning on about whatever disease they're suffering from.

DOROTHY
Gary, there's hidden nastiness everywhere. I dread to think what's under this sofa.

GARY
Nothing.

DOROTHY
(*Getting up*) Let's have a look then. Get up.

GARY
Dorothy, I forbid you to touch this sofa.

DOROTHY
Tony, help me to turn this over.
Cowed by her no-nonsense expression, Tony gets up. Gary is perched on the back of the sofa, as though guarding it.

GARY
Tone, mate, I'll be very disappointed if you . . .
Dorothy and Tony turn the sofa over on to its back. Gary is catapulted out of sight.

GARY
(*Offscreen*) Right, now I'm very angry.
Where the carpet was covered by the sofa there is now a neat rectangle of filth and mess: a mouldy sandwich and plate of food, the inevitable pair of pants, playing cards, crushed cans of lager, a sex novel, possibly a dead mouse. Gary emerges from behind the sofa. The three of them stare at the mess.

GARY
All right, I'll get a cleaner.

3. KITCHEN

The following morning. Gary is sitting on his own at the kitchen table, smoking irritatedly. He adopts the hunch and voice of an ancient Fag-ash Lil cleaning lady.

GARY
'No, I've got a suppurating leg, I can't clean anything below waist height . . . Ooh, these

biscuits are a bit disappointing, haven't you got any hand baked by the Roux brothers . . .?'

The doorbell rings. Gary gets heavily to his feet and goes out.

GARY

'Hello, I'm your cleaner. Yes, I've had all me insides out. I'm hollow inside . . .'

4. COMMUNAL HALLWAY

Gary opens the front door. Standing outside is Elena, a very attractive and cheerful young Portuguese woman. Her English is rather broken. Gary's mouth drops open.

ELENA

Hello. Cleaner!

Gary is lost for words. He tries to say something but manages only to whimper.

ELENA

I am from the agency.

GARY

(*Weedily*) I'm Gary.

5. KITCHEN

A moment later Gary is leading Elena into the kitchen. He stares at her, gauche and tongue-tied. She smiles.

GARY

I'm sorry it's so dirty.

ELENA

I am here for cleaning!

GARY

Oh, plenty of time for that.

He continues to stare at her.

ELENA

Are you going to staring at me through all the day?

GARY

(*Still staring*) No, no. No, no. No.

He carries on ogling, hopelessly besotted.

ELENA

You have a squeegee mop? Yiff cream? Jellow dusters?

GARY

(*Flirting boyishly*) I'm getting a tiny hint of an accent here.

ELENA

I have come from Portugal to study English.

GARY

(*Gabbling*) Lovely country, gorgeous. Famous for its . . . port. And of course it's . . . ugal. Ha ha ha.

ELENA

You are silly.

GARY

What's your name?

ELENA

Elena da Silva.

GARY

(*Mimicking her*) Elena. Or Elena da Cleaner, as you now are. No, I'm being foolish.

Elena stares back stonily.

ELENA

And you are . . . Carry?

GARY

Gary.

ELENA

Carry.

GARY

Gary.

ELENA

(*Making an effort*) Carry.

Her pronunciation is no better. A pause.

GARY

Exactly! Brilliant!

ELENA

I am working to pay my English lessons.

GARY

(*Instantly*) I'll pay for them!

ELENA

You are silly!

Gary laughs manically.

GARY

(*Calming down*) Yes.

6. THE CROWN

That night. Tony is standing behind the bar with a broad, stupid smile on his face. Gary comes in.

TONY

(*Smiling*) Hey, guess what happened to me today?

GARY

You went bungee jumping with Douglas Hurd.

TONY

No.

GARY

You bought a pencil.

TONY

No. I got a job as a model. I went into this modelling agency, they liked how I looked and said they could easily find me work.

Tony beams as he serves Gary his pint of lager.

GARY
Tony, none of this happened, you're hysterical, and I'm going to have to slap you.

TONY
You're just jealous!

GARY
(*Jealous, tight-lipped*) I'm not, actually.

TONY
See, you said that in a jealous way.

GARY
(*Looking around the dismal pub*) This is a great job, you shouldn't throw it away.

TONY
You said it was a crappy job earning crappy wages serving crappy people in a crappy pub.

GARY
(*Pause*) Yes, but . . . it's regular.

TONY
I can't wait to tell Deborah, she'll be dead impressed. Mind you, it'll break Les's heart, he's kind of treated me like the son he never had.

GARY
He's got a son.

TONY
Yeah, but he treats me like the one he never had.

GARY
Oh, right.

TONY
Here, how was the cleaning lady?

GARY
(*Evasive*) Oh, fine, nothing special. I asked her to come round again tomorrow. I have to be at home anyway. You'll probably want to be out.

TONY
Why's she coming two days running?

GARY
She . . . missed a bit. (*Nodding*) Yup.
Tony looks up to see Les coming in with another man. They hang up their jackets.

TONY
Oh, no, here comes Les. I'd better tell him.

LES
Lads, this is my brother, Les.
Standing next to him, Les's brother is amusingly similar to Les himself: identical T-shirt, hair at similar mad angles, identical gormless expression.

TONY
Hi. Um, Les?

LES/LES'S BROTHER
Yes?

TONY
I've got some bad news . . .

LES
Me too: Les asked me for a job, and blood being thicker than water, especially ours, I said, yes, so I'm going to have to let you go.

TONY
Oh.

LES
What's your bad news, son?

TONY
Um, Gary?

GARY
Our young British tennis players still aren't breaking through at international level.
Tony nods in agreement.

7. GARY'S FLAT: LIVING ROOM

The next morning. Gary is with Elena, who is taking off her coat as though just arrived. The flat is now immaculately clean. Gary himself looks scrubbed and smart.

GARY
I've, er, had a bit of a tidy up so you won't tire yourself out. I hope that's all right.

ELENA
For sure. What do I do?
They look around. There is obviously nothing to do.

GARY
Well, I thought you could do a few seconds of gentle dusting – if that's acceptable, no obligation obviously! And then we could have some light refreshments.
He goes over to the table.

GARY
I've prepared some things for you. Hot coffee, Portuguese newspaper, some chocolates, crusty rolls . . .
He gives her a new duster. She starts to dust in the living room. Gary folds his arms and watches her.

ELENA
You don't have job?

GARY
Me? Oh, I go in when I like, you know. I'm the manager.

ELENA
It is a big company?

GARY
Yes, I have two hundred people working for me.
He nods vigorously, convincing himself.

ELENA
They don't need you?

GARY
No, I've told them both I'm at the dentist.

ELENA
Who both?

GARY
(*Improvising*) Both the hundreds of people.

ELENA
There, I have dust.

GARY
Okay, well done, let's have a bit of a sit-down, shall we?
Elena sits down.

GARY
So, do you have a boyfriend?

ELENA
Yes.

GARY
Oh.

ELENA
In Portugal.

GARY
Oh, good.

ELENA
You live here alone?

GARY
No, I share with another man. (*Winsomely offering her a chocolate*) Little choccy?

ELENA
Many English men are homosexuals, I think.

GARY
No, you're thinking of the French.
A silence. Gary shrugs and gives her a smile.

ELENA
So, you have a girlfriend?

GARY
No. No, I'm looking . . .

8. TRENDY RESTAURANT

A bistro-type place, dimly lit by candles in bottles. Several people are eating lunch. Deborah is walking among the tables, checking everyone is happy. She is obviously the manageress. Tony comes in, looking like a caricature of a male model: dark glasses, designer clothes, jacket slung over his shoulder. He walks in, vaguely looking around, doing a few cat-walk turns. Deborah watches him for a moment, sighs heavily and goes over.

TONY
Deb, hi!

DEBORAH
Hello, Tony.
He lifts up his sunglasses, trying to stick them in his hair. They keep falling back down on to his nose. He cavalierly throws them down on the table.

TONY
So, this is your new restaurant. It certainly is important to have a good job.

DEBORAH
Uh huh.

TONY
A person in a glamorous job really, you know, looks the business, doesn't he.
He tosses his hair and swings round again like a fashion model. His jacket knocks over all the crockery on one of the tables. Deborah clears it up.

DEBORAH
Tony, you know I'm going out with Ray. There's no point in you trying it on.

TONY
No, no, I came for a reason.

DEBORAH
What?

TONY
I've . . . started working as a model, and I might invite my new mates round. Do you do grub that'll appeal to, like, glamorously tall, good-looking and sophisticated people?

DEBORAH
No, we only cook for dwarves and lorry drivers.
Tony is tossing his hair again, not listening.

TONY
Great.

DEBORAH
Why are you doing that?

TONY
That's what we do, models, we kind of toss our hair.

DEBORAH
(*Genuine*) Congratulations, Tony. I'm glad you're doing well for yourself.

TONY
It's weird, isn't it? Only the other day I was saying you could be a model.

DEBORAH
(*Smiling, flattered*) Well . . .

TONY
I was just flattering you for the sake of it, but here I am actually doing it.

DEBORAH
(*Tetchy*) Have you actually worked yet?

TONY
I'm booked in for a few jobs, you know. Soon you probably won't be able to drive along without seeing my face on a billboard, all big.
He measures the width of his nose with his fingers and holds the inch-wide gap up to Deborah.

TONY
See that distance? That'll be about four-feet wide, that.

DEBORAH
(*Smiling politely*) I'd better go—

TONY
(*Not listening*) My face will be up there, as big as your living room, and you'll go: 'Ooh, look, there's Tony advertising aftershave, I wonder how he is?' And: 'Ooh, look, there's Tony again, I could be going out with him if I hadn't gone a bit mental and chosen that sonofabitch the estate agent—'

DEBORAH
(*Wearily*) I'm going out with Ray, I'm very happy.

TONY
I bet his face has never been as big as your living room.

DEBORAH
Tony, why don't you get a girlfriend of your own and stop bothering me?

TONY
I've got one.
This is obviously a lie, but Tony is pleased to notice a pang of jealousy on Deborah's face.

DEBORAH
Oh, well, I look forward to meeting her.

TONY
No problem, we'll probably drop round some time.

DEBORAH
Lovely.
She turns on her heels and heads off. Tony now realises he has a problem.

9. GARY'S FLAT: BATHROOM

The next morning. Through the slightly ajar door we can see Tony examining his face in the mirror. He is about to start a complicated face-cleansing ritual. There is a series of lotions laid out in front of him and a book of grooming tips for men propped up next to the mirror.

TONY
(*Reading*) 'To bring the blood to the surface, slap the face.'
Tony slaps his face heavily, first with one hand, then the other. Unseen by Tony, Dorothy appears in the doorway. She looks still half asleep. She stares at Tony slapping his face, until he overdoes it and hurts himself. Looking confused, Dorothy wanders back to bed.

TONY
(*To himself*) Okay, done that.
He picks up the first lotion and reads the back.

TONY
'Contains pulverised bark and extract of caribou's placenta for the hormonal balance a working face needs.' Brilliant!
He puts a tiny amount on some cotton wool and gingerly dabs it on to his face. Gary appears in the doorway. He watches Tony.

TONY
(*Reading on, frowning*) 'Apply the pre-cleansing emulsion, using a bold sweeping action going with the grain of the face.'
Tony attempts this and manages to knock a couple of the bottles off the shelf into the sink.

GARY
Little bit girly, isn't it?

TONY
I've got to look after my skin now. That's got caribou's placenta in it.

GARY
You'll want to send that back, then.

TONY
No, it's good – it treats your pores gently but firmly, caressing and cajoling them individually to maximum performance.
Gary is about to scoff but changes his mind.

GARY
Oh, does it?
Tony carries on his cleansing routine.
Gary tries to read the grooming book over Tony's shoulder.

GARY
Good for pulling birds, then.

TONY
Must be, it cost me twenty-eight quid. It's especially good for sensitive skins – bugger, it's gone in my eye.
Tony winces at the pain and, his eyes closed, reaches out for his towel. Instead he knocks over all the remaining bottles laid out on top of the shelf. Gary takes away the grooming book and leaves Tony to his agony.

10. KITCHEN

A moment later Gary comes in, reading the book with interest. He sits down at the kitchen table.

GARY
(*Reading*) 'How many times have you looked at another guy and thought, his partner's more attractive than mine – what's he got that I haven't? The answer is often, Grooming.'
Dorothy shuffles in behind Gary. Gary looks at his watch, realising it is late.

GARY
(*Reading*) 'Make your motto: I am, therefore I groom.' (*Nodding in agreement*) Okay.

DOROTHY
Too bad you already have a motto: 'Drink beer, talk drivel'.

GARY
(*Embarrassed*) Hello!
She sits down blearily at the table next to Gary.

DOROTHY
What's all that about?

GARY
It's Tony's book. You know me, I'm happy just to have a quick wash every Christmas, if I've got time.

DOROTHY
(*Rubbing her eyes*) You're being shifty, but I haven't got the energy to find out why.
Gary looks at his watch again.

GARY
Bye, then. See you at the end of the week.

DOROTHY
Oh, bye.
Dorothy slumps down on the table sleepily. Gary looks awkward.

GARY
No, I mean you have to go.

DOROTHY
I'm not on shift till midday. You don't mind if I spend the morning here, do you?
Dorothy rests her head on her arms. Gary looks agitated. He surreptitiously tips up her chair to make her leave. She looks up and glares at him. Gary tries to laugh it off.

GARY
I'm sorry, you can't stay here.

DOROTHY
Why not?

GARY
Um, the cleaner's coming round.

DOROTHY
So?

GARY
You don't want to be here with her, she's hideous. Drunk, terrible hair. (*Shuddering*) Great open sores all over her.

DOROTHY
Poor thing, perhaps I should take a look at them.

GARY
No, they're clearing up. The real problem is . . . she jabbers away, complete gibberish.

DOROTHY
It can't be worse than you. I'll stay in the bedroom.

GARY
No, she screams through the door. I'm going

to sack her today, that's why I have to be here. There'll be a scene. I'll probably have to strap her down until the agency come and take her away.

DOROTHY
(*Looking around*) Keep her, she's obviously good at her job.

GARY
Ah, but she steals things. I came back yesterday and found her stuffing her handbag full of pillows and shoes and things, tragic.
Tony comes in and hears all this. Gary brings over Dorothy's jacket and starts to put her arms into it. She frowns but complies.

GARY
I was just saying to Dorothy – I need to be on my own in the flat this morning.

TONY
I've got to be out anyway, I'm up for a couple of jobs.
Tony is frowning as he watches Gary bringing over Dorothy's shoes and handbag. He lays her shoes by her feet and puts her handbag round her. Dorothy sits there, looking at Gary as though he is mad. Gary smiles weakly

11. KITCHEN

The same day, a couple of hours later. Gary is sitting cross-legged on the kitchen table, watching Elena doing some very light dusting. He is obviously still infatuated with her and has been manically 'grooming' himself: his hair weirdly gelled, his skin glowing with unguents, possibly an obviously fake, streaky tan.

GARY
Good. Try another one: 'My boyfriend in Portugal is cheating on me.'

ELENA
My boyfriend in Portugal . . . was cheating on me. My boyfriend in Portugal has been cheating on me. My boyfriend in Portugal will be cheating on me.

GARY
Excellent. One more: 'I need a new boyfriend in England.'

ELENA
No, I am tired.
Elena is dusting the (already clean) mantelpiece. She turns over a photograph and looks at it.

ELENA
Who is the woman?
Gary comes over and looks at it.

GARY
(*Uneasy*) My sister.

ELENA
You are together in the bed.

GARY
Yes, we . . . grew up in a very small house.

ELENA
You are both naked.

GARY
Yes, it was small but very hot.
Gary moves closer to Elena.

ELENA
You are greasy and smelly, I think.

GARY
Sorry? Oh, yes, I've been using my new lotions.
She looks at the photograph again. We see it: Dorothy and Gary bare shouldered in bed.

ELENA
I think she is your girlfriend.

GARY
(*Looking again at the photo*) Oh, sorry, her. Yes. She died. Sad. (*Tutting*) Never mind, I'm over it now.
He smiles brightly, then becomes nervous.

GARY
Um, I have to go to work now, but I wondered if you'd come round tomorrow evening for some . . . special cleaning.

ELENA
(*Surprised*) But . . . it is clean!

GARY
No, the . . . chairs needs . . . rinsing. I'll pay you double. Please. Please.

ELENA
I think you are lonely and . . . what is the word?

GARY
Pathetic?

ELENA
Yes, pathetic.
Gary gazes at her devotedly.

ELENA
I need money so . . . okay.

GARY
Thanks.
The door is heard to slam. Gary reacts. He stands in front of Elena, pathetically trying to shield her. Tony comes in. He is wearing another set of trendy-model clothes. His sunglasses are now held in his hair by a piece of string.

TONY
Who's that?

GARY
There's nobody here.

ELENA
Hello.

GARY
Apart from her.

TONY
(*Enthusiastically*) Hel-lo. And you are . . .?

ELENA
I am Elena, the cleaning girl.
Tony looks a little put out.

GARY
(*Stiff smile, to Elena*) Excuse us one moment.
Seconds later Gary and Tony are standing outside in the hall, deep in a heated exchange.

12. HALL

TONY
(*Accusingly*) You said she looked like a cross between Winston Churchill and a bag of potatoes.

GARY
She's just . . . smartened herself up a bit.

TONY
You've been hiding her from me. You knew I needed cheering up.

GARY
You're supposed to be a successful model, you meet women all the time at your successful models' get-togethers.

TONY
I haven't had any work yet! They keep turning me down.
A pause. Tony looks genuinely depressed. He leans his head, a little theatrically, against the wall.

GARY
Oh, sorry about that.

TONY
Yeah, well.

GARY
Um, it's just that, well, I'm a bit . . . obsessed with Elena. The last couple of days I've woken up sweating.

TONY
That's just . . . because you're sweaty.

GARY
Yeah. Still, I just want to ask you this once, as a mate, not to ask her out.

TONY
I only want Deb, you know that.

GARY
Cheers.

TONY
Right.
They go through a bit of matey arm slapping. They are about to go back into the kitchen when Gary stops Tony, still apprehensive.

GARY
Only you've, you know, got a bit of a reputation.

TONY
Look, you're my best mate, best mates don't do that to best mates.

GARY
Okay.
They go back in. Elena is still there. She has started to wash a chair. Gary puts on his jacket.

GARY
(*To Elena*) Right, I'm off then. See you . . . soon.

ELENA
Bye-bye.
Gary looks at Tony suspiciously. Tony rolls his eyes to reassure Gary. Gary leaves. Tony and Elena smile at each other. A nervous pause.

TONY
Um, are you doing anything this afternoon?

13. TRENDY RESTAURANT

Later that day, back at Deborah's workplace. Tony and Elena have just arrived and are sitting down at a table.

ELENA
Why you want me here to teach you Portuguese?

TONY
(*Anxiously looking around for Deborah*) I learn faster in restaurants.

ELENA
I don't mind. You pay the lessons.
Tony spots Deborah, who heads over. He immediately leans romantically close to Elena.

ELENA
I told you, I have a boyfriend in Portugal. We have a big love.

TONY
(*Under his breath*) Yeah, can you not mention your big love for the next three minutes.
Deborah arrives. She sees how pretty Elena is and shows a hint of jealousy.

DEBORAH
Hello.

TONY
(*Casually*) Oh, hi. Deborah, this is my . . . special friend, Elena.

ELENA
Hello.

DEBORAH
Hi, there. Do you want me to get you a menu?

TONY
No, coffee'll do. (*To Elena*) Won't it, darling?

ELENA
Darling?!

TONY
(*Shy and goofy*) I still love it when you call me darling.

DEBORAH
Where did you meet?

TONY
Modelling.

ELENA
You lie!

TONY
(*Smiling manically*) She's brilliant! Great sense of humour. Sometimes we laugh so much we . . . burst.
Tony puts his arm round the back of Elena's chair. She looks vaguely behind her to see what is going on.

DEBORAH
So, you've managed to take time off from your busy modelling schedule, then?

TONY
Yeah. I've just heard I've got an assignment tomorrow. It pays the bills, you know.

DEBORAH
And, you're a model too, Elena?

ELENA
No, in this country I am cleaner.

TONY
(*Forced smile*) That is so Portuguese. Fantastically humorous.

ELENA
I don't understand.

TONY
(*To Elena*) Deborah's boyfriend at the moment is an estate agent.

ELENA
What is that?

TONY
They wear too much aftershave, they'd sell their own mother a holiday home in Chernobyl, and they go around nicking your girlfriend.
Deborah looks at Tony sharply.

DEBORAH
I'll get a waiter to bring you your coffees, shall I?
Deborah heads off. Tony, realising this may have backfired, winces as he watches Deborah go.

14. GARY'S FLAT: KITCHEN

Early morning. The kitchen is deserted.

TONY
(*Offscreen, shouting*) Oh, God, it's really bad!

GARY
(*Offscreen, shouting*) What!
Gary comes in from his bedroom via the hall. Tony emerges from his bedroom.

TONY
I've got a bloody spot.
Gary comes over.

GARY
Let's have a look.
Gary studies the rather large spot on Tony's nose.

TONY
My first modelling job, and I look like I'm balancing a bloody strawberry on my nose.

GARY
No, it's tiny. You'll be all right.

TONY
(*Reassured*) Yeah, supermodels get the odd spot all the time. Apparently, they just cover them up.

GARY
Yeah. A bucket should do in your case.
Tony looks panicky.

GARY
No, I'm only joking.
Tony seems reassured again.

GARY
A big saucepan would do just as well.

TONY
Oh, God—

GARY
I'm joking, I'm joking.
Gary goes over to the fridge. Tony stands in the middle of the room, gingerly fingering his spot. We can now see clearly that he is wearing a khaki nylon safari suit.

GARY
(*Serious, his back to Tony*) Um, Tone, mate, I don't want to be negative here, but what exactly are you wearing?
Gary turns round. Tony looks at Gary evenly, trying not to rise to the bait.

TONY
(*Patiently*) It's for work.

GARY
That'll be modelling the Action Man off-duty range, will it?

TONY
(*Subdued*) It's for a mail-order catalogue, I've got to start somewhere. I didn't take the piss out of you when you were being such a sad-arse about Elena.

GARY
We happen to have something intense and beautiful going actually.

TONY
That's not what she said when I took her out this afternoon.

GARY
You bastard.

TONY
At least I'm not a dork, that's what she called you.

GARY
(*Triumphant*) Ah, ah! She doesn't know the word 'dork'.

TONY
She looked it up in her dictionary. She couldn't decide between 'dork', 'jerk' and 'berk'.
It is Tony's turn to smirk. Gary's lower lip quivers just perceptibly.

15. LIVING ROOM

That evening. Gary is wearing lounge-lizard clothes, his hair slickly brushed etc. He has put on some soft music and is drifting around, humming suavely and rearranging the decor minutely. The doorbell goes. Gary leaves the room to answer it, and moments later comes back in with Elena. They look at each other.

ELENA
You are smart.

GARY
Thank you.

ELENA
Nice dress!

GARY
(*Unsure how to react*) Whatever.

ELENA
Okay – to clean.
She is about to head off into the kitchen.

GARY
(*Stopping her*) No, let's have a drink first. Tony's away for an overnight shoot. Um. I'm here, ha ha. (*Looking around*) Oh, look, here's a bottle of champagne!
On the table, under a cloth, is champagne in an ice bucket. Elena gives Gary an old-fashioned look.

GARY
(*With feigned spontaneity*) Tell you what, off the top of my head, feeling crazy, why don't we just drink this, forget about the cleaning and then go out for the evening?

ELENA
(*Sighing*) Gary, you are silly.

GARY
Oh, I don't know . . .
He goes over and starts to open the champagne. The front door is heard slamming. Gary freezes.

GARY
What?!

ELENA
Perhaps it is Tony?

GARY
(*Determined*) Right.
Gary considers, looks around and smiles at Elena, gently positioning her behind the open door. He picks up the champagne and goes to stand with her, listening out for Tony.

GARY
We'll sneak out quietly after he's come in.
Tony enters. He has an Elastoplast on his nose and is wearing another tacky mail-order-type suit. Obviously in a bad mood, he slams through the door, which hits Gary in the face, knocking him back. The bottle in Gary's hand simultaneously erupts, showering him in champagne. Tony closes the door to reveal the two of them hiding there, Gary in a bit of a state.

TONY
(*Stiff smile, to Elena*) Excuse us one moment.
Gary and Tony go out into the hall.

16. HALL

Seconds later Tony and Gary stand facing each other, Tony with a plaster on his nose, Gary holding a streaming nosebleed.

TONY
You can't go out with her. I've already introduced her to Deborah as my girlfriend.

GARY
So what?

TONY
I claimed her first.

GARY
She's not the bloody moon, you can't stick a flag on her and say she's yours. Anyway she's mine, I've stuck my flag in her.

TONY
That is so cheap.

GARY
You just used her to make another woman jealous. That isn't cheap?

TONY
No, it's traditional.

GARY
Oh, is it?

TONY
Yeah.
Both of them nursing their noses, they do a bit of pushing and shoving and laddish 'Yeah?' 'Yeah!' 'Yeah?' etc.

GARY
You shouldn't even be here. What's that on your nose?

TONY
My spot got worse. They sent me home. I'm packing in the modelling, I can't stand the humiliation.

GARY
(*Instantly laddishly supportive*) Oh, sorry, mate.

TONY
Cheers, appreciate it.
They pause, having lost their place in the argument.

GARY
Where was I . . .?

TONY
Er, 'That's so cheap . . . Deborah jealous . . . traditional . . . Yeah? . . . Yeah! . . . Yeah?'

GARY
(*Angry again*) Yeah. Anyway I'm taking her out tonight.

TONY
No way.

GARY
It's either that or I'm throwing you out of this flat.
Tony considers. They drift back to the door.

TONY
Okay. But don't come to me expecting to borrow my knobbly jumper again.
They go back into the living room.

17. LIVING ROOM

Elena is sitting down watching the television when moments later Gary returns, all smiles again.

GARY
Right, that's all cleared up. Shall we go?
Elena does not look overjoyed at the prospect but gets her coat anyway. Then the front door is heard slamming again. Gary and Tony stop and listen.

18. COMMUNAL HALLWAY

Outside in the hallway Dorothy and Deborah are coming in. They have had an early evening drink and are in party mood, laughing.

DEBORAH
I'd better not come in.

DOROTHY
Don't leave me alone with Gary and Tony. When they're together it's like 'Carry On, Vegetable' in there.

DEBORAH
I don't know. Tony might be with his new girlfriend.

DOROTHY
I thought you wanted him to find someone and leave you in peace.

DEBORAH
Well, it's like your virginity – you hate it when it's there, but you kind of miss it when it's gone.
Dorothy raps on the door.

Tony and Gary have been listening to this. Gary looks agitated.

TONY
(*Tutting, amused*) So, Dorothy's home, and you're with Elena.

GARY
Tell you what, why don't you pretend Elena's your girlfriend?
Gary hurriedly takes off his jacket, tries to look casual by ruffling his hair and clothes etc.

TONY
Oh, that suits you fine now, doesn't it?

GARY
Come on, you said she was your girlfriend. You're a lovely couple.
Gary hastily positions Tony and Elena together. He looks at them, then goes back and puts their arms round each other.

GARY
See – lovely.

ELENA
What about me?!

GARY
I'm sorry?

ELENA
(*Raised voice*) I am not the girlfriend of anybody here! Who thinks so? Who?!
Another knock at the door. A pause.

GARY
Excuse us for one moment.
They lead her out into the hallway.

20. HALLWAY/BATHROOM

Smiling at Elena, they put her in the bathroom.

ELENA
Why are you putting me here?

GARY
Um. Tony – think of something.
Tony shuts the bathroom door with him and Elena inside. Gary hurries to the main door and opens it, all smiles.

GARY
Ah, good evening. How pleasant!

DOROTHY
What took you so long?

GARY
I was in the bathroom – not that there's anything going on in the bathroom!
Deborah and Dorothy look at him queryingly. He steers them into the living room.

21. LIVING ROOM

GARY
Tell you what – you two sit down here, stretch your legs out. I'll bring you . . . something to nibble.

DOROTHY
Why are you wearing that and acting oddly – what have you done to your nose? And what's that bottle of champagne doing over there?
A pause while Gary tries to think of an answer.

GARY
Perhaps I should start with the nose question.

DOROTHY
Go on then.

GARY
(*Pausing*) I ran upstairs too quickly.

DEBORAH
You haven't got any stairs.

GARY
(*Pausing*) No . . . Excuse me.
He backs out of the room, smiling.

22. BATHROOM

Gary joins Tony and Elena in the bathroom. Tony is standing in the bath, explaining. Elena is frowning at him as though he is mad.

TONY
But for that really deep-down dirt, I find you can't beat a lotion with bark in it, um, dabbed on to a sponge. Then, using a bold sweeping action—
The door opens, and Gary comes in, shutting the door behind him. The three of them stand there. A pause.

GARY
Okay, to sum up: I've told Dorothy the cleaner is a grouchy old witch, and I've sacked her anyway. I've told Elena that Dorothy is an old, dead girlfriend. Deborah thinks Elena is your girlfriend—

ELENA
(*Indignant*) It's not true. I tell her!

GARY
—but Elena won't go along with that. We could make a run for it—
There is a rap on the door.

GARY
—but the three of us are trapped in the bathroom . . .
The door opens. Dorothy and Deborah are standing there. A long awkward pause.

TONY
Deb, this is my girlfriend's twin sister, she's the new cleaner.
Dorothy, Deborah and Elena look sceptically at Tony.

TONY
No?

23. LIVING ROOM

Late that evening. We pan across the coffee table, Tony's grooming book and lotions are laid out on the coffee table, surrounded by empty lager cans and half-eaten kebabs. The flat is starting to look a mess again. Gary and Tony are sitting on the sofa, slightly drunk, vaguely watching the television. Gary's face is smeared in one of Tony's lotions. Tony has on a mud pack, which looks odd with the pink Elastoplast stuck over his nose.

GARY
See, the thing about your Mediterranean bird is her urges have been brought gently to the boil by the hot sun and basically left to simmer and bubble away over many years.

TONY
Yeah, right.

GARY
Whereas your average British girl—

TONY
Bless her!

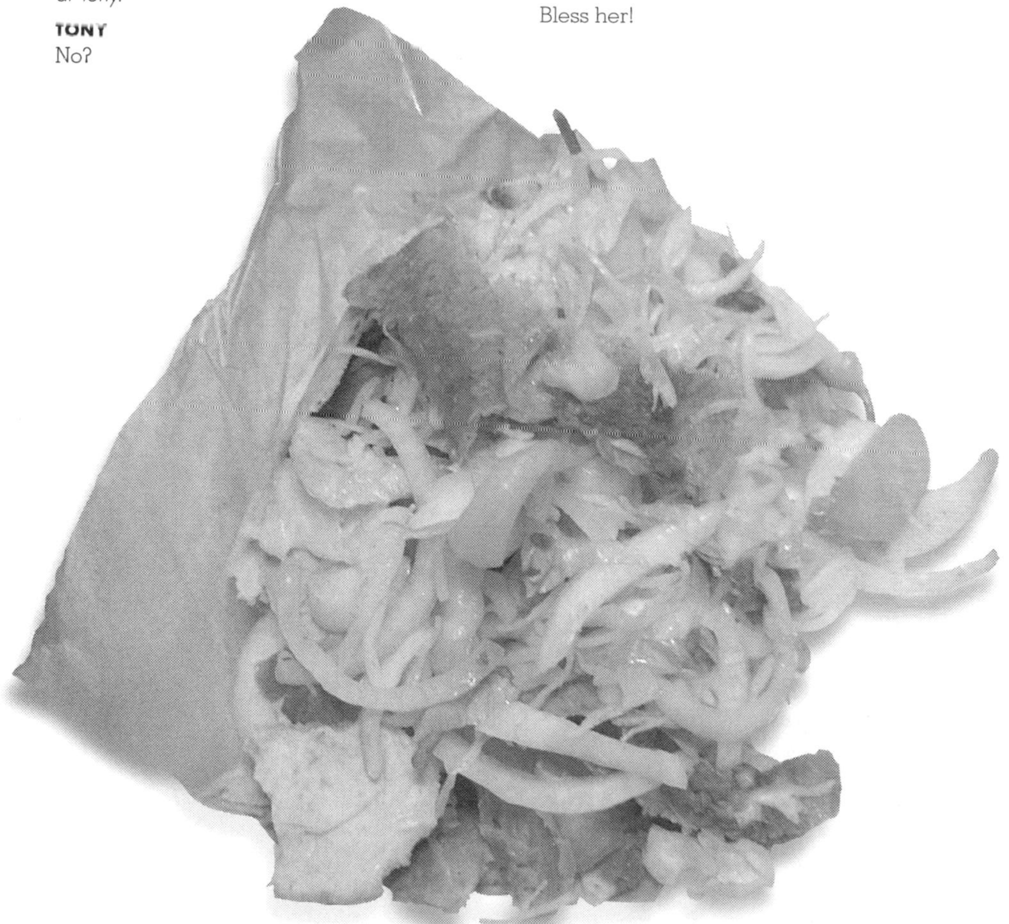

GARY
Bless her! She's spent most of her life under woolly tights and a couple of thick cardigans, shivering at bus stops. She's in no fit state to abandon herself sexually.
A pause. They look around.

TONY
I prefer the flat dirty, don't you? It's more natural.

GARY
Yeah. I mean, there's a lot of nonsense talked about dirt.

TONY
Yeah, what is it anyway? It's just, like, bits of dark stuff, isn't it?

GARY
Yeah. So, which supermodel would you go out with if you had the chance?

TONY
It's got to be Cindy Crawford, hasn't it.

GARY
Cindy, yeah. Why?

TONY
Well, because years ago I went out with this girl called Barbie, so I've always wanted a Cindy to, you know, complete the set.
Gary nods, understanding completely.

GARY
So, what job are you going to look for now?

TONY
I thought maybe . . . dentist.

GARY
Yeah, good choice.

TONY
Apparently you get all these free samples, so you never run out of toothpaste, ever.

GARY
Great.
A pause.

TONY
What's the biggest spot you ever had?

GARY
My first date, I was sixteen. This huge sod came up on my forehead. I tried to cover it up by pulling my hair down over it, but it wasn't long enough, so I cut some hair off the back of my head and glued it to my forehead.

TONY
Uh-huh. I once got two big ones, one on each cheek, they were there for ages. My Mum used to call them the Two Ronnies.

They nod. Another pause. They sit there in their face packs.

TONY
Hey, it's great, isn't it? At the end of a pretty difficult day, you can't beat a serious, free-ranging conversation, can you . . .
They carry on watching the television and drinking lager.

SERIES THREE: EPISODE SIX

MARRIAGE

In this episode Gary gets very drunk and proposes to Dorothy, who tortures him by pretending to take him at his word. Writing about marriage is a dodgy business. You don't want to suggest that the little ladies are all sitting at home just waiting to be proposed to (although there is a fantastic episode of *Friends*, in which all three women end up in wedding dresses, based unapologetically on the assumption that deep down all women love the idea of marriage).

How rude should we allow the show to be? In this episode we discussed snappier alternatives to Gary's coy line in scene three: 'Maybe he's gigantic in the trouser department.' Martin Clunes suggested, 'Maybe he's got a huge cock.' Beryl felt cock left a nasty taste in the mouth, so we compromised on knob. I like to think Shakespeare had similar discussions.

This episode contains a typical office plot. In America Anthea and George would be there to mop up middle-aged viewers, on the grounds that people only watch programmes containing someone like them. If I was even more pretentious than I already am I would suggest that the office scenes operate like the Greek chorus, reflecting on the events of the main plot.

1. GARY'S FLAT: LIVING ROOM

Early evening. Tony and Deborah sit slumped, glumly listening to an irritatingly buoyant Gary. They have drunk their way through a bottle and a half of wine. Gary is referring to a clipboard.

GARY
Item fifteen: the house dustbin.
Deborah groans with boredom.

GARY
It's been stolen again, so as part of the Neighbourhood Watch scheme I'll be wiring up the handles of the new one with a powerful electric charge. Any objections?

DEBORAH
(*Wearily*) It'll electrocute the dustmen.

GARY
Well, you can't make an omelette without breaking eggs.
Deborah narrows her eyes at Gary, who concedes her point.

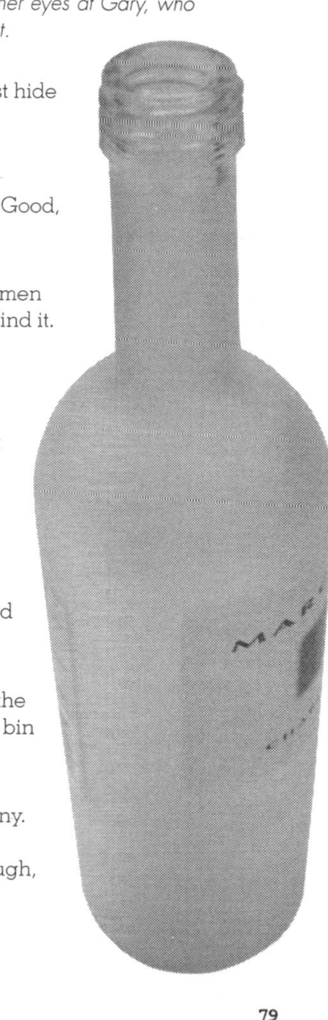

TONY
Why don't we just hide the bin?

GARY
(*Nodding encouragement*) Good, Tony.

DEBORAH
Because the dustmen won't be able to find it.

GARY
Yes, stupid, Tony.

TONY
We could leave a note saying it's in the shed under a blanket or something.

GARY
Now that is a good idea.

DEBORAH
People will read the note and find the bin and steal it.

GARY
Yes, very poor, Tony. You hadn't really thought that through, had you.

DEBORAH
Yeah. And, Tony, will you stop going through my rubbish, please.

TONY
I haven't!

DEBORAH
I saw you. Where did you get that old blouse you're wearing?

TONY
It's a shirt.
Deborah reaches over and pulls out the collar of the shirt that he is wearing under his jumper. The large, frilly ruff of a very feminine blouse cascades down his front.

TONY
I like it, it's got your smell on it.

DEBORAH
It's not mine, I saw the old Greek woman next door putting it into our dustbin.
Tony looks down at the blouse queasily.

GARY
(*To Deborah*) Can I just apologise for that gross invasion of privacy.

DEBORAH
You were with him, you went off with a ball of my hair.

GARY
Harmless souvenir, I don't see the problem.

TONY
I wanted to find out what makes you tick. I can't believe you prefer (*Mocking*) Ray to me.

DEBORAH
Oh, not again, Tony.

TONY
He's got a face like an arse!

GARY
(*Swigging wine*) That's true actually.

TONY
A horrible arse. Not even a nice arse.

DEBORAH
(*Defensive*) Ray and I have . . . stimulating conversations.

TONY
I can do conversations, try me: girl vicars, global heating—

DEBORAH
Warming.

TONY
Whatever, vans, anything. Come on, ask me a subject.
He does a laddish come-and-get-me gesture. Deborah has already got up to go.

DEBORAH
If you were a tenth as interesting as Ray I'd have gone out with you months ago.
Tony reacts. Gary also gets to his feet, swallowing yet more wine. Deborah heads for the door.

GARY
I'd better go, too. Dorothy's waiting for me.

TONY
Where?

GARY
Italian restaurant. Pasta Pig. We're having a candlelit supper. (*Tottering a little as he exits*) We couldn't get anywhere with proper lighting.
Deborah also leaves. Tony is now sitting there alone.

TONY
(*Calling after them*) Come on, ask me anything . . . What about VAT on fuel, eh? Shocking. That Channel Tunnel, eh, that's a hell of a hole. Eh? What d'you reckon . . .?
The door slams shut. Tony looks forlorn.

2. ITALIAN RESTAURANT

Later that night. A romantic, candlelit restaurant. Dorothy and Gary are finishing off their meal. Dorothy is pleasantly merry but appears sober compared to Gary, who is being an amusing drunk.

GARY
You know what I like about you, Dorothy?

DOROTHY
My car.

GARY
No.

DOROTHY
The fact that I'm prepared to sleep with you?

GARY
Oh . . . close enough.

DOROTHY
Maybe we should get home before your breath

catches light, and the whole place goes up in flames.

GARY
No, seriously, you're very lovely, um . . .

DOROTHY
Dorothy—

GARY
I know, I know, it was a dramatic pause. We've been through a lot together in, in . . .

DOROTHY
In galoshes?

GARY
No, in . . .

DOROTHY
In-spector Morse?

GARY
No, in four years.
They both smile nostalgically.

DOROTHY
Mm. Remember what my Mum said when I first introduced you?

GARY
'What's wrong with his ears?'

DOROTHY
No, after that.

GARY
'I'll eat my hat if you're still together at Christmas.'
Gary gives an amused grunt.

DOROTHY
You shouldn't have made her.

GARY
A deal's a deal. It was only a small hat.
He reaches out and clasps Dorothy's hands romantically.

GARY
Do you know what I like about you, Dorothy?

DOROTHY
You've already done that one.

GARY
Oh, fine.
Gary looks around at the other tables, where various couples are gazing into each other's eyes. One pair is in an especially close clinch.

GARY
Oh! Isn't it romantic? I think he's proposing. Ah.

DOROTHY
No, they've had their hands in each other's trousers since the melon balls.

GARY
(*Ignoring her*) Lovely. What's your opinion of marriage? (*With a supreme effort*) Are you in favour or do you regard it as an institution that has outstayed its welcome in contemporary society?
He blows out his cheeks.

DOROTHY
Why, are you going to propose to me?
Gary smiles. He looks around, drunkenly considering.

GARY
Yeah, why not?

DOROTHY
(*Casually, sipping her wine*) Go on then, do it properly. On your knees.
Gary sniggers but gets down on his knees. As he does so he hits his chin on the table. He winces. Dorothy remains seated. Only Gary's head is visible above the table, and even this is obscured by an empty bottle of wine. Dorothy moves it to one side.

DOROTHY
Oh, there you are.

GARY
Will you marry me, Dorothy?

DOROTHY
(*Smiling, casual*) Of course I will, Gary. (*Turning to the menu*) What do you want for pudding – lemon tart or profiteroles?
As Dorothy studies the menu, we focus on the still kneeling Gary. He now has a slightly perturbed look on his face.

3. GARY'S FLAT: KITCHEN

Early the next morning. Gary is sitting at the kitchen table, looking hung over and glassy eyed with alarm. Tony comes in, going over to the fridge.

TONY
How was Pasta Pig?

GARY
Fantastic. Dorothy opted for the linguini with squid in its own ink, I plumped for the proposal of marriage.

TONY
(*Smiling*) You asked Dorothy to marry you? (*Smile fading*) Why?
Tony bangs a cereal bowl down on the table. The noise jars Gary's hangover. He tries to cope.

GARY
Because I'd drunk a litre and a half of Chianti,

and at that point I was very much in love with Dorothy

TONY
Ah, nice—

GARY
I was also very much in love with the waiter, my country and my cutlery. I probably would have proposed to Yasser Arafat if he'd been sitting there.
Tony sits down next to Gary.

TONY
You could do worse than Dorothy, you know.

GARY
I don't want to get married. I've got my whole life ahead of me. Except what I've had already, obviously.

TONY
Can I be your best man? In my speech I can tell that story about when you fell asleep on the train and those kids stapled your hair to the curtains.

GARY
(*Snapping*) It wasn't funny! I lost about half a pound of hair.

TONY
All right! My problems are just as bad as yours.

GARY
Oh, I didn't realise your girlfriend was lying in your bed wondering whether to walk down the aisle to the Wedding March or 'Funky Weekend' by the Stylistics.

TONY
Listen, the woman I love has just told me that I'm a tenth as interesting as the estate agent she's going out with.

GARY
(*Serious, shuddering*) Sorry, that must be horrible.

TONY
Why does she enjoy being with him more than me?

GARY
Maybe he's gigantic in the trouser department.
Tony just looks at Gary.

TONY
I wonder what they talk about that's so interesting.

GARY
Find out, bug her flat.
Tony's eyes light up.

GARY
We're going to be testing a few listening devices at work. I'll bring you one back.

TONY
Brilliant! Hang on, though, I mean, I'd be hearing exactly what goes on in a young woman's home. Let's think about the, like, moral issues here.
A brief pause as they consider.

GARY/TONY
Seems okay./Yep, no moral problems there.
Gary gets to his feet.

GARY
So, what am I going to do about Dorothy?

TONY
You just have to tell her it was the drink talking. It must have happened before.

GARY
No, actually.

TONY
What about last week, you promised her you'd shoot your parents and buy her a Toyota Land-Cruiser with your inheritance.

GARY
Oh, I think she knew I was getting carried away.

TONY
Or you could pretend she misheard you. Like, instead of, 'Will you marry me?', you said, 'Will you merry me?'

GARY
Will you merry me?

TONY
Yeah, like, will you make me merry.
A pause, while the idiocy of this sinks in.

GARY
Thanks, Tony.

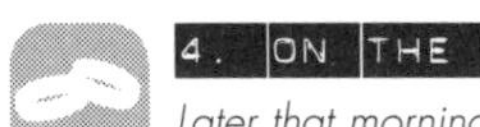

4. ON THE BUS

Later that morning. Gary is sitting next to Dorothy, who is looking out of the window cheerfully. Gary seems nervous.

GARY
Dorothy, maybe we should talk about last night. I, um, said a few things.

DOROTHY
Mm.

GARY
(*Laughing*) I'd certainly had a lot to drink!

DOROTHY
Yes, I can still picture you down on your knees asking me to marry you.

GARY
Oh, did I do that?

DOROTHY
I think it was a mistake to spend the rest of the meal there, but that's probably just me being conventional.

GARY
My knees had gone.
Dorothy looks out of the window again.

GARY
Yes, most of the things I said were wise and fascinating, as always, but some were probably, in the light of day, you know, if we're honest, um, foolish.

DOROTHY
Which was it when you asked the taxi driver if he wanted a cuddle?

GARY
Um, foolish. (*Tutting*) Me asking you to marry me, eh?
He tuts again, as though amused by the suggestion. Dorothy now notices how edgy he is. She smiles mischievously to herself, clearly only interested in goading Gary.

DOROTHY
Well, you obviously wouldn't do that without meaning it.

GARY
Ooh, God, no. Because it's . . . a big step, isn't it?
She turns to him and begins to play with his hair 'romantically'.

DOROTHY
You'd been bottling it up, hadn't you?
Gary smiles uneasily.

DOROTHY
How long had you been planning to ask me?

GARY
Ooh, let me see. Goodness, seconds, ha ha!
She laughs along with him.

DOROTHY
No, seriously. Was there one moment when you suddenly knew you wanted to spend the rest of your life with me, or did it sort of sneak up on you like a delicious dream?

A pause while Gary thinks of an answer.

GARY
(*Tight-lipped, subdued*) Delicious dream.

DOROTHY
Sorry?

GARY
(*Loud*) Delicious dream!

DOROTHY
Me too.

GARY
We'll probably have all sorts of doubts and end up breaking it off.

DOROTHY
No, you've made that commitment. This is it. We're on our way.

GARY
You've never actually said you wanted to get married before.

DOROTHY
(*Pulling his cheek affectionately*) You just don't understand us girls, do you?

GARY
Maybe we should have a, a—

DOROTHY
Full church wedding with organ? Yes, I think so.

GARY
No, a cooling-off period while we think about it.

DOROTHY
No. We need to do it straight away. You've made me very happy.
She clasps his hand and turns away, gazing out of the window with a sly grin on her face. Gary looks dismayed.

5. GARY'S OFFICE

Later. George is wandering around the office, watering plants. Gary is at his desk, unpacking various surveillance products.

GEORGE
Oh, I think marriage is tremendous.

GARY
I hate to be cynical, George, but you think Croydon's tremendous.

GEORGE
No, all that sharing.

GARY
I hate sharing. It's what people do when they can't afford one each of something.

He puts one of the surveillance kits on George's desk.

GEORGE
You know what I think you need for a successful marriage?

GARY
I don't know – enormous nipples?

GEORGE
(*Frowning*) No.

GARY
Two desperate people with nothing else to look forward to?

GEORGE
No, plenty of things in common.

GARY
So what did you and Marjorie have in common? No, don't tell me: you're both members of the North Surrey Association for the Almost Completely Barmy. Anyway, I'm not getting married, it's simply a ghastly misunderstanding.
Gary presses a button on his desk intercom and speaks into it.

GARY
Anthea, will you come in, please? Oh, and can you bring your fez and a large pair of pliers.
Anthea puts her head round the door, looking confused and alarmed.

GARY
Ignore me, it was a feeble attempt to cheer myself up.
She comes in.

ANTHEA
Why what's the matter?

GARY
Anthea, why haven't you ever been married?

ANTHEA
Well, I was asked once but . . .
She starts to look tearful.

GEORGE
Don't talk about it if you don't want to.

ANTHEA
No, no, I'm fine.
Gary and George dutifully look concerned.

GARY
(*Gently*) What happened?

ANTHEA
Well, I said yes, but then he just started being beastly, and I realised it wouldn't work out.

GARY
What did he do?

ANTHEA
Well he kept . . . pulling my hair.

GEORGE
Pulling your hair?

ANTHEA
Yes. It was all over by the time we went to big school.
Gary sighs and gets up. George goes back to his desk. Anthea does not know what she has said wrong.

GARY
Right, I'd like you to take that bugging device home and test it around the house.

GEORGE
Why?

GARY
Because we sell security equipment. I apologise if this wasn't pointed out when you joined the company twenty-three years ago. (*Handing Anthea a box*) It says these can be installed and operated by a child, so I immediately thought of you two.
Anthea leaves. George sees Gary still looking morose.

GEORGE
(*To Gary*) What is it you don't like about marriage?
Gary is suddenly serious.

GARY
It's not marriage as such. It's no secret that I've written to Michelle Pfeiffer in her Malibu home offering sole use of my loins in perpetuity. But settling down, I mean it's – it's such a grown-up thing to do, isn't it?

GEORGE
But, you are a grown-up.

That evening Gary is sitting alone in the room, watching television. He has a large Shreddies packet wedged upside down on his head. In another attempt to recapture his youth he is wearing a T-shirt from the early 1980s. The front door is heard to shut. Tony comes in. Gary bounces around like a teenager.

GARY
Hey, Tone, let's play.

TONY
It's a bit juvenile, isn't it?

GARY
No, we're larking around, you know, single guys, having fun.
Gary hands Tony a huge pile of scrunched-up balls of newspaper and goes to stand in the middle of the room. During the conversation that follows Tony throws the paper balls at the cereal packet on Gary's head, trying to knock it off.

TONY
So, have you told Dorothy you only proposed because you were out of your head?

GARY
No, I . . . forgot.

TONY
But, you're not just going to drift into this, are you? Cos, you've got to ask yourself: will I be happy with this person until we're, like, divorced?

GARY
No, I'll tell her. Anyway, thanks for being a mate, you know.

TONY
Well, I don't want to have to find a new place.

GARY
Oh, right.

TONY
You don't think she's, like, having you on.

GARY
Tony, I think I know Dorothy well enough by now to know when she's being sincere. Okay?
Gary smiles smugly. Tony stops throwing paper. They sit down and talk.

GARY
I need to put her off me. It's like chucking someone – it's sort of easier if you make it look like it's their decision. I wonder if there's something I can do to make me less attractive?
He stands there looking goofy and unattractive in his cereal packet.

TONY
No, I don't think so.
Gary looks at Tony evenly. The front door is heard to slam. Gary takes off his 'hat'.

TONY
Hey, that's Deborah, did you get that bug thing?

GARY
Yeah.
He goes to a bag and gets it out.

TONY
What do I have to do with it?

GARY
Hide it in her flat.

TONY
How am I going to do that? I mean, she's not stupid. I'm going to have to come up with something pretty ingenious.

7. DEBORAH'S FLAT

Later. Deborah is sitting watching the television. There is a knock at the door. She gets up and opens it. It is Tony, carrying a sickly potted daffodil.

TONY
Hello! I've brought you a plant!

DEBORAH
Why, Tony?

TONY
To apologise.

DEBORAH
What for?

TONY
Um, I'm not sure, I've usually done something I need to apologise for.
He holds up the plant, keeping one hand over the soil, where he has obviously put the eaves dropping device. Deborah looks damningly at the sorry specimen.

TONY
It's a special variety that looks like it's about to die. They all look like that. It was actually very expensive.

DEBORAH
It's an old daffodil. I saw you just now digging it out of the garden.
Tony just gazes back at her shiftily.

DEBORAH
(*Sighing*) I'll get a plate to put it on—
Tony stops her before she can head off.

TONY
No, it's okay, I've brought my own.
He gets a plate out of his pocket, puts the pot on it and looks around for a place for it.

TONY
Let's see, why don't I put it here, where you can see it and think of me?
He puts it on the coffee table in front of the sofa, near the TV. We see him checking that the bug is still in the soil.

DEBORAH
Tony, how many times do I have to tell you: I'm going out with Ray.

TONY
Yeah, how is Mr Fascinating and his Amazing Prize-winning Conversations?

DEBORAH
Do you have to be such a child?

TONY
(*Serious*) Sorry. All I'm saying is—

DEBORAH
(*Sympathetically*) What?

TONY
—he's got a face like an arse!

DEBORAH
Look, I don't claim he's perfect, I don't even agree with most of what he says. I mean, okay, he's an estate agent and a bit superficial but . . .

TONY
But what?

DEBORAH
But . . . somehow he's still more interesting than you.
Tony frowns.

8. GARY'S OFFICE

The next day. Gary and George are at their desks. Gary turns on a cassette player.

GARY
Home tests, listening-device number one. (*Briskly making notes*) Ease of use, out of ten?

GEORGE
Twelve.

GARY
Out of ten.

GEORGE
Eight.
On the tape, a general buzz of women's conversation is heard.

GARY
Location of device?

GEORGE
The living room. I positioned the device at approximately nineteen hundred hours and made my getaway on foot through our kitchen facility—

GARY
Yes, thank you, George.
Wild, cackling laughter is suddenly heard on the tape.

GARY
Who's that?

GEORGE
Marjorie. That was what first attracted me: her infectious laughter.

GARY
(*Under his breath*) Love really is blind.

GEORGE
She was having some of her friends round from the Choral Society. You may remember, Marjorie invited you to their workshop production of *Starlight Express*, but you were unexpectedly taken hostage by your next-door neighbour at the last minute.

GARY
Ah, yes.
Gary looks contemplative. He paces around.

GARY
George, when you married Marjorie did you stop wanting to go to bed with other women?

GEORGE
Ooh, no, not entirely. I am only human.

GARY
(*After studying him*) Yes, I suppose you are.

GEORGE
Marjorie and I made an agreement: if either of us has an unfaithful thought we have to put ten pence in a box.

GARY
You've been married for four hundred years – must have cost you a bit.

GEORGE
Fifty pence. I was doing quite well until 1982 then I came over all funny in the Post Office, and before I knew where I was I'd blown thirty pence.

GARY
What about Marjorie?

GEORGE
Two-thousand three-hundred and eighty-six pounds. I suppose I should say something to her, but it has paid for five caravanning holidays.
On George's tape there is a sudden blast of 'The Age of Aquarius', sung by a reedy chorus of mainly middle-aged women.

GEORGE
(*Shouting over the noise*) They're rehearsing *Hair*. It's their next production, perhaps you'd like to come and see it?

GARY
(*Also shouting*) Ah, unfortunately, I've got an . . . evening class, Yoga for Middle Managers.
Gary turns down the volume. 'The Age of Aquarius' continues thinly in the background.

GARY
Um, George, the object of the exercise was to see if the product could record a normal conversation, not a dozen mad middle-aged women screeching about 'letting the sunshine in'.
He presses the intercom button on his desk.

GARY
Anthea, will you bring your tape in, please?
On the tape machine there is a sudden clunk, and the singers come to an abrupt, ragged end.

GARY
What happened there?

GEORGE
Um, one of the ladies got overexcited and started to take her clothes off. It's happened before. Marjorie was standing by with a blanket.
Anthea has entered, carrying her cassette. Gary puts it into the machine and goes back to his notes.

GARY
Home tests, listening-device number two. Ease of use out of ten, Anthea?

ANTHEA
Oh, yes.
Gary tosses aside his pen in despair. They listen to the tape, which is silent.

GARY
I can't hear anything. Where did you put it?

ANTHEA
I left it on the sideboard, where it wouldn't get lost.

GARY
It's a covert audio-surveillance device, Anthea. It's not very covert if it's on the sideboard, is it?

ANTHEA
I didn't think it mattered, I was on my own, reading. My sister's away for the week at a moped rally in Norfolk.

GARY
So you've recorded the sound of yourself, sitting down reading?
There is the sound of a tiny cough

ANTHEA
That was me coughing.
Gary walks away in despair.

ANTHEA
I think I cough again in about twenty minutes.
George and Anthea stand by the cassette player, listening with expectant faces to the silence.

That evening. Tony is sitting in his room, listening to the receiving device, which is relaying sounds from Deborah's flat: the end of an episode of EastEnders. The EastEnders theme tune comes on. Tony starts to dance inanely to the music. Gary enters the kitchen, looking greasy haired and dirty, and wearing the ugliest items in his wardrobe. He is holding a can of lager. Tony sees him and shouts through from his room.

TONY
Deborah's been watching *EastEnders*. Dougie's just had a bit of a barney with Sharon and Michelle's acting peculiarly.
Gary grunts. Deborah turns off the TV.

TONY
I can hear it really clearly. (*Turning childish*) During *Newsroom South East* Deb did this, like, burp.

Gary and Tony snigger together juvenilely.

GARY
Hey, do you like how I look?

TONY
(*Offscreen, uneasy*) Yeah, very nice. I mean, you're not my cup of tea or anything—
Tony drifts into the kitchen and stops in mid-sentence when he notices Gary's appalling appearance.

GARY
Dorothy's coming round, I've got to put her off the idea of marrying me.

TONY
(*Looking at him*) Yeah, great, you can't beat charity-shop clothes for that really crappy look, can you?

GARY
No, these are mine.

TONY
Oh.
They hear a distant phone ringing.

TONY
Debs' phone.
He dashes back into his room and listens to the speaker.

DEBORAH'S VOICE-OVER
(*Slightly distorted*) Oh, hi, Mum. Yeah, all right. How's your head?
A pause, Tony listens. Gary stays in the kitchen, getting another beer out of the fridge.

TONY
She's asking her Mum how her head is.

DEBORAH'S VOICE-OVER
Go to the doctor you saw before when you had that dizzy turn.

TONY
She's saying go to that doctor she saw before when she had that dizzy turn—

GARY
(*Offscreen*) You can just give me the highlights if you like.

DEBORAH'S VOICE-OVER
Yeah, Ray's coming round later. (*Pausing*) Mm, I'm sure it'll be nice.

TONY
(*Mimicking*) Ray's coming round later. (*Rolling his eyes theatrically*) 'Worst luck', she says.
In the kitchen, Gary hears the doorbell. He looks suddenly nervous. He goes and stands in Tony's doorway.

GARY
How do I look?

TONY
Disgusting.

GARY
(*Genuine*) Thanks.
Gary heads for the door.

10. LIVING ROOM

Seconds later. Dorothy comes in with Gary. It should be clear to the audience that she is winding him up.

DOROTHY
So, how are you, darling?

GARY
Oh, you know me: thick as pigshit. I must say, it's a brave woman that wants to marry me.

DOROTHY
And I am that brave woman.
She gives Gary a gooey smile. Gary stands over her, frantically smoking and swigging alternately from the can of lager in each hand. His flies are visibly undone.

DOROTHY
Your flies are undone.

GARY
Well, let's face it – if it moves, I'll hump it.

DOROTHY
(*Smiling*) I love your wry sense of humour.
Gary looks put out by her relaxed attitude.

GARY
How was the hospital?

DOROTHY
The usual. At one point we ran out of kidney bowls and had to use a Sainsbury's bag, then a man came in with a horrendously swollen—

GARY
I've never told you before Dorothy, but I'm violently opposed to the National Health Service. I'm sorry if that makes you not want to marry me, but, well, there you are.
Dorothy gives Gary a twinkly smile.

DOROTHY
No, I find your plain-speaking amusing and refreshing.

11. TONY'S ROOM

Meanwhile. Tony is still listening in to the upstairs flat. Through the speaker we hear Deborah shutting the door, having let in Ray.

DEBORAH'S VOICE-OVER
(*Coming nearer*) Hello.

RAY'S VOICE-OVER
Hi, babe.
They kiss audibly.

RAY'S VOICE-OVER
Mm, eat me . . .
Tony snarls.

DEBORAH'S VOICE-OVER
Good day at work?

RAY'S VOICE-OVER
Yep, we're taking price hikes pretty much across the whole residential shooting match. The commercial sector still needs some freeing up, but the helicopter view's fabby.

TONY
(*Scornful*) You what?

RAY'S VOICE-OVER
Hey, sugar, my love, what's that wanky little plant doing on the telly?

DEBORAH'S VOICE-OVER
(*Getting fainter*) Oh, Tony brought it up. He wanted to apologise for something.

RAY'S VOICE-OVER
(*Close to microphone*) Hey, come on, you're going out with me now. I'm dumping this in the bin.

DEBORAH'S VOICE-OVER
(*Distant*) That's not fair. Tony's okay.
Tony desperately tries to hear what she is saying.

RAY'S VOICE-OVER
(*Loud*) I don't agree, I think he's a complete—
The sound goes abruptly dead. Tony looks cross. He gets to his feet.

12. DEBORAH'S FLAT

Ray and Deborah come back from the kitchen. Ray reclines arrogantly on the sofa. There is a knock at the door. Deborah goes and answers it. It is Tony. Deborah looks friendly but uneasy.

DEBORAH
Hello, Tony.

TONY
Hi.

DEBORAH
What can I do for you?

TONY
Um, I was wondering how my plant was.

RAY
No plants here, mate. You want to try a garden centre.

DEBORAH
It really was looking dead, so I'm afraid we threw it out.
Tony adopts a look of shock and surprise.

TONY
Excuse me, that was a present.

RAY
Yeah, I could tell it was from you because it was scrawny, it served no obvious purpose, and neither of us liked it.

TONY
Well, I'll have it back if I may, thank you.

DEBORAH
Um, why?

TONY
I . . . want to take some cuttings from it.

DEBORAH
How do you take cuttings from a daffodil?

TONY
You, um, make incisions in the green sticky-up thing, put it in the airing cupboard and then a couple of days later, hey presto . . . tulips.

DEBORAH
(*Shrugging*) Okay.
She heads off to get it. Alone, the men trade rapid insults out of the corners of their mouths.

TONY
Creep.

RAY
Bastard.

TONY
Prick.

RAY
Jerk.
They stop instantly as Deborah reappears with the plant. She hands it to Tony. They smile at each other.

TONY
Anyway, you're looking great.

RAY
Thanks—

TONY
I was talking to Deborah. (*To Deborah*) So, how are your Mum's headaches these days?

DEBORAH
How do you know she's got headaches?

TONY
They're . . . doing the rounds. My Mum's thinking of getting one.

With his back to the camera, Tony removes the bug from the soil. We see him clean it on his trousers. He backs away towards the door and discreetly puts the bug on a shelf. They wonder what he is doing.

TONY
(*Pointing to them*) Shelves.
He opens the door and leaves.

13. GARY'S FLAT: LIVING ROOM

Gary is still smoking and drinking, and trying to put off Dorothy.

GARY
No, the way I see it, the only kind of marriage that works is the kind where the bloke goes to the pub every night with his mates, they get pissed, talk about who they'd like to shag, slag off their bird, then come back and have a huge row to clean the air.
Dorothy is smiling and nodding patiently.

DOROTHY
Well, I know you lads need to enjoy yourselves.
Gary runs his hands through his hair, getting increasingly frantic. In the background Tony walks through irritably, tossing the plant in a bin, heading for his room.

GARY
Yes, let's get it all out in the open, before we commit ourselves. Um, have I told you my controversial views on how society should cope with the menace of little stray dogs?

DOROTHY
No, you haven't.

GARY
I reckon – this might sound harsh – they should be rounded up and roasted, alive if necessary, and fed to the homeless.
A pause. Dorothy is no longer smiling. Gary thinks this might have done the trick.

DOROTHY
Actually that's probably quite sensible—

GARY
For God's sake, Dorothy – I'm talking about roasting pets here. How can you want to marry me?!
Dorothy smiles contentedly again, reaches into her bag and brings out a copy of Brides *magazine.*

DOROTHY
Well, you're the boss.

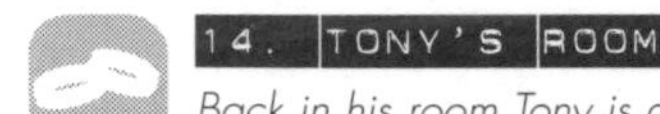

14. TONY'S ROOM

Back in his room Tony is already listening to the conversation in Deborah's flat. He looks goggle-eyed with boredom.

RAY'S VOICE-OVER
At the weekend I thought we could go for a drive in the Mazda.

DEBORAH'S VOICE-OVER
Yeah, if I'm not—

RAY'S VOICE-OVER
(*Not listening*) The thing about the MX3 is you can ask a lot of her, and she'll give you a hundred and ten per cent.

DEBORAH'S VOICE-OVER
Uh-huh.

RAY'S VOICE-OVER
I'll probably chamois her down before I come on over. You might want to pop over and watch.

DEBORAH'S VOICE-OVER
Mm.
Tony yawns and looks at his watch, amazed at this banality. Deborah also sounds fed up.

RAY'S VOICE-OVER
The Mazda benefits from a surprisingly advantageous mpg actually—

DEBORAH'S VOICE-OVER
Shall we go out and watch a film?

RAY'S VOICE-OVER
Could do, parking wouldn't be a problem, I can get the old Maz into a space the size of . . . well, you know, a very small space.
Tony pretends to loll asleep, waking up abruptly. Gary comes in, looking rattled, holding another can of lager.

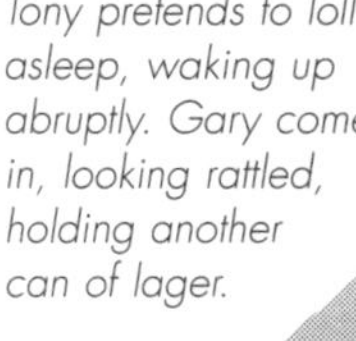

GARY
It's not going well in there.

TONY
(*Preoccupied*) He's not even interesting! I'm more interesting than that even on my uninteresting days.

GARY
Yeah, shut up. (*Swigging lager*) One more try then I'm going to have to tell her.

TONY
(*Not listening*) I'm going to have to go up and say something.

GARY
Yeah, right. Of course, you can get banged up for bugging someone illegally.
Gary takes a deep breath and heads back into the living room. Tony is frowning with frustration.

15. LIVING ROOM

Meanwhile we see Dorothy alone, looking like she is enjoying this. Gary comes back in, and she adopts an adoring smile.

16. TONY'S BEDROOM

Simultaneously, with mounting irritation, Tony is listening to the conversation that continues upstairs.

RAY'S VOICE-OVER
I presume Tony hasn't got a car.

DEBORAH'S VOICE-OVER
He had an old van for a while.

RAY'S VOICE-OVER
Sounds like a fitting epitaph: 'Tony. He had an old van for a while.'

DEBORAH'S VOICE-OVER
Oh, leave him alone.
Tony is getting more and more steamed up.

RAY'S VOICE-OVER
Have you noticed how he's always got his mouth open.
Tony indeed has his mouth open. He shuts it self-consciously with his hand.

RAY'S VOICE-OVER
Apart from the fact that he's got a face like an arse—

TONY
Right, that's it.
He gets up and storms out. We are left listening to the conversation coming out of the speaker.

DEBORAH'S VOICE-OVER
Shut up, Ray.

RAY'S VOICE-OVER
What?

DEBORAH'S VOICE-OVER
I'm sorry, I don't want to go out with you any more.

RAY'S VOICE-OVER
Why?!

DEBORAH'S VOICE-OVER
Tony may be a bit of a jerk, but he's considerate and gentle. You're just boring.

17. DEBORAH'S FLAT

As the surveillance device records them in Tony's room, Deborah and Ray are sitting unawares at opposite ends of the sofa, embarrassed. Ray looks aggrieved. A lengthy silence.

RAY
How d'you mean boring?
There is a sudden almighty splintering crash as Tony charges down the door. It comes off its hinges. Tony is standing there. Having been fired up with anger he is suddenly unsure what to do, aware that he can not reveal why he is so furious. Deborah and Ray sit there with their mouths open.

TONY
Hi!
Looking apologetic, Tony backs towards the door. As he does so he discreetly picks up the bug from where he left it.
At the door he gingerly tries to piece together the door frame. A still gob-smacked Deborah and Ray watch him leave.

18. GARY'S FLAT: LIVING ROOM

At the same time Gary is still trying to put off Dorothy, now at the end of his tether.

GARY
So, those are my conditions if we were to get married – (*Counting them off on his fingers*) total obedience at all times; I'm allowed to sleep around when I feel like it, including with members of your family; Tony to live with us, for ever, and you will be expected to agree to any sexual acts I deem fit, even if they involve, er, enormous vegetables. (*Looking at her nervously*) Got that, um, minge bag?
Gary winces. A pause while Dorothy appears to waver. Gary looks hopeful.

DOROTHY
No, that all sounds pretty standard—

GARY
(*Blurting*) I don't want to get married!
Dorothy looks at him mildly.

GARY
I was drunk, it's all been a hideous mistake. Forgive me.
A tense moment. Tony enters, nursing a bruised shoulder. They all nod at each other sociably.

DOROTHY
Nice evening, Tony?

TONY
Great, thanks.
Dorothy turns to Gary.

DOROTHY
Gary. Can I just say that I've enjoyed making you suffer for forty-eight hours but why would I want to marry a man who, though sometimes innocently entertaining, never grew up, always puts himself first, shows no interest in the world, and whose idea of an elegant lifestyle is buying the most expensive lager in the off-licence?
Gary looks hugely relieved.

GARY
Thanks.
He smiles. Then the smile starts to fade.

GARY
Hang on a minute. Actually I'm a bit of a catch.
Deborah comes in, looking confused.

DEBORAH
Tony, why have you destroyed my front door?
A pause. Tony tries to think of something.

TONY
(*Romantic*) Because even doors won't keep our love apart.

DEBORAH
Maybe not.
She smiles, apparently won over.

DEBORAH
I wonder if this will.
She kicks Tony in the balls. He doubles up, falling to his knees. He clutches at Gary's legs for support. Gary is still brooding. He barely notices Tony hanging on to his knees, eyes watering, groaning.

GARY
(*To Dorothy*) No, I mean it. I'd be a good husband. I'm tall, humorous. I've got a respectable job, I've tracked down your G-spot after years of looking. I'd take our children to the zoo and so on.

A lengthy pause.

DOROTHY
You're right.
Gary smiles at Tony, who has got back on to his feet.

DOROTHY
I will marry you.
Dorothy's expression is inscrutable. She, Tony and Deborah stare at Gary, who is panicking again, unsure whether she means it . . .

19. LIVING ROOM

Later, the end of the evening. Gary and Tony are sitting on the sofa, rather drunk. Tony is nursing his bruised groin. The coffee table in front of them is as usual awash with dead lager cans.

GARY
Stag nights, eh. (*Frowning*) That can all get pretty sleazy, can't it.

TONY
Yeah. Brilliant.

GARY
Brilliant.

TONY
I went to my Dad's stag night, actually.

GARY
How come?

TONY
Well, you know how some people have a second honeymoon—

GARY
(*Dubious*) Yeah.

TONY
—He decided to have a second stag night.
They nod, taking this in.

GARY
Mate of mine had one. We got him legless, chained him to the roof rack of this car and took him through half a dozen car washes. (*Pause*) He'd come up quite nicely by the end.

TONY
Bloke I know, we stripped him naked, poured axle grease on him, shaved this big stripe down the middle of his head and dropped him off on the hard shoulder of the M25.

GARY
He must have been a bit shaky at his wedding.

TONY
No, he wasn't getting married, we just didn't like him.
Gary glances at Tony's groin.

GARY
Still throbbing?

TONY
Yeah. I'll have a big bruise in the morning. Last time a girl did it to me I had every colour of the rainbow down there. I took a polaroid of it, actually, do you want me to dig it out for you?

GARY
(*Considers briefly*) Nah, it's all right.

GARY
I remember the first wedding I went to, my cousin married this great Dane.

TONY
Is that allowed then?

GARY
No, no, not a Great Dane, a big Dane, you know, tall bloke.

TONY
Oh, yeah.

GARY
The moment came when he had to say 'I do'.

TONY
Yeah.

GARY
And instead he starts humming the Danish entry in the 1974 Eurovision Song Contest. I think the pressure of the occasion got to him, you know.

TONY
Yeah.

GARY
Interesting.

TONY
Yeah.
They sit there in silence, vaguely smiling.

GARY
You see, the trouble with marrying a bird is you're not going to get conversations of this sheer quality, are you.

TONY
No.
They sit there shaking their heads and drinking lager.

PREMIUM LAGER BEER
ANNO 1366
STELLA ARTOIS
LEUVEN
Strong Continental Lager

SERIES FOUR

SERIES FOUR: EPISODE ONE

BABIES

This series was probably the best and happiest of the seven, coming at that point when I had got to know the characters but there was still a lot to say. And Neil's hair had calmed down. Headlines were starting to appear in the papers along the lines of 'Bletchley Newsagents Behaving Badly'. Viewing figures climbed above the psychologically important 10-million level, overtaking *Home and Away* or something. Now with the confidence of the author of a hit sitcom, I bought a small second-hand car.

I'm not as fond of the opening 'nightmare' scene as I once was. Now it seems just to hold up the action. I stole the visual joke about the bride's half of the church differing wildly from the groom's half from *Raising Arizona*. It's okay to steal if you do it in a loving way. The scene in which Tony goes through Deborah's underwear drawer and puts her knickers on his head seems to have struck a chord. Nobody believes me when I say I have never done it myself, yet.

This script formed the basis for the first episode of the American *Men Behaving Badly*. Executives at NBC, the broadcaster, refused to allow condoms to be seen unwrapped on air, so goodness knows what they would have made of Gary putting a Dutch cap into his mouth. (For days after our episode went out I worried someone out there would copy Martin and die a horrible and unusual death by contraceptive asphyxiation.) One of the problems for the American series was that their episodes are only 21 minutes long, so the languid drunken conversation on the sofa at the end lasted about ten seconds.

When I wrote this we had just had our first baby, so children were on my mind, and I could bandy about technical terms like perineum and breasts like footballs. Because I am sensitive I really like the ending, in which Gary and Tony curl up and fall asleep to womb music.

1. AT CHURCH

Mid-afternoon. Gary is standing at the altar in full wedding regalia. Tony is in the best man's position, smiling happily. The groom's side is thinly populated by a few cronies of Gary's, including Les, Anthea and George. By contrast, the bride's side is full of respectable, rather elegant people. Deborah is among them, in a stunning dress. Standing next to Gary, Dorothy turns round to smile to her side of the church. She glances at Gary's motley crew with a look of undisguised disappointment. We are in the middle of the service. The vicar is young and handsome.

VICAR

Do you, Garfield Benji Digweed take Dorothy Bianca to be your lawful wedded wife?

Gary does an ooh-shall-I expression.

GARY

I do.

VICAR

Do you have the ring?

GARY

Yes, your Grace.

Tony steps forward and gives Gary a ringing mobile phone. He does an only-kidding gesture and produces an inflated swimming ring instead. Gary pulls the ring over Dorothy's head. She looks slightly perplexed.

VICAR

You may kiss.

Dorothy leans forward and gives the vicar a passionate kiss on the mouth. Gary looks mildly put out. The organ launches into an upbeat, baroque version of, perhaps, 'Stayin' alive'. The organ is being played by a celebrity.

We focus on Gary's face. Behind him, Anthea and George are kneeling opposite each other, imitating Torvill and Dean starting their 'Bolero' routine. Les is in the pulpit, pulling pints. Tony is giving Deborah a piggy-back round the church. Gary looks increasingly worried. Next to him, Dorothy is smiling serenely. We pan down and see that they are both enormously pregnant. Panicking, Gary turns to Dorothy to speak to her. Fade to black.

2. GARY'S FLAT: HIS BEDROOM

Early morning. Gary is writhing under the duvet, jabbering away in his disturbed sleep, watched by Dorothy, who is dressing.

GARY
Dorothy. Not, no. Ha-ha, telephone. Piggyback vicar.
He quietens down. Dorothy comes and sits down next to him.

DOROTHY
(*Repeating*) 'Dorothy. Not, no. Ha-ha, telephone. Piggyback vicar.' Well, I suppose it's no worse than when you're awake.
Gary's eyes snap open in alarm.

GARY
I've just had a nightmare.
It is still dark outside. Dorothy puts on the bedside lamp.

DOROTHY
What about?

GARY
I'd . . . rather not say.

DOROTHY
One of your usual ones?

GARY
(*Guiltily*) Yes.

DOROTHY
Was it the one where I've nailed you to a tree, and I'm whipping you with wet towels?

GARY
No.

DOROTHY
The one where . . . you think the Pope's stolen your bus pass?

GARY
I don't want to talk about it—

DOROTHY
You're sharing a houseboat with Noel Edmonds?

GARY
No! If you must know we were getting married, and you were pregnant.

DOROTHY
Is me being pregnant such a nightmare?
Gary does a pained look.

DOROTHY
Oh, of course, it's one of the taboo subjects. We can spend two days arguing about the name of the fifth Osmond, but we can't talk about whether we should give life to another human being.

GARY
Brian. Brian Osmond. Trust me.

DOROTHY
No, it's good, we've got to talk about this.
Gary whimpers.

DOROTHY
Obviously I'd rather not have to have sex with you at all let alone have your kids, but these are the pitiful, dog-eared cards fate has dealt me.

GARY
What's the hurry? You've got a good ten years left in you.

DOROTHY
Thanks, I've always wanted to be described like a slightly rusty Volvo estate.
The radio alarm comes on suddenly. It is Chris Tarrant at his most cheerful. Gary takes his pillow and forcefully smothers the radio until it goes dead. He lies back. Dorothy glances over at Gary's pillowslip.

DOROTHY
I suppose the big question is, do I really want to have children with a man who has a Fungus the Bogeyman pillowcase?

3. KITCHEN

Tony enters in his dressing gown, vigorously brushing his teeth with an electric toothbrush. He takes it out of his mouth and sensuously runs it over his face, then experimentally up one nostril. He opens the fridge, pours himself some milk, adds some Nesquik and dips the toothbrush in. The milk froths into a milkshake. He drinks it. There is a knock at the door. He goes to answer it, smoothing his hair down as he goes.

4. HALL

Tony opens the door to Deborah, who is in her jacket, ready to go out. Tony has an absurd milk ring round his mouth and a trail of toothpaste over his face. Deborah does not bother to point this out.

DEBORAH
Hi, Tony.

TONY
Hi, Debs.

DEBORAH
How are you?

TONY
Um, I haven't had a woman for three months because I can't get you out of my head, so I'm in this real spiral of depression alleviated only temporarily by these huge, long binges of self-abuse.

DEBORAH
Great.
Deborah is rummaging in her bag, not listening.

DEBORAH
Can I ask you a favour? I need to have my boiler serviced today, but I've got to go in to work.

TONY
Sure, I'll have a go. I can't guarantee it won't explode afterwards.

DEBORAH
(*Patiently*) No, can I leave you my keys so you can let the man in?
Deborah holds out her house keys. A smile appears on Tony's face.

TONY
You want to leave me the keys to your flat?

DEBORAH
You won't need to go up there except when he's there.

TONY
Course not, no. Um, can I ask for a favour in return?

DEBORAH
Sure, what?

TONY
Will you sleep with me?

DEBORAH
You don't think that's a bit of an uneven bargain?

TONY
Okay. Will you sleep with me and lend me a hundred quid?

5. GARY'S BEDROOM

Gary and Dorothy are lying in bed as before.

GARY
You know test-tube babies. I always wanted to know, do they keep putting the baby in bigger and bigger tubes as it grows or do they start with, like, one really big one?

DOROTHY
I hope you're joking, Gary.
Gary realises he has made a mistake.

GARY
Yeah, course.
Gary adopts a smug expression.

GARY
Isn't it funny how girls' ability to reproduce peters out pathetically in their forties whereas blokes can do it into their seventies.

DOROTHY
Not if their girlfriend has battered their genitals to a pulp with their radio-alarm clock.

GARY
Do you know, a yoghurt pot full of my semen could repopulate the whole of Ireland?

DOROTHY
Haven't they had a tragic enough history without you turning up at the border with your yoghurt pot?

GARY
What's the matter with you?

DOROTHY
This is serious, Gary. If I can't decide to have children with you I might as well look for another man.
They both ponder this, frowning.

DOROTHY
I suppose we'd have to live together.

GARY
Would we have to if we had a baby? Couldn't you just pop round occasionally with it?
Dorothy gives him a look and gets out of bed. She finishes pulling on her clothes.

GARY
What's so great about children anyway?

DOROTHY
I just want them. It's like you and pints of lager.
Gary adopts a 'concerned' expression.

GARY
Would you like a dog? They're quite like children.
Dorothy carries on getting dressed.

GARY
Or you could sponsor a panda.
Dorothy sighs and goes on ignoring him.

GARY
Is it really fair to bring a child into a world full of . . . pestilence and disease and war and . . . pestilence and disease. And war?

DOROTHY
Oh, sorry – are you still talking?

GARY
I'm not really sure I feel ready to abandon my bachelor lifestyle. Do you see?

DOROTHY
Bye-bye.
Now dressed, Dorothy heads for the door.

GARY
(*Calling after her*) They wet themselves, you know.

6. KITCHEN

As Dorothy leaves, she passes behind Tony, sitting at the table, eating a piece of toast.

TONY
Bye, Dorothy.
Dorothy departs for work. The door slams as Gary wanders in wearing his dressing gown.

TONY
What's wrong with Dorothy?

GARY
(*Yawning*) She wants a baby.

TONY
Here, guess what – Debs just given me the keys to her flat. I've got to let her gasman in.
Gary sits down.

GARY
Nice to know she trusts you.

TONY
Yeah, it's a bit of a vote of confidence, isn't it?

GARY
So, what are you going to do first – look in her photo album or check out her knicker drawer?

TONY
Neither!
For a moment they concentrate on their breakfast.

TONY
Still, a quick look can't hurt, can it?

GARY
No.
They are already on their feet and on their way out.

7. DEBORAH'S FLAT: LIVING ROOM

The room is empty. Tony puts his head round the door. He and Gary appear, both in their dressing gowns. They stand in the middle of the room, then fan out, looking for items of interest.

TONY
Did you ever have this fantasy that everyone else's been killed in a neutron bomb, but you've survived and can roam freely in people's houses?
Gary is looking at him as though he is odd.

TONY
First I'd go round to Paul McCartney's house and play the guitar he used in *A Hard Day's Night*. Then I'd pop over to Princess Di's and put on one of her swimming costumes, then I'd—

GARY
Tony, Tony. Too weird, Tony.

TONY
Oh. Okay.
Gary goes into the kitchen area, Tony examines Deborah's bookshelves.

TONY
Debs has got *Lady Chatterley's Lover*.
He takes it off the shelf and lets the pages fall open.

TONY
Hey, look, it falls open at the dirty bits, even though she's a girl.

GARY
That's your copy, you made her borrow it.

TONY
Oh, yeah.
He reads the page that has fallen open, with difficulty.

TONY
'An' what I get when I'm i'side thee, and what tha gets when I'm i'side thee; it's a'as it is, all on't . . . Tha mun goo, let me dust thee.'
He frowns in confusion, then does his moronic laddish expression.

TONY
Wey-hey! Brilliant.
He tosses the book aside and studies Deborah's ornaments.

TONY
What d'you reckon's the point of china horses?

GARY
Company?

TONY
Yeah, probably.
From under the sink Gary produces a box. He takes out some vaguely dildo-like electric curling tongs

GARY
Is this what I think it is?

TONY
No, I think it's for making hair all bendy.

GARY
What about this?
He produces a hair-crimper.

TONY
That's for making it kind of corrugated.
He produces another fancy device.

TONY
Steam-brushing.
He produces a fold up drier.

TONY
Drying it on the move.
He produces a drier with a fancy diffuser.

TONY
Drying it in the home.
He produces an epilator.

TONY
Removing it.

GARY
And they wonder why they're not in positions of power in British industry. Too busy buggering around with their hair.
Gary picks up a box of cereal and sits down on the sofa. Tony has found some photo albums.

TONY
Aha!
He joins Gary on the sofa. Gary puts his hand into the box and eats some dry cereal.

GARY
So what do you reckon – should I impregnate Dorothy or not?

TONY
I don't know – kids, it's the biggest decision you'll ever make, isn't it. That and whether to be a lager or a bitter drinker.

GARY
You know what I don't like about babies? They're all small. It's like those new five-pence pieces, they're all sort of fiddly.

TONY
Mind you, they are, like, a celebration of this explosive power we have in our loins.

GARY
That's true.

TONY
It's amazing, when you think about it, that this simple act, which can be over in as little as a few sec—

GARY
(*Joining in*) Seconds, yeah.

TONY
It can lead to the creation of a complete . . . little chap.

GARY
Yeah, it is amazing.
They sit in wonder, Gary still absent-mindedly scooping cereal into his mouth.

GARY
They are fiddly, though, aren't they.

TONY
Fiddly, yeah. God, look at that.
Gary and Tony go quiet as they scrutinise a photograph.

GARY
You can't beat the old red-string micro-bikini, can you.

TONY
Just think, you might have a kid who turned out like Deborah.

GARY
I can't think about that, it's too complicated.

TONY
Look at the jerk she's with.
They both snort but then sigh, hopelessly jealous.

GARY
Still, maybe he's just a casual acquaintance, eh.

TONY
Yeah.
Tony turns the page. They go quiet again.

TONY
So . . . he's not a casual acquaintance then.

GARY
No.

TONY
Still, it's pretty clear she's only left these photos lying around to make me jealous.

GARY
Yeah, sure.

TONY
On the outside she acts as though I'm a toolhead, but on the inside she's quivering with suppressed desire. (*He does a little quiver*) Like that.
Brief tableau of the two of them, squeezed together on the sofa, both lost in thought.

8. GARY'S OFFICE

Late morning. Gary is sitting at his desk, still lost in thought. George is working at his desk.

GARY
George, were you there when your son was born?

GEORGE
(*Trying hard to remember*) No, it was a Saturday.

GARY
No, not there at your desk, there at Marjorie's bedside.

GEORGE
Oh, no, men didn't attend the birth in those days.

GARY
Why?

GEORGE
I think because the baby comes out of a lady's rude area.

GARY
Ah.

GEORGE
We were encouraged to go home and relax by sort of pacing. She was in labour for thirty-six hours, so I managed to pace to Reigate.

GARY
So, overall, are you happy about how your son turned out, George?

GEORGE
Oh, yes. Sometimes we wish he'd, you know, not keep stealing our furniture and selling it, but generally we get nothing but joy from Biff.

GARY
Why did you call him Biff?

GEORGE
Well, he was supposed to be Bill, but the clerk at the Town Hall dropped her lunchbox on the F when she was typing the birth certificate.

GARY
So a few inches the other way, and he could have been called . . . Bipp.

GEORGE
No, that would have been silly.

GARY
I don't know – kids – what's in it for me? I'm a sexy bachelor-type person.

GEORGE
Well, doesn't it worry you that you could die tomorrow without leaving anything of lasting value?

GARY
Oh, I think you're underestimating the impact of my humorous speech to this year's Security Fencing Manufacturers' Gala.

GEORGE
The only disadvantage I can remember is that Marjorie didn't feel like sexual intercourse for two years after the birth.
A pause while Gary takes this in.

GARY
Right, that's it. We're not having children.
Anthea comes in, carrying her usual bits of paper. Gary is breezy and confident again.

GARY
Anthea, remind me what's so good about being a child-free single person.

ANTHEA
Um, well, you can keep everything neat and tidy and smart around the home.

GARY
Exactly.

ANTHEA
And people don't often visit, so there's lots of time to sit and read my gardening magazines and nod off with Melody Radio on.
Gary is losing his confidence.

ANTHEA
And, of course, although I sometimes have a bit of a cry, that usually makes me feel slightly better, and then I go mad and have sardines on toast to really cheer me up.
Gary gazes glumly into the middle distance.

9. DEBORAH'S FLAT: LIVING ROOM

Later that morning. Tony has made himself at home. He is sitting on the sofa, leafing through the last of the photo albums. He is wearing one of Deborah's girly cardigans and sipping a vile-coloured cocktail studded with cherries. Bottles of spirits from her drinks cabinet are lined up on the coffee table. He shuts the last photo album and pours some chartreuse into his

cocktail, turning it an even fiercer green.
He gets to his feet, surprised by the potency of the alcohol.

10. BEDROOM

Tony enters, sipping his cocktail. He looks around and grins mischievously. He puts the glass down and jumps on to Deborah's bed. He does an exuberant, drunken backflip, which does not quite work. He gets off the bed and picks up his glass again. He spies the chest of drawers and goes over to it. He nervously looks round, hesitates guiltily, then gingerly opens one of the top drawers.
It is a well-stocked underwear drawer. He takes out some expensive-looking silky knickers and wonders what to do with them before he puts them on his head. Delving further into the drawer, he finds a leather-bound book – a five-year diary. He examines it with a mixture of triumph and guilt. Agonising over whether or not to read it, he opens it an inch, then another inch, until he is reading it.

TEENAGE DEBORAH'S VOICE-OVER
Bought the Bay City Rollers' new single. I feel all funny when I think of Woody.
Lisa came over, and we played it thirty-seven times. She is horrible. I hate her. She is horrible.
He throws the diary into the drawer and gets out another one. He turns to a page.

DEBORAH'S VOICE-OVER
Went to see *The Terminator* with Mike. I wanted to see *The Color Purple*. He made us sit in the cheap seats.

TONY
(*Sympathetic*) Ah.

DEBORAH'S VOICE-OVER
Afterwards, feeling romantic, we went back to his place and made—
Tony stops and looks over his shoulder guiltily. He turns over the page.

DEBORAH'S VOICE-OVER
—pasta.
Tony turns to another page at the end of the diary. He reaches for his cocktail, which is on the chest of drawers.

DEBORAH'S VOICE-OVER
Tony behaved like a complete arsehole today—
In surprise he knocks the full glass into the open knicker drawer.

TONY
Aaarrghh!

He jumps about, wondering what to do. In panic, he removes the drawer and empties it out on the pastel duvet, which is instantly spattered with stains. Tony stands there turning this way and that in panic.

11. HOSPITAL CANTEEN

Dorothy and Gary are getting their lunch.

GARY
I think we should do it.

DOROTHY
I don't know. What's made you change your mind?

GARY
Oh, you know, we're okay together, other people do it. I'd have someone to do my shopping for me when I'm old.

DOROTHY
You dear, sweet, romantic man.

GARY
No, I mean, let's face it, one of these days I'm going to die.

DOROTHY
Hopefully.

GARY
(*Ignoring her*) I've got lots to pass on.

DOROTHY
This will be your collection of mugs in the shape of different parts of the body, will it?

GARY
No. My experience and knowledge.

DOROTHY
Well, it would certainly be a catastrophe if all your knock-knock jokes were to die with you.

GARY
I'm serious.

DOROTHY
Gary, you have the maturity of a boy of seven.

GARY
Well, it's something to build on, isn't it?

DOROTHY
A child is a huge responsibility. You're the least responsible person I know. And I know Tony.

GARY
That's because I've never had to be. Parenthood calms you down, doesn't it. Look at your Dad – I've seen the photographs, he had the biggest winkle-pickers in Finchley before he had you.
She looks at him seriously, then she sighs. Cut to Gary and Dorothy sitting down.

DOROTHY
Sometimes I find it all a bit daunting. Your body's never the same after having a child.

GARY
I'll be all right.

DOROTHY
Me, Gary, me!

GARY
Sorry. Don't worry, I'd be there for you, with the hot towels.

DOROTHY
That'll be handy if I give birth in a Chinese restaurant.

GARY
No, you know, towels, boiling water. Cigars.

DOROTHY
And what happens when I get varicose veins, stretchmarks, crying fits, breasts like footballs—

GARY
Now you're talking . . .

DOROTHY
—which are too tender to touch.

GARY
Oh.

DOROTHY
Collapsed pelvic-floor muscles. Sex might feel different afterwards.

GARY
Well, we probably need a change anyway.

DOROTHY
And things can go wrong. How would you feel if your perineum tore in half?
Gary thinks about this.

GARY
Disappointed?

DOROTHY
Not to mention post-natal depression. No doubt your remedy would be lavish use of the whoopee cushion.

GARY
Still, they're great, aren't they? Running around with their little nappies on.
Gary looks genuinely keen. Dorothy softens.

DOROTHY
Oh, maybe it would be okay.

GARY
I've never thought about children before. Then this morning George showed me a photograph of his little niece. She was so sweet.
Gary smiles indulgently. Dorothy melts.

DOROTHY
Oh, Gary. You are an old softie.

GARY
She's nineteen as it happens. Fantastic arse.
Dorothy glowers at him.

GARY
But the point is, I wasn't interested, she didn't mean anything to me. I've changed. I want you to have our baby.
Dorothy sighs, impressed with his sincerity.

DOROTHY
I'll come round tonight. Maybe we should just do it.
Gary kisses her. He gets to his feet and walks away, leaving Dorothy deep in thought. She looks down and sees that Gary has left his briefcase behind. She looks out for him, but he has gone.

12. LAUNDRETTE

Early afternoon. Tony sits, reading Deborah's most recent diary while his washing goes round in the machine. His lips move, silently voicing what he is reading.

DEBORAH'S VOICE-OVER
Watched *Terminator 2* on video with Ray. I'd wanted to watch *Gob with the Wino.*
Tony frowns and tries to decipher her writing again.

DEBORAH'S VOICE-OVER
Gone with the Wind. Went down to Tony and Gary's to complain about them singing 'Happy Talk' at the tops of their voices. Tony

wearing his sexy denim shirt. Can't make up my mind if he's stupid and irritating or just misguided.

TONY
I'm misguided!
He turns over the page.

DEBORAH'S VOICE-OVER
Tony is definitely stupid and irritating.

TONY
Damn.

DEBORAH'S VOICE-OVER
Caught him trying to wedge a big carrot into Ray's exhaust pipe.
Tony looks up and sees that his washing is ready. He goes over and opens the machine. He cheerfully pulls out the contents: Deborah's duvet and her silky underwear. It is all stained a sludgy green.

TONY
Oh, my God!
He removes the offending article: a pair of dark pants. Holding up the underwear, he runs around with it like a headless chicken.

That evening. The door is pushed open, and Gary comes in, looking happy. He is carrying three huge carrier bags. He manhandles the contents of the first bag on to the kitchen table: a black-and-white rabbit – lifelike but freakishly large. He gets a new book on childbirth out of the second bag, sits down next to the rabbit and starts to read. Tony comes in from the hall, looking harassed. He has changed into his denim shirt. He does a double take when he sees the rabbit. Gary looks up from his book.

GARY
Apparently, after the birth you can cook the placenta and eat it.

TONY
(*Distracted*) What do you have it with?

GARY
It doesn't say. I suppose you could have it in a bap.
Tony grunts.

GARY
Did you know that to aid fertilisation the temperature of the scrotum is several degrees lower than the rest of the body?
Tony grunts again.

GARY
Mind you, that could just be bollocks.
Gary does a knowing laugh. Tony goes over to a bowl of washing soaking in the sink and snaps on rubber gloves. Gary has gone goofy and bashful.

GARY
Dorothy and I have decided to make a baby. (*Looking at watch*) I reckon if we start in an hour or so we might squeeze a small one in before Christmas.
Tony is glancing at his own watch, not paying much attention.

TONY
Yeah, can you do it quietly? I've had a bit of a difficult day.
Tony puts his hands into the bowl and lifts out an article of clothing. The bleach has made big holes in an expensive-looking bra.
Tony despairs.

GARY
I've been thinking of names. What do you think of Ivor?
Tony is holding up a succession of underclothes, whimpering at their tattered state.

GARY
Or how about Martin?

TONY
That's a bit crap, isn't it?
Gary decides to ignore him.

GARY
Look what I've bought.
He removes three boxes from the third bag.

GARY
F-14 Tomcat Seek-and-Destroy fighter plane model. A Death Ray gun, that comes with three death rays. And a Policeman Set.

TONY
What if it's a girl?

GARY
Tony, the progressive parent doesn't encourage gender stereotyping.

TONY
Fair point.

GARY
(*Reaching down for the last box*) But if it is a girl, I think this Ironing Board and Iron Set will go down a bit of a storm with the little lady, don't you?

TONY
You know when you find you've dyed loads of your best clothes a sludgy colour in the wash by mistake?

GARY
Been there, mate.

TONY
That's sort of . . . annoying, isn't it?

GARY
Is it annoying?! Is Luciano Pavarotti a fat bloke?

TONY
Supposing someone else did it to your clothes. Would you be able to kind of laugh it off?
He demonstrates a rather lame 'carefree' laugh, which eventually peters out.

GARY
No.

TONY
(*Heading off*) I'd better have a rethink.
Tony exits in the direction of Deborah's flat. Gary heads off to his bedroom.

14. GARY'S BEDROOM

A little later. Gary has turned his bedroom into a romantic grotto. Soft music is playing. He is searching for something in his chest of drawers, delving into the back of one of them.

GARY
(*In triumph*) Ah!
It is a battered, opened packet of condoms. He examines it nostalgically.

GARY
(*Calling out*) Hey, Tone, I've found another packet.
Tony comes in, looking a bit more relaxed. His denim shirt has white patches and holes in it where the bleach has splashed.

GARY
This packet's pre-Dorothy. I used to take it to parties, in case I needed it. Six years' worth of parties, if I'm honest.

TONY
Oh, well, it looks like you've used a couple.

GARY
No, we ran out of clingfilm at my Dad's retirement do.
He tosses the packet into a metal bowl containing various other contraceptives.

TONY
What are those?

GARY
Got them out of a machine when we were on holiday in Morocco. Turned out to be bubble gum. Still, it seemed to do the trick all right.
He picks up a Dutch cap, looking nostalgic again.

GARY
Ah. One of Dorothy's early caps. We had to stop using this one, it kept shooting out across the room.
There is a knock at the door. Looking nervous, Tony goes to answer it.

15. COMMUNAL HALL

Tony opens the door to Deborah. He attempts to look casual.

TONY
Hi!

DEBORAH
Hi, Tony. Did the engineer come?

TONY
Yup.

DEBORAH
Great. Did he service it okay?

TONY
Not unless he managed to do it through the letter box. He called while I was at the laundrette. Sorry.

DEBORAH
Tony. Couldn't you have done that another day?

TONY
Not . . . that specific washing, no.

DEBORAH
Tony, is it any wonder I keep rejecting you if you let me down like this?

TONY
No. Still, look, I'm wearing my sexy denim shirt . . .
He poses in a would-be seductive manner, looking ridiculous in his shirt. Debs looks confused.

DEBORAH
I'll just have my keys back, shall I?
He gives Deborah back her keys. She opens the door to her own flat and heads upstairs. Tony hangs about guiltily, listening out for her reaction. As he waits he notices that his shirt is ruined. There is a muffled cry of anguish from Deborah.

DEBORAH
(*Offscreen*) Oh, no!

TONY
(*Calling out weakly*) Anything wrong?

16. DEBORAH'S FLAT: LIVING ROOM

Some of Deborah's possessions have been artfully left hanging out of drawers etc.

17. BEDROOM

Moments later. Deborah is still checking her possessions.

TONY
So . . . we're looking for a burglar who breaks into people's houses and steals their duvet and their underwear.

DEBORAH
Looks like it.

TONY
Sounds like some kind of dirty old man.

DEBORAH
You said you thought it was kids.

TONY
Mm. Maybe it was . . . dirty old kids.

Deborah turns her back on Tony and gets out one of her diaries. She opens it with difficulty – the pages are gummed up. She ponders. Tony watches out of the corner of his eye.

TONY
Oh, well, there's not much more I can do here, so I'll just be on my way now—

DEBORAH
Tony, have you been reading this?

TONY
No, I don't read other people's diaries.

She turns menacingly.

DEBORAH
How do you know they're diaries?

Deborah is feverishly checking her possessions. Tony is tutting energetically.

TONY
The sods, eh.

DEBORAH
There seems to be nothing missing.

TONY
Um, I think there probably is.

DEBORAH
They've taken my camera!

TONY
No, they haven't.

DEBORAH
(*Finding it*) No they haven't. Tony, did you come up and leave the door open?

TONY
Deb, I think you're underestimating me slightly.

DEBORAH
So how else did they get in?

TONY
Actually, now you mention it I think I did see some kids scampering through the back garden carrying a big bag. Kids, eh?

He tuts again. Deborah is watching him closely.

TONY
In my day we were too busy helping old people and . . . flying kites to break into people's flats.

She heads off towards her bedroom. Tony winces and follows her.

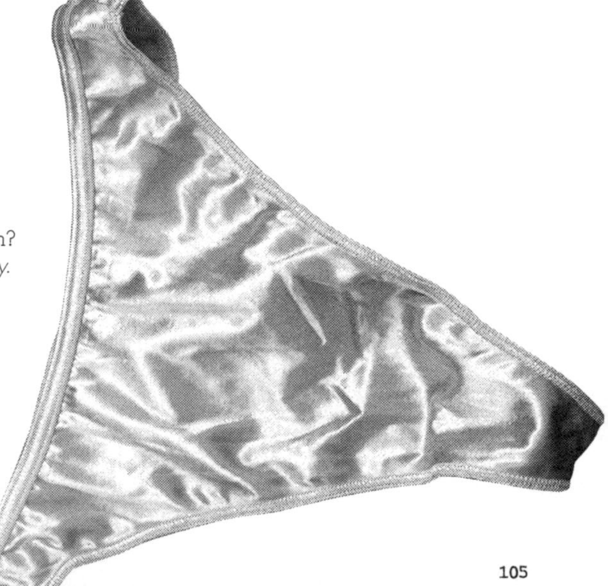

TONY
(*Improvising nervously*) Well, you're not going to keep old copies of Exchange & Mart at the back of your undies drawer, are you? Unless you want to, like, order up a lawnmower while you choose your pants.
She looks at him evenly.

DEBORAH
You're behind this, aren't you?
He struggles visibly to come up with an excuse.

TONY
Yes.

DEBORAH
And what are you going to do about it?

TONY
Apologise a lot?

DEBORAH
Yes. And?

TONY
Pay you loads of money to make good any financial loss?

DEBORAH
Yes. And?
Deborah's hand is on the knob of the open drawer. Tony's eyes flicker with apprehension between the drawer and her angry face.

TONY
Put my hand in the drawer?

DEBORAH
Yes.
He puts his hand wrist deep into the drawer. Deborah casually slams it shut hard on his hand. Tony tries not to show any pain.

TONY
Thank you.

18. GARY'S FLAT: BEDROOM

Tony's blood-curdling scream is heard from downstairs. Gary looks up momentarily, then goes back to blowing up a condom. He lets some air escape, making various amusing noises. He ties up the condom and adds it to a very poor sausage-dog 'balloon sculpture'. The front-door bell rings. He places the condoms with the other contraceptives in the metal bowl and goes to answer it.

19. KITCHEN

Gary leads Dorothy in. She lags behind, looking sombre and pensive.

GARY
Do you like the rabbit?

DOROTHY
Mm. Not so much a bunny, more a . . . huge bastard.

GARY
Well, I may have my faults—

DOROTHY
No, no . . .

GARY
—but when I buy my kid a cuddly toy, I buy my kid a cuddly toy, know what I mean? They had a four-foot hamster, but frankly it scared the shit out of me.

DOROTHY
Gary, this is all a bit . . . premature.

GARY
Well, obviously, we might take a while, but the way I see it, conception's a bit like a coconut shy. If you chuck enough balls at enough coconuts you win the goldfish.

DOROTHY
(*Wintry smile*) Another winning simile, Gary, if I may say so.

GARY
Cheers. Come through, watch this.
He has already headed off.

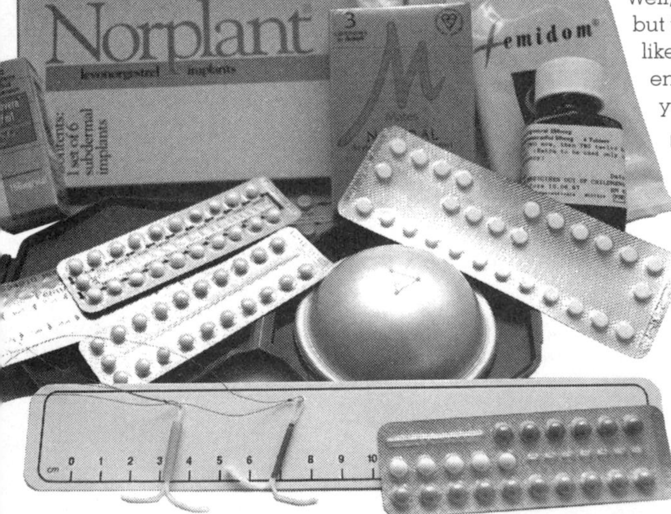

20. GARY'S BEDROOM

Moments later Gary is pouring paraffin into the metal bowl containing the contraceptives. He stands there with the matches. Dorothy comes in a little wearily, carrying – we now see – Gary's briefcase. She arrives in time to see Gary putting a match to the bowl.

DOROTHY
Gary, no—
They watch the bowl light up. Through the flames we see that Gary is smiling happily, whereas Dorothy is looking bleak.

DOROTHY
Gary, I'm sorry, but I don't want to have children with you.
A moment while this dawns. Gary looks desolate.

GARY
I've just set fire to all our favourite contraceptives.
Dorothy looks embarrassed.

GARY
Why, what's wrong with me?

DOROTHY
Nothing, I just—

GARY
No, come on, I can take it.

DOROTHY
Okay.
She puts Gary's briefcase on the bed, opens it.

GARY
I kept Anthea and George behind after work looking for that.

DOROTHY
You made the fatal mistake of giving me a glimpse into your private world.

GARY
Go ahead, I have absolutely nothing to hide.
Dorothy removes a couple of Curly-Wurly bars, some strings of liquorice and a paper bag of sweets.

DOROTHY
I was only slightly concerned that the potential father of my children still goes into sweet shops and orders wine gums by the quarter . . .
She takes out a four-pack of lager.

DOROTHY
I decided to turn a blind eye to his passion for cheap lager and the effect that might have on an impressionable young person . . .
She removes a scrap book with a picture of Michaela Strachan stuck on the front.

DOROTHY
I could even cope with the fact that he seems to keep a scrapbook of pictures of an attractive woman TV presenter, torn out of magazines and newspapers . . .

GARY
(*Wheedling*) She's very professional.
Dorothy icily removes an entry form cut out of a local newspaper.

DOROTHY
An entry form for a wet T-shirt competition, filled out on my behalf?

GARY
You don't have to enter if you think it's in any way slightly tacky.

DOROTHY
You're so kind. But I suppose this was what worried me most.
Dorothy takes out a sheet of paper and holds it up: on it is a sketch by Gary of a baby with an alarming resemblance to himself, complete with distinctive ears. Underneath is a caption: 'My son'.

DOROTHY
Do you see my problem?
Gary and Dorothy look at each other.

GARY
I think you're being a tiny bit negative.
Dorothy remains resolute. Gary looks upset.

GARY
But . . . I've bought things for him. We're all going to have fun together.

DOROTHY
I'm sorry, Gary.
Dorothy gives Gary a kiss on the cheek and leaves. Gary watches her go, sadly.

21. LIVING ROOM

Gary and Tony are sitting on the sofa, drinking Gary's cans of lager, watching the TV with the sound low. It is late and they are showing signs of drunkenness. Tony's wrist is bandaged.

GARY
Have you ever thought of donating sperm?

TONY
Yeah, I went to one of those sperm banks once. Bird in a white coat shows me into a little room, and there's these magazines in there, you know, for you to use.
They make laddish noises.

TONY
Yeah, funnily enough there were quite a few copies of *Caravanning Monthly*. Anyway, there were a couple of *Cosmopolitans* so I started to, you know . . .

GARY
Choke the chicken.

TONY
Yeah.
A pause.

TONY
Anyway, it turned out to be a dentist's waiting room.

GARY
Nasty.

TONY
Mm. The sperm bank was next door.
They take a swig of lager.

GARY
Did that really happen?

TONY
No.
They take another swig of lager.

TONY
So, who'd you like to have kids with, ideally?

GARY
Kylie.

TONY
Kylie?

GARY
Kylie.

TONY
Why?

GARY
Because if we were having trouble getting the little baby off to sleep, who better to sing 'Away in a Manger' than Kylie, with her infallible ear for rhythm and her distinctive Aussie brogue? And, although she's quite petite, I get the impression she's as strong as an ox.
Tony shoots Gary a quick, perturbed look.

TONY
So you're not disappointed about Dorothy then?

GARY
God, no. I mean, if we'd gone ahead with it, you would have had to move out for a start.

TONY
Yeah, you'd find it a bit of a struggle without my rent coming in, wouldn't you?

GARY
No. You've never paid me any. Any chance of some this month?
Gary gets up and goes over to the hi-fi.

TONY
Sorry, mate. I owe Deb a couple of hundred quid's worth of underwear.

GARY
Bit steep, isn't it? How much do you reckon your pants drawer's worth?

TONY
(*Calculating*) Six pounds fifty?

GARY
Me, too, tops.
Gary turns on a tape. Loud gurgling sounds follow. He sits down.

TONY
What's this?

GARY
The Womb.

TONY
Oh, yeah, they're good.

GARY
No, no, the womb – you know, where babies come from. The sound of it's supposed to make the little chap feel comforted, like he's back in safety.
The womb recording begins to lull Gary and Tony, who slowly curl up on the sofa.

GARY
So, what does Deb say about me in her diary?

TONY
She says you're a bit of a pompous twat sometimes.
Gary's thumb has been hovering near his mouth.

GARY
What about the times she likes me?

TONY
Those are the times she likes you.

GARY
That's a bit unkind.
Gary puts his thumb into his mouth.

GARY
How's your hand?

TONY
My fingers have gone blue.
He and Tony are now both curled up separately in foetal positions, Tony clutching his can of lager protectively. The womb music plays on.

GARY
Still, it's all part of growing up, isn't it?

SERIES FOUR: EPISODE TWO

INFIDELITY

Paranoia is always funny, especially when it's justified. Dorothy's infidelities gave this series its strongest moments, providing what we in TV call the 'series arc' and what normal people call 'the story'.

The whole of scene two here was cut because we were overrunning. If an episode was long we usually managed to trim it to length by taking out the weaker jokes. In the old days if your episode overshot the half-hour (some episodes of *Fawlty Towers* are over 35 minutes long) they broadcast it at that length and just made the News shorter.

There's a lot of location footage in this episode. It helps to have a few minutes of pre-shot film when you go into the studio, if only because you are more likely to achieve the holy grail of sitcom production: getting to the bar after the show by nine-thirty. But OB (outside broadcast) inserts can be clumsy. The studio audience is watching a tape and often laughs over a joke, and it can interrupt the rhythm of what is otherwise a live performance.

I always promise myself I will not ridicule real people, but then an opportunity comes along and I can't help myself. Tony: 'Did you know there's a one-in-four chance you'll end up having to be looked after by a carer?' Gary: 'Well, as long as it's not Bill Oddie, I don't mind.' It is not as though I even dislike Bill Oddie. And what did they make of that joke in Finland, for example, where *Men Behaving Badly* is so huge? The only time I have actively tried to get at someone was a couple of barbed references in the show to Roy Hattersley, who moonlighted as a hopeless TV critic in the mid-1990s before his peerage came through.

I like the closing scene with Gary and Tony mulling over their future without girlfriends, against a backdrop of slides. It's helpful to have two simultaneous chances to make people laugh, although sometimes even that is not enough.

1. GARY'S FLAT: LIVING ROOM

A lazy Saturday. Tony and Deborah are watching the afternoon movie. Gary has dozed off. Comically dated, clipped-forties British dialogue is heard.

MAN'S VOICE-OVER
How long have people been living in these conditions?

WOMAN'S VOICE-OVER
(*Brisk*) Sufficiently long to get used to them. Cigarette?

MAN'S VOICE-OVER
But . . . the flies, the stifling atmosphere, the beastly surroundings – this is no kind of life.
Tony looks around at the untidy flat guiltily. On screen, a blood-curdling scream reclaims his attention. Deborah is watching, empathising.

MAN'S VOICE-OVER
What was that?

WOMAN'S VOICE-OVER
A scream. Haven't you heard a scream before? Now if you'll excuse me, I have a beating to attend to.
Dialogue gives way to mood-setting music.

TONY
Who's the bloke in the hat?

DEBORAH
He helps run the leper colony.
A pause. Deborah is completely absorbed.

TONY
Who's the woman in the big shoes?

DEBORAH
The villager who's trying to close the hospital down.

TONY
Who's the hairy chap eating the sausages?

DEBORAH
A dog. It's not important.
Another pause.

TONY
What's going on?

DEBORAH
(*Still calm*) I'm about to scream in your face.
Another pause while Tony wonders if he dare risk it.

TONY
Who's the—
Without tearing her eyes from the screen, Deborah picks up a copy of GQ magazine from the coffee table and slaps Tony in the face with it. The noise wakes up Gary. He gradually focuses on the film, yawning.

GARY
Who's the bloke in the hat?

DEBORAH
(*Into his face*) Shut up! Shut up! Shut up!
Gary frowns, looks bewildered.

GARY
There are some very good remedies for PMT on the market these days—

DEBORAH
The only PMT I've got is . . . Pathetic Men Tension.

TONY
That's clever, the way you took the letters PMT and changed the words round—

DEBORAH
Don't be a creep.

TONY
Sorry.

DEBORAH
You invited me down. It's a lovely film. About this man who mends his broken heart by going off and healing the sick in the jungle.
Gary and Tony both curl their lips in disdain.

liar liar...

We all do it and we'd like to do more of it if we thought we'd get away with it. So why is deceit condemned by decent society? Story: Norman Mailer and Stephen King. Additional material: John Naughton

TONY
So . . . not many car crashes then?
Deborah continues to watch the film. Gary is looking at the cover of GQ.

GARY
Load of nonsense in these magazines. 'Danny DeVito – Not Just a Fat Short-arse'. (*Tutting, he turns to the contents page*) 'All You Need to Know about Your Penis'.
Gary looks at Tony pointedly.

TONY
I bought it for the short story.

GARY
'Infidelity – Is Your Girlfriend a Two-timing Slut?' (*Muttering*) No, she's not, thank you very much.
He starts to read the article.

GARY
Apparently there are six symptoms if your girlfriend's having an affair. 'One: she can't help slipping her new lover's name into the conversation.' Difficult to tell with Dorothy – she's always talking about the men she wants to sleep with. 'Two: in case she is about to dump you, she tapes your LPs. 'Three: she makes ridiculous excuses for cancelling dates.'

TONY
Yeah, why didn't Dorothy come over last night?

GARY
Um, she had to stay at home and put her books into alphabetical order. 'Four: she loses interest in sex, at least with you.' Well, we've both been very tired . . .
Gary is becoming quiet and thoughtful.

TONY
What are the other two?

GARY
Oh, the usual drivel.
Gary is perturbed but trying not to show it. Tony snatches the magazine. He reads.

TONY
'She will become evasive when holiday plans are being made.' Where are you going this year with Dorothy?
Trying to think of somewhere, Gary's gaze comes to rest on the coffee table.

GARY
Um, the Table Mountain. Yeah, I'll probably be booking it tomorrow.

DEBORAH
(*Still staring at the TV*) Oh, I heard her say you were going to play it by ear.

GARY
Play it by ear, ah, yes, that's right, we changed our minds.

TONY
'Finally: the errant girlfriend, to assuage her guilt, will bring you flowers and small presents.'
All eyes turn to the room divider, where there is a vase of fresh flowers and a presentation pack of lagers with a red bow round it. Tony and Deborah look at Gary. Gary does a painfully forced laugh.

GARY
Ha. I hope you're not suggesting that Dorothy would be capable for a moment of cheating on me.
Deborah and Tony both look uneasy.

DEBORAH/TONY
No, I'm sure she wouldn't./No way, mate.

GARY
I mean, how many of us here have actually been unfaithful, as opposed to just thinking about it, day after day on an hourly basis?

DEBORAH/TONY
I have./Loads of times.
Gary tries to control his alarm.

2. HALL
A few minutes later. Gary is on the phone, looking tense.

GARY
Hi, Pat! It's me, your old Mr Chipolata. Ding ding, plenty of room on top!
He laughs at this shared joke. A pause. Gary's face falls a little.

GARY
Gary. We went out together for two years.
He smiles, then his face falls again.

GARY
Tall, blondish, leggy, distinguished. (*Nodding*) You've got it, good, good, we're there. (*Listening, frowning*) Is that a parrot?
He listens politely.

GARY
Your children? Ah, lovely. Anyway, my friends and I were joshing around, you know, and, um, we got to talking about the people we've been out with, and, well, basically . . . did you ever . . . see anybody while you were seeing me?
He listens, smiles.

GARY
No, seriously. (*Listening, swallowing*) Was that a team, or eleven separate people? (*Listening*) No, I'm just a bit . . . surprised, that's all.
The front door is heard to slam. Gary looks around, flustered.

GARY
(*All smiles*) Anyway, great talking to you, Pat. Yeah. (*Going through the motions*) We must, you know, if you're up my way, or I'm up down your way, or, yeah, great talking to you. Shall I give you my new address? No? Oh, okay. Take care now. Okay, bye.
Gary puts down the phone as Dorothy comes in, carrying a bag of shopping. She kisses him.

DOROTHY
Hello, darling. I got you another little present, your favourite wine gums. And I've brought back those albums I borrowed.
She hands them to him and goes into the kitchen. Gary looks bleak.

3. KITCHEN

A moment later Dorothy exchanges hellos with Tony and Deborah, then starts to unpack her shopping bag. Gary saunters in, an edge in his voice.

GARY
So, did you successfully put your books into alphabetical order?

DOROTHY
No, actually, I didn't get round to that in the end.

GARY
You didn't get round to that. Oh, how disappointing. I've got some holiday brochures, maybe we should have a flick through them, decide where we're going.

DOROTHY
Can we do that another time? I'm not in the mood.

GARY
Not in the mood. Okay. How about popping into my bedroom for sexual intercourse?
She gets out the paper and starts to read it.

DOROTHY
Do you mind if we don't? I've tried it, I'm not sure I like it.

GARY
Fine, whatever.

DOROTHY
Can we eat early tonight? I need to be back home, there's a programme that Tim, this friend at work, has recommended.

GARY
Tim, uh-huh. (*Lightly*) So, what's he like in bed?

DOROTHY
Sorry?

GARY
Nothing. Are you happy with me, Dorothy?

DOROTHY
Of course I am, Gary, you give my life substance and meaning.

GARY
What's your opinion on infidelity?

DOROTHY
Oh, I think it's okay if you lock up your pets first.

GARY
What would you say if I was having a bit on the side?

DOROTHY
I'd say it's a shame that now there are two of us women who have to put up with your feet.

GARY
Uh-huh. Interesting.

DOROTHY
(*Finally looking up from paper*) Is there a problem, Gary?

GARY
No, no.

DOROTHY
You're acting rather strangely, even for you. Are you wearing your tight pants?

GARY
No.

DOROTHY
(*Smiling*) Funny thing happened yesterday – Tim's just got this—

GARY
Tim. Tim again. Shall we phone Tim and ask him over? Maybe you'd like to jiggle around on Tim's todger while I bring you in a series of tasty snacks.
Dorothy gives Gary a long, hard look.

DOROTHY
Won't it disturb the others while they're watching the film?
Gary reacts.

DOROTHY
Are you suggesting I'm sleeping with somebody, Gary?

GARY
Well, it's a bit bloody obvious, isn't it? You might as well have a bloke walking ahead of you waving a pair of knickers on the end of a pole.

DOROTHY
Gary, it's hard enough going out with you as it is, don't make me dislike you more than absolutely necessary. I'm going home.

GARY
So . . . are you sleeping with somebody?

DOROTHY
That's for you to find out, isn't it?
She gathers up her things and leaves.

4. LIVING ROOM

Meanwhile. Tony and Deborah are still sitting on the sofa. Deborah is absorbed in the movie, Tony is bored. He sighs heavily and looks around the room. He pulls his finger joints, making them crack. Then he does the same with his neck, which finally produces a resounding crunch.
Still bored, he pulls his arms out of his sleeves and sits with them inside his jumper. He arranges the empty sleeves across his body and puts one arm back into its sleeve. He glances over at Deborah and then arranges the empty sleeve round her shoulders.

DEBORAH
Tony.

TONY
I'm not touching you!
They carry on watching.

TONY
He's got a bit of a nasty cough.

DEBORAH
Yes, he's dying.

TONY
He probably regrets going out to the jungle to heal the sick now.
Deborah ignores him.

TONY
I bet he's thinking: Sod it, if only I'd stayed at home instead of going out to the jungle to heal the s—
Deborah snaps, getting to her feet.

DEBORAH
Tony, do you know what I hate about you most?

TONY
Oh, I know this . . . Um, the way sometimes I cough and some spit comes out?

DEBORAH
No. You look okay, and when I haven't got a boyfriend, sometimes I think, why don't we get together. And then you remind me that you're the most selfish, self-centred person in the country.

TONY
So – just to talk about me for a second – if I started to think about people other than myself, I might have a chance of going out with you?
Deborah is on her way out.

TONY
(*Calling after her*) I've got a very caring nature as it happens. I shaved my legs once for charity, you know. (*Sound of the door slamming*) I've got the hairs in an envelope if you don't believe me.
Tony thoughtfully toys with his empty sleeve.

5. DOROTHY'S HOUSE

Wide shot of Tony and Gary sitting in a small red hire car outside a fairly posh suburban house.

TONY
We're staking out her house anonymously, right.

GARY
Yeah.

TONY
So . . . why did you hire a bright red car?

GARY
It was the cheapest. They said it'll be all right if I park in front of a pillar box.

TONY
Does the radio work?
An astonishingly loud blast of rock music. Muffled screams from the two men, then silence.

GARY
Yes.
Cut to inside the car. Tony is dressed like a social worker, complete with caring, mainly home-made lapel badges such as 'Vote Dolphin' and 'i ♥ old people'. Gary is peering out at the house through

binoculars. He has a camera round his neck. Tony quietly adjusts the angle of his passenger seat, reclining more and more as he speaks.

TONY
Why does Dorothy still live at home with her parents?

GARY
Her mother keeps threatening to kill herself if she moves out. I think she should risk it.

TONY
(*Offscreen*) Yeah.

GARY
Can I see your disguise?
Tony gradually reappears, winding the seat back into the upright position. He is now wearing a black balaclava. Gary is not impressed.

GARY
A bank robber. How subtle and ingenious. If Dorothy walks past with a bloke she obviously won't find that suspicious at all.

TONY
What's yours, then?
Gary produces a sombrero from under the seat and puts it on, hiding under its brim.

TONY
A Mexican? Oh, you really blend in dressed like that.

GARY
I may be foreign, but at least I'm not a bloody urban terrorist wearing a badge that says, 'Pets Are People Too'.

TONY
It's for my Samaritans interview. I want to look compassionate.
They sit there, wearing their disguises.

TONY
I should have thought of this before, impressing Deborah by showing my caring side. My raw masculinity's scared her off.

GARY
Well, it's like Dorothy, isn't it? If she is having an affair it's probably because she feels threatened. I'm not a psychologist, as you know—

TONY
No.

GARY
No.

TONY
No.

GARY
But when I look at Dorothy these days I see one scared little girl. To be honest, I think she's crying inside.

TONY
You don't think she just . . . fancies the arse off another bloke?
Gary looks at Tony blankly, then turns back to Dorothy's house. They take off their disguises.

TONY
So what'll you do if you see her with her new shag?

GARY
Well, I'm not a psychologist, as I said.

TONY
No.

GARY
No.

TONY
No.

GARY
But she's obviously in denial, so I'll present her with all the evidence, calmly, and we'll talk it through in an adult way. Then I'll go round to the bloke's house and make him regret ever messing with my chick.
Gary thumps the dashboard aggressively, then tries to hide how much he has hurt his wrist.

TONY
Well, whether we like it or not, there is a place for violence in the modern world.

GARY
No, I thought I'd shout something through his letter box, what do you think?

TONY
Yeah, that can be effective.
They suddenly notice a man going up the garden path. He rings the bell.

TONY
The Eagle has landed.
They scramble into action, hurriedly getting out of the car. Gary locks the doors with the remote device before Tony has shut his door, and when he does so it sets off the alarm. Gary and Tony panic, desperately trying to muffle the noise without alerting Dorothy's mystery caller. Finally they manage to switch off the alarm.
They rush over and hide behind a fence. Dorothy answers the door and lets in the man. From Gary's point of view – the camera shaky, a parody of foot-in-the-door journalism – he and

Tony run up the garden path and flatten themselves against the wall either side of the front door.

The door opens again a little, and the man starts to come out. Gary realises he will be spotted unless he hides. There is a small tree nearby, into which Gary climbs, scratching himself in the process. He encourages Tony to do the same. Tony tuts and does so, reluctantly.

The two of them hang precariously in the foliage while Dorothy emerges with the man. They have a banal, muttered conversation.

DOROTHY
Yes, I think they wanted a quote to tarmac the drive.

BUILDER
Do you know if it was to include just the drive or round the back, too?

DOROTHY
I don't know really. Um.

BUILDER
I could do you two if you like.

DOROTHY
Yes, that might be an idea.

They step out a little further into the drive. Unseen behind them, Gary and Tony continue to hang in the tree. As Dorothy and the builder mutter on, Gary's camera drops down below the line of the foliage, dangling there. He pulls it back up. A handkerchief falls out of Tony's pocket, followed by his keys, then a slow, regular stream of coins. Dorothy and the builder wander round to the side of the house. Gary and Tony drop out of their perches like dead birds.

A day or so later. Tony is sitting, cheerfully reading a magazine. Gary comes in, lugging a carrier bag.

TONY
There's loads of fascinating stuff in here.

GARY
You're not still getting to know your penis, are you?

TONY
No.

GARY
Good. Because, ironically, I'd have said that of all your organs it's the one you know the best.

TONY
No, this is *The Carer* magazine. Did you know that there's a one-in-four chance you'll end up having to be looked after by a carer?

Gary wearily plonks himself down on the sofa.

GARY
Well, as long as it's not Bill Oddie, I don't mind.

TONY
Yeah. Or, I tell you who'd be bad. Who's that chubby bloke who runs Germany?

GARY
Chancellor Helmut Kohl?

TONY
Yeah, imagine having him wiping up your dribble.

GARY
Nightmare.

TONY
Nightmare.

GARY
That's the good thing about going out with a nurse. You might have your ups and downs, but you'll always get the best medical care.

TONY
So, did you catch out Dorothy having a snog?

GARY
No, but I'm collecting some pretty conclusive evidence against her. I discovered the perfect disguise today – nobody notices anyone in a uniform.

Tony leans forward and yanks a Day-Glo orange-and-white uniform out of Gary's bag. Gary looks slightly embarrassed.

TONY
Even if you're holding a six-foot orange lollipop?

GARY
It's great for meeting women actually. Mind you, you have to take them across the road.

Tony gets up and prepares a pot of tea, calling through from the kitchen. We cut between them.

TONY
It's pretty sad, isn't it, though, standing around on street corners snooping on your own bird?

GARY
No, it happens in all the great, stormy relationships. I bet . . . Paula Yates couldn't go

shopping without finding Bob Geldof outside in the bushes with his Instamatic.

TONY
It's normally guys that screw around though, isn't it.

GARY
Well, the hormones are in our make-up. Not literally make-up.

TONY
I used to be like that. I thought of joining Sex Addicts Anonymous at one stage.

GARY
Well, you're not telling me you don't meet a lot of birds there who are up for it.

TONY
Exactly. I used to say, some men express themselves through the things they say, or by inventing penicillin, or whatever, and I express myself by having sex with a lot of women.
Tony comes through with a tea tray. Gary picks up the letter from the coffee table.

GARY
What's this?

TONY
Rejection letter from the Samaritans.

GARY
(*Reading*) 'Unfortunately, we thought your comment that "These people just need to pull themselves together" betrayed a lack of understanding. Nor could we agree that the best antidote to depression is "drinking lager until your head spins".' (*Throwing down the letter*) It's nit-picking, isn't it.

TONY
Still, sounds like I was that close.

GARY
Oh, well, bad luck, mate. So how're you going to impress Deborah with your compassion now? Or are you going to fall back on your cheese impressions?

TONY
No, I've got a placement as a volunteer at an old folks' day centre. They've got this 'companion scheme' where we chat informatively to the old-timers about the issues of the day, and in return they sort of tell us stories about rationing and how chicken used to taste like chicken.

GARY
I tell you the only good thing about being old.

TONY
Cardigans?

GARY
No. You get to carry a stick.

TONY
Yeah, that's good that. Anyway, apparently old people get on well with us unemployed.

GARY
Why's that?

TONY
Because we're both regarded by an uncaring world as an underclass. And we both eat a lot of soup.

GARY
And you both potter a lot, don't you?

TONY
Yeah, we do a lot of pottering. There's so much they can teach us though. They've got a lady there who can remember Lincoln being assassinated.

GARY
Wow.

TONY
She's lying, apparently, because it happened fifty years before she was born. But still.

GARY
Yeah, still.

7. DAY CENTRE

Tony is sitting with an elderly lady, sipping tea. He is nodding and listening in a 'caring' way. He is dressed rather like a Playschool presenter.

ELDERLY LADY
That's why historically an elected body is the only way to run a metropolis like London. You can tinker around with residuary bodies and quangos, but that's like trying to fix a sucking chest wound with little pieces of kitchen towel. How do you see it, Tony?
Tony looks clueless.

TONY
Did you see *Gladiators* on Saturday?

ELDERLY LADY
I think television is the most disastrous single invention of the twentieth century.
A pause. Tony looks less sure of himself.

TONY
They had this great competition where one of them had to hit the other one with this big padded thing. Brilliant.

They sit in embarrassed silence. Tony's elderly companion looks disappointed in him.
Fade to some time later. Tony is in full flow. The elderly lady has fallen asleep.

TONY
. . . then another night I'm cooking Deb one of my meals – pot-noodle-in-a-kebab, very tasty – we're having a real laugh, and I think, I'm in there, right, she's begging for it. Then I tell her my joke about the page three girl who goes into the greengrocer's, and Deb flies off the handle, and I'm back to square one again. Then another time, we're having this cracking evening in the Crown, and we've got eight bevvies on the go, and we're doing real snogging. I'm thinking, I'm in there again, and these banana-flavoured ribbed condoms fall out of my pocket – well, from her reaction you'd think I was carrying a severed hand or something. Then another time . . .

8. STREET OUTSIDE DOROTHY'S HOSPITAL

Third man spy music. Gary is standing on a street corner in a Bogart-style raincoat. He has some scratches on his face from the tree. Round his neck is a camera with a long telephoto lens. Obviously into the romanticism of being a private eye, Gary lights up a cigarette, puts it in the corner of this mouth and lines up his shot.
The smoke goes into his eye as Dorothy emerges with a group of mainly male friends. They head in

Gary's direction. With his eyes watering painfully, Gary manages to take a few pictures and scribble something in his notebook. Realising they are getting close, Gary steps back into the shadows. He plummets from view, falling down some steps into a basement.

9. DAY CENTRE

Same day. An elderly man is sitting on his own, happily reading a book. Tony suddenly appears at his shoulder, beaming with exaggerated friendliness.

TONY
Hello! I'm Tony, the others may have told you about me. I'm here on the Happy Companion scheme. I've come to chat!
The man looks distressed. Tony sits down anyway.

TONY
So, what shall we talk about? Shall I give you a run-down of what's in the pop charts . . .
Cut to a wide shot of Tony talking to the man, who gets up and goes to sit in an armchair on the other side of the room.

10. HIGH STREET

Daytime in a crowded street. We pick out Dorothy, walking along on her own towards us. She stops to look in a shop window, then walks on. We eventually pick out Gary some distance behind her. He is wearing dark glasses and is following her doggedly . . .

11. DAY CENTRE

Later that day seven or eight pensioners are sitting around in chairs facing an unattended microphone. Tony bounds on in best Ben Elton style, grabbing the microphone.

TONY
Thank you. Hello, Sunnyside Day Centre! How're you doing! Great to be here! Yo!
He whoops enthusiastically and surveys his audience, who are polite but unsure.

TONY
Post-office queues, they're slow, aren't they? Slow? Queues? I queued at one the other day, the person at the head of the queue finally picked up her pension. She was a bit surprised – she was only forty-seven when she went in.
One person smiles.

TONY
Post-office queues, terribly slow. Hey, money these days, it doesn't go very far, does it? Never mind 'spend a penny'. It's more like 'spend three pounds eighty'!
He waits for the non-existent laughter.

TONY
Inflation, that certainly is a terrible thing. Hey. I'll tell you the best thing about being old. You get to carry a stick.
Tony's audience is starting to talk among themselves. He is beginning to lose confidence.

TONY
A stick, that's the best thing. Hey, have you noticed how difficult it is to get the tops off jars these days? I'll tell you what I do. I . . . tend to eat out.
The audience is now chatting away, becoming oblivious to Tony. He looks forlorn but forces himself to go on.

TONY
Steps – they're everywhere, aren't they? Far too many.
Nobody is paying any attention. Tony looks around, quietly replaces the microphone in its stand and backs off the stage.

12. OUTSIDE A CINEMA

Gary now has a camera with an obscenely long telephoto lens. He manages to manhandle it so he can focus on a distant cinema. Looking through the lens, we see Dorothy emerging with a couple of men and a woman. The men's faces are obscured. The view is suddenly blocked. A couple of tourists are standing in the way. Gary urgently gestures them aside. They wave back. Gary gives up and moves the cumbersome camera. Through the lens again we see that Dorothy has gone. Gary desperately points the lens this way and that but can not find Dorothy. The camera picks up a couple smooching in a doorway and does a double take. Gary now lingers on the pair as they get into some heavy petting. The view is obscured again. Gary looks up furiously to see a policeman standing there, looking disapproving. Gary does a cheesy smile.

13. COMMUNAL HALL

Deborah is coming in. Tony suddenly appears, as though by chance. He is continuing to make an effort to look like a nerdy do-gooder.

TONY
Hi, Deb.

DEBORAH
Hello, Tony.

TONY
How are things?

DEBORAH
Fine, I'll just go upstairs now—

TONY
I just thought you might want to know, after the conversation we had, I'm doing a lot of charity work now.

DEBORAH
Oh, good for you.

TONY
In the community, you know. I'm a bit of a hit down at the day centre.

DEBORAH
Great.
An awkward pause.

TONY
If you could see the look of gratitude I've had from some of those lovely crumblies, you'd understand why I feel so fulfilled.

DEBORAH
Lovely.
She edges towards her door, trying to leave.

TONY
Look at these. I had some photos taken.
Deborah wearily looks over at them. We see a polaroid of Tony's elderly woman, ducking behind a pillar.

TONY
She's brilliant, always mucking around, pretending to hide from me.
He shows Deborah another, of a man scowling, arm raised in the classic 'No-photos' pose.

TONY
He's great too. Big pigeon collection. Fantastic.
Tony tosses the snaps aside.

DEBORAH
Well, thanks for sharing that with me, Tony.

TONY
Pleasure. I mean, my caring side's really, you know, motoring now. Non-threatening, that's me.

DEBORAH
Mm, at this rate I might come to like you. What are you going to do next to impress me?

TONY
No, that's it. I've finished now.
Deborah gives him a sceptical smile and puts her key in the lock.

TONY
So will you go out with me now?

DEBORAH
Oh, I think you've still got a little way to go to prove you're not a self-centred bastard.
Deborah disappears upstairs.

TONY
Bugger.

14. GARY'S FLAT: LIVING ROOM

Night-time. Gary opens the door to Dorothy.

GARY
Good evening.

DOROTHY
Hi.
Dorothy does an embarrassed, affectionate smile.

DOROTHY
I'm sorry we had to row last time. I hate it when we argue. (*Pausing*) Unfortunate, really, as we do it two or three hundred times a year.
She goes to give Gary a kiss on the cheek, but, looking unmoved, he stops her.

GARY
I don't think kissing's really appropriate, do you, Dorothy?

DOROTHY
It was only a peck on the cheek. I wasn't going to force you to show affection against your will.

GARY
Perhaps you'd like to step into the kitchen. I've got something to show you.
He flounces off into the kitchen. Dorothy frowns.

15. KITCHEN

Seconds later Dorothy comes in. Chairs have been set out to face a screen for a slide show.

DOROTHY
Oh, no. Not your slides of the major intersections of the M25.

GARY
No.

DOROTHY
Your office outing to the World of Leather in Guildford?

GARY
No.
Dorothy reluctantly takes a seat. Gary gets his notebook out and ceremoniously turns to the first page. He will conduct the slide show like a police presentation.

GARY
Okay. The background of this whole operation was suspicions arising from circumstantial evidence and conversations with Dorothy, to wit that she did commit with malice aforethought acts of indecency with another, you know, bloke.

DOROTHY
What are you talking about?
Using a remote-control device, Gary activates the first transparency. It shows Dorothy leaving an Ann Summers-type lingerie store.

GARY
This.
Dorothy's mouth has fallen open.

GARY
This is as upsetting for me as it is for you.

DOROTHY
How long have you been snooping on me?

GARY
Since we last met. Except Thursday – I had to go into the office, George was panicking because he'd lost the stapler.
Dorothy continues to look incredulous.

GARY
On Wednesday at one-thirty p.m. you were seen leaving this lingerie shop, presumably with a number of items bought to titillate the disgusting appetites of your—

DOROTHY
Gary, I was taking back the peep-hole bra you bought me at Christmas.

GARY
Why?

DOROTHY
Because most women dress for comfort, not to look like a milking machine.
Gary clicks on another slide. It shows Dorothy with a group of friends outside the hospital.

GARY
Notice the ratio of men to women, nearly two to one.
He produces a pointer and taps the men on the screen.

GARY
I would remind you that the ratio in the population as a whole is roughly equal.

DOROTHY
I can't believe it – you've bought a pointer.
Another slide comes up – the same group – but this time Dorothy is talking and laughing with two of the men.

GARY
(*Indicating with his pointer*) Notice the lascivious expressions here and here.
Dorothy rolls her eyes.

GARY
At this point investigations began to focus on these two men, whom I shall call A and B.

DOROTHY
Or Tim and Jeff, as everyone else calls them.
Tony comes in.

TONY
Hi, have I missed anything?

DOROTHY
Yes, Gary being an arse.

TONY
Oh, damn.

DOROTHY
Don't worry, he hasn't finished being an arse yet.
A new transparency comes up – a bought one in bright technicolor of some landmark.

GARY
Sorry.
Another slide appears. Taken with a long lens through a window of the hospital, it is a fuzzy image of a couple kissing.

GARY
A bona-fide hanky-panky situation, clearly.

DOROTHY
Gary, it isn't me.

GARY
How can you be so sure?

DOROTHY
I would have remembered.

TONY
Hey, it's great this, isn't it? Like *Crimewatch* but with your mates.
A new slide: Dorothy smiling at the milkman as he delivers milk to her house.

GARY
Friday, eight-thirty. Another apparently innocent encounter.

DOROTHY
It's the bloody milkman!

GARY
All right, I'll let that one go.
The next transparency, taken with a telephoto lens again, shows an attractive woman in an office, bending over. Gary is flustered.

GARY
Ah, that was a test shot.
He quickly moves on to another woman in her home adjusting a bra strap.

GARY
It's surprisingly difficult to get the, um, focal . . . lengthening factorisation right.

DOROTHY
Gary, I can either leave now or break some furniture over your head. Do you have a preference?
A slide comes up of a young Gary on a boozy holiday with a pint glass stuffed down his trousers.

GARY
Ah, some private ones have got mixed in.

TONY
(*Gesturing at the screen*) Good gag, mate.

GARY
Thanks, mate.

DOROTHY
Tony, please get lost.

TONY
Okay.
Tony leaves the room. The last slide: Tim is giving Dorothy a kiss on the cheek. He has his arm round her. Gary turns on the light.

GARY
So, there you have it – it's a pretty sleazy story of temptation and submission.

DOROTHY
He was just being affectionate! If you must know, he's gay.

GARY
Oh, how convenient.
Dorothy tuts with irritation and starts to search through the slides.

GARY
Yes – I thought I had a straight-talking girl, turns out I've just been a crazy fool. But I've decided that there's no place for vindictiveness in my life and, with counselling, you'll—

DOROTHY
Shut up, Gary.
She crossly puts the slide back into the projector. It is the second slide we saw.

DOROTHY
You will notice that A has his hand on B's bottom. A has lived with B for several years, they have a little dog called Liberace. Okay? If you really want to know, I've started to see C.
She is pointing to one of the other men in the group, his face barely visible in the background.

GARY
(*Stunned*) You've started to see C?

DOROTHY
His name's Jamie. He's a radiographer.

GARY
(*Disbelieving*) I've never heard of him. Which radio station's he on?

DOROTHY
Radio Dorothy. (*Gary remains blank*) Radiography, he does X-rays.

GARY
Have you slept with him?

DOROTHY
Yes.

GARY
No, you haven't.
Dorothy shrugs. Gary looks sorry for himself.

GARY
What's wrong with me, am I so disgusting?
A very long pause.

DOROTHY
Well, that's part of it, obviously.

GARY
What?!

DOROTHY
No, I'm doing it because . . . well, I'm sorry, Gary, but I love him.
Dorothy looks guilty. Increasingly desperate, Gary turns back to the image on the screen.

GARY
You can't love him, he's all grey and smudgy. That's no basis for a relationship.
Dorothy prepares to leave.

GARY
He's exploiting you, Dorothy. I know these medical guys, it's three points for screwing a nurse, two points for a patient, if she's not too

ill, and the first one to twenty wins a set of steak knives.

DOROTHY
(*Nettled*) I was dreading having to tell you, Gary. Thanks, you've made it easy for me.

GARY
So what does this mean?

DOROTHY
It means we're not going out with each other any more.
She leaves. Gary sits in open-mouthed silence.

16. COMMUNAL HALL

Later that night Tony is waiting for Deborah. He has made himself look even more like a staid do-gooder. He puts a pipe in his mouth to enhance the effect, then reconsiders.

TONY
No, that's too much.
As he puts the glasses away, Dorothy passes on her way in.

TONY
Bye-bye, Dorothy, mate.

DOROTHY
Bye-bye, Tony, mate.
Deborah comes out of her flat, slightly testy.

DEBORAH
Yes. Hello. What?

TONY
Just thought we could have a chat, you know.
Deborah looks long-suffering.

TONY
I've got some more badges, look. 'Respect Whales' – that's the huge fish things, not the country, 'More Drinking Fountains Now'—

DEBORAH
Tony, you don't think these badges are a bit . . . nerdy.
Tony looks at her blankly.

TONY
Anyway, what I really wanted to talk to you about is this.
He hands her a piece of paper. She reads it.

TONY
You see, I've already shaved my legs once for a good cause, as I mentioned, so I was looking for a new challenge.

DEBORAH
You're offering to shave your pubic hair for charity.

TONY
Shall I put you down for a tenner? You don't have to watch or anything, I'll be putting it on video to show my sponsors I'm not hiding anything.
Deborah, lost for words, hands Tony back the sponsorship form.

TONY
Or we could both do the shave, if you like—

DEBORAH
Tony, I appreciate that you're doing this to impress me.

TONY
Cheers.

DEBORAH
But it's pointless.

TONY
No, I'm doing it to raise money for Friends of the Earth, 'cos the way I see it, the survival of the earth, our home, is more important than my personal hair. Probably.

DEBORAH
It's pointless because I've got a new boyfriend.
A shocked silence while Tony takes this in.

TONY
You can't – I've been caring, like you told me to be.

DEBORAH
I'm sorry, Tony.
He leans against the wall and whimpers.

TONY
It's so unfair!
Deborah smiles apologetically and goes back into her flat.

TONY
(*Calling after her*) Charity begins at home, you know. I've been to hell and back for you.

17. GARY'S FLAT: KITCHEN

Later that night. Gary and Tony are sitting at the kitchen table, both looking sad and dazed. Empty lager cans litter the table. The projector and screen are still set up, showing a blank rectangle of light, which dominates the otherwise dimly lit room.
Gary idly presses the slide-changer button, bringing up an in-your-face picture of Gary and Tony, heads together, smiling hugely. The image contrasts with how they now look. Gary and Tony do not even bother to turn and look at the slides.

They take a swig. Another slide comes up: Gary and Dorothy in pyjamas, larking about on a double bed, bending over and looking back between their legs at the camera.

GARY
Five years, we've been going out. Do you know, back then when we first met, chicken really tasted like chicken.

TONY
Yeah.

GARY
We've seen . . . John McCarthy reunited with lovely Jill Morell.

TONY
You've seen the unexplained disappearance of Rick Astley from the pop charts.

GARY
Yup. We've seen prime ministers come and go.

TONY
Well, one—

GARY
Yeah, one.
Another slide comes up, of fruit and vegetables arranged on a table in the shapes of a male and a female torso, complete with genitalia.

TONY
You've both grown wiser.

GARY
And a little sadder.
Another slide: an old photo of a boy of about eight, recognisably Gary, looking daft and happy.

Same night. Deborah and Dorothy are sitting on the sofa, nursing glasses of wine, looking thoughtful. The moody lighting matches that of the lads' flat.

DEBORAH
How did Gary take it?

DOROTHY
Oh, he went through the usual stages: aggression and disbelief, deviousness and gibbering desperation, then back to aggression again. What about Tony?

DEBORAH
I felt sorry for him in the end. He really thinks one day I'm going to drop everything and sleep with him.

DOROTHY
Will you?

DEBORAH
Probably. Well, it's not every day a man offers to shave off his pubic hair to make you go out with him.

DOROTHY
No. Gary dyed his red, white and blue during the 1990 World Cup, but that's not quite the same thing. Many's the evening I spent back then, watching him touch up his roots.
They both smile wistfully.

DOROTHY
You don't get that kind of entertainment from every boyfriend.

DEBORAH
Mm. Going out with Tony must be like being on a rollercoaster – lots of screaming and a few laughs. You keep wishing you could get off and think you're going to be sick a lot.

DOROTHY
It's so sad, when you think of all Gary and I've been through together.

DEBORAH
Mm.

DOROTHY
Occasionally it was even quite enjoyable.

DEBORAH
I suppose it'll all be different with our new men. It'll just be plain good conversation, evenings out and lots of uncomplicated sex.
They sit there sadly, then break out into grins. They keep on grinning.

The scene as ten minutes earlier. A slide is showing a dog with its head cocked. Gary and Tony continue to drink lager.

GARY
To be honest, I'll be surprised if I even notice she's gone.

TONY
Who?

GARY
Who, exactly. There's a lot of nonsense talked about monogamy. If God had meant men to stick with one woman, He wouldn't have invented other women, would He?

TONY
No.
Gary clicks on a new slide: a young woman sunbathing. Another slide quickly comes up:

Tony with about twenty unlit cigarettes stuffed in his mouth.

TONY
Yeah, I can't be chasing after Deb all my life. She's dented my confidence a bit. I used to only have to do that (*Snapping fingers*), and I'd have women running after me.

GARY
Wasn't that inconvenient if you were just calling over a waiter or something?

TONY
Yeah, it was actually.

GARY
Was it one woman per click running after you or several clicks per woman, or—

TONY
The point is, from now on I'm a free agent again.

GARY
Me too. Isn't it great?

TONY
Yeah. Brilliant.
A moment's silence. Gary changes the slide one last time, bringing up a picture of the four of them, Gary, Tony, Dorothy and Deborah. They are posed together, smiling happily.

GARY
Anyway, Dorothy'll come back. She needs me.

TONY
Yeah, maybe I'll just have one more crack at Deborah.

SERIES FOUR: EPISODE THREE

PORNOGRAPHY

Our rudest episode, until the controversial 'sticky tissue' episode, 'Performance', broadcast on Christmas Day 1998. Well, a post-watershed sitcom about two men sharing a flat has to deal with masturbation at *some* point. I like the idea of using a sitcom to tackle contemporary themes and dilemmas, although in practice the memorable bits are usually people falling over or banging their heads. *Roseanne* used to be great at handling issues, for example its episode on dope-smoking.

Miscellaneous production notes. A handy tip: use yoghurt to get the bird-droppings effect in the park scene . . . Note how director Martin Dennis poked fun at my script by filming to the letter my stage instruction: 'Slow-motion, worm's-eye shot of the Scotch egg thudding across the floor . . .' A special actor-safe chain saw was built for the sawing-kitty's-head-off scene . . . Lovely, innocent stage manager Mary Motture never really recovered from being sent down to the newsagent to buy two dozen porn mags to dress the set . . . Leslie Ash is on great form as she tries gently to dissuade Gary from gate-crashing her dinner party . . . Neil was very grateful for his bed scenes, as well he might be . . .

I added some lewd dialogue to the last scene during rehearsals – believe me, when you are in the mood there is nothing more fun than writing a conversation about sex between two pissed-up blokes. Neil and Martin improvised 'The Wanker's Song', which worried me at the time, but in fact it provides a brilliant, chaotic, obscene ending to the show.

1. GARY'S FLAT: KITCHEN

Morning. Gary is sitting at the kitchen table, morosely smoking, looking terrible. From another room comes the sound of an acoustic guitar being played very badly. Gary winces.

TONY
(*Offscreen, singing badly*) 'We had joy we had fun, we had seasons in the sun, But the hills that we— (*Missing the chord*) we . . . we . . . we'?
To shut the noise out, Gary picks up a towel and wraps it round his head. There is a pause while Tony finds a new chord.

TONY
(*Offscreen, still singing*) 'Goodbye, Michelle, my little one, You gave me love and helped me find—' (*Missing the chord again*) 'find . . . find . . . find'? (*Breaking off*) What d'you reckon? It's in my book – *A Hundred Best Busking Ballads.*
Not getting a reply, Tony comes in with his guitar, wearing a harmonica stand round his neck. He finds Gary with his head completely wrapped in a towel, a cigarette wedged in the gap where his mouth is. Tony reaches into the towel and frees one of Gary's ears, so he can hear if not see.

TONY
This is it with a mouth organ.
He starts strumming again, this time leaning forward and blowing into the harmonica. Gary removes his towel and watches Tony.

TONY
'We had joy we had fun, we had—'
Gary snatches the guitar and harmonica and throws them to the floor.

GARY
Tony, how can I put this? Take your joy and your fun and bugger off.

TONY
It's very popular in the subways actually.

GARY
So's mugging and urinating. At least people don't urinate and then expect you to give them your small change.
Tony looks hurt.

TONY
I'm just trying to earn a living.

GARY
(*Sighing*) Sorry, mate. It's this Dorothy stuff.

TONY
I know, mate. Try to think about something else.

GARY
You know what hurts the most?

TONY
Having your testicles squeezed between two bricks. Got to be.
Gary stares at Tony evenly.

GARY
You know what hurts the most about Dorothy going off with this bloke?

TONY
Oh, right. No, what?

GARY
She says she's in love. She's never told me that.

TONY
She doesn't love him. She probably just likes bonking him more than you.

GARY
(*Even more depressed*) Thanks, Tony.
Tony sits down close to Gary, smiles kindly.

TONY
Listen, I've never told you this before but one night when we were in the Crown, you were at the bar, Dorothy leaned over to me and said, 'I really don't deserve Gary.' See? (*Prodding him for emphasis*) That is respect, mate. She respected you, and she loved you, and she respected you.

GARY
Are you sure she didn't say: 'What have I done to deserve Gary?'
Tony considers this.

TONY
Oh, yeah, that was it. (*Getting up*) Still, there's a positive side to all this.

GARY
(*Brightening*) Is there?

TONY
Yeah – at least I've got a girlfriend. It was about bloody time, I hadn't had a woman for so long I'd forgotten which end to start at.
Gary looks glum. Tony goes into his bedroom.

TONY
(*Offscreen, calling through*) I tell you, chicks come on to me all the time while I'm busking.
Tony reappears with a tom-tom.

TONY
I'm thinking of varying my act. What do you think of this?
He sits down with the tom-tom between his knees. As he sings he bangs it haphazardly.

TONY
'We had joy we had fun, we had seasons in the—'

GARY
Tony, Tony.

TONY
'Sun'. What?

GARY
You're not too old to be beaten senseless and sent to your room.

TONY
All right. I was thinking of doing some performance art. How about this, this is me walking in the wind.
He does a bad version of someone doing just that. Gary watches, then gets to his feet menacingly.

GARY
How about this? This is me slapping you in the wind.

TONY
Hey, Gaz, lighten up. Look, do you trust me?

GARY
'Course.

TONY
Right – do what I say, and I think I know how to get Dorothy back.

GARY
How?

TONY
Well, the first thing is, you've got to play hard to get. Don't go and see her or phone her.

GARY
Okay.

2. HALL

A sharp cut to Gary on the phone, some time later.

GARY
Dorothy, hi.

DOROTHY'S VOICE-OVER
Hello, Gary.
Gary has a tray by him. On it are an empty wine bottle and two cassette players.

GARY
How are you?

DOROTHY'S VOICE-OVER
Okay. What about you?

GARY
Me. Great.
With a remote control, Gary activates his hi-fi. Lounge-lizard music comes out.

DOROTHY'S VOICE-OVER
Gary, why are you phoning me from a brothel?

GARY
No, no, I'm at home. Lazing around, you know.
He presses a cassette player, and we hear a woman giggling. He puts the phone close to the speaker.

DOROTHY'S VOICE-OVER
Have you got someone there with you?

GARY
Oh, nobody special.
He presses the other cassette player. The sound of very loud licking and sucking comes out.

GARY
Um, I wondered if we could meet for a chat.

DOROTHY'S VOICE-OVER
Okay.
Gary is holding a cork in a wine bottle. He pulls it out, making a popping sound, then clinks two glasses together.

DOROTHY'S VOICE-OVER
Sounds like you've got people round.

GARY
People, person – pouting, dripping love-slave, whatever, you know. Why, I'm not making you jealous, am I?
The giggling is repeating monotonously, clearly on a loop.

TONY'S VOICE-OVER
(*Distant, on cassette*) Can I stop doing sucking noises now, Gary? Me lips have packed up.

DOROTHY'S VOICE-OVER
Gary, how about you phone me another time, when you don't need to rely on a tray of props, a BBC sound-effects tape and your friend making sucking noises.

GARY
Ah. Okay.

3. THE PARK

Later that week, daytime. Gary and Dorothy are walking in the park.

GARY
I've been thinking about our situation, and I wondered – I'm obviously not going to embarrass us both by, you know, begging you to reconsider—

DOROTHY
No, I understand.

GARY
So I wondered if you'd reconsider if I . . . paid you to go out with me again.
Dorothy looks at him damningly.

DOROTHY
Would that be a lump sum or regular instalments?

GARY
Well, how about a small one-off payment of—

DOROTHY
Gary. I don't think so.

GARY
Oh.

DOROTHY
Why couldn't you have been this keen when we were going out together?

GARY
I was. I've showered you with presents this year.

DOROTHY
What?

GARY
That thing for scraping the dirt off celery.

DOROTHY
So – just to be boringly technical – you've showered me with a celery scraper.
Gary looks depressed.

DOROTHY
I gave enough hints I thought there was something missing in our relationship.

GARY
When?

DOROTHY
When I kept begging you to find another girlfriend. Didn't that set any alarm bells ringing?
They walk through, out of shot.
Cut to Gary and Dorothy sitting on a bench.

GARY
So what's so great about your new bloke?

DOROTHY
Jamie? (*Smiling warmly*) Oh, he's lovely, he's got this lovely way of—

GARY
I don't want you to tell me, for God's sake! Are you mad? Five years, Dorothy, doesn't it mean anything to you?

DOROTHY
Of course it does. You're part of my life.
They both gaze into the distance miserably. Something plops on Gary's shoulder. They don't react.

DOROTHY
A bird just, um . . .

GARY
Yes, what a surprise.
Dorothy reaches into her bag, takes a tissue out and wipes the bird shit off Gary's shoulder.

DOROTHY
Some of my things are still round at your place.

GARY
I know. There's a cheese sandwich of yours in the fridge. If you want it I can post it.

DOROTHY
No, you can have it.

GARY
Thanks. Tony broke your facial sauna, I'm afraid.

DOROTHY
How?

GARY
He cracked it while he was steaming his genitals.

DOROTHY
Why was . . .?
They consider this for a while.

DOROTHY
Oh, never mind.

GARY
I'm keeping the things we bought together.

DOROTHY
That's not fair.

GARY
Well, as you pointed out – if life was fair, Michael Portillo would have a big wart on the side of his face.

DOROTHY
Look, you have the tent, I'll have the sunlamp and the Scrabble.

GARY
Oh, so I get to huddle under some damp canvas while you and Mr Lovely have all over tans and play an entertaining and informative word game.

DOROTHY
All right, the other way round then.

GARY
Who am I going to play Scrabble with?

DOROTHY
Tony?

GARY
It's not the same. He keeps altering his letters with a felt pen.
A pause. They sit there in silence.

DOROTHY
Please don't make this difficult, Gary.
Another silence. A dollop of bird shit falls on Gary's other shoulder. He tuts.

4. GARY'S FLAT: KITCHEN/TONY'S BEDROOM

Night-time. From the kitchen we hear love-making sounds – gentle moans from a woman and excited gasps from Tony, getting louder.

TONY
(*Offscreen*) Whoaa! Whoooaaagh!
Some items fall from the mantelpiece.

TONY
(*Offscreen, ecstatic*) Bananarama!
A moment's silence, apart from heavy breathing. Cut to Tony and Jill – attractive, affectionate – lying in Tony's bed.

TONY
Well, it beats busking, that's for sure.
Jill smiles. Tony reaches for his guitar.

TONY
I've learnt the chords to 'The Birdie Song', shall I play it for you?

JILL
No, don't spoil it, we've had such a nice time.
She runs her hand across his chest sensuously.

JILL
So, what's your secret? You've been like a stick of rock all afternoon.
Tony smiles bashfully, then looks perplexed.

TONY
Minty?

JILL
Er, no.

TONY
Oh, yeah. Well, I've had a bit of a gap from women.

JILL
Why?

TONY
I've been sort of saving myself for the girl upstairs. My fluids have been building up for quite a while now. It's like when you open the washing machine in the middle of the cycle, and all this stuff comes pouring out, over your feet.
Jill has put a cigarette in her mouth.

JILL
So why didn't she want to open your machine for you?

TONY
Deborah? Oh, I think she's got a fixed idea about the kind of guy she wants.

JILL
What kind is that?

TONY
Um, someone she likes.
Jill tries her box of matches but finds it empty.

TONY
Well, she sort of likes me, but it's like a swingometer, you know. (*Miming a swingometer*) She likes me, she likes me, she likes me less, less, less, she likes me a bit more, a bit more. (*Miming violent swing*) She hates me, she really hates me—

JILL
(*Opening the bedside cupboard, no longer listening*) Have you got a light, Tony?

TONY
No, don't open that . . .
He trails off as a stash of soft-porn magazines cascades out of the cupboard. Jill holds several magazines up accusingly. Tony struggles to think of an excuse.

TONY
How many times have I told Gary not to leave his stuff in my room!
He takes the magazines from Jill and scornfully reads a cover.

TONY
'Bollock Bare in Burnley', 'Open Wide and Say Ahhhh'. I mean, is it just me or is that offensive and degrading to women?!

JILL
Don't bother, Tony.

TONY
No, I'll have a word with Gary. It's the shock of Dorothy dumping him. These are the only women he can trust.

JILL
I mean, does that really turn you on?
She holds up a centre spread for him to see.

TONY
(*Lying*) No way, who could possibly find that . . . Yes, it does actually.

JILL
How can it?

TONY
Well, she's naked.

JILL
Yes, but she's obviously freezing to death, she's sitting on a fork-lift truck feeling exposed and stupid and like a piece of meat. How can that turn you on?

TONY
(*After a pause, in a small voice*) She's naked, look.
Jill turns away, looking pissed off.

TONY
I mean, be fair, we do come into the world nude.

JILL
Yeah, we don't come into it on our hands and knees clutching a cucumber and pretending to have an orgasm.
A pause. Tony looks chastened.

TONY
So . . . you're not a big user of pornography yourself, then?

JILL
I'm serious, Tony. If you don't get rid of these I don't want anything to do with you.

TONY
No problem. I'll just put these here in the bin, there we go.
He carefully puts the magazines he is holding in the wastepaper basket next to the bed and smiles at Jill.

5: LIVING ROOM

One night later that week. Gary is leading Deborah in. She looks happy. He is smoking and drinking, a wreck.

GARY
Drink, Deborah?

DEBORAH
No, thanks. I'm in the middle of cooking.

GARY
Oh. Can I have some?

DEBORAH
No.

GARY
Okay.
They sit down. Gary is hyper, a little lost.

GARY
Deborah, you're a girl.

DEBORAH
No, I was a girl, now I'm a woman.

GARY
(*Confused*) How does that work then?

DEBORAH
Never mind.

GARY
Anyway, thanks for coming down, I thought that as a girl you might have an insight into how I could get Dorothy back.

DEBORAH
I know it's hard to accept, but maybe she doesn't want to come back.

GARY
Good. Very sound.

DEBORAH
Perhaps you should think about finding somebody new.

GARY
Okay. Yes.
Gary is nodding. A sticky pause.

GARY
How do I do that?

DEBORAH
Well, you need to meet some new people.

GARY
Meet some new people. Like your thinking.

DEBORAH
Do you meet anybody at work?

GARY
Yep, a mad middle-aged bloke and a mad middle-aged woman.

DEBORAH
Oh. Well, you could, I don't know, do some evening classes?

GARY
Won't I be too busy meeting people?

DEBORAH
You meet people there.

GARY
Good, got it. What should I study, fridge maintenance, something like that? Basketball?
Deborah studies Gary closely.

DEBORAH
This has hit you quite hard, hasn't it, Gary.

GARY
No, bit of freedom, just what the doctor ordered.

DEBORAH
You could do what I'm doing tomorrow night, have a dinner party.

GARY
Or should I . . . come to yours?

DEBORAH
No, I've got enough guests.

GARY
I could squeeze on to the end of the table.

DEBORAH
No, there really isn't room—

GARY
I could bring my own little table, put it next to yours.

DEBORAH
(*Getting tetchy*) You can't come, Gary.
A pause. Gary seems to have got the message.

GARY
I could bring my own cutlery and food – I wouldn't be any trouble.
Deborah sighs.

DEBORAH
You wouldn't want to come – I've invited Dorothy and her new boyfriend.

GARY
(*Getting up*) Oh, I get the picture. Well, thanks for your advice. I'll probably be having a dinner party of my own then.
Deborah gets up and edges towards the door.

GARY
Tomorrow night seems a good time.

DEBORAH
Won't you need more time to prepare?

GARY
I can see you haven't organised as many sophisticated dinner parties as I have.

6. GARY'S OFFICE

Gary – a bit more together than the night before – is looking anguished as he tries to start a list. George is sitting at his desk.

GARY
George, remind me what you need for an elegant dinner party.

GEORGE
Guests.
Gary ponders, then reaches for his list.

GARY
(*Adding to it*) Guests.

GEORGE
Food.

GARY
(*Writing*) Food.

GEORGE
Drink.

GARY
(*Yet more writing*) Drink. Anything else?

GEORGE
I find a bowl of nuts often puts a smile on people's faces in the early stages.

GARY
Nuts as well? (*Tutting and writing*) This is all starting to get complicated.
Anthea comes in, carrying her now traditional typed letters.

GARY
What sort of people shall I invite to my dinner party, Anthea?

ANTHEA
Well, Peter Ustinov's very chatty, isn't he? He'd make it go with a swing.
George nods sagely in agreement.

ANTHEA
Or . . . comedian Tom O'Connor, he'd probably have a ready quip.
Unimpressed, Gary starts to dial a number.

GARY
Any other suggestions – Whitney Houston perhaps? The Birmingham Six?

ANTHEA
Do you have enough chairs for the Birmingham Six?
Gary stares at her for a moment in disbelief.

GARY
No, you're right. Better make that the Guildford Four. (*Speaking into the phone*) Clive? Hi. Gary. What's happening your end tonight?
Gary listens. Anthea and George are standing there, watching him. Gary realises and shoos them away. Anthea exits.

GARY
(*Into the phone*) Great. I'm having a dinner party. Can you bring a couple of birds and a bottle? Magic. Dorothy? No, I chucked her. Well, you know how it is, mate, if you've got the keys to the whole sweetshop you don't want to just stuff your face with Crunchies the whole time, do you?
Gary cringes at what he has said, then is suddenly all genteel smiles.

GARY
Super. See you at eightish.
He puts down the receiver and crosses off 'Guests' from his list.

GARY
That's the guests. Food. Is there any point in asking you for suggestions, George?

GEORGE
Well, at our last supper party we had vegetarians over so Marjorie cooked as an hors d'oeuvre some rather nice leek and mushroom dumplettes.

GARY
What's a dumplette?

GEORGE
It's Marjorie's recipe. It's half way between a dumpling and an omelette. Sometimes we call them omml—

GARY
(*Joining in*) Ommlings, yes.

GEORGE
The main course was vegetarian strogamatouille.

GARY
Half way between stroganoff and ratatouille?

GEORGE
And taramasalata.

GARY
Of course.

GEORGE
The only problem was it tasted like—

GARY
Shit?

GEORGE
Yes.
In despair Gary tosses his pen aside. He sighs.

GEORGE
Why are you having a dinner party?

GARY
To celebrate me being free again. Bachelor boy, that's me, like Cliff Richard. Not exactly like Cliff Richard, obviously.

GEORGE
She's one in a million, Dorothy.

GARY
Thanks, George.

GEORGE
I don't suppose you'll ever find anyone as special as her again.

GARY
Thanks. Thanks a lot. (*Sadly*) I dreamt about her again last night. She was at this dinner party upstairs, I was having mine downstairs. Mine went so well I was awarded a prize by Delia Smith, some kind of golden frying pan, on a plinth. Then there was a hammering at the door, and it was Dorothy, shouting, 'I love you, Gary. I want to be with you for ever at your award-winning dinner parties.' Then I woke up, and it was Tony knocking on my door, wanting to play me 'The Birdie Song' on his guitar.
Gary gazes bleakly. George has left his desk and come over to Gary's. In a clumsy gesture of sympathy, George puts his hand on Gary's shoulder and leaves it there. Gary smiles at George but looks uneasy.

7. GARY'S FLAT: KITCHEN/LIVING ROOM

Early evening. In the kitchen Tony, wearing a smart white shirt, is tidying up and dusting. He calls through to the living room.

TONY
You know masturbation?
Gary is in the living room, dressed in an equally smart white shirt and laying out a sheet on the table as a tablecloth. We switch between the two men.

GARY
Vaguely, yeah.

TONY
And you know women.

GARY
Women. Yeah.

TONY
When they do it, right, they imagine Richard Gere or Linford Christie or whoever lying on top of them, probably on a mountaintop.

GARY
Or in a leafy glade.

TONY
Right, somewhere with a girly atmosphere – anyway, doing the business to them.

GARY
Right. Whereas we just turn to our favourite mag, and, you know, Bob's your uncle.

TONY
Exactly, it's quicker, you don't have to use your imagination, and it's good for local newsagents.
Gary is aligning the sheet with fanatical precision.

GARY
Actually, I haven't bought any since Dorothy found my collection.

TONY
Cross?

GARY
Not really. Well, she waited until I left the flat, then sent a magazine to every address in my Filofax, with a covering note.

TONY
That's a bit awkward.

GARY
Yeah. Mind you, some of my relatives were quite grateful for the mags actually.
Tony grunts supportively.

GARY
I know my branch of Barclays were pretty surprised when the Christmas issue of *Minge* plopped on to their doormat.

TONY
They must have been.
Gary is tearing sheets off a kitchen roll.

GARY
Do you know how to fold paper serviettes into roses?

TONY
No.

GARY
Nor do I. I'll do aeroplanes.
He starts to fold paper planes out of the kitchen roll. Tony comes through into the living room.

TONY
What we need is more pornography but better, so girls can enjoy it too.

GARY
Yeah, so we've got *Titbits* and *Muff*. They should have magazines called . . . *Bollocks* and *Wang*.

TONY
Yeah, the ladies, bless 'em—

GARY
Bless 'em—

TONY
They should be able to go into the newsagents and say, 'I'll have *Hello!* and *Knitting Weekly* and, oh, give me a copy of this month's *Foreskin*.'

GARY
That would be true equality.

TONY
Brilliant!

GARY
So if someone offered you five hundred quid to pose naked, in *Wang*, would you do it?

TONY
I would if it was, you know, artistic.

GARY
Me too.
Tony adopts a pose, leaning in the doorway 'artistically'.

TONY
Like this, maybe.
Gary grunts, not paying attention.

TONY
Or I could be, like, sitting down on a chair.
He adopts an awkward seated pose, legs raised

GARY
(*Not looking*) Yeah, sexy.

TONY
Then if they wanted something a bit cheekier I could do this.
He adopts another ridiculous girly-mag position and puts his finger in his mouth 'sexily'. Gary gives him a long look.

GARY
No.

TONY
No?
Tony takes a dustbin liner and heads for his bedroom.

TONY
I'd better get rid of my mags before Jill arrives.
Gary surveys the table and gets little card name tags out of his pocket.

GARY
(*Calling through*) Hey, Tony, I got Anthea to do place names. She couldn't read my writing, so I'm afraid you're down as Totty.

8. TONY'S BEDROOM

Tony takes the magazines out of the wastepaper basket and is about to put them in the bin-liner. He stops and cradles them lovingly. He opens one and glances at the photographs with fondness and nostalgia. The doorbell goes. Struggling with his conscience, Tony looks around for somewhere to hide the magazines.

9. KITCHEN

Moments later. Gary is showing Jill through, trying to be a posh host.

GARY
Um, coats in my room, lavatory there if you need to freshen up – not that you don't look fresh, obviously. (*Chuckling*) I'll be serving some nuts shortly, I thought maybe some witty conversation with the other guests initially, then . . .
Jill smiles politely and heads off to Tony's room.

GARY
Oh, you're going to visit Tony in his bedroom, fine.

10. TONY'S BEDROOM

Tony is putting on aftershave. Jill comes in. They kiss enthusiastically.

JILL
Mm, that's nice.

TONY
You're looking great.
She does a little twirl. She does look great. Tony does a gravelly groan of desire. They go into another clinch.

JILL
It's a shame we have to have supper.
Tony glances at his watch, then at her body, then in the direction of the living room, then back at her body, horribly torn.

JILL
Your flatmate's made quite an effort. He seemed excited that we were going to be having a candle—

TONY
Yeah, he's my best mate, we should really get out there and . . .
They start to kiss again, obviously bound for bed.

JILL
Who needs those horrible magazines?
Tony looks shifty. They fall on to the bed.

11. COMMUNAL HALL

Same night. Deborah opens the front door to Dorothy and Jamie, her hip, good-looking boyfriend. He and Dorothy are both wearing leather jackets and carrying full-face crash helmets.

DEBORAH
Hi, there.

DOROTHY
Hi. Shall we do the introductions upstairs?
Dorothy glances anxiously at Gary's door, which now opens. Gary appears.

GARY
Oh, hello. I thought that might be the catering for my dinner party.
The others look awkward.

DOROTHY
Hello, Gary. This is Jamie.
Jamie nods hello convivially. Gary notices their impressive motorbike gear.

GARY
Ah, yes. I used to have a moped.

JAMIE
It's a Harley-Davidson actually.
Gary searches, almost visibly, for a suitably caustic riposte.

GARY
(*Childish imitation*) It's a Harley-Davidson actually.

DOROTHY
Gary, if that's the juvenile level you want to conduct this—

GARY
Juvenile level? Sorry, did you say juvenile level? Juvenile as in what?

JAMIE
Juvenile as in—

GARY
I know what juvenile means, thank you. I did go to university.

DOROTHY
(*Quietly*) No, you didn't, Gary.
Jamie is smirking. Deborah ushers her guests to her door.

GARY
And I'd be grateful if you'd keep your voices down, I'm having a sophisticated dinner party. I'll ask my guests whether they find me juvenile. We can discuss that over the five-course meal, washed down with a choice of fine wines from around the world.
The front door is pushed open, and Les appears. He is carrying a tray and is looking sleazier than ever.

LES
Hello, catering! Hi, Gary. I'm afraid we're having the oven sandblasted so I've had to do you some cold cuts instead.

Les removes the tea towel from the tray, revealing various unappetising items. Watched by the others, Gary does an embarrassed laugh.

GARY
I'll just take this inside and—

LES
Funnily enough nobody's ever asked me to do outside catering before so I made a hasty study of nouvelle cuisine. Here we have organic pilchards in a *jus*. Over here smoked-salmon hexagons drizzled with Malibu.

GARY
Thanks, Les, I'll just—

LES
Here (*Pointing to grapefruit centrepiece*), a variation on the always popular cheese-and-pineapple cubes: kiwi-fruit cubes with pork scratchings. Bit of a bugger to get on the cocktail sticks.
Gary looks humiliated. Dorothy gives him a sympathetic look. She, Deborah and Jamie exit into Deborah's flat. Les is now alone with Gary.

LES
I made the Scotch egg myself, with the finest Scotch. Be careful, though, the egg's still got the shell on.
Gary has taken the tray. He looks at Les blankly and shuts the door in his face.

12. GARY'S FLAT

Gary walks disconsolately through the hall, carrying the tray. The phone rings. He answers it.

GARY
Hello? (*His face falls*) You can't have had a better offer. What about the two girls you were bringing? (*Listening*)

What do you mean they're the better offer. (*Listening*) Of course I can't get anyone else this late! No, I don't have any other friends, you know I don't.
He whimpers, looks down at the tray.

GARY
I've spent days preparing the food. Right, that's it. Don't come to me next time you want someone to take your Mum round Harrods.
He slams down the phone and walks sadly into the kitchen. He listens out for signs of life in Tony's bedroom.

GARY
(*Gently*) Hello, supper is served in the living room.
There is no reply. Gary edges towards Tony's bedroom door. Smoochy music is playing.

JILL
(*Offscreen, muffled giggles*) Don't force it, Tony. Let me just put my leg— Ooh. Yesss.
Gary grimaces and tiptoes away from the door. He stands in the middle of the kitchen, clears his throat and calls out.

GARY
Um, bit of a setback on the guests front. Anyway . . . any time you're ready . . .
A pause, then the music is turned up louder. Gary walks through into the living room and puts the platter of food down on the table. Everything is set out neatly. He stands there, looking forlorn. The sound of bright laughter drifts down from upstairs. Gary morosely raises his eyes to the ceiling. We go into a montage.

13. DEBORAH'S FLAT

Upstairs, an elegant dinner party, shot in After Eight-style gloss. Vivaldi is playing. Deborah, Dorothy, Jamie and Deborah's boyfriend, Peter, are sitting round a candlelit table.
They are chatting animatedly and drinking wine from gleaming glasses.

14. GARY'S FLAT: LIVING ROOM

We focus on a piece of card typed 'Girl Guest 2', then a serviette poorly folded into a paper aeroplane. The room lighting is harsh, but there is a single candle sticking up out of a beer mug. Plaintive mouth organ or lonesome-cowboy guitar is playing.
We open out to find Gary clutching a wine box that he is trying to open, using a knife to free the plastic-tap device. The knife slips and slashes open the container. Three litres of red wine spew

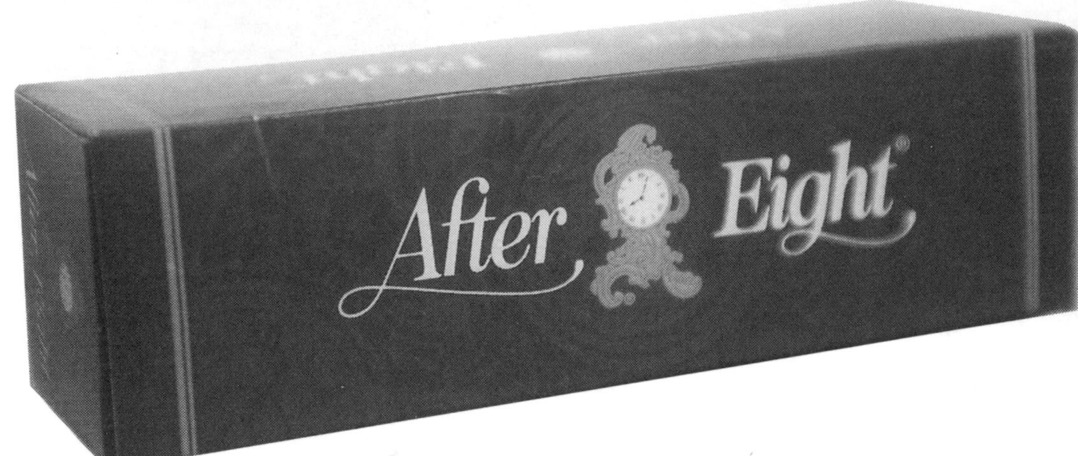

out over the white tablecloth, despite Gary's attempts to push the wine back in. His white shirt is spattered.

15. DEBORAH'S FLAT

Jamie is telling an anecdote to the others, who are smiling and joining in as they eat their plates of sumptuous, steaming-hot food.

16. GARY'S FLAT: LIVING ROOM

The table is a mess of paper napkins sodden with red wine. Gary – now wearing a paper hat and swigging from a can of lager – nibbles at the food dubiously. He picks up a cracker and strains to pull it on his own. As it finally tears, he knocks the candle and Scotch egg across the room with his elbow. Slow-motion, worm's-eye shot of the Scotch egg thudding across the floor.

17. DEBORAH'S FLAT

The lights dimmed even lower. Deborah brings in an ambitious pudding, which is flambéeing spectacularly. Appreciative comments follow a ripple of understated applause.

18. GARY'S FLAT: LIVING ROOM

Gary is carefully munching some Scotch egg. Empty cans of lager are arranged in a pyramid on the table. He is trying to construct the plastic necklace that came with his cracker. He winces suddenly as he chews, gingerly puts his fingers in his mouth and tries to remove some shell.

The plastic necklace disintegrates in Gary's hands. He sighs heavily and tries to remain calm. He finishes his can of lager and tosses it at the pyramid of cans, which collapses. Musical montage ends.

19. DEBORAH'S FLAT

Dorothy, Deborah and their boyfriends are still at the table, talking over cups of coffee. They are slightly merry with drink.

JAMIE
So, what's it like living above Beavis and Butthead?

DEBORAH
That's not fair. If anything they're more like Fred and Barney, only not quite so well dressed.

DOROTHY
They'd take that as a compliment – Wilma won their Cartoon-Woman-They'd-Most-Like-to-See-Naked Competition.

PETER
Oh, I'd have gone for Lady Penelope. She was this great sexual icon.

DOROTHY
I don't know about icon. She won in Gary and Tony's Best-Babe-with-her-Own-Car section.

PETER
They're keeping pretty quiet downstairs.

DEBORAH
At this time of night it could go either way: they'll either collapse in an alcoholic coma or start singing 'Lady In Red' very unmusically.

JAMIE
I'm a bit worried about that Scotch egg – shall I have some paramedics on stand-by in case someone tries to eat it?

DOROTHY
I'm not going to sit here while you make fun of my ex-boyfriend.

DEBORAH
(*Amused*) Where are you going to sit?

DOROTHY
(*Pointing*) I thought maybe over there in that armchair.
Laughter.

JAMIE
It must be a relief to go out with someone whose ears don't look like they were welded on by a drunk Albanian.

DOROTHY
(*Suddenly not amused*) I mean it, Jamie, leave him alone.
A pause, then the others do amused ooh-sorry-I-spoke noises. Dorothy looks nostalgic.

DOROTHY
He's . . . unhappy. I never wanted that to happen.

20. GARY'S FLAT: KITCHEN/LIVING ROOM

Tony creeps out of his bedroom in his dressing gown. Trying not to be noticed, he quietly opens the fridge door and removes a four-pack of lager. He is about to tiptoe away when he realises that Gary is sitting alone at the table, looking maudlin and rather drunk as he goes through the contents of a large plastic bag. Looking guilty, Tony sits down next to Gary.

TONY
Hi, there.

GARY
Oh, hi.
He sees Tony's dressing gown and bare legs.

GARY
I thought we agreed on smart–casual for this evening. I think you're edging into casual–casual there.

TONY
Where are the others, in the toilet?

GARY
Yes, I'm going to join them in a minute. We're going for the European record for the most people in a toilet during a dinner party. The current record dates back to a dinner party held in Oslo in 1976.

TONY
Sorry about me and Jill. We were feeling, you know, a bit sexy.
He grins goofily. Gary frowns.

GARY
Feeling a bit sexy. No, sorry, doesn't ring any bells.

TONY
Anyway I'm here now. (*Smiling puppyishly*) What can I do to help?

GARY
You could wring the tablecloth out into that wine box.

TONY
Maybe I'll just . . . sit here and chat.

GARY
Don't worry, mate, I don't need company, I've got all of life's essentials – a beer, a cake and a broken plastic necklace.

TONY
What's in the bag?

GARY
What's left of me and Dorothy.
Gary gets a sunlamp out of the plastic bag and plonks it down on the table.

GARY
We bought this when we were about to go to Majorca and realised that with our clothes off we both looked like two pieces of raw cod. (*Getting out a cat basket*) We got this when we rescued a stray cat and nurtured it back to health. (*Producing a scrawny toy cat from inside*) And this is the replacement cat we got when the one we nurtured back to health was run over by next door's Campervan.
He gets out a game of Scrabble.

GARY
We bought this together in a shop in Ipswich. I accused Dorothy of flirting with the shop assistant, so she made me travel in the boot on the way home. Happy days.
He puts everything back in the bag.

GARY
That's just a selection of items from our relationship, which is now over.

TONY
Well, all credit, you're taking it really calmly.
Laughter drifts down again from upstairs. Still apparently calm, Gary gets up.

GARY
Excuse me, I'm just going out to the shed.

TONY
Okay, mate.
Carrying the plastic bag, Gary leaves the room. Tony looks confused.

JILL
(Offscreen) Tony!
Tony smiles suavely and swaggers off towards the bedroom.

21. TONY'S BEDROOM

Jill is holding Tony's guitar, looking accusing. Tony comes in.

TONY
What?
She turns the guitar round and pulls off the back. Inside is Tony's stash of girly magazines. He affects surprise.

TONY
So that's why 'The House of the Rising Sun' sounds so crap!
Jill starts angrily to pull on the rest of her clothes.

JILL
You couldn't do that one thing for me, could you?

TONY
But you might chuck me, then what am I going to do for company?

JILL
Ah, the ideal chance to find out.

TONY
These girls are my friends!

JILL
Well, you obviously prefer friends with staples through their breasts.
She leaves, furious.

22. KITCHEN/HALL

Tony pursues Jill through the kitchen, holding some of the magazines.

TONY
They have excellent articles and short stories. Surprisingly educational.
Jill reaches the door and lets herself out into the communal hall.

TONY
Tell you what, just let me keep the one with Nikki and Kimberly playing snooker, it means a lot to me.
They are now in the communal hall. Jill lets herself out of the front door and is gone. He calls after her.

TONY
Hey, maybe you've got the problem, not me, pal.
He shuts the door.

TONY
(*Sadly*) Sod, you then.
He looks disappointed but is distracted by the sight of Deborah's door being open.

23. DEBORAH'S FLAT

Moments earlier. Deborah and her guests are now sitting around in armchairs and on the sofa. A knock on the door, which only Deborah hears. She gets up. She enters her hall and opens the door. Gary is standing there, brandishing a cordless power saw. He turns it on. Deborah steps back in alarm, and he walks in. Gary appears in the flat, brandishing the saw. Deborah follows him in, looking alarmed. Dorothy, Jamie and Peter watch with their mouths open.

GARY
Okay, sorry to interrupt. Don't get up, ex-boyfriend here. Dorothy and I have one or two possessions to divide up, so I thought I'd do it in the fairest way possible, down the middle, to show there's no bitterness.
He empties the contents of the plastic bag on to the coffee table.

GARY
Right, what shall we start with? How about our tent.
He saws the tent in half cleanly.

GARY
Maybe it'll be less of a bastard to put up now it's in handy sections. Lovely. What's next? The cat basket.
The four of them watch as he slices that in two.

GARY
Now the cat.

DEBORAH/DOROTHY/PETER
No!

GARY
Let's put it this way, Dorothy, either you go out with me again or the cat gets sawn in half.
A tense pause. Nobody says anything.

GARY
Okay.
He saws in half the toy cat, cutting deep into the table. As he finishes, Tony comes in. He goes up to Gary and caringly turns off the power. Gary,

calming down, realises everyone is looking at him. A pause follows, in which he tries to push the two halves of the cat together again. As the others stare at him, Gary smiles apologetically and leaves with Tony. Alone, Dorothy, Deborah and the guests sit in stunned silence. Gary reappears suddenly. Jamie looks frightened, but Gary merely picks up his half of the possessions and leaves with them.

24. OUTSIDE THE FLATS: STREET

Wide shot of three or four houses in darkness, apart from a light on in one downstairs room. Gary and Tony are having a late-night drinking session.

TONY/GARY
(*Offscreen, singing*) 'Lady in Red! Lady in Red'!
A pause while Tony plays a heavy, jarring chord on his guitar.
They repeat the refrain again and again, until eventually they stop. A pause.

TONY
(*Offscreen*) Hey, why are we sitting in the dark?

GARY
(*Offscreen*) I don't know.
After a moment a light goes on downstairs in one of the houses which is otherwise in darkness.

TONY
(*Offscreen*) Oh, you're over there.

25. GARY'S FLAT: LIVING ROOM

Tony walks across the room to sit down next to Gary on the sofa. Gary is stroking his half of the cat and is sitting in front of half a Scrabble board. He has pitched his tattered half of the tent, with guy ropes nailed into the floor.

TONY
Can I be honest with you, mate?

GARY
I'd be shocked if you weren't, mate.

TONY
I've been a bit worried about you.

GARY
Why's that?

TONY
Well, let's face it, you don't power-saw your bird's stuff in the middle of a dinner party unless you're a bit stressed.

GARY
Oh, you don't want to worry about me. I will survive.
They start to sing, occasionally together, tragically unsure of the words.

GARY
'I will survive . . . creeping out that door . . . survive . . .'

TONY
(*Overlapping*) 'I, I will survive . . . door, I will survive . . .'
They peter out.

TONY
What a bastard, eh?

GARY
Who, Jamie? Yeah, little piggy eyes.

TONY
No.

GARY
My mate Clive? Yeah.

TONY
No.

GARY
Les?

TONY
No. Tony Blackburn.

GARY
Yeah, bastard.

TONY
Bastard.
A pause. Gary continues to stroke the remains of his cat.

GARY
This is supposed to be good for alleviating stress.

TONY
What, stroking your pet? Yeah.

GARY
Of course, it's better if you've got, you know, the whole pet.

TONY
Yeah.

Embassy
NUMBER 1

I wrote this on holiday in the Caribbean and worried that this was not the right place to write an episode in praise of the British pub. But it came out well, I think. I had planned a stripped-down episode with Gary and Tony at the bar getting gradually more drunk. In the end I threw it all in: video footage, bad dancing, singing, location filming, Tony naked (again) and a host of extras. A historical note: the after-hours 'We are Sailing' rowing sing-along actually took place in the Crown pub in Camden Town in 1983.

Making up names is one of the joys of comedy writing. Having in the previous week wiled away happy minutes inventing names for porn mags (I'm still disappointed nobody was inspired by the episode to start up *Foreskin* magazine), now it was the time for lager brands (Binky, Plop). The word 'smingey' appears here and in a couple of other episodes. This was my tragic, doomed attempt to introduce a new word into the English language.

For once I was reasonably happy with the scenes with Dorothy and Deborah alone together. I always found them a bitch to write, even though in other projects I have enjoyed doing all-women dialogue. Ultimately perhaps, vital though Dorothy and Deborah are, when they are on everyone is wondering where the daft blokes have got to.

I love writing drunks. Their dialogue has a sort of submerged logic and is usually shot through with a mad, touching optimism, as here when Gary tries out his hopeless excuses to Dorothy. I am particularly fond of Neil's drunken Tony – benign and cheery but with that unhinged look in his eye. Incidentally, it is supposed to be a bad idea to write under the influence of alcohol, but I've had a go, and I have to say a couple of glasses of wine can really help. But do stop before you get completely rat-arsed.

1. THE CROWN

Lunchtime. Gary, Tony and Dorothy are sitting at a table drinking. Dorothy looks subdued.

GARY
I've, um, got a surprise for you.
He smiles and nudges Dorothy, encouraging her to guess.

DOROTHY
(Bored) You're half man, half-fish?

GARY
No.

DOROTHY
You've invented a new kind of banana?

GARY
No.

TONY
I like surprises. Is it a . . . pet beaver?

GARY
No. Anyway, you know what it is, you helped make it.

TONY
Oh, yeah.

DOROTHY
It's not something unpleasant like a presentation set of your bodily fluids, is it?

GARY
No, I'll give it to you later. It'll cheer you up.

TONY
Yeah, what's up, Dorothy?

DOROTHY
Isn't it blindingly obvious? I'm going out with Gary again.

GARY
You don't have to.

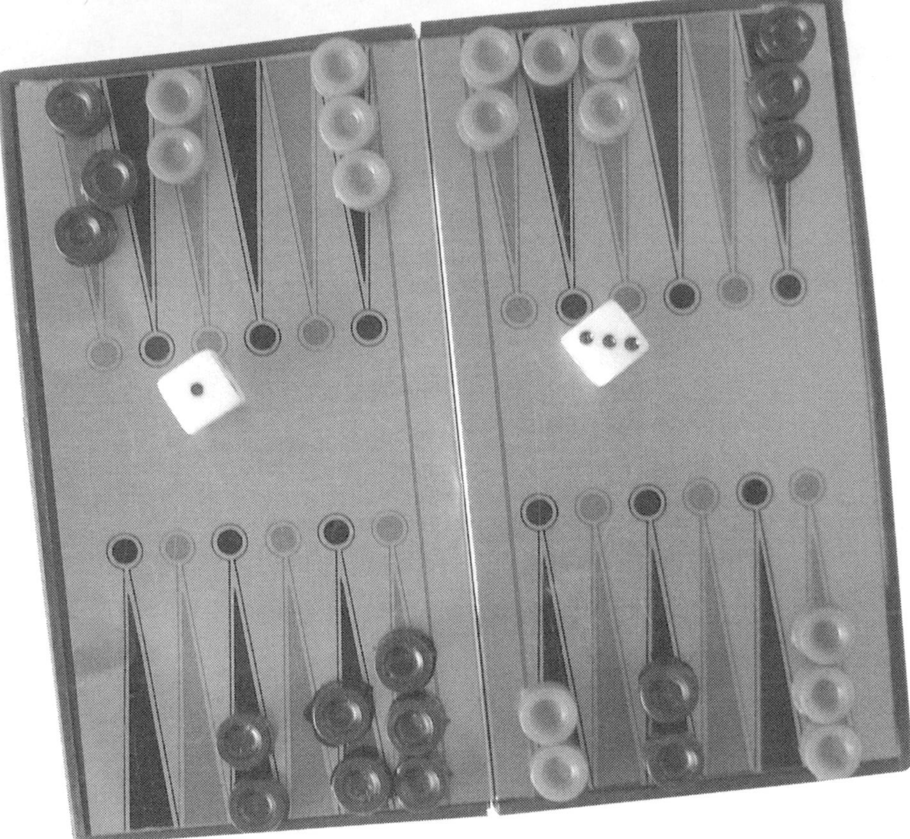

DOROTHY
I do. I've obviously been condemned to perpetual misery by the god of abysmal boyfriends. I'll probably get Bill Wyman next. Or Mr Bean.

GARY
You're supposed to be happy. I know some girls who'd physically assault other women in order to go out with me.

DOROTHY
I'm sorry. It's lovely to be going out with you again. I just feel we've been here before, and we're going round and round in circles. And the more we—

GARY
Yeah, you've made your point, shut up.

DOROTHY
See? I want us to have a proper relationship, where we talk about things, other than . . . what kind of knickers Betty Rubble wears in *The Flintstones*.

TONY
Yeah, I phoned up this mate, apparently they're—

DOROTHY
Tony, it doesn't matter.
Dorothy is looking at them in despair.

GARY
Look, love, this is our new start. We'll have a nice meal tonight . . .

DOROTHY
I know, I'm cooking it—

GARY
Exactly, each of us brings our special strengths to the relationship.

DOROTHY
So mine seems to be cooking, what's yours?

GARY
Eating. See? It's uncanny. Just one example of the two of us working together in perfect harmony.
Dorothy still looks doubtful. Gary punches her playfully on the shoulder, a gesture of affection. Dorothy smiles. Gary does it again.

DOROTHY
(*Suddenly po-faced*) Don't, that hurts.

GARY
Sorry.
They gaze at each other affectionately, then realise that Tony is looking lost.

TONY
No, you have a great romantic evening. I'll keep out of your way, probably stay in here and play backgammon with Les.

DOROTHY
Les plays backgammon? Next you'll be telling me he's stopped signing his name with a big shaky cross.

TONY
No, we just like to get the board out and sit with it, to look like two dandies. Les has got this dream of being nominated for the Pub of the Year competition.
They look around the dismal room. Les is behind the bar, trying to look smart in a very old suit.

DOROTHY
As long as the year's 1942 he might have a chance. Shall we go?
She has got up. Gary escorts her towards the exit. Tony heads for the bar.

LES
Dorothy. (*Holding out a bowl to her*) As part of the Crown's continuing search for excellent service, can I offer you a goodbye gherkin?

DOROTHY
No, thanks, Les, it's my month for not eating poisonous bar snacks.

LES
Can I bend your bloke's ear for a second?

DOROTHY
If you're going to do it properly it'll take more than a second.

GARY
Sorry, Les, my lady and me are off for a candlelit supper at home – together, obviously – and nothing is going to get in the way of that.

DOROTHY
You can finish your pint if you like—

GARY
(*Instantly*) Okay.
They stop in the doorway. Gary takes her hand.

GARY
Everything's going to be different from now on, okay?

DOROTHY
Yes.
They kiss tenderly. Dorothy leaves. Gary turns round to find the pub's entirely male clientele frowning at him in stern silence.

GARY
Sorry.
He joins Tony, who is nodding earnestly as he listens to Les behind the bar.

LES
So I reckon they should release Barmby forward, capitalising on his speed across the park.

TONY
Park, yeah.

LES
That'll free up Klinsman to fulfil his roving brief up front, feeding off loose balls.

TONY
Balls, yeah.
Les goes off to serve a customer.

GARY
What's he talking about?

TONY
I don't know. Sounds like it might be football.

GARY
Yeah, what a cliché barman. Do they think all blokes can talk about is booze, birds and football? (*Rapid fire*) How's your pint?

TONY
Brilliant.

GARY
Where's Deborah tonight?

TONY
Her place.
They sip their lager.

TONY
I reckon I've got a real chance of cracking her this time.

GARY
Magic.

TONY
In the past, if I'm honest, I haven't always come on to her very subtly.

GARY
No.

TONY
Mooning her in Waitrose when she was with her mates – if I'm really hard on myself, that was probably a misjudgement.

GARY
Yeah.

TONY
And buying her that monk doll with the pop-up erection.

GARY
Yeah. Still, you've always been there for her, haven't you? Downstairs.

TONY
Yeah.

GARY
Often pissed-up and seeing other birds—

TONY
But always there for her.

GARY
Yeah.
Les finishes serving and drifts over.

GARY
What did you want me for, Les?

LES
Oh, yeah. The brewery's bunged me these guest lagers I wanted your opinion on. This one's from Bulgaria, it's called Sod.

GARY
(*Getting up*) Sorry, Les, I can't, I've got a special lady waiting at home for me.

LES
What does Dorothy feel about that?

GARY
It is Dorothy, Les.

LES
Oh. I thought you'd been going out with her for five years.
Gary considers.

GARY
(*Sitting down*) Yeah, give me a cold Sod, will you?

Later that evening. Dorothy is sitting waiting, fed up. A full meal is set out on the elegantly laid kitchen table. She gets up and wanders around, looking for distractions. She opens the fridge and gets out a bottle of white wine. Inside we can see lots of lager and a joke-shop severed hand. Dorothy drifts out to the hall and switches on the answerphone. She listens to the old messages as she walks round the kitchen, looking for a corkscrew.

GARY'S VOICE-OVER
Tony, I'm running late, can you record *Baywatch*? Cheers.
Dorothy tuts. A beep follows.

HEATHER'S VOICE-OVER
(*Terse*) Tony, I've still got your Nirvana CD and watch. This is me smashing them with a hammer.
A distant smashing sound, then a beep. Dorothy opens a cupboard door, revealing the freakishly large rabbit from episode one.

TONY'S VOICE-OVER
Hey, Gar, if you get in can you record that documentary about king penguins and their fascinating wintry world. Ta. Oh, and *Baywatch*.
A beep. Looking increasingly depressed, Dorothy picks up the telephone and dials.

WOMAN'S VOICE-OVER
Message for Gary Strang. You requested information on the Sun and Skin Naturists Club. Unfortunately single men aren't eligible to join, I'm sorry.
Dorothy sighs heavily and turns the machine off.

DOROTHY
(*Into the phone*) Quick, come and rescue me, I think I'm going to kill myself.
With the phone wedged under her chin, Dorothy opens a drawer. A bendy jack-in-the-box toy catapults out across the room. Dorothy does not even look surprised. She takes out a corkscrew.

3. THE CROWN

Later. The pub is in full swing. Gary and Tony are standing at the bar, on which a backgammon set is out, the counters placed in absurd positions.

GARY
What's this one?
Tony turns his bottle round so he can read the label.

TONY
Binky. I think it's Indonesian.

GARY
It's not as good as Sod, but it's better than that Russian one. What was that called?

TONY
(*Turning round label*) Plop.

GARY
I'd better go back, Dorothy'll be waiting.

TONY
Yeah.
They carry on drinking.

TONY
So, Deborah, right. I'm not going to rush in like before. I'm going to really, like, woo her as if we've just met.
Les finishes serving and comes over.

LES
Where was I – oh, yeah, so either the guv'nor goes with lobbing it high into the big feller, or he drills it in to feet on the carpet . . .

GARY
Yeah, or the apricot man does a passover across the nutmeg, off the sock. Am I right, Tony?

TONY
Yeah, 'cos if you play the sock-master, like you say, then you've got three points written blind.

GARY
Uh-huh. I've been looking at the shoulder stats, Les, and – this'll tickle you – you've got to go all the way back to West Ham for the diagonal counter-rabbit.
Les is trying to look like he understands.

TONY
Or do you reckon that's bollocks, Les?

LES
Um. I've – I've got to go and serve someone.
Les wanders off. Tony and Gary pick up where they left off.

GARY
Woo her.

TONY
Woo her, yeah. I was reading this book about chat-up lines, and you know what works?

GARY
Um, 'Run along, darling, I want to talk to your pretty friend'?

TONY
It didn't mention that one.

GARY
Or how about this, I came up with this one: 'Is that your chest or are you keeping two really big round things warm for a friend?'

TONY
No, this book says women respond to three things: flattery, the protection that only a bloke can offer and a sense of humour.

GARY
So your best chat-up line would be: 'Hello, gorgeous tits, I've got a shooter in my pocket. How many prostitutes does it take to change a light bulb?'

TONY
No.

GARY
Too much?

TONY
Too much. It's something like, 'Can I just say how much I love your eyes. By the way I'm a doctor. (*Smirking suavely*) So, can I buy you a glass of the old fire water?'

GARY
(*After considering*) Bit wanky, isn't it?

TONY
Yeah, I'm going to adapt it to Deborah, so it's, 'Deborah, can I just say how much I love your hair. I'm thinking of training to be a doctor. Isn't it funny how the last chocolate in the box is always a coffee cream?'

GARY
Observational humour, lovely.

TONY
Then we advance to the next stage.

GARY
That'll be penetration, will it?

TONY
No.

GARY
Heavy potting leading inevitably to mutual masturbation?

TONY
No, asking if she's free perhaps to go to a restaurant.

GARY
Oh, okay.

TONY
Then, gradually—

GARY
(*Drinking up*) Sorry, mate, you're taking too long, I've got to go. You don't keep Dorothy waiting. Not more than a couple of hours anyway.

TONY
Yeah, you're right. Have a good meal, you two deserve it, mate.

GARY
Well, I may sound like a hardball-playing, dog-whipping, take-me-as-you-find-me kind of bloke – which I am – but when you've got something as precious as Dorothy and me . . .
Two attractive women have come in and are waiting to be served at the bar. Tony is openly staring at them. Gary appears not to have noticed them.

GARY
. . . you don't jeopardise it by— (*Spotting the women out of the corner of his eye and turning*

to face them) two more Binkys for us and something for the ladies, please, Les.

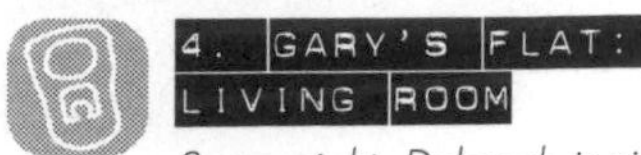

4. GARY'S FLAT: LIVING ROOM

Same night. Deborah is sitting with Dorothy, working their way through a bottle of wine. Dorothy has cheered up a little.

DEBORAH
Bloody hell, though. Are you sure you don't want to ring the pub?

DOROTHY
No. That's the good thing about going out with Gary, you know you're going to be disappointed. It's just a question of how often and how much.

DEBORAH
The trouble with Tony is, if he tries it on I feel sordid, if he doesn't I feel unattractive.

DOROTHY
Which is worse?

DEBORAH
(*Instantly*) Unattractive.

DOROTHY
What d'you think would happen if you said, 'Come on then, let's do it, show us your policeman.'

DEBORAH
I did once. He thought I was joking.
They snigger, at length.

DEBORAH
I think he was still a bit wary from when I told him to take all his clothes off and wait for me in the shed.

DOROTHY
(*Remembering*) Oh, yeah. How long did he wait?

DEBORAH
Three and a half hours.
They both look a bit wistful.

DOROTHY
Quite tempting, though.

DEBORAH
No, there wouldn't have been room anyway, the lawnmower was in the way. One of us would have had to sit on the thing that collects the grass.

DOROTHY
Gary and I once did it in my parents' shed. It became a phrase of ours for a while: 'Fancy a quick shed?' We went through this phase of trying to make love in unusual places.

DEBORAH
What was the most unusual place?

DOROTHY
(*On consideration*) Dudley.
They mull this over.

DEBORAH
It's Tony's fault, sod him. If he was a bit more thoughtful, just once, I'd think what the hell.
Dorothy is opening a present.

DEBORAH
What's that?

DOROTHY
Gary's getting-back-together present.
She removes a video with a blank cover.

DOROTHY
I hope it isn't *Jurassic Poke*. He kept begging me to allow him to get it out of the video shop.
Dorothy reaches forward and puts the video in the machine. They watch.

DOROTHY
Oh, my God.
We switch to their point of view. On the TV screen, made out of plastic letters stuck on the fridge, is: 'Gary & Dorothy: The Video'. The camera pans down to: 'made with the assistance of Tony'. Someone opens the fridge door, then another hand hastily shuts it. Cuts ad lib from watching the video on the TV set to full-screen.

5. STREET

Daytime. Gary is standing on the pavement, self-consciously talking into a hand-held camcorder, like a guest on This Is Your Life.

GARY
Hello, Dorothy! Do you remember, this is where we first met, at Barry Best's party? I was doing my interesting dancing. I'd had quite a lot to drink, and you told me to put my trousers back on. We've had many a chuckle about that since!
Gary gestures for Tony to pan the camcorder round to film the house. For a few seconds the camera points soundlessly at the house – where a man and woman are standing in the window, frowning – then pans back to Gary, whose words fade back in.

GARY
. . . on each nipple. Still, we must away now, because the journey we are about to go on is a long one, full of—
Sharp cut to:

8. STREET IN FRONT OF DOROTHY'S HOUSE

Gary is standing outside as before. Tony remains in charge of the camcorder.

GARY

Hello, Dorothy! This is where you live with your parents, still, well into your thirties. Do you remember, you took me home to meet them shortly after we met? Well, two years after, they were very busy.

Gary attempts some Whicker-style walking towards the camera. The hand-held camera backs away.

GARY

It was on this lawn that—

Tony obviously trips, and the camera is suddenly shooting skywards, then pointing obliquely across the lawn at Tony's face. We go immediately into a retake. Gary is now standing still again.

GARY

It was on this lawn that you played as a child with your childhood pals and many years later you played as an adult with me, your new pal—

Cut to a close-up of Gary, doing his serious bit.

GARY

Your bloke, your buddy, your shipmate on life's heaving love boat.

As the camcorder stays on Gary's face – longer than he feels comfortable – we hear Tony's voice quietly in the background.

TONY

(*Offscreen, weedily*) I think that's Dorothy's mum coming out of the house, she looks a bit cross.

We cut back to:

7. GARY'S FLAT: LIVING ROOM

Dorothy and Deborah are watching the video, open-mouthed.

GARY

(*Offscreen*) This is where we had our first date. You had a lamb korma, I had . . . something brown in a smingey sauce, and after two hours I knew I'd never look at another woman lustfully again.

Meanwhile Gary and Tony are trying to chat up the two women who came in earlier. The women look unimpressed. Gary is nervous and inept.

GARY
I'm in security equipment. We handle all the major burglar-alarm systems, um, we've actually just taken an order from Ostende, in Belgium, so as you can see we're really . . . pushing out . . . into Europe. I took the order myself, in fact. Processed the whole shooting match within three working days. Quite good going.

Gary is nervously tracing his finger through some lager on the bar. An awkward silence follows.

GARY
Tony?

TONY
Yeah, so, what do you girls do in the evenings?

WOMAN
We go out.

TONY
Great. So how did you chance on Les's watering hole? Two girls in a pub on their own, to me that spells d-a-n-g-e-r.
He chuckles knowingly.

WOMAN
To us it spelt M-a-r-l-b-o-r-o.

TONY
(*Nodding*) Uh-huh. (*Frowning*) Middlesbrough?

WOMAN
We needed some fags.
Another awkward silence.

GARY
Can I just say how much I love your nose?
The women look at him with damning blankness.

WOMAN
Yeah, well, we're off now so you'll have to love somebody else's.

GARY
No problem.
She and her silent friend hastily finish their drinks and head off.

WOMAN
(*Leaving*) Thanks for the drinks.

TONY
(*Calling after them*) Cool!

LES
Here, girls, you haven't had your goodbye gherkins!
Tony and Gary avert each other's eyes in embarrassment. A hiatus.

TONY
Who do you fancy for the European Championship next year?

GARY
Yeah, it's going to be interesting, with the new, whatsit.

TONY
Yeah.
They gulp their lager, beginning to show signs of drunkenness.

TONY
Shouldn't you be back at the flat by now?

GARY
Yeah, I should. The trouble with girls is, they don't understand the place the public house has in the cultural fabric of our nation.

TONY
It's not something you can learn, is it?

GARY
It's not, it's not.

TONY
You can get a book about it—

GARY
You can get a book about it, from a shop, or a library . . .

TONY
But you can't learn it.

GARY
But you can't learn it. Because it's . . .
A long, drunken pause. They both remain frozen.

GARY
. . . the blending of a thousand years of . . .

TONY
Blokes sitting around talking—

GARY
—king. Dorothy, for example, doesn't understand that lager is a metaphor for life itself. The beer mats are the, if you like, springy ground beneath our feet. The glass . . .

TONY
. . . is . . . the clothing around the body. Only, like, glass clothing.

GARY
Yeah, and the lager is the body with its foamy little, fuzzy little hair on top.

TONY
And the peanuts are . . .
They stare at the bag of peanuts, their invention exhausted.

TONY
They're just peanuts really.

GARY
Yup.

TONY
I've tried to explain to Deborah that there's more to pubs than drunk blokes talking crap and telling jokes.

GARY
Yeah, well, sometimes when you're going out with someone you have to show who's the boss, and in my case—

TONY
Dorothy is.

GARY
Ah, but is she? Actually. You see. Is she?

TONY
Yes, she is.

GARY
Yes, she is. But not tonight, because tonight is the start of a new phase in our relationship, in which I call the sho— (*Looking at his watch*) Christ, is that the time!
Gary downs the rest of his bottle.

GARY
Right, that is it. I'm on my way.

TONY
Hang on, I've got a joke before you go.
Gary forces a smile.

TONY
Bloke goes into a pub—

GARY
Yeah.

TONY
Asks for a pint.

GARY
Asks for a pint.

TONY
The barman says, do you want me to liquidise you up a live parrot with that. The customer says, 'Isn't that a bit cruel?' And the barman says, 'I said liquidise him, I didn't say I was going to make him watch *Beadles About* first.'
Tony thinks it is hilarious. Gary smiles thinly.

GARY
Yeah, that's good that.

TONY
Two babies sitting on a park bench—

GARY
Yeah, that's enough now, Tony.
A silence.

TONY
Welsh bloke goes to buy a lottery ticket—

GARY
Shut it, Tony.
Gary finishes off Tony's bottle of lager and slowly gets off his bar stool.

GARY
Right, that's me done.

TONY
Yeah, you get off home, my son.

GARY
Yeah, have a good night.

TONY
Cheers, mate. Don't do anything I wouldn't do.

GARY
So it's okay if I have sex with a couple of ostriches then.

TONY
Good one. Cheers.

GARY
Be good. Cheers.

TONY
Catch you later.

GARY
Cheers.
Les appears with a plate of sausage rolls.

LES
Tasty bar snacks! Freshly made on the premises.
Gary immediately goes back to his bar stool.

TONY
Another couple of cold Sods with that, please, Les.

Meanwhile at home. Dorothy and Deborah still have their eyes glued to the TV screen, watching the video.

GARY
(*Offscreen, on video*) Do you remember, Dorothy, this is where we celebrated a year of knowing each other?

Gary is standing in front of a kebab house, pointing to the gutter. Tony is recording it all with the camcorder.

GARY
Afterwards I vomited here, and you had to put me into a minicab over there.
The camera swings wildly to point at a minicab office, then swings back to Gary.

TONY
(*Offscreen, sulky, barely audible*) I want to be in it. You said I could be in it.

11. PARK

Later that day. The camcorder is obviously on a tripod, pointing at Tony and Gary.

GARY
This is Tony.

TONY
Hi.

GARY
As you know.
A pause, Tony clears his throat, then they talk at once.

GARY/TONY
Do your stuff, Tone./I met you, Dor—
Tony recomposes himself and starts again.

TONY
I met you, Dorothy, ooh, two years ago, and I knew then I was in the presence of a super person. I was carrying a pig's head in a plastic bag, do you remember? Can't recall why. I had long hair then.

GARY
(*Muttering*) Long girly hair.
A ball bounces across the field of vision. Tony and Gary follow it with their eyes.

TONY
Do you remember the time you stayed over, and I saw you coming out of the bathroom after a bath. When the towel fell off, and I saw you in the nude, partly?
Tony grins. Gary's eyes flicker over at Tony dubiously.

TONY
Then there was the time I came back early and found you and Gary doing the business on the living-room table, and you tried to pretend you were just sort of stretching out.
Tony is grinning. Gary's eyes flicker over at him again with irritation.

TONY
Then there was the time—
An abrupt cut to:

Night-time. Gary is talking in a low voice to camera, obviously trying not to wake up the house.

GARY
Hello! Do you remember, Dorothy, when you and me came back early one night and found Tony on the sofa watching a video with his trousers round his ankles . . .
There is a knock at the door.

TONY
(*Offscreen, muffled*) Who are you talking to? Is it—
Another abrupt cut to:

13. GARY'S OFFICE

Daytime. Anthea and George's smiling faces are filling the screen, frighteningly.

ANTHEA/GEORGE
Hello!

ANTHEA
Ahh, Dorothy, lovely! I'm so glad you and Gary are back together, at a time when so many of our royal couples are finding the stain of living under each other's feet intolerable. Not that you're royal.
A pause. Gary, the cameraman, prompts.

GARY
(*Offscreen*) George!

GEORGE
Shall I talk? (*Clearing throat*) Yes, speaking as someone who got married when you could still buy quite a sturdy bicycle for a matter of shillings, can I say that I hope you remain 'an item' at least as long as Marjorie and I. (*Pause*) Have.
The lens zooms in experimentally, then pulls out again.

GEORGE/ANTHEA
Bye!
They relax their faces.

ANTHEA
Can we try that again? I think I said stain instead of strain. I was overexcited.

Night-time. The telephone is ringing. Dorothy, still agog at the contents of the video, gets up to answer it. Deborah continues to watch with the sound on low.

DOROTHY
(*Coming in with the phone*) Hello? Oh, it's you. Hello. (*Humouring him*) Yes, hello, I know I'm lovely. (*Rolling her eyes*) Lovely person, yes. I'm – You're telling me I'm lovely, I understand, yes. I'm watching the video. What can I say – (*Grimacing*) thank you?

Gary is speaking into the payphone. Tony is with him, both of them pretty drunk. There is a noisy, festive atmosphere in the pub. We intercut between the pub and the flat. As Gary speaks Tony is dancing madly to juke-box music in the background.

GARY
Tony's mate needed the camera back to film his wife's hip-replacement operation, so it was all done in a bit of a hurry.

DOROTHY
(*In the flat*) Well, you can't tell. So, are you coming back this evening or have the brewery finally given in and allocated you a table to live under?

GARY
(*In the pub*) Yes, I'm sorry I've been a bit delayed this evening. First we had to help an old chap who got a Scampi Fry stuck in his throat and stay with him until the ambulance arrived. Then there was a power cut, and we couldn't find the exit for some time, then—

DOROTHY
(*In the flat*) Gary, I don't care. Just come home now, have some of the meal I lovingly cooked with fresh delicate ingredients for you three hours ago, and we'll go to bed.

GARY
(*In the pub*) Bed? No, beds are for sleepy people, we should all have a kebab and go to a disco.
In the flat Dorothy is agog at the video:

16. OUTSIDE A SECOND CHEAP RESTAURANT

Gary stands in front of another cheap restaurant.

GARY
This is me outside the restaurant where we celebrated our second anniversary of knowing each other. Unfortunately I drank something that didn't agree with me and was sick, here.
The camcorder duly points at the gutter.

GARY
(*In the pub*) We must always be together, Dorothy. Will you promise you'll never leave me?

DOROTHY
(*In the flat, depressed by the video*) Do you mind if I don't, Gary.

GARY
(*In the pub*) Oh. Anyway, it's nearly closing time – time, gentlemen! Haven't you got homosexuals to go to?! – so we'll be back shortly. I think Tony wants to say hello.
Tony stops dancing and takes the receiver.

TONY
Hello.
A long pause.

TONY
Bye, then. That's all I wanted to say.
In the flat Dorothy hangs up.

DOROTHY
They're coming back.

DEBORAH
How drunk are they?

DOROTHY
I've heard worse. I can tell when Gary's seriously pissed – he starts singing or telling me he loves me. I know I'm really in trouble when he sings that he loves me.
Dorothy sits down on the sofa with Deborah.

DEBORAH
Maybe I'll wait to see if Tony comes in in a romantic mood.
Fade to:

17. THE CROWN

Some hours later. In the otherwise virtually deserted pub, a bleary Les is at the bar serving afters to a seedy drunk. Gary, Tony and two or three other severely drunk men are sitting on the floor as though in a rowing boat. They are singing and 'rowing' in time, their pints beside them on the floor. It is clear from the expertly synchronised choreography that these late sessions have happened before.

DRUNK MEN
(*Singing*) 'We are sailing, we are sailing, far away, across the sea . . .'
The actions become more elaborate: on 'stormy waters' they jiggle about as though in stormy waters. The scene fades out.

18. GARY'S FLAT: THROUGHOUT

Meanwhile back at the flat Dorothy is lying on the sofa, asleep. Deborah has left. On the TV, Gary's video is ending. A hand is pulling a roll of kitchen paper on which the credits – accompanied by stirring Elgar – are written out:

Script editor: Tony
Shoes: Gary
Hair: Gary & Tony
Camcorder lent by: A mate of Tony's
Technical so-called advice: George

Dorothy wakes up and stares across sleepily at the screen as more credits come up.

Cinematography: Tony
Produced & directed: Gary
© 1995 Gary

A longer gap – the hand still pulling the kitchen roll – then:

Filmed in Garyrama.

Dorothy turns off the video and gets to her feet. She looks at the clock, which says half-past twelve. She sighs heavily and goes through into the kitchen, checking that the flat is deserted. The food is still on the table. She brings Gary's briefcase and shoes over and puts them on the table. More in sorrow than anger, Dorothy slowly tips the plates of food into the briefcase and shoes. She goes out into the hall, turns the deadlocks on the front door and smashes the door bell with a broom handle. Yawning, she goes back into the flat and heads off to bed.

19. OUTSIDE THE CROWN

Tony and Gary are finally leaving, shown out by Les. All three are very drunk. Tony and Gary come out of the door backwards, feeling their way gingerly. They are carrying a bag that obviously contains bottles. Les stands on the doorstep.

GARY
I love you, Les. I do.

TONY
I love you, too, Les, big time.

GARY
You're quite a portly man, but somehow – God knows I don't know how – you've managed in your own way to make me love you. And you've got a stock of very drinkable wines and beers.

TONY
(*Singing*) 'I am walking, I am walking, home again, across the . . . little bit of road here.' Do you want a lift home, Les?

LES
Okay, where are you heading?

TONY
Nowhere is too far for you, Les. Apart from Romford. I'm not going there.

LES
No, disrespect, but I'd better not.

TONY
Why?

LES
I live here.

TONY
What, here on the doorstep? Isn't that a bit cramped? You've only got, what: ten inches by thirty-four.

GARY
No, I think it'd be all right, if he squeezes his legs up really tiny, so they're tiny-tiny-tiny. And at least it's flat – it's a good flat surface – a good small, flat surface.

LES
I don't think you lads should drive.

TONY
(*Astonished*) Why?!

GARY
(*Astonished*) Why?!

TONY
Why?

GARY
Why ever not?

TONY
I drive better when I've had a drink to soothe me.

GARY
It's true. After a drink, if necessary, he can park on the end of a biro. The thin end, not the fat end. It's not always necessary, but he can do it.

TONY
Mind you, after two drinks, I'm . . . a hazardous driver, it has to be said. But that's okay, because I haven't got a car!
They both laugh inordinately. Les has come out and is locking the door with his bunch of keys. Tony looks in vain for handholds in the wall so he can climb up.

GARY
All those keys, doesn't the responsibility weigh you down, Les? Don't you wake up some days (*Miming a yawn*) and say to yourself: 'Blast, I can't stand the pressure of supplying very drinkable wines and beers day in, day out, and carrying these heavy keys around at my belt'?
Les has locked the door with himself outside. He turns, looking confused.

TONY
I think you'll find you're the wrong side of the door.

GARY
Easily done, Les.

TONY
If I was given a pound for every time I've done that I'd . . . be incredibly surprised, because I'd think, Who is giving me these pounds? I've done nothing to deserve this kind of money!
Les turns round again and starts to open all the locks again to let himself in. Tony and Gary head off down the street, their voices fading as Les struggles with all the locks.

GARY
(*Offscreen*) Look at those stars! Is that the Plough? What does a bloody plough look like anyway?

TONY
(*Offscreen*) 'I am kneeling, I am kneeling!'

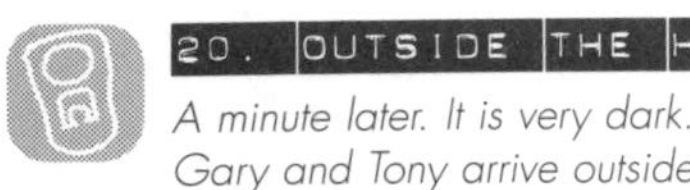

20. OUTSIDE THE HOUSE

A minute later. It is very dark. Gary and Tony arrive outside. They try to keep their voices down. The jingle of keys in pockets.

GARY
They're here somewhere, they're here somewhere. Come on, out you come. Here they are. (*Pause*) No, they've gone back in.

TONY
Shall we use my keys?

GARY
Keys! That's a good idea. I was looking for my bollocks.
They snigger. They are standing in the porch, propping themselves up.

TONY
Hey, I'm going to knock on Deborah's door.

GARY
Can't do any harm, can it? That's the convenient thing about calling in the middle of the night – everyone's in.

TONY
Well, I think I'm ready to seduce her now. I've planned it all, in the minutest detail.

GARY
What are you going to say?

TONY
Say? Oh, I don't know that. (*Pausing*) Oh, say! I'm going to compliment her on her hair, as we discussed—

GARY
Hair, discussed, yeah.

TONY
Then I'm going to tell her I love her, and I'll protect her, and I want to go out with her until we're old and grey.

GARY
Oh, that's lovely, mate, really lovely.

TONY
Or bald, if we go bald before we go grey.

GARY
So, until you're old and bald.

TONY
Yeah.
After several attempts Gary manages to get his key in the lock.

TONY
I'm going to subtly ask her out to tea, for a scone, and then we'll be sitting there, and I'll say how much I love her, and she'll smile sweetly and – Oh, sod it, I'll just shout out. (*Shouting up at her window*) Deborah! I fucking [*Bleeped out*] love you! Come down, I want you!
Gary shushes Tony. Tony shushes himself. Gary is having trouble with the lock.

GARY
I think Dorothy's locked the door.

TONY
Why would she do that?

GARY
I don't know, I can't understand it.
He rings the bell, but nothing happens.

GARY
It's not working.

TONY
Here, I'll make it ring. (*Pressing the button*) Ring! Ring! Ring!
Gary gets down on his knees, opens the letter flap and looks in.

GARY
(*Calling gently*) Dorothy, it's me, Gary. Your boyfriend. Please let me in.
Tony holds up the clinking carrier bag.

TONY
There's a couple of Plops in it for you.

GARY
(*Still gently*) Dorothy, I've got my flap open, and I'm asking you to let me enter.
Tony joins Gary on his knees.

TONY
Maybe a weenie bit louder?

TONY
(*Shouting*) Dorothy!

GARY
(*Shouting still louder*) Dorothy!
They carry on yelling through the letterbox for some time. Then stand up, disappointed.

TONY
Have we got the right house?
They drunkenly stand back to look at the door.

GARY
Yeah.

TONY
Seems all right.

GARY
We'd better break in.

TONY
How?

GARY
Well, what I'm going to do is – is this: carefully tap a pane of the door, with precision tapping, and break it and put my hand inside and open the door.

TONY
I'll do it, I'd be good at that.

GARY
No, I want to, it's my door.
He gets a bottle of lager out of the bag and, like a safe-cracker, gently taps the pane with the neck of the bottle. The bottle shatters. He gets another bottle and does it with the base. It smashes again. Tony disappears.
He is about to do it with a third bottle, but Tony has reappeared with a huge breeze block that he unceremoniously throws through the door pane. When the crashing noise has subsided Gary shushes Tony, then reaches in and turns the lock. He and Tony enter.

21. COMMUNAL HALL

Gary and Tony try to act as though sober.

GARY
Honey, we're home!

TONY
Hummy, we're hone! Hun, we're homey!
Gary unlocks the inner door into the flat.

GARY
Sorry about the noise, we experienced a glass hazard in the foyer.

TONY
(*About to knock*) Right, wish me luck.

GARY
Are you sure, it's half-past two in the morning?

TONY
(*Checking his watch*) Yes, it's definitely half-past two in the morning. She'll be feeling nice and rested and mellow.

GARY
Good luck, mate

TONY
How do I look?
He looks very much the worse for wear.

GARY
Never better!
Gary heads inside.

GARY
(*Offscreen, to Dorothy*) Sorry I'm a bit later than I said . . .
Tony, drunker than ever, straightens out his clothes, carefully trains a lock of hair back in place and rehearses his lines under his breath. He is about to knock on Deborah's door when it opens. Deborah is standing there, looking furious.

TONY
Hello. I'm glad I've caught you up.

DEBORAH
You didn't catch me up, you woke me.

TONY
Oh. (*Taking a deep breath*) Would you like a scone, and some protection? And I'd like to go out with you until we're grey and bald, please.
Deborah stares back at him.

TONY
(*Reaching out to touch it*) Lovely hair.
Deborah knocks his hand away.

DEBORAH
Why do I have to live above two drunk morons?

TONY
You don't! Who says you do?! Stay here in your flat.

DEBORAH
Are you always going to be this stupid?

TONY
No, it'll probably vary.

DEBORAH
God, you're irritating.

TONY
I just want you to know that I'll always be here for you, waiting for the call, standing by, totally devoted.

DEBORAH
Okay.
She looks at him meaningfully.

TONY
(*Grinning*) What?

22. GARY'S FLAT: HIS BEDROOM

The lights are dimmed. Dorothy is in bed, her back turned to Gary, who is being a cheerful drunk.

GARY
So then we were about to leave again, but this woman called in at the pub and asked us to try to get her car going. Well, would you believe it, it turned out her car needed a

whole new gearbox, so there we were trying to put these little cogs in by the light of Les's torch until—

DOROTHY
Shut up, Gary.
Gary reaches down and picks up a bottle of lager.

GARY
(*Swigging*) I don't know what the matter is, we just went for a quick drink.
Gary leans over and feels around for the drawer in his bedside cabinet.

GARY
I'll have a quiet read while you think of an apology.
He manages to open the drawer. Dorothy has filled it with the remains of the stew. Gary puts his hand in and splashes around before realising what it is. Unperturbed, he extracts his slimy paperback, sits up and tries to ungum the first page.

23. BACK GARDEN

The garden and surrounding area is in darkness. We become aware of humming that is coming from the shed at the bottom of the garden. As we approach the shed, the humming turns into singing.

TONY
Mmmm, mm. (*Singing*) 'I am sitting, I am sitting, far away, across the thing, do de dye de, do de dye de.'
It goes quiet. We can now see inside the shed, through a grubby window. Tony is sitting on the lawnmower, surrounded by garden tools and assorted junk. He is waiting, naked apart from a strategically placed flower pot. He sniffs, sobering up.

TONY
Ready when you are, Debs.
We cut to a wide shot of shed, garden and house. A pause.

TONY
(*Offscreen*) You're not coming, are you?

SERIES FOUR: EPISODE SIX

IN BED WITH DOROTHY

This is one of my favourite episodes, although it loses its way slightly towards the end. The plot about Tony needing glasses is all about the importance of mockery in men's relationships. Male friendship is based squarely on taking the piss out of each other.

And there had to be a lot of laughs in the stresses that illness puts a couple under. One of the best moments in the episode was not my idea: a bored Gary jabbing Dorothy on her appendix wound to wake her up. I worried it was too cruel but it's a measure of how forgiving an audience is to a character who engages them (Gary), however bastardly his behaviour.

Lots of the script had to be cut because it was over length. I used to keep a file of cut gags in order to use them later, but they never fit. It's funny how you never the miss the jokes when they are gone.

1. GARY'S FLAT: HALL/KITCHEN

Daytime. The door to the flat bursts open. A groggy Dorothy is sitting in a hospital wheelchair, clutching her bag. Gary, manic with power, is pushing her.

DOROTHY
You just broke my knee on the door.
Gary chuckles patronisingly.

GARY
(*As though to a child*) Do you want to be sick in a bag?
Dorothy has her head in her hands.

GARY
Are you oozing or leaking at all? (*No reply*) Shall we pop you under the duvet? (*No reply. Louder*) Shall we tuck you under the—

DOROTHY
(*Snapping*) Yes, yes, anything.

Gary wheels Dorothy through the hall. We switch view to the empty kitchen. Gary wheels Dorothy across the arch from right to left.

GARY
You'll soon be as right as rain again.

DOROTHY
Shut your face.

2. GARY'S BEDROOM

Gary wheels Dorothy into his bedroom, positioning her by the bed. Dorothy's eyes are closed. Gary wonders how he is going to get her on to the bed.

GARY
Okay, what I'm going to do now is lift you gently. You may experience a slight twinge.
He tries to lift her but can not get an easy hold. He ponders for a while, then up-ends the wheelchair sideways on to the bed. Dorothy screams with pain, then slithers groaning to the bed, watched by Gary.

GARY
Did you experience a slight twinge at all?
Dorothy is lying half on the duvet. Gary grabs the ends of the duvet and positions himself to yank it from under her in one swift movement.

DOROTHY
Don't even think about it.
Thinking better of it, Gary brings over a jumper and lovingly drapes it over her, trying in vain to position it so it covers her.

GARY
I'll let you get some sleep, then I'll come back and entertain you.
Another groan of distress from Dorothy. Waking up a little, she pulls herself under the duvet.

GARY
I know it hurts when you laugh so I'll be careful.

DOROTHY
Don't worry, you haven't made me laugh since 1991. And even then I was laughing at you.
Gary just smiles patronisingly.

GARY
As a bit of a treat I had a word with the hospital, and they've allowed us to have your appendix as a souvenir.
Gary produces a jar containing a pink thing floating in fluid. He lovingly places it on the bedside table.

GARY
I asked if they had anything else, and they gave me this spare spleen.
He produces another, larger jar containing a huge spleen.

GARY
Bookends, I thought. If I ever get any books.
He smiles at her, then rummages in his jacket pocket and gets out a small jar.

GARY
And a paperweight, for small paper. That's a bit of bowel.
He puts it next to the other two jars and crouches down 'caringly' at Dorothy's bedside.

GARY
Now, the removal of any organ is a serious business—

DOROTHY
I know, I remember when they took your brain out.

GARY
So I've checked in the medical books, and apparently you may experience some slight, can't-quite-put-your-finger-on-it sense of discomfiture.

DOROTHY
(*Forcing a smile*) Well, I'll certainly look out for that then.

GARY
Good, good. Anyway, I want you to know that I'll be here for you over the coming days.

DOROTHY
(*Genuine*) Thanks.
Gary looks at her lovingly for a moment.

GARY
Can I quickly photograph your stitches?

DOROTHY
No, Gary.

GARY
Okay. Can I get anything for you – magazine? Jigsaw? (*Getting no response*) Stiff gin and tonic? Grape?
She has fallen asleep. Gary hovers over her, looking sympathetic.

3. KITCHEN/TONY'S BEDROOM

Later same day. Tony comes in, glancing around furtively. He listens out for anyone in the flat. He gets a smallish plastic bag out of his jacket and is about to open it when he suddenly thinks he hears something. He hurriedly hides the bag in the kitchen drawer and acts casual. Nobody comes in so he gets the bag out again and scurries off into his bedroom. He shuts the door and is about to open the bag when he thinks he hears someone outside. Same hiding of bag and acting casual.
He sits on the bed and opens the bag under his duvet, then burying himself beneath it too. He emerges, looking anxious, wearing a pair of Michael Caine-style glasses. Tentatively he gets up and looks at himself in a mirror. He practises taking the glasses off and putting them on, whipping them out of his pocket increasingly fast like a gunslinger. He goes through spectacle-wearers' tics: blinking wildly and pushing them back up his nose with the tip of his finger, taking them off to make a point in a conversation, polishing them enthusiastically etc. Distant noise of a door slamming. Tony instantly takes off the glasses and hides them.

4. GARY'S BEDROOM

Dorothy is asleep. A line is stretched across the bed a few feet above her head. A small mirror is already dangling from it. Gary, humming happily, is now attaching a bell. Finally he reaches into a shopping bag, produces a bunch of grapes and hangs them on the line. Gary sits by her bed, attentively checks Dorothy is not awake. Bored, he picks up her appendix jar, gazes in at the organ and taps the glass as if it were a tropical fish. He unscrews the top and fishes out the appendix. He holds it against his abdomen in its correct anatomical position, then under his nose like a moustache. He sniffs it and seriously considers taking a little nibble, but it slithers out of his hand. Gary gets down on his knees, finds it and picks it up. He wipes the appendix on his trousers and puts it back in the jar. Dorothy stirs. Gary positions his face close to hers. Dorothy's eyes snap open in alarm.

GARY
Hello.

DOROTHY
It hurts.

GARY
That'll be your operation.

DOROTHY
(*Disoriented and in pain*) What?

GARY
They've separated you from your Siamese twin. You were joined at the bottom to Kevin Keegan.
Dorothy looks momentarily upset.

GARY
Only joking. I've been out and bought you a copy of *Hello!*. Roger Moore relaxing at home at his Scottish baboon sanctuary, intriguing.
Dorothy is waking up, focusing on her mirror, bell and grapes.

DOROTHY
Would you like me to lie on some old newspaper, so I really feel like a budgie?

GARY
No, it's an activity centre. At this stage of your recuperation you're obviously still a bit pathetic.
Dorothy stares at Gary blankly.

GARY
Bell to ring for my attention, grapes for nutrition and mirror to check you're not bleeding repulsively.
With a flannel Gary is dabbing Dorothy's forehead.

DOROTHY
What are you doing?

GARY
I've seen this on *Casualty* – you have to blot the head.
Gary pulls down her bottom lip and dabs inside her mouth with the flannel. Dorothy reaches up and rings the bell.

GARY
Hello, how can I help?

DOROTHY
Will you stop doing that, please?

GARY
Okay, you're the boss.

DOROTHY
And will you take away my bloody baby mobile.

GARY
Ah, you see, can I just say here, what you're showing is the sick person's classic aggression towards her carer, who is devoting himself often without thanks (*Sickly smile*) but always with a cheery smile.

DOROTHY
I know (*Doing an even more sickly smile*) I've been a state-registered nurse for ten years.

GARY
Oh, yes.

DOROTHY
(*Very reasonable*) Gary, I'm very grateful for your help, but I suppose what I'm saying is, I'm tired and in pain, and I want you to bugger off.
Gary looks at Dorothy evenly, his caring manner under threat for the first time.

GARY
(*Getting up*) Okay, you're not yourself, I understand.

5. LIVING ROOM

Meanwhile, Tony is watching the television, sitting in the seat closest to the set. He squints slightly at the picture. Gary comes in, settling down to watch the TV.

TONY
How's Dorothy?

GARY
Fine. I'll go back in in half an hour and check she hasn't gone purple. (*Glancing at Tony*) You're sitting a bit close, aren't you?

TONY
(*Shifty*) Me? No, I'm just . . . soaking up the atmosphere in the *Tomorrow's World* studio.

GARY
Another couple of inches and you'll be able to stick your tongue down Carol Vorderman's throat.
They watch the TV for a moment.

TONY
Do you reckon the presenters get off with each other after the show?

GARY
Well, they always seem in a hurry to go home.

TONY
Mm. I reckon a typical Friday evening for them would be: chat on air about some amazing new bendy plastic or what have you, pile into the *Tomorrow's World* minibus, and shoot off to Carol's place to splash about naked in her jacuzzi, see what develops.

GARY
Mm.

TONY
I got a new CD today. Kylie's latest.
He hands it to Gary.

TONY
I see she's, um, wearing glasses.

GARY
Yeah. (*Looking at the TV*) Plus of course, working on *Tomorrow's World*, they'd know about state-of-the-art contraceptive devices and creams.
He goes back to watching. Tony glances across at Gary nervously.

TONY
I think the glasses make her look quite good.

GARY
Well, let's face it, Kylie'd look foxy in a welder's mask with a parsnip strapped to her head. (*Pointing to the TV*) That's good, look. Something to stop your tie from flapping up over your shoulder when you're running along. Excellent.
Gary is absorbed. Tony still looks edgy.

GARY
I don't suppose that'll hit the shops until the year 2004. I'm still waiting to buy that rubber car that makes parking so easy.

TONY
(*After a pause*) A lot of people look sexy in specs, though, don't they?

GARY
Sure, if you think it looks sexy to have two bits of perspex and a tangle of ugly metal dangling from your face.

TONY
Oh, I don't know. Warren Beatty wears his quite a lot nowadays.

GARY
Yeah, and you're not going to tell me he'd have done half as much knobbing if he'd had his bins on during his major chatting-up years. 'Hello, Julie Christie, my name's Warren Beatty. Excuse me while I just pause to clean my glasses on this tiny little piece of yellow cloth, like a librarian.'
'Get lost, four-eyes.'
There is a knock on the door. Gary gets up to answer it. Tony sits there looking depressed.

6. HALL

Gary answers the door to Deborah, who is holding a bunch of flowers.

GARY
What can I say! Little yellow flowers, wrapped in paper.

DEBORAH
They're for Dorothy.

GARY
(*Disappointed*) Oh. Thanks. Got any fruit?

DEBORAH
No.

GARY
Okay, your decision.

DEBORAH
So, what's the news?

GARY
Well, to be honest I don't think I realise how tired I am. I suppose I'm just taking it one hour at a time.

DEBORAH
And . . . Dorothy?

GARY
Bit off colour. Well, she has had a rather large organ taken out of her body. (*Chuckling*) Not for the first time.

DEBORAH
Can I see her?

GARY
I'd rather not, she's very frail.

DEBORAH
Oh.

GARY
You can come and sit with Tony and me. We've got a couple of lagers on the go. The chat's racy but never oversteps the mark.

DEBORAH
Maybe another time. So how did the operation go?

GARY
Very well. The surgeons at the hospital know her pretty well. Still, I'm sure they did a good job anyway.

DEBORAH
I remember after I had my appendix out, it hurt so much I thought they'd left a little burrowing animal inside.

GARY
Uh-huh. Had they?

DEBORAH
No.

GARY
(*Nodding*) Good, good. (*Eventually*) Nice neat scar?

DEBORAH
Yup.

GARY
Quite low down, just above your . . .

DEBORAH
(*Sighing*) Yes.

GARY
(*Eventually*) Can I see it?

DEBORAH
No.

GARY
Okay.

DEBORAH
So, can I do anything to help?

GARY
You could show me your scar.

DEBORAH
Anything to help Dorothy?

GARY
No, thanks, I'll shoulder the burden of caring for her.

DEBORAH
Oh, well, maybe later, when compassion fatigue sets in.

GARY
Oh, you know me, once I commit myself to something . . .

Deborah turns to go.

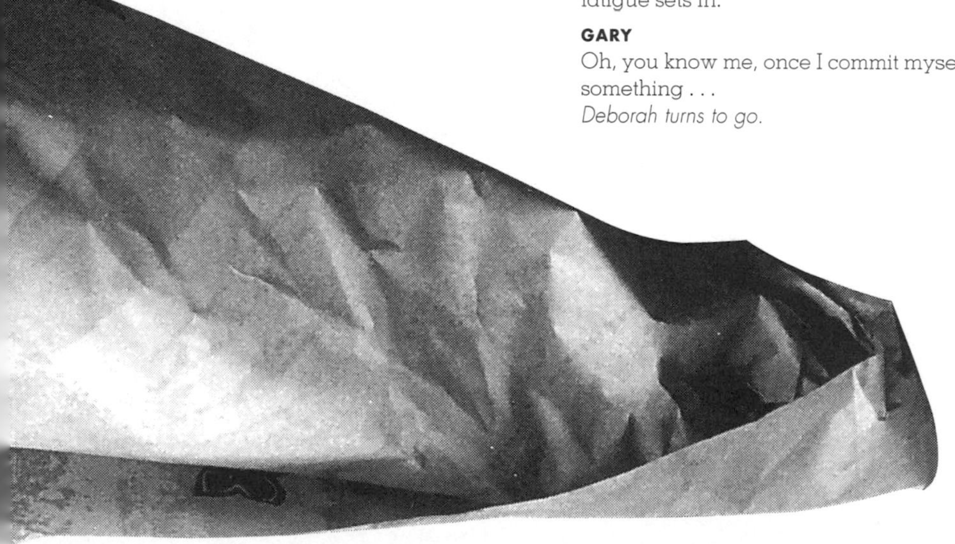

GARY
Um, do you have any photographs of your scar at all?

7. KITCHEN

Next morning. Tony is sitting at the table, reading the Daily Mirror. He glances around him and gets his glasses case out of his pocket. He opens it, removes his glasses and starts cleaning them earnestly with the piece of yellow cloth inside. He puts them on.

TONY
(*Trevor McDonald impersonation*) This is Tony, reading the news.
He gets up and goes over to the refrigerator.

TONY
Hello, fridge. My name's Michael Caine.
He gets out some milk, shuts the fridge door and launches into an Ian McCaskill impersonation, using the fridge door as his weather map.

TONY
Hello. Here we have a cold front. These letters will be coming in from here and here, making the word (*Peering at letters*) 'shmemley' and colliding with these fridge magnets here, here and here.
He does not realise that Dorothy has been making her way painfully into the room in her dressing gown and is watching him. Tony puts on his glasses upside down, takes a broom and uses it as a snooker cue, à la Dennis Taylor. As he 'pots' an apple he sees Dorothy. He hastily pockets his glasses.

DOROTHY
Er, Tony?

TONY
What?

DOROTHY
Were you wearing glasses?

TONY
No.

DOROTHY
Um, yes, you were.

TONY
Oh, these. They're not mine. I found them. I don't need glasses. Look, see that pin over there?
Dorothy follows his gaze. Tony walks over to the other side of the room, picks up something small from the floor and holds it up.

TONY
Look at that. Twenty-twenty vision.

DOROTHY
Um, Tony, you haven't got anything in your hand.

TONY
Ah. How are you feeling, can I mix you up a poultice or something?
Dorothy sits down very carefully.

DOROTHY
No, thanks. Tony, I get the impression you're slightly embarrassed about glasses.

TONY
No, I think they're great . . . for seeing well, if you're into that. It's just that nobody in my family wears glasses. We go straight from brilliant eyesight to dead.

DOROTHY
What does that postcard on the mantelpiece say?
He screws his eyes up and looks over at the mantelpiece.

TONY
'Hi, gang. Having a great time, so you can all sod off.' It's from Gary.

DOROTHY
There isn't a postcard on the mantelpiece. I threw it away.
Tony swallows hard.

TONY
You won't ever tell people I've got glasses, will you?

DOROTHY
Where are you planning to wear them, just in the toilet? Alone in darkened rooms?

TONY
Please, Dotty—

DOROTHY
(*Deadly*) Don't call me Dotty.

TONY
Please, Dorothy, I'm the good-looking outdoor type. We used to call the kids who wore glasses 'speccy'. Or 'furniture-face'. Or . . . (*Less convinced*) 'short-sighty'.

DOROTHY
Put them on.

TONY
We used to snatch off their glasses and stick chewing gum on the lenses so they couldn't see properly and bumped into things.

DOROTHY
Put the glasses on, Tony.

TONY
Don't want to.

DOROTHY
Tony.

TONY
I'm ashamed.

DOROTHY
I'll tell Gary.
Tony immediately gets the glasses out and puts them on.

DOROTHY
See, I don't know what all the fuss was about. You look very nice.

TONY
Do you think so?

DOROTHY
Of course. I doubt if anyone will even notice. It's like people who spend their lives worrying that they've got a big nose.

TONY
Yeah, at least I haven't got a bloody great schnozzle like them.
Dorothy sighs.

DOROTHY
Just wear the glasses and stop worrying about it.

TONY
What about the style, though, you don't think I look too, I don't know, too—

DOROTHY
Too much like a git?

TONY
Yes.

DOROTHY
(*Late and unconvincing*) No. Not at all.
Tony looks undecided. Dorothy winces with pain.

TONY
Ooh, is it your operation?

DOROTHY
(*Getting up*) No, I accidentally swallowed a chair on my way to the bathroom.
Tony watches Dorothy hobble out.

TONY
(*Calling after her*) So you think I look very nice then?
He puts his glasses back on, smiling uncertainly.

8. GARY'S BEDROOM8

That night. Dorothy is dozing in bed. Gary, clothed, is sitting at her bedside in the wheelchair, looking bored.

GARY
(*Softly*) Dorothy. (*No reply*) Dorothy, your bed's on fire.
Still no reply. He goes for a spin round the bedroom, doing wheelies, finally crashing into some furniture painfully. He limps back and lies on the bed next to Dorothy, bored again.

GARY
Dorothy?
Again no reply. He nudges her so she half wakes up.

DOROTHY
What?

GARY
Can I get you anything?

DOROTHY
(*Dozy*) A big rusty nail. To drive through your head.

GARY
It's been three days now. I don't suppose you fancy a quickie?
Dorothy looks daggers at him.

GARY
Nothing strenuous. You could lie down on your good side and I could gently slide my—

DOROTHY
Gary, if you so much as touch me anywhere below the neck I'll sue you for grievous bodily harm.

GARY
It's ironic, isn't it, the word 'patient'? It's a bit like calling a mass murderer an 'old soppy'.
Dorothy sighs and manages to prop herself up in bed.

GARY
Sorry, love, it's just that I'm bored. I was looking forward to looking after you but, I don't know, you seem a bit ill.
They hold hands affectionately.

DOROTHY
You did invite me here to recuperate. You know you're no good with sick people. I've had a temperature of a hundred and three before, and all you can think about is trying to fry an egg on my forehead.

GARY
It did work . . .

DOROTHY
I know! Go and play with Tony.

GARY
I can't, he's shut himself in his room.

DOROTHY
(*Smiling*) I caught him this morning wearing glasses.

GARY
Sunglasses?

DOROTHY
No.

GARY
Joke glasses with veiny eyeballs that fall out on springs in a humorous way?

DOROTHY
No, real glasses.

GARY
Tony?! Real glasses?! But he's a normal person, he's never read a book in his life. It's like expecting a sheep to wear complicated breathing equipment.

DOROTHY
Don't make fun of him, he's obviously got a complex about it.

GARY
Don't make fun of him?! Are you mad, of course I'm going to make fun of him! Peering out behind his glinty little windows, always getting out those horrid little snappy cases.

DOROTHY
Try to be sympathetic. I thought you were best mates.

GARY
Well, I might have to reconsider, now he's turned out to be a speccy. This is probably just the start – next week he'll pitch up with a hearing aid, the week after it'll be braces round his teeth and a zimmer frame, before I know where I am it'll be like sharing a flat with a shopping trolley.

DOROTHY
Do you enjoy being mindless and offensive?

GARY
You know I do.

DOROTHY
Well, don't.

GARY
Sorry.

DOROTHY
Peel me a grape.
He does so.

9. AT THE OPTICIAN

A day or so later. A young female optician – personable and helpful – is behind the counter. Tony comes in.

TONY
Hello.

OPTICIAN
Hello.

TONY
I came in and chose some glasses last week, for a friend—

OPTICIAN
Friend, yes.

TONY
Yeah. He can't get out to choose for himself because he's in pris—

OPTICIAN
Prison, I remember. You realise that the prescription is for your eyes, not his.

TONY
Yeah, he doesn't mind. He only wants a rough idea of what's going on.

OPTICIAN
Did he like your choice of frame?

TONY
He's a bit worried they make him look like a . . . git. When he's slopping out.
Tony puts on the glasses.

OPTICIAN
You haven't actually got a friend in prison, have you?

TONY
No.

OPTICIAN
Good, shall we try on some other frames?

TONY
No, it's all right. I've cut some glasses out of magazines.
Tony gets out a selection of mask-shaped magazine cuttings. He holds the first up to his eyes – red-frame glasses.

TONY
Elton John. What do you think?

OPTICIAN
I think we're still in git territory.
He swaps the 'glasses' for another, half-moon pair, in grainy black and white.

TONY
Emperor Hirohito of Japan.

OPTICIAN
Those are reading glasses.

TONY
(*Tossing them aside*) Oh, I won't need them, then.
He puts on some large, women's glasses.

TONY
Bit of a long shot: Sophia Loren.
The optician just stares.

TONY
Maybe not. I like these. Stevie Wonder.
He puts on a cutout of some very dark glasses.

OPTICIAN
For everyday use possibly better on a blind person?

TONY
Good point.

OPTICIAN
What image are you looking for?

TONY
Well, I want to look kind of fashionable but intelligent. And humorous and sophisticated. And sexy.

OPTICIAN
Have you thought of . . . reincarnation?
A pause, then Tony smiles. They both chuckle.

OPTICIAN
What about contact lenses?

TONY
No, I don't like the idea of having something resting on my eye. Right there, you know, staring at me.
He does a ghost-type scary noise.

OPTICIAN
I imagine it's no more uncomfortable than wearing a condom, say.

TONY
How would you get a condom on your eye?

OPTICIAN
No, on your penis.
They catch each other's eye and look away in embarrassment.

OPTICIAN
Um, you might want to soften the shape of your face—

TONY
Softer shape, great . . .

OPTICIAN
—by choosing some round glasses.

TONY
Hang on, hang on, I've got some John Lennons here somewhere.
He finds an above lifesize cutout of John Lennon's round glasses and applies them to his face. He looks absurd. The optician chews her lip.

TONY
(*Hidden by his 'glasses'*) Shall we go with these, then?

10. GARY'S FLAT: LIVING ROOM/KITCHEN

Evening. Deborah, Gary and Dorothy are watching the TV. Dorothy is still dressed for bed and is covered in blankets.

DEBORAH
Is he coming in yet?

DOROTHY
(*Glancing towards Tony's bedroom*) No.
Deborah picks up a sofa cushion to put under her head, revealing a picture of Nana Mouskouri in her distinctive specs. Dorothy and Deborah scowl at Gary.

GARY
Just a bit of fun.

DOROTHY
Gary, don't draw attention to him.

GARY
Relax, I won't!
Tony enters the kitchen, not wearing his glasses. Deborah quietly scrunches up Nana Mouskouri.

TONY
(*Calling through*) Anybody want anything to drink?

DEBORAH
No, thanks.

DOROTHY
No, thanks.

GARY
Lager, please, mate. I'll have it in one of those, um, silly *glasses*.
The women glare at Gary. Tony looks through the hatch at them, slightly suspicious. They smile back innocently. Tony comes in, hands Gary a can of lager and a novelty tumbler and sits down.

DEBORAH
How are you, Tony?

TONY
Great, thanks.
Deborah and Dorothy smile at Tony encouragingly. As they all watch the TV, Tony's hand goes surreptitiously to his shirt pocket. The others' eyes drift over. His hand goes back to his lap. The others look at the TV again. The same happens again, more quickly.
Finally Tony gets out the glasses and holds them. Unbearable tension, then he puts them on. The frames are still not quite right for him, possibly a little too trendy. Tony determinedly watches the TV while the others snatch discreet glances. Gary starts smirking first, then Deborah and Dorothy. Tony looks over pointedly, but they manage to look serious.

TONY
How've you been feeling today, Dorothy?

DOROTHY
Better, thanks. I'm all right if I don't laugh.
Gary starts weeping with suppressed laughter. Tony ignores the sense of growing hysteria.

TONY
It was quite chilly today, wasn't it?
Finally they all burst out laughing. Tony jumps to his feet.

TONY
Don't be so bloody immature.

DEBORAH
Sorry, Tony.

DOROTHY
Sit down, Tony.

GARY
Don't move, Tone, mate, there's something on your face.
Tony storms out. Deborah and Dorothy look at Gary accusingly. Finally Gary dutifully gets to his feet and heads for Tony's bedroom.

11. TONY'S BEDROOM

Tony is lying on his bed, sulkily turning the pages of a comic. A small knock on the door.

GARY
(*Offscreen*) Sorry.

TONY
Go away.
A silence. Tony goes back to his comic.

GARY
(*Offscreen*) I'm very sorry.
Gary opens the door and comes in.

GARY
Sorry about that just now.

TONY
Nah, it's all right.

GARY
No, it was unfair, making a spectacle of you like that.

TONY
Get out.

GARY
No, I'm sorry, I'm sorry. Put your glasses on, they looked nice.

TONY
No, you'll only take the mickey.

GARY
I won't.

TONY
You will.

GARY
I won't.

TONY
(*Wavering*) You will.

GARY
I won't.
Tony reaches for his glasses and is about to put them on.

TONY
You will, won't you?

GARY
I won't.
Tony puts them on. Gary nods appreciatively.

GARY
Yeah, nice. Nice bins.
Tony looks relieved.

GARY
How do they stay on?

TONY
They sort of go round your ears, here.

GARY
Practical, excellent. I expect you can play football in them and everything.

TONY
Oh, yeah. As long as I don't, like, move my head suddenly.

GARY
Great. So, are you . . . myopipic or . . . the other one?

TONY
Short-sighted. I'm brilliant on near objects. The optician said I was the best she's ever seen on near objects.
Gary is managing to maintain a straight face, but the strain is starting to show.

GARY
So, will you be getting wipers fitted?

TONY
Get out.
Gary turns and slowly exits.

12. LIVING ROOM

Meanwhile, Deborah and Dorothy are musing on the sofa.

DEBORAH
Is Gary looking after you all right? He seemed very attentive.

DOROTHY
He was at first, when he was doing his

impression of Florence Nightingale on a Club 18–30 holiday.

DEBORAH
That's the trouble with men, their sympathy never lasts as long as the illness.

DOROTHY
I think Gary's got a chart with how long he's prepared to be sympathetic: two days if I've had major surgery, an hour and a half if I've got flu and four seconds if it means he misses *Baywatch*.

DEBORAH
Mind you, it's not much fun sharing a bed with a sick person, is it? You don't know whether to lean over and say something comforting, or soak them in Dettol and put them out in the garden.

DOROTHY
Mm. Gary had bronchitis once. It was like trying to sleep while lying on top of a speeding combine harvester.

DEBORAH
Do you think Tony's all right? He's so vain about his glasses, it's ridiculous.

DOROTHY
Yeah, as if it matters.

DEBORAH
Mind you they're boring, aren't they, men in glasses?

DOROTHY
Sadly. No, they make some men look sweet, you want to take their glasses off, tell them everything's okay and bury their face in your cleavage. Not for very long, obviously.

DEBORAH
Still, poor Tony. There must be something we can do.

Later that night. Tony is splayed out on his bed. A gently rotating shot from the ceiling of his supine form. He is wearing both his pairs of glasses, depressed.
Voices filter in from the kitchen.

DOROTHY
(*Offscreen*) Tea, Debs?

DEBORAH
(*Offscreen*) Yeah, thanks, Dorothy. Where's Tony?

DOROTHY
(*Offscreen*) He must have joined Gary in the pub.

DEBORAH
(*Offscreen*) Joking aside, I really like his glasses actually.
Tony's ears prick up.

DOROTHY
(*Offscreen*) Yes, they give him a sort of dignity, don't they? In a funny kind of way they're the missing piece in the jigsaw of his personality.

DEBORAH
(*Offscreen*) Yes. They are.
A pause. Tony creeps towards his door so he can hear better.

DOROTHY
(*Offscreen*) To be honest I think Gary's jealous.

DEBORAH
(*Offscreen*) Well, I know when I was at school it was always the boys in glasses we went for first. Because they were always gentlemen.

DOROTHY
(*Offscreen*) Absolutely. And even today, when I see most men in glasses I experience a rush of, well, of almost sexual excitement.

DEBORAH
(*Offscreen*) Me too.
A silence. Tony is looking happier. He puts his ear to the door. Another silence. He opens the door and tiptoes out towards the kitchen.

14. KITCHEN

Dorothy and Deborah are convulsed and tearful with silent laughter.
Deborah is on her knees trying to creep away into the living room. Dorothy is lying on the kitchen table, the laughter occasionally making her grimace with pain. Tony sees them, glares angrily and storms back into his bedroom. Deborah and Dorothy see him go but can not stop laughing.

DEBORAH
Come back, Tony.

DOROTHY
We were only trying to help.

15. GARY'S BEDROOM

The next morning. Gary is standing by his bed, putting on his tie. He is already wearing his pinstripe-suit jacket but no trousers. Dorothy is in bed.

DOROTHY
Please, take the day off, I hate being here on my own.

GARY
I'm sorry, the domestic and business markets for high-quality security equipment don't stand still just because you claim you're feeling a bit poorly.

DOROTHY
You took a week off when you had a cold.

GARY
It wasn't a cold, it was a particularly vicious strain of killer flu. Probably from one of those dangerous Asian countries.

DOROTHY
Mm. Unusually for a killer flu, the symptoms disappeared when you had a Lemsip.

GARY
Have you seen my trousers?

DOROTHY
Yes, they're dark blue, and like most of your wardrobe they set British men's fashion back thirty-five years.
Gary searches everywhere for his trousers.

GARY
Why don't you get some friends over?

DOROTHY
Because they're working during the day, and they won't come in the evening in case you smarm up to them in your usual way calling them 'toots' and offering them phallic-shaped nibbles.

GARY
Okay, where have you hidden my trousers?

DOROTHY
Nowhere! Stay. I'll be fit enough to leave in a couple of days.

GARY
You're perfectly well now. Look at you, you could hop in a taxi and lead an expedition across the North Pole.

DOROTHY
I feel dizzy, I'm still bleeding and swollen, and my temperature is still over a hundred.

GARY
Well, you'll feel nice and warm then.

DOROTHY
I'm a nurse, Gary, I've seen patients get up too soon. One minute they're saying 'Oh, maybe I could do a bit of light gardening', the next they're lying in a large metal filing cabinet with a label round their big toe.
Gary tugs back the duvet to reveal Dorothy wearing his suit trousers.

DOROTHY
My God, how did that happen!

GARY
(*Getting furious*) Give me the trousers, Dorothy.

DOROTHY
Please stay, Gary, we'll have a nice day. We can tell each other things we've always wanted to tell each other but haven't had the time.
He grabs the trousers at the ankle. She holds the belt. He pulls the trousers, managing only to drag Dorothy slithering across the bed. Gary gives up, seething.

GARY
(*In a rush*) Go and die somewhere else, you're driving me mad, you silly malingering tart. I'm a bloke. I need my freedom!
Dorothy looks genuinely shocked and hurt. Gary angrily grabs the first trousers that come to hand – and leaves.

16. AT THE OPTICIAN

Daytime. Tony comes in. The optician is behind her counter.

TONY
Hi.

OPTICIAN
Hi.
Tony puts two glasses cases on the counter.

TONY
Thanks, but I think I'll have my money back. I've decided I like it blurry.

OPTICIAN
Ooh, we can't do refunds.

TONY
(*Pathetically*) But, I've spent all me money.
The optician winces sympathetically.

TONY
My friends laugh at me when I put them on. I'm losing all the admiration and respect I've built up.

OPTICIAN
Sorry. Maybe you should overcome your doubts about contact lenses.
Tony looks undecided.

TONY
So, it just feels as comfortable as wearing a condom?

OPTICIANS

OPTICIAN
Yes.

TONY
Except you put them in your eye.

OPTICIAN
Yes.

TONY
(*After pondering*) All right.

OPTICIAN
Do you have a preference between hard, gas-permeable, tinted, soft daily wear or disposable lenses?

TONY
(*Rummaging in pocket*) You'd better give me your cheapest.
He puts a handful of coins and the odd screwed-up fiver down on the counter.

TONY
No, what the hell, make that two.

17. GARY'S FLAT: KITCHEN

Later that day. The door slams. Gary comes in, carrying his briefcase and a puny bunch of pink flowers. He is wearing his pinstripe jacket with colourful tartan trousers. He calls out to the flat in general as he gets a lager out of the fridge.

GARY
Hi, babe, sorry about this morning. I don't know what came over me. As the actress said to the— Dorothy?
He is peering round in the direction of his bedroom. No reply. He goes off into the bedroom, leaving the kitchen empty, then reappears.

GARY
Dorothy? Come on out, I've bought you some flowers. They match your appendix.
He opens a cupboard, making sure she is not there. Then he checks the fridge again, peering into the icebox. He glances around, looking worried, then finds a piece of paper on the table. He reads it, looking even more concerned.

18. STREET OUTSIDE OPTICIAN

Same day. Tony leaves the optician. He is very shaky and disoriented, obviously wearing his new contact lenses. As though wearing ice skates, he hangs on to the shop door for a while. He looks up and gazes around quickly, making his head spin.
Blinking wildly and wiping the tears from his eyes, he walks the short distance to the nearest lamppost, taking exaggeratedly high steps. He clutches the lamppost. The optician pokes her head out of the shop to check Tony is okay. Tony instantly pretends everything is all right. She waves goodbye and goes back into the shop.
Tony goes back to the serious business of trying to walk, making his way clumsily down the street as though wearing snowshoes. He walks into a nun, knocking her over.

19. DEBORAH'S FLAT: LIVING ROOM

Meanwhile, Deborah is showing into her flat a distracted, agitated Gary.

DEBORAH
Well, have you tried everywhere she might be?

GARY
Yes – her parents' place, the hospital, all her friends, her disgusting ex-so-called boyfriends, her favourite clothes shops.

DEBORAH
What did they say?

GARY
They said: 'No, we don't appear to have a slightly deranged woman dressed in pyjamas tottering dizzily through Mixed Separates, you stupid bastard.'

DEBORAH
Do you know why she's run off?

GARY
No! I may jokily have called her a malingering tart but—

DEBORAH
(*Shocked*) Gary, how could you!

GARY
That's the way we talk to each other. I didn't realise she'd come over all bonkers.
Deborah sits down calmly. Gary paces up and down.

GARY
Let's just . . . not panic. Let's . . . draw up a psychological profile, to find out her state of mind.
He puts the tips of his fingers together in a thoughtful, Cracker-like pose.

GARY
So, she's wearing ill-fitting pyjamas, she nearly died of a burst appendix a week earlier—

DEBORAH
Her boyfriend's just called her a malingering ta—

GARY
(*Joining in*) Tart, so she's just been rejected by the one person she should be able to trust. So, what's her frame of mind?
Deborah rolls her eyes and crosses her arms. Gary is getting into his role, slipping gradually into a Robbie Coltrane impersonation.

GARY
A little unhappy? Let's come back to that, shall we? What kind of a person is Dorothy? A scary person, a brown-haired person, a person with a history of volatile behaviour.
Gary gets out a scrap of paper from his pocket.

GARY
But the note she left. (*Reading*) 'Feeling a bit odd – have gone for a walk.' Doesn't that sound like someone who is actually quite sane? I don't think I need to blame myself over this.

DEBORAH
She's spelt 'odd' with five Ds.

GARY
Oh, yes. Well, that's it then, she's probably wandered on to a major road. I've killed her.

DEBORAH
Gary, you're getting hysterical, pour yourself a drink.
Gary goes over to a long sideboard. He opens the end door, revealing Dorothy's head, made up to look extremely ill. A momentary pause, then Gary shuts the door again and tries to look dignified.

GARY
Right, you've both made your point, thank you very much. I take it my nursing services aren't required any more. Thank you.
Gary leaves. Deborah smiles to herself and walks over to release Dorothy.

DOROTHY
(*Offscreen*) Can you help me out, Debs? It's pulling my stitches.

20. GARY'S FLAT: LIVING ROOM

Later. Gary and Tony are sitting on the sofa, drinking lager, vaguely watching the TV. Tony's eyes are shut.

GARY
Put it this way, if a bloke's pain threshold is here, right?
He holds his hand some three feet above the ground.

TONY
Right. (*Unable to see*) Where?

GARY
Up here.

TONY
I can't see, it hurts when I open my eyes.

GARY
Oh, yeah. (*Grabbing Tony's hand*) If a bloke's pain threshold is up here.

TONY
Right.

GARY
Then your average girl's threshold is down here.
He lowers his and Tony's hand to an inch above the floor.

TONY
That's quite low.

GARY
Low, that's what I'm saying. That's the difference. (*Moving Tony's hand up and down*) High, low. High, low. The reason, obviously, is that in olden days the women stayed at home – chatting – whereas the blokes went out and about, running barefoot on thorns and sharp stones, and you can't tell me that doesn't raise your pain threshold. Are you all right there?

TONY
Yeah.

GARY
So, it's not a good idea to clean your lenses with Fuzzy Peach shower gel and then put them back in your eye, then?

TONY
No.

GARY
Do you want a hand with your lager?

TONY
No, I'm okay.
Tony raises his can to his mouth but misses by and inch and pours the lager down his face.

GARY
You see, look at all the fuss women make about childbirth. I'm not saying it doesn't smart a bit, but if blokes did it I reckon we'd be looking at, what – give birth, have a couple of paracetamol, maybe a quick kip and back to work within the hour?

TONY
I'm going to do it, I'm going to open my eyes.

GARY
Good luck, mate. Count of three.
Tony breathes heavily, psyching himself up like a weightlifter.

GARY
One. Two. Thr—

TONY
(*Panicking*) No, I'm not ready, I'm not ready.

GARY
Okay, in your own time. So what's it like with your lenses in?

TONY
Great. Everything's really clear. I was walking up the street, and I could see all the tiny leaves on the tree, and ants crawling along branches. Brilliant!

GARY
Ants. Brilliant.

TONY
I mean, it hurt to buggery, obviously.

GARY
I bet. Do you want to go again?

TONY
Yeah, let's do it.
Tony does his weightlifter's breathing again, grabs Gary's shirt for support, whimpers with pain and forces his eyes open. He keeps them wide open, staring wildly.

GARY
Do you know, you wouldn't know you were wearing them.

TONY
Yeah, that's the beauty of lenses.

GARY
Are they comfortable?

TONY
Yeah, except when I blink. So, would you look after Dorothy again?

GARY
Well – this may sound harsh – but I think women lose a lot of their femininity when they're ill, do you know what I mean?

TONY
(*Still staring wildly*) Yes.

GARY
I suppose it's an old-fashioned view, but I find it difficult to completely respect a woman who's dribbling, groaning, bleeding and wingeing on about some ache or other.

TONY
Still, bless 'em.

GARY
Bless 'em, exactly.
Tony has to turn his whole head to see where his lager can is. He picks it up, knocking things over on the coffee table and raises the can to his lips. He overshoots his mouth again and pours the lager down his face once more.

TONY
Cheers.

GARY
Cheers.
Gary looks over at Tony thoughtfully. He reaches down and brings out the jar containing Dorothy's appendix. Tony is not able to see anywhere but straight ahead.

GARY
Fancy a pickled chilli with that?

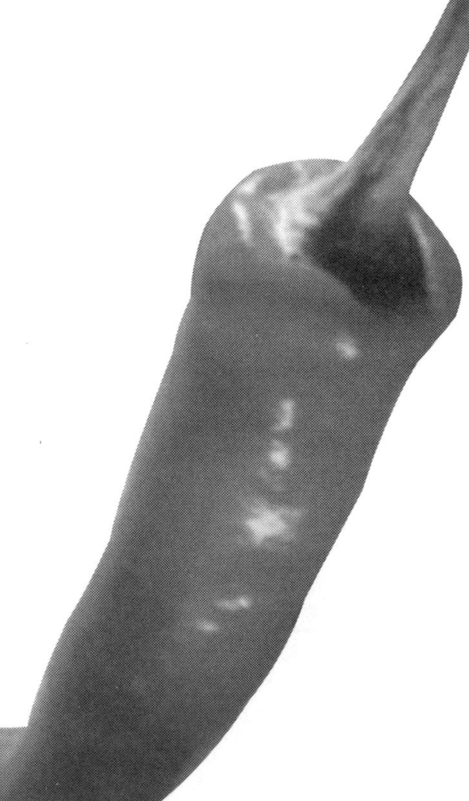

SERIES FOUR: EPISODE SEVEN

PLAYING AWAY

I thought first about having Gary sleep with Deborah, but somehow I couldn't see that happening. The problem was not making us believe that Tony would be prepared to have sex with his best mate's girlfriend – or anyone with a pulse – it was making it credible that Dorothy would sleep with Tony. To make her behaviour more palatable, I made sure Gary was at his most self-important in the other plot, in which he goes away on a writing course with Deborah.

The script overran again so we had to cut lots of stuff, mainly about students. I always think students are going to be good comedy material, but they are hard to mock convincingly (see 'Home-made Sauna', Series Five, Episode Five).

There is some great acting in this episode: Caroline and Martin unsure what to do, and particularly Neil's *tour de force* as he loses his tooth. The love scenes were very odd for Caroline and Neil – lots of 'Ooh, this is weird . . .' Apparently after this show was broadcast, men in white vans kept stopping and leaning out of the window to shout at them: 'You shouldn't have done it!'

1. GARY'S FLAT: LIVING ROOM

Night-time. Tony and Gary are on the sofa, gormlessly watching the TV with their mouths open. Dorothy is sitting in an armchair reading a book. Dorothy looks up at them, then back to her book. Without taking their eyes off the screen, the men eat some cheese puffs from a bowl.

DOROTHY
Are you going to turn it on?

TONY
(*Eventually*) It is on.

DOROTHY
It might as well not be. What's the programme?
They look over at her, confused, then back to the TV screen.

TONY
Dunno.

GARY
Something about . . . Dunno.

DOROTHY
Rearrange these words to make a sentence: Tony, and, Gary, are, witless, morons.

TONY
Morons are witless Tony Gary . . . and?

DOROTHY
Nearly. When did either of you last read a book?

TONY
Last week.

DOROTHY
Oh. What?

TONY
That little floppy book that comes with the gas bill.

DOROTHY
A few adverts for log-effect fires stapled together – it's not exactly *Tess of the D'Urbervilles*, is it?

GARY
May I remind you I am about to go on a creative-writing course.

DOROTHY
May I remind you that that's like Barbara Cartland going on a hang-gliding course.
Gary and Tony continue to watch blankly.

DOROTHY
Gary, you did invite me round. I don't expect you to hire a top juggler to entertain me, but it would be nice to have some attention.

GARY
We're having fun. You've got your . . .
He can't think of the word.

DOROTHY
Book?

GARY
. . . book. And we've got an interesting programme about . . . whatever this is about.

DOROTHY
Do you know how many hours a week you spend in front of the television?

TONY
Two and a half?

GARY
One?

DOROTHY
I counted recently, Gary. Fifty-two hours.

GARY
Come off it, I'd have to get in from work, turn the TV on immediately and watch it every night until after midnight, then put in twelve hours a day at the weekend.
A pause.

DOROTHY/GARY
Exactly./Yeah, probably about right then.

TONY
You learn a lot though, don't you? I've got all my knowledge of the world through the TV.

DOROTHY
Where's Bosnia, Tony?

TONY
No, that's news. I don't watch the news, too depressing. Except the funny story at the end, you know: And finally, they wheeled out the biggest sausage in the world in Luton today . . . for charity!
There is a knock at the door.

ALL
It's open!
Deborah comes in.

ALL
(*Á la* Cheers) Debs!

DEBORAH
Who wanted the painkillers?

TONY
Me. Ta.

DEBORAH
(*Handing them to him*) What's wrong with you?

TONY
Toothache. Little son of a bitch tosser at the back.

DEBORAH
Is it a wisdom tooth?

TONY
No, we don't get them in my family.

DOROTHY
(*Still reading*) What a surprise.

DEBORAH
Have you seen a dentist?

TONY
(*Swallowing the pills*) Yeah.

DEBORAH
What did he say?

TONY
I can't really remember, it was in 1986. The only thing I can remember is, he told me to rinse out, and I thought he said mince out, so I bit him.
Gary and Tony deliberately make a space for Deborah between them on the sofa. She reluctantly sits down.

GARY
So, Deborah, all set for our weekend course?
He gives her a wink and does that clicking sound.

DEBORAH
(*Grumpily*) Yes.

GARY
Hope you don't mind me tagging along. Don't worry if you want to get off with someone. I won't stand in your way.

DEBORAH
That's not why I'm going.

GARY
Oh, we all know what happens at these residential courses. Young people away for the

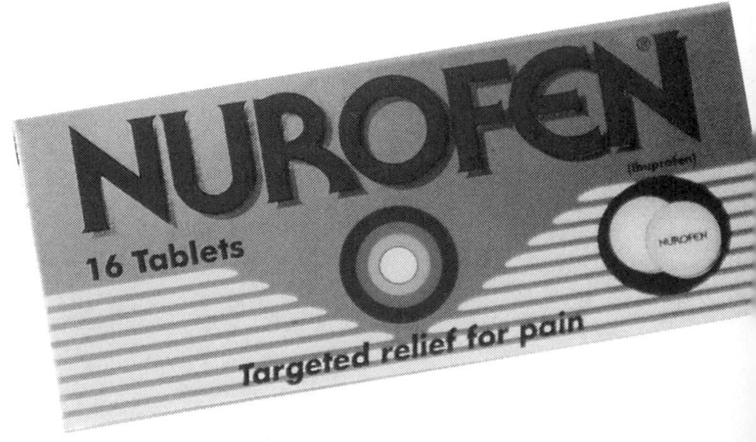

weekend – they have a few lagers, invite each other into their rooms for an Ovaltine, and before you can say 'neatly trimmed pubic hair' it's a bit less of the Chekhov and a bit more of the pants-off.
Dorothy gives Gary a heavy look.

GARY
That's if you're not in a loving relationship like me.

DOROTHY
You're not even interested in creative writing.

GARY
I am. Before you squeezed all the romance out of me I seem to remember writing you a rather touching sonnet.
Dorothy smiles nostalgically.

DOROTHY
No, it was a limerick. It started, 'There was a young nurse from Hever'. And you tried to rhyme 'marvellous' with 'great arse'.

GARY
I've always got my head in a novel.

DOROTHY
When?!

GARY
What's that long one – disabled chap, church, terrible back problem.

DEBORAH
The Hunchback of Notre Dame?

GARY
I finished that.

DOROTHY
Yes, after three years. On cassette. It's not quite the same thing. Especially as you taped over the moving finale with the Simon Bates Show and didn't even notice.

TONY
Maybe I should go on the course instead. I was always good at poetry at school. (*Lyrically*) 'I wandered lonely as a clown, that flows on high o'er . . . shoes and . . . grass. When all of the once I espied a crone, a hostess of goldey . . . daffs.'
A respectful silence.

GARY
Mm, sends a shiver down your spine, doesn't it? (*Shivering with the thrill of it*) The distinctive cadences of Shakespeare, of course.

DOROTHY
Wordsworth. Obviously in his dyslexic years.
Gary disappears out to the hall.

DEBORAH
I'm not sure about poetry. All those pale men going all quivery about roses. I'm more interested in writing short stories.

TONY
Yeah, there was a TV programme on this – the classic short story has . . . no, it's gone.

DOROTHY
A big explosion?

TONY
I'm not sure. I think we turned over to the indoor bowls.
Gary returns wearing a smoking jacket, complete with a row of pens in the top pocket.

GARY
I think this'll strike the right literary note, what do you reckon?
Tony and Dorothy smirk. Deborah cringes.

2. KITCHEN

Next morning. Tony is making breakfast, assembling a plate of cheese, bread and crispy rashers of bacon. He gingerly takes a nibble. Relieved that the tooth is not hurting, he takes a bolder bite and is suddenly in agony. He dances round the room in pain. Gary enters, dressed like a 1950s beat poet in dark glasses and a black rollneck sweater under a jacket. He watches Tony's agonised dance, joining in facetiously with his movements.

TONY
It's my tooth, I'm not a well man.

GARY
(*Opening fridge*) Cheer up, at least you've still got your health.

TONY
What are you dressed like that for?

GARY
It's for the writing course, my beat-poet look.

TONY
Just as well you told me, I thought it was your beat-me-up-I-look-annoying look.

GARY
Trust me, mate, the place'll be littered with girls trying to get off with the first bloke who looks sensitive and can hold a pencil.

TONY
You're not going to cheat on Dorothy, are you?
Gary does an extended laddish chuckle, then is suddenly serious.

GARY
Probably not. No, I've got serious ambitions as a writer, money for old rope. Look at Jeffrey Archer, all the imagination of a piece of bark.

TONY
(*Wincing*) Will you have a look in my mouth?

GARY
Do I have to?
Tony opens his mouth wide. Gary reluctantly peers in, from a distance.

TONY
Can you see the problem?

GARY
Yeah.

TONY
What?

GARY
On the left at the back. Somebody's parked a rusty old bike.

TONY
Please, help.
Tony pulls Gary closer so he is holding his face, able to see into his mouth properly.

TONY
What can you see?

GARY
There's the dangly thing at the back that looks like a sand-papered testicle.
Unable to speak, Tony grunts with frustration.

GARY
And you appear to have a big, pink and spongy chap in the middle surrounded by various hard, white and knobbly bits.
Tony shuts his mouth crossly. Gary grabs his face back.

GARY
Okay, okay. (*Peering in again*) Dentists always say things like: rear seven occluded, upper left rupture. Why don't they just come out with it and say: crap teeth.

TONY
There's nothing wrong with them!

GARY
I'm not knocking it, mate. If I'd been sitting around in your mouth for twenty-five years I'd look a bit sorry for myself too.

TONY
(*Laddish*) It's seen some sights, though, this mouth.

GARY
(*Equally laddish*) Yeah, I bet.

TONY
I tell you what, if this mouth could talk it'd have some pretty interesting things to say.

GARY
It can talk, of course.

TONY
Yeah, good point.

GARY
What's the most interesting thing you've ever sucked?
They ponder this in all seriousness.

TONY
Girlfriend of mine put her nose in my mouth once.

GARY
What did it feel like?

TONY
Well, it's more substantial than a nipple but not as satisfying as a Twix.

GARY
(*Shutting Tony's mouth*) Mm. Can't see anything, mate, you'll have to go to a dentist.
He playfully slaps Tony on the cheek. He yelps.

GARY
Sorry.

TONY
No, I hate dentists. It's not natural, paying some mad bloke in a white coat twenty-eight quid to drill away bits of your head.
Gary grunts in agreement. Tony gets up and forks the food into a blender, adding ketchup, milk and for good measure a banana.

TONY
I hate the way they always ask if you floss every day, in that really accusing voice.

GARY
Yeah, I floss every day, sure, and Barry White works in Burger King in Willesden High Street.

TONY
Anyway, I'm going to let my teeth grow old gracefully, like Stonehenge.

GARY
Your problem, mate. In a couple of days I'll be on my writing course—
Tony turns on the blender, instantly drowning out what Gary is saying. Gary carries on talking animatedly for some time, with us and Tony not able to hear a word. Tony humours him, pretending to show an interest. To illustrate what he is saying, Gary makes increasingly sexual

gestures, thrusting his hips. Tony switches off the blender.

GARY
—begging me to show them my Longfellow.
Tony picks up the blender bowl. Gary watches with distaste as Tony drinks the murky fluid. Tony emerges happily with scum on his top lip.

3. GARY'S OFFICE

Later. George is sitting at his desk. Gary is at his, reading a letter, wearing a toned-down version of his beat-poet garb. George has his tongue out and is concentrating as he tries to separate two paper clips. Gary watches as George tries everything: shaking them free, teasing them apart, biting them, using brute force, shaking them again.

GEORGE
It's almost as though paper clips have a life of their own, isn't it?

GARY
Yes, and sadly it's probably more interesting than yours.

GEORGE
I'm rather upset, I've mislaid my favourite paper clip. I've had it for eighteen years. He became a bit of a friend to me.

GARY
You have a friend who is a paper clip. Do you find that at all worrying, George?
George frowns, not understanding the question.

GARY
This is a letter from Head Office asking me if the London office would function effectively if I were suddenly called away. The answer that immediately springs to mind is: would it, bollocks.

GEORGE
Oh, I think Anthea and I could cope.

GARY
Mm, until morale was suddenly destroyed by the loss of one of your friends the drawing pins.

GEORGE
Oh, we're very experienced. You'd have to get up pretty early to get one past us.

GARY
Really? I'd say you could get up some time after lunch and still get a couple of London buses and a Trident submarine past you.
Anthea comes in, carrying paperwork.

GARY
Anthea, if I suddenly ran off to Brazil with Winona Ryder would you have the mental toughness to cope with running a modern office?
Anthea thinks about it then does a scared ooh-er expression.

GARY
Ah, yes, the confidence and poise of a born coper.

ANTHEA
Wouldn't they send someone down from head office, like when you go on holiday?

GARY
Do you two really want to be nannied for the rest of your lives?

GEORGE/ANTHEA
Yes./If it's not too much trouble.

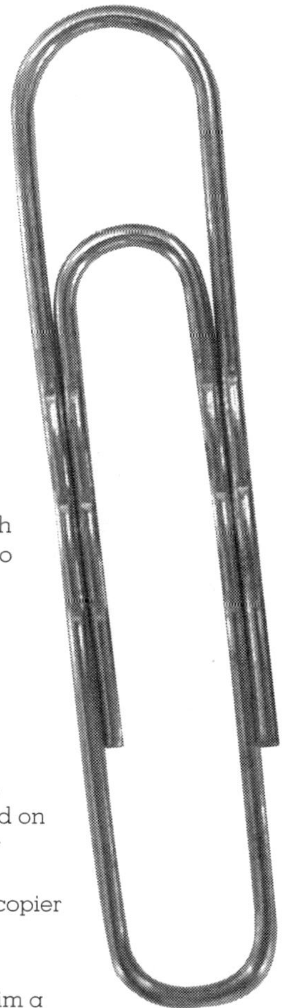

GARY
Yes, of course you do. I mean, look at you.
George and Anthea are looking even more mousy and woolly than usual.

GARY
This may sound harsh, but I'd rather put a biro in charge of my office than you two.

GEORGE
We have other abilities.

GARY
Really, what would those be? Ability to sit down with a nice cup of tea? Ability to put on a cardy in a crisis?

GEORGE
We're very dogged.

ANTHEA
And we don't wander off.

GARY
Dogged, don't wander off, lovely. Now let's try to build on those skills. Anthea, in my absence how would you handle a persistent photocopier salesman?

ANTHEA
Win his trust by offering him a chocolate-coated biscuit?

GARY
And if that fails, unlikely though it seems?

ANTHEA
Agree to buy the photocopier?

GARY
Well done, Anthea, almost heroically inept. George, one of our burglar alarms fails to go off resulting in the theft of ten thousand pounds worth of golfing umbrellas. The customer turns up demanding the money. What do you do?
George looks anguished.

GARY
Go into the foetal position, yes, then what?

GEORGE
Um. Offer him a chocolate-coated b—

GARY
No, no biscuits.

GEORGE
A doughnut?

GARY
No. Tough, George. If you can, think, 'Hell-cat mother-sucking bastard'.

GEORGE
I could suddenly shout, 'Ooh, what's happening outside!?' in an excited voice and in the ensuing mayhem rush out the back way?
Anthea is nodding in agreement. Gary considers.

GARY
Right, you're both going on a course this weekend.
He gets out a file containing details of business courses, scans through the leaflets.

GARY
It so happens I'm going on one too. Mine will be a never-ending round of delirious pleasures, probably involving an element of sexual fulfilment, yours will be a gruelling lesson in modern commercial methods, probably involving a good slapping. Here's one.
Gary dials a number on one of the leaflets.

GEORGE
I can't go away this weekend. Marjorie and I are having some creosote delivered.

ANTHEA
I was planning to reorganise my apron drawer.

GARY
(*Into the phone*) Hello, your training course this weekend: 'Assertiveness and Interactive Strategies in the Business Workplace'. Would you still have room for two rather nervous underachievers?
Anthea and George look nervous.

4. GARY'S FLAT: KITCHEN

Saturday, a day or two later. Tony enters from his bedroom. He is in toothache hell, whimpering, the traditional scarf wound tightly round his jaw with a big bow on his head. He opens the fridge and gets out the tray of ice cubes. The cubes will not come out. Tony, frantic with pain, desperately tries to free them. They fly out everywhere. He grabs as many as he can, tears off the scarf and crams them into his mouth. He stands there, feeling the benefit. He applies two hot-water bottles he prepared earlier, one to each cheek. The pain hits him again. He tears at his face, grabs a hand mirror and snarls at his tooth.

TONY
Right. See how you like this.
He rummages in a drawer and brings out some string. Growling all the while with pain, he ties the string round his tooth and goes over to his bedroom door. He attaches the string to the door handle and goes to the middle of the room. He realises that he does not have anyone to slam the door. He picks up a chair, grimaces in anticipation and throws it at the door but misses, breaking something.
He hooks the string round the leg of the kitchen table so it is taut. He goes to the door, grimaces and slams it. The string pulls the leg off the table, which falls over. Things slide off the table and break. He winds the string round the handle to make it taut. He grimaces again and slams the door.

Nothing appears to have happened. Tony waits to see if he is in pain. Blood comes flooding out of his mouth. A look of relief passes over his face. Seconds later a wave of even worse pain hits him. To stop the bleeding he crams great wedges of kitchen roll into his mouth, then the whole roll. In desperation he goes over to the telephone, looks down a list of numbers and dials one. He removes most of the kitchen paper to speak.

TONY
(*Distorted, barely intelligible*) Can I speak to Dorothy, please? (*Listening*) Dorothy! (*Not able to be understood*) No, Dorothy! (*Ditto*) D, O— No, D, like in dog. No, dog! D, O, G. (*Listening*) No, G, like in . . . giraffe. (*Listening, smiling*) Yes, exactly. (*After a pause, shouting*) No, Dorothy, you arse, I'm in pain. Dorothy! Dorothy!
A pause. His face is becoming smeared with blood.

TONY
(*Suddenly reasonable*) Hello, Dorothy, how are you? (*Taking it slowly*) I've pulled my tooth out, and I wondered if you had some very strong painkillers you could bring round from the hospital after your shift. (*Listening*) Yes, I feel a bit faint, so I'm going to have a lie-down. Okay. Bye-bye.
Tony hangs up, his face bloodstained like in a horror movie, and faints.

5. STUDENT BAR

Evening. Gary is standing at the bar with Deborah. Gary has gone for the Chekhovian look – rumpled linen jacket, neckerchief and waistcoat. One or two other course members are hovering. Gary glances behind the bar at a noticeboard with studenty messages, announcing a 'Skimpy Swimwear and Anorak Party', a 'Grants in crisis' meeting, a gig or two ('Colin Birch & the Wankers') and a notice: STUDENTS MUST FULLY VACATE THEIR ACCOMMODATION DURING THE HOLIDAY PERIOD.

GARY
Students. (*Tutting*) The so-called intellectual heart of the nation, most of them studying for degrees in Feeling Sorry for Themselves and Going on Pointless Demonstrations.

DEBORAH
Oh, I think they're sweet.

GARY
Sweet, huh. When I was at university we were too busy living life to the limit to be sweet. We used to talk on and on through the night about, I don't know, just crazy things, I guess. Crazy notions. Then we grabbed a couple of hours sleep and got up, stretching our lean young bodies like Greek gods, and went out and talked about crazy things all over again. Great days.

DEBORAH
Gary, you didn't go to university.
Gary ignores her.

GARY
I mean, do they really think that's funny?
Cut to a wide shot of the bar, dominated by its The Dog's Bollocks sign.

GARY
What's wrong with 'The Red Lion' or 'Pencils Wine Bar'? And have you noticed how easy the questions are on the new University Challenge? (*Proudly*) In my day we couldn't answer any of them. Huh.

DEBORAH
There's no need to feel so threatened. They're just starting out on life's great adventure.

GARY
Yes, the great adventure of how to spend all their housing benefit during their annual ten months of holiday while slagging off us poor bourgeois suckers who are forced to work in boring offices to keep them in Ecstasy and duffel coats.
A pretty student working behind the bar, wearing a Don't Squeeze Grants Badge, smiles innocently at Gary. Gary is suddenly all timid smiles.

GARY
Mind you, there's a lot of nonsense talked about students, trying to make ends meet on a grant of – what is it now? – about three pounds seventy a year.

DEBORAH
So what do you think of our teachers?
They gaze over to two burly, bearded Celts who are drinking heavily at a table.

GARY
They're all right. I had hoped there'd be a little more about how to write a bestselling novel and a bit less about how to enjoy a poem about a mining disaster.

DEBORAH
Maybe you'd like them more if you hadn't been told off for calling out, 'Oh, get a bloody move on' in class.

GARY
He said he wanted contributions from the class.

DEBORAH
Yes, contributions, not someone shouting out, 'Shut your face, beardy.'
Cut to Gary and Deborah sitting down at a table, gazing around the room.

GARY
You get all sorts doing these courses, don't you? Look at him, holding forth.
They are looking at a man dressed rather like Gary. Gary does a florid imitation of him.

GARY
'Yes, I'm of the opinion that Agatha Christie is actually a post-modern narrative genius.' Oh really, what's your opinion of this post-modern chair leg I'm about to insert in your face?
We scan the room, from a consumptive-looking poet-type . . .

GARY
(*Offscreen*) Scary chap.
To a pair of animated elderly women . . .

GARY
(*Offscreen*) There's always two mad old biddies, have you noticed?
To an anoraky man in his thirties.

GARY
(*Offscreen*) Overspill from the train-spotters course.
To two ethereal, attractive women . . .

GARY
(*Offscreen*) Seem very nice. (*In vision*) I reckon we'll probably end up chatting in their room tonight.

DEBORAH
Well, you can count me out, I'm going up to work on my short story for tomorrow.

GARY
Oh, I've finished mine.

DEBORAH
That was quick. Let's have a look.
Gary hands her a piece of paper. Deborah reads.

DEBORAH
'Barry was in his early thirties and blond, the kind of blond that made people with brown hair really jealous of. Barry's best friend was Toby' (*Heavy look at Gary*) 'Toby. They were like chalk and cheese, really different, the chalkiest chalk as opposed to the cheesiest cheese. Really different, as I mentioned earlier. One day Toby accidentally shampooed his hair in . . . bleughh?'

GARY
Bleach.

DEBORAH
'. . . bleach, making his hair blond. "Not so different now," Toby opined. "We could almost be brothers, like those two who used to be in the group Bros." '
Gary grins proudly. Deborah turns over the page, looking in vain for more.

DEBORAH
Little bit short, isn't it?

GARY
It's a short story.

DEBORAH
Where's the characterisation and plot development? The theme or the twist in the tale?

GARY
(*Vaguely peering over*) Um . . . (*Breezily*) So, shall I come up later and tuck you in?
He does that laddish clucking sound.

DEBORAH
No. You could phone Dorothy and tell her you're missing her.

GARY
Oh, she understands that I've got m'needs. We've got a bit of an arrangement.

DEBORAH
You arrange to try it on with every woman you meet?

GARY
Good one. Um, no, I think she realises that in the heat of literary creativity (*Burping*) people get carried away and, sadly, do things with other people, rubbing their private parts together and so on.
He downs his lager, starting to get drunk.

GARY
And if it happens, sadly, I'm pretty sure she'll realise it didn't mean any more to me than if I was posting a letter. Although hopefully it would take a bit longer. (*Sipping lager*) And I wouldn't be using a letter. (*Another sip*) And the slot thing wouldn't be so high up.

DEBORAH
(*Getting up, long-suffering*) Good night.

GARY
Oh, are you off?
Deborah leaves. Gary gazes round the bar hopefully.

6. GARY'S FLAT: LIVING ROOM

Late that same evening. Dorothy and Tony are sitting on the sofa, laughing. They have nearly finished a bottle of wine.

DOROTHY
Has the pain gone?

TONY
Yeah, cheers. Are there any side effects?
Dorothy picks up the packet of painkillers and reads the back.

DOROTHY
Yes, apparently any moment now you may start to believe you're a member of the Swedish royal family.
They chuckle. Tony takes the packet.

TONY
(*Reading*) 'Do not operate heavy machinery, drink alcohol or exceed the stated dose.' Oh, well, at least I'm not operating heavy machinery.
Tony fingers the manky tooth dangling round his neck on a string.

TONY
Better out than in, eh? I think I'll get it made up into a ring.

DOROTHY
Mm. Nearly as attractive as the bracelet Gary made out of his toenails. That was a waste of three years.

TONY
It's weird him not being here.

DOROTHY
Mm. Quite nice really.

TONY
Why, aren't you happy with him?

DOROTHY
Would you be happy going out with a cross between Oliver Reed and Forrest Gump?

TONY
Yeah, I wouldn't mind. I think we'd get on.

DOROTHY
It's not as though I want anything complicated. A birthday card instead of a 'Sorry, I forgot your birthday' card. A holiday with someone who doesn't sit on the beach dividing women up into 'totty' and 'non-totty'. The odd bit of excitement.
Dorothy looks bleak.

TONY
Still, at least . . . (*Long pause*) he's got all his own hair.

DOROTHY
What about you?

TONY
I'm experimenting with celibacy at the moment.

DOROTHY
How's it going?
Tony winces. Dorothy tuts sympathetically.

TONY
Well, it's not natural, is it? That's why they've put the sexual organs in front, to keep reminding you to have sex, instead of tucking them away behind, just above your bottom, where you can't see them.

DOROTHY
You and Deborah still not getting it together?

TONY
No, I asked her out again yesterday. It's painful getting rejected, you know.

DOROTHY
I know. Where did you invite her?

TONY
Jelly-wrestling.

DOROTHY
That'll be women in bikinis wrestling in jelly, presumably?

TONY
Yeah. At the Bear. You've probably seen the posters: 'YOU AND THE NIGHT AND THE JELLY'.

DOROTHY
Mm, odd that Deborah didn't want to go along.

TONY
You get to eat the jelly afterw—

DOROTHY
I don't want to know, Tony.

TONY
Well, I tried being a New Man. Deborah just laughed in my face.

DOROTHY
Pretending you like doing a bit of knitting doesn't make you a New Man, Tony.

TONY
Yeah, but she's always turning me down. I'm never asking her out again, and she'll never ask me, so I guess that's it.
Dorothy looks sympathetic.

TONY
Still, Saturday night, eh. Weh-hey! Makes you think – all round the world, billions of people snuggling up, taking their gear off.

He and Dorothy think about this, dreamily.

TONY
At this moment, half a million women in Germany are being fondled.

DOROTHY
Frightening. As we speak enough Parisian men to fill Wembley stadium are lying in beds with their bottoms going up and down.
They continue to think about this, dreamily.

TONY
Have you missed your last bus?

DOROTHY
I think I have actually.

TONY
Is the door locked?

DOROTHY
Yes.
They turn to each other and kiss. After a bit of this they throw their legs over each other. Moments later, still kissing, they are on their feet and heading for Tony's bedroom.

DOROTHY
Is this a good idea?

TONY
Yeah. I mean, it's only exercise, isn't it?

7. STUDENT BAR

A barman is (e.g.) pulling down the grille to indicate closing time. Gary is propping up the bar. He is now wearing his dressing gown and is fairly drunk. A few fellow course members are still milling around.

GARY
So, who wants to come back to my room for a chat, talk about life, no obligations?
Nobody listens. The two ethereal, attractive women walk past.

GARY
Hello. I've got some little sachets of Ovaltine and a kettle, if you're interested in—
They smile politely and walk away.

GARY
Maybe another time, eh? Peace! See you in class tomorrow. I think you'll like my short story.
A couple from the course are finishing their drinks.

GARY
I was just saying to those ladies, fancy a warm beverage? I've brought some mugs up specially from London. We could all sit on my bed and—
They ignore him.

GARY
No – okay, cheers, I'd better turn in too.
He sees the two bearded teachers at the far side of the room having a heated argument.

GARY
(*Raising his hand*) Good night, bearded blokes!
He puts down his glass on the bar.

GARY
(*To the barman*) Nice pint, mate. I'll just turn in. This is me turning in. Nighty-night.
Gary makes his way slightly drunkenly towards the exit. As he goes he sees that the two teachers have started to brawl violently. One of them breaks his glass over the other's head. Gary watches for a moment, then heads off to bed.

8. GARY'S FLAT: TONY'S BEDROOM

The next morning. Signs of someone under the duvet waking up. Tony's head emerges. He does an inane waking-up smile, then grimaces as his mouth pains hits him. The duvet moves. He opens his mouth in horror, remembering. He gingerly lifts the corner of the quilt, revealing Dorothy's face, her eyes wide open, as anguished as him. He gently replaces the duvet on her face. They lie there, not daring to move. Tony eases himself up until he is sitting up. He clears his throat.

TONY
Um. Dorothy. You know last night—

DOROTHY
(*Face under duvet*) I don't want to talk about it. It didn't happen.

TONY
Gary's me best mate.
Dorothy pulls the duvet away from her face.

DOROTHY
Maybe you should have thought about that last night when you started whispering sweet nothings to me. Like, 'Blimey, this is a turn-up for the book.'

TONY
What about you!

DOROTHY
I know!

TONY
I had a lethal cocktail of drink and drugs inside me. I didn't know what I was doing!

DOROTHY
You seemed to know exactly what you were doing as it happens.

TONY
(*Unsure how to react*) Oh. Did I? So . . . I was pretty good then?

DOROTHY
I don't care! I've slept with— Oh, God, it's all too horrible.
She pulls herself up. They sit propped up in bed like a married couple.

TONY
Are we going to have to tell him?

DOROTHY
Of course. And I thought we could put an advert in the *Independent on Sunday*: 'Dorothy and Tony wish to announce that they had sex together several times on Saturday night. Dorothy wishes to be branded a complete trollop and dragged in shame through the streets of London on some kind of cart thing.'

TONY
You don't think we should tell him—

DOROTHY
No, I bloody don't.

TONY
(*Miffed*) Why, are you that ashamed?

DOROTHY
(*Softening*) No, Tony. I mean, I enjoyed it. But it's like waking up the next morning after eating a whole box of chocolates.

TONY
(*Smiling, shyly*) Thanks. (*Earnestly*) You were really excellent.
Dorothy shuts her eyes in anguish, then opens them.

DOROTHY
(*Vulnerable*) Really, was I okay?

TONY
Brilliant!
Dorothy bites her lip. Tony glances over at her shiftily.

TONY
If you want to do it again, I'm only too—

DOROTHY
No, I don't!

TONY
(*After a pause*) I'm here if you want me.

DOROTHY
Poor Gary. He trusted me. What are we going to do?

TONY
Game of 'Monopoly'?
Dorothy groans. The front door slams. They freeze.

DOROTHY
What was that?

TONY
It can't be Gary, he won't be back till tonight.

GARY
(*Offscreen, shouting distantly*) Tone, you'll never guess what happened.
Tony and Dorothy are instantly out of bed, panicking. Tony runs across his bed a couple of times. Their eyes fall on the wardrobe. Tony yanks the door open, too viciously: it comes away in his hands. He attempts in vain to mend it.

GARY
(*Offscreen, getting nearer*) Last night, our two teacher guys start knocking the crap out of each other. One's taken in for GBH, the other's in casualty with— Hey, have you got a bird in there?
Dorothy's only hiding place seems to be on top of the wardrobe. With his hands Tony makes a foothold for Dorothy to climb up. She hops around a bit then gives up. They look around desperately.

9. KITCHEN

Gary is wearing his outfit from last night, plus a writer-type floppy hat. He approaches the door to Tony's bedroom in cheerful mood.

GARY
So we were all sent home with a refund. I'm quite glad to be back, to be honest. Are you awake?
He knocks.

TONY
(*Offscreen, edgy*) No. I'm sleeping. On my own. Without anyone else.

GARY
You all right?
He opens the door.

10. TONY'S BEDROOM

Tony is in bed. Although apparently alone, his body bulks absurdly large under the duvet.

GARY
Hi, matey.

TONY
Matey.

GARY
How's your tooth?

TONY
(*Shifty*) What tooth, there's no tooth here, mate, I'm all on my own. Oh, tooth. Yeah, I pulled it out.
Gary sits down on the bed. Tony looks uneasy.

GARY
So what did you do last night?

TONY
(*Blurting at random*) Reading. Pub. Television. Pub. Bath. Whatever.
Gary sees an opened packet of condoms. He smiles approvingly.

GARY
What've you been using those for then, rain hats?
He does a dirty laugh. Tony joins in nervously.

GARY
I've got to hand it to you, mate. How do you do it?

TONY
Um, right place at the right time, I suppose.

GARY
So, what's she like?

TONY
I can't remember. It was dark.

GARY
(*Looking around*) Where have you hid her?

TONY
She had to leave early. She's a . . . milkman.

GARY
What, on a Sunday?
Gary notices slight movement under the duvet.

TONY
You're right. Actually she's . . . under here. She's very shy.
Gary sees a shirt on the floor. His smile freezes.

GARY
That's Dorothy's shirt.

TONY
No, it isn't.
Gary swallows hard and pulls back the duvet. Dorothy is cowering between Tony's legs. A chilling silence. Gary is too shocked to speak. He takes off his hat, turns and slowly walks out. Dorothy looks guilty. Tony looks appalled.

11. GARY'S OFFICE

The next morning. Gary is sitting at his desk, still looking shocked. His shirt is crumpled. He has bags under his eyes. The telephone rings. Still lost in his thoughts, Gary picks up the receiver. He holds it the wrong way round, putting the mouthpiece to his ear. After a moment he hangs up. George comes in, completely transformed – wearing his sharpest suit, carrying a hi-tech briefcase. Gary does not notice.

GARY
I have a problem, George.

GEORGE
There are no problems, only challenges.

GARY
Something terrible has happened.

GEORGE
Let's utilise it as a jumping-off point, shall we?
Gary now watches with growing fascination as George opens the endless, loud security clips on his briefcase and unlocks the combination.

GEORGE
I was working on some new targets and strategies on the train.

GARY
You always fall asleep on the train. You're known as Mr Snoozy from East Croydon.

GEORGE
My personal goals were insufficiently focused, with the result that my—

GARY
(*Anguished*) George, George, shut your face. I'm upset, I have a personal crisis on my hands.

GEORGE
The effective manager doesn't let his or her domestic situation prejudice his or her commercial performance.
Anthea enters, power dressed, bringing in the post.

GARY
Thank God, you're here, Anthea, this business course has turned George into a speak-your-weight machine.

ANTHEA
I think fear of change is at the heart of your misgivings.

GARY
(*Putting his head in his hands*) Oh, bloody hell. Please, just make me some tea. And bring me two chocolate-coated biscuits.

ANTHEA
No, from now on chocolate-coated biscuits will be productivity-linked on the basis of—

GARY
Yes, yes. Sit down.
Anthea does so, sitting down stiffly. She gets out her shorthand pad.

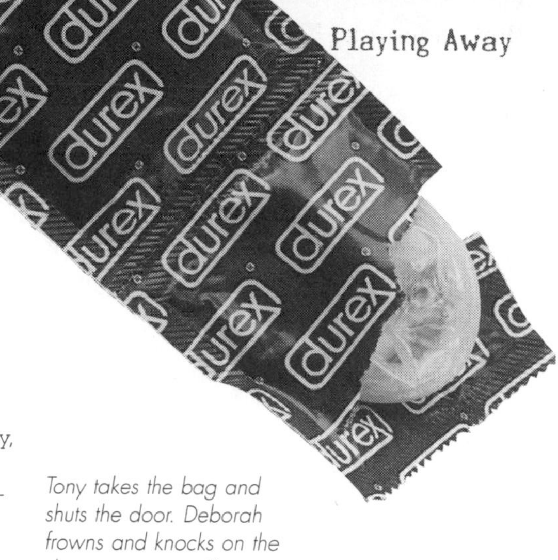

GARY
Dorothy slept with Tony while—
He stops. Anthea is taking it down in shorthand.

GARY
Put the pad away, Anthea.
She does so. Gary gets up and paces, agitated.

GARY
Dorothy slept with Tony while I was away. I don't know what to do. I mean, am I such a bad guy? I don't want to split up with Dorothy, and Tony seems really sorry but basically how can I share a flat with someone who's—

ANTHEA
I'm sorry, this isn't in our job description.
Anthea gets to her feet and goes back to her office.

GEORGE
Frankly, I'm worried that in your current mind-set you're ill-equipped to provide a meaningful agenda. You'll excuse me, I have to dictate some draft business proposals to my colleague.
George picks up a file and joins Anthea, leaving Gary on his own. He manages to control his anger for a moment, then presses the intercom.

GARY
Would you two care to step back into my office, please?

Same day. Deborah comes out of her flat and knocks at the door. While she is waiting she checks she looks nice and clears her throat nervously. The door opens a few inches, so we can just see Tony's face. He is looking paranoid, dressed in black.

TONY
Oh, it's you.

DEBORAH
Are you all right?

TONY
Why? What have you heard?

DEBORAH
(*Confused*) Nothing. Gary left one of his bags in my car.
She holds the bag up. It clatters.

DEBORAH
(*Smiling*) Sounds like coat hangers. I'm sure he took them by mistake.

TONY
Thanks.
Tony takes the bag and shuts the door. Deborah frowns and knocks on the door once more. Tony opens it a few inches again.

DEBORAH
Tony, are you sure you're okay?

TONY
Yeah. I just . . . had a lot on over the weekend.

DEBORAH
(*Nervous*) So, what are you up to?

TONY
Did he send you to check up on me?

DEBORAH
Who?

TONY
Gary.

DEBORAH
No. What's going on between you?

TONY
I . . . used something of his.

DEBORAH
What?

TONY
His . . . eggs. He's threatening to stab me in the back with our breadknife, then tie me down and, like, repeatedly jump off the table on to my balls in his climbing boots.

DEBORAH
Seems a bit of an over-reaction.

TONY
No no, fair do's, he's within his rights.

DEBORAH
Oh. Anyway, I wondered if you'd like to go out somewhere this week. You're always asking me out, and I always say no, I suddenly thought, maybe you're not such a bad guy.
Deborah gives him a friendly smile. Tony is still standing behind a half-closed door.

TONY
No, I'm not seeing women any more. It's too dangerous.
He shuts the door. Deborah sighs, cross with herself.

DEBORAH
(*Turning to go*) Sod you, then.

13. OFFICE

Later the same day. Gary is on his own, looking a bit lost. Dorothy appears, looking contrite.

DOROTHY
Hello.

GARY
(*Matter of factly*) Oh, hello.
An awkward pause. Gary shuffles paper, trying to be businesslike.

GARY
Pull up a bed. Sorry, I mean chair. Can I get you a brimming cup of libido? Sorry, I mean coffee.

DOROTHY
I'm sorry, Gary. Tony and me, I don't know, we were in a funny mood.

GARY
Oh. Well, I'll remember to be in a funny mood the next time I'm offered sex. 'Gary, my boyfriend's gone away for a nano-second, will you bonk my brains out?' Or 'Wait a minute, let me check if I'm in a funny mood. Yes, I am. Jump on.'

DOROTHY
If it's any consolation, he's not my type.

GARY
Really. I shudder to think what you'd have done if he was your type. Offered yourself up as a living sacrifice presumably.

DOROTHY
You must admit, your motives for going away weren't entirely innocent.

GARY
That is an outrageous accusation!
Dorothy sits down.

DOROTHY
Maybe we shouldn't go out together any more.

GARY
No, you're not getting off that lightly. You'll go out with me until you bloody well start enjoying it.
She does a relieved half smile. Gary feverishly shuffles papers, avoiding her eyes.

GARY
So, did you enjoy it?

DOROTHY
(*Lying*) No.

GARY
I imagine he's, what, pretty useless?

DOROTHY
Completely.

GARY
Little bit embarrassing for him, sharing a flat with someone who knows he's shite in bed.
They smile at each other bashfully.

DOROTHY
(*Serious*) You don't have to tell him of course.

GARY
No, no.
She hands him a present.

DOROTHY
I've, um, bought you a peace offering.

GARY
(*Opening it, excited*) What is it?

DOROTHY
Something for the long evenings at home.
Gary unwraps a large hardback. He tries to hide his disappointment.

GARY
War and Peace. Great. Plenty to enjoy there.
He tries to flick through the pages, but the inside is hollowed out. He pulls out something floppy.

GARY
(*Happy*) Whoopee cushion. Thanks.

DOROTHY
I know your other two are wearing out.
They look at each other, still tentative. They embrace lovingly.

DOROTHY
Where are George and Anthea?
Without breaking the embrace, Gary reaches out and opens the slats of the venetian blind. Anthea and George are now visible outside, their noses forlornly pressed up against the glass. Gary shuts the venetian blind.

GARY
Harsh but fair, I think.

14. OUTSIDE GARY'S OFFICE BUILDING

The reverse view. Two middle-aged office staff, looking suspiciously like Anthea and George, are standing marooned on a wide ledge on the first floor, their noses pressed against the glass.

15. GARY'S FLAT: LIVING ROOM

That night. Gary and Tony are sitting some distance apart: Tony on the sofa, Gary in an armchair, drinking lager. There is still a slight frostiness between them. Tony glances across at Gary nervously.

TONY
Sorry, mate.

GARY
No problem.

TONY
Next time I get a girlfriend – I'll explain the situation to her, if she's willing, any time you want a lend . . .
Gary does an airy gesture of dismissal.

TONY
It didn't mean anything, honest. We were both a bit out of it.

GARY
(*Knowing*) That probably affected your performance then?
Tony looks at Gary, obviously torn.

TONY
Yeah. Oh yeah.

GARY
So, would you say you were averagely useless or totally pathetic?
Tony bites his lip, even more torn.

TONY
Totally pathetic.

GARY
Uh-huh.
Gary is happier now. He gets up and sits next to Tony on the sofa, back in their usual places.

TONY
Does Dorothy always do that thing with—

GARY
Tony, Tony. No, Tony.

TONY
Sure, sorry.
A pause.

GARY
Yeah, she does.
They drink from their cans of lager. Gary idly studies his can.

GARY
Funny old business.

TONY
Yeah, a few hops and a bunch of water, boil it all up, and Bob's your uncle.

GARY
(*Momentarily confused*) No, not lager – sex.

TONY
Oh, sex, right.

GARY
We blokes think about it all the time. We talk about it a lot. We do it quite a bit. As you know. And yet . . . (*Holding his fingers only half an inch apart*) it's only a tiny word.
He shows Tony the tiny space his fingers are making.

TONY
Tiny, yeah. And it doesn't take any time to say. (*Lightly*) Sex. See? You start saying it, and you've immediately finished saying it.
They think about this, emptying their cans of lager. They crunch their cans and throw them over their shoulders. Freeze frame on the cans in mid-air.

PREMIUM LAGER
STELLA ARTOIS
LEUVEN
PREMIUM LAGER BEER
ANNO 1366
STELLA ARTOIS
LEUVEN

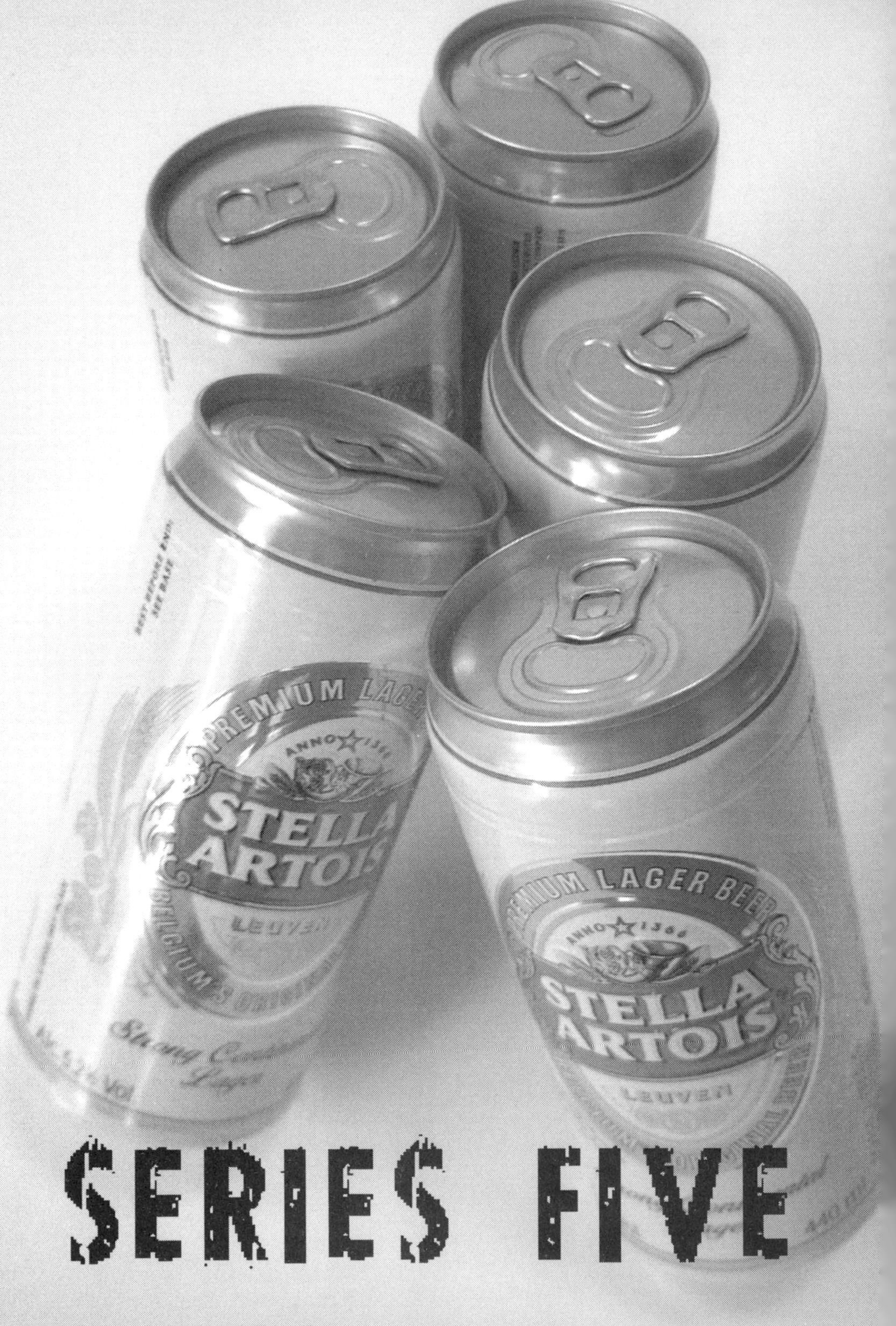

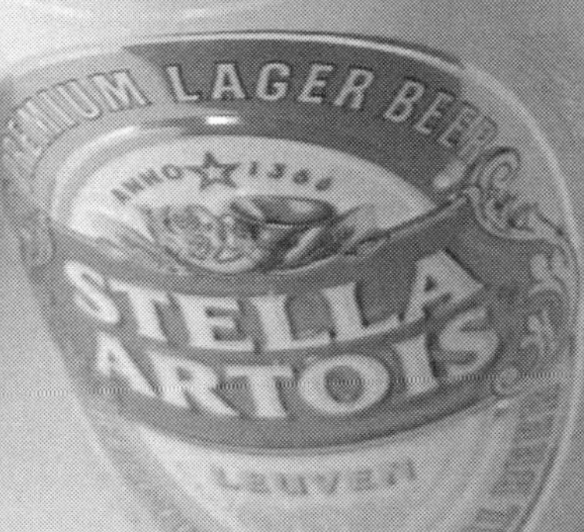

SERIES FIVE

SERIES FIVE: EPISODE TWO

THE GOOD PUB GUIDE

I decided it was time to tackle male grossness head on – the groin-scratching, the throat-clearing, the farting – and if anyone asked I would call it 'Chaucerian'.

I enjoyed writing Dorothy and Gary's tirades against the opposite sex. For once Gary gets a proper right of reply. I often felt I was giving men too much of a hard time but in the end the show is called *Men Behaving Badly* rather than *An Even-handed Examination of the Way Men and Women Both Sometimes Possibly Go Too Far*.

There is a comedy device whereby a scene ends with a character saying, 'You'll never catch me on that bicycle', and then you cut to the character riding the bicycle. It is probably the kind of cartoony mechanism that gives sitcoms a bad name but I often can't resist them. Hence here Gary's 'We're not stepping inside your place until you agree to reinstate him', then we cut to him and Tony standing in the pub. Always gets a laugh, trust me. But I draw the line at other traditional sitcom set pieces, like the 'tortuous misunderstanding' in which two characters talk at cross-purposes for five minutes. That is just silly.

This was John Thomson's first outing as the Crown's new landlord. I meant Ken to be a simple man confused by life, but in this episode he just comes across as mentally ill.

1. GARY'S FLAT: BEDROOM

Saturday morning. Gary and Dorothy are idly reading in bed – Gary Saturday's Sun, Dorothy the Independent. The remains of breakfast are on a tray. Gary farts, with undisguised relish. Dorothy looks long-suffering, then goes back to her paper.

GARY

'Plastic surgeons in Brazil are developing implants that allow breasts to be pumped up or deflated, according to the mood of the Latino lady or her lucky lover.'

Gary does a dirty, Sid James laugh. Pauses, then does it again.

GARY
I don't think you can go wrong with hugely inflated.
He sticks his finger in his ear and starts digging about. He takes his finger out, looks at it and wipes it in his hair. Dorothy rolls her eyes. Gary farts again.

GARY
Sorry.
Then again. Dorothy keeps her eyes on her newspaper.

DOROTHY
'On Saturday morning a woman lying in bed next to her boyfriend Gary suddenly broke off a piece of her bedside table and stabbed him with it over and over again.'

GARY
I said sorry.

DOROTHY
'As she was led away, Dorothy explained: "I don't fear prison. It will be far more civilised than my current lifestyle." '
Gary gazes at her evenly, then frowns and peers at the item she is pretending to read.

DOROTHY
Why do you have to do that in bed?

GARY
Because it's what blokes do.

DOROTHY
Why do you think women don't do it?

GARY
Lack of confidence?

DOROTHY
No, because it's not very nice for the other person.
Gary gazes at her uncomprehendingly.

GARY
Sorry, you've lost me. (*Turning back to his paper*) Sounds like you're a tiny bit scared of the human body.

DOROTHY
Gary, I'm a nurse. I've seen and heard things emerge from the human body that would make you scream with terror.

GARY
Well, there you go then.

DOROTHY
This is about respect.

GARY
I respect you. Vaguely.

DOROTHY
What would you say if I farted in bed all the time?

GARY
I'd be absolutely delighted.

DOROTHY
You wouldn't—

GARY
Absolutely delighted.

DOROTHY
You'd say I was being unfeminine.

GARY
Would I, though, actually? Would I?

DOROTHY
It's not just the farting. Since I've moved in you've been outrageous.

GARY
Thanks.

DOROTHY
No, it's a bad thing.

GARY
Oh, a bad thing.

DOROTHY
At least you used to make a tiny effort, now you're a twenty-four-hour slob. No wonder Deborah's so depressed, after five years living above men like you and Tony.

GARY
Men. It's always men, isn't it, getting it in the neck? There's my neck, I'm a bloke, go on – get it in there. What do we do that's so bad? Name one thing.

DOROTHY
You're always . . . rummaging around in your pants, adjusting yourselves.

GARY
It's complicated down there. Things need freeing up.

DOROTHY
You stare at women's chests. You sit on the tube with your legs wide open as though you're displaying some . . . rare species of giant plum—

GARY
We are!

DOROTHY
You think road rage is a brilliant idea. You go to football matches so you can shout out 'You're a total wanker' to the little umpire man. You clear your throats with that horrible

scraping sound. You think women are endlessly intrigued by ironing, and you're always going (*Laddish*) weh-hey-hey . . .
She finally runs out of steam. A pause.

GARY
Name one thing.

DOROTHY
I'm just disappointed, Gary.

GARY
What about you women? You think the most important thing in the universe is chocolate. You put on a skirt the size of four teabags and complain when men look at you. You're always saying things like, 'Ooh, ooh what lovely curtains.' You think you're pretty damn sensual, but woe betide any bloke who wants sexual intercourse more than three times a week, oh, no. You complain blokes can't find birds' clitorises, but you know as much about our tackle as you do about how to wire a plug.
A cool silence.

GARY
You blame us when you have your period, and you blame us when you don't—

DOROTHY
Shhh-shh.
They sit there in silence.

GARY
Fancy a bit of . . .

DOROTHY
Yeah, okay.
They start to take off their clothes and roll about together. Tony bursts in, looking distressed and out of breath. Gary and Dorothy break off hurriedly.

DOROTHY
What?!
Tony tries to speak but is too upset. He starts pointing in the direction of the road.

GARY
Accident?

TONY
(*Breathless*) No . . .
Tony shakes his head and points again.

GARY
Big tidal wave coming this way?

TONY
(*Still breathless*) Pub . . .

GARY
(*Alarmed*) The Crown? What's happened?
Tony snivels.

DOROTHY
Shall I slap you, Tony?

TONY
No.
The threat finally calms him down enough to speak.

TONY
They're redecorating the Crown.
Tony and Gary look anguished.

2. STREET OUTSIDE THE CROWN

Later that day. The pub is being completely gutted. The sound of hammering and sawing inside. Workmen are bringing out faded, tacky pictures and bits of ancient decor etc. Gary and Tony are standing outside with their mouths open. They stop a workman.

GARY
Is Les here?

WORKMAN
What does he look like?

TONY
He's quite dribbly.

GARY
Usually got a couple of gherkins on the go.

TONY
Looks a bit stained.

WORKMAN
Wino, is it?

TONY
No, he's the landlord.

WORKMAN
You want Ken. (*Shouting*) Ken!
He heads inside. Gary and Tony lean into the doorway to see what is going on. Tony is hit on the head by a tall slab of porcelain urinal being carried out by a workman. Ken comes out. He is deadpan, impassive and liable when under pressure to bullshit. His clothes suggest someone who is trying to make an impression but is failing.

KEN
This is Ken.

TONY
What's happening, Ken?

KEN
Exciting new interior.

TONY
What was wrong with it before?

KEN
The brewery did some market research on it, and it was classified in the category of . . . crap hole.

TONY
It might have been a crap hole to you, mate, but it was our home!
Ken blinks, a sign that he is bullshitting.

KEN
You'll like how we're doing it up. They're flying wallpaper in specially from Malta, to be here.

GARY
Why?

KEN
It's the wallpaper capital of the world, for wallpaper.

TONY
Who are you?

KEN
Ken. I'm the new . . .
He is searching for the word.

GARY
Landlord?

KEN
Landlord, yeah.

GARY
What happened to Les?

KEN
The brewery sacked him.

TONY
Why? He was a brilliant landlord.

KEN
He kept forgetting to open at lunchtimes.
A pause.

GARY/TONY
Yes, that's very Les./Yeah, he liked his sleep did Les.

GARY
Well, we're not happy.

TONY
We loved Les.

GARY
No, we didn't.

TONY
No, we didn't. But we felt sorry for him.

GARY
And I'll tell you something, mate, we're not stepping inside your place until you agree to reinstate him.

TONY
Absolutely.

3. INSIDE THE CROWN

Seconds later. Tony, Gary and Ken are obediently sitting at bar stools in the gutted, dusty interior.

KEN
Yeah, at first the brewery wanted to rename this place Mobiles, the pub for people who like using their mobile phones in public places. Then they were going to turn it into a Showaddywaddy theme pub called Showaddywaddys. Um, then they thought about a darts theme pub called Tossers.

TONY
Yep, I could go with any of them.

KEN
But then the brewery decided to recreate the Crown how it was. I found an old black-and-white photograph of here before the war.

TONY
What was it like?

KEN
Terrible apparently. Lots of people killed.

TONY
What was the pub like?

KEN
It had the authentic pub feel that people are now looking for as we approach the end of one millennium and the beginning of a new millennium. And there'll be horse brasses. To preserve the authentic pub atmosphere. Pink ones.

TONY
I always wondered, what are horse brasses for?

KEN
Nobody knows.

TONY
Oh.
Tony nods obediently, buying all this. Gary is more sceptical. He gets off his stool.

GARY
Right, well, thank you. Obviously we'll have to consider other premises in the area, check out the facilities they offer, and we'll get back to you. Come on, Tony.
Gary and Tony get down off their bar stools. They look around nostalgically.

GARY
I suppose it's the end of an era.

TONY
Yeah.
As they make to leave, a workman comes through carrying a pile of dingy items.

TONY
Look, Gary, the towel out of the gents.

GARY
Ahh.
Gary picks a filthy, threadbare towel off the pile. It is stiff with dirt. They stare at it nostalgically. They turn to Ken.

GARY
Can we have this?

4. DEBORAH'S HALL

A little later that day. Deborah opens the door to Tony, who is carrying a large present wrapped in newspaper.

TONY
Hi, Debs.

DEBORAH
Hello, Tony.

TONY
I've bought you a present, as you've been so depressed.

DEBORAH
I'm much better now, thanks.

TONY
Oh. Okay I'll keep it then.
He turns to take the present away.

DEBORAH
I don't suppose it was a . . . nice present?

TONY
They're all nice, my presents to you.

DEBORAH
Well, to be honest, I wasn't that thrilled with the chocolate knickers. Or the carrot you found in the shape of a penguin. Or the piece of wet bark.
Tony holds the present out to Deborah. She sighs and tears the newspaper away to reveal a battered and rusty vending machine.

TONY
It's a condom machine. We rescued it from the Crown.
Deborah looks disappointed.

TONY
Oh, have you got one already?

DEBORAH
I haven't actually.

TONY
I thought it was something we could enjoy together, you know.

DEBORAH
No, Tony.

TONY
You don't have to use it with johnnies. Gary and me have just been using bits of cheese in it. Whenever you fancy a bit of cheese you pop in your two quid, turn the handle and, hey presto, a slice of cheese.
Deborah looks unhappy with the idea.

TONY
You get your money back—

DEBORAH
I know, Tony.

TONY
Or you could use it for spoon-size mini-wheats.

DEBORAH
Do you mind if I don't, Tony?

TONY
Okay.
He puts it down and wanders in, unasked. Deborah rolls her eyes and lets him in.

Tony strolls in behind Deborah, immediately making himself at home.

TONY
So, what's been happening?
He does some pointless, frisky sparring around Deborah, which she ignores.

DEBORAH
I've been getting into astrology actually.

TONY
Oh, yeah, the moon is in Uranus, that sort of thing.
She gives Tony a cold look.

TONY
Make sure you don't go shopping on the sixteenth of the month or you'll be sucked to death by guinea pigs.

DEBORAH
Real astrology has a strong basis in scientific fact actually. What sun sign are you?

TONY
I'm a Solero.

DEBORAH
That's an ice cream.

TONY
Oh, okay, I'm a Leo.

DEBORAH
I thought so. You see – the sign exactly fits your personality.

TONY
I'm a Capricorn actually.

DEBORAH
So why did you say you were a Leo?

TONY
(*Snorting*) Well, which would you rather be – a great big roaring lion with a shaggy mane or a goat?
Tony snorts again. Deborah is losing her patience.

TONY
I mean, guys don't believe in all that bollocks, do they? Unless they want to get off with a girl who thinks it's—
He stops himself as he looks across and sees Deborah eyeing him with resentment.

TONY
Real astrology, though, that I do believe in. In fact astrology, tarot cards, palm-reading, you name it, I believe in it.
He sits down next to Deborah. She looks at him sceptically.

DEBORAH
You're just saying that.

TONY
Get out of here! I've always got my head in books about astronomy—

DEBORAH
Astrology.

TONY
Astrology. Gary's always having a go at me, you know, saying, 'Come on, let's go bowling, let's do this and that,' and I'm always saying, 'No way, mate. I'm staying in to . . . check if my ascendancy's in Pluto. Or not.'

DEBORAH
Have you done a full natal chart?

TONY
(*Bluffing*) Yeah, oh, yeah.

DEBORAH
It's fascinating, isn't it?

TONY
Mm.

DEBORAH
You must show me it.

TONY
You show me yours, I'll show you mine.

DEBORAH
Okay.
They smile. Deborah turns away. Tony does a what-the-hell's-she-talking-about? expression.

Daytime. Fade in music that perhaps suggests a consumer programme. Gary and Tony are standing, looking up at the facade. Gary is writing businesslike notes on his clipboard.

GARY
Brewery?

TONY
Acceptable.

GARY
Access?

TONY
Small step could prove problematic on departure.

GARY
Proximity of takeaway facility?
Tony glances down the street.

TONY
(*As appropriate*) Poor/average/good.
The music fades up over the dialogue. A brief montage follows.

Dusk, later that day. Tony and Gary emerge from a pub. They are showing some signs of drunkenness. Tony attempts a leapfrog over a bollard and then swings round a lamp-post. He falls over but tries to hide the fact. Fade to:

Early evening. They arrive at the next pub. Tony goes in straight away. Gary gets his clipboard out and, swaying slightly, repeats his note-taking procedure.

Later still that night. The door of the pub opens, and a clipboard is thrown out. It is shortly followed by a completely pissed Gary and Tony. Tony is crawling on his knees. Gary has trouble negotiating a non-existent step on to the pavement. Tony gets to his feet and, to stay upright, hugs the wall of the pub. Gary totters about, then launches into a very badly co-ordinated dance.

Early evening, some days later. Gary is on the sofa, and Tony is sitting up at the table. Propped up by them are two stained porcelain urinals mounted on a slab of wall. Tony is concentrating, tongue out, as he draws on a huge piece of card in coloured pencils. Gary is the same as he scribbles notes on his clipboard. Beside him is a folder marked 'Pub.' Gary idly puts his hand down the front of his tracksuit bottoms, jiggles a bit and leaves it there. He looks up at the urinal.

GARY
You don't think it makes the room too . . . toilety?

TONY
(*Looking up and pondering*) Nah.

GARY
No, okay. Happy days, eh? Standing at that urinal.

TONY
Happy days. How long do you reckon we've each spent standing there since I moved in here?

GARY
Ninety-eight hours. I got Anthea to work it out for me at the office the other day.

TONY
So it was quite a quiet day at the office.

GARY
It was, yeah.

TONY
I'll tell you a funny word.

GARY
Spankathon?

TONY
No, karzi.

GARY
Mm. What did you call your toilet at home?

TONY
Trevor.

GARY
Eh?

TONY
Yeah, we had this family thing, we used to say, 'I'm going to see Trevor.' You know: 'Where's our Tony?' 'Oh, he's seeing Trevor.'
Gary stares at him. Tony is losing confidence.

TONY
'Is Dad around?'
'No, he's in with Trev—'

GARY
No, I meant did you call it a toilet or a lavatory or what?

TONY
(*Eventually, feebly*) Trevor.

GARY
You know what—

TONY
And we used to call our garage Steve. (*Pause*) And our shed was Nikki.

GARY
You know a word I hate?

TONY
Um, 'discharge'? 'Dangly'?

GARY
No, no – 'loo'.
They both grimace.

GARY
It's one of those girly words, isn't it? Like . . . 'doobrie'.

TONY
Mm. And 'oops'.

GARY
Yup.

TONY
And 'potty'.

GARY
'Potty', yeah, very girly. And . . . 'flip-flops'.

TONY
Girly—

GARY
Girly, frighteningly girly.

TONY
Then you've got your guys' words, like . . . 'carburettor'.

GARY
Yeah, and . . . 'sweat'.
The sound of the front door shutting. Gary focuses again on his clipboard.

GARY
How did you rate the snacking amenities in the Green Man?

TONY
Don't know. I tried to order up some dry roasted peanuts, but I must have been pretty out of it by then because the barman came back with matches and a little bar of soap.

GARY
Not quite the same, is it?

TONY
No. I ate them though—

GARY
You did, didn't you?
Dorothy comes in from work, taking off her coat.

DOROTHY
You're not still doing that stupid chart? It's only a pub. Anybody would think you were choosing the venue for the next Olympics.
Gary turns to her solemnly.

GARY
Let me tell you about pubs, Dorothy.

DOROTHY
Oh, God.

GARY
The local pub is . . . like a cathedral. It's where blokes go, to be with other blokes and chat about life as they see it over a pint.

DOROTHY
So it's not really like a cathedral, is it?

GARY
No, no, it isn't. Okay. The local pub is like . . . a library. You don't commit yourself to the first library you see. You examine it coolly, you see what booze it does, you check that it smells right, you get a feel for the bar snacks. And then, only then, do you make the emotional commitment to it.

DOROTHY
So, it's not like a library either then.

GARY
(*On consideration*) No. Pass me the purple pencil, Tony.
Tony passes it. Gary fills in a purple column on his graph.

DOROTHY
What's purple?

GARY
Purple is how long it took the bar staff to serve us two lagers, a tequila and blackcurrant, and a slim Panatela.

DOROTHY
Who was the quickest? Let's pretend I care.

GARY
(*Consulting his clipboard*) The Duchess of Kent. Except they incurred a ten-second penalty for calling Tony, what was it?

TONY
'A complete and utter drunken bastard.'

DOROTHY
I don't suppose you'd think of judging a pub by what really matters. Comfortable chairs, reasonable prices, decent range of wines, clean toilets . . .
Gary and Tony give Dorothy a long, withering look.

DOROTHY
So what do you go by then? Presumably whether the barmaid allows you to bury your head in her breasts at the end of the evening.
Gary gives her another dismissive look, then discreetly adds it to the bottom of his list. Dorothy sits down in an armchair and picks up a book. Gary concentrates on his notes. Dorothy watches him. He fiddles in his crutch area, does a big sniff and clears his throat gutturally, then farts. Dorothy looks despairing and opens her book.
Tony farts. Gary puts his hand down the back of his trousers and scratches. He clears his throat again and carries on colouring in. Dorothy goes back to her book. Gary makes some more adjustments in the groin area. In desperation Dorothy turns on the television. Tony and Gary look over. They do laddish wey-heys at what they see.

GARY
Look at the top bollocks on that!

TONY
Wey-hey!

GARY
You couldn't get many of those in a suitcase.

DOROTHY
For God's sake, it's a cartoon.

GARY
Mm, still.

DOROTHY
(*To Gary*) Are you doing this deliberately?

GARY
What?

DOROTHY
Acting boorishly like this so I react and feel I have to say something, and then you can call me a nagging witch?
He and Tony think about this.

GARY
No, that's too complicated for me.

TONY
(*Overlapping*) Too complicated.

DOROTHY
It's not just that – you expect me to do all the work around the flat.
Tony takes the opportunity to slip away into the kitchen.

GARY
I'm sorry, love. (*He holds his hand out to her, wheedling*) It's just that . . . you're better at it than us.
Smiling 'encouragingly' he takes the side of Dorothy's face and waggles it.

GARY
You're just too damn good at it.
Dorothy waits until Gary has finished waggling. Taking a can of lager, she quietly shakes it and opens Gary's mouth. Positioning the can over it, she pulls. Gary convulses.

DOROTHY
(*Genuinely sad*) We're living together now, Gary, please don't treat me like your personal slave.

GARY
Okay.
They kiss.

DOROTHY
I want us to be like a proper couple.

GARY
We are.
He gazes into her eyes. Then brusquely gets up.

GARY
I'm off to the pub.
He leaves, taking his clipboard with him. Dorothy blows out her cheeks, depressed. Alone in the room, she looks around at the urinal, at the bar towels acting as antimacassars, then at the set of pub optics that we now see for the first time, mounted between the kitchen and the living room. Dorothy drifts out to the kitchen.

11. KITCHEN

Tony is quietly working at the kitchen table as Dorothy mooches in. She looks at the six optics, which hold bottles of whisky and vodka, a carton of milk, a large tube of toothpaste, a can of lager and an unmarked bottle of thick white liquid.

DOROTHY
I hesitate to ask, but what's this one?

TONY
Lotion for athlete's foot.

DOROTHY
Lovely.

TONY
I get it quite a lot.

DOROTHY
Oh.

TONY
It's a nasty little fungus—

DOROTHY
Yes, yes, it is.
Dorothy wanders around, fed up.

TONY
I quite like having athlete's foot actually.

DOROTHY
Why, Tony?

TONY
I suppose it . . . makes me feel wanted. You know, this fungus has chosen me, Tony, to live on.

DOROTHY
Yes, that's nice. I can see that now. You've got quite low self-esteem, haven't you?
Tony grunts. Dorothy sits down next to him.

DOROTHY
What's this?

TONY
My birth chart.

DOROTHY
Must have taken you a while. Don't you have to calculate the exact position of the stars?

TONY
You can do it that way, yes.

DOROTHY
Or you can . . .

TONY
Make it up.

DOROTHY
Uh-huh.

TONY
Debs is into astrology so I thought I'd, you know, exploit her.

DOROTHY
A little cynical maybe?

TONY
How d'you mean?

DOROTHY
Well, she's going through a career crisis and feeling a bit worthless, so she's a bit vulnerable.

TONY
Yeah, it's great, isn't it?
He gathers up his big chart, about to go.

DOROTHY
Tony, maybe instead you should be reassuring Deborah that she's a worthwhile person who doesn't need to believe in astrological mumbo jumbo.
Tony looks torn.

DOROTHY
It's just a crutch.

TONY
Yeah, but it's a really nice crutch. Anyway, I don't just think of Debs like that—

DOROTHY
(*Patiently*) Astrology is a crutch.

TONY
Oh, astrology.
Dorothy looks at Tony sternly. He whimpers.

TONY
But this has taken hours. I've coloured it in and everything.

DOROTHY
Well, I'll leave it to your conscience.

TONY
(*Brightening*) Oh, great. Bye, then.
He leaves with his chart. Dorothy sighs and sits down at the kitchen table.

12. THE CROWN

Mid-evening. The pub after its refurbishment. It looks remarkably like it has always looked, apart from the pink horse brasses. Gary is sitting on a stool at the bar, one of very few customers. The landlord, Ken, is serving someone. He comes over.

KEN
Pretty nice, eh?

GARY
Yeah, very authentic.
They look around. Ken runs his hand along the bar.

KEN
See that?

GARY
Yeah.

KEN
That's piranha pine, from Guatemala.

GARY
Lager, please, mate.

KEN
It's the piranha-pine capital of the world. They carry it chest high through the jungle, by hand.
Gary nods, then glances down at the bar.

GARY
It's not plastic, then?
They look at the bar more closely.

KEN
Plastic, yes.
Ken shakily serves Gary half a pint of lager in a pint glass.

KEN
How're you getting on with your urinal?

GARY
Fine.

KEN
That's seventy-six of your Earth pence, please.
He does a rather forced chuckle.

GARY
(*Perplexed*) A pint.

KEN
All the way up. Okay.
Ken pours the rest of the glass.

GARY
Can I have a look at your old photograph of the Crown?
Ken hands Gary the slightly out-of-focus framed photo hanging behind the bar.

KEN
Check the guy at the back with the weird hat.

GARY
Mm. You mean Tony, balancing the plate of gherkins on his head.

KEN
It was a less self-conscious age. The tram was king. People thought nothing of— Eh?
Ken peers at the photograph.

GARY
There's me standing next to him. Les took this at his Free Nelson Mandela evening last year. Before we told him he'd been free for five years.
They look around at the decor. Ken manages to remain expressionless.

KEN
Oh. Still . . .
He discreetly throws the photo into the bin. Gary reaches down for his clipboard.

GARY
Anyway, that's enough chitchat, Ken. Just one or two questions.
Gary is at his most officious. Ken blinks.

13. DEBORAH'S LIVING ROOM

Same evening. Deborah comes in, followed by Tony, who is carrying his birth chart in a plastic bag.

DEBORAH
Do you want a coffee?

TONY
It's okay, thanks, I've brought some beers along.
He gets some cans out of his plastic bag.

TONY
I checked, and according to the co-ordinates Saturn's in conjunction with Pisces, so it's all right to get pissed.
Deborah gives Tony a sharp look.

TONY
(*Handing her a lager*) What sign are you? No, don't tell me. Let me think, I'm getting it, I'm getting it. You're one of the air signs, aren't you?
She nods.

TONY
Yes! (*Closing his eyes to concentrate*) Let me see, you're feisty and plucky, you're good fun without being silly. Let me look at you. (*Looking at her*) You're a Sagittarius, aren't you?

DEBORAH
Yes.

TONY
I knew it!
He whoops.

DEBORAH
You have sent me a birthday card for the last three years.

TONY
(*Forcing a smile*) Mm?

14. GARY'S FLAT: KITCHEN

Later that evening. Dorothy is still sitting at the table, reading a magazine. She gets up and retrieves the kettle from the crockery-filled sink. It has a yellow Post-it note stuck on it. Dorothy reads it and looks peeved. She fills the kettle, puts it on, picks up a mug and gets some milk from the milk optic. Waiting for the kettle, Dorothy wanders about, holding her Post-it note. She opens the fridge. A springy thing or two flies out. She ignores this. Inside the fridge is another Post-it note, which she reads. She is even more annoyed. She wanders out into the hall. In the empty kitchen, the milk optic falls off its mount. From the hall we hear Dorothy.

DOROTHY
(*Offscreen, furious*) Right.

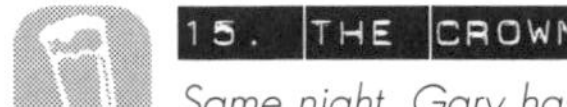

15. THE CROWN

Same night. Gary has started to audition a rather perplexed Ken, noting his answers on his clipboard.

GARY
(*Pen poised*) If we do decide to become regular patrons, will you be offering flexible-payment options?

KEN
No.

GARY
(*Noting this*) Oh. Little bit disappointing. Will you be stocking dairy-based snacks along the lines of Cheesy Moments, or do you favour fish-based products such as the Scampi Fry?

KEN
I don't know.

GARY
Will you be doing lock-ins?

KEN
Is that a dairy-based snack or a fish-based product?

GARY
Lock-ins, Ken. Afters.

KEN
Afters? No, we're not doing any food.
Gary gives Ken a long look.

GARY
Have you worked in a pub before, Ken?

KEN
Of course. (*After a pause*) No, I haven't. My brother works at Head Office. He got me this.
Gary gazes at him, getting his measure.

GARY
I'm afraid that pint was off, Ken. I'll be needing another one on the house.
He hands Ken his empty glass. Ken looks uncertain.

GARY
(*Brazenly*) Completely standard practice, Ken.

KEN
Oh, okay.
He pours Gary a pint. Gary lays aside his clipboard and relaxes.

GARY
Yup, I think this'll make an acceptable local.
Dorothy comes in, looking angry.

DOROTHY
Hello.

GARY
Oh, hi. Vodka and tonic for the little lady. She likes it on the rocks. (*Chuckling*) Still, that's enough of our sexual problems.
Dorothy glares at him. She takes three Post-it notes out of her pocket.

DOROTHY
'Dorothy: please fill this kettle with water when you have the time.'
She viciously slaps the Post-it pad on Gary's forehead. She peels off the second note.

DOROTHY
'Dorothy: before you sit down, please defrost the fridge.'
She slaps this Post-it note on Gary's cheek, peels off the next.

DOROTHY
'Dorothy: please iron by Tuesday.'
She slaps that on to his other cheek, hard.

GARY
(*Tentatively*) Do you want to make that Thursday then?

DOROTHY
Do you know what it's like, being with you, Gary?

GARY
Like white-water rafting – a bit of a challenge but ultimately rewarding?

DOROTHY
Not really. Shall I show you?

GARY
Okay.
Ken comes back with Dorothy's vodka and Gary's pint.

DOROTHY
All right, mate? (*Staring at Gary's groin*) Look at the gristle on that.
Gary looks shocked. Ken stops in his tracks. Á la Gary, Dorothy adjusts her breasts. Gary and

Ken watch her. She looks over at a man quietly nursing a pint on his own.

DOROTHY
(*Raising her voice*) Don't know about you, but I wouldn't kick his tush out of bed.

GARY
Um. Maybe we should leave.

DOROTHY
Oh, no, I've only just started.
She throws the drink down her throat, burps hugely and sits with her legs wide apart. Gary surreptitiously tries to ease Dorothy's legs back together. Dorothy throws a tenner on to the bar.

DOROTHY
Line 'em up, mate. Another pint for my little gentleman. Not that he'll be ready for it for half an hour. Still, that's enough of our sexual problems—
Gary puts his hand over Dorothy's mouth, laughing nervously.

KEN
I must hereby issue you a verbal warning that—
Dorothy stares at Ken's groin. She manages to shout through Gary's hand.

DOROTHY
Nice todger. You couldn't get many of those in a biscuit tin.

KEN
You're outlawed.

GARY
What?

KEN
You two are outlawed. (*Pondering*) No, barred, sorry. You have to leave.
Gary looks upset. Dorothy climbs down off her bar stool. They exit, Dorothy looking triumphant.

16. DEBORAH'S FLAT: LIVING ROOM

Tony is having trouble staying awake, his eyes glazed. Deborah is explaining her birth chart.

DEBORAH
My mid-heaven aspect at my natal point was in Aries with Mercury a strong presence and Jupiter in opposition. This means that, where am I . . .?
She turns a page of what she is reading, to another page of dense type. Tony's elbow slips off the sofa armrest, waking him.

DEBORAH
Jupiter signifies my career, obviously, so in opposition that points to why I keep losing my job. On the other hand Venus trined to Mercury could indicate the opposite. What do you think, Tony?
Tony wakes up again with a start.

TONY
Can I show you mine now?

DEBORAH
Oh, okay.
Tony reaches down for his chart. We can see from a cursory glance that his 'chart' is a mess of scrawled words and pictures.

TONY
Okay. Well. I was born . . . under a wandering star. Um, but with the Sun basically . . . shining in my face the indications are that I am destined to have . . . congress with a Sagittarian lady.
Deborah looks at him levelly. Tony falters.

TONY
If you look here, on my chart, you can see—

DEBORAH
A rabbit. You've doodled a rabbit.

TONY
(*Small voice*) No, it's a badger.

DEBORAH
Okay a badger. What's a badger got to do with astrology?

TONY
It's the . . . sign of the badger, symbol of . . . thing. So, according to the planets I must lie down here, now, and you must . . . lie here, in conjunction with me.
A pause.

DEBORAH
Well, that's odd because according to my chart if you don't leave immediately I call the police.

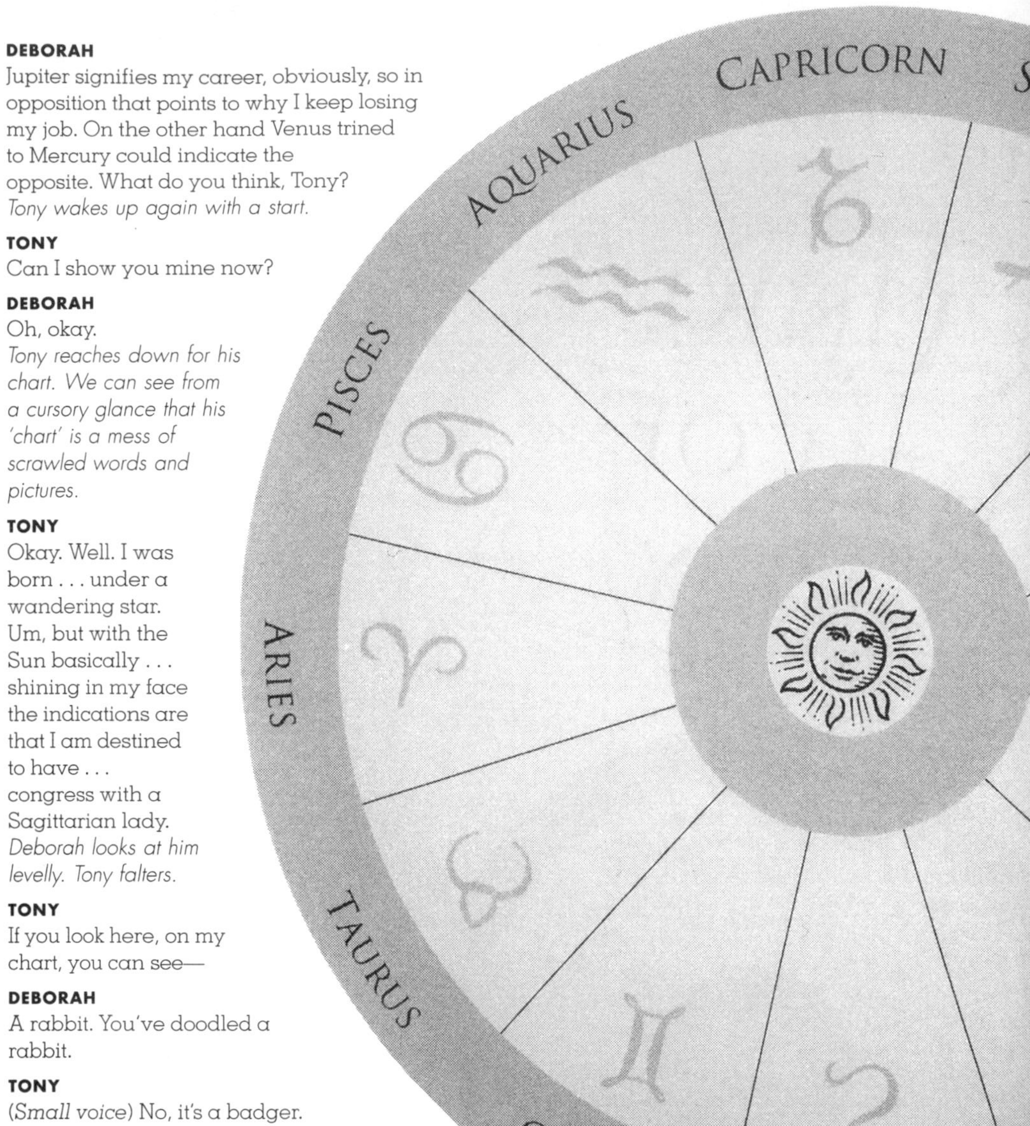

TONY
(*Nodding*) Mm, interesting.
(*Pause*) So I'll head off then.

DEBORAH
Yes.
He gets up and goes. Then comes back.

TONY
I'm better at palm readings—

DEBORAH
(*Brittle*) No.

TONY
No.
He leaves again. Deborah shuts her eyes. Tony returns again.

TONY
I'm Chinese year of the hedgehog, what are y—?

DEBORAH
(*Finally snapping*) Get out!
He gets out.

17. GARY'S FLAT: LIVING ROOM

Later. Gary and Tony are on the sofa, getting drunk.

GARY
Yeah, I mean, I suppose there could be something in it. We shouldn't just slag it off.

TONY
No. 'Cos, nobody really knows, do they, if they're honest? And a lot of people swear by it.

GARY
They do. They do.
They mull this over.

TONY
How did we get on to Marmite?

GARY
I don't know.

TONY
So, bad luck about the old Crown.

GARY
Yeah, I don't know what came over Dorothy. I've never been barred from anywhere in my life.

TONY
Apart from the swimming pool.

GARY
True, yeah.

TONY
And the video shop.

GARY
The video shop, that's true. And the Piccadilly Line.

TONY
How do you get barred from the Piccadilly Line?

GARY
Oh, shoelaces, bucket of sand . . . It's a long story.

TONY
Oh, okay.
Tony gets up and goes over to the condom machine, which is now on the wall. He puts in some coins.

TONY
Why do you reckon girls are more interested in astrology than men?

GARY
Ooh, I think it's because they're not very rational, are they, really? Not really.

TONY
They weren't at home when the Logic Monkey called.
Gary shoots Tony a brief look of concern.

GARY
No, they weren't. I'm not knocking the ladies, bless 'em—

TONY
Bless 'em. Although it has to be said that we've both got our Lucky Pants.

GARY
We have.

TONY
And you've got your Happy Shoes. And I've got my Magic Pebble.

GARY
Yeah, how is your magic pebble?

TONY
Magic.

GARY
Brilliant.

TONY
If I had to predict the future, though, do you know how I'd do it?

GARY
No.
Tony turns the handle of the machine. Nothing comes out. He bangs it on the side. The machine flies off the wall and falls with a crash. Tony goes back to his seat on the sofa, tottering slightly.

TONY
Phrenology.

GARY
Phrenology?

TONY
Phrenology.

GARY
Phrenology?
A pause.

TONY
Phrenology.

GARY
Phrenology?

TONY
Phrenology. Telling the future by feeling the bumps on a person's head. I saw a programme about it once. Fascinating.

GARY
Does it work?

TONY
Does it work? God, no. How could it? Total nonsense.

GARY
The thing is, though, do we really want to know the future? Stretching on and on.

TONY
Like the M6.

GARY
Yeah. Or stopping dead suddenly. Like that little road by the station in Yeovil.
They sip their lager, considering this. Abrupt cut to black.

SERIES FIVE: EPISODE THREE

cowardice

This is a ropey old episode, despite the timeless fascination of lesbianism. It probably reads better, though, than the more visual first episode of this series (not included here), which had two glorious musical montages and the hauntingly marketable lager mitt.

As in the previous episode, this starts with a discussion about differences between the sexes. It's all a bit self-conscious. Generally in this series there was too much theorising: 'The trouble with you men is . . .' and not enough showing. At the end of it the actors took me to task for not having moved the action on dramatically enough. They may have had a point, but the essence of sitcoms is that nothing changes. *Dads' Army* would never have worked if they had got twitchy after ten episodes and promoted Sergeant Wilson to Captain.

The script shows the original ending, in which Dorothy finds out that Gary hired someone to beat up. We decided it was only fair sometimes to let Gary win.

1. GARY'S FLAT: LIVING ROOM

Mid-evening. Gary, Tony, Dorothy and Deborah are watching the television, absorbed. Moody background music.

DOROTHY
She's got to tell Dominic, hasn't she?

DEBORAH
Mm. But can you imagine how, you know?

DOROTHY
I know. Horrible – your parents killed in the same car as your best friend.

DEBORAH
She's such a good actress, isn't she?

DOROTHY
Mm. It's true, though, isn't it? The way we all want people to think we're resilient and independent but hate it when they don't realise we're, you know, falling apart.
Gary and Tony are concentrating.

GARY
She's going to take that top off any minute.

TONY
It's coming off.
They watch for a bit.

TONY
Come on, come on, you can do it, it's only a top.

GARY
Don't be shy, nobody's watching.
She obviously does not take it off. Gary and Tony tut. Gary realises the women are looking at him and Tony accusingly.

GARY
Thank goodness BBC2 isn't scared to tackle thought-provoking drama.

TONY
Thank goodness. Thought provoking.
They watch a bit more.

TONY
Have you noticed on telly, you never see people just sitting there, hour after hour like us, watching the telly?

GARY
No. Or doing their shoes up. When was the last time you saw a person on television really do their shoes up properly?

TONY
1987. *Howard's Way.*

GARY
Exactly.

TONY
And on telly you never see people walk past a door handle or a cupboard knob, and the handle or knob catches on their trouser pocket and sort of pulls the person back.
They are looking at him.

TONY
You never see that, do you?

GARY
No. No, you don't.
Deborah and Dorothy slowly turn back to the television.

TONY
And you never see people cough—

DOROTHY
Stop, please, stop!

GARY
(*Reacting to the TV*) It's off!

TONY
It's off! The top is off.

DOROTHY
It's always the women, isn't it? Never the men. 'You're a bloke – slip under the sheets with your pants on. You're a bird – take all your clothes off and walk around for ten minutes.'

DEBORAH
No, I think he's going to as well.

TONY
Don't do it, mate! Maintain your dignity!

GARY
Keep your pants on!

DOROTHY
See.
They look relieved.

GARY
Good, he's decided just to watch.
They watch some more.

GARY
The bottom is off! Her bottom is off!
Tony and Gary go strangely quiet.

TONY
(*Swallowing hard*) The bottom's off.

DEBORAH
What an incredible body.

DOROTHY
Absolutely.

DEBORAH
Magnificent breasts.
Tony and Gary smirk like schoolboys.

DOROTHY
What?

TONY
She said . . . Nothing.

DEBORAH
What?

TONY
You said magnificent breasts.
Tony and Gary snigger.

DEBORAH
Well, she has.

TONY
Yeah, but you're a girl.

DOROTHY
Gary, do you know one of the least attractive things a man can do?

GARY
Um, keep using the word 'stiffy' on a first date?

DOROTHY
No, snigger.

GARY
Well, I think you'd be a bit taken aback if me and Tony were watching the footie and out of the blue one of us said to the other one: 'I see the big number seven's got a magnificent bottom.' I don't think you'd find that very attractive.
He snorts triumphantly.

TONY
I think you've uncovered a major double standard there, mate.

GARY
Thanks, mate.

DOROTHY
Well, maybe you should say he's got a magnificent bottom, if he has got one.

GARY
Well, maybe I won't, if that's all right with you.
A pause. Tony is still glued to the TV.

TONY
Oh, she's popped them back in.
They watch a bit more.

TONY
No, they're out again.

2. KITCHEN

The next day, early evening. Tony is doing up a tie, looking smart. The sound of the front door shutting. The pub optics are still up from last week's episode. Acting the barman, Tony takes a mug out of the sink of opaque, dirty water and prepares to serve himself a 'shot' of lager.

TONY
A large lager, sir? In a straight mug, sir or (*Trawling the sink water, finds at random*) in a *Neighbours* souvenir egg-cup?
A mug, okay.
He applies the mug to the optic. It shoots off its mount. Tony struggles to fit it back. Gary comes in, from work.

TONY
Good day at work, mate?

GARY
The usual. George talked for four hours about pencils. Anthea left early to have her moped exorcised, or something.

TONY
I've had a really exciting day.

GARY
Not another minor commotion down at the library?

TONY
No, I've got an interview for the bar job at the Crown, with the new landlord. And guess what I saw today, right? I hear Deborah leaving her flat, so I go to the window, and I'm watching her with my nose pressed up against the glass.

GARY
Minding your own business—

TONY
Minding my own business. And she comes out with this girlfriend.

GARY
Which one, the stocky redhead with the big knees?

TONY
No, a gorgeous new one. And they go out to this bird's car, and they both get in. And they give themselves a little peck on the cheek and drive off.
Tony looks triumphant. At first Gary shares his excitement, then looks politely interested and then confused.

GARY
Have I missed something?

TONY
Well, it's obvious, isn't it? Debs is going through a lesbian phase.
Gary looks at Tony in astonishment.

GARY
No!

TONY
Oh, maybe not then.

GARY
No, no, don't say that. I like the idea, stick with it.

TONY
Well, look at the evidence. (*Counting off on fingers*) A: Debs has been much happier recently. B: She was going on last night about that woman's brilliant bosoms. And C . . .
He pauses, thinking hard.

GARY
You over-reached yourself with the C haven't you—?

TONY
(*Joining in*) Yeah, over-reached myself there on the C. Still, lesbianism, eh?
They think about this, smiling, obviously letting their minds wander.

GARY
(*Finally*) What do lesbians do exactly?

TONY
I don't know. I suppose they just sort of . . . rub each other.

GARY
(*Thoughtful*) Yeah. Doesn't seem enough somehow, does it?

TONY
And lie on top of each other and then . . .

GARY
Get off again.

TONY
Yeah.
A pause.

TONY
Brilliant!

GARY
Brilliant!

3. THE CROWN

Later. The pub is very empty. Tony is at a table, being interviewed by Ken, the eerily deadpan new landlord. Ken himself is clearly feeling his way into the job.

KEN
So, have you worked in a pub before?

TONY
Yeah, I worked here actually.

KEN
Here at this table?

TONY
No, in the whole pub.

KEN
Do you live locally?

TONY
Yeah, over the road.

KEN
So, you've basically just got a road to cross to get here, then?

TONY
Yeah.

KEN
Do you want a Flake in that?

TONY
Eh?

KEN
No, sorry. Bit of a flashback to my last job. Okay, um. Are you good with cash?

TONY
Yes, very good.

KEN
Are you good with customers?

TONY
Very good, yes.

KEN
What about drinks. Are you good with serving drinks?

TONY
Yes, I am.

KEN
Well, you seem to be quite a good barman. Would you like the job?

TONY
Yeah, great! Can I ask you a few questions?

KEN
Okay.

TONY
Will there be a uniform? I've always wanted a job with a uniform.
Ken blinks slightly, a sign that he is bullshitting.

KEN
Yeah, um, I'm going to be ordering them. They'll have gold piping, probably.

TONY
Where?

KEN
(*Pointing, vaguely*) Probably here, somewhere at the top of the arms. And here.

TONY
Great.

KEN
And pockets, here.
He mimes putting his hands into jacket pockets.

KEN
Substantial pockets.

TONY
Brilliant. Is there, like, a staff rota?

KEN
A rota?

TONY
Yeah, you know, when we're on shift.

KEN
Um. Yeah, why not? I'll ask my brother at Head Office, he'll know.

TONY
Great. So, when shall I start?

KEN
Well, there's no time like the present. Tuesday?

TONY
Okay. What's your rule on smoking?

KEN
(*Looking around at the few customers*) Well, I think they can if they do it quietly, don't you?

4. DOROTHY'S CAR

Early evening. Dorothy is driving through London traffic with Gary, who is perusing the film section in Time Out. *They are getting on well, arms hanging out of windows.*

GARY
So which film shall we see?

DOROTHY
Oh, you know me – anything with terrorists holding a building hostage. Or your other favourites, *Lethal . . . Cop Buddy Car Chase 3.*

GARY
What about you? You're only interested if it was filmed in China using a piece of string. Or if everyone calls each other old *sausage* and spends the whole film worrying they've got the wrong hat on.

They are stuck behind a car. Dorothy glances over at the films.

DOROTHY
Isn't there a new film called *Red Beans*?

GARY
Red Beans. Don't tell me – the touching story of some Chinese people who grow beans.

DOROTHY
Yes, actually.

GARY
If it's all right with you I think I'll wait for *Red Beans 2: The Nightmare Continues*.
The car ahead is still negotiating a narrow gap between two parked vehicles.

GARY
Parp him, go on.

DOROTHY
No.

GARY
Parp. He deserves a parping.

DOROTHY
He's waiting for the other car to move.
Gary leans over and presses the horn, holding it down for some seconds until Dorothy pulls his hand away. She looks very cross.

GARY
Well, what do you think it's there for?

DOROTHY
It's for emergencies, and alerting stray sheep.
The door of the car in front opens, and the driver gets out. He is small but scarily aggressive.

DOROTHY
Well done, Gary.
Dorothy locks her door and winds her window up so it is only an inch open. The driver puts his head in the gap.

ANGRY DRIVER
Did you beep?

DOROTHY
Yes, sorry.
Gary's window is going up slowly as he very discreetly winds it. He is obsessively immersed in the A to Z.

ANGRY DRIVER
Why? Why? Why?

DOROTHY
Um. Gary?
Without looking up, Gary does a little shrug.

ANGRY DRIVER
I've got a crowbar in my boot. I'm going to come back and shove it through your window and . . .
His voice fades and is silenced as Dorothy winds up the rest of the window. He continues to threaten scarily, unheard.

GARY
(*Low key*) You could cut down Sunnyside Road, that would avoid that nasty sticking-out bit by the thing.
The angry driver, realising they can not hear him, starts to make ugly, distorted faces in the windscreen. He presses his face against the glass, amusing but psychotic.

GARY
Or down Tavistock Road, which I believe, I believe, is now a one-way street.
Dorothy is embarrassed at Gary's inaction. The driver stares at Dorothy aggressively, looking ready to lash out. He bangs her window then slouches off back to his car. Dorothy sighs heavily.

DOROTHY
Thanks, Gary.
In spite of herself, Dorothy looks upset.

GARY
(*Shiftily*) Sorry, you were saying?

DOROTHY
Nothing. (*Under her breath*) Fine, if you want to be a wimp.

GARY
What?

DOROTHY
Let's go.

GARY
What did you say – wimp?

DOROTHY
All right, yes. You parp, and then you leave me to sort it out – you should have told that bloke to get lost.

GARY
So I'm a wimp.

DOROTHY
No, I didn't mean—

GARY
(*Looking around*) Okay, drive after him. You want me to go and beat him up, I'll go and beat him up.

DOROTHY
Okay.

Dorothy drives off, in the same direction as the angry driver. Gary looks uneasy.

GARY
Yes, I'm a guy, that's what we do. Chicks are the first to complain when their bloke gets into fights, but it seems we're wimps if we turn the other cheek.
Dorothy has to stop at a junction or some lights.

DOROTHY
It's okay. He's gone.
She smiles ruefully. Gary looks shifty.

5. GARY'S FLAT: KITCHEN/HALL

The next morning. Gary is sitting alone at the kitchen table, depressed and twitchy. Dorothy comes in, looking for her shoes. She glances at Gary and walks out. Gary sees this and looks paranoid. Tony enters, from the bathroom. He looks over at Gary, then heads out again. Gary looks even more paranoid. Dorothy reappears, holding her shoes.

GARY
I am not a coward.

DOROTHY
Nobody said you were.
Gary follows her as she leaves for the bathroom. Tony re-enters. Gary switches to him. Tony buries his head in the fridge.

GARY
I was playing it cool, like Clint Eastwood in *Unforgiven*.

TONY
Oh, right, only the way Dorothy described it you were more like Bernard Bresslaw in *Carry On Camping*.

GARY
What?
Gary follows Tony as he takes a carton of orange juice and heads for his bedroom.

TONY
(*Averting his eyes*) I'm not knocking it, mate. We all lose our bottle sometimes.

GARY
I did not lose my bottle. I'll show it to you, I've still got it— Why's nobody looking me in the eye?
Dorothy crosses in from the bathroom. Gary follows her.

GARY
I've been in fights.

DOROTHY
I know, most of them were with me.

GARY
No, real fights, with nosebleeds.

DOROTHY
Sure. Look, it doesn't matter.

GARY
Anyway, I thought there was supposed to be sexual equality these days.

DOROTHY
Exactly.
Dorothy goes to the fridge and gets something to eat. Getting desperate, Gary picks up an old lager can.

GARY
See that, I can crush that on my forehead.

DOROTHY
Don't be silly, Gary.
She takes it from him and puts it down. Gary picks up a fork.

GARY
All right, watch this. I'll put this fork through my hand. I'm not scared. I've done it before.

DOROTHY
Not intentionally.

GARY
No, not intentionally, but—

DOROTHY
Gary, look, for the last time: you acted in completely the correct way.
Tony has wandered back in.

TONY
Absolutely, mate. There's no shame in what you did.
Gary scans their faces for sincerity.

TONY
Or didn't, in this case.

GARY
See!

TONY
I'm off out to buy a paper.
He leaves. Gary turns to Dorothy.

GARY
See, he never buys papers. You've turned him against me. You've brought dishonour upon me.

DOROTHY
Dishonour? Sorry, did we miss a turning last night and end up in Sicily?

GARY
No, bloke dishonour. We live by a complicated code, you know. In fact, we don't

even know the rules ourselves. Except the one about not drinking Malibu in pubs.

Gary still looks tortured. Dorothy is putting her coat on, ready to leave.

GARY

Go on, admit it – you think I should have done more to protect you.

DOROTHY

(*Serious*) Okay. I suppose. Yes.

GARY

What? Oh, fine, if that's where we stand. (*Putting hands on hips*) It's not easy being a man in the 1990s, you know!

Dorothy rolls her eyes and leaves. Gary sits down, looking depressed. He picks up the lager can and prepares to crush it on his forehead. He rams the can against his head, but it does not concertina. A pause, then Gary winces with the pain. He starts to live out revenge fantasies.

GARY

(*Imitating road-rage man*) I've got a crowbar in my boot. I'm going to— (*In his own voice*) Hey, you, back off, or I'll shove your head so far down your neck you won't be able to . . . (*Faltering*) Well, it'll be nasty. See those?

With two outstretched fingers Gary does a none-too-convincing poking-in-the-eyes gesture. Depressed again, he picks up a freebie magazine from the table and flicks through it. He sees something that cheers him up. He takes the magazine out to the hall, picks up the phone and dials.

GARY

Hello, I'd like to book someone please. (*Listening*) No, not a Gorillagram. (*Listening*) Mm, Stripping Socialworker, funny— (*Listening*) Yup, Fatbloke-o-gram, yeah, that is quite good but— (*Interrupted again*) Be quiet, please!

Gary composes himself. He drifts into the kitchen and lowers his voice in embarrassment. He does not see Dorothy returning.

GARY

Listen, I want to hire a large man. (*Listening*) I'll just ignore that. I want to hire a large man to threaten and abuse me in public. Yes, then I step in and, in a scene reminiscent of *Death Wish* – I don't know if you saw it – I show incredible bravery and—

Gary hears Dorothy shut the door behind her. Without missing a beat he changes tack.

GARY

On second thoughts I'll go for Kitchen Table at the one fifteen at Haydock Park, with a double on Bandy Mistress in the, um, Five Whippets Handicap Stakes. Thanks.

He hangs up. Dorothy frowns but has not taken in what he said.

DOROTHY

Gary, I don't want you to take this badly. Come here.

She gives him a hug. Gary surreptitiously throws down his magazine with the Strippogram numbers.

6. THE CROWN

Tony is standing behind the bar. Ken is next to him. They both have their hands on the bar counter, waiting.

TONY

Bit slow.

KEN

Yeah, that's normal. It's the quarter-past one lull. It's a well-known catering phenomenon. Nobody's ever explained it.

TONY

The problem is that just from walking past nobody knows the place has been carefully remodelled from old photographs for that authentic feel of . . . crappy old pub.

KEN

No.

A wide shot reveals the all too authentically stressed decor.

KEN

Yeah, these days you've got to appeal to all the socio-economic . . . groupages.

TONY

Yeah, you want a look that says, 'We don't care who the hell you are, you can drink in here.'

Deborah and an attractive woman enter, laughing. Deborah spots Tony.

DEBORAH

Oh, hi.

TONY

Hi, Debs.

DEBORAH

Are you working here now?

Ken is nodding.

TONY

Yes.

DEBORAH

Judy, this is Tony.

Ken solemnly offers them his hand.

KEN
Hello, Judy, I'm Ken, or Kenneth, the new landlord. Hello, Debs, I'm Ken, or Kenneth, the new landlord.
They shake hands, bemused.

KEN
Drinks?

DEBORAH
Yes, please, Ken.

KEN
We do all sorts. Have you tried beer?

JUDY
Yes.

KEN
Anyway, I'll leave Tony here in charge of getting your drinks.

JUDY
Okay, Ken.
Ken wanders off.

DEBORAH
Is he all right?
Tony's eyes are flicking between Judy and Deborah, obviously speculating.

DEBORAH
Hello, public house to Tony?

TONY
(*Coming out of reverie*) Sorry.

DEBORAH
Large orange juice for me, please.
She heads off to the loo.

JUDY
I'll have a half of lager.
Tony stares at her as he pours her drink.

TONY
So, how are you two lesbians? (*Correcting himself*) Ladians. Ladies.
Judy was rummaging in her purse and did not realise what he was saying.

JUDY
Eh?

TONY
Are you sleeping with Deborah? Sleeping in Deborah's flat at the same time as she is, on whatever basis?

JUDY
Yes, for a few days.

TONY
What . . . kind of thing are you getting up to?

JUDY
Oh, you know, running around the flat.

TONY
(*Dry mouthed*) Naked?

JUDY
Naked?

TONY
Sorry, I have this disease that makes me say the wrong word.

JUDY
Oh, what's it called?

TONY
(*Weedily*) I don't know. (*Pausing*) I live underneath Deborah.

JUDY
Lucky you. Must be nice and warm.
Tony's eyes widen, his suspicions confirmed. Judy lights up a cigarette.

TONY
Do you eat food?

JUDY
Why?

TONY
I wondered if you'd be interested in going out with me for a meal or something?

JUDY
Not really.

TONY
Any particular reason?

JUDY
Question of taste, I suppose.

TONY
Okay. That's your lifestyle choice.
Deborah comes back, all smiles. She gives Judy a brief, happy hug. Tony watches, mesmerised.

TONY
That's one pound sexy. Sixty.

7. GARY'S FLAT: KITCHEN

Early evening. Tony is standing on a precarious pyramid of chairs in the kitchen, his ear to a cup that he is holding to the ceiling. Dorothy comes in from her bedroom. Tony looks down on her from his great height.

DOROTHY
Oh, has that mouse come back?

TONY
No.

DOROTHY
Look, if you're so obsessed why don't you just go up and ask them if they're sleeping together?

TONY
I can't. It's a private thing between the two of them.
Dorothy idly searches for a mug. She looks thoughtful.

DOROTHY
You know this paranoia Gary's got?

TONY
What, about people hanging on to his ears on the tube in the rush hour to stop themselves falling over?

DOROTHY
(*Brief frown*) No, this fighting business. He wants to prove himself all the time.
From under the dirty water in the sink she brings out a large old lamb bone. She hastily drops it and abandons the washing up.

DOROTHY
Has he talked to you about it?

TONY
No.

DOROTHY
What do you talk about? Sometimes I get, I know this sounds stupid, I get jealous about your late-night chats.

TONY
Well, it varies. Last night we talked about how on two days a year they should convert the Channel Tunnel into, like, a massive bowling alley.
Dorothy manages to show polite interest.

TONY
Then we talked about how great it must be to have breasts, but what a responsibility it is. That's quite a recurring theme actually.
Dorothy's smile fades.

TONY
Then we talked about why on TV they don't read the news standing up, and if they did whether they'd wear special trousers.
Tony puts his ear back to the ceiling. Dorothy sits down.

DOROTHY
(*Heartfelt*) Sometimes I think I'll overhear you and Gary one night and you'll be talking about . . . how to bake bread or something. Then you'll have this really normal conversation about how you try to do the right thing as blokes, but you're just as much a victim of stereotyping as—

TONY
Shhhh! I can hear panting. (*Pause*) No, it's me.

DOROTHY
(*Sighs, giving up*) And then I think, Oh, bugger off. (*To Tony*) Why are you so interested anyway?

TONY
Well, two women, I mean, it's sexy, isn't it? It's a bit different. A bit sexy. And the thought that you might turn up and find them at it, naked and smeared with vegetable oil, and they say: 'Come on in, Tony, join us, we're not really really definite that we just like other women.' And they lead me in, and I pretend to be nervous at first, but eventually they coax me down on to the bed among all the little bits of white under-wear they've discarded . . .
He peters out as realises Dorothy is gazing up at him.

TONY
I don't know, I haven't really thought about it.

DOROTHY
Obviously.

TONY
Will you help me get down?

DOROTHY
Sure.
She casually pulls out one of the bottom chairs and walks away. We hear a crash of chairs and a small whimper.

8. HALL

A moment later. Dorothy wanders out to the hall to hang up her coat. Gary comes in from work in aggressive mood.

GARY
You should have seen me on the tube. I was sitting opposite this big bloke, and I outstared him!

DOROTHY
Did you, dear? Well done.

GARY
I could sense the fear in that carriage.
He gives the wall a flurry of punches.

DOROTHY
Fear? Jolly good, love.
She goes back into the kitchen. Alone, Gary cringes, crouches down in pain and holds his injured fists between his legs.

9. KITCHEN

Meanwhile, Tony is putting back the chairs. Gary walks in, all smiles again. Dorothy has sat down and is reading the newspaper.

GARY
Dorothy, I thought we could, you know, go to the Crown this evening, about eight?

DOROTHY
You can. There's a telly programme I want to watch.

GARY
(*Perturbed*) Oh, what?

DOROTHY
Something about the NHS.

GARY
We could video it. I'd be interested to see it too actually. The old NHS. Health issues. Fascinating.

DOROTHY
No, I don't fancy the Crown.

GARY
Yes, you do.

TONY
I'm behind the bar tonight, Dorothy. I might be able to sneak you a peanut.
Gary sits down. Dorothy is now sitting between Tony and Gary, turning from one to the other.

GARY
It'll be fun. I can tell you the new joke I've been working on.

TONY
Yeah, and Ken said he might open a tin of cocktail sausages and put them out. In a bowl.

GARY
And after I've had a few drinks and can't speak properly, we can have a singsong round the jukebox.
Dorothy takes this in. She slowly gets up.

DOROTHY
I'm just going to my room for a bit of a cry.

Minutes later. Deborah opens the door to Tony.

DEBORAH
Evening.

TONY
Hi.
He peers in, scanning for signs of lesbianism.

DEBORAH
Can I help?

TONY
Yes I . . . thought I could smell burning.

DEBORAH
What kind of burning?

TONY
A sort of burny smell. Of burntness. Burnt things . . . that had been burning.

DEBORAH
I'm pretty sure it's not us.
Judy walks past in a dressing gown. She smiles politely. He cranes round to see where she is going.

TONY
Should I come in and check your rooms anyway?

DEBORAH
No, it's all right. If I see flames I'll ring you.

TONY
Okay.
She gently shuts the door. Fade.

11. DEBORAH'S HALL

Minutes later. More knocking. Deborah reappears and opens the door, to Tony.

DEBORAH
What?

TONY
So, no burning then?

DEBORAH
Yes. I'm on fire. Still, never mind.
Tony thinks, then grins.

TONY
Brilliant.
She makes to shut the door.

TONY
Can I borrow some vegetable oil?
Deborah sighs and lets him into the flat.

Tony peers around for evidence while Deborah rummages in a kitchen cupboard.

TONY
So, how's your mate Judy enjoying her stay?

DEBORAH
Fine, I think. I'm afraid we're out of vegetable oil.
Tony swallows hard.

TONY
So she's not finding the spare bedroom too lonely? (*With a break in his voice*) Or is she sleeping in your bed?

DEBORAH
I don't think that's any interest of yours, do you?

TONY
(*Desperate*) Yes, yes it is.
Judy wanders in, her hair wet from a shower. She smiles politely.

TONY
Hi.

DEBORAH
Okay. Anything else you want to borrow? Vinegar? Half a banana?
She starts to show him out.

TONY
Some Elastoplast, please.
Deborah grits her teeth and goes to get it. Judy is flicking through a magazine. Tony approaches her nervously.

TONY
I hope I didn't disturb you up here.

JUDY
Why, what were you doing?

TONY
My room's just below your spare room and I was . . . playing my bongos until three in the morning.

JUDY
It's all right, I was sleeping with Debs in her bed. Why were you playing the bongos till three?
Tony has gone catatonic with excitement.

TONY
Bongos.

JUDY
What?

TONY
(*Coming round*) Can I just say, that if you and Debs decide that you'd like a man to join you in your sex play, I am standing by to assist you in any way.
Deborah has reappeared, with Elastoplast. She has heard what Tony said and is fuming.

13. DEBORAH'S HALL

Moments later. Tony enters the hall on his way out. He looks back towards the living room. He has a broad strip of heavy-duty Elastoplast over his mouth and other strips over various parts of his face. He exits, looking reproachful.

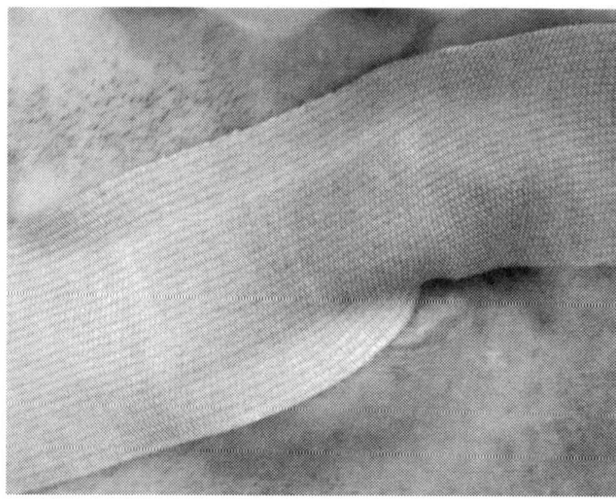

14. THE CROWN

Evening. Tony is serving behind the bar. He has red marks where he has ripped off the Elastoplast. Ken is also serving. For once the pub is relatively busy. Gary and Dorothy come in. Gary looks jittery. Standing at the bar is a large, thuggish-looking man wearing a red scarf. Gary's eyes meet his, meaningfully. Gary indicates a table to Dorothy.

GARY
Let's sit here.

DOROTHY
No, why don't we sit—
Gary pushes the chair under her, forcing her to sit down. He goes to the bar. Tony knows Gary's order without asking.

GARY
What have you been doing to your face?

TONY
Tearing Elastoplasts off it.

GARY
(*Paying*) Well, why not, eh?
He looks pointedly at the man at the bar with the red scarf. Gary winks and looks round the bar nervously.

GARY
(*Under his breath*) Ready?

MAN AT BAR
(*Raised voice*) What's up with you?

GARY
Nothing. What's up with you?

MAN AT BAR
I said what's up with you?

GARY
Listen, mate, I've just come here to have a quiet conversation with my lovely girlfriend.

MAN AT BAR
A quiet conversation – with those ears?
Other customers are starting to look over and go quiet.

GARY
Steady on, mate.

MAN AT BAR
Where did you get them – at a Massive Ear Sale?

GARY
(*Quietly*) No, I mean it. Don't go on about the ears, okay.
Gary very deliberately takes his drinks and heads for Dorothy's table. The man watches him go, then calls out after him.

MAN AT BAR
I thought you said you had a lovely girlfriend.
Several sharp intakes of breath, becoming a hushed silence. Gary pushes his chair back and gets to his feet. Ken and Tony are watching from behind the bar.

KEN
If you're going to fight can you, um . . .
He has forgotten.

TONY
(*Prompting*) Do it outside—

KEN
(*Joining in*) Do it outside.

DOROTHY
(*Anxious, calling over*) Gary—

GARY
Don't, Dorothy, I'll do what I have to do.

DOROTHY
I know. I was going to remind you to hit him.
Gary frowns at her then gets eyeball to eyeball with the man, who is considerably taller than him.

GARY
When you insult my girlfriend, you insult me.

MAN AT BAR
Why's that?

GARY
Um. I don't know. I suppose it's traditional.
The man shapes up to hit Gary, who punches him in the midriff. He doubles up and collapses to the ground. Gary looks around in triumph and slowly walks back to Dorothy. Another man approaches Gary – he is tall, nervous and slightly effete, and is wearing clothes almost identical to the winded thug's. The new arrival – obviously the hired 'assailant', recognises Gary and gives him a weedy, ineffectual signal of acknowledgement. Unseen by Gary, the man from the bar gets up and launches himself at Gary, who chooses this moment to pull back his chair with a flourish. It goes in the man's midriff again. He collapses to the ground again. Customers in the pub applaud and whoop. Gary looks around and sees what has happened.

GARY
Okay, floorshow's over.
He sits down and takes a swaggering gulp from his lager. The beer mat sticks to the bottom of his glass, lessening the impact. In his moment of triumph Gary finally notices his official 'assailant', who is doing small fighting gestures in an attempt to be recognised. Gary blanches. Looking a little faint, he glances down at the thug, who is starting to get up off his knees, grabs Dorothy's arm and heads for the exit.

GARY
Let's go, Dorothy. I've proved my point.
Dorothy lets herself be dragged out. Gary determinedly keeps his head down as he exits. The tall thin man looks perplexed.

15. GARY'S FLAT: LIVING ROOM

An evening at the end of the week. A reprise of the opening scene: Deborah, Tony, Dorothy and Gary are watching the TV.

TONY
(*After a while*) Have you noticed how on telly, people never go into a room, forget what they went there for, so leave again—

DEBORAH/DOROTHY/GARY
Please be quiet!/It's not interesting./Shut up, Tony.
They watch some more.

GARY
I think she's about to get her T-shirt off.

TONY
It's coming off, it's coming off . . . No, she's put a cardy on.
As they watch, Deborah and Dorothy's eyes widen. Tony and Gary grimace.

DEBORAH
So, Dominic finally gets his pants off.

TONY/GARY
That's disgusting, that./Gratuitous.
They watch some more.

GARY
Did you see how I pulled the chair back in one swift move, aiming directly at the big guy's solar plexus?

DOROTHY
Gary, we all think you're very brave, but do we have to relive your fight every eight minutes?

GARY
He'd gone down, and he's whimpering a bit, little groans, and I've walked away, and he's got up, and—

DOROTHY/DEBORAH/TONY
No more!/Please, shut up./Shut up, mate.
The TV programme's closing music starts up and credits begin to roll. They all relax and stretch, apart from Tony.

TONY
So, Debs, um, any plans to see Judy?

DEBORAH
Oh, I expect so.

TONY
She mentioned that you, um, shared the same bed.

DEBORAH
Mm, the heating wasn't working properly.

TONY
(*Relieved*) Oh, I see.

DEBORAH
(*Getting up, stretching*) And you know us girls, we had a lot to talk about so it seemed a good place to chat.

TONY
Yeah, true.
She heads for the door.

DEBORAH
(*On her way out, serious*) And, anyway, how are we going to make love if we're sleeping in separate beds?
She has gone. Tony and Gary turn and call after her.

TONY
What?

GARY
Sorry?
They follow Deborah out. Dorothy, now alone, smirks and gets to her feet. She goes out to the hall.

16. HALL

The men have gone out into the hall in pursuit of Deborah. Dorothy yawns. On her way to the bedroom she picks up a magazine. Under it is the magazine Gary used earlier, open at the Strippogram page. Dorothy sees his handwritten notes on the margin.

DOROTHY
(*Reading*) 'Fight-o-gram forty-nine pounds plus VAT. Wearing red scarf. Don't punch his nose because he has a sinus condition.'
Dorothy looks shocked. She puts the magazine back. Gary reappears. He sees Dorothy's face and looks perturbed.

GARY
Anything the matter?
She looks over at him, torn.

DOROTHY
No.
She smiles gently at him.

GARY
Do you want to come to the pub? Tony was saying you wanted to sit in on one of our interesting chats.

DOROTHY
Maybe another time.
She kisses him goodnight and wanders off to bed.

DOROTHY
(*Pointedly, with her back to us*) Don't get into any fights.
Gary freezes, wondering if she knows . . .

17. THE CROWN

After closing time. All the chairs are up on the tables, the place seems closed. We pan across and find one table still occupied: Gary and Tony are sitting there with a sleeping Ken. There is a forest of beer glasses on the table in front of them.

TONY
I'll tell you what's brave.

GARY
What's brave, mate?

TONY
Going up to Rod Hull and his emu, in a bar, and saying to Rod, 'I know how you do it. Your real arm goes inside the emu neck, and the arm round the emu is a false arm.' And seeing if he tries to peck you.

GARY
Yeah, that's brave. And I'll tell you what's brave. Going up to Arnold Schwarzenegger.

TONY
In a bar?

GARY
Yeah, still in a bar, or in a shop, and saying 'That film *Twins* with Danny DeVito, what was that all about then? You looked nothing like twins.'

TONY
Nothing.

GARY
Brave.

TONY
Brave.
A pause follows.

TONY
So, lesbians.

GARY
Lesbians.

TONY
To recap.
Gary has been leaning back in his chair. He suddenly falls backwards. Tony, partly out of sympathy, also falls backwards. They stay there.

SERIES FIVE: EPISODE FOUR

Your MATE v. Your BIRD

This theme is the crux of *Men Behaving Badly*: who do you love most, your best mate or your girlfriend? The show is, of course, the story of a passionate affair between two men, Gary and Tony, and how their love is occasionally thwarted by others, like Dorothy.

I had a sweet, guilt-inducing letter from a viewer complaining about the two Tarantino-esque nightmare scenes, which shocked and nauseated his family. Maybe we did overdo the blood, although we thought the more excessive the gore the more patently artificial (and therefore less shocking) it would all look. Dream sequences are of course a cheap trick, but I liked the way they illustrated Gary's paranoia about losing one of his loved ones.

Over the years we have badgered countless gorgeous celebrities, especially Kylie Minogue (repeatedly). Gary had already admitted to keeping a Michaela Strachan Scrapbook. In this episode we paid homage to Emma Forbes. I rather hoped that, overwhelmed by the mention on the show, she would ring me and ask me out for tea. In fact she probably felt, rightly, that being the object of Gary's adolescent affection would not exactly help her get a gig presenting *Newsnight*.

1. GARY'S FLAT: KITCHEN/HALL

Early morning. Gary enters, dressed for work apart from his shirt, which he is carrying. He is harassed, greasy haired and in a bad mood. He rattles the bathroom door.

GARY
How much longer are you going to be?

TONY
(*Offscreen, eventually*) What, how much longer in time?

GARY
Yes.

TONY
(*Offscreen*) I'm being as quick as I can.
Gary seethes. Tony starts singing, slowly.

TONY
(*Offscreen*) 'Is this the real thing? Is this just fantasy? Caught in a real—'

GARY
(*Shouting*) And stop singing!
Gary struggles to put up the ironing board, getting increasingly irate. It will not go up. He traps his fingers. He gives up and lays the folded-up ironing board on the kitchen table. He turns on the iron and waits for a second.

GARY
(*To the iron*) Come on!
Dorothy emerges from the bedroom, dressed for work apart from a skirt, which she is carrying. She is also late and in a bad mood. She eyes the ironing board in despair.

DOROTHY
Isn't it a bit early for surfing? I need to use the iron.

GARY
I'm using it.

TONY
(*Singing*) 'World, or escape from reality. Momma—'

DOROTHY
Stop singing!

TONY
(*Offscreen, spoken*) 'Just killed a man.'

DOROTHY
(*To Gary*) I thought you'd know by now that the kind of shirts you buy melt if you iron them.
He starts to iron. Dorothy sits down heavily, fed up. She gratuitously reaches out and knocks a cereal packet off the table.

GARY
What's wrong with you?

DOROTHY
I didn't get much sleep because at half-past one in the morning you and Tony were congaing through our bedroom. Why exactly?

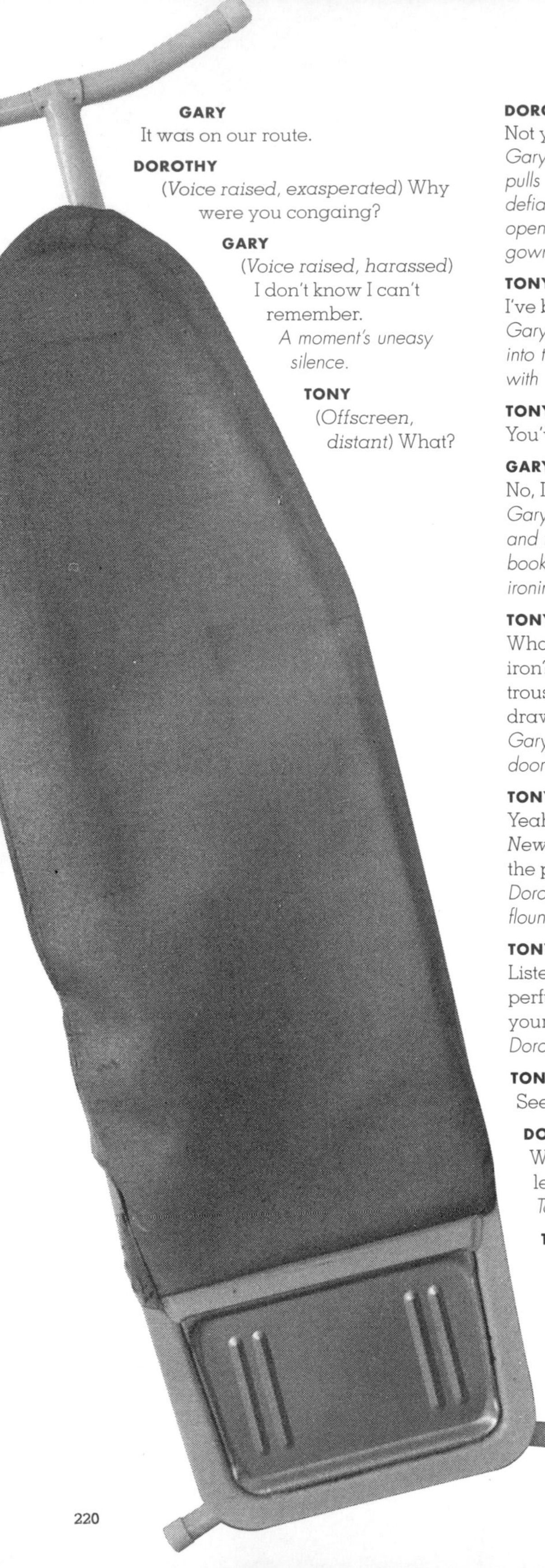

GARY
It was on our route.

DOROTHY
(*Voice raised, exasperated*) Why were you congaing?

GARY
(*Voice raised, harassed*) I don't know I can't remember.

A moment's uneasy silence.

TONY
(*Offscreen, distant*) What?

DOROTHY
Not you!

Gary lifts up the iron. His shirt is sticking to it. He pulls it away. An iron-shaped hole is left. Gary defiantly puts on the shirt. The bathroom door opens, and Tony comes out, wearing a dressing gown and carrying a book.

TONY
I've been reading this book, it's really great.

Gary and Dorothy glare at him. Dorothy goes into the bathroom. Gary realises and screams with frustration. Tony is looking at Gary's shirt.

TONY
You've made a hole in your shirt.

GARY
No, I haven't. It's a designer vent.

Gary stomps about putting things in his briefcase and finding his jacket. Tony wanders around, book in hand, getting in Gary's way. He sees the ironing board.

TONY
What do you reckon's the hardest thing to iron? I reckon it would be a pair of heavy trousers that's been, like, crumpled up in a drawer since Tudor times, don't you?

Gary just grits his teeth. He goes to the bathroom door and shakes the handle pointlessly.

TONY
Yeah, this book's called *Free as a Burp: The New Age Bible*. It's great for people like me, the poor but happy people.

Dorothy has emerged from the bathroom. Gary flounces into it. Tony turns to Dorothy.

TONY
Listen to this: 'Nobody needs aftershave or perfume. Smell lovely for free by rubbing yourself with a lemon.'

Dorothy starts to iron her skirt.

TONY
See, simple but effective.

DOROTHY
Where are you supposed to get a free lemon from – the New Age lemon fairy?

Tony frowns and flicks through the book.

TONY
Ah, yes: 'Fruit and vegetables can often be had for free by stealing from large supermarket chains, who expect to have things nicked anyway.'

Dorothy goes on ironing.

TONY
Do you think Deborah would like me more if I smelt more of lemon?

DOROTHY
No, I think she'd like you more if you moved to New Zealand.

TONY
Oh. (*Glancing at the book*) What about if I built her some 'shelving made from the plastic trays frequently discarded by bread manufacturers, if you just ask'.
Dorothy just looks at him damningly. He looks even more crestfallen.

TONY
So, what do you reckon would work then?

DOROTHY
(*Sympathetic*) Oh, I don't know, Tony. Have you thought of appealing to her sense of pity?

TONY
Yes—

DOROTHY
Yes, you have, haven't you.

DOROTHY
Maybe she just needs some sign of genuine commitment.
Tony thinks, then starts to look down the book's index.

TONY
Commitment. Commitment, genuine. The nearest they've got is Compost. What about Cobbling Tips? – she might need something cobbling.
Dorothy has already grabbed her bag and is on her way out.

TONY
Colonic Irrigation? Climbing Frame – I could build one for her, that might swing her behind me.

DOROTHY
Bye.
Gary emerges from the bathroom. He has obviously given his hair a quick wash without taking off his clothes: his jacket and shirt are wringing wet around the neck.

GARY
Right.
Gary picks up his briefcase and heads for the door.

2. COMMUNAL HALLWAY

As Gary exits he meets Deborah leaving her flat, about to call.

DEBORAH
Morning, Gary. Has Dorothy left?

GARY
(*Frowning*) Oh, Dorothy – little snappy thing, lies next to me in bed? I don't know.
He leaves. Deborah picks up her post – several large envelopes – and goes to the men's door. She listens at it gingerly. Tony opens it, grinning. Deborah winces slightly.

TONY
Hello.

DEBORAH
Hi.

TONY
Hi.

DEBORAH
I wondered if Dorothy was in.

TONY
Oh, right.
He stands there, happily looking at her.

DEBORAH
Is she in?

TONY
No. I am though. Come in for a cup of tea.

DEBORAH
No, I'd rather not—

TONY
A mug of water?

DEBORAH
No.

TONY
A cracker with jam?

DEBORAH
Really, I'm—

TONY
(*Blurting, all pride gone*) Please spend some time with me!

3. GARY'S FLAT: LIVING ROOM

Twenty minutes later. Deborah is sitting in an armchair, looking bored. Tony is on the sofa, reading from his book.

TONY
Here's another good one. 'Who needs pencils? Just collect discarded lolly sticks, split

in half and burn in a workmen's brazier. The result: charcoal you can use on most types of paper.' Um, what else . . .?
Smiling contentedly, Tony looks for another one. Deborah seizes her chance.

DEBORAH
I have to go now.

TONY
No, stay. We were really communicating.

DEBORAH
(*Holding up her envelopes*) I've got to read these college prospectuses.

TONY
Why?

DEBORAH
I'm becoming a full-time student. Why do you think I sent off for them?

TONY
To get some post?

DEBORAH
No.

TONY
Oh, well, there's lots of useful stuff for students here. Look, um: 'Keep food costs low by going fishing, or sleeping for long periods.'

DEBORAH
Thanks, I'm leaving now.
Tony follows Deborah to the door. The sound of the door shutting.

TONY
(*Calling after her*) 'Show someone you love them, for free, by tattooing yourself, using only a pen, needle, matches and some herbal pain relief . . .'
Alone, Tony glances down at the book.

4. GARY'S OFFICE

An hour later. Gary is sitting on George's desk, shoulders slumped, looking depressed. He idly scratches himself through the iron-shaped hole in his shirt. George is sitting behind him, partially obscured.

GEORGE
Um, you're sitting on my biscuit.

GARY
Oh. Sorry.
Gary gets up and wanders around.

GARY
So what do I do, George? I'm living with my bird and my best mate, and it's about as much fun as being stuck in a cable car with Roy Hattersley.

GEORGE
Maybe you should organise some games.
Gary just gives George a look.

GARY
No, one of them's got to go. How do you decide between your mate and your bird?

GEORGE
I once lived with a woman and a man. We got on rather well.
Gary looks over at George.

GARY
You're talking about your parents, aren't you?

GEORGE
Yes.

GARY
Did you stay up late singing drunkenly with your dad, then go off and sleep with your mother?

GEORGE
Not as far as I can remember.

GARY
Well, you can't really appreciate my position then.
Anthea enters. For once, she is cheerful.

GARY
Anthea, you're grinning. I don't know about you, George, but I find that a little spooky.

GEORGE
Yes, little bit spooky.

ANTHEA
I've just opened the mail.

GARY
Yes, if you remember you do that every morning. After checking your hair.

ANTHEA
We've had a circular from the Security Equipment Manufacturers Association.

GARY
Well, life's just one long party in this company, isn't it?

ANTHEA
They've organised a five-a-side football competition for local firms, and they're short of teams.

GEORGE
Oh, I think we should play.

ANTHEA
Yes let's. I've never been asked to play football before.

GARY
Really? Well, I expect you were out at the shops when Graham Taylor was phoning round for a middle-aged Dorking woman to shore up his back four.
Gary snatches the leaflet.

GARY
I'm sorry, but I've got an important decision to make in my private life. I can't afford the time to manage the most tragic team since Peter Purves joined *Blue Peter*.
He glances up and sees them looking downcast.

GARY
Don't try the old looking-pathetic trick.

That evening. Gary is sitting on the sofa, looking nervous. Tony wanders in, all smiles.

TONY
Hi.

GARY
Hello, um, Tony. Have a bit of a sit-down here for a second.

TONY
Sure. Why?

GARY
Just being friendly.

TONY
Oh, okay.
They sit in silence. Tony hugs himself and rocks contentedly.

TONY
So, what shall we talk about?

GARY
The flat, Tony.

TONY
Oh. Okay.

GARY
How long have you been living here?

TONY
Four or five years. Great years. Brilliant.

GARY
Yes, don't – don't say any more, Tony.

TONY
Okay.

GARY
Well, you've probably noticed that Dorothy lives here now as well.

TONY
Yeah, still nothing's really changed, has it?

GARY
No. No, no. Or rather yes and no. More specifically: yes.
Tony swallows hard, starting to realise.

TONY
(*Shakily*) How?

GARY
It's changed in so far as . . . you have to leave.

TONY
You can't do this to me. I'm your mate. You're my mate. We're mates. (*He does some shadow boxing*) We're always kidding around together, mate to mate.

GARY
Still, you've got to leave.
Tony is on his feet, reaching for the nearest weapon to hand.

TONY
I'll stab myself if you make me go.

GARY
Put the Thames Barrier souvenir mug down, Tony.
Tony throws it down and rummages blindly in a jar of pens, penknives etc. He brandishes one.

GARY
Put the banana-shaped biro down, Tony.
Tony throws it down, leans over into the kitchen sink and picks up a knife.

TONY
I mean it, Gary. I model myself on you. You're brilliant. I love you.
Gary moves forward to disarm Tony, who stabs himself in the stomach. A huge arc of blood gushes out, going over the walls and Gary.

GARY
God, what have you done!
Tony screams, groans and doubles up. A genuinely horrific moment. Gary rushes towards him but goes straight past, to where the blood is dripping down the wallpaper.

GARY
This wallpaper was new when I moved in here. I'll never be able to match it up.
Gary tries to wipe it off with his sleeve, then a cushion. Abrupt cut to next scene.

6. GARY'S BEDROOM

Saturday morning. Gary wakes up, bathed in sweat, thrashing around. Dorothy is already awake, lost in thought.

GARY
God, that was horrible.

DOROTHY
Well, if you will fall asleep.

GARY
This . . . stuff shot out across the room.

DOROTHY
That's stuff for you.

GARY
I'm sweating like a horse.

DOROTHY
Unfortunately that's where the similarity ends.
Gary looks over at her.

DOROTHY
Sorry.

GARY
Before you moved in you would have shown some sympathy. You used to mop my brow.

DOROTHY
Well, I used to wipe your face with the sheet, it's not quite the same thing. No, you're right, things seem to have changed since I moved in.
They gaze into space, sadly, lying affectionately close.

GARY
That's the worse thing about nightmares, you're at the mercy of these mad, uncontrollable thoughts.

DOROTHY
And how does that differ from your waking life?

GARY
Yes, I see what your driving at. What's the worst nightmare you've ever had?

DOROTHY
Is was quite recently actually. Tony was being incredibly cheerful, and we were both throwing cutlery at him.

GARY
That wasn't a dream.

DOROTHY
. . . wasn't a dream, no. Do you dream about me much?

GARY
No, but I think you crop up in symbols, you know. Fierce animals. Speeding lorries. Big dark bushes.
Dorothy looks at Gary, then they gaze into space again.

GARY
So why isn't it working out, the three of us living together?

DOROTHY
Well, there's a well-known phrase for our predicament.

GARY
Um. 'Ooh-er, Mr Grimsdale'?

DOROTHY
No.

GARY
'They don't like it up 'em'?

DOROTHY
Mm, close enough. No: 'Two's company, three's a crowd'.
They lie there, thinking about this.

DOROTHY
We don't even have sex as much as before.

GARY
Well, there's another well-known phrase: 'If there's always biscuits in the tin, where's the fun in biscuits?'

DOROTHY
That isn't a well-known phrase.

GARY
Well, it ought to be.
There is suddenly a scream and groan from Tony, much like the one in Gary's nightmare. Gary looks alarmed.

7. KITCHEN

Tony is tattooing himself on his thigh. He is sitting by the cooker, holding a needle under the burner. In his other hand is a fountain pen. To ease the pain he is biting on a wooden spoon. Tensing, he applies the needle to his thigh again. He cries out in agony. The wooden spoon in his mouth splits. He feverishly puts a thicker one into his mouth and bites on that. Gary comes out, in his dressing gown, and sees what is happening.

GARY
Do you know what you're doing?
Tony nods vigorously and goes into a long, pained explanation – holding up his New Age Bible *– all of which is muffled by the spoon in his mouth. Gary knocks it out.*

TONY
—surprisingly painful.

GARY
Let's have a look.
Tony reveals the bloody wound on his thigh.

TONY
Looks all right, doesn't it?

GARY
That's a tattoo, is it?

TONY
Yeah, I've had a bit of a rethink, and instead of DEBORAH I LOVE YOU, I think I might do: DEB.

GARY
So why've you started with a P?

TONY
No, it's a D.

GARY
Looks like a P, mate.

TONY
(*Whiny*) Oh.

GARY
Do you know anybody you quite fancy whose name begins with P?

TONY
No!

GARY
You've always quite liked Prince.

TONY
No, it's for Deborah, to show my genuine commitment to her. I've got to sleep with her. D'you know – I think it's becoming a bit of an obsession with me.

GARY
Really? Well, you've kept that very quiet.

TONY
At this rate I'll live here five more years and the nearest we'll have got to sex was when she dozed off during *Rocky IV*, and I put my finger in her mouth.
Gary looks uneasy about his bad news.

TONY
Or when I was doing it with Jill, and her hair fell over her face, and she looked like Debs. I managed to keep her hair in place till the end. I don't think she minded.
Gary's eyes flicker towards Tony, even more uneasy.

TONY
Or the time Debs and me won that sack race in the garden, and I lost control of my bodily functions.

GARY
Just backtracking to your comment about you living here for five more years . . .

TONY
Well, I'm bound to, aren't I?

GARY
Yeah. Let's say yeah. Um . . .

TONY
Hey, Gaz, why don't you do a tattoo like me? You could do: I DIG DOROTHY.

GARY
No, I'm busy this morning.

TONY
Oh, what are you doing?

GARY
I've got to . . . Oh, it's all too depressing.

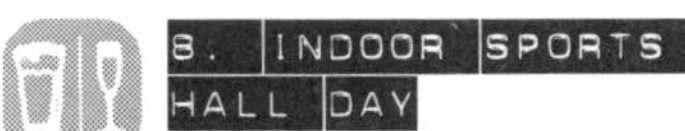

8. INDOOR SPORTS HALL DAY

Later. A five-a-side football match is in progress, watched by a few motley spectators. Gary is looking embarrassed as he leans on the goalpost, smoking. Anthea is in goal, looking rather refined in a beige tracksuit.

GARY
Me, a mad middle-aged clerk from the Croydon area, Tim and Brian, the disturbed cleaners, and a lady goalkeeper in a beige leisure suit. Yes, welcome to the super-charged world of inter-office five-a-side football.

ANTHEA
I think George is doing terribly well.
We pick up the game: George is using the minimum of energy, fiddling around with the ball ineffectually. His team mates – a weedy middle-aged cleaner and a chubby younger one – are hanging around looking clueless. They are all dressed in a ragbag of football kit.

GARY
(*Offscreen*) Really? I'd say he couldn't do less well if he lay on a lilo in the middle of the pitch and quietly went to sleep.

ANTHEA
(*Offscreen*) Nice to see George running off his excess energy.

GARY
(*Offscreen*) 'George' and 'excess energy', not words you'd normally expect to find in the same sentence.
The opposing team look like members of a master race by comparison. They watch George for a moment, then one of them barges him aside and takes the ball.

ANTHEA
Shouldn't you be taking the opportunity to get puffed out?

GARY
No, I've got too much on my mind.
The ball flies into the net past Anthea. She picks it out of the net.

GARY
(*Ignoring it all*) You see, the tragedy is that a bloke gets different things from his bird and his best mate. Ideally, of course, you want something between the two – a bird who doesn't faint after three cans of lager or a mate who looks good bending over in a bikini. But I suppose you have to say, how many blokes coming up to their mid-thirties still share with another bloke?

ANTHEA
Batman and Robin?

GARY
(*Reassured*) Yes, I suppose that's quite encouraging.
The ball flies past again into the goal. Anthea retrieves it again.

GARY
Mind you, there's something a bit odd about those two, isn't there? (*Pondering*) One of them dresses up as a bat, maybe it's that.

ANTHEA
Still, who hasn't at one stage or another?
Gary reacts. He takes a drag on his cigarette. George joins them, picking up a towel and using it to shine his trainers.

GARY
How are you feeling, George?

GEORGE
Quietly confident.

GARY
You're not in any way daunted by the twenty-three two scoreline then?

GEORGE
Oh, no. It's not over till the fat lady sings.

GARY
Oh, didn't you hear? She started singing in the middle of the first half.

GEORGE
Bye, bye.

GARY
Bye.

ANTHEA
Bye.
George dutifully trots back into the action.

GARY
I suppose it can't be that bad, just living with your woman. George has been happily shacked up with Marjorie for twenty-eight years.

ANTHEA
Oh, I think they've had their bad times.

GARY
Yes, he brought the photos in.

ANTHEA
I get the impression there was quite a battle of wills when they first moved in together. George . . . well he lost really, didn't he?

GARY
Mm.
We focus on George again. He is standing mid-pitch, looking typically dazed and confused.

GARY
(*Offscreen*) Well, that's helped me make up my mind.
The final whistle blows. Gary immediately heads for the changing rooms.

GARY
Okay, Anthea, into the shower. Let's get that sweaty kit off you.
Anthea looks frightened.

Tony is sitting by the oven again, finishing off his tattoo. Gary is watching, calmly sipping tea. Tony screams and whimpers.

TONY
Aaaaghhrr!
He pauses to relax himself and wipe his tears.

GARY
So that's painful, is it?
Tony reapplies the needle, bracing himself.

GARY
Of course, you could have just stolen a car for her. That's commitment.
Tony looks at Gary, not appreciating him.

GARY
Or stood at a by-election as the candidate for the Desperate to Hop in Bed with Deborah Party. She would have had to take you seriously then, standing up there in some town hall wearing a big rosette with her face in the middle . . .

Tony does more painful tattooing, building to a crescendo of gurgling, grunting and screaming. It is over. Intensely relieved, Tony hugs Gary, sobbing.

GARY
It's okay, it's all over, it's all over. Well done.
Tony wipes his thigh. We see it: a livid, bleeding, bluish wound. The word DEB can just be made out.

GARY
That's crying out for a full stop.

TONY
(*Grabbing him, begging*) No, no, no.

GARY
Okay.
Tony pulls up his jeans, wincing as they go over his thigh.

TONY
Right, I'm off.

GARY
Good luck, mate. I'll be rooting for you. Try not to bleed on the stairs.
Geeing himself up, Tony slaps his thighs. He screams with pain. Gary wanders into the hall yawning.

Deborah opens the door. Tony is there. She holds the door half open, protectively.

TONY
Hi.

DEBORAH
Hi.

TONY
Can I come in?

DEBORAH
You're not going to read me out any more tips about how to get things for free?

TONY
No.

DEBORAH
Okay.
She lets him in.

Deborah leads Tony in.

DEBORAH
Did I hear . . .? Have you been screaming?

TONY
Oh. Yeah, I was just watching the TV, and Roy Hattersley came on unexpectedly.
Deborah ponders this but lets it go. Tony looks down at the coffee table, which is strewn with college and university prospectuses. He picks one up.

TONY
More college brochures.

DEBORAH
Well, prospectuses . . .

TONY
It's like going on holiday, isn't it? Even better really because you don't need any jabs.

DEBORAH
No, not normally.

TONY
(*Trying to be serious*) What are you thinking of studying?

DEBORAH
I'm not sure. Either a degree in business studies or something more academic like psychology.

TONY
How about PE?

DEBORAH
Why?

TONY
Well, you could, like, mess about on the wall bars all day.

DEBORAH
I'll bear it in mind.

TONY
Or you could study the history of clothes and hair. That'd be good.

DEBORAH
Mm.
He glances at a couple of prospectuses.

TONY
(*Solemnly*) I think you should go here.

DEBORAH
(*Glancing over*) Why?

TONY
Look at the length of that student bar.

DEBORAH
The college doesn't have the course I want.

TONY
Oh, right. Still, have you seen how long the bar is?

DEBORAH
No, no I haven't . . .

TONY
(*Opening another prospectus*) No, this bar's even longer! Go here – look at the length on that. And it's wider too. Longer and wider. Room for more drinks.

DEBORAH
Was there any particular reason you came up to see me or are you just in the area giving careers advice?

TONY
No, I just . . .
He sighs, reaches forward and caresses her shoulder 'romantically'.

DEBORAH
Don't smooth my shoulder, Tony.

TONY
Sorry.
He touches under her chin.

DEBORAH
Or my chin.

TONY
I just wanted to tell you how much I love you.

DEBORAH
You don't love me. You just want to have sex with me.

TONY
(*Po-faced*) Well, we could start there, and from that acorn maybe love will grow into a big . . . thicket.

DEBORAH
(*Kindly*) I don't really want your acorn, Tony.

TONY
What if I proved how serious I am about you? You know I was talking about tattoos . . .

DEBORAH
That's all I need, you getting DEBORAH tattooed across your knuckles.
She smiles. Tony forces a laugh. He looks down at his thigh and sees that the letters DEB have started to seep through his jeans. He covers the patch up by awkwardly leaning on his thigh.

TONY
Still, that'd be quite a nice gesture, wouldn't it?

DEBORAH
No, I think it's tacky.

A pause. Tony gets up.

TONY
Well, I'll be off then.

DEBORAH
Okay. What's that on your thigh?

TONY
Nothing.

DEBORAH
Are you all right? I thought I saw—

TONY
(*Airily dismissive*) It's nothing. Bye.
He leaves hurriedly. Deborah is left alone, looking slightly guilty.

DEBORAH
Bye.

12. GARY'S FLAT: HIS BEDROOM

Night. Gary is sitting on his bed, looking pensive. Dorothy comes in.

DOROTHY
You're looking depressed. What's happened – has the European Court of Human Rights banned farting?
She smiles at Gary and gives him a kiss.

DOROTHY
I bought you a lump of your favourite cheese.
Gary takes the bag, guiltily.

GARY
Thanks.

DOROTHY
Gary, I don't want to nag, but please take down the girlie pictures. They make the flat look like a garage.

GARY
They're not girlie pictures, they're art.

DOROTHY
I don't remember seeing many pictures of women in rubber knickers at the Tate Gallery.

GARY
Yes, they're in a back room. Quite tucked away.

DOROTHY
Really.

GARY
Listen, Dorothy, it's not really working out, the three of us living here.
Dorothy looks shocked.

DOROTHY
Oh. That's taken the wind out of my sails a bit.

GARY
Yes, well.

DOROTHY
So . . . how do you feel about this?
She picks up a pair of scissors from the dressing table and throws them at Gary, who is standing in front of the wall. The scissors embed themselves in Gary's throat, skewering him to the wall. Blood starts to glug from his neck.

13. LIVING ROOM

Gary wakes up with a start from this latest nightmare. He is lying on the sofa, having dozed off. Tony comes in, limping, a big patch of blood on one thigh. He takes off his jeans, throws them down in a fury and kicks them across the room. He sits down, fuming.

GARY
So, did Deborah like your tattoo?

TONY
She thinks they're tacky.

GARY
It is tacky, look. All sticky. And crusty.

TONY
Not sticky tacky – tacky tacky.

GARY
Oh, tacky tacky.
Tony lies down on the sofa and shuts his eyes. Gary winces, steeling himself.

GARY
Tony, sorry to add to your problems but I've been having a bit of a chinwag with Dorothy, and – well, would you believe it! – she doesn't think it's working out with the three of us living here. In fact she thinks, maybe, you'd like to move out. What can you do, eh?
Gary tuts. Then again, more elaborately.

TONY
Okay.
Tony is obviously upset. He gets up.

GARY
No hurry, you know. Go and have a swim or whatever, mull it over.

TONY
No, if you want me out I'm going.

GARY
Don't rush into it, though, as I say. Take a couple of weeks, get some sturdy cardboard boxes together.

TONY
There's a room going above the Crown for bar staff. Ken offered it me anyway.

GARY
That's handy. Is it nice?

TONY
No, it's got a rat in it. And no windows.

GARY
Oh. Still, that's . . . one less thing to look through, isn't it?

TONY
So, who're you going to get lagered-up with and have interesting chats with on the sofa late at night?

GARY
I'll try it with Dorothy. Train her up.

TONY
Yeah.

GARY
Yeah.

TONY
I'll get some things together and go over now.

GARY
Okay.
Tony goes off to pack. Gary is miserable. Fade to later.

14. KITCHEN/HALL

Gary is wandering around. He has made the place nicer for Dorothy, tidied up etc. He opens a cupboard door and removes the picture of a model wearing rubber knickers. He scrunches it up and puts it into the bin. He sits down, looking depressed. He pulls the tablecloth off the kitchen table, to reveal a huge poster of Emma Forbes stuck to it. He tears it off, gets up and bins it too. The front door is heard to slam. Gary goes over to the wall and takes down a Kylie Minogue calendar. He replaces it with Dorothy's calendar of country crafts. This month: dry stone walls. Dorothy comes in, looking heavy hearted.

GARY
Hi, I've been . . . making the place nice for you.

DOROTHY
Oh.

GARY
I've scrunched up Emma Forbes.

DOROTHY
That's sweet of you, Gary—

GARY
(*Not listening*) Poor love, been flat on her back on our kitchen table for six weeks, that's no life for a young woman . . .

DOROTHY
Gary, I'm moving out. I'm really sorry.

GARY
What?
Dorothy looks apologetic.

GARY
Where are you going?

DOROTHY
Deborah's spare room. She's going to need the rent money, being a student. (*Smiling*) Got to pay for those drugs and duffle coats somehow. We get on, you know—

GARY
We get on. We're a super couple. Everybody thinks so.

DOROTHY
It hasn't been brilliant living together, though, has it? Especially with the three of us.

GARY
Exactly – I've just told Tony to move out. He's found a place.
She wavers a moment.

DOROTHY
I . . . think we get on better if we don't live together. You did say it frightened you, seeing my bras hanging up to dry.

GARY
I was getting used to it.

DOROTHY
I'm not going far. You won't need to put your shoes on to visit me. I'd rather you did put your shoes on, obviously. From a hygiene point of view.
Gary is standing there, lost for words. Dorothy looks upset.

DOROTHY
Tony'll come back.

GARY
(*Raised voice*) Maybe I don't want him back. Maybe I'll put an ad in . . . *Young and Sexy Londoner* magazine for a gorgeous girl flatmate.

DOROTHY
You're getting angry. I'll get some things together and head upstairs.
She disappears in the direction of their bedroom. Gary shouts through to her.

GARY
That'll give you something to think about – me sharing with a bird running around in her bra and pants.

DOROTHY
(*Offscreen*) Won't you look a bit odd?

GARY
No, her – her in her bra and pants, actually. As you well know. Or in a T-shirt, and not caring if it rides up when she's looking in the fridge.
Dorothy says nothing. Gary edges nearer.

GARY
Or her calling me into the bathroom to hand her the shower gel and then saying, 'Oh, well, now your hand's got wet you might as well hop in with me and give me a boffing and a half.'
Dorothy reappears, carrying a bag.

GARY
That sort of thing.

DOROTHY
So. I'll be upstairs.

GARY
Don't go, Dorothy. If I can't live with you, I don't want to live with anyone.

DOROTHY
I'm sorry, Gary.
She kisses him and leaves. Gary watches her go, looking upset. We hear the door shut. Looking lost, Gary drifts out to the hall, apparently to follow her. The room is empty for a few seconds, then Gary reappears holding the phone he has already dialled.

GARY
Hi, Tony? Oh, Ken, is Tony there, please?
A pause. While Gary waits he goes over to the bin and retrieves the crunched up poster of Emma Forbes. He tries to flatten it out.

GARY
(*Cheerfully*) Hi, Tone, mate. Great news! You can come back. I've told Dorothy I've changed my mind, she's got to move out. She didn't take it too badly.
Gary goes over to the rural crafts calendar, tosses it aside and replaces it with Kylie. His face falls as he hears Tony.

GARY
No, you were never second best— (*Listening*) Yeah, I know it must be brilliant living in a pub but— (*Listening*) Oh. All right then. No, fine. Bye. Bye.
He hangs up. He looks around at the silent, empty flat.

GARY
Ah. Bugger.

15. DEBORAH'S FLAT: LIVING ROOM

Later that night. Deborah and Dorothy are sitting on the sofa, relaxed and drinking wine. Dorothy looks settled in.

DOROTHY
So, how do you feel about Gary sleeping over here?

DEBORAH
(*Calmly*) No, I'm pretty, you know, um (*Nervously*) panicky actually.

DOROTHY
I'll only do it if he's in a civilised mood.

DEBORAH
How often's that?

DOROTHY
Every four years. So are there any house rules I should know about?

DEBORAH
Yes, if you hear Tony coming up the stairs you have to quickly turn off all the lights and hide under the bed with me.

DOROTHY
Gary and Tony had house rules. You had to be obsessed with at least ten female TV presenters, and you had to be able to do the noise of the doors opening in *Star Trek*.
Dorothy successfully imitates this noise.

DEBORAH
How did Gary take you leaving?

DOROTHY
Quite well, actually. I think he'd been trying to tell me for days himself. I caught him mouthing the words in the hall mirror.
Dorothy perhaps imitates Gary mouthing, 'Dorothy, I want you to leave. Please,' into a mirror.

DOROTHY
Can you ever hear them downstairs?

DEBORAH
Yeah. Singing mainly, late at night. They seem to have finally moved on from 'Crazy Horses' to 'Bermuda Triangle' by Barry Manilow. And every now and again one of them throws a lager can in the air and tries to head it.

DOROTHY
I hope Gary's all right.

DEBORAH
He'll be fine. I bet he's already got his friends round.
They sip their wine.

DOROTHY
What friends?

16. GARY'S FLAT: LIVING ROOM

Mid-evening. Lager cans litter the coffee table. Gary is sitting on the sofa. Next to him is a blow-up doll dressed in Tony's clothes. Gary has drawn on the doll's face to make it look even more like Tony. Like Gary, the doll has a can of lager in its hand. Gary is getting drunk.

GARY
You see, living with your girlfriend's all very well, but in a funny kind of way I would liken it, Tone, to living with your parents. Because you have to keep your room quite tidy. You can't put up the posters you want. And you can't invite girls back.
He swallows some lager.

GARY
Or you can invite them back, but all of you have to sit around making conversation and drinking tea, pretending she's just a friend and trying not to sound pissed, and then you have to call a cab for her. Am I right, mate? (*In Tony's voice*) Spot on, mate. (*In his own voice*) Thanks, mate.
The door to the flat slams. Gary hears it and freezes. He hurriedly picks up the blow-up doll and wonders where to hide it. There is nowhere obvious so he grabs the knife and fork from the used supper plate in front of him. He stabs at the doll, which deflates partially. He hastily hides it under the sofa cushion he is sitting on. Tony enters.

TONY
Hi.

GARY
(*Trying to be cool*) Oh, hi.
The following conversation is accompanied by the sound of air wheezing out of the doll.

TONY
I thought maybe I'd live here after all.

GARY
Oh, okay.
Limping slightly, Tony sits down on the sofa and picks up a can from the table.

TONY
What have you been doing?

GARY
Had a kebab, watched a documentary about how housewives are turning to stripping to make ends meet and sat here drinking lager.

TONY
So a pretty successful evening then?

GARY
Absolutely. Text-book evening. What have you been doing?

TONY
Sweating.

GARY
Oh. Well, it's something to do, isn't it?

TONY
Yeah. I think I've given myself blood poisoning, doing this tattoo.

GARY
Still, even if you have to spend a couple of days in hospital, you've ended up with a lovely piece of work. And that tattoo will still be looking good long after the ceiling of the Sistine Chapel's started to look a bit tatty.

TONY
Yeah. What's that noise?

GARY
Noise?

TONY
Yeah, it's like air coming out of something.

GARY
It's . . . me.

TONY
Oh, cheers, mate.
They swig some lager. Tony suddenly pulls the still half-inflated doll out from under Gary.

TONY
It's me! You made a Tony doll!

GARY
I didn't!

SERIES FIVE: EPISODE FIVE

cardigan

The theme of encroaching middle age struck a chord with me. Ostensibly speaking for a generation of outrageous, lagered-up lads, I was sitting at my computer listening to Radio 2 and thinking of upgrading to a slightly roomier family car. Like George, my late Dad was a big fan of the Seekers, and I have to say Radiohead could learn a thing or two from them about how to carry a nice tune.

Deborah's student friend here is a reminder of the danger of creating an irritating character: that they are merely irritating to watch. But this episode is worth seeing for Gary's spectacular vomiting at a rave, which we recreated in a 10-square-foot corner of Teddington Studios.

This show was to have ended with one of Tony and Gary's typically meandering chats on the sofa. These had only come about when I kept delivering the episodes a few minutes short so I had to add some dialogue somewhere. I discovered they don't work if Gary and Tony are drinking tea, and anyway it was funnier to show them reverting to lager-frenzy in the pub.

1. DEBORAH'S FLAT: HALLWAY

Mid-evening. The hall is empty. A knock from outside. A pause.

TONY
(*Offscreen, laddish*) When you were a kid, did you ever knock on doors and run away?

GARY
(*Offscreen, equally laddish*) Yeah.
A pause.

TONY
(*Offscreen*) Why did we do that then?

GARY
(*Offscreen*) Dunno.
Another pause.

GARY
(*Offscreen*) Actually I never did it, but I knew people who did, you know.

TONY
(*Offscreen*) Hey, do you ever do that thing where you're waiting for someone to open the door and you make, like, a silly face and hold it till the last possible moment?

GARY
(*Offscreen*) No, I don't.

TONY
(*Offscreen*) Oh. Okay.
Dorothy arrives and opens the door. Tony and Gary are making ridiculous faces, which they change instantly. Dorothy frowns but says nothing.

GARY
Hello. We were a bit bored.

2. LIVING ROOM

Tony and Gary enter, followed by Dorothy. Deborah is working at a table, surrounded by files and books.

TONY
Hi, Debs.

DEBORAH
Hi.

TONY
So, what's it like being a mature student?

DEBORAH
Really good.

TONY
(*More to himself*) A mature student. Mature.
He rolls it around his mouth, annoying Deborah. She forces a smile and goes back to her work. Tony hovers beside her. Dorothy goes back to the sofa, where she is watching TV. Gary mooches around.

GARY
Feels weird.

DOROTHY
(*Not interested*) Breaking in some new pants?

GARY
No, weird, you two living upstairs – just the same as us, only girls.

DOROTHY
Just the same, except we've never had a 'Last One to Vomit's a Nancy Boy' competition.
Gary sits down. Tony is still hovering near Deborah, to her obvious irritation.

TONY
(*Peering over her shoulder*) How's your homework going?

DEBORAH
It's not called homework.

TONY
In class do you ever take an empty biro tube and use it to fire off little balls of inky paper?

DEBORAH
Tony, I'm in my thirties. I'm doing a psychology degree. We don't play with inky paper.

TONY
(*Losing confidence*) So how do you unwind?

DEBORAH
(*Getting tetchy*) I don't.
He idly flips open a ring file. Deborah slams it shut on his hand. He stays there, showing a polite interest. Deborah gives up. She goes over and sits down in front of the TV. Tony wanders over to a radiator where bras and knickers are hanging up to dry.

TONY
Can I have some of these, please?

DEBORAH
(*Long-suffering*) No.
He sits down. All four of them are now sitting watching the TV.

GARY
It's all bollocks, isn't it? Studying.

DEBORAH
Thanks, Gary.

GARY
Except Psychology, obviously, that's terribly useful—

TONY
Crucial—

GARY
Vital. Yep. I've learnt everything I need at the University of Life. In the faculty of Hard Knocks. Special subject: Life As It's Lived. Grant cheque supplied by the Hard Graft Education Authori—

DOROTHY
Yes, yes. God, Gary, you're so middle-aged. All you need now is a cardy and slippers. (*Looking over at him*) Oh, you've got them.

TONY
I'd like to help, though, Debs. Can I test you on anything? I'd be good at testing.

DEBORAH
No, it's okay.

TONY
I could sharpen your pencils. Go round making them all sharp—

DEBORAH
I don't use pencils.

TONY
I could wax your satchel.

DEBORAH
(*Losing patience*) I haven't got a satchel.
He sits quietly.

TONY
I could help you buy one. Go satchel shopping togeth—

DEBORAH
Tony, look, I know you want to help but I have new interests now and a new set of friends, and I don't need you hanging around me like a poodle.
Tony looks hurt. He goes quiet.

DEBORAH
Sorry . . .

TONY
Poodle. Fine.

DEBORAH
I didn't mean—

TONY
(*Ignoring her*) I'm a poodle. No, that's very clear.
An awkward silence.

GARY
(*Sympathetic, to Tony*) Do you want me to . . . take you out for a walk—?

TONY
Shut up.

DOROTHY
(*Kindly*) Tony—

TONY
It's okay.

DOROTHY
Tony, really—

TONY
(*Not listening*) No, I'm a poodle—

DOROTHY
(*Angrily*) Tony will you pass the bloody paper!

TONY
Oh, sorry.
He passes the newspaper.

TONY
Okay, I'm not a student, so I'm not good enough for you.

DEBORAH
I never said that.

TONY
(*Histrionic*) I would have got some O levels, I just forgot to send in the form.
He gets up, upset. The others looks guilty. On his way out Tony pauses by Deborah's underwear again.

TONY
Could I just borrow some of these then?

DEBORAH
No!

TONY
Oh, I suppose I'm not clever enough.
He leaves.

3. GARY'S OFFICE

Next afternoon. George and Gary are working quietly at their desks. The ambience is particularly homely. A radio-cassette player on George's desk is playing 'Georgy Girl' by the Seekers. George is humming along to the music. A draughtboard is laid out between them so they can both play from their desks. George makes a move and takes a wine gum from a little paper bag next to the board. Gary sees the move and does an ooh-er-I'm-in-trouble expression. He takes a wine gum himself and ponders.

GARY
(*Taking off his jacket*) I'll have a little think about that.

Gary joins in the humming. George gradually starts singing.

GEORGE
'Hey, there, Georgy Girl, de-be de-be de de de be-de.'
Gary involuntarily joins in.

GARY/GEORGE
'Could it be you just don't care, or is it the clothes you wear? You're always window shopping de de de dum . . .'
They peter out.

GARY
They certainly knew how to write a tune in those days. They obviously couldn't do words, but they could do tunes.

GEORGE
She was always smashingly turned out, wasn't she? The lady in the Seekers.

GARY
God, yes. You wouldn't catch her with egg on her blouse. Or grease from sausages.

GEORGE
I can still remember the day the Seekers split up. I came home and Marjorie was in tears and we just . . . hugged.

GARY
Mm.

GEORGE
Of course, after the Seekers there was the New Seekers, but I found them rather raucous.

GARY
Well, to be fair, I don't remember the New Seekers being raucous.
George has got up to sharpen his pencil. Gary gets up too, to file a letter. They are standing next to each other. Gary glances at George. He swallows hard and turns off the music.

GARY
(*Looking away, trying to remain calm*) George, will you reassure me that I'm not dressed the same as you.
They turn to assess each other. The awful truth dawns on Gary: he is wearing virtually the same clothes as George – staid shirt and cardigan, sensible trousers, Hush Puppies.

GEORGE
Oh, yes. That's rather splendid. Marjorie buys most of my clothes, shall I ask her to buy two of everything?
Gary puts his head in his hands.

GARY
What's happening to me?
Anthea comes in with a watering can to water the plants. George is hidden behind the door. Anthea sees Gary with his head in his hands.

ANTHEA
George—?

GARY
(*Shouting over her*) I'm not George I'm Gary! (*Considering*) I'm turning into George.
Anthea and George smile benignly.

ANTHEA
Oh, that's nice.

GARY
No, it's not nice.

ANTHEA
Well, they always say people start to look like their dogs.

GARY
(*Frustrated*) I don't mind looking like a dog! I just don't want to look like George!

ANTHEA
Actually, you have started to say the same things as George too, like 'Whoops-a-daisy' and 'What's the biscuit situation?'

GARY
I have not.

GEORGE
And you know all the words to my favourite songs.

ANTHEA
I think it's super that we're all growing middle-aged together.
Gary looks bleak. They sip their tea.

GARY/GEORGE/ANTHEA
(*In unison*) Ooh, that really hits the spot.

4. THE CROWN

That evening. Tony and Ken are behind the bar, chatting.

TONY
So, have you always wanted to run a pub?

KEN
Oh, yeah, ever since I was, um. No I haven't, no, I never wanted to run one. I thought you were going to say, '. . . wanted to run a Dormobile.'

TONY
You know what I like about pubs?

KEN
Is it the way you can walk in and get drinks?

TONY
Yeah. Yeah, I suppose it is. And the way you get all sorts together. You've got a newsreader talking to a lumberjack over there, you've got a scaffolder having a chinwag with Dame Judy Dench over here.
Ken gazes around, seeing nobody.

KEN
Have they all popped to the toilet?

TONY
No, generally.

KEN
Oh, generally. Okay.

TONY
Oh, yeah, the brewery guy dropped off the signs you wanted. There's some for the toilet doors.

Tony produces a bag from under the bar.

TONY
We've got a choice.
He gets out a piece of card. Mounted on it are two little signs. In elegant writing one says BLOKES, the other TOTTY.

TONY
What do you reckon?

KEN
It's quite classy, isn't it?

TONY
'Tis, yeah.
Tony produces the next ones: a pair of Regency silhouettes of a woman holding a parasol and a foppish man holding a handkerchief at a camp angle.

KEN
(*Considering*) It's not really us, is it?

TONY
No.

KEN
That's more for places with, you know, clean toilets.

TONY
Yeah.
He rummages in the bag and brings out a single sign: the symbol does not make sense. Tony turns it round: it is a simplified line drawing of male genitals. They look at it gravely, then Tony rummages in the bag for its counterpart. It shows a pair of breasts.

KEN
That's a bit of a relief—

TONY
(*Joining in*) Relief, yeah.
Into the pub comes Deborah and four students: a woman and three men, all in their early twenties. Deborah – now dressed in jeans and trainers, more like a student – sees Tony and goes up to the bar, a bit embarrassed.

DEBORAH
Hi, Tony. We were around, and I thought I'd show you that my friends are, you know, normal.
Adam, one of the students – good-looking, rather earnest, obviously keen on Deborah – has been asking the others what they want.

ADAM
Hi, two halves of your cheapest bitter, please, two glasses of tap water, and what are you having, Debs?
Deborah is about to answer.

TONY
It's all right, I know what she likes.

DEBORAH
Actually I'll have a half of bitter too.

TONY
Oh. Okay.
Tony, eyeing Adam suspiciously, starts to get the drinks.

DEBORAH
This is my friend Tony, everyone. He's a neighbour.
They all mutter hello etc.

TONY
Hi. We had a snog once, you know.
They look awkward. Deborah squirms.

DEBORAH
It was a while ago now.

TONY
Still, a snog's a snog. So you're all students.
Mutters of agreement.

TONY
I would have got some O-levels, but I forgot to send in the form.
Obliging mutters of sympathy.

TONY
I left it on the sofa and it . . . fell down the back of the cushions and . . . dissolved.

ADAM
I didn't think you needed to send in any fo—

TONY
(*Sharply*) You did at our school.
Deborah and friends are comprehensively embarrassed. They now have their drinks.

TONY
Have you noticed how easy the questions are on *University Challenge* these days?
An awkward pause, then the others all mutter their agreement.

TONY
They're very easy. That's one pound ninety-five.

DEBORAH
I'll get this.

ADAM
No, this is my round.
They wait while he painstakingly gets out his cheque book.

ADAM
I'll have to pay by cheque.

TONY
(*Under his breath*) Tosser.

5. GARY'S FLAT: LIVING ROOM

Same night. Dorothy and Gary are slumped on the sofa, watching the TV. Gary looks depressed.

GARY
So that's it, then, that's my youth gone.

DOROTHY
Oh, well.

GARY
One minute I'm learning what the big hand and the little hand do, the next I'm padding round Marks and Spencer with a basket buying old man's shoes.

DOROTHY
Well, go to a trendier shop.

GARY
No, it's good, you can always take your purchases back if you change your mind. Do you remember those long hazy summers when it felt like life would last for ever?

DOROTHY
I remember feeling that on our holiday together in Corby.

GARY
Bob-a-job week. Little nametags sewn into your socks. The lemonade van coming round every Wednesday, bringing bottles of pop. We'd take the empty ones out, and they'd give us tuppence for each one.

DOROTHY
The lemonade van? When was this, 1931?

GARY
I wouldn't mind if I'd really done something with my life.

DOROTHY
You've done things, love.
A pause while Dorothy thinks.

GARY
What . . .?

DOROTHY
I'm trying to think.

GARY
And look at us.

DOROTHY
What's wrong with us?

GARY
We're watching *Hetty Wainthrop Investigates*, that's what's wrong with us. We should be watching something violent and unpleasant.

DOROTHY
So what do you want to do?

GARY
I don't know, wild stuff. Something I've never done before.

DOROTHY
Sat quietly with a book, occasionally looking up and making a sensible comment?

GARY
No. I've never been part of a 'scene'. Even George was part of the Croydon folk-club scene. Apparently they used to cruise up and down Croydon High Street in Fair Isle sweaters.

Tony enters, looking unhappy. He sits down in an armchair.

DOROTHY
You're back early.

TONY
Ken sent me home for challenging one of Debs' student friends to a duel.
Gary and Dorothy look at him pityingly.

TONY
Yeah, I meant to say 'fistfight', but I couldn't think of the word. They wind me up, you know, I lose all my legendary poise and confidence.
Gary and Dorothy look even more baffled.

TONY
I'll never get Deborah back now.

DOROTHY
They're only students. She hasn't been kidnapped by religious fanatics.

TONY
She has! They're like that. They sit in a huddle and roll their own spitty little fags, looking smug and evil. And they won't let me join in, they kept spreading out and pretending there wasn't room at the table.

DOROTHY
Maybe you should have done one of your cheese impressions.

TONY
I offered actually. They just sort of did that in their seats.
Tony mimes someone turning their back.

TONY
(*Whimpering*) I love Deborah, and I want to sleep with her.

DOROTHY/GARY
(*Wearily*) We know.
A silence. Tony and Gary sulk. They sigh.

DOROTHY
Well, thanks for inviting me down—

GARY
Tony, did you do crazy things when you were younger?

TONY
(*Cheering up*) Yeah.

GARY
What was it like?

TONY
Brilliant.

GARY
Why didn't, you know, why didn't I do crazy things?

TONY
I don't know, mate, maybe you were . . . dull.

GARY
Mm, maybe.

TONY
Yeah. I went through the lot – punk, New Romantic, Goth, New Hairy.

DOROTHY
Me too.

GARY
Oh, you too, oh.
Dorothy realises Gary is upset.

DOROTHY
You must have been something.

GARY
Yes, I was a schoolboy, then I was an office junior, then I became a New Office Manager, then I joined the Floppy Knitwear scene.
Dorothy and Tony try to give him encouraging looks.

TONY/DOROTHY
That's not bad, is it?/See, that's lovely.

GARY
Right, that's that. We're going clubbing.

6. THE CROWN

One night later that week. Gary is standing at the jukebox choosing some music. He is dressed in a very eighties suit. He puts in some money, and something very electronic and techno starts playing. Gary is not sure how to dance to it. He has a stab at it, eventually hitting some kind of rhythm. He jigs over to the bar, where Tony and Ken are serving.

KEN
Er, sorry. New sign.
Ken refers Gary to one of the new signs up behind the bar – a roadsign-style silhouette of a man dancing with a diagonal line through it, alongside a similar one outlawing spitting and a Lost Property Not Returned sign.

TONY
Come on, Ken, he's my best mate.

KEN
Oh, all right, go ahead.

GARY
Thanks.
Gary self-consciously does a bit more jigging, watched by Tony and Ken.

GARY
It's all right, I'll stop now. (*Rubbing his hands together*) So, let's get out of our heads and go crazy! We're young, and we don't give a shit!
Everyone in the pub goes quiet and looks over at him.

GARY
(*To the pub*) Sorry. Sorry.

TONY
Don't take this the wrong way, mate, but . . . you're dressed like an arse.

GARY
This? No, it's a classic suit. I tell you, mate, the last time I went dancing in it Lionel Ritchie came on the record player, and
I could have had any woman in that scout hut.

TONY
Yeah, I really think this is the night for me and Debs. Picture it, right. We're all sticky from dancing.

GARY
Both sticky, yeah, that's good.

TONY
We've had a bit to drink.

GARY
Out of her head, can't do any harm.

TONY
My Horn aftershave's playing, like, mind games with her hormones.

GARY
(*Pondering, then*) Whatever, yeah.

TONY
I reckon at the end of the night she's going to look me in the eye, or both eyes, and say, 'Tony, if you don't make love to me right now, I'm going to call the police.'
Gary gives Tony a long look.

GARY
You're quite an optimist, aren't you, Tony?

TONY
Yeah.
Tony wanders off to serve someone. He does not see Dorothy enter with Deborah and Adam. They exchange vague hellos with Gary.

DEBORAH
Gary, this is Adam, we're studying together.

GARY
Hi, student bloke.

ADAM
Hi. I'll just . . .
Adam motions vaguely to the gents and heads off. Gary looks over at Tony and winces. Dorothy kisses Gary, then looks at his suit.

DOROTHY
Ah, yes, the suit.
Gary proudly straightens his lapels.

GARY
Well, you know what they say.

DOROTHY
'Why are you wearing that crap suit?'

GARY
'Style never goes out of fashion.'

DOROTHY
Gary, we'll be dancing in some sweaty warehouse. We're not going to the 1984 Building Society Employee of the Year Show.
Adam has come back to the bar. Tony sees him for the first time.

ADAM
Um, I found this on the floor.
He puts the sign to the ladies toilet – the breasts motif – on the bar. Ken has wandered over.

ADAM
I think it might be a bit sexist. No pressure, you know.

KEN
Maybe he's right. Let's see what else we've got.
Tony is fuming. Ken gets the remaining signs out of the bag.

KEN
(*Consulting Adam*) Dogs and Bitches, or Tarts and Vicars?
Tony turns to Deborah, aggrieved.

TONY
(*Under his breath*) What's he doing here?

DEBORAH
Adam? He just turned up and asked to come out with the four of us, I couldn't really say no.

TONY
Right, if he comes with us, I'm staying here.

DEBORAH
Oh, Tony—

TONY
I mean it, take it or leave it.

7. DOROTHY'S CAR

Later. Adam is in the back seat, sitting between Deborah and a sullen Tony. Dorothy is in the driving seat, with Gary next to her. Gary is studying a couple of maps. We see Tony's arm go round behind Adam and feel about for contact with Deborah. He succeeds only in patting her head. Deborah removes his hand.

8. AT A CROSSROADS

We can now see where Dorothy's car is parked: on a verge at a crossroads in semi-rural surroundings.

GARY
(*Offscreen, breezily*) Okay! Let's see.
A long pause.

GARY
(*Offscreen*) Where are we?

Another long pause.

GARY
(*Offscreen*) Wait, this is a town map of Dieppe.
Sighs of impatience from everyone.

GARY
(*Offscreen*) Roman road, look. (*Pausing*) Oh, no it's a fold in the map.

9. DOROTHY'S CAR

As before.

ADAM
It's interesting, isn't it, how the original rave scene shifted leisure out of towns into the suburbs or even the countryside? It was sort of the first time the entertainment industry with a small 'e' – (*Amused*) if you'll pardon the expression – had challenged the received notion of urban supremacy.

TONY
Oh, shut up.

DEBORAH
Tony, don't.
Deborah smiles at Adam apologetically, clearly rather keen on him.

TONY
I just don't see why he should sit next to you. It's so unfair.

ADAM
What does it matter?

TONY
So let me sit next to her.

ADAM
No, I've . . . made the seat all nice and warm now.

DEBORAH
I'm sick if I don't go by the window.

ADAM
That's interesting, isn't it—?

TONY
Oh dear! Another interesting thing . . .

ADAM
It confirms everything we know about how the irrational psyche determines wellness.

GARY
What's he on about now?

DOROTHY
(*Trying not to lose her temper*) Gary, where are we, please, before I beat you to death with the *Reader's Digest Book of the Road*?

GARY
(*Scrutinising map*) Well, I'm sticking my neck out hugely here, but we seem to be at . . . a junction. Of two roads.

DEBORAH
(*Slightly flirty*) What's so irrational about my psyche?

ADAM
Well, there's obviously nothing in the glass of the window per se that's making you not feel not well, as it were—

TONY
(*Abruptly opening the door*) Right, get out, I'm going in the middle.

10. CROSSROADS

Tony gets out and waits for Adam to get out and let him sit in the middle.

ADAM
(*Offscreen*) Actually I feel sick if I don't sit in the middle.

TONY
Good

ADAM
(*Offscreen*) No, I'm not moving.

TONY
Okay, I'm going to count to three and—
He can not wait. In irritation Tony tries to pull Adam out of the car. Adam resists by planting his feet on the frame of the door.

11. DOROTHY'S CAR

We are looking through the windscreen again. In the foreground Gary is frowning over the map, while behind him Tony and Adam tussle undignifiedly. Gary quietly gets a bottle of vodka out and drinks from it as he studies the map. Dorothy gives up waiting and takes the map. In passing she sees Gary's bottle and frowns disapprovingly.

GARY
Come on, we're having a night out!
Dorothy studies the map, quickly sees where they are, puts the car into gear and drives off. Behind her Tony and Adam continue to tussle, with Tony sitting on Adam, trying to shift him. Adam holds his ground. Deborah rolls her eyes, trying to ignore them. Tony gives up but refuses to go back to where he was so remains sitting on Adam's lap.

12. COUNTRY LANE

An hour later. The car is parked in a quiet, narrow lane in deep countryside.

13. DOROTHY'S CAR

Dorothy is poring with increasing exasperation over a map. Gary takes another slug of vodka. He is very drunk. Behind them, Tony and Adam obviously have not resolved their differences: Tony is still perched on Adam's lap.

DOROTHY
I've had enough, let's turn back.

GARY
I've had enough turn back? Are you mad? Are you madder than . . . Brian Mad of Madcastle? Are you?

DEBORAH
Yes, come on, it's two o'clock in the morning.

GARY
No! Absolutely no! We're having a great night out. It's two o'clock, and we haven't even got there yet. That's very fashionable. I read it somewhere. In a magazine. Of some kind. Or other. (*Peering at the map*) Make sure you've got the right map. I was working from that map of Dieppe for some time, with disastrous consequences.
Tony tries again to squeeze in next to Deborah. Adam will not let him in. Gary looks round to see what is going on.

GARY
Oh, are you two friends now? Careful, I once had someone on my lap in a car and— (*Giggling*) no, I can't say, I'm too embarrassed. Still, she was a girl.
As they tussle, Gary maunders on.

GARY
This is it, isn't it? Pleasure, at the cutting edge. We'll go anywhere for a good time. Distance no object. Just give us a map, and we'll find it. Eventually.

DEBORAH
Oh, for God's sake.
Deborah manoeuvres herself into the middle. She now has Tony and Adam on either side of her.

DOROTHY
Who did you get these directions from, Tony?

TONY
Ken.

DOROTHY
Right that's it, we're going home.

GARY
No!
Dorothy puts the car into gear.

14. COUNTRY LANE

A very wide shot of the car pulling away from where it was parked. In the distance we can see a glow of lights. This is clearly where the rave is.
The car drives out of shot.

GARY
(Offscreen) Hang on a minute, what's that over there?

DEBORAH
(Offscreen) Stop the car, I feel sick.

ADAM
(Offscreen) Me too actually.

15. WAREHOUSE VENUE

A small section of the dancefloor full of off-their-heads revellers, thudding music and lights. We see the dancers from a low angle. Tony comes across our line of vision, dancing with his usual mad enthusiasm. Seconds later Gary's face crosses our line of vision. He is creeping on his knees on the floor, and looks very much the worse for wear. Fades to next scene.

16. BACK HOME: COMMUNAL HALLWAY

The dawn chorus is heard from outside, then voices.

ADAM
(Offscreen) Is he all right?

DOROTHY
(Offscreen) Yes, it was a bit too much for him, that's all. He got overexcited.
The sound of keys jingling.

DEBORAH
(Offscreen) Tony, shall I look for my keys?

TONY
(Offscreen) No. I may not be a student, studying Keys, or have an A-Level in . . . Key Studies, but I can open a door.
More jingling of keys.

ADAM
(Offscreen) How long does it normally take?
The sound of a scuffle, then of Deborah and Dorothy intervening.

SMIRNOFF

DEBORAH/DOROTHY
(*Offscreen*) Stop it, you two./ Tony, leave him.

GARY
(*Offscreen, incoherent bellow*) GetMeInsideHomeHomeTummyUnder-TheCabbage.
The front door opens. A brief tableau: Gary is propped up, a blanket round him, his face squashed against the door frame. He is out of it, hungover and drunk. Tony and Adam, their hair sweaty and matted from dancing, look tense. Deborah and Dorothy have obviously enjoyed themselves. They walk in, Gary only with the help of Dorothy. He is coming round, starting to make sense.

GARY
What's been happening?

DOROTHY
You passed out.

GARY
That's not very me.
Gary lurches from one side of the hall to the other, bumping into the hall table. Dorothy follows him.

DOROTHY
We lost you for half an hour and found you outside hugging the wheel of a car. Gary, I'm over here.

GARY
Clubbing . . . ridiculous idea . . . What's wrong with tea? What's wrong with tea and a nice night in?!

DOROTHY
Shhh.

GARY
Oh, it's shush now, is it? What happened to, Speak your Mind, Get It Off Your Chest Area?!
Dorothy is keeping Gary upright with one hand and opening the door with the other.

DEBORAH
(*To Dorothy*) Can I help?

GARY
Yes, you can get Kajagoogoo to reform. Or you can invent a fridge that doesn't make a noise when it goes on and off.

DOROTHY
It's all right, I'll put him to bed.

GARY
Oh, cheeky.
Dorothy leads Gary into the flat.

GARY
(*Offscreen*) I'm in considerable pain, you know.
Deborah, Tony and Adam are left in the hall. Deborah has opened the door to her flat. Awkwardness.

DEBORAH
So, boys, thanks for a great night out.

ADAM
I'll see you up.

TONY
No, mate, there's nothing more to see. On your way now, go on.
Tony tries to usher Adam to the door. Adam looks to Deborah, who seems torn.

ADAM
I've got some book stuff I need to talk to you about, Debs—
Tony tries to ease Adam out of the front door. Adam resists. Tony picks him up, but Adam hangs on to the hall table, then the door frame.

DEBORAH
Tony, put Adam down. Put him down.
Adam frees himself. Deborah smiles at him.

DEBORAH
Come on up.
Tony looks upset. Deborah gives Tony a sympathetic look. Adam and Deborah head up to her flat. Alone in the hall, Tony whimpers.

17. DEBORAH'S FLAT: LIVING ROOM

A moment later. Deborah comes in, followed by Adam. Deborah takes off her shoes and her ear rings.

DEBORAH
Ooh, that's better.
Adam is trying to look cool but is obviously keen and nervous.

ADAM
Ha. Anything else coming off?

DEBORAH
Not just yet.

ADAM
It's a sort of ceremony, isn't it, the stripping away again of the social trinkets? The sort of . . . return to self.

DEBORAH
No, I was just taking off my earrings.

ADAM
Ha. Yeah, right.
Deborah puts the kettle on.

DEBORAH
Well, that was a bit of a laugh. How do you take your tea again?

ADAM
Um, in the bedroom.
A silence. He laughs nervously. Deborah winces apologetically.

DEBORAH
Oh, Adam, do you mind if we don't?

ADAM
Hey, no, whatever, traditional bed question.
He picks up an ornament and immediately drops it.

ADAM
Would that be the permanent 'Do you mind if we don't,' or is that the interim holding position?

DEBORAH
(*Kindly*) Well, apart from the fact that I don't always understand what you're saying, I just think we're a bit . . . too different.
Deborah puts a friendly hand on his shoulder. Tony bursts in, carrying a pile of books under his arm and a big packet of Corn Flakes. He is wearing his glasses.

TONY
Hey, is it too late for me to join your discussion group? I've brought Corn Flakes and some intriguing books.

ADAM
(*To Deborah*) Bye, then.

TONY
Oh, are you off?
Adam leaves. Deborah watches him go, with regret. She throws herself into a chair and groans.

TONY
Has he got to go and do his paper round?

DEBORAH
I may have to hit you if you say anything else.
She looks up at Tony's books.

DEBORAH
The Guinness Book of Records and *Watership Down* – that would have been a fascinating discussion.

TONY
So what was wrong with him?

DEBORAH
I suppose I realised he was a bit too young and intellectual for me. (*Getting to her feet*) Sadly, and I do mean sadly, I've probably got more in common with you than him.

TONY
Oh, ta.
They are standing close. Deborah smiles ruefully at Tony. Encouraged, Tony whips off his glasses, half closes his eyes and puckers up for a kiss.

DEBORAH
Not that much in common, I'm afraid.
She picks up the packet of Corn Flakes and hands it to him. She heads off.

DEBORAH
(*On her way out*) My bedroom door will be locked.
Tony stops. He stands there alone, not unhappy. He holds the Corn Flakes by the top of the packet. The bag inside is obviously upside down and its contents begin to fall on to Tony's feet. We watch until the last of the Corn Flakes have fluttered to the ground.

18. GARY'S FLAT: LIVING ROOM

That evening. Tony and Gary are on the sofa, sober, sipping tea, wearing slightly George-type clothes. A middle-of-the-road CD is playing. Gary is going through his photo album, smiling nostalgically, showing Tony the photos.

GARY
That's me on my first day at work.

TONY
Ahh – shiny shoes.

GARY
Very shiny.

TONY
Look at the row of pens in your top pocket. (*Peering at the photo*) How many, um . . .?

GARY
Seventeen pens.

TONY
And a couple of rulers.

GARY
Yeah. I had to keep my jacket on all day because it was too heavy to take off.

TONY
What's your mum doing?

GARY
(*Peering at photo*) Sprinkling holy water on my briefcase. She thought it would help my career.

TONY
And you've . . . got a dog on your head.

GARY
No, that's my hair. Hair was like that then.

TONY
Yeah, I reckon that's why men go bald – it's nature's way of stopping them have any more bad hairstyles.

GARY
Mm. (*Smiling at another photo*) Look at me! What have I got on?!

TONY
Um, Dorothy.

GARY
No, not that one, that one.
They stare at a photo.

GARY
Oh, yeah, the office fancy-dress party. I went as Anthea. That's not something I'll rush into again in a hurry. How's your hangover?

TONY
Bit better.

GARY
Me too.

TONY
I think I'm ready to tackle walking and talking at the same time again.

GARY
I tell you, I'm in no hurry to go out again.

TONY
Well, let's face it, mate – what is wrong with staying at home, popping on a song with a proper tune—

GARY
A proper tune.

TONY
—and resting up with a nice cup of tea.

GARY
Yeah. Half the country's out and about, doing this.
He does a mad flapping-about gesture. Tony looks intrigued, if bewildered.

TONY
Oh, are they? I've never seen that.

GARY
While canny old dogs like us are sufficiently at ease with ourselves to stay in and have a nice dignified evening in—

TONY
Watching programmes about antiques and gardening.

GARY
Mm.
They sip their tea. Another jaunty-but-dull song comes on. They try to look contented, but boredom is already creeping into their features. They gaze around.

19. THE CROWN

Late that evening. Gary and Tony are dancing madly to a song on the jukebox – something half way between techno and the Seekers. They dance alone, then gradually go into something more coordinated, linking arms, until they are dancing together. Other customers in the pub watch and start to clap in time to encourage them. Freeze frame and colour fades to match the closing titles.

SERIES FIVE: EPISODE SEVEN

Home-made Sauna

I really like this episode, which seems to prove the point that the more serious the subject matter – in this case cheating on a long-time partner – the funnier it is.

Martin brilliantly conveys male adolescent joy and surprise at having persuaded a woman to have sex with him. (Women should be warned: this joy and surprise never really goes away.) And although pathos is a very risky area for sitcoms, Caroline pulls it off as the woman who wants to know – but doesn't – if her boyfriend has been screwing around.

Martin Dennis, our director, did a fine job filming the wooden barbecue catching fire. I am not a very hands-on writer – during location filming I believe in turning up, offering in a barely audible voice to change lines anyone is not happy about, then going off for a big free meal. This may look like a lack of professionalism, but I prefer to see it as a demonstration of how much I trust everyone to do a good job.

As the script shows, in this episode I fell in love with the word 'shed', which appears several hundred times. I have fallen in love with other words in my time: 'tops', 'cheese', 'pants' (obviously), 'cake' and 'totty', but 'shed' is probably the single luxury word I would have on my desert island.

More miscellaneous production notes. It was drizzling on the day of filming, so I had to hastily rewrite the 'girls sunbathing' scene as a 'girls bringing in washing' scene . . . The script contains the made-up name Dave Tuffin, and a Dave Tuffin wrote to me, asking me who gave me his name . . . For some reason my Australian relatives thought Gary and Tony's 'dates' were trying to do Australian accents . . . Gary's one-night-stand was played, beautifully, by Neil Morrissey's then girlfriend Liz Carling, so rehearsals were punctuated by Neil shouting, 'Stop him – he's kissing my bird!'

1. GARY'S FLAT: LIVING ROOM

Early Friday evening. Gary and Dorothy are lying on the sofa, happy together, their legs lazily intertwined. Gary's hands are clamped on Dorothy's breasts.

GARY
They must be the two scariest words in the English language.

DOROTHY
What?

GARY
Sailing weekend. Let's go on a sailing weekend. I'd actually rather go on a having-your-nose-pulled-off weekend, or a sitting-in-sick weekend. (*Begging*) Don't go.

DOROTHY
I have to.

GARY
Why?

DOROTHY
I've bought one of those shiny yellow hats that sailing people wear.

GARY
What's the point of sailing? Silly little wobbly boats with silly wobbly people in them.

DOROTHY
There's nothing silly or wobbly about me and Deborah.

GARY
Well, I don't know where you got that idea from. In fact, there's only one thing more pointless than sailing.

DOROTHY
Asking you to shut your face?

GARY
Flying kites. You stand in a wind, you get some dreary slave to run along with it, it flaps about a bit then plops down. You spend an hour winding up the string, and you go home.
A pause.

GARY
No, tell a lie, there is one thing more pointless. Puppet shows. Staging your own puppet show, and doing the voices of the little figures while waggling them about.

DOROTHY
(*Eventually*) You're an incredibly joyless character, aren't you?

GARY
Not me, I'm built for fun.

DOROTHY
Really? Everyone I know thinks you're built for pointing at and slapping.
Gary starts to nuzzle her. Dorothy enjoys it. He playfully puts her nose in his mouth.

GARY
Come to my bedroom and make love.

DOROTHY
Why, who's in there?

GARY
No, with me.

DOROTHY
I can't, Deborah's coming down in a minute.

GARY
She'll understand. She knows that people have sex.
They are collapsing, giggling, to the floor.

DOROTHY
She doesn't! She has no idea!
They quieten down, sigh heavily. Dorothy disentangles herself from Gary, who remains lying on the floor.

GARY
So what am I supposed to do for sex this weekend?

DOROTHY
Well, I don't need to draw you a picture.
Dorothy starts to get her weekend bag ready.

DOROTHY
Anyway, you know how cramped you felt when I lived here. You kept going on about needing 'quality bloke time' and 'lager space'.

GARY
Yeah, but that was last week. I'm changeable. That's why I'm so fascinating.

DOROTHY
It's good for us to do our own thing. What's tragic is that your thing is watching TV, drinking beer and talking to Tony in an unusual homemade grunting language.
Tony comes in. He duly gives Gary a grunt of greeting. Gary responds. Dorothy smiles, vindicated. Tony is carrying an eccentric, very homemade stool made out of sawn-up planks. He puts it down on the coffee table.

TONY
Look. It's brilliant, isn't it?
They look at it.

DOROTHY
You'll have to help us out on what it is.

TONY
A stool. I made it out of wood.
To steady it Tony puts an old crushed lager can under one leg.

DOROTHY
Why?

TONY
Bloke I served in the pub had lots of timber going. Didn't you hear me banging away in the shed?

GARY
Yeah, we thought you'd locked yourself in.

TONY
So why didn't you come and rescue me?

DOROTHY
Because we liked the idea of you trapped in the shed getting more and more desperate. Didn't we, Gary?

GARY
Yes, we did.
Tony looks at them, frowning. He lets it go.

TONY
Yeah, this is good. I'm doing the garden up for us. (*Indicating the stool*) This is one of the stools for my wooden seating area.
Then there'll be a wooden barbecue and a little wooden wheelbarrow with a wooden wheel.

DOROTHY
So wood very much the theme, then, Tony?

TONY
Yes.
Gary has rummaged in Dorothy's overnight bag and taken out a lifejacket. He puts it on, looking ridiculous. Dorothy snatches it off him and throws it back in the bag.

TONY
(*Shifty*) And I'm converting the shed into a sauna.

DOROTHY
A sauna. Really.

TONY
What do you mean?

DOROTHY
So you won't be begging and pleading with Deborah to hop in the converted shed with you dressed only in a tiny towel?

TONY
It hadn't even entered my head!
Gary has taken a shiny yellow hat and a whistle out of Dorothy's bag. He poses with them. Dorothy snatches them from him and throws them back into the case. She picks up her bag and puts it down on Tony's stool. It collapses.

TONY
(*Hysterical*) It's not built for bags!

A few minutes later Deborah leads Tony in. She is distracted with packing her own weekend bag.

DEBORAH
What sort of plans?
From a serious-looking attaché case Tony removes a sheet of paper.

TONY
Well, there'll be a seating area here, with stools – well, stool, now. This will be a barbecue I'm building, you know, for barbies. (*Bad Australian accent*) 'Ere, toss me over one of those chop guys, will you, cobber. And a tinny from me tucker bag.'
Deborah just gives him a confused look.

TONY
And if there's any wood left over I'll probably build a wishing well.

DEBORAH
Don't, Tony.

TONY
Oh, okay.
Deborah glances over at the plans.

DEBORAH
Why have you drawn people lying down in the shed?
Tony peers and strains to look casually at the plans.

TONY
Yeah, I think that's now . . . a sauna.

DEBORAH
A sauna?

TONY
It's a Swedish thing—

DEBORAH
I know. But where's the shed going?

TONY
I'm converting the shed into the sauna. I guess technically it'll be a . . . shedna.

DEBORAH
What happens to all the stuff in the shed?
Tony hesitates, then ploughs on.

TONY
Anyway I'll get it all done over the weekend so by the time you get back from your sailing weekend we can, you know, pop straight into the sauna.
He mimes 'popping in'.

TONY
Apparently you go in, like, all tense, and you come out all floppy.

DEBORAH
Yes, so I hear.

TONY
It's really healthy. After half an hour in the sauna they say you can see the dirt oozing out of you.

DEBORAH
So it sounds just like being in the shed.
Tony takes a moment before realising it is a joke.

TONY
(*Laughing supportively*) Good one. Excellent.

DEBORAH
I might argue with you about this if I thought for a minute you'd actually do it.

TONY
No, I'm serious. I've already decided on the towels, look.
He removes a tiny pink towel from his attaché case and holds it to his waist.

DEBORAH
Little bit on the small side?

TONY
No, I checked in *Sauna* magazine. That's pretty standard.

DEBORAH
Can you really imagine me wearing that?
Deborah is ready with her weekend bag. Tony is pondering at length.

TONY
(*Small voice*) Yes. Very much so.

The next morning: sunny and summery. Tony and Gary are in the garden. Tony is trying cluelessly to adjust the rudimentary table he has constructed. The garden is littered with planks, off-cuts and sawdust. Tony is wearing handyman's overalls. Gary is in shorts and a sun hat.

TONY
Is that straighter now?
They look at the table. It is tipping wildly.

GARY
Yeah.
Gary looks over at the dilapidated shed.

GARY
So you reckon the old sauna's the answer with Deborah, then?

TONY
Yeah. She once said that the heat makes her feel sexy.

GARY
And you reckon she'll still feel sexy lying basically in a warm shed?

TONY
No, I'll kit it out like a proper sauna. You know, with a picture of Scandinavian people.

GARY
What, like Abba?

TONY
Yeah, they'd be good.

GARY
Or a photo of an open sandwich. That's very Scandinavian.

TONY
Right. Hey, you know Abba's made up out of their initials.

GARY
Yeah.

TONY
I was thinking. That means if Agnetha or Anni-Frid had been called Betty, say, Abba would have had to call themselves Babb.

GARY
Mm.
Gary is being distracted by the sight next door of two attractive young women emerging from the back door wearing shorts and bikini tops.

TONY
(*Offscreen*) Or if Benny had been called Sven, they'd have had to have been called Saab.
The two women sit down to read paperbacks on the patio in the sun. Tony remains oblivious to them. Gary wanders over to them.

TONY
(*Offscreen*) Yeah and if Abba had teamed up with the Bee Gees – Barry, Robin and Maurice – they could have called the band . . . Brabbam. Gary?
Gary is leaning on the fence. The women are in their twenties, with northern accents. Paula is more overtly sexy and upfront than Carol. They look up and see Gary struggling at length to come up with a chat-up line.

GARY
So. What are you girls . . . (*Long pause*) doing?

PAULA
Water-skiing.

GARY
Water-skiing? So where are your . . . skis?
He realises his banter is not going well. By this time Tony has come over.

GARY
(*To Tony, under his breath*) Some girls.

TONY
(*To them*) Hi.

PAULA/CAROL
Hi.
Tony seems marginally more self-assured.

TONY
Are your books . . . good books?

PAULA
Yes.

TONY
Good.

GARY
Good.
A long, awkward pause. Gary and Tony try desperately to think of something to say. Paula and Carol gaze back mercilessly.

GARY
Tony and me are great readers. We sometimes read a book a day. Or more.

TONY
One in the morning and one in the evening.

CAROL
Oh, what are you reading at the moment?

They obviously are not reading anything at all.

GARY
(*Inventing*) We're both reading . . . *Hang On To Your Heads.*

TONY
By . . . Christopher Timothy.
Another pause.

GARY/TONY
Have you ever been scuba d—/ So where did you get—
They grind to a halt.

GARY
Go on, mate.

TONY
Okay. Where did you get your shorts? My . . . mum's got a pair just like them.
He cringes at how lame this sounds.

CAROL
Which of us are you asking?

TONY
Either.

PAULA
I thought you said your mum's got some just like them. They can't be like both of them.
Tony freezes.

TONY
(*Conceding*) No.

GARY
Do you want to come to a barbecue tonight?

PAULA
Who'll be there?

TONY
Just us.
Tony and Gary grin over the fence. Paula and Carol gaze back, understandably hesitant.

4. GARY'S FLAT: BATHROOM/KITCHEN

Later, early evening. 'Night Fever' is playing on their radio-cassette player. Shades of Saturday Night Fever *with Tony and Gary vaguely jigging along to it as, squeezed round the bathroom mirror, they get ready for an evening out. Tony is organising his hair. Gary checks his tongue, then smooths his ears down against his head. They spring back. Tony sprays anti-perspirant liberally under his arms. Then he puts it down his trousers and sprays for ages – perhaps as long as ten seconds. Gary stops what he is doing to stare. Tony finally stops. He quickly sprays his bottom.*

GARY
I wouldn't go too near a naked flame for a while, mate.

TONY
Cheers, mate.
As they talk, they continue to pat their faces, pluck hairs and generally prepare themselves.

TONY
Hey, we'd better allocate birds, we can't just go in mob handed. We've got to give them the respect they deserve as two, you know, separate chicks.

GARY
Yeah.

TONY
And I reckon Paula's the right person for me.

GARY
Why?

TONY
Well, it could be her smile.

GARY
Smile, yeah.

TONY
Or the little sort of tinkle in her laugh.

GARY
Little tinkle, yeah.

TONY
But it's probably because . . . she's obviously more up for it.

GARY
Thanks, so while you're off playing 'Whose Bush?' with your sexy piece, I get to chat to her librarian friend about what the weather's been doing?

TONY
Well, I'm a single guy. You've got Dorothy.

GARY
Yeah, well, who knows what she's up to. Give us a handful of your Horn.
Tony hands his traditional huge bottle of Horn aftershave to Gary who splashes it on.

GARY
It wouldn't be the first time one of us has gone away for the weekend and Dorothy's ended up shinning up some bloke's mast and . . . hoisting the giblet or whatever.

TONY
(*Supportively bolshie*) Yeah!

GARY
It was with you.

TONY
Yeah, sorry, mate. You know how it happens – you're sitting on a sofa with a girl and before you know what's going on, you've got your—

Gary blurts out an indiscriminate noise to stop hearing what Tony is saying.

TONY
Sorry.

GARY
Okay.

TONY
All right, you have Paula. I quite fancy Carol anyway, and they say it's always the quiet ones . . .

GARY
No, I'll have Carol.

TONY
Okay.
Tony leaves the bathroom, looking happy. Gary looks annoyed with himself. In the kitchen Tony does some more posing and preening. He calls through to Gary.

TONY
I've had a great day making stuff. I always wanted to be a carpenter. (*After a pause*) I don't mean in the group the Carpenters—

GARY
(*Entering*) No, sure.

TONY
I built this tree house when I was a kid. Only we didn't have a tree in our garden so I had to build it on the ground.

GARY
Well, it's probably safer.

TONY
Yeah.

GARY
I once built my own Wendy House – I called it a Gary House, obviously. I used to have all my meals in there. I didn't want to actually but my parents insisted.

TONY
We started doing woodwork at school, but I was chucked out for nailing Dave Tuffin to the workbench. If it wasn't for that I'd have probably been a carpenter now. (*After a pause*) I don't mean I'd have been in the group the Carpenters—

GARY
No, sure.

5. GARDEN

Dusk. A pan round the garden, taking in various rickety wooden objects that Tony has had a stab at making – another shaky stool, a wobbly bird table, something too badly made to be identifiable and a useless wheelbarrow. Gary and Tony are struggling to get the barbecue alight. It is built on a large but unsound wooden frame. They fiddle around self-importantly.

TONY
What are we doing wrong?

GARY
I don't know. Aren't we supposed to blow on it or something?
Tony crouches down and does so gently for a while.

GARY
What's wrong?

TONY
I've blown it out.
They stare at it.

TONY
Maybe we need to buy some kind of lighter fluid.

6. GARDEN

Sharp cut to minutes later. The barbecue is a raging fireball. Tony and Gary are desperately poking at it with sticks, trying to get nearer. They look round to find Paula standing there, watching. Carol is behind her clambering over the fence.

PAULA
Evening.
Gary and Tony go into hearty, men-in-charge-of-barbecue mode.

GARY
Howdy!

TONY
Pull up a sausage!

GARY
Let's barbie!

TONY
Get down! Yo, chops!

PAULA
(*Eyeing the raging fire*) Shall I blow on it. It looks like it's going out.

GARY
Yup, what we're doing here is letting the flames build up really quite substantially to sear in the juices.

PAULA
Sear them in? I reckon you'll scare the crap out of them.
The fence behind the barbecue is starting to

catch fire. Tony desperately tries to stop the flames spreading by hitting the smouldering fence with a plank of wood. Gary tries to remain calm.

GARY
(*To Carol, sweetly*) Hi.

CAROL
(*Warm smile*) Hi.

GARY
And what Tony's doing here is just going round and nicely ensuring that the barbecue stays under control.
A crack as Tony pushes a whole section of the fence over and puts the flames out by kicking soil over them.

GARY
Thanks, Tony. (*Rubbing hands*) So, let me fix you a beverage. What can I interest you in?
He turns to the drinks, which consist of a large case of lager cans.

PAULA
Have you got anything other than lager?

GARY
Yeah, sure.
From behind the cans of lager he produces a small can of juice.

GARY
Tomato juice.

CAROL/PAULA
Maybe a lager?/Lager, then.

GARY
Okay, you've gone for the lager.
He hands them cans. Tony rejoins them, his face rather blackened with smoke.

TONY
Hi.
Gary is standing closest to Paula, Tony closest to Carol. In a neatly choreographed move, Gary and Tony swap places.

TONY
The burgers are already on.
He looks over at the still raging fire.

TONY
They might be nearly done actually.

GARY
So, welcome! (*Indicating next door*) I tell you, you're an improvement on the last tenant, she was a squalid old tart.

PAULA
That's my auntie actually. She still lives there.

GARY
(*Winsome*) Will you give her my love?

CAROL
We're down staying with her till tomorrow, having a crazy time in London, you know. I can be a bit of a wild child.

GARY
Oh, good.

TONY
What about you, Paula?

PAULA
I've left my husband looking after our kids.
Tony tries to hide his disappointment.

TONY
Oh.
From another angle we see Tony edging towards Carol.

PAULA
He's great. You'd really like him.
Tony makes a definite move towards Carol. There is an unseemly tussle as Gary shoulders him back towards Paula.

7 GARDEN

Later. Night has fallen. The barbecue is now a blackened shell, glowing faintly. The couples have paired off. Paula is with Tony, half way through a huge stack of photos. Tony is struggling to show a polite interest. In front of them are two paper plates, on them some carbonated burgers and nearly raw chicken legs with a small bite taken out of each of them.

PAULA
And this is Jessica on the lawn. It's a bit out of focus, but she looks cute, doesn't she?

TONY
Yes.

PAULA
You can see how she's grown.

TONY
Yes. Upwards.

PAULA
(*Flicking back through pile*) You've only got to compare her with her a few months earlier, shall I go back—

TONY
(*Alarmed*) No.

PAULA
Oh, okay. This is Jessica with Hayley standing by the swing.
Tony glances at the photo and puts his hand out

for the next. Paula makes him wait.

PAULA
And this is Jessica pushing Hayley on the swing.
Ditto. Tony barely looks this time.

PAULA
Here's Hayley pushing Jessica on the swing.
Ditto. Tony takes a massive swig of lager.

PAULA
And this is . . . the swing. Hayley took that.
We pan across to Gary and Carol. By contrast, they are having a good time – so much so that they are tucking into their undercooked chicken legs, their mouths wreathed in blood and bits of raw flesh. Gary is grinning, like a lapdog.

CAROL
I don't mind being tickled.

GARY
No, nor do I.

CAROL
It's like, half way between pleasure and panic, isn't it? Really sexy.

GARY
(*Swallowing*) Mm.

CAROL
Have you ever had an orgasm without being touched?
This is all too exciting for Gary. He shakes his head, then regains the ability to speak.

GARY
So how does that work then?
Carol laughs. Gary remains serious.

GARY
No, I need to be touched. But not always for very long.
Carol laughs some more. Gary, obviously getting tense, checks the others are not looking.

GARY
(*Murmuring, self-consciously*) Do you want to go inside and, you know?

CAROL
Yeah, okay—

GARY
Sure, never mind, I understand, you've got your own sense of right and wrong.

CAROL
I said yes.
She starts to get up.

GARY
Oh. Right.
Carol leads the way indoors. Gary sidles in after her. Tony realises what is happening. He frowns, then watches them go longingly. Paula moves on to a wallet-type photo album and holds it up. It concertinas open, revealing several feet of new photos. Tony whimpers.

8. GARY'S FLAT: LIVING ROOM

Carol enters, followed by Gary, who is nervous but trying to swagger.

CAROL
Nice place.

GARY
Oh, you know, it keeps the rain off.
Carol sits down on the sofa. Gary searches feverishly for a smoochy CD.

CAROL
What work do you do?

GARY
You know the wings of aeroplanes?

CAROL
Yeah.

GARY
I design them.
Gary does a what-am-I-saying? expression.

CAROL
So what's going to be big in aeroplane design, then?

GARY
Everything's going to be . . . fatter and more pointy.

CAROL
Uh-huh.
Gary puts on a CD and goes to perch on the arm of the sofa. He smiles at Carol as suavely and sexily as possible.

GARY
You're a lovely lady, Carol.
'Rabbit' by Chas and Dave strikes up. Gary leaps back to the hi-fi and changes the CD.

CAROL
Gary are you going out with anyone?
Gary does an elaborately dismissive snort.

CAROL
Is it serious?

GARY
Good God, no. No-no, no-no. No, no.

CAROL
Why are you going out together then?
Gary sits down next to her. Some suitably smoochy music comes on.

GARY
I don't want to talk about her, I want to talk about you.
They are getting close. Gary tries a compliment.

GARY
Your lips are like . . . liver.
Carol pauses but decides not to let this put her off. They kiss, lingeringly. Gary does not know what to do with his spare arm. Eventually he leans it on his hip, his wrist cocked elegantly. They resurface.

CAROL
I think we should go to bed.

GARY
(*Overly hearty*) Yup, bed, sounds good. Bed it is. Let's do the old bed thing. Bed-bed-bed!
They head off. At the doorway Gary stops Carol, not able to believe his luck.

GARY
So, why are you doing this? It's a joke, isn't it?

CAROL
No.

GARY
So what's in it for you?

CAROL
Women like sex too, you know, Gary.
They head off for Gary's bedroom, rather sweetly holding hands.

GARY
(*Offscreen*) Oh, do you?

9. STREET TELEPHONE BOX

Later that night. Deborah and Dorothy are sitting on a bench on some attractive shoreline, gazing out at the water. A red telephone box is near by.

DEBORAH
So are you going to phone Gary?

DOROTHY
I don't know. (*Looking at watch*) We've entered the lager zone. He may feel the need to tell me over and over how much he loves me.

DEBORAH
At least he says it. I've had boyfriends who needed nine pints to announce that they think they might be edging towards liking me.

DOROTHY
Gary once rang me from a pub and told me he loved me thirty-two times, I counted.

DEBORAH
Ahh.

DOROTHY
He spoilt it slightly by turning up an hour later with some woman he'd picked up at the chip shop.

DEBORAH
Oh, he's very loyal, though.

DOROTHY
He is, he's lovely, but it's partly because he's no good at talking to women. He's got two chat-up lines – 'Hi, my name's Gary. Can I stand here?' and 'Hello, you smell brilliant.'

DEBORAH
Mm. I overheard one of Tony's – 'Hi, you must be from the planet Top Totty.'
They both wince.

DEBORAH
Mind you, I always think having a steady boyfriend's like owning your own flat. You spend ages making it nicer, and then you realise you want to move—

DOROTHY
(*Joining in*) You want to move, yeah. Then sometimes, I don't know, I look over at Gary in bed, and he looks all sleepy and gentle – his tongue lolling – and I think, I could have done a lot worse.
She means this. They gaze out at the water for a sentimental moment.

DOROTHY
And then I think, How exactly could I have done a lot worse . . .?

10. GARDEN

Tony and Paula are still sitting by the remains of the barbecue. Tony is now doing the talking. He is starting to get drunk. He has perhaps started to whittle, cowboy-style.

TONY
Then Deborah says: 'Oh, you don't love me, you just want to sleep with me.' So I said to her, 'That's nonsense,' and she says 'No, it isn't nonsense.' So I said to her, 'Okay, you're right – sex always gets in the way. So let's get it out of the way, by having it. Then it's had, it's been had, and it's forgotten, out of the way and over.' (*After a pause*) Anyway, that was in 1992.

Tony pauses. We see now that Paula has fallen asleep, wrapped in a blanket.

TONY
And in the autumn of that year – I had quite long hair then, by the way, people used to stop me in the street, and I had to let them touch it – I tried to snog her during *Emmerdale Farm*, as it was then still known—
Tony stops and glances over at Paula.

TONY
Oh, you've dozed off.
He pushes her to wake her up.

TONY
Wake up, Paula. You're in somebody else's garden.
She will not wake up. He lifts her into his arms, then wonders what to do with her. He puts her handbag over her shoulder and totters back with her towards the house. He looks into her serenely sleeping face and goes, 'Ahh.' But after struggling several yards, she is getting heavy. Realising there is a simpler solution, Tony walks over to the fence. He looks around to check nobody is watching, then holds Paula over the fence and lowers her into next door's garden. He peers over to check she is all right, then heads indoors.

11. GARY'S FLAT: HALL/KITCHEN/LIVING ROOM

Tony comes into the hall. He looks around gingerly, calling out.

TONY
Gary? Gary and Carol?
He pokes his head into the living room.

TONY
Carol? Your friend was a bit tired so I popped her back over into your garden. I hope that's all right. We had a nice chat.
He drifts out into the kitchen, still looking for them.

TONY
I'm jealous, Gary. I want to be with someone, like you. In a bed. (*A pause, warning*) I'll tell Dorothy.
The phone goes next to him. He starts, alarmed, and scrambles for the receiver.

TONY
Hello? Oh, hi, Dorothy.
He listens to her. Panicking visibly, he cranes his head towards Gary's bedroom.

TONY
Very quiet. Yes. We had a barbecue, but it was just the two of us so nothing happened at it, and now we've come back inside, and nothing's still happening, very much so.
We intercut with:

12. TELEPHONE BOX

Deborah and Dorothy are in the call box.

DOROTHY
Can I have a word with Gary?

TONY
(*Wooden*) Yes, I'll just get him.
Tony stands there, frozen. He twice shapes up to answer then realises that will not do.

TONY
Why do you want Gary? I know what he'd say, I can say it.

DOROTHY
I've just realised, we've been going out for exactly seven years. I feel a bit, you know, sentimental.

TONY
Oh, okay, I'll tell him. (*After a pause*) So, bye, then.

DOROTHY
Oh, bye. How's the—
Dorothy hears the dialling tone. She hangs up, looking thoughtful and upset.

DEBORAH
Everything all right?

DOROTHY
Yes. Except it sounds like Gary's either passed out, or he's with a woman.

13. GARY'S FLAT: HIS BEDROOM

The next morning. Carol is getting dressed. Gary is lying in bed. He is ultra-languid, content.

GARY
So that was rather jolly, then.

CAROL
Mm.

GARY
I very much enjoyed it.

CAROL
Me too.
A pause.

GARY
Thank you very much.
Carol smiles at Gary's gaucheness.

GARY
I've got this funny feeling. I can't explain it.

CAROL
Guilt?
Gary ponders this.

GARY
Remind me what that feels like.

CAROL
Well, I think you underestimated how strong your relationship with your girlfriend is.

GARY
No no. Horribly shaky. Flimsy.

CAROL
When we were making love you said things like, 'Dorothy lifts her legs up for that,' and 'Dorothy and I tend to save that till the end.'

GARY
Oh, still—

CAROL
And 'You might want to make a kind of mewing noise now, Dorothy usually does.'

GARY
Was that a problem?

CAROL
Well, it did make me feel a bit like an impressionist.

GARY
Oh, sorry. Thanks for having a stab at the mewing anyway.

CAROL
You're welcome.

GARY
It's actually more of a squeak. No, it's a mew. No, a squeak. No, maybe it is a mew. I ought to get a recording of it really. Then I could have played it to you, and you could have—

CAROL
Gary, you're making it worse—

GARY
Worse, okay, I'll stop.
Carol sits down on a chair by the bed. Gary crosses his hands on his stomach. It looks like a psychotherapy session.

CAROL
So, you don't do this often?

GARY
Well, not for lack of offers, I can tell you. If I had a quid for every time I've been propositioned—

CAROL
(*Rapid fire*) How much?

GARY
Two quid.

CAROL
Does that include me?

GARY
(*Trying to remember*) Does it include . . .? Yes, yes, I think so.

CAROL
What happened the other time?

GARY
In the end she had to . . . go downstairs and take more fares or something.

CAROL
Well, I didn't want to mess up your relationship.

GARY
Oh, no, it's pretty robust. It's survived screaming rows, vomitings, mutual humiliation, bollard-throwing . . . And that was just last Tuesday.
He does a hearty laugh. Then sighs.

CAROL
(*Smiling, ready to leave*) So.
Gary gets to his feet. They look at each other affectionately.

GARY
Don't go.

CAROL
I have to.

GARY
You're right. Best to go now and leave it as something perfect.

CAROL
No, I have to go because we're off to Madame Tussaud's.

GARY
Oh, well, that's a good reason too.
It is now strangely formal.

GARY
Have you got everything?

CAROL
Earrings, underwear, slight sense of awkwardness. Yup.
They go to give each other a peck on the cheek. Their faces clash awkwardly, confusion over whether to kiss on both cheeks. Gary watches her go.

14. KITCHEN

Later that morning. Gary is sitting at the kitchen table, looking happy if slightly dazed. Tony is sitting with him, wearing his woodworker's overalls.

GARY
So that's that, then. Ships that pass in the night.

TONY
You didn't just pass in the night, though, did you? You were more like ships that got under the duvet together and gave each other a pretty good seeing-to in the night.
Gary just gazes. A pause.

TONY
You see what I'm saying about ships—

GARY
Yes. Yes.
A pause. Gary smiles to himself.

GARY
She had a little mole.

TONY
You're going to have to pull yourself together, mate. You've committed adultery.
Gary thinks about this, then looks rather proud. He snaps out of his reverie and gets up.

GARY
Oh, well, hey, it happens.
He goes over to the fridge, walking with a John Wayne swagger.

TONY
Still, you had some catching up to do, didn't you, mate—?

GARY
Yes, yes I did.

TONY
'Cos you'd only slept with three women, which is very few—

GARY
Yes, thank you—

TONY
And since you've been going out, Dorothy's gone off with one or two blokes.

GARY
Yes, shut up.
They stand there, thinking.

GARY
You see, I'm not a moral philosopher . . .

TONY
No . . .

GARY
No . . .

TONY
No . . .

GARY
Never have been, probably never will be, not full-time . . .

TONY
No.

GARY
But I reckon it's okay to cheat on your loved one if that person . . . (*Searching for the phrase*)

TONY
Is on a sailing weekend?

GARY
No, if the other person . . . doesn't find out about it. (*Getting up*) Now, I'm not proud of what I've done, so let's keep it under our hats, eh?
Still strutting proudly, he leaves the kitchen, whistling.

15. GARDEN

That evening. The sound of banging. We pan down the garden, past the detritus of the previous night's barbecue, to the shed. The banging stops. The door eventually opens, letting out a shaft of light and billows of steam – very Close Encounters. A figure emerges spectrally amid the vapour – it is Tony, holding a hammer, looking rather hot and moist but happy.

16. COMMUNAL HALL

Later that evening. Dorothy and Deborah come in, carrying their week-end bags, looking healthy. Tony opens the door to their flat.

TONY
Welcome Home!

DOROTHY
Thanks.

TONY
I've finished the sauna!

Deborah looks underwhelmed. Gary appears at the door, cockier than usual.

GARY
Hello, girls.

DOROTHY
Oh, hi.

Dorothy kisses Gary and smiles at him affectionately.

DOROTHY
You should have come with us.

GARY
Oh, I had things to do, you know.

TONY
I had to clear out the shed and everything.
Tony pushes back the door to their flat. The hall is full of the contents of the shed: the lawnmower, several garden tools, a bike, a space hopper, a large amusing roadsign and a few flower pots.

TONY
I've put up pictures of Abba inside.
Tony looks desperate. Deborah relents.

DEBORAH
Oh, okay. I'll go and get ready.
She heads into her flat.

TONY
Me too.
Tony disappears off into the flat. Gary and Dorothy are left alone in the hall. Dorothy looks untypically vulnerable.

DOROTHY
So, how was your weekend?

GARY
Phuff. Mad.

DOROTHY
What's been going on?

GARY
Well, you know, lads will be lads—

DOROTHY
Gary, you seem to want to tell me something.
Gary stops swaggering. Tension.

DOROTHY
I rang last night, but you weren't around.

GARY
Hey, when the cat's away—

DOROTHY
Shut up, Gary.

GARY
Okay.

DOROTHY
What happened last night?
They gaze at each other. Gary realises finally that he can hurt Dorothy.

GARY
I passed out, and Tony slept with a girl from next door.
Dorothy relaxes a little. She smiles.

DOROTHY
Good. I thought maybe you'd, you know . . .

GARY
Good God, no, me?

DOROTHY
If you want to come up I'm, you know, that would be nice.

GARY
Okay, I'll be up.
She heads up to her flat. Gary watches her disappear. He adopts the suave pose of a confirmed womaniser.

DOROTHY
(Offscreen) Gary?

GARY
(*Instantly obedient*) Coming!

17. GARDEN

Pitch-dark night. The back door to the house opens, and Deborah comes out, wearing a dressing gown and holding a towel, ready for the sauna. Tony emerges behind her, wearing only one of the tiny towels he showed Deborah earlier. We follow their gaze to the shed. They start to walk across the lawn towards it.

DEBORAH
Are saunas allowed to have windows?

TONY
Yep. Oh yeah. And we had a bit of a fire yesterday so for safety, I used gas—
A pane of glass shatters, and the shed explodes massively, blowing out the windows. In slow motion we see fire engulf the shed. Shards of wood flutter down on Tony and Deborah through the night sky. In the aftermath Deborah looks upset and very pissed off. Tony looks awkward.

TONY
I'll go and get a broom.

SERIES SIX

SERIES SIX: EPISODE ONE

STAG NIGHT

I had decided this series was going to be the last full one, so I thought we could afford to throw Tony and Deborah together. Useful as Unresolved Sexual Tension is, after five series Tony had suffered enough. He had earned a shag. And I thought that by now it was believable that Deborah would go for him. Evidence was mounting that, like him, she was not coping well with life: she was a depressive who believed in astrology, lived in a slightly twee flat, could not hold down a job for more than a couple of episodes and changed her hairstyle with psychotic regularity. I got a bit of media attention – and questions were asked in my own home – because of Tony's line: 'What's good is how in their thirties women start to lower their standards.'

I rarely use incidents from my own life, largely because nothing ever happens to me. But my girlfriend, Claudia, and I did have a birthing pool for our second baby. Even as I was desperately trying to get the bloody water pump to work as dilation reached ten centimetres, like a true pro I was wondering how I could use this in an episode of *Men*.

The birthing pool was supposed to explode when inflated, but it decided instead to bulge and mutate, which was much spookier and funnier. Then its air feed kept getting clogged, jeopardising the under-water fart jokes. You have not worked in TV until you've heard a director screaming, 'Go farting, go! Now! Where's the bloody farting!?' to a tearful special-effects guy.

Late evening. Gary and Dorothy are sitting up in bed. Dorothy is reading a book. Gary is watching TV. We switch the angle to reveal that the TV is in fact a tiny, four-inch, portable one. Gary chuckles. He squints at the screen, then chuckles again.

DOROTHY
What's on?

GARY
I can't tell, the screen's too small.

DOROTHY
We always said if we became the kind of couple who watched TV in bed we might as well split up.

GARY
Okay. Close the door quietly on your way out.
They concentrate on their TV and book.

DOROTHY
(*Not looking at him*) When I went away on that sailing weekend did you sleep with anyone?

GARY
(*Shifty*) Sorry?

DOROTHY
When I went away did you sleep with a woman?

GARY
How do you mean 'woman'?

DOROTHY
A woman. They're the ones who have what you and Tony call 'chest puppies'.

GARY
Absolutely not! Absolutely not, love! No! No way! Ask Tony—

DOROTHY
You did, didn't you?
Gary hesitates.

GARY
It was the most meaningless thing I have done in my entire life. I might as well have been . . . putting a tortoise into its box for the winter.
Dorothy takes this in, obviously hurt.

GARY
You said yourself, love, sex without commitment is just two people stuffing bits of body into each other. And to be fair, you've done quite a bit of stuffing yourself.

DOROTHY
Gary, let's not do any more stuffing with other people.

GARY
Well, it's out of my system. You could put me in a room full of women wearing only tiny little pants, and I'd probably just want to chat.

DOROTHY
Maybe we should get married.
Gary scoffs, assuming she is joking.

DOROTHY
No, I mean it—

GARY
Yes, why not. Yes. Well, we've tried everything else.

DOROTHY
You know what I mean, though. Perhaps we need something to show that we're serious about being together.

GARY
Or would buying a dog make the same point in a slightly more fun way?

DOROTHY
No, and this might help us relax more together. No more looking over our shoulders for someone better.

GARY
Mm. (*On consideration*) And . . . could we have a proper TV in bed?

DOROTHY
Yes.

GARY
Okay. Let's get married.

DOROTHY
Propose to me properly.
He reaches over and takes a wrapped condom out of a packet. He unwraps it and bites off the tip. They look into each other's eyes affectionately, and Gary puts the rolled-up condom on Dorothy's engagement finger.

DOROTHY
Oh, Gary. You've bought me a ring.

2. LIVING ROOM

A few weeks later. Tony and Gary are sitting in their familiar position on the sofa watching the TV, lager probably in hand. Gary is idly leafing through a copy of Brides *magazine.*

TONY
You know Mark Phillips married Princess Anne in his uniform. Do you reckon he'd forgotten to pick his suit up from the dry cleaners so he thought, Oh, bugger, I'll have to wear what I had on yesterday?

GARY
Yeah. Still, it could have been worse, he could have ended up in a tank top.

TONY
Yeah. And you know Princess Di's dress was all creased when she went up the aisle, I reckon that was because the Queen had been hogging the iron.

GARY
Uh-huh.

TONY
'Cos you're not telling me, when you're nineteen odd, you've got the confidence to barge over to a Queen and say, 'How long are you going to be ironing that . . . top, Queen?'

GARY
No.

TONY
So is Dorothy going to wear white?

GARY
No, she said she was thinking about grey or brown. (*Starting to flick through the magazine again, suddenly he stops and looks more closely*) Wedding-night lingerie.
Gary goes quiet. Tony leans over and stares. Gary quietly puts a cushion on his lap. Tony does the same. Gary turns the page, to even raunchier lingerie adverts. Gary and Tony replace the small cushions on their laps with bigger ones. They reach over for a DIY magazine and a copy of the Radio Times *(e.g. Patrick Moore on the cover) and gaze at them. After a moment they throw aside their cushions.*

GARY
So are you ever going to get married?

TONY
Yeah, I'd marry Debs tomorrow.

GARY
Course.

TONY
Oh, no, I can't make tomorrow, they're doing free teas down at the library.
They watch TV.

GARY
No, it's great, marriage. No more messing around. As the saying goes, You don't go out for a steak when you've got hamburger at home.
They think about this.

TONY
No, the other—

GARY
Other way round, yeah.

TONY
(*Glancing at lingerie ads*) Although sometimes you really want to wolf down a hamburger, don't you?

GARY
Yeah, you do. Still, the great thing is, nothing will change. I'll still be the same Gary, and she'll still be the same unique . . .
He peters out, watching the TV.

TONY
Dorothy?

GARY
Dorothy.

TONY
Gary, if I was a girl, with a girl's bottom and everything, would you marry me?
Gary looks across at Tony, who seems rather needy.

GARY
Yes, mate.

TONY
Ta, mate.
Tony picks up a well-thumbed book: The Best Man's Duties.

TONY
Okay. The stag night.

GARY
The stag night. Can I just say, I don't want anything too sleazy. That's all a bit of a cliché.

TONY
Yeah, right.

GARY
Strippers though, obviously—

TONY
Obviously.
They think about this for a bit. Then they reach for their big cushions and put them back on their laps.

3. DEBORAH'S FLAT

Daytime. Dorothy and Deborah are sitting on their sofa, pensive, an echo of the previous scene. Dorothy obviously lives here too.

DEBORAH
So, are you looking forward to it?

DOROTHY
(*Brave smile*) Yes. I suppose I'm just a bit sad that . . . I'm not marrying somebody else.

DEBORAH
Come on, Gary's sort of special. What other man would offer to pierce his nipples as a wedding present?

DOROTHY
Ton—

DEBORAH
Apart from Tony.

DOROTHY
Mm. Maybe that's the trouble. You never felt that if Humphrey Bogart had married Lauren Bacall in *Casablanca* he would have been happy to spend the honeymoon dabbing disinfectant on his nipples.

DEBORAH
Well, it's a different era, isn't it?

DOROTHY
(*Gloomily*) Yes, it is.
A knock on the door. Deborah gets up.

4. HALLWAY

Deborah comes through and answers the door. For no particular reason Tony has pulled his head inside his jacket and is holding under his arm a ball with a childish face painted on it, as though carrying his own head.

DEBORAH
(*Not reacting*) Hello, Tony.
She goes inside. Tony takes a hesitant step after her, unsure where he is.

5. LIVING ROOM

Deborah comes in, followed by Tony, now looking normal.

DOROTHY
Hi, Tony.

TONY
Hello, Dorothy. Or should I say, Hello, Gary's future little lady.

DOROTHY
Yes, you can say it, but then I'll have to kill you.

TONY
It's weird, isn't it, that in a week's time you'll be Gary's other half?

DOROTHY
I thought we'd already established that Gary's two halves are Homer Simpson and Christopher Biggins.

DEBORAH
So what have you been up to, Tony?

TONY
(*Proudly*) Well, did I tell you Gary's asked me to be his Best Man—

DEBORAH/DOROTHY
Yes, you have mentioned it . . ./Yes, we've gathered that . . .

TONY
I have to organise the stag night. It says in my book (*Getting out his Best Man book*) 'Allow the groom to have fun but take care not to let his behaviour destroy the marriage.' So I wanted to know if there were any things, you know, that you didn't want us to do?

DOROTHY
I'll just leave that to your own conscience, shall I?

TONY
So where does that leave us on sucking whipped cream off a—

DOROTHY
I don't want to know the details!

TONY
Oh, fine. How's the studying going, Deborah?

DEBORAH
Really well.

TONY
Can I help you with any stories?

DEBORAH
We don't do stories, we do essays.

TONY
Oh, okay.

DEBORAH
Tony, put the bra back.
Tony wordlessly takes out of his pocket the bra of Deborah's he has surreptitiously taken out of a washing basket. He puts it back. Deborah gives Tony a long look.

DEBORAH
Tony, you seem a bit . . .

TONY
(*Smiling*) What? Groovy?

DEBORAH
No . . .

TONY
Snazzy?

DEBORAH
No, a bit pathetic. (*With sympathy*) Do you think you're keeping your mind active enough these days?

TONY
Yeah, I work two nights a week at the Crown. That keeps my mind as sharp as a . . . (*Long pause*) stick.

DEBORAH
What do you do during the days?

TONY
Well, in the mornings I tend to sit and . . . just sit. Then I make lunch – a cheese sandwich on Mondays, Wednesdays and Fridays, a baked-bean sandwich on Tuesdays and Thursdays. Then I . . . sit down again, until the Children's Programmes come on, when I have a cup of tea and a biscuit, except on Friday, when I have a small cake.
Everyone takes this in.

DOROTHY
So it's a full life, then?

TONY
Yeah, brilliant.

DEBORAH
Why don't you try to get a regular job?

TONY
Well, routines, you see. I'm no good at routines.

DOROTHY
There's a job advertised on the noticeboard at the hospital, in Obstetrics. They need agents for birthing pools. You work from home.

TONY
What's a birthing pool?

DOROTHY
For women who have their babies at home and want them to be born in water.

TONY
That's a bit weird, isn't it?

DOROTHY
Never mind.

TONY
No, I'm interested.
Tony looks at Dorothy with a self-consciously 'interested' expression.

DEBORAH
Knickers, Tony.
Tony automatically puts some of Deborah's knickers back in the basket and goes back to his 'interested' expression.

6. GARY'S OFFICE

Morning. George is sitting at his desk, Anthea is filing. Gary is finishing an irate phone call.

GARY
Yeah, you too mate, sit and swivel.
He hangs up.

GARY
(*Mildly*) So, that was a no.

George smiles at Gary, who goes back to the Rolodex of phone numbers on his desk.

GARY
Did you have a stag night, George?

GEORGE
Yes. Some chums and I went to see the film *Whistle Down the Wind* starring Hayley Mills.

GARY
That was it, was it?

GEORGE
We had a sherry beforehand.

GARY
Oh, that's all right then. For a moment I thought it might all have been rather tame.
Gary has dialled another phone number.

GARY
(*Into phone*) Hello, is that Colin Attwater? It's Gary Strang, how are you? We met briefly at the Happy Eater just outside Taunton in 1992. Yup. Well, I'm getting married and wondered if you'd like to come to my stag night. How do you know you're busy? I haven't told you when it is. Okay, well, your decision. Bye, specky.
He flicks through the Rolodex again for another number, then looks up to find Anthea and George looking at him.

GEORGE
Are you having trouble finding chums for your stag night?

GARY
No.

ANTHEA
At least you can count on Tony and George.
George smiles again. Gary looks uneasy.

GARY
Oh, I don't think it's something George would enjoy.

ANTHEA
Why, what will you be doing?

GARY
Oh, you know.

GARY
(*Seeing Anthea's expression*) No, you don't, do you? (*Dialling another number*) Well, certain traditions have grown up whereby the groom is allowed to drink alcohol till he bleeds and indulge in, um . . .
George and Anthea are all ears. Gary is grateful for the interruption.

GARY
(*Into phone*) Hello, Simon Watkins! It's Gary Strang, how are you? We met at the Barnet Sales Forum in 1989— Oh, when did he leave? How about you, do you want to come to my stag night? Okay, fine.
He puts down the phone, deflated. George is looking expectant.

GARY
Okay, you can come.

ANTHEA
Oh, thanks.

GARY
Not you.

7. GARY'S FLAT: KITCHEN

Tony has pushed back the kitchen table and spread out what looks like a paddling pool and various accessories. He has the telephone cradled under his chin as he studies an instruction booklet and is meanwhile using a foot pump to inflate the pool. In his other hand he has a leaflet advertising a sleazy nightclub.

TONY
(*Into phone*) Hi, is that Cheeks? Can you tell me if your club would it be suitable for a small group of men on an outing? Great. So do the girls, like (*Voice breaking*) take everything off? Brilliant. And then . . . They . . . (*Joining in*) put them back on again, right. No, fair do's. One of the gentlemen isn't as young as he was so could he be excused individual lap-dancing? He'll be the one in

the cardigan. Okay, bye. See you tomorrow.
Tony hangs up but is still pumping. He looks at various accessories: a large metal strainer, plastic tubing, surgical rubber gloves . . . The pumping appears to be making no difference. He gives up and finds an electric pump. He tries to get a hand in the rubber gloves but fails. Unable to resist, Tony attaches the glove to the electric pump. The glove balloons to a huge size and explodes. Impressed, Tony looks around for something else to inflate. He attaches the pump to the pool. It quickly inflates. Gary comes in, from work, in time to see the pool explode.

GARY
(*Taking in his stride*) Nice one.

TONY
Ta, mate.

GARY
What are you doing?

TONY
It's this new job I've got, hiring out these pools to, like, knocked-up women.

GARY
That's a bit weird, isn't it?

TONY
That's what I said.
They look at a long piece of plastic tubing.

GARY
What's that?

TONY
I don't know. Umbilical cord?

GARY
Mm. (*Holding strainer*) I suppose that'll be for . . . straining the baby.
They nod cluelessly and gaze for some time at the various items.

TONY
I'd better go on the training course—

GARY
Yeah.
They wander around the kitchen.

TONY
So, I've arranged tomorrow night.

GARY
Great. (*Lewd smile*) So will it be, you know?

TONY
(*Laddish*) Yeah.

GARY
(*Sober*) Without being, you know.

TONY
(*Sober*) No.

8. COMMUNAL HALLWAY

The following evening. Deborah emerges from her flat, wearing elegantly understated clothes. She checks herself in the hall mirror while she waits.

DEBORAH
(*Shouting upstairs*) Dorothy!
Tony and Gary come out of their flat. They are dressed for a real lads-on-the-town night out, Tony in a shirt open to the navel etc. Deborah gazes at them.

GARY
What?

DEBORAH
Just a wild guess, are you off on your stag night?

GARY
Few quiet drinks, yeah.

DEBORAH
Tony, I hear you took the job Dorothy told you about. That's great.

TONY
Well, I was thinking over what you said about stretching my mind.

DEBORAH
I just think you've got this potential.

TONY
Yeah, because the mind's like a loaf of bread, isn't it? It needs the yeast of experience to rise—

GARY
Excuse me, excuse me,
can we stop being sensitive here? It's my stag night.

TONY
Sorry, mate.

DEBORAH
A friend of mine's interested in a pool actually. Let me give you her number.
She gets a pen out of her bag and writes a telephone number on Tony's hand. He watches with his usual blind adoration.

TONY
Do you want to come with us?

GARY
No! No girls!

DEBORAH
I can't come anyway. It's Dorothy's hen night.

Dorothy arrives finally, also elegantly dressed. The contrast between the couples is complete. Dorothy gazes at the men.

DOROTHY
Where are you two off to, Las Vegas?

GARY
(*Very macho*) Listen, I'm not apologising, on my last proper night of freedom, for doing what men do. It's a stag night, so I'm going to be acting like a stag.

DOROTHY
(*Affectionately*) Don't overdo it, though, will you, love?

GARY
(*Suddenly meek*) Course not, love.
They kiss and leave.

9. GARY'S FLAT: LIVING ROOM/KITCHEN/HALLWAY

The next morning. Gary is waking up on the sofa. He bears the scars of the night before: a furry mouth, terrible hangover, the odd smear of gaudy lipstick. He struggles to an upright position.

SALLY-ANNE
(*Offscreen*) I don't understand why we couldn't use your bed.
We – and Gary – realise there is a half-dressed woman sitting up on the other end of the sofa. From her businesslike attitude and appearance it looks more than possible that she is a prostitute. She has obviously slept with Gary on the sofa. Gary's reaction is fear and some confusion.

SALLY-ANNE
Which is your bathroom?

GARY
It's the quite small room with the bath in it.
Sally-Anne gives him a blank look and gets up to find it herself.

GARY
Hello, I'm Gary.

SALLY-ANNE
Hi, Gary.

GARY
Can I just warn you that I'm getting married in a few days.

SALLY-ANNE
Oh dear!

GARY
What I mean is, you're lovely, as far as I remember, but we probably haven't got a long-term future.

SALLY-ANNE
Well, that's my life in ruins.
She heads for the bathroom.

GARY
(*Calling after her*) Only fair to warn you. (*To himself*) Oh, God, what have I done?
Gary gets to his feet, his blanket draped round him and heads for the kitchen. He has to wade through empty cans of lager and remnants of takeaway food. In the kitchen, Gary finds Tony face down on the floor near his door, asleep in last night's clothes.

GARY
(*Nudging Tony with his foot*) Tony, Tony.
Gary stands there, looking apprehensive and cornered. Tony starts to stir.

TONY
You should have put me to bed.

GARY
Don't you start.
Tony gets up. He looks down at his utterly crumpled trousers and shirt.

TONY
Do I look creased in this?

GARY
Dorothy mustn't find out I had sex with a woman last night.

TONY
Why?

GARY
Because . . . it's not nice! How would you like it?

TONY
Well, it would have been great, but I could only afford one woman.

GARY
You paid for her to sleep with me?!

TONY
To be fair, mate, why do you think she was here when we got in?

GARY
I thought she'd seen me and followed me home, in a nice way.

TONY
Why would she have done that?

GARY
Because she liked me!

TONY
Oh, I'm sure she liked you, but not in a sexual way. (*Confused*) No, hang on a minute—

GARY
Dorothy won't marry me if she finds out I slept with a prostitute the weekend before our wedding.

TONY
You said you wanted to enjoy yourself.

GARY
Not that much!

TONY
You could have said no.

GARY
Of course I couldn't have said no! (*After a pause*) No wonder she kept calling me 'Dearie'.

TONY
Sorry, mate.
An awkward silence. Tony looks contrite.

TONY
What was it like . . .?

GARY
I can't remember! I don't think she was very . . . involved—

TONY
Well, she wouldn't be, would she? It was a job of work to her.

GARY
I know.

TONY
She didn't get any pleasure out of it—

GARY
(*Snapping*) I know.

TONY
When I rang round I tried to pick someone you'd like. Her parents come from the West Country, like yours.
Gary is too troubled to react.

TONY
Dorothy said she didn't want to know what you were up to—

GARY
Believe me, she'll want to know if I spent the night with some tart— so, I gather you're familiar with Central Somerset.

Sally-Anne has emerged from the bathroom, ready to leave. Gary is all polite smiles.

SALLY-ANNE
Well, more Devon really.

GARY
Uh-huh. Well, that was great! Can I ask you to leave fairly quietly . . .?
He ushers her towards the hall, then stops. From Deborah and Dorothy's flat we hear a sound, e.g. of footsteps or a floorboard.

GARY
In fact, don't take this the wrong way, but would you mind leaving under a blanket?

SALLY-ANNE
Yes, I would.

GARY
I'm sure I could find you a nice one.

SALLY-ANNE
I'm going now.

GARY
Okay. Ah, actually the front door's been playing up. We've been using the front window to get in and out. It slides up quite nicely—

SALLY-ANNE
Bye.

GARY
Bye.
She opens the flat door and leaves. Gary ducks out of view in case anyone's in the hall. He goes back into the living room. Tony is standing there, looking subdued.

TONY
Sorry, mate.
Gary goes over to the half-drawn curtains and peeks out.

10. STREET OUTSIDE THE HOUSE

Gary peers cautiously out of the curtains, anxious not to be seen. He watches until Sally-Anne has disappeared from view. He is about to turn away when he sees a man emerging from his front door. Gary watches as the man – young and good-looking, more hunk than brain surgeon – turns back and looks up at the upstairs window. All bedroom-eyed, he smiles, waves goodbye and walks away. Gary looks extremely suspicious.

11. GARY'S FLAT: LIVING ROOM

Gary turns back and staggers, slightly dazed, away from the window.

TONY
What's the matter, mate?

GARY
It was a man.

TONY
(*Tutting*) Honestly, you pay good money and you get a bloody transsexual!
Gary stares at Tony.

GARY
No. It looks like Deborah or Dorothy slept with a bloke last night.

TONY
I hope it was Dorothy.
Gary looks furious.

TONY
Sorry, mate.

12. DEBORAH'S LIVING ROOM

Later that day. Dorothy leads Gary in. She busies herself tidying up the flat. Suppressed tension.

DOROTHY
So, how was last night? Anybody throw up?

GARY
George felt dizzy at one point, but I think that was from clutching his train timetable too tightly.

DOROTHY
Were you stripped naked, covered in treacle and left tied to railings?

GARY
No, that's dying out. How was your evening?

DOROTHY
Oh, lots of girl talk. Relationships, holiday plans, hair care.

GARY
So, what did you get up to?

DOROTHY
Oh, you know – pub, restaurant, club, the usual. What about you?

GARY
Oh, you know – circus, laundrette, bat cave, the usual.
Slightly tense laughter from them both.

GARY
Where's Deborah?

DOROTHY
She spent the night with her friend Claire.
Dorothy sees from Gary's expression that he knows what has happened.

DOROTHY
Gary, I've got a confession to make.

GARY
Really.

DOROTHY
I had a . . . thing last night. I'm sorry. It was completely meaningless.
Gary wonders how to react.

GARY
I guess that's that, then.
Hurt, he leaves. Dorothy bites her lip.
Gary returns.

GARY
Well, you'll be pleased to hear that I also had someone to stay last night, someone rather special.

DOROTHY
How is Clive?

GARY
No, actually, not Clive, actually. A woman. And out of respect for you I wouldn't let her sleep with me in our bed. Now that is commitment.

DOROTHY
At least when I have a silly little fling I don't claim it was like putting a tortoise away in its box for the winter.
They glare at each other.

DOROTHY
Well, this whole idea's obviously a terrible mistake, isn't it.
Dorothy walks away, out of the room. Gary waits for her to come back. She doesn't.

13. DEBORAH'S FRIEND'S HOUSE

Afternoon. A large bedroom in a fairly trendy house. Tony is on his knees, demonstrating the birthing pool, like a slightly larger paddling pool with sides up to four feet high, which he has half inflated. Beside him stands Deborah's timid friend, who is extremely pregnant. Tony now knows more or less what he is doing.

TONY
So the water supports and soothes during the stages of labour, providing drug-free relief and a calming environment.

DEBS' FRIEND
Oh. Good.

TONY
Do ask any questions. I have done a course.

DEBS' FRIEND
Okay. Um—

TONY
I love Debs, you know.

DEBS' FRIEND
Yes, she said you were quite keen. So what temperature should the water be maintained a—

TONY
It started out as something sexual, but over the years it's kind of changed into a general obsession.
Tony goes out. Deborah's friend experiences a twinge. Water starts to gush out of the tube into the pool.

TONY
(*Offscreen, calling through*) I was beginning to give up to be honest, but what's good is how in their thirties women start to lower their standards.

DEBS' FRIEND
(*Wincing*) Tony, can you come in—

TONY
(*Coming in*) It's like footballers, isn't it? They start off by only wanting to play for Manchester United, but by the time they're Debs' age it's kind of, Ooh, Stenhouse Muir, brilliant. Or, Well, actually, I've always had a lot of respect for Basildon Athletic.
Oblivious, Tony fiddles with the hose while Debs' friend feels her contractions.

TONY
Because in the end— Are you all right?

DEBS' FRIEND
It's starting, Tony.
Tony takes full control of the situation.

TONY
What is?

14. GARY'S OFFICE

Later that afternoon. Gary is at his desk, smoking, in a bad mood, banging drawers open and shut. George is sitting at his desk, still shell-shocked from the stag night.

GARY
Oh, snap out of it, George, that's what happens on stag nights. It was a nightclub with a few nice topless ladies, not the last days of Sodom and Gomorrah.

GEORGE
What's happening to the world?

GARY
Oh, I think there have always been places where men are encouraged to bury their faces between women's jiggling breasts.

GEORGE
I didn't know where to put myself.

GARY
If it's any consolation, she was as embarrassed as you to find you'd wedged your briefcase in her cleavage.
George has got up, still dazed.

GEORGE
I'm going to buy some biscuits.
He exits as Anthea comes in.

ANTHEA
Is he any better?

GARY
A bit. He's stopped doing that scary humming. (*Sighing, upset*) Anthea, can I confide in you?

ANTHEA
Of course.
Anthea makes to sit down on a chair.

GARY
What are you doing?

ANTHEA
Sorry.
She puts the chair back and stands.

GARY
George is right, these days everything's cheap and sleazy and dirty.

ANTHEA
I thought that was what you liked.

GARY
It is, but . . . maybe I'm moving away from all that. I mean, look at George, he's got his picture of his wife on his desk, he's got a packed lunch with the special cold sausage he and Marjorie like, he's got a model village set out in his loft. I want that.

ANTHEA
Maybe he'll let you borrow it.

GARY
No, not the model village, the lifestyle, the togetherness.

ANTHEA
I'm sure you and Dorothy can patch it up.

GARY
No, we can't. It's all spoilt. It would be like marrying . . . a great, rutting rabbit.

ANTHEA
What have you fallen out about? I know soft furnishings are often a flashpoint when you're setting up home.
Gary wonders whether to break it to Anthea.

GARY
Yes, we've fallen out over soft furnishings.

15. DEBORAH'S FRIEND'S HOUSE

Still later that day. Shaky point of view, hand-held camera. Someone tossing aside an old-fashioned bicycle and entering the house at a run. We dip into the kitchen – deserted – then up the stairs. As we go we start to hear the sound of a baby crying. We go on to a landing, then push open a bedroom door. The baby's crying is louder still.

MIDWIFE
(*Offscreen*) That sounds like a healthy pair of lungs.
We finally locate the still only half-inflated birthing pool. Tony and Deborah's friend are sitting in it in two feet of murky water. Tony stops crying like a baby.

TONY
Thanks.
An emotional Tony is cradling a very new-born, slightly suspicious looking baby as the mother looks on, exhausted but happy.

TONY
It's a boy!

DEBS' FRIEND
No, it's a girl.

TONY
It's a girl!

16. DEBORAH'S LIVING ROOM

The next day. Tony is with Deborah.

DEBORAH
What are they going to call him?

TONY
They're thinking about Tony.

DEBORAH
Oh, how nice.

TONY
Or Bilbo.
They both do not-sure-about-that grimaces.

DEBORAH
God, you must be so proud.

TONY
Well, you know.

DEBORAH
You did everything right. I'm really proud of you, Tony.

TONY
(*Bashful*) Oh, stop it.

DEBORAH
No, really.

TONY
Stop it.
Deborah looks at him with affection. They are sitting close together.

TONY
Actually, don't stop.

DEBORAH
No, I'm bored now.
To their mutual surprise, they kiss.

DEBORAH
Anyway . . .

TONY
Anyway . . .
They part, slightly dazed.

DEBORAH
So how are we going to get them back together again?

TONY
Who?

DEBORAH
Dorothy and Gary.
They kiss again, then Deborah pulls away.

DEBORAH
I can't concentrate until this is sorted out.
Tony instantly breaks off, businesslike, calling out towards Dorothy's bedroom:

TONY
Dorothy, we're going downstairs to sort this out.

17. GARY'S FLAT: KITCHEN/LIVING ROOM

A little later. The living room is empty. The door to the hall opens, and we see Deborah's hand pushing Dorothy in. She enters grudgingly. Gary is pushed into the room from the kitchen by Tony. Gary and Dorothy look at each other coolly.

GARY
So, are we going to get married?

DOROTHY
I don't really see much point, do you?

GARY
No.

DOROTHY
At least we can agree that sleeping with other people doesn't do anyone any good.
Gary hesitates.

GARY
No.
Tony stands in the kitchen listening. Deborah joins him from the hall. We cut back to the living room.

GARY
Still, I don't suppose I'm the first bloke to send his old policeman out on special duties the week before his wedding.

DOROTHY
That's the difference, isn't it. I apologise, but you have to boast about it.

GARY
I wasn't boasting.

TONY
(*Offscreen*) He wasn't boasting.

DOROTHY
Tony, get out.
We cut back to the kitchen. Deborah walks Tony away from the living room. They stop at the door to Tony's bedroom.

DOROTHY
Get right out, Tony—

TONY
I'm going.
We cut back to the living room. Gary and Dorothy weigh each other up.

18. TONY'S BEDROOM

Moments later. Tony and Deborah stand there, waiting, conscious there is a bed in the room. Deborah peers into a plastic bag on the bed.

DEBORAH
What's that?

TONY
Oh, nothing.
Tony tries to grab the bag, but Deborah manages to remove its contents.

DEBORAH
(*Amused*) Put it on.

TONY
No.

DEBORAH
Come on – you've bought it, put it on.
Tony reluctantly puts on a brand-new doctor's white coat. He has already lined up pens in the top pocket.

DEBORAH
You don't think you're taking your medical triumphs a bit seriously?

TONY
It's just to wear about the house, you know.
Deborah is amused. She and Tony are on the bed. They start to kiss, then roll on top of each other.

DEBORAH
(*Muffled*) Your row of pens is sticking in me.

TONY
Sorry.
They kiss some more and are edging towards love-making when Deborah stops them and sits up.

DEBORAH
We can't do this. Our best friends' lives are being decided in the next room.
Deborah gets up. Tony whimpers with frustration. She leaves the room.

19. KITCHEN/LIVING ROOM

Tony joins Deborah. They listen out. Silence. They walk quietly across to the living room. Dorothy and Gary are semi-naked on the sofa, in a flagrantly sexual position.

TONY
So, how's it going—

DOROTHY/GARY
Get out!

20. LIVING ROOM

A birthing pool, unoccupied but filled with water, is set up where the sofa normally is. Tony and Gary suddenly burst up out of the water, spluttering, and go into their homemade synchronised-swimming routine – grinning fixedly and doing various would-be balletic moves. We switch to a view of the pool from a ceiling-mounted camera, watching four legs flail about, the odd arm etc. They possibly end with some synchronised lager-drinking and lager-can tossing. They stop and recover their breath.

TONY
And they say synchronised swimming doesn't deserve to be in the Olympics!
They reach over and put a raft made of empty lager cans into the water. On it is the tiny battery TV, which they now watch.

TONY
So Debs and I have agreed that we shouldn't rush into it.

GARY
Well, it's only been five years, hasn't it? You're not warmed up.

TONY
It's like you and marriage, isn't it? You've taken a cool, calm look at marriage and decided that, Yes!

GARY
Yes . . .

TONY
Yes.

GARY
Yes—

TONY
Yes. Marriage is for you.
As they stand there air suddenly bubbles to the surface behind them. Neither draws attention to it.

GARY
I was reading in *Brides* magazine, the average wedding costs eight thousand pounds.

TONY
How much is yours going to cost?

GARY
Seventy-three quid.

TONY
After you're married is Dorothy going to take your name?

GARY
No, I think she's quite attached to Dorothy.
More air bubbles up to the surface.

TONY
I wouldn't mind changing. (*Musing*) Tony Minogue.

GARY
Gary Minogue.

TONY
Tony Minogue.

GARY
Gary Binoche.

TONY
Tony Binoche.
Air bubbles to the surface, on and on intermittently for a spectacularly long time. A pause.

GARY
Shall we get out . . .?

TONY
Yeah.

SERIES SIX: EPISODE TWO

Wedding

I played Clive, Gary's Only Other Friend, though we got a proper actor in to do his voice. Writers should be made to take (very) small parts once in a while, to be reminded how hard acting is.

The episode has an attack of sentimentality two-thirds of the way in when I realised I was being horribly mean-spirited about weddings, which are, after all, joyful occasions for which people spend years saving up. I liked the idea of getting everyone who had been in the show back for this episode, but it didn't really work out. The episode overran so Neville, Tony's fellow stallholder in Series Two, was squeezed out. We also filmed a whole scene with Dorothy's mother (scene 16, played by Delia Lindsay), which had to be cut. I was sorry to see it go, not least because it suggested one of the reasons why Dorothy had stayed with Gary for so long: because it really annoyed her scary mother.

I like jokes involving banal objects and am childishly fond of the moment when the toast bursts out of the wrapped-up toaster. If I have one sitcom writing tip to pass on it is this: make sure there is at least one visual joke in every scene. Even if it is not funny it will create a welcome diversion if the dialogue is rubbish.

Biggest studio laugh in all of *Men Behaving Badly*: Tony's 'I was just wondering what colour your bush is.' I still want to know who changed my 'Wee Willy Winkie' to 'Betty Boothroyd'.

1. GARY'S FLAT: TONY'S BEDROOM

Daytime. Tony is half-dressed in a smart – if slightly spivvy – suit. He is reading from a series of index cards, woodenly but with enthusiasm.

TONY
When Gary asked me to be his Best Man I was reminded of the joke: How many Best Men does it take to change a lightbulb? Two. The first to remove the old lightbulb, the second to have sex over and over again with the prettiest bridesmaid. (*To himself*) That'll work.
He turns over to the next index card.

TONY
Not very popular at school . . . (*Flicking to next card*) . . . lying face down in a gutter . . . (*Next card*) . . . foot stuck in a chicken . . .
He turns to the next card.

TONY
But, seriously. (*Wooden gesture*) Gary's a great guy, and in Dorothy (*Another gesture*) he has met a lovely person, though scary. I once slept with Dorothy, but we all laugh about it now . . .
He looks up. A warm glow lights up his face.

TONY
Ah. Weddings. Romantic.

2. KITCHEN

Meanwhile, Gary is also half dressed in his wedding suit, his hair uncombed. He is smoking as he disconsolately rehearses his speech, scrawled on a crumpled scrap of paper.

GARY
So, thanks for coming. I'd like to thank my wife, who is as lovely now as . . . who is lovely, though perhaps not quite hitting her 1990 peak, when she was of course considerably younger. Still, we've all lost some bounce since then . . .
Gary morosely lays the speech aside. Tony enters. He comes up behind Gary and ruffles his hair exuberantly.

TONY
Hello, Groomy!

GARY
Don't call me Groomy.

TONY
Hey, have you noticed, I'm the Best Man, right – of all the men I'm the best. Whereas you're just a groom, like a stable boy, brushing a horse. (*Gary looks at him heavily*) So that's an interesting little . . . thing to say.
Tony nods, rapidly losing confidence.

GARY
I don't want to get married.

TONY
Why?

GARY
I haven't slept with enough women.
Tony looks at his watch.

TONY
Do you want to try to squeeze one in before—

GARY
No, no!

TONY
—no, no, course not.

GARY
Dorothy doesn't deserve that.

TONY
No.
Gary sneaks a look at his watch, wondering.

GARY
No.

TONY
Listen, you wouldn't be human if you didn't have doubts. You're marrying an amazing lady who thinks the world of you.

GARY
You're quoting from that Best Man book again, aren't you?

TONY
Yes, I am.

GARY
It's true though, isn't it? On his deathbed a man never looks back at his life and says, 'Ooh, I really wish I'd slept with fewer women.'

TONY
Mm. Wouldn't it be terrible if your last words on your deathbed were something really stupid. Like . . . 'Can you get your bottom off my foot?'

GARY
Yeah, or 'Will you video *The Bill* for me?'

TONY
Or 'Who farted?'

GARY
Or 'Is there any more cake?'

TONY
That's why I've got it all planned. My last words are going to be: 'Don't be sad. I did it My Way.' The problem is I might say it, then need a tissue or something so my last words would be, 'Can I have a tissue, please?' Unless I then repeated my previous last words. Or I suppose I could just mime, 'Can I have a tissue please?' And that would be my last mime.
Gary is lost in thought.

TONY
An-y-way. What were we talking about?

GARY
I want to call off the wedding.

TONY
Listen, think of Dorothy upstairs, getting into her dress, all smiley.

GARY
(*Encouraged*) Mm.

TONY
And when you get down to it, what's the point of sleeping with lots of girls? It's like eating pies, isn't it? Okay, it's nice to eat a few varieties of pies, experiment with pies, but in the end, you know where you are with your old pie.
Gary nods.

TONY
You . . . won't tell Dorothy I compared her with a pie?

GARY
No.
Won round, Gary smiles ruefully. Tony gives him a playful punch. Gary returns it. Gary starts to put on his tie.

TONY
Did I tell you? At the pictures last night Deborah let me put my hand on the top bit of her bottom. (*Voice cracking*) After five years, I think we might be going to sleep together.
Jealous and frustrated again, Gary gives up knotting his tie and throws it down.

GARY
You see? That could be me. I haven't slept with enough women!

TONY
Cheer up, mate. Open your wedding present.
Tony hands a wrapped gift to Gary. Gary cheers up slightly again. He touches the side, and two slices of cold toast burst out of the top, through the wrapping paper.

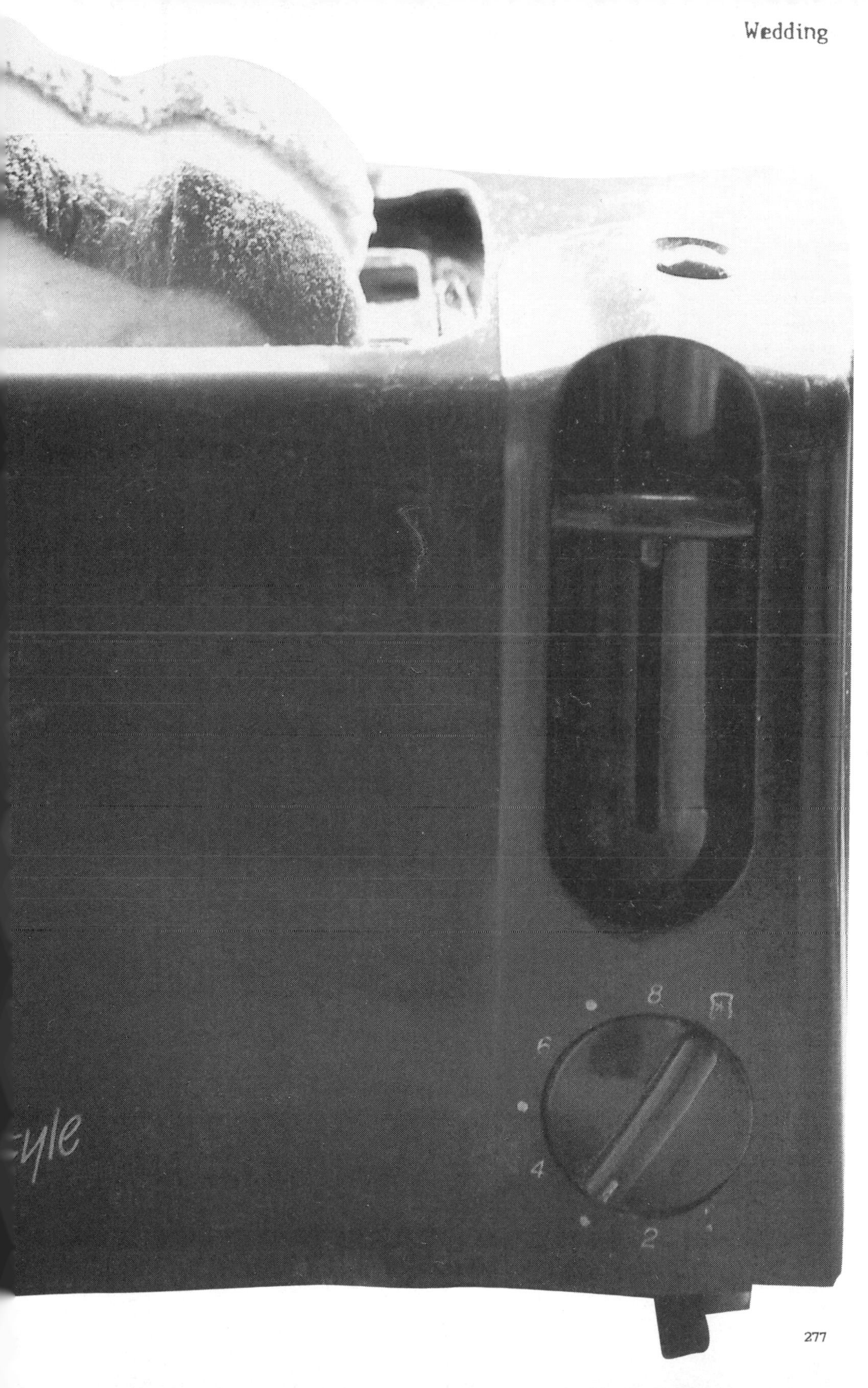
8
6
4
2

TONY
I put some toast in it for you.

3. DEBORAH'S FLAT: HALLWAY

A few minutes later. Deborah opens the door to Tony. She is in a bathrobe, still getting ready.

DEBORAH
Hi, Tony.

TONY
Hi, Debs.
She gives Tony a quick kiss. He is strangely excited.

DEBORAH
Anything happening down there?

TONY
(*Dry mouthed*) Very much so.

DEBORAH
We're running a bit late up here. I'm having a shower. I think Dorothy's in the living room.
Deborah exits to the bathroom. Tony ponders, then starts to take off his shirt with a view to joining Debs in the shower.

DEBORAH
(*Offscreen*) Tony?

TONY
(*Freezes*) Yes?

DEBORAH
(*Offscreen*) It wasn't so long ago you would have tried to get in here with me. I'm really glad you've changed.
Tony puts his shirt back on. He heads for the living room.

4. LIVING ROOM

Dorothy is sitting on the sofa, looking much as Gary did – disgruntled, hair over her eyes etc.

TONY
Hello, Dorothy.

DOROTHY
Hello, Tony.

TONY
I just came up to say I couldn't get little white roses for the buttonholes, so we've got to make do with dandelions.

DOROTHY
How symbolic.
Tony sits down next to Dorothy on the sofa.

TONY
So, today's your big day. How're you feeling?

DOROTHY
Giddy. Giddy with happiness.

TONY
Giddy. Good.
Tony has brought Dorothy a wrapped present. He hands it to her.

TONY
Your wedding present. I got one for Gary too. In case you split up.

DOROTHY
Thanks.

TONY
Be careful with it. There's toast in it.

DOROTHY
Right. (*After a moment*) I'm sorry, it's just, when I was twelve I imagined more than a wedding in a concrete Registry Office with a few gherkins passed round afterwards in a pub.

TONY
They're the big gherkins, the nice ones.

DOROTHY
(*Looking him in the eye*) 'They're the big gherkins, the nice ones.' Why don't I find that reassuring?

TONY
You did leave all the arrangements to us.

DOROTHY
I know. I suppose if I'm honest, I don't want many people to know I'm getting married.

TONY
Why?

DOROTHY
Because I'm marrying Gary!

TONY
Oh.

DOROTHY
Even my parents have refused to come.

TONY
Why?

DOROTHY
Because I'm marrying Gary!
Dorothy's eyes mist over. Tony hesitates, then gathers her affectionately in his arms.

TONY
Clive's going to be recording it. You can send them a video. If you get a long enough tape you can record a movie on the end.

DOROTHY
Mm, how about that movie *God Almighty, What the Hell Happened to My Life?*

TONY
Oh, I don't know that one.
Dorothy continues to look upset. Tony casts around for something to say.

TONY
There's always *Free Willy* . . .

DOROTHY
Yes, there is that.
Tony narrows his eyes, not understanding. Dorothy still looks unhappy. They sit there. Tony tries again.

TONY
So, do you think Debs is going to let me hump her?

5. STREET OUTSIDE THE REGISTRY OFFICE

We are in camcorder mode and will be for almost all the wedding scenes. The operator, Clive, is at best adequate. The camcorder has a powerful zoom, which Clive is not afraid to use. We pick up dialogue in bits and pieces. We are watching a tacky TV programme, very shaky. The zoom pulls back to reveal a TV shop window, then pans rapidly across to a very unglamorous Registry Office. A modest blue-saloon car, incongruously decked with wedding ribbons, pulls up. Gary and Tony get out.

GARY
Hi, Clive!

CLIVE
(*Offscreen, muffled*) Hello.

GARY
That's a suit, is it?

CLIVE
(*Offscreen*) What's wrong with it?

GARY
It's bright green.

CLIVE
(*Offscreen*) What's your point?
Gary looks put out before a sharp cut to the next scene.

6. A ROOM IN THE REGISTRY OFFICE

The camcorder pans round the room, which is crowded with guests, half of whom have dandelions in their buttonholes. We recognise George, Anthea and Tony's ex-colleague Neville. The panning stops as the camcorder hits one of the guest's heads. He glares.

CLIVE
(*Offscreen, grudging*) Sorry.
Gary and Tony are at the front. Dorothy and Deborah enter, looking stylish, and go to the seats Tony has kept for them. Gary and Dorothy smile at each other, a touch ruefully. The registrar and her assistant appear.

REGISTRAR
Good morning, everyone. Especially Michael and Julie, if you could step forward.
A couple in the front seats stand up and step forward.

REGISTRAR
So, we are here today to join in marriage—

TONY
Um, excuse me. We're next.
Tony goes forward to talk to the registrar. We pan round to Gary, Dorothy and Deborah, who look awkward. Behind are Gary's ploddy middle-aged Uncle Steven and Aunt Anne.

UNCLE STEVEN
He's gone up to see the woman . . . She's telling him something . . . She's looking in her little book . . .
The camcorder jerks back to the front. Tony coughs to get his wedding party's attention.

TONY
Um, I'm afraid—
A guest moves his head, blocking the camcorder's view and sound. Clive unceremoniously knocks the head aside with the camera. A muffled 'Ow'.

7. STREET OUTSIDE REGISTER OFFICE

Jagged cut to a few minutes later. Gary and Dorothy's wedding party are milling about. Tony is explaining into the camcorder, reporter-like.

TONY
So it's at one o'clock instead of eleven. You see, Gary and me wrote down one one, I mean a one – you see, it's confusing – and somehow—
Bored, Clive switches from Tony in mid-sentence to Deborah and Anthea.

DEBORAH
So what's Gary like at the office?

ANTHEA
Oh, he's lovely really.

DEBORAH
Dorothy told me he locked you out on a ledge once.

ANTHEA
Yes, he did.

DEBORAH
And pinned you up on the noticeboard?

ANTHEA
Yes.

DEBORAH
And made you call him 'Gary, Prince of Darkness' for a week.

ANTHEA
(*Face clouding*) Yes—

8. OUTSIDE THE REGISTRY OFFICE

Sharp cut to the programme in the TV shop window, then shaky pull-back to the thinning group outside the register office. Gary is clapping his hands to get everyone's attention.

GARY
(*To the gathering*) Okay, so we'll all pop quickly back to the Crown, where the reception's being held – keynotes very much simplicity and homeliness. There's limited room available in our official cars, but you're very welcome—
Guests are already drifting towards the official wedding cars. Gary joins in the stampede. Clive realises belatedly what is happening, then starts to run towards the cars, camcorder running.

9. OUTSIDE THE REGISTRY OFFICE

Cut to moments later. Clive is trying to get a lift. He goes between the three cars: Tony and Gary's car contains them, the driver and Gary's 'friends' Peter and James. Clive bangs on the window, but they will not let him in. Same story at the girls' car, already containing Deborah, Dorothy, her two best friends, Cath and Imogen, the driver and an aunt. He rushes to George's small car, which is crammed full with George, Anthea, Neville, Uncle Steven and Aunt Anne. It is already driving off. The camcorder pans round. All the cars have left.

CLIVE
(Offscreen) Bastards.

10. THE CROWN: SALOON BAR

From the point of view of the camcorder we enter. The guests from the three cars are already milling. Others are arriving. The pub is only very slightly more festive than usual. The camcorder zooms in on Ken – unshaven, in a vest – having a quietly urgent conversation with Gary.

KEN
I'm not ready, mate.

GARY
Ready with what?

KEN
I haven't washed my nibble plates.

GARY
Where are the wedding decorations?
Ken turns to a sad-looking tinsel banner that reads NGRATULATIO.

KEN
There. Quite weddingy.
Gary's humourless uncle and aunt are hovering.

GARY
Uncle Steven, Auntie Anne. Thanks for coming. Did you bring a present?

UNCLE STEVEN
Yes, it's a juicer.

GARY
Well, we've been together eight years, we can always do with a bit of help!
The uncle and aunt just stare blankly.

AUNT ANNE
I don't understand.
Jerky pan across to Dorothy, talking to George.

DOROTHY
I was hoping to meet Marjorie.

GEORGE
Yes, she wanted to come, but she's busy rehearsing *Dr Zhivago* for the local dramatic society.

DOROTHY
Gosh, isn't that a bit ambitious?

GEORGE
No, they've reset it in Guildford.

DOROTHY
Right.

GEORGE
So that cut down on sets.
An awkward pause.

DOROTHY
Piss off, Clive.

11. SALOON BAR

Half an hour later. People are standing around, being served drinks by a morose waiter. Clive stands half hidden and eavesdrops on Gary, who looks anguished again.

GARY
I want to be faithful to Dorothy, and I love her and everything, but I just feel I haven't . . . seen enough women naked . . .
We come round a pillar and find he is talking to Anthea, who looks terrified.

GARY
I haven't touched enough wom—

ANTHEA
That's a lovely suit, Gary.

GARY
I haven't lain on top of en—

ANTHEA
I'm not sure I'm the right person – maybe I should get Tony—

GARY
Yes, where is he? You see, he's off somewhere with Deborah. It's not fair.

ANTHEA
Well, I'm sure every man, and woman, feels the same when they're about to get married. Maybe not on the day itself, but . . .
Gary is distracted. We follow his gaze. He is watching Dorothy's attractive friend Imogen adjusting her bra. We zoom in as though from Gary's viewpoint, into slow-motion, a genuinely erotic moment.

GARY
I can't do it.

ANTHEA
What?

GARY
Get married. I'm sorry.
He brushes past Anthea and heads for the door. Clive follows, knocking guests out of the way where necessary. But at the door he catches sight of a female guest some yards away with a nice bottom. He stops and zooms in on it. We hold it in vision for several seconds.

12. OUTSIDE THE CROWN

As seen by the normal camera Gary walks out without looking back. A few yards on he finds Dorothy coming the other way. He turns on his heel, but Dorothy has seen him.

DOROTHY
Where were you going?

GARY
Um. I left some Rolos in the car.

DOROTHY
So you've changed your mind?

GARY
No. No. No. No. Marriage, that's the grown-up thing to do, cement our love, get a certificate.

DOROTHY
I meant changed your mind about getting the Rolos.

GARY
Yes. I probably eat too many anyway.
A pause. Dorothy gives Gary a brave smile.

DOROTHY
It's scary, isn't it.

GARY
Yes, you eat one, and you want the whole packet. Zjhummm. Gone.

DOROTHY
No, getting married's scary.

GARY
Oh, yes.
An awkward pause.

DOROTHY
So, are your parents going to make it?

GARY
No, they had to go to the village fête.

DOROTHY
Is your Dad organising the 'Guess the Weight of the Vicar' competition again?

GARY
No, they're changing it this year, apparently.

DOROTHY
What to?

GARY
A 'Guess the Width of the Vicar' competition.

DOROTHY
Uh-huh.
An awkward pause.

DOROTHY
Shall we go back in?

GARY
Yeah.
They wander slowly back towards the pub, hand in hand. A taxi passes by. Unseen by Dorothy, Gary puts out his hand to hail it, but it doesn't stop. Gary gives a two-finger salute.

As seen by the normal camera Tony comes in, followed by Deborah.

DEBORAH
She looks so nice, doesn't she?

TONY
Yeah. Really nice.

DEBORAH
I hope she's okay.

TONY
(*Caring*) Mm, she'll be okay. (*After a pause*) Who?

DEBORAH
Dorothy.

TONY
Oh, yeah. You look great too.

DEBORAH
Thanks.
He pulls Deborah gently to him.

DEBORAH
(*Nervous*) New aftershave.

TONY
Yeah.

DEBORAH
I thought you only wore Horn.

TONY
Yeah, but this bloke was selling Toss down the market, so I bought half a pint.
They kiss.

DEBORAH
I thought we were coming back for the wedding cake.
They kiss passionately.

DEBORAH
It looks like you've worn me down.

TONY
Oh, sorry.
With his fingers he puckers Deborah's lips again to full plumpness.

TONY
So, how come you turned me down for so long?

DEBORAH
Well, I always liked the look of you, I just had a problem with the things you did and the things you said.
Tony looks uneasy.

DEBORAH
I suppose if Dorothy's prepared to marry Gary I might as well give you a try.
They smile at each other dreamily.

DEBORAH
What are you thinking about?

TONY
(*Without thinking*) I was wondering what colour your bush is.

DEBORAH
What?

TONY
I was wondering . . . what car rubbish is.

DEBORAH
What does that mean?

TONY
(*Swallowing*) Nothing. It's nonsense. Let's have a look at the cake.
Tony gets the cake out of the fridge. Deborah stares at it: a reasonably accurate, lifesize little dog in white icing, standing on four legs.

DEBORAH
So . . . a wedding cake in the shape of a dog.

TONY
Dorothy said she didn't want anything too traditional. We asked for an owl, but the lady said it would look stupid. (*Picking up two little figures*) There's the little bride and groom riding him, look.
They are close again. They kiss. Tony eases down the zip of Deborah's dress.

DEBORAH
We should get back, or we'll miss the wedding.

TONY
But we've been waiting five years.

DEBORAH
Exactly, so let's not rush it. We can't do it in ten minutes.

TONY
Speak for yourself.

DEBORAH
Tony, let's wait till after the wedding.

TONY
Oh, no! You'll change your mind, then I'll have to wait another five years.

DEBORAH
I won't, I promise.

TONY
Write down that you promise you'll make love with me.

DEBORAH
No—

TONY
Okay, just sign.
Tony has scribbled on a scrap of paper. He pushes it across the table to Deborah.

DEBORAH
(*Sighing, reads*) 'I promise I will make love with Tony shortly after Gary and Dorothy are married.'
Tony looks desperate. Deborah takes pity and signs. Tony looks delighted. He rests his hand on the cake dog. The back legs collapse so the dog looks like it is sitting.

TONY
Sit. Ha.

14. REGISTRY OFFICE

A pan round the room in camcorder mode. All Gary and Dorothy's guests are there again, merrier and less well behaved, vaguely reading the Order of Service. Clive lingers on Neville, who is talking to George.

NEVILLE
I got married in Vegas. You don't have to book in advance, you just turn up with a girl, and they'll marry you. In fact if you don't have a girl, or she's backed out, they'll supply you with one—
Clive puts the camcorder down on his knees for a second, then holds it out and points it back on himself: for a joke he has covered his face with the Order of Service, held in place by his glasses. His suit is a violent green. He swings the camcorder back to the guests. He zooms in for a super close-up of one of Gary's ears.

15. REGISTRY OFFICE

Jagged cut to a little later. The registrar and her assistant are standing out front. The registrar looks a little pale.

REGISTRAR
Good afternoon, everyone. Especially Gary and Dorothy, if they could step forward.
Gary and Dorothy, smiling shyly, step forward.

REGISTRAR
So, we are here today to join in marriage—
Her voice fades out as Clive swings the camcorder round to the window. He zooms in on (e.g.) a busker over the road, whose music is just audible. A policeman comes up and obviously asks the busker to move on. Meanwhile we pick up one of the wedding guests, who is focusing on Clive himself.

UNCLE STEVEN
(*Offscreen*) Now he's pointing it out of the window, I don't know what he's doing . . .
The busker tries to run away, and the policeman runs after him, out of shot.
Clive reluctantly pulls back and pans back across the room. He hits the guest in front on the head again – a cry of pain – then refocuses on Tony, who is smiling at Deborah goofily. Tony gives her a coy little wave.

REGISTRAR
(*Offscreen*) . . . the ring. (*Pausing, annoyed*) The ring, please.

TONY
(*Realising*) Oh, the ring.

16. REGISTRY OFFICE

Cut to minutes later. Dorothy and Gary are slightly glazed as the service continues. The registrar now looks decidedly ill.

REGISTRAR
Forsaking all others. Do you, Dorothy take Gary to be your lawful wedded husband, to have and to hold, from this day forward?
A big moment. Dorothy exchanges a look with Gary. She turns to say 'I Do,' but the registrar is holding her head.

DOROTHY
Are you okay?

REGISTRAR
No, I feel a bit faint.

DOROTHY
Have a sit down.

REGISTRAR
I'll be all right in a minute.

17. REGISTRY OFFICE

Cut to minutes later. The registrar is now lying down on the floor, tended by Dorothy. Tony is to one side having a quiet word with the registrar's assistant.

TONY
You don't understand. They have to get married now.

ASSISTANT
We may have to ring round for another registrar.

TONY
Prop her, up and I'll read it. I'm a good reader.

ASSISTANT
No, the ceremony has to be carried out by a properly licensed official.
Tony looks anguished. He calls round to the room.

TONY
Anyone here got a marrying licence? It's an emergency.

18. OUTSIDE THE REGISTRY OFFICE

Still in camcorder mode Gary is addressing the assembled guests, again.

GARY
So the situation is that we'll go back to the pub and have the reception before the wedding, while they sort out another registrar. As before, there's limited room available in our official cars, but you're very welcome—
The race is already on to get to the cars. Clive runs, camcorder on. Clive is close to getting in when he runs into a parking meter and is sent flying. The camcorder continues recording on the ground for a few seconds. Cut to moments later. As before, Clive has picked himself up and is trying to get a lift. The cars, all full, turn him away and drive off.

19. THE CROWN: SALOON BAR

In camcorder mode, a little later. The guests are politely drinking and eating from plates of rather basic-looking nibbles. Dorothy is trying to be a good host. We circulate or cut between the guests. Cath is talking to Peter and James.

CATH
So, are you friends of Gary or Dorothy?

JAMES
Gary. Actually we don't really know him. We work in the off-licence.
A painful silence. The camera lingers on them, waiting for something. Clive's hand appears and takes a half of lager off a tray. Seconds later the glass is replaced on the tray, now empty.

JAMES
Um.
Finally the camcorder moves off, lingering on Tony, who is in a corner, nervously pacing and rehearsing his speech. George and Anthea are sitting down talking.

ANTHEA
I wonder why people throw confetti.

GEORGE
I suppose throwing anything heavier than little pieces of paper might cause a nasty eye injury.

ANTHEA
Yes, because even rice can get in your eye, can't it.

GEORGE
Oh, yes, a little sharp grain of rice.

ANTHEA
I used to cook the rice first, then throw it. Although then it tends to stick on clothing. And in hair.
A long pause. They look into the camcorder.

ANTHEA/GEORGE
Piss off, Clive.
Gary's aunt, Anne, has been cornered by a typically earnest Ken.

KEN
All I'm saying is, in a straight fight, your squirrel could take on a beaver and win. Squirrel against a cat is an interesting one.
As Ken is talking Clive's arm appears, holding a full glass of wine.

KEN
If the squirrel goes in strong at the beginning, you'd be mad to bet against him. I once saw—
Ken is distracted as Clive's hand shakily puts his empty glass back on the tray. Clive's hand emerges again, and he snatches Aunt Anne's hat off her head. Clearly becoming drunk, Clive runs around with it playfully, waving it about. He runs into Dorothy, who gives him her best damning stare.

CLIVE
(*Offscreen, slightly slurred*) Sorry, Dorothy.

20. THE CROWN

Cut to later. Gary and Tony are having a conversation they obviously believe is private. Clive eavesdrops on them. He is swaying slightly.

GARY
I reckon: blonde. No question.

TONY
Well, you say that, but it's a tricky customer, pubic hair.

GARY
Absolutely.

TONY
I'm sticking my neck out here, but I'm going to say brown with a hint of ginger.

GARY
Well, that's just crazy talk.

TONY
Well . . .

GARY
Anyway, it's all a bit academic, since, let's face it, you'll never get Deborah into bed.

TONY
(*Smugly*) Really. Okay. Well, it's your day, mate. Hey, so, you're going to be married in a couple of hours!
Tony looks wildly enthusiastic. Gary tries to put on a brave face.

GARY
Yeah.
The camera pans round, and we see a depressed Dorothy gazing at Gary. We pan back to Gary, who tries to shake off his gloom.

GARY
Hey, one last cheese impression as a bachelor. I've been working on it.
He scoops up a handful of crisps, crushes them slightly in his hand. He rubs his head against his arm, letting flakes of crisp fall as though from his head.

TONY
Parmesan! Brilliant.
We pan back rapidly to Dorothy, who has been watching this, more depressed than ever. She picks up her jacket and bag and discreetly heads for the door. Clive starts to follows her, not entirely stable. A small child suddenly snatches the camcorder and runs off with it, our point of view now at knee level.

CLIVE
(*Offscreen*) Come back, you little bastard.

Still from the boy's viewpoint, we run into the gents and to frowns from the one guest drying his hands in the hot-air drier. The boy is finally caught by a flailing green-sleeved arm, followed by the sound of Clive unceremoniously slapping a child.

21. OUTSIDE THE CROWN

Now in normal camera mode Dorothy runs into an impressive, smartly dressed middle-aged woman. Awkwardness.

DOROTHY
Oh, hello, Mum.

MOTHER
I decided to come.

DOROTHY
Thank you. Actually, I was—

MOTHER
Just because we hate Gary that's no reason to—

DOROTHY
Oh, don't start.

MOTHER
You could have had Sebastian Lord.

DOROTHY
Mum, he's the gayest solicitor in North London. He drives a pink car.

MOTHER
Well, you obviously like a challenge, or you wouldn't be going out with Gary. He still calls me Dave, you know.

DOROTHY
Yes, I do. Look—

MOTHER
What about Ken Ooms? I'm sure I could persuade his girlfriend to stand aside.

DOROTHY
(*Sighing*) Right, that's it. I'm going back in. (*To herself*) I knew there was a reason I was marrying Gary.
Dorothy heads back into the pub.

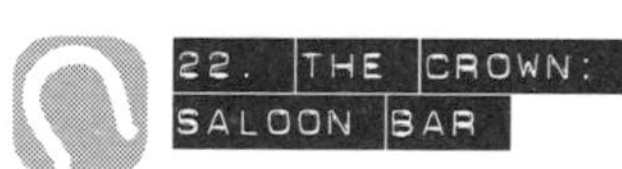

22. THE CROWN: SALOON BAR

Still in normal camera mode Dorothy re-enters the bar, brushing past Ken, who is talking to (e.g.) James.

KEN
So what have we got: a badger and a fox would give an otter and a beaver a sound wupping. Fox and beaver beats ferret and squirrel . . .
Gary appears.

GARY
It's time for the speeches. Where's Clive?
We see Clive emerging from the gents, his face obscured by the camcorder, which he has to his eye. He has a pint in his other hand. We cut to camcorder mode, Clive's point of view. Panning round the room rather wildly, he finally focuses on Gary, who looms up threateningly in his viewfinder.

GARY
Speeches, Clive, speeches.
Gary takes Clive's pint out of his hand and, for good measure, slaps him. The camcorder swings round to a nervous Tony, who is holding his index cards, about to make his speech.

TONY
Hello!
Various 'Hellos' are returned.

TONY
So, who would have thought that Gary (*Turning to another card*) would get married!
Polite laughter. Tony turns to the next card. Deborah gives Tony a smile of encouragement.

TONY
It seems like only yesterday that he was wondering whether to stay in and watch *Blue Peter*, or put on his flares and go on the pull. (*Pause*) In fact, it was yesterday. (*Trying again*) In fact it *was* yesterday.
More obliging laughter. Tony smiles, encouraged by this response, then drops his index cards into his pint of lager. Cut to a little later. Tony is trying to make sense of his soggy, smudged index cards. He is severely flustered. He teases apart two stuck cards and tries to decipher one.

TONY
How many Best Men does it take to change a light bulb? (*Peering*) Ten. The first to . . . (*Giving up*) I'll come back to that.
He pulls off the top index card. With a loud unsticking sound.

TONY
Gary wasn't very . . . popple at . . . scroom?
The pub telephone goes. Widespread relief. Dorothy is nearest the phone and answers it. The others start talking and drinking again. Tony tries to carry on, but nobody is listening:

TONY
Ah, I've got it: wasn't very popular at school . . .
He gives up. Clive's swaying behind the camcorder has become alarming. He now slowly keels over. The camcorder is pointing along the floor, at shoes. Camcorder mode ends. Cut to moments later. In the foreground is the slumped figure of Clive, passed out. It is Gary's turn to get to his feet.

GARY
My turn. I'm not going to attempt to top Tony's speech.
We see Tony, standing to one side, looking ashamed. Deborah tries to cheer him up by putting her hand on his sleeve. He pulls his arm away, inconsolable.

GARY
Thanks for coming, some of you from as far away as Fulham. I just want to say, Dorothy and I have been together for many years, so we must be doing something right. And she's as lovely now as she was then.
He means it, giving Dorothy a warm smile. Dorothy stands up, looking serious.

DOROTHY
I just want to say something.
A hush. Gary looks worried, Dorothy guilty.

DOROTHY
Um. Hello everyone, I'm afraid the phone call was from the Registry Office. They can't marry us today.
Ahhs of disappointment from the guests. We focus on Tony, looking pale and panicky.

DOROTHY
Never mind, we'll fit it in later on in the week. We can still cut the cake – (*Pointedly*) the cake in the shape of a dog – and have a great party.

23. THE CROWN

Some time later. The party is in full swing, people really enjoying themselves. A glitter ball is on, making even the pub look festive. Gary and Tony are leading the dancing, a semi-organised group knees-up. Tony suddenly finds himself facing Deborah.

TONY
(*Shouting, to be heard over the music*) Debs, you know you promised to sleep with me after Gary and Dorothy got married. What happens now they're not married?
Deborah looks enigmatic, teasing Tony. They get mixed up in the melee of dancers. All the guests are involved except Clive, who remains slumped on his chair in a corner. Of the cake only the dog's head remains, a slightly macabre sight. We fade out on a high, wide shot of everyone having a good time.

24. OUTSIDE THE CROWN

The end of the party, guests starting to leave, tired but happy. Gary finds himself alone with Dorothy for the first time. They hold hands and watch the other guests talking and horsing around.

GARY
(*All smiles*) It wasn't the Registry Office on the phone, was it?

DOROTHY
No. I didn't want to disappoint anyone. We can tell everyone in six months that we weren't ready to get married.
Gary looks pleased. He and Dorothy hug, a romantic moment.

DOROTHY
Well, it's been eight years. We don't want to spoil everything by rushing into it.

GARY
Mm, and this way we get to keep the wedding presents.
Tony appears, his chirpy self again.

TONY
Your car's ready.
Dorothy heads off, smiling at Gary.

TONY
Ahh. All happy?

GARY
Yeah. (*Dreamily watching her*) We're not getting married.

TONY
(*Confused*) Ah. Good.

GARY
I think Dorothy's enough for me, you know.

TONY
Mm.
He and Gary watch the other guests. Gary sees a piece of paper sticking out of Tony's pocket. He sneaks it out.

GARY
(*Reading*) 'I promise I will make love with Tony even though Gary and Dorothy haven't got married.'
Tony looks coyly proud.

TONY
You're not jealous.

GARY
Signed: Wee Willy Winkie.
Tony snatches the paper and stares at it. Gary wanders off.

TONY
Oh, no!
Dorothy is already in the car, ready to leave. Gary joins her. Anthea throws some confetti. Cries of 'Have a nice time' ring out as the chauffeur starts the car. Tony looks a little downcast until Deborah comes up and kisses him enthusiastically. As the car pulls away, to whoops and cheers, Gary watches Tony and Deborah kiss, his mouth open in surprise. Dorothy brusquely shuts his mouth with her hand. Tony watches the car disappear from view. He turns to Ken.

TONY
Um, Ken, I thought you were going to decorate the car.

KEN
I did.
George's car pulls up. It is festooned with blown-up condoms, tin cans trailing on strings and good-luck messages including HAPPY SHAGGING and JUGS ♥ DONKEY. George is in the driving seat, with Anthea beside him. They both look ill at ease.

KEN
Oh. Sorry.

25. GARY'S FLAT: KITCHEN

Later. Tony and Deborah come in. A moment's awkwardness.

DEBORAH
So, here we are.

TONY
Yep.
After some hesitation, they kiss.

DEBORAH
Shall we go to bed together?
Tony swallows.

TONY
(*Gravely*) No, I don't want to.
Deborah looks shocked and disappointed.

DEBORAH
Oh.

TONY
Ha ha. See, that's what it's like!
They kiss and edge towards Tony's bedroom.

26. COUNTRY LAY-BY

Wide shot of a road with a telephone box in the foreground. Gary and Dorothy's chauffeur-driven car appears.

GARY
(*Offscreen*) Pull over, pull over!

DOROTHY
(*Offscreen*) Why?
The car turns into the lay-by.

GARY
(*Getting out*) I promised I'd tell my Mum and Dad how it went.

DOROTHY
(*Calling after him*) I know what you're up to, you know.
Gary goes over to the call box. Some intercutting between Gary in call box and:

27. TONY'S BEDROOM/KITCHEN

Tony and Deborah have just got into bed and are about to make love. The bedroom door is half open. The phone rings. Tony and Deborah both groan slightly, then ignore it, going into an embrace. The sound of the answering machine clicking on.

GARY
(*Offscreen, telephone distort*) Hello, this is Gary, checking in. Tony? Oh. Just wondered if you and Deborah had, you know.
Without interrupting his kiss, with one hand Tony rips his radio-alarm out of the socket.

GARY
(*Offscreen, telephone distort*) So, ring me if you've got anything to report. Especially on the question of what colour Deborah's—
The radio-alarm, flying through the air, hits the door and shuts it. Gary is silenced. We cut to the deserted kitchen.

GARY
(*Offscreen, telephone distort*) Anyway, it's not important.
A pause, then the sound of someone banging on the door of the phone-box. Gary calls out:

GARY
(*Offscreen, telephone distort*) I'm coming!
Half way through the closing credits dancing we fade into Tony and Deborah in bed. Deborah is asleep, but Tony is sitting up in bed, a look of dazed wonderment on his face. We hold his expression until the end.

JUGS ♥ DONKEY.

HAPPY SHAGGING

SERIES SIX: EPISODE FOUR

WATCHING TV

It is an unwritten rule that sooner or later a sitcom writer must attempt an episode that takes place in real time. This is mine. If I'd had any sense I would have seen the potential of a bunch of people slumped watching the TV for half an hour and spun it off into The *Royle Family*.

Star Trek might seem an uninspired choice of programme, but there are reasons why I chose it rather than *University Challenge*, say: *Men Behaving Badly* is watched all over the world, and I couldn't bear to think of viewers in Majorca or Croatia scratching their heads over jokes about Jeremy Paxman.

I don't usually sub-contract dialogue, but Dorothy and Deborah's pet hates about men were supplied by my partner, Claudia. Like Gary, I was a bit surprised to find 'asking if he can kiss you' on the list, but that's the beauty of the opposite sex, you never know what the hell they're thinking.

Note the reappearance of the word 'shed', vying with 'bush' for comedy supremacy in this series . . . Another failed attempt to introduce a catch phrase: Tony's 'I feel like a king.' I was sure that would catch on . . . Difficult Endings, part 13: the last line we ended up with, 'Beam Us Up, Scotty' is all wrong, but it's too late to change it now . . .

1. GARY'S FLAT: LIVING ROOM

Early evening. Gary and Tony are watching Star Trek. *Dorothy is slumped, snoozing. Tony is especially perky.*

TONY
On the Starship *Enterprise*, on the bridge, when no one's looking do you reckon they swivel round in their chairs really fast?

GARY
Yeah.

TONY
Maybe not Mr Sulu.

GARY
Oh, I think he'd be the first to swivel. Knowing old Mr Sulu.

TONY
Or maybe there's times, like late on a Friday, when they all put the kettle on and do it together. You know, all swivelling.

GARY
Yeah. Or they have a special word that any of them can shout – probably, 'Swivel!' – and that's the signal to all swivel for a few minutes.

TONY
Mm. Like at our school. If the teacher left the room, and one of us called out 'Shoes!' we all had to swap shoes. We tried it with 'Pants!' but some of the girls objected.

A pause. They watch TV.

GARY
How do you think they clean their windscreen?

TONY
The big windscreen at the front?

GARY
Yeah.

TONY
They've probably got . . . a device.

Dorothy has opened her eyes. She watches them blankly.

GARY
Although, it's not like you go on a long space trip, and you get back and there's loads of midges stuck to your windscreen.

TONY
No, although there is space debris, isn't there.

GARY
Yeah, what is that?

TONY
Bits of . . . old helmet? Little run-over space creatures? You get a dead space-badger coming at your windscreen at warp factor two, that's going to leave a nasty smear.

GARY
Good point.
Tony and Gary peter out as they realise Dorothy is gazing at them pointedly. She gazes back at the TV.

TONY
How many ears are there in space?
No answer.

TONY
Anybody know how many ea—?

DOROTHY
(*Shouting*) No, I don't know, how many ears!

TONY
Three. The right ear, the left ear, and the final frontear.
They ignore him.

TONY
'Space, the final frontier'. Makes you think. Wouldn't it be weird if it wasn't the final frontier, if there was space and space and space and space, space space space, and then . . . milk. Milk going on for ever and ever. So then it would be, 'Milk, the final frontier'.
Now even Gary is looking at Tony.

DOROTHY
Tony, you know you were depressed a lot before you somehow persuaded Deborah to sleep with you?

TONY
Yes.

DOROTHY
Would you be depressed again, please?

TONY
No, I can't. I feel like a king.
They watch the TV.

TONY
Do you reckon they've got a glove compartment?

GARY
What?

TONY
Do you reckon Kirk's got a glove compartment just in front of him there, like in a car?
Gary is about to answer Tony.

DOROTHY
Don't answer him, Gary.

TONY
A glove compartment would be handy on a long journey, wouldn't it, on a five-year mission. For a really big tin of travel sweets. Or a map. Or a manual.
Dorothy quietly despairs.

TONY
Or, as it's a glove compartment: a glove.
A little knock.

DOROTHY
(*Almost pleading*) Please come in, please.
Deborah enters. She and Tony kiss.

DEBORAH
What's happening?

TONY
Dr McCoy's gone mad from injecting himself with Cortrazine by mistake, and he's running wild on the ship with his eyes all stary.
Deborah sits down. A moment, then Tony leans across to her.

TONY
I was just saying to the others, a glove compartment would be handy on a long journey, wouldn't it, on a five-year mission.
Depression settles on Deborah.

DEBORAH
Why do we have to watch this?
Dorothy has obviously heard Gary's answer before.

GARY/DOROTHY
(*Reciting in unison*) Because it's a classic. It's as fresh now as . . . when it was made thirty years ago . . .
Gary gives Dorothy a look.

GARY/DOROTHY
(*Continuing, in unison*) . . . anticipating many technological advances.

DEBORAH
(*Already very depressed*) Let's go out.

GARY
Too late, we've phoned for the pizzas.

DEBORAH
How do you know what I want?

TONY
Thin-crust Peking duck with extra raisins.

GARY
If it takes more than forty-five minutes to deliver we get it free. We figured it would take them valuable seconds to find some raisins.

DEBORAH
I'm not eating that.

TONY
Okay, love, you can have my Four Seasons.

DEBORAH
Thanks.

TONY
With peach.
They watch the TV.

DEBORAH
Who's he, he's quite sexy—?

TONY
(*Instantly*) Shall we turn this off and play a game?
The others groan.

TONY
No, it would be good. How about 'Postman's Wok'? The snogging-and-cooking game.

DOROTHY
How about 'Dead Tony'? The three-people-sitting-on-Tony's-head-until-he-passes-out game.
Tony gets up.

TONY
Don't say anything interesting while I'm in the toilet.

Tony exits to the hall. They watch the TV in silence. Tony comes back in, obviously to check.

TONY
You haven't said anything inter—

DEBORAH
No!
Tony leaves again.

DEBORAH
Tony's quite . . . chirpy.

GARY
Mm.

DEBORAH
It's nice, isn't it?
A long pause.

GARY/DOROTHY/DEBORAH
Not particularly./Horrible./Maybe not.

DOROTHY
We could play that game Clive told us about.
They look at each other.

DEBORAH
Alright.

GARY
Okay.
Tony re-enters, at speed. He glances at his watch. Distant sound of the toilet flushing.

TONY
Seventeen seconds. Do you know how I was so quick? I reach over and wash my hands while I'm, you know, and I start flushing a bit before I've finished. So I can zip up and go immediately.
He sits down.

TONY
(*More to himself*) That's how I do it so quick.

DEBORAH
Tony, we've decided to play a game.

TONY
Okay.

DOROTHY
How about the one where we all go to our rooms and dress up as historical characters, using whatever we have in our rooms. Then we come back here and judge who has the best costume.

TONY
It's a bit girly, isn't it.

DEBORAH
No, it's a good game.

TONY
Okay. Great, let's do it.
He gets up, followed by the others. They exit in the direction of their rooms. Seconds later Deborah, Gary and Dorothy re-enter and sit down. They watch the TV. The sound of the Star Trek teleporter machine.

DEBORAH
What's happening now?

GARY
They're teleporting down to the planet to find Bones.
Deborah tries to understand this.

DEBORAH
What do they want bones for?
Gary just looks at her damningly then back to the screen.

DEBORAH
(*Whispering to Dorothy*) What do they want bones for?

DOROTHY
Bones is the name of the doctor.

DEBORAH
(*Whispering*) Why's he called Bones?

GARY
Because he's a doctor!

DEBORAH
Is he a bone doctor?

GARY
No.

DEBORAH
So why did they call him B—?

GARY
I don't know! Where've you been for the last thirty years?

DEBORAH
(*Snapping*) Out.

GARY
This is part of our cultural heritage, it's taught a whole generation.

DEBORAH
What?

GARY
Science. The Klingon language. How a crew made up of different nations can work together in harmony. Particularly when there are no bloody Italians.

DOROTHY
What is Lieutenant Uhuru wearing?

GARY
There's nothing wrong with looking a bit sexy.

DOROTHY
It's a bit of a worry though, isn't it? Probably the most popular TV show ever, and they give the only woman a desk job and a skirt that only just covers her knickers. What's that taught a whole generation?

GARY
She probably just forgot to pack more than one skirt. You're going on a five-year mission, you've got to cancel the papers and stuff, you're bound to forget something.
Dorothy gives Gary a pitying look.

DEBORAH
That must be boring, mustn't it, wearing the same thing every day. Do you think they could add accessories?

GARY
What?

DEBORAH
You know, a nice belt. Or a little waistcoat.

GARY
Oh, so you haven't seen the episode 'Scottie Goes Shopping for a Nice Little Waistcoat'?

DOROTHY
Maybe they had that thing like in some offices where on Fridays you can wear something more casual.

DEBORAH
Mm. They'd probably want to wear something a bit looser.

DOROTHY
Yes, that's quite clingy, that fabric, isn't it.
Gary now gives them a pitying look. They watch some more.

GARY
(*Amused*) When you first see the show, when you're young, you always think the captain's log's an actual wooden log, don't you, which he keeps in his office.

DOROTHY
You thought the captain's log was an actual wooden log?
Dorothy and Deborah smirk. Gary realises his confession was a mistake.

DOROTHY
So how would that have worked then? Did you think he wrote on the log?

GARY
(*Tight-lipped*) I don't know.

DEBORAH
Did he just have one log or did he have lots of logs all piled up?

DOROTHY
Or did you think it was one long log? Gary?

GARY
I can't remember.

DOROTHY
Did it still have the bark on—?

GARY
Can we just drop it please?

DOROTHY
Okay.
They watch, smirking.

CAPT. KIRK
(*Offscreen, from TV*) Captain's log, stardate—
Deborah and Dorothy snigger.

GARY
(*Getting up*) Right, I'm going to get my friend Tony—
Dorothy eases him back into his seat.

DOROTHY
I'm sorry, I'm sorry. Stay, stay.

GARY
At least I never thought this was a Mexican wave.
He mimes a silly wave.

DOROTHY
That was a joke!

GARY
I don't think it was.

DOROTHY
You promised you wouldn't tell anyone.

GARY
Ah, yes, suddenly my 'captain's log' doesn't look so stupid.
A pause, then Gary stands up in his seat, doing the Mexican wave. Deborah does the same. Then Gary imitates Dorothy's mistaken idea of the Mexican wave.

DOROTHY
Okay, yes, thank you.
They settle down, watching some more.

DEBORAH
Who do you think Tony's going to come in as?

DOROTHY
I just hope it's not Flipper again.

GARY
He's very fond of his bedside lamp. I wouldn't be surprised to see Florence Nightingale.

DOROTHY
We shouldn't make fun of him. He's just in a great mood because he's going out with you, Deborah.

GARY
Yeah, I'd be the same. (*Aware of Dorothy's look*) . . . if Dorothy sadly were no longer alive thereby freeing me up. Yeah, you make a great couple. So what do you like about him?

DEBORAH
(*Smiling*) Oh, I don't know.
Her face starts to cloud as she tries to think of something.

GARY
(*Referring to TV*) Ah, they've landed on the planet.

DOROTHY
Ah, they've landed on the same corner of the studio they land on every week containing those three plastic boulders.

GARY
Well, that's what planets look like.

DOROTHY
Absolutely, and there's that plastic bush that planets always have.

GARY
(*To Debs*) Have you come up with anything that you like about Tony yet?

DEBORAH
I'm still thinking.

DOROTHY
A blonde woman in a robe will wander in in a moment.

GARY
Well, very popular throughout the universe, the robe.
Deborah is still thinking, getting desperate.

DEBORAH
Tony's got . . . a lovely smile.

GARY
I chose it, you know.

DEBORAH
What?

GARY
He took ten Polaroids of him smiling, and I had to pick the best one. Give me some numbers from one to ten.

DEBORAH
Eight.

GARY
This was his number eight.
Gary does a hopelessly weedy smile. Deborah looks depressed.

DEBORAH
Number three?
Gary mimics another smile – sleazy. Deborah looks even more depressed.

DEBORAH
Seven?
Gary does Tony's smile.

DEBORAH
That's his smile.

GARY
Exactly, that's the one I picked. I created Tony. He wanted to go with his number-two smile.

DEBORAH
What was that?
Gary does an over-the-top grin.

GARY
What else do you like about him?

DEBORAH
Um. (*Eventually*) His little phrases?

GARY
I taught him them. You know (*As Tony*) 'I feel like a king.' That was mine. I sold it to Tony for twenty quid. He used to say (*As Tony*), 'I feel marvellous.' Hopeless.

DEBORAH
All right, it's not what Tony says. I just like it when he's all . . . lost.

GARY
I taught him that. You know that little break in his voice, I coached him. (*As Tony*) 'I'll . . . (*Voice faltering*) just leave, shall I?'

DOROTHY
Ignore Gary, he's jealous.

GARY
I'm not.

DOROTHY
He's always wanted to be Tony. It's a suppressed homoerotic relationship.
Gary gives Dorothy a chilly look.

DOROTHY
If you were living in classical Greece you two would've curled up naked in bed together every night.

GARY
Don't be disgusting! Right, that's Classical Greece off the holiday list.
Tony enters. He is dressed in his version of Mel Gibson's Braveheart *– wrapped in a tartan blanket, his hair mussed up, blue war paint on his face. Two jumpers are lashed to his feet with electric flex. Tony stares blankly at the three of them, who manage to keep straight faces.*

GARY
Are you Winston Churchill?

DEBORAH
Are you . . . a Flintstone?

TONY
Where are your costumes?

DEBORAH
We, um, we were playing a trick. Sorry, Tony.

TONY
So, you (*Break in voice*) think this is funny?
A solemn moment. The others look solemn.

GARY
(*Quietly to Deborah*) See, I taught him that.

TONY
What?

GARY
Nothing.

DOROTHY
It's a really great costume, Tony.

TONY
Thank you.

DOROTHY
Are you . . . Julius McCaesar?

TONY
(*Histrionic*) No, I'm *Braveheart*. Mel Gibson in *Braveheart*. The Scottish film with the sheep.
Tony sits down, still offended.

TONY
I look foolish now.
The others mutter belated, half-hearted 'No, you don'ts'.

TONY
I made old-fashioned Scottish boots out of two jumpers wrapped round with flex.

DEBORAH
They're really nice boots, Tony. Really authentic looking.
Gary gives him a smile of encouragement. Tony looks away.

GARY
So, is anything worn under the kilt?

TONY
(*Dutifully*) No, it's all in perfect working order.

GARY
Sorry, mate.

TONY
It's okay. I nearly came as Florence Nightingale.
He is perking up. The others smile at him, humouring him.

TONY
I had the lamp, you see.

DOROTHY
Yes, Gary said.
Gary picks up a can of lager and quietly shakes it. He hands it to Tony as a peace offering. He and Gary open their cans at the same time. Tony's sprays lager in his face. He jumps up, furious.

TONY
Oh, for God's sake, grow up.

GARY
I'm sorry, I'm sorry.
Tony wipes the lager off his face.

DOROTHY
Shall I fetch you a wee clothy?

TONY
Why are all you being so horrible?

GARY
Because you're too happy.

DOROTHY
We feel uncomfortable with happy people.

GARY
We've never known any before.
Tony sits down again. They watch the TV.

TONY
How far have we got?

DEBORAH
The one who overacts has jumped through the big donut thing, and it's all gone black, so the chubby one and the one with the face like a sad donkey have jumped through the donut as well.

GARY
Bones has crossed through the Guardian of Forever's time portal and interfered with the course of history, thereby eradicating the *Enterprise*. So Jim and Spock have gone back into history to unfreeze time.

DEBORAH
That's what I said.

TONY
You know Time?
Dorothy and Doborah look weary. Nobody responds.

TONY
You know Time?

DEBORAH/DOROTHY
(*Long-suffering*) Yes.

TONY
Wouldn't it be great if you could revisit moments from your past?
Nobody responds.

TONY
Wouldn't it be great if you could revisit moments from your past—?

DEBORAH/DOROTHY
(*Long-suffering*) Yes.

TONY
I'd go back to the day I learnt how to, you know.

DOROTHY
What?

TONY
You know. Satisfy myself, on my own.
General embarrassment.

TONY
That was quite a day, I can tell you—

DEBORAH
Anyway—

TONY
My Mum and Dad didn't see much of me that weekend—

DOROTHY
Thank you, Tony.

DEBORAH
I'd go back to when I was eighteen. I could have been anything and gone anywhere.

GARY
Mm. Or you could . . . go back slightly earlier and tell us about when you first learnt how to satisfy yourself—

DOROTHY
No, Gary.
They watch the TV. Tony is cheerful again.

TONY
It's nice, isn't it? The four of us, watching telly, intelligently discussing issues thrown up organically by our television viewing. Although we're all sitting in a line, it's actually quite an intense form of communicatio—

DEBORAH
No more talking, Tony.

TONY
Okay.

CAPT. KIRK
(*Offscreen, on TV*) Captain's log, stardate . . .
Deborah and Dorothy snigger. Gary glares at them. Tony looks puzzled.

TONY
Can I say something?
They don't reply.

TONY
Can I say something—?

DOROTHY/DEBORAH
Yes!/Go on . . .

TONY
If you were Jim Kirk and you were picking a crew for your own five-year voyage on the *Enterprise*, which top TV personalities would you take?

GARY
Ooh, nice one. Um.

DOROTHY
(*Under her breath*) Oh, God.

TONY
I'd replace Mr Chekov with . . . Bianca from *EastEnders*.

GARY
Good choice.

TONY
I'd have Emma Forbes sitting here in the Mr Sulu position.

GARY
She'd be cheerful on a long voyage.

TONY
. . . on a long voyage. Carol Smillie in the engine room.

GARY
Safe pair of hands.

TONY
. . . pair of hands. Ship's doctor: the Spice Girls.
Dorothy sighs pointedly, gets up and heads out to the loo.

GARY
Hey, Tone, why don't you get your own back. While Dorothy's in the toilet, we'll all hide.

DEBORAH
Oh, that's a good idea.

TONY
Oh, okay.
They get up and rush around like headless chickens for a while. Gary and Deborah exit via the kitchen. Tony tries to hide somewhere ridiculous, then realises it will not work. He leaves by the hall door. The living room is empty for some moments, then Gary returns, followed by Deborah, then Dorothy.

DOROTHY
He fell for it then.

DEBORAH
Yep.
They resume their seats, put their feet up and watch the TV. A clattering sound from upstairs.

GARY
What's that?

DEBORAH
Tony trying to hide in our broom cupboard.
A further clattering, then a heavy thud.

DOROTHY
Tony falling out of our broom cupboard.
They concentrate on the TV.

GARY
You see, there are some interesting issues being addressed here. How would the course of history have been changed if one peace protester hadn't been accidentally run over crossing a street in America in 1930? You see it's all very . . .

He does a hand gesture implying incredible complexity and ambivalence.

DOROTHY
. . . crap?

GARY
Funny how the actors never really worked again.

DOROTHY
Yes, funny that.

DEBORAH
No, I've seen the actor playing Spong in something else.
They look at Deborah, who is serious.

GARY
Spong?

DEBORAH
What?

GARY
You called him Spong.

DEBORAH
No, I didn't.

GARY
What's his name then?

CAPT. KIRK
(*Offscreen, on TV*) What are we going to do, Spock—?

DEBORAH
Spock.
Gary and Dorothy smirk at Deborah. They go back to the TV.

GARY
Although of course William Shatner played maverick cop T. J. Hooker, which ran for two series between 1979 and 1981.

DOROTHY
Shall I fetch your special Trivia Anorak?

GARY
Okay, here's one, TV-cop football team. What's your strongest line-up?
They look at him.

GARY
Come on, we've all played this. (*They are still blank*) Okay, I'll go first. In goal: Starsky. Sweeper: Taggart. Wingbacks: Regan and Carter. Midfield: Wycliffe, Tosh Lines out of *The Bill*, and Columbo. Up front Spender, Dannio from *Hawaii Five-O* and Hutch. Manager: Frank Cannon.
A heavy pause.

DEBORAH
Do you sometimes think you watch too much TV, Gary?

GARY
How d'you mean?
They watch.

DEBORAH
How did the theme tune go to *Starsky and Hutch*?

GARY
Da, da-da, da dum. Dum dee doo dum dee do oo oo o oo. (*Pause*) Dum de doo de dum, diddle-ee da, bup-de bup bup bup.
He stops. The others are looking at him.

GARY
No, that's 'All around My Hat' by Steeleye Span.

DOROTHY
Isn't it, Doo, do doo, da doo do do doo, do doo dooh do do—?
Gary joins in, gradually drowning Dorothy out and veering off into something else completely.

DEBORAH
Isn't that *The Good Life*?

GARY
Quite possibly.

DOROTHY
No, *The Good Life* is (*Correct version*) da da-da dee, dum-di, doo . . .
They all join in, getting increasingly raucous. Then they remember Tony and shush each other.

GARY
You know Felicity Kendal?

DEBORAH
Yes.

GARY
She was deliciously pert, wasn't she?

DEBORAH/DOROTHY
(*Heard it all before*) Yes.

GARY
I've got one for you – top three women's arses on British TV in the last twenty-five years, what do we think?
Dorothy and Deborah gaze at Gary, who falters.

GARY
Okay, that's more one for Tony and me.
They watch TV. Gary glances at his watch. He holds up a kitchen timer.

GARY
Nine minutes away from free pizza.

DOROTHY
Don't make Tony jump out in front of the pizza moped this time, love.

GARY
He volunteered. You know what he's like when he smells a free pizza.

DEBORAH
Do you think he's all right? He might have hidden somewhere small and got stuck.

GARY
No, he's an experienced hider.

DEBORAH
Mm. It was on his last job application actually, under Hobbies he'd put 'Hiding'.

GARY
The only problem with *The Good Life*, though, was it wasn't realistic, was it?

DEBORAH
I don't know. A lot of people were into self-sufficiency back then.

GARY
No, I mean in real life if you'd stayed at home with Felicity Kendal, you wouldn't have let her get out of bed, would you. You'd have said, Bugger broccoli, I'm staying upstairs in bed playing with these puppies.
He does a laddish expression. Dorothy looks irritated.

DOROTHY
Wait, let me write that humorous observation down on my captain's log.
In retaliation Gary stands up and does the Mexican wave. Deborah half-heartedly does the same. Gary then does Dorothy's version of the Mexican wave. Dorothy ignores him. Gary sees Deborah's smirk.

GARY
What's Mr Spong up to—?

DEBORAH
I said Spock!

DOROTHY
Spong.

GARY
Spong.

DEBORAH
Spock!

GARY
Spong.
A pause.

DEBORAH
(*Quietly*) Spock.

GARY
Spong—

DOROTHY
Okay, stop it now.

GARY
You know *The Magic Roundabout*?

DOROTHY
Mm.

GARY
What the hell was that all about?

DOROTHY
I've no idea.
They watch on.

DEBORAH
What did you use to do when you were watching TV with your parents and someone took their clothes off?

GARY
Well, if it was my Dad we—

DEBORAH
Someone on TV took their clothes off.

DOROTHY
My Dad used to study the ads in the *Radio Times* very thoroughly. At one point he usually said, 'These sheds are very reasonable.'

DEBORAH
Mm. My Mum's knitting always got a bit manic. She knitted a whole bobble hat during the first episode of *The Borgias*.

GARY
My Dad was okay until we were watching the cricket once, just before dinner, and this woman streaker came on, and my Dad said 'Mm, I wonder what's for nipples?'
They all wince, then turn back to the TV.

DOROTHY
Ooh, Captain Kirk's falling in love. That's going to end in tears.

DEBORAH
It must be difficult to form a relationship if the only new people you meet are from other planets, mustn't it?

DOROTHY/DEBORAH
Mm.

GARY
(*Muttering*) Ah, relationships, what a surprise.

DOROTHY
Although in the early stages it gives you a lot to talk about.

DEBORAH
Mm.

DOROTHY
Instead of 'So, how long have you been working for British Gas?' it would be— 'So, what does that green scaly flappy thing on your head do?'

DEBORAH
Mm.

DOROTHY
It would be nice to be asked something new as well, wouldn't it. Instead of 'Can I kiss you?' it would probably be 'Can I squeal at you?' or something.

DEBORAH
I bet they still go on about how they were hurt by their last girlfriend from the planet Dweeb, so they find it hard to make a commitment . . .

DOROTHY
. . . make a commitment, mm.

DEBORAH
Don't you hate it when you've been on a date, and men ask your permission to kiss you?

DOROTHY
Oh, yeah. Either that or they suddenly pounce on you while you're saying something funny and interesting—

DEBORAH
Or you've got a mouthful of nuts.

DOROTHY
I tell you what's worse, though, when you've just had sex, and they hand you the box of tissues.
They both do a theatrical shudder.

DOROTHY
Or they pay two quid for a bunch of sad old carnations, and you have to spend half an hour finding a vase and making them look a bit less crap while they put their feet up in front of the telly—

GARY
Hello? Excuse me. Man in room. Man in room.

DOROTHY
Sorry.

GARY
(*Hurt*) I asked your permission to kiss you. I thought I was being sensitive. (*On reflection*) No, tongue—

DOROTHY
'Tongue me', exactly. 'Dorothy, can I tongue you?'

GARY
Well, little bit of plain speaking on a first date never does any harm.
A pause. In the silence Tony enters the room, looking very tight-lipped, still in his Braveheart *costume and now very dusty and wet, his blue war paint smeared. The others gradually notice him. They keep straight faces.*

DEBORAH
Where were you hiding, Tony? We looked everywhere.

TONY
You didn't hide, did you?

GARY/DEBORAH
Yes.

TONY
Where?

DOROTHY
Um, Gary was in the oven (*Tutting damningly*) and Debs was . . . on top of a cupboard.
Tony doesn't know whether to believe her.

DOROTHY
So where were you?

TONY
In the attic, inside the water tank.

DOROTHY
Oh, good place.
Gary and Deborah nod earnestly.

GARY
Good hiding place.

DEBORAH
Clever.
They sit down to watch.

TONY
What's been happening—

GARY
So, you were crouching in the shallow end, were you?
Tony looks at them sharply.

TONY
No, there was a little ledge.

GARY
Sorry, mate.

TONY
I hate practical jokes.

GARY
We just needed to get it out of our cistern.

One of them can't help smirking.

TONY
Well, I'm obviously a figure of fun now. Maybe I should make a badge with FOF on it, for figure of fun, and wear it.
A respectful silence.

DOROTHY
So . . . foff.

TONY
(*Snapping*) Foff. Yes. Foff. Exactly.

DEBORAH
Tony, how does the theme tune to *Starsky and Hutch* go?

TONY
I'm not telling you.
Tony discreetly shakes a can of lager and hands it to Gary.

GARY
Cheers.
Tension as Tony watches out of the corner of his eye as Gary prepares to open the can. Gary looks at the timer.

GARY
Free pizza in four minutes. I reckon we've cracked it this time, mate.

TONY
I don't care. I'm not interested.

DEBORAH
(*To Tony*) Spock's making a rudimentary computer out of coat hangers—

TONY
I don't care.

GARY
Come on, let's do the *Star Trek* doors.

TONY
I don't want to do the doors.
A pause.

GARY
You know you like doing the doors . . .

TONY
I'm not doing the doors.
They look at Tony. Finally, conceding, Tony does the noise of the Star Trek *doors opening. Gary does it too.*

GARY
You girls have a go.
Dorothy and Deborah do the door noise, with less success. Gary and Tony do not-bad-could-be-better faces. Tony smiles, then realises he is supposed to be sulking. Gary puts down his lager can. As he looks away Tony discreetly snatches the can again, shakes it up and puts it back on the coffee table. Tension as Tony watches Gary finally open his can. The lager explodes out at an angle into Tony's face. Tony sits there, dripping, trying to look dignified. In the awkward silence Tony gets up and slowly walks out of the room. His exit is spoilt by his home made footwear making a squelchy noise and his tartan blanket snagging on something and coming off. His bedroom door slams. The others look guilty. They go back to the TV. Gary's ears prick up.

GARY
Can you hear it?

DOROTHY
What?

GARY
(*Very Clint Eastwood*) The pizza moped. It's coming.
Gary holds up the timer.

GARY
Three minutes. I'm not going to let this happen.
He gets up and starts to turn off the lights.

DEBORAH
What are you doing?

GARY
Turning the lights off. We're going to pretend this is the wrong house.

DOROTHY
What's the point?

GARY
The pizza guy has to go back and get them to phone. We say, Where's our pizza, we've been here the whole time.
They are now in pitch dark apart from the flickering TV.

GARY
Hide under this blanket.
The moped is heard pulling up outside.

GARY
We'll have to turn the TV off.

DEBORAH
No!

DOROTHY
We want to know what happens!

GARY
They stop history being altered, the world order's restored, blah blah, complete nonsense. Shush, quiet.
The living room is pitch dark.

DOROTHY
(*Offscreen*) That's it, Gary. I'm not going out with you any more.

GARY
Sshh.
Outside, footsteps approach, then someone rings the doorbell. A moment of silence, then the TV flickers into life. We hear a snatch of the Star Trek *theme tune.*

GARY
(*Offscreen*) Deborah, give me the remote.

DEBORAH
(*Offscreen*) I want to know what happened—
The sound of Gary snatching the remote control and turning off the TV. More silence. Tony appears from the kitchen, still only in his boxer shorts, vaguely lit by the light from his bedroom. He finds his tartan blanket.

TONY
Where's everybody gone? I'm lonely.
He turns on the light, revealing Gary, Dorothy and Deborah huddled in one armchair and the pizza delivery man standing at the window holding boxes of pizza, peering in.

PIZZA MAN
(*Muffled*) Pizza!
The timer goes off.

GARY
Bugger.
General embarrassment. In the armchair Gary, Deborah and Dorothy acknowledge the confused-looking pizza man with a little wave, muttering, 'Hi.'

GARY
I'll just . . . go and pay then.
Gary exits. The others sit down again. Deborah turns the TV back on, in time to hear the end of the theme music for Star Trek. *Tutting, rolling of eyes etc. A silence.*

TONY
That was good. What's on next?

DEBORAH
No, we're going to talk for a change.
She snatches the remote away and turns off the TV. They sit in silence, trying to think of something to say. A long silence.

DEBORAH/DOROTHY
Okay./Go on then.
Tony gratefully turns on the TV again. Gary comes in with the pizzas. They watch TV. Gary puts a Coke down on top of the TV, then tips it accidentally into the back of the set. It explodes, hugely. The smoke clears.

TONY
Well, we don't watch much telly anyway . . .

SERIES SIX: EPISODE FIVE

TEN

Gary and Tony are famously in touch with their 'little boy inside', so it seemed a good idea to make the metaphor blindingly obvious and have a little boy staying with them. I wanted to suggest that maybe Gary and Tony are wise to be ten, spiritually, so it would have backfired if Zak McGuire, who played the boy, had not been so innocent and winning.

I may be deluded about the power of TV, but I was a bit reluctant to lampoon 'relationship therapy'. In the end I persuaded myself that we are laughing *near* it rather than at it. There is a whiff of American-style 'learning' in this episode, as Gary and Tony come to respect and understand a child, having previously made him clean their flat.

This episode tackles the archetypal scene: Meeting Your Girlfriend's Mother. There is another in the next episode: Person Back from Pub Trying Not to Look Pissed in Room Full of Sober People. Neil is fantastic in both. Give him a BAFTA.

1. DEBORAH'S FLAT: LIVING ROOM

Evening. Tony, Gary, Dorothy and Deborah are watching the TV. The Star Trek theme tune is playing. Gary and Dorothy are sitting as far apart as possible.

DEBORAH
You know my Mum's coming to stay on Friday.

TONY
Mm. I'm looking forward to meeting her.
A moment, then Tony does an exaggerated grimace of horror.

GARY
I tell you who I'd like to have as my mother.

DOROTHY/DEBORAH
(*Bored*) Dolly Parton.

GARY
Have I said that before?

DOROTHY/DEBORAH
Mm./Yes.

DOROTHY
And you know my nephew's coming to stay.
Tony and Gary look put out

GARY
Why can't he stay at a hotel like normal people?

DOROTHY
Because he's ten.

GARY
Isn't there a kiddies' hotel he could go to?
Dorothy glares at Gary.

TONY
I think Gary's point is that we're a bit worried about letting a child into the mature environment of our flat.

DOROTHY
Mature.

GARY
Yes, mature.

DOROTHY
That'll be the mature environment in which you play your homemade boardgame 'What's That Stink?', will it?

GARY
'What's That Smell?'

DOROTHY
Believe me, you are the last resort. I'd have thought you'd be grateful for the company.

GARY
What's that supposed to mean?

DOROTHY
You know very well.

GARY
Do I? Really. Do I?
They face each other off.

GARY
(*Humbly*) Seriously, what does that mean?

DOROTHY
Nobody wants to spend any time with you these days, least of all me.
A shocked silence. Deborah and Tony look embarrassed.

TONY
(*Jollying along*) Mambo – that's a funny word, isn't it—?

GARY
(*To Dorothy*) At least I didn't live with my parents until I was technically old enough to be a grandmother.
Deborah and Tony wince. Another silence.

DEBORAH
So, have you two still got plans to get married?
Dorothy and Gary snort derisively. After a moment Tony smiles at Deborah dreamily and strokes her coyly with one finger.

GARY
I don't know why you two are looking so smug. I'd like to see you after eight years. We used to be like you. We had sex everywhere, you know.
Dorothy and Gary look nostalgic. Tony frowns slightly.

TONY
Where?

GARY
You name it.

DOROTHY
It's true.

TONY
(*On consideration*) In a shoe shop?
Gary and Dorothy ponder.

GARY
No.

DOROTHY
(*Enjoying herself*) In that supermarket, though, do you remember?

GARY
Yeah. Aisle 7, Sainsbury's, Camden Town. Cereals. Rice. Pasta. Quickie sex. Dried Fruit.

DOROTHY
During *Starlight Express*.

GARY
In a wheelie bin.

DOROTHY
Oh, yeah.

GARY
That's commitment.
Dorothy and Gary look nostalgic. Deborah is grimacing slightly at the thought. Tony is obviously intrigued.

2. GARY'S BEDROOM

Later. Dorothy and Gary are sitting up in bed reading, wearing sturdy, unsexy night clothes.

GARY
Do you want to have sex?

DOROTHY
No, thank you.
They read on.

DOROTHY
Did you turn the heating off?

GARY
Yes.
More reading.

GARY
Nightmare.

DOROTHY
What?

GARY
(*Referring to his magazine*) Those trousers.
He holds the page out for her to see.

DOROTHY
Mm.
They read on.

DOROTHY
I hope Tony gets on with Deborah's mother.

GARY
Yeah.

DOROTHY
That hasn't helped, you and my parents hating each other.

GARY
Oh, I don't think we actually hate each other.

DOROTHY
Well, they hate you.

GARY
(*Hurt*) Oh. Okay. Mind you, I always find it a bit creepy when guys get on really well with their in-laws.

DOROTHY
Mm, people getting on, having nice conversations. What an ordeal. Thank God, we didn't have to go through that. Quite a blessing.
Gary gives her a look.

DOROTHY
We're well out of that—

GARY
Yes, you've very much made your point.
They read on. Without looking up:

DOROTHY
What's gone wrong, Gary?

GARY
Is something wrong? (*Referring to magazine, muttering*) Shocking hat.

DOROTHY
Don't you think we should talk about it?

GARY
Okay. You start. I'll join in if I understand what the hell you're banging on about.

DOROTHY
I want us to see someone about our relationship.

GARY
Okay. How about Freddie 'Parrotface' Davies?

DOROTHY
A relationship counsellor.

GARY
Oh, no, love. We'll perk up. Just having this chat's helped no end. Or whatever.

DOROTHY
They use someone at the hospital. He's supposed to be really good.

GARY
If he was that bright he wouldn't be spending his life listening to couples whingeing. He'd be out . . . shopping.
Dorothy gives him a cock-eyed look.

DOROTHY
What have we got to lose?

GARY
Our dignity. Our pride. Our patience. A precious hour of our dwindling lives. Our sense of self-determination—

DOROTHY
I'll book us in.

GARY
All right.
Gary turns a page of his magazine. Dorothy turns out the light.

10 3. DEBORAH'S FLAT: HER BEDROOM

Meanwhile, Tony and Deborah are in bed. They have just made love. Deborah is snuggled up to Tony, dozing.

TONY
So where have you had sex, then?

DEBORAH
Oh, you know, only the usual places.
Tony looks relieved.

DEBORAH
On a beach.

TONY
(*Jealous*) You've done it on a beach? That must be great.

DEBORAH
Not really. Sand was still appearing two boyfriends later.

TONY
I've had lots of sex. How come I haven't been as adventurous as everyone else?

DEBORAH
Oh, you know, people exaggerate. (*Pause*) And I did it in a skip once.

TONY
A skip? It's not fair. What was it like?

DEBORAH
Big, yellow, rusty—

TONY
No, the sex.

DEBORAH
I can't remember. I know while we were doing it someone threw in a broken old ironing board.

TONY
I want to do it in interesting places.

DEBORAH
Why?

TONY
It's exciting.

DEBORAH
It's not. You try reaching an orgasm in a wardrobe.

TONY
I want to! I want to try! (*Pause, whiney*) Oh, you've done it in a wardrobe! I want to do it in a wardrobe!

DEBORAH
Well, everyone experiments when they're young. What's the big deal?

TONY
I want to do more things, I want to do everything before I die. Except get something in my eye. And fall into icy water.
A pause. Deborah snuggles up to Tony and shuts her eyes. Tony is thinking.

TONY
(*Tentatively*) Can I ask a favour?

DEBORAH
Mm.

TONY
Can we make love in a tree?

DEBORAH
No.

TONY
In a summer house?

DEBORAH
No. Isn't it just nice having normal sex with me in a bed?
Deborah rolls on top of Tony, who looks dry mouthed with excitement.

TONY
Very much so.

4. LONDON BUS

The next day. Dorothy is sitting on the bus with her 10-year-old nephew, Jonathan – heartbreakingly innocent, fresh faced and smartly dressed.

DOROTHY
Are you okay?

JONATHAN
Yes.

DOROTHY
What did you do at school?

JONATHAN
Fractions.

DOROTHY
Uh-huh.

JONATHAN
Will I ever use them?

DOROTHY
No.
They look out the window.

DOROTHY
I'm sorry I've got to leave you with Gary and Tony while I'm working.

JONATHAN
It's all right.

DOROTHY
You have to remember that they've lived on their own for a long time, and they're a bit set in their ways.

JONATHAN
Okay.

DOROTHY
They're really nice. Deep, deep down.
He smiles and looks out of the window. Dorothy looks over at him apprehensively.

DOROTHY
Jonathan, you know how important it is to grow up to be thoughtful and interested in the world.

JONATHAN
Yes.

DOROTHY
Don't grow up to be a bit of a wanker.
Jonathan looks perplexed. Dorothy gives him an affectionate, protective look.

5. KITCHEN

That evening. Gary and Tony are sitting at the kitchen table, in unaccustomed silence, uneasy. We widen out to see why they are feeling awkward: Jonathan is sitting to one side, reading a book. Gary and Tony exchange looks.

GARY
Isn't it your bedtime?

TONY
Sonny Jim.

GARY
Sonny Jim.

JONATHAN
It's only half-past five.

GARY
Nice early night.

TONY
Auntie Dorothy won't be back for a while.
A silence.

TONY
Do you like *Thomas the Tank Engine*? He's good, isn't he? With his . . . face all flat and blue.
Jonathan smiles politely.

GARY
Parp, parp!
Tony gives Gary a querying look. Gary shrugs. Jonathan has gone back to his book.

GARY
Old Pooh.

TONY
Sorry, mate?

GARY
I always thought Piglet was a bit creepy.

TONY
Yeah, creepy.

JONATHAN
No, I like Piglet.

GARY
Oh, okay, fair enough.
A silence.

GARY
Tigger. He's good.

TONY
You know you're in for some fun when Tigger's around.

GARY
Do you like Tigger, Jonathan?

JONATHAN
Yes.

GARY
Yup, we all like Tigger. (*Pause*) But we're split on Piglet.
A silence.

TONY
Paddington Bear.

GARY
Ant and Bee.

TONY
Noddy.

GARY
Postman Pat.

TONY
And his black-and-white cat.
Another silence. Communication has broken down.

TONY
Hey, Jonathan, get us a beer.
Jonathan happily trots to the fridge, hands Tony a can of lager and sits down again. Tony and Gary exchange a look.

TONY
(*Side of mouth, to Gary*) He did what I said.

GARY
(*Side of mouth*) I know, I saw.
Gary looks at Jonathan speculatively.

GARY
Would you get me one, Jonathan?
Jonathan gets another can out and hands it to Gary.

GARY
Do you know how to work a duster, Jonathan?

JONATHAN
Yes.

GARY
There's one under the sink. It's great fun.
Jonathan gets the unused duster out.

JONATHAN
Where's it dusty?

TONY/GARY
Everywhere.
Jonathan starts to dust the kitchen, going about it with great seriousness, standing on chairs where necessary. Gary and Tony start to relax.

TONY
So, Johnny, you must know about mothers. What would you do if you were meeting your best-friend's mum for the first time, and you were a bit nervous?

JONATHAN
Um. I'd just . . . be nice.
Gary and Tony look confused.

JONATHAN
I'd wear my best shorts.

GARY
There you go, mate, you'll have to go and buy some shorts.
Gary is smirking. Tony reacts.

TONY
At least I don't have to go to the totty doctor.

GARY
The what?

TONY
The totty doctor, the therapist, 'Hello, I'm Gary, I'm a crappy boyfriend—'

GARY
I'd rather see a therapist than my girlfriend's mother.
They take this in. They do it's-a-close-call expressions. As he dusts, Jonathan unearths a soft-porn mag. He holds it out.

JONATHAN
Somebody's book of ladies.
Guiltily, Tony takes it.

TONY
Thank you.

10

6. CONSULTING ROOM

A day or two later. Leaflets and posters indicate that this is the office of a Relate-type organisation. Gary and Dorothy are sitting with Ben, the relationship counsellor. He is languid, youngish and good looking, and knows it. Dorothy is obviously attracted to Ben, to Gary's great irritation.

BEN
When something goes wrong, a couple – or *two people*, which is the term I prefer – can adopt one of two positions. The A position is what I call Ostrich, the B position is what I call Mongoose. I don't know if you've ever watched a mongoose . . .?
Dorothy nods, smiling flirtatiously.

BEN
Good. They're always alert and tireless, constantly maintaining what's theirs.
Gary puts his hand up.

BEN
Gary?

GARY
I think we should be like Mongeese rather than Ostriches.
Ben scrutinises Gary for irony.

BEN
Yeah, I think you're right.

GARY
(*Getting up*) Well, thanks for your help—

DOROTHY
Sit down, Gary.
He sits down. Dorothy smiles conspiratorially at Ben.

DOROTHY
(*Half serious*) What are you doing tonight? Ha.

BEN
So in our relationships we have to be a bit like—
He stops. Gary has elongated his neck and is peering round the room jerkily.

BEN
What are you—?

DOROTHY
He's being a mongoose. Ignore him.
Gary continues intermittently to be a mongoose. Ben looks at him blankly.

BEN
Okay, let's talk about anger.
Gary rolls his eyes.

BEN
Do you consider yourself an angry person, Dorothy?

DOROTHY
I suppose I am, yes.

BEN
Why are you angry, do you think?

DOROTHY
If I'm honest, because I feel I can do better than Gary, but I'm still going out with him.
Gary reacts.

BEN
Gary?

GARY
Will we be getting a plate of sandwiches?

BEN
Do you think sandwiches are important?

GARY
Do you only ever ask questions?

BEN
(*Rapid fire exchange*) Does that make you angry?

GARY
Why do you say angry?

BEN
Were your parents angry?

GARY
Were yours?

DOROTHY
Stop it, you two.

BEN
Okay, here goes. I'm going to suggest that the two of you go away and fill in this compatibility questionnaire as honestly as you can.

He hands the form to Gary.

GARY
Thanks, Bill.

BEN
Ben.
Dorothy gives Ben a see-what-I-have-to-put-up-with smile.

10 **7. RESTAURANT**

That evening. Deborah and her mother are sitting at a table, chatting and studying the menu. Deborah's mother is in her mid-fifties, glamorous but fairly stern. Tony enters. He has made an effort to look smart, although his hair keeps flopping over his face. He spots Deborah's table.

TONY
(*Willing himself on*) Okay: charm charm charm, respect, lovely daughter, show an interest, very respectful . . .
Clearly nervous, he goes over to their table.

DEBORAH
Hi.

TONY
Hi.
They give each other a quick kiss on the lips.

DEBORAH
This is my mother. Mum, Tony.

TONY
Hello!

DEBS' MOTHER
Hello.
Tony and Debs' mother exchange looks, unsure how to greet each other. Tony leans forward and hugs her, for several seconds too long. She looks embarrassed. Tony sits down. Smiles all round. General awkwardness, silence.

TONY
So, Deborah came out of your body.

DEBS' MOTHER
Yes.
Tony nods, making an effort.

TONY
What's your name?

DEBS' MOTHER
Penny.

TONY
Like the tiny coin?

DEBS' MOTHER
Yes.

TONY
Or shall I call you Mum?

DEBS' MOTHER/DEBORAH
No.

TONY
Have you come far?

DEBS' MOTHER
Yes, Yorkshire. I don't enjoy London much any more.

TONY
Is that because you're fairly old now?

DEBS' MOTHER
(*Acid*) Possibly. (*To Debs*) I'll have the mushrooms, then the duck. I'm just going to powder my nose.

TONY
You can do it at the table if you like. We're very informal.
She smiles crisply and heads off.

TONY
Lovely lady.

DEBORAH
Tony, you don't need to go overboard on the polite questions.

TONY
Oh, okay. Are there any areas you don't want me to discuss with your mum?

DEBORAH
I think you've covered them already. Maybe you should experiment with saying nothing.
Tony is not listening. He is gazing around the restaurant.

TONY
We could have sex behind those plants, look.

DEBORAH
Oh, Tony, not this again, please.

TONY
It'll just look like our belts have got caught up, and we're trying to shake them free.

DEBORAH
You've got such a sleazy side.

TONY
It's not sleazy, it's erotic.

DEBORAH
No, Tony. Erotic is . . . making love under a deserted waterfall, or in a field of swaying corn. It's not just about . . . having sex up against things.
Tony looks bitterly disappointed. Deborah gives in.

DEBORAH
Okay, anything for a quiet life. Next week we'll . . . do it somewhere.
Tony looks euphoric.

TONY
Up against a big truck—?

DEBORAH
(*Instantly*) No.

Meanwhile, Gary and Jonathan are sitting at a table playing an absorbing but mindless game such as 'Crocodile Dentist' or 'Ker-Plunk'. They are both wearing similar baseball caps. Every so often they dip into a huge jar of sweets. Gary is opening his heart out.

GARY
The thing about Dorothy is, she needs to think she'd like to go out with a brainy guy who'll take her to art galleries all day – like Sting. But the truth is – and you can't tell a girl this – it's tiring being intelligent, and they don't

want to be tired any more than we do. You know what I'm saying.

JONATHAN
Yes.

GARY
When you're going out with someone one of you has to be the policeman, and one of you has to be the silly one. Otherwise there's anarchy. Look at the great couples. John and Yoko – policeman: John. Anthony and Cleopatra – policeman: Cleopatra. Mork and Mindy – policeman: Mindy. Well, in our case, Dorothy got the policeman part. Mainly, it has to be said, because when we first met, at a party, I was dribbling and dancing with my trousers off.
They play on.

GARY
Are you seeing anyone?

JONATHAN
No.

GARY
You know what I love about Dorothy?

JONATHAN
Charlies.

GARY
Yeah, okay, I'm moving the discussion on from that now. What I love about Dorothy is . . . You know, most of us have one . . . big thing. Well, Dorothy's my big thing. What's your big thing?

JONATHAN
Sweets.

GARY
Good choice. Well, if I've only learnt one thing in life, it's this: (*On the tip of his tongue*) Oh, what was it? Oh, never mind.
Dorothy comes in, just off shift.

DOROTHY
Thanks, Gary. How's it been, Jonathan?

JONATHAN
Fine.

DOROTHY
Did Gary tell you a horrible joke about two barmaids and a travelling salesman with a rude monkey?
Gary mimes, 'No' to Jonathan.

JONATHAN
No.
Dorothy automatically takes the big jar of sweets and hides it in a cupboard.

GARY
(*To Jonathan*) Policeman, you see? (*Pointing alternately*) Silly person, policeman.

DOROTHY
What?

GARY
Nothing.
Dorothy sits down at the table with them, watching the game. A happy group.

DOROTHY
(*To Gary, tentative*) Have you filled in that questionnaire?

GARY
Yes.

DOROTHY
So, do you think we're compatible?

GARY
Well, I am.
Dorothy suggests a move to Gary, who does what she says. A disastrous move – he loses.

DOROTHY
Funny, Tony believing we'd had sex in all those places.

GARY
Mm.
Jonathan smiles at Dorothy, all innocence.

DOROTHY
Seriously, you haven't been teaching Jonathan any bad habits have you?

GARY
(*Aggrieved*) He's ten. Give me some credit.
Jonathan does a full-throated burp. Gary pretends not to notice.

JONATHAN
Better out than in, eh, Gary?
Dorothy looks at Gary, disappointed.

9. DEBORAH'S FLAT: LIVING ROOM

The next morning. Deborah leads Tony in. He is carrying a newspaper, his hair a mess. Deborah is preparing breakfast.

TONY
Where's your mum?

DEBORAH
Probably hiding.

TONY
Why?

DEBORAH
You should have heard yourself last night.

TONY
What did I say?

DEBORAH
Let me see. Things like: 'Penny, have you ever been running along and swallowed a bee by mistake?' Or, 'Penny, where did Deborah get her lovely bottom from?' And, 'Which would you rather be, Penny, a horse or a fish? I'd rather be a horse.'

TONY
I should have said fish, shouldn't I?

DEBORAH
No! You should have . . . said normal things.

TONY
I wanted to make an impression. I was being bubbly.

DEBORAH
Do me a favour, Tony. When my mum appears – don't say anything.

TONY
Oh, okay. I just wanted to be part of your family. I've never had one of my own.

DEBORAH
What about your mother, father and brother?

TONY
All right, I've got one, but I'm bored with them.
Deborah's mother appears.

DEBORAH
Morning, Mum.

DEBS' MOTHER
Morning.
Tony just does an airy wave, his lips sealed. Debs' mother gives Tony a polite smile.

DEBS' MOTHER
Anything in the paper?
By way of an answer, Tony opens the paper and turns the pages for her.

DEBS' MOTHER
Got a . . . busy day ahead?
Tony does a detailed but incomprehensible mime. Deb's mother sidles up to Deborah in the kitchen area.

DEBS' MOTHER
(*Aside, to Debs*) Is he okay?

DEBORAH
I think so. Why?

DEBS' MOTHER
He's not talking. And can't he do something with his hair?
Tony has wandered nearer and heard this. He looks hurt.

DEBORAH
He can do what he likes with it, Mum, he's a grown-up.
They glance over at Tony who, covering up the fact that he was listening, is intently doing something very ungrown-up, such as hiding behind a tiny pot plant. He flashes a self-conscious grin.

10 10. CONSULTING ROOM

Two or three days later. Gary and Dorothy are waiting. They give each other a tense smile. Ben enters. Dorothy's face lights up. An attractive young woman enters. Gary's face lights up.

BEN
Hi. Sorry to keep you. Karen's a trainee, I hope you're okay with her sitting in on this consultation.

GARY
Sure.
Dorothy looks slightly put out. For Karen's benefit Gary nods in Dorothy's direction and does her eye-rolling, look-what-I-have-to-put-up-with expression.

BEN
We've evaluated your questionnaires. Great. Let's focus in on some of your responses.

DOROTHY
Thanks, Ben.

BEN
Okay. To the question 'What are major areas of disagreement?' Dorothy, you've put 'Behaviour, drinking, attitudes to women, respect, my friends, farting, attitude to my parents. Loud music, television watching, refusal to cook, bad clothes. Sex'. Gary, you've put: 'Nothing. Everything seems okay'.
Gary is too busy trying to flirt with Karen to listen. She is trying to ignore him. Gary chews his tie 'seductively'.

BEN
On the question 'What are your partner's strengths?' Dorothy, you've answered: 'Profound if misguided self-confidence, capable of great kindness'. Gary, you've put: 'Bouncy'.
Karen is still gamely ignoring Gary. Getting frustrated, Gary deliberately drops something. As he picks it up he tries to look up Karen's skirt.

BEN
'Preferred time for love-making?' Gary: 'Night-time'. Dorothy: 'Morning'. 'Ideal

environment?' Gary: 'City'. Dorothy: 'Countryside'. 'Religious beliefs?' Dorothy: 'None'. Gary: 'Reincarnation, lucky pants'.
We fade down, then up minutes later.

BEN
. . . 'Political allegiance?' Dorothy: 'Labour'. Gary: 'Monster Raving Loony stroke Lib-Dem'. 'What first impressed you about your partner?' Dorothy: 'His child-like exuberance'. Gary: 'Her car'. 'Motto?' Dorothy: 'Be kind', Gary: 'If it's wet, drink it'. I could go on.
Dorothy looks grave.

BEN
More worryingly, perhaps, you've both been flirting with the very people working to help you focus on your relationship.
Dorothy looks guilty. Gary is still paying more attention to Karen.

GARY
(*Leaning towards her*) So, Karen, Capricorn, am I right?

BEN
I've never said this to two people before, but I seriously urge you to consider splitting up.
Dorothy looks shell shocked.

DOROTHY
Oh. All right.
Gary is still trying to flirt with Karen. He points to his thigh.

GARY
Feel that. That's like steel. Go on, feel it.
Gary does that clicking noise with his mouth, then realises belatedly that the others are looking at him.

GARY
Okay, how did we do?
His smile gradually fades.

10 **11. DEBORAH'S FLAT: LIVING ROOM**

Meanwhile, Jonathan is sitting on his own on the sofa. He is wearing one of Tony's T-shirts with something unsuitably rude on it.

TONY
(*Offscreen*) You see, Jonathan, you have to make sacrifices for the one you love.
He emerges from the kitchen, bringing over soft drinks. He has had his hair permed, to tragic effect.

TONY
Especially with your girlfriend's mother. Fortunately this has turned out really well.
He pats his curls.

JONATHAN
Like a clown.

TONY
(*Unsure*) Yeah.
He sits down. He and Jonathan sip drinks contentedly from straws. Tony takes out a sheet of paper.

TONY
Okay, see what you think of this. 'Debs and Tony out-and-about love-making schedule'.
Jonathan sips his drink and listens obediently.

TONY
On the fifteenth: Selfridges, probably in carpet department. Eighteenth: weather permitting, London Zoo. Bad-weather alternative: Odeon, Leicester Square. Here's a romantic one – twenty-third: in a big green bush. Can you think of anywhere else nice?

JONATHAN
Sweet shop?

TONY
(*Writing it down*) Good one.
Deborah and her mother have come in in the background, obviously from shopping. They are looking, open mouthed, at Tony's new hair. Tony looks up to see Deb and her mother.

DEBORAH
What have you done to your hair?

TONY
It's great, isn't it? Like your mum said, it was really untidy. So we've (*Quoting hairdresser*) taken the hair off the forehead and created a fun shape on the top of the head.
Deborah and her mother continue to stare. Tony is losing confidence.

TONY
As it grows out, the curls will travel down the head and create a cascading effect . . .

DEBS' MOTHER
You can't go out with him, darling, he looks like spaniel.

DEBORAH
Mum—

TONY
Well, make up your mind, you stupid bloody woman—
An icy silence. Deborah's mother makes a dignified exit to her room. Deborah glares at Tony, who realises his mistake.

TONY
You see, mutual respect, very important.

10

The next day. Jonathan is sitting at the table, neatly dressed in a clean shirt. Gary and Tony are flitting around, putting on his tie and shoes, getting him ready. They obviously now have a lot of affection for him. Gary brings over Jonathan's little satchel.

GARY
I've put your favourite sandwiches in, okay.

TONY
(*Putting on his shoes*) Now, we want you to take care out there.

GARY
And grow up to be a decent member of society.

TONY
Play lots of sport.

GARY
(*Running out of ideas*) Eat fruit and . . . celery, that kind of thing. Help old people across the road.

TONY
Unless it's Debs' mother.

GARY
Yeah, don't help her.

TONY
Hinder her—

GARY
Hinder her from crossing the road.
Jonathan sees Gary smoking.

JONATHAN
Can I try a cigarette?

GARY
Ooh, no, you don't want to get into all that. If you're going to take up anything take up . . . golf.

TONY
Yeah, smoking's a mug's game.

GARY
Absolutely.

TONY
Dirty, smelly.

GARY
Yup.

TONY
Only inadequate people smoke—

GARY
Okay, steady, steady.

TONY
Sorry, mate.

The doorbell rings. Gary gets up and goes to answer it. In the hallway, Gary opens the door to Dorothy. She hands Gary some flowers, obviously in conciliatory mood. They smile nervously.

GARY
You must be Dorothy, interests – what was it? – 'Reading, conversation, travel'.

DOROTHY
Hello, you must be Gary. Interests – what was it? – 'TV, lager and lager products, thinking about ladies' bottoms'.

GARY
You see, loads in common.

DOROTHY
I think I've worked out what our relationship needs.

GARY
Great.
He looks anxious. Dorothy indicates a large, wrapped object behind her in the communal hall.

DOROTHY
A ceiling mirror.
Gary looks relieved.

GARY
I've got something for us too.

DOROTHY
What?

GARY
(*Producing wrapped box*) A special Girls' Edition of my boardgame 'What's That Smell?'

DOROTHY
Thanks.

GARY
Fancy a quick game? It's made out of proper cardboard.

DOROTHY
No, I'd better take Jonathan back to his mum. You've been a bit of a hit with him. Maybe you're more innocent than I thought.

GARY
Well, we're all children under the surface, aren't we?
They smile. Then:

DOROTHY
No.

GARY
Oh.
They head back into the kitchen. Tony is teaching Jonathan lager techniques. They are sitting at the

table holding empty drink cans. Jonathan is copying Tony.

TONY
And finish (*Downing lager*) and crush (*Squashing can*) and burp (*Belching*) and throw.
He and Jonathan throw their cans over their shoulders in synch. The cans clatter.

TONY
He's got it, Gary! He's got it.
Tony turns round to see Dorothy watching, very unamused. She comes into the room.

DOROTHY
Thanks for your help.
She takes Jonathan's hand and leads him off, giving Gary a jaundiced look.

GARY
It was lemonade!
Gary holds up the crushed lemonade can as evidence. Gary and Tony drift out into the hall, watching Jonathan go sadly. They call out after him.

TONY
Remember, eat plenty of celery.

GARY
Help old ladies across the street!

TONY
Except Deborah's Mum!

GARY
Except Deborah's Mum!
Tony realises too late that Deborah and her mother have emerged from Debs' flat, obviously to get a lift in Dorothy's car. Tony wonders what to say.

TONY
Because she isn't old.

GARY
. . . not old.

TONY
In the slightest.

GARY
In any way.

TONY
At all.

13. LIVING ROOM

Tony and Gary are sitting on the sofa, having the traditional late-night chat.

GARY
How's the hair?

TONY
(*Defensive*) Fine.

GARY
You, um, look quite like—

TONY
Kevin Keegan, I know.

GARY
No, I was going to say a clown. Actually I read somewhere that men's perms are very much in.

TONY
Really?

GARY
Yeah. It was in the March 1976 edition of the *Hairdresser*. Or was it this last month's *Clowns and Clowning*?

TONY
Deborah says she won't have sex with me outdoors until my perm grows out.

GARY
Do you want me to try to iron it flat?

TONY
Wouldn't that burn my head?

GARY
I think it's worth it.

TONY
No!

GARY
Or you could pretend to be a motorcycle messenger for a couple of months.

TONY
Yeah, I might do that.
They sip lager.

TONY
How are you and Dorothy?

GARY
Great.

TONY
So, it doesn't worry you that you got professional help, and they told you to split up?

GARY
No, I was quite encouraged. The so-called experts, eh?

TONY
Yeah. If we believed the so-called experts we'd all still be . . . sitting on rocks.
They frown at this patent nonsense, but let it go.

TONY
I wouldn't mind being ten again, I can tell you.

GARY
Oh, me too. You could suck your thumb in public.

TONY
You could shout things out. Nobody minded.

GARY
The whole boy-girl thing was a lot simpler, wasn't it?
As Tony speaks, Gary wanders out to the hall and comes back with a holdall.

TONY
God, yes. You only had to lend a girl your bike, and you could more or less do what you wanted. Unless that was just Tracey Simmonds.

GARY
Not that you wanted to do anything.

TONY
Absolutely.

GARY
So, have you ever fancied your girlfriend's mum?

TONY
Yeah, you always do till you're about nineteen, don't you?

GARY
Yeah, why is that?

TONY
I suppose because they say sexy things like, 'Do you want to come in and take your jacket off?'

GARY
Yeah, and they look a bit like your girlfriend, only you know they've had sex at least three or four thousand times.

TONY
A mate of mine split up with his girlfriend and married her mum. And his dad married my mate's old girlfriend. And they both had kids. So my mate's kid is . . .
He stops, confused.

TONY
. . . something.
They sip lager. Gary reaches into his holdall and take out a battered motorcycle helmet. He puts it on Tony's head, covering up his perm.

GARY
See you in a couple of months.

TONY
Thanks, mate.

When I wrote this I thought it would be the final *Men Behaving Badly*, hence the closing image when Gary and Tony muse about what it is to be a man, while sitting on the sofa on top of the Giant of Cerne Abbas in Dorset. Their rolling down his massive erection is obviously a symbolic act of . . . something or other.

They say flashbacks in a sitcom indicate that you've run out of ideas. On the contrary, they are a sign that the writer fancies seeing the cast wearing a bunch of ridiculous wigs and clothes. I loved the scene with Gary's first day at the office; his ideals and enthusiasm still touchingly intact.

We thought we would get lots of angry letters about the scene where Young Gary takes a run-up to kick his tortoise, but I don't remember anybody writing in. Honestly, what do you have to do to get a few letters these days? The most hate-mail we ever received was in Series Three when Gary lists the nightmare people who might move in if Deborah sold her flat, culminating in: 'Welsh people!!' Someone from Wales threatened to burn down my house, which seemed a bit harsh. I noticed afterwards that the Welsh had indeed become everybody's comedy punchbag, down there with mothers-in-law and social workers, estate agents and Prince Philip, so I'm sorry if I added to their pain.

Special thanks to the boy playing Young Gary, who put up with having his ears pushed forward painfully . . . The first prosthetic snake was rubbish (kept turning up late for rehearsals, complained about his dressing room, looked like a hose), so another one was run up hastily but never quite looked the part either . . . My final attempt at a catch phrase: 'Too weird, mate.' Nobody went for it. Well, sod you then . . .

1. GARY'S FLAT: LIVING ROOM

Deborah and an entwined Gary and Dorothy are sitting on the sofa, watching a late-night film on TV. Deborah scratches the inside of her thigh. Gary looks over at her.

DEBORAH
I think your sofa's got fleas.

GARY
You got a problem with that?
Deborah gives Gary a look.

GARY
All right, come here, I'll scratch you—

DEBORAH
No!

DOROTHY
Haven't you got a pub to go to?

GARY
Yeah, I really like standing in a smoky room drinking a third my weight in liquid till some fat bloke shouts at me to leave, then spending the next day feeling like my head's clamped between a sheep's thighs.

DOROTHY
Yeah, you do like that.

GARY
Yes, I do, but not tonight.
Dorothy and Deborah are now both quietly scratching.

DEBORAH
There really are fleas in this sofa.

GARY
There aren't!

DEBORAH
There, look! One jumped on me.
Dorothy and Deborah hastily stand away from the sofa. Gary sits there.

GARY
Well, there may be the odd one.

DEBORAH
How long have you had this sofa?

GARY
It's nearly new. Twenty-five years. Mind you, my parents kept the polythene on for six years.

DOROTHY
Look at it, Gary, it's got some horrible stains on it.

GARY
Where?

DOROTHY
(*Finding and pointing*) There. There. There. There.

DEBORAH
There. Here. There.

DOROTHY
There. There.
A pause. They turn over a cushion.

DOROTHY
There.

DEBORAH
There.

DOROTHY
There.

GARY
I can't see any.

DEBORAH
I mean, look at that stain. What is it?
They gaze at it, appalled and impressed.

GARY
Yup, that is a bit of a worry.
The sound of the door slamming.

GARY
(*Calling out*) We're in here, mate!

TONY
(*Offscreen, clearly drunk*) Evening!

DEBORAH
Did you have a nice time?

TONY
(*Offscreen*) I had a very nice time! I'm just popping to my room.

DEBORAH
Can you remember where it is?

TONY
(*Offscreen*) Yes, it's here. (*After a moment*) No, it isn't. Here it is.
The sound of Tony going into his bedroom. Dorothy and Deborah are still standing.

GARY
Are you going to sit down?

DOROTHY
No, I'll catch a disease. My mum's throwing out their sofa, I could get it brought over tomorrow.

GARY
No, this sofa's part of me.

DOROTHY
I know, that's why it must be destroyed. I shudder to think how many gallons of bodily fluid there are in this sofa.

GARY
A couple of pints are yours—

DOROTHY
I don't want to know!
Dorothy and Deborah pointedly go and sit on armchairs. Tony comes in. He is trying desperately not to look drunk, but clearly is.

DEBORAH
Did you have much to drink?

TONY
No, no, I was very . . . not much . . . drinking.
He manages to position himself over the sofa and lower himself. The others smirk.

DOROTHY
Nice evening?

TONY
Oh, yes! Very nice! Lots of . . . people?
He giggles childishly, then tries to looks serious.

TONY
Anything interesting on the . . . BG? The TG? The VT?

GARY
TV?

TONY
TV? (*No reply*) So . . . good?

DOROTHY
Good what, Tony?
He blows out his cheeks.

TONY
Evening?

DOROTHY
Yes.

TONY
Excellent!

DEBORAH
Did you bump into anyone?

TONY
God, yes, I kept bumping into people. Give me a hug! Sit here.

DEBORAH
No, I'm not sitting on the sofa.

TONY
I know that! You're sitting on the chair! With your bottom all nicely tucked away. But we know it's there. Lurking.

DOROTHY
We were talking about—

TONY
Dorothy, hello!

DOROTHY
Hello.

TONY
Give me a hug. Go on.

DOROTHY
No, thank you.
Tony leans forward to Deborah. Conspiratorially.

TONY
Actually, I've got something exciting to show you.

DEBORAH/GARY/DOROTHY
I've seen it./Seen it, mate./We've all seen it.

TONY
No, something I bought in the pub.
He tries to put his feet up on the coffee table but misses.

TONY
It's not crisps!

DEBORAH
Night-night, Tony. I think I'll sleep upstairs.
She kisses him and heads for the door.

TONY
No, stay! We must make love all night. Until we're all sore!
She leaves. Without looking, Tony casually slaps his arm, obviously to kill a flea.

2. TONY'S BEDROOM

The next morning. Tony in bed. Daylight is shining in his pained face, his hair severely askew. The duvet is in a pile under him. He moves his head and groans. Realising how hungover he is, he does a couple of sobs. He rolls over into a crouch, teetering on the edge of the bed, then falls off. He groans and struggles to his knees. On his bedside table he sees a packet of Resolve. He gets out a sachet and looks around. There is a bottle of water but no glass. Fighting the nausea, he tears off a corner of the sachet and pours the powder into his mouth, chokes, then takes a swig of water. He tries to swallow. Fizzy stuff erupts out of his mouth. He eventually swallows it all down.

TONY
That's better.
He sees a large holdall and looks even more miserable. He lifts it on to the bed, takes a deep breath and opens it. Inside is a snake – at least three feet long, very much alive. Tony stands back. The snake starts to slither out. Tony wags his finger sternly.

TONY
Stay. Stay!
He tries to shut it back in, but the snake moves sinuously across the bed and away. Tony vaguely looks for it, alarmed, then exits.

3. LIVING ROOM

Meanwhile, Gary is sitting on the sofa, running his hand lovingly along the upholstery. Tony enters. Gary grunts hello. Tony grunts back.

GARY
How are you feeling?
Tony does a complicated grunt that conveys great nausea and discomfort.

GARY
My last day on my sofa. I've agreed to get rid of it.
Tony sits down next to him.

GARY
Look what I found in the lining.
Gary reaches down behind a cushion and puts an unpleasant-looking object on his knee.

GARY
Bacon. Must be eight years old.

TONY
(Queasy) Can you get rid of it, please, mate?

GARY
Sorry.
He puts the rasher back in the sofa.

5 SACHETS RESOLVE FOR THE MORNING AFTER Fast headache relief gently settles stomach CONTAINS PARACETAMOL

TONY
Gary, have you ever fancied an unusual pet?

GARY
Well, my Uncle Todd had a beaver. That was the talk of Tiverton for a while.

TONY
How about a long thin pet? That would be fun, wouldn't it?

GARY
I used to have a tortoise. I loved him actually. We got him about the same time as the sofa.

TONY
But—

GARY
Sshh, I'm reminiscing.

TONY
Sorry, mate.
Fades to next scene.

4. GARY'S GARDEN

A slightly sepia tone conveys the year: 1970. The sounds of a summer morning, birds singing. We hear conversational murmurs from an eightish-year-old boy – unmistakably Gary – and his mother. She is florid, in her mid-thirties, wearing the depths of seventies fashion. They are sitting, reading a book. Gary junior is smiling and listening cherubically. Mrs Strang is distracted by the gate opening and two men coming in, carrying a new sofa, wrapped in polythene. She gets up to supervise them. Now unwatched, Gary finishes his carton of orange squash. He crunches it and tosses it over his head, lager-style. He gets up and goes over to a pet tortoise that is eating a pile of leaves. Checking his mother is not looking, Gary picks up the tortoise and puts it on its back. He watches it look confused, waving its limbs.
In the background, the delivery men are manoeuvring the sofa into the house. Meanwhile, Gary gets a large handful of soil and builds a tee. He carefully places the tortoise on it, still upside down, and steps back a few yards. He starts a run-up, preparing to boot the tortoise out of the garden. It falls off its tee just in time. Gary replaces it and steps back, to take an even longer run-up. He accidentally reverses too far, trips up and falls backwards into a bush. Fade back to the present.

5. GARY'S FLAT: LIVING ROOM

Tony and Gary on the sofa as before. Seeing Gary is in a reverie, Tony quietly gets up and leaves.

6. TONY'S BEDROOM

Tony enters cautiously, looking around. He stands in the middle of the bed and dials a number on the roving phone.

TONY
(*Into phone*) Hello, Zoo? Can I speak to someone about snakes, please. Thank you.
He looks around for the snake. Still on the bed, he leans over to his wardrobe and quickly opens the doors. Nothing there. A female showroom dummy falls out.

TONY
(*Into phone*) Oh, hi. Last night my girlfriend bought a snake off this bloke in the pub. (*Listening*) I don't know why, she was very drunk. (*Listening*) Illegal? Sorry, did I say snake, I meant dog. So . . . how are the animals—? (*To himself*) Oh, she's gone.
He hangs up and gets off the bed. With his toe he carefully turns over some pants on a huge pile of dirty underwear. He jumps back. Nothing there. He turns to a Yellow Pages, finds a number and dials.

TONY
(*Into phone*) Hello, pet shop? I've got a snake, I wondered if you wanted to buy it. It's very nice. (*Listening*) Sort of pinky with a zigzaggy line down the back. (*Listening, swallows*) 'Can be fatal?' Uh-huh. Yes, it's in a secure place.
Tony is gingerly climbing back on to the bed. He stands there, very scared.

7. LIVING ROOM

Moments later. A cushion is off the sofa, exposing bits of crud and various items: coins, crisp bags, pants etc. Gary is reaching his arm down the lining of the sofa. Tony comes in, looking shaky.

GARY
I've found some great stuff down the lining.
He retrieves a greasy, hairy metal comb.

GARY
My old comb. Ahh.

TONY
Well done, mate.

GARY
I lost it in 1978. I used to comb my hair every six minutes.

TONY
(*Sitting down*) Me too. Well, we were all punks then, weren't we?

GARY
(*Bluffing*) Punks, yeah. With our . . . bondage slacks and everything.

TONY
You need to rebel, don't you?

GARY
Oh, God, yes.

TONY
(*Shaking fist*) Ban the whale! (*A moment's thought*) No, save the whale!

GARY
(*Shaking fist*) Ban other things!

TONY
Yeah. We used to argue into the night, putting the world to rights. Then we'd look out the window and see—

GARY
A fox?

TONY
No, that the sun's coming up, and we'd been talking all night.

GARY
Yeah.

A sixteen-year-old Tony – it is 1978 – is hanging out with two mates. They are wearing school uniform but trying to look as punk as possible with spiky hair and generally dishevelled. They are all smoking and posing, trying to impress each other. Tony is inexpertly smoking a cigar.

TONY
You going to Tim's party?

MATE 1
Nah, he's a wanker.

MATE 2
Yeah, wanker.

TONY
Terry's going to be there.

MATE 2
He's a wanker.

MATE 1
Tosser.

MATE 2
Wanker.

TONY
And Mike.
A pause.

TONY
Wanker.

MATE 1
Wanker.

MATE 2
Tosser.

TONY
Tosser.

MATE 1
Wanker.

MATE 2
And Mike's mate Cliff.
They look at each other, unsure.

TONY
Wanker?
Relieved, they all agree.

MATE 1
Tosser.

MATE 2
Wanker.

TONY
Toss-pot.

MATE 1
Tosser.
Tony chokes on his cigar. One of the mates takes a run-up and pogo head-butts the side of the bike shed. He tries to hide the fact that he has hurt himself.

MATE 1
The Clash, they're great.

TONY
Yeah.

MATE 2
Yeah.

TONY
Brilliant.
A pause. They do heavy guitar-riff noises.

MATE 1
Genesis, they're pathetic.

MATE 2
Pathetic.

TONY
Yeah.

MATE 1
Yeah. Wankers.
They all get their combs out and do their hair.

TONY
Hats, they're pathetic.

MATE 1
Yeah.

MATE 2
Wankers.
A nice, innocent schoolgirl of about fifteen appears.

GIRL
Excuse me, have you seen my bicycle?
The boys immediately stop posturing and are gauche and willing.

TONY
Um.
They all look around helpfully for it.

GIRL
Are you going to Tim's party?

TONY
(*Goofy*) Might be quite jolly.

GIRL
I might go too then.

TONY
(*Taking a big puff on his cigar*) Great.
They are smiling sweetly. Tony looks suddenly queasy.

GIRL
Are you all right?

TONY
Yeah.

GIRL
I think that cigar might be making you ill.

TONY
No, I always smoke cigars.
Tony is suddenly sick down the girl's shoulder. She looks quietly appalled.

TONY
So, do you want to go to the party with me?
Fade to the present.

As before. Tony's turn to be in a reverie. Gary has his arm down the back of the sofa again. He brings out a battered mid-eighties tie, thin orange leather with a piano-key motif.

GARY
Ahh, my first work tie. (*Holding it up*) They were stylish, weren't they? The eighties.

TONY
(*Unsure*) Yeah.

GARY
You've never really taken to the work thing, have you? It's never really gelled with you . . .

TONY
. . . gelled, no. Well, it's not natural, is it? Man was born to fish and hunt and forage in the open air.

GARY
So why aren't you doing that then?

TONY
Well, I get a bit chesty in the open air.

GARY
I tell you what's weird about work.

TONY
All the pencils?

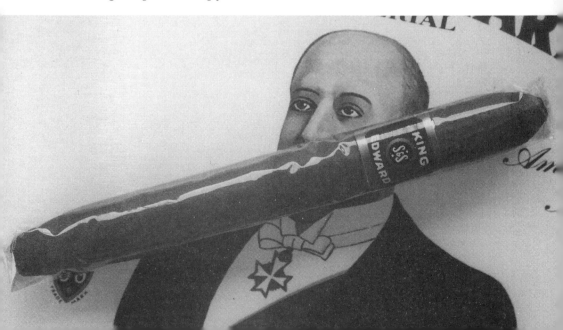

GARY
No.

TONY
The way you have to sign big cards all the time for people you don't know who are having an operation?

GARY
No. What's weird is, how some people end up with brilliant careers and other possibly more gifted people get sidetracked.

TONY
Yeah.

10. GARY'S OFFICE

It is about 1984. George, unchanged apart from a full head of dark hair, is sitting at his desk. An almost girlish Anthea enters with Gary. He is about twenty-two, keen, idealistic and smartly dressed in the orange tie. It is his first day.

ANTHEA
And this is where we put the post, in the tray marked POST. The little piece of card with POST written on it came off last year, but we stuck it back on with Sellotape, didn't we, George.

GEORGE
Little bits of Sellotape, yes.

GARY
Right, okay. Thanks for showing me the ropes. Great stuff. I am actually keen to make a fair number of changes to—

GEORGE
Your predecessor Mr Innes encouraged us all to nibble a Rich Tea biscuit at a quarter-past ten.

GARY
Yes, well, lovely. I have to say it all looks fairly sleepy here.

ANTHEA
Oh, thank you.

GEORGE
Thank you.

GARY
I'm going to be setting up some new systems and procedures. So, any input from yourselves at this juncture?
Anthea and George just smile serenely.

GEORGE
Sorry?

GARY
Any input from yourselves, as we enter this exciting period of change?
A pause.

ANTHEA
(*Still smiley*) Hmm?

GARY
The way we do business with Bristol, for example, you're duplicating paperwork generated by two departments.
A befuddled pause from George.

GEORGE
We've done you a card.
From a filing cabinet Anthea retrieves a plastic bag. She hands Gary a large card. He opens it and reads.

GARY
'Welcome, Barry'. That's great, except I'm Gary, not Barry.

GEORGE
Oh. I wonder how that happened.
Anthea hands Gary a huge box of business cards.

ANTHEA
Some business cards . . .

GARY
(*Reading*) 'Manager: Barry Strange'. That's actually Gary Strang.

ANTHEA
And your door sign. I'm afraid it's in the name of Barry—

GARY
Barry, yes, never mind.

GEORGE
Rather than redo the sign could we perhaps call you Barry?
Gary is starting to look weary.

GARY
No. Anyway, the important thing is, work should be about commitment and energy. So, are you out, or are you in?
Gary is fired up again, glowing with ambition.

GEORGE
In what?

ANTHEA
That's a fun tie.

GEORGE
Yes.
Gary sits back in his chair, already looking disillusioned.

ANTHEA
So, time for our Rich Tea biscuit, I think.
Anthea opens a filing cabinet and removes a plate with some dull biscuits already fanned out on it. She offers the plate to Gary, who considers, then takes one.

GARY
(*A broken man*) Thank you.
Fade to the present.

As before. Gary, tie slung round his neck, is looking depressed. He opens a can of lager. A knock on the door.

TONY/GARY
It's open!
Deborah enters. She kisses Tony.

DEBORAH
Hi!

GARY
Hi!

DEBORAH
I thought you were getting rid of the sofa today.

GARY
Yes, well, it might just be a sofa to you, but to me it's like an old girlfriend.

DEBORAH
A rather grubby girlfriend, presumably.

GARY
Well, in many ways that's the best kind, of course.
Tony is nodding. As Deborah turns to him he immediately stops.

DEBORAH
I need my watch from your bedroom, Tony.
She is already in the kitchen, nearly at Tony's door. Tony runs ahead of her, barring her way.

TONY
You can't go in.

DEBORAH
Why?

TONY
Because . . . basically . . .
A long, painful pause while he invents.

TONY
. . . there's been a fire.
Deborah just looks at him, damningly.

TONY
No? Okay. Private party?
Deborah makes to enter.

TONY
All right, there's a poisonous snake running loose in there.

DEBORAH
(*Humouring him*) Well, you always said if I got bitten you wanted to suck out the poison.
She pushes past him and into the bedroom. Tony calls anxiously through a gap in the door.

TONY
Yeah, I've had a bit of a rethink on that—
Deborah comes out, businesslike.

DEBORAH
See you later.

TONY
Yeah, bye, love.
She exits. Tony glances into his bedroom and shuts the door. He goes back into the living room. Gary swigs some lager, already much perkier.

GARY
This sofa's seen some arse, I can tell you, mate.

TONY
I bet, mate.

GARY
You know what it's like, when you get a lovely girl back to your bedsit . . .?

TONY
(*Laddish*) Yeah . . .

GARY
And you sit down on the sofa . . .

TONY
Yeah . . .
Gary's smile fades.

GARY
(*Insincere*) It's great isn't it, all that?

12. GARY'S BEDSIT

One late night, 1984. The classic first London bedsit – small, hideously decorated, very visible fridge. On the wall is the famous poster of the tennis player scratching her bottom. 'Relax' (Frankie Goes to Hollywood) is playing on a record player. Gary is sitting on the sofa with a shy young woman. He is struggling to open a bottle of Asti Spumanti.

GARY
Do you like Spumanti?

SHY WOMAN
It's okay, yes.

GARY
Me too.
He puts one arm round her while trying to open the bottle with his other hand.

GARY
Did you understand that bit in the film where—
The cork shoots out and hits the woman in the eye.

GARY
God, I'm sorry, are you all right?

SHY WOMAN
Ow. No!

GARY
I'm sure it'll be all right. Shall I put some butter on it?

SHY WOMAN
How does that help?

GARY
I think it makes the swelling . . . all buttery.
She continues to hold her eye, in some discomfort. Gary is not sure what to do. Seductively – as he sees it – he puts his hand on one of her breasts and leaves it there, awkwardly. She purses her lips in irritation. Realising it is not working, Gary moves his hand to her other breast and leaves it there.

SHY WOMAN
Take me home, please.

GARY
Okay.
Obviously expecting this, Gary removes his hand and gets up.

13. GARY'S BEDSIT

A night in 1986. Same bedsit but with two years' more grime. New poster: the follow-up version of the tennis player/bottom poster. 'Do They Know It's Christmas?' is playing on a cassette player. Gary is sitting with a rather fierce, trendy girl. He hands her a bottle of lager.

GARY
I've got us this new Spanish lager. You're supposed to drink it straight from the bottle, which is an interesting new approach.

COOL WOMAN
I know.
She takes a swig. Gary looks offended.

GARY
Aren't you going to say 'Cheers'.

COOL WOMAN
Cheers.
She takes another swig.

GARY
What about clinking?

COOL WOMAN
What?

GARY
Clinking.
He clinks his bottle against hers. She just looks at him. Gary pounces without warning, burying his face in her neck wetly. She carries on smoking, looking faintly disgusted.

GARY
Ooh, this is good!
She looks down at him.

COOL WOMAN
This isn't going to work—

GARY
(*Instantly on his feet*) Okay, no problem.

14. GARY'S BEDSIT

1988. Another night, same bedsit, now even grimier. A new, classier poster: a classical standing nude, rear view. 'Together Forever' (Rick Astley) is playing on a CD player. Gary is on the sofa with a serious, slightly odd-looking girl. They are sipping tea. A chilly silence. He hums 'casually' and starts to slide his arm along the back of the sofa.

SERIOUS WOMAN
I know it's old fashioned, but I don't actually believe in sex before marri—
Gary is already on his feet, handing her her coat. Fade to the present.

15. GARY'S FLAT: LIVING ROOM/KITCHEN

Gary comes out of his reverie, alone on the sofa.

GARY
Tony?
We cut to Tony, who is crouching out of Gary's view in the kitchen, putting on oven gloves. He is wearing a hat, two heavy coats and boots and has a scarf round most of his face.

TONY
(*Muffled*) Be right back.
He makes a dash for his bedroom door.

16. TONY'S BEDROOM

Tony looks around for the snake, getting down on his hands and knees.

TONY
(*Friendly*) Hello, snake, mate!
He spots it on the bed, looking at him. He tries to grab it, but it escapes. He eventually finds it and makes another lurch for it, this time catching the tail. It wriggles alarmingly, but he hangs on. He tries to stuff it in a holdall, which keeps closing.

TONY
Get in, you skinny bastard.
He wedges the snake under his arm, enabling him to open the holdall. Finally he manages to get the snake into the holdall and shuts it. He holds up the bag, staring in through the air holes.

TONY
Are you okay?
He ponders, then heads for the door.

17. KITCHEN

Seconds later Tony tiptoes towards the bathroom. He reaches the hall.

GARY
(*Offscreen*) Hey, Tone. Come here, I haven't finished reminiscing. Look at this.
Tony tuts. He starts long-sufferingly to take off all his protective clothing.

18. LIVING ROOM

Moments later, a normally dressed Tony joins Gary on the sofa. Gary, starting to get drunk, is holding up a bra.

GARY
An early Dorothy!

TONY
Great.

GARY
Girls' bras, eh.

TONY
Girls' bras.

GARY
What do you reckon it's like to put one on?

TONY
I suppose it's a bit like . . . parking.

GARY
Yeah.

TONY
Sexy parking.

GARY
Sexy parking. You know some bras open at the front and some at the back?

TONY
Yeah.

GARY
They're both great ways, aren't they?

TONY
Yeah. Taking your bra off. That must be like . . . taking your pants off. Only more so.

GARY
Yeah. I think Dorothy was wearing this when we first met.

19. AT A PARTY

1989. A late-night student party in an emptied-out sitting room. Half a dozen guests are dancing half-heartedly to bassy rock music. A few more are chatting, including Dorothy. Gary comes in, clearly drunk. He has his trousers on his head. He scans the room.

GARY
You all need livening up. Let's conga!
The guests are reluctant, but Gary starts to organise them into a line.

GARY
Come on! Hold his waist. Don't be shy, it's only a bottom. We're having fun!
He grabs the man Dorothy is talking to and forces him into the conga line. He forms an arch with a wincing Dorothy and makes the conga go under their arms. Then, putting himself at the head of the line, he leads them towards the door.

GARY
Everybody go, 'Ooh!'

GUESTS
(*Reluctant*) Ooh.
They exit, leaving Dorothy on her own. Seconds later Gary comes back in and shuts the door behind him. He and Dorothy are now alone.

DOROTHY
I think just wearing your trousers on your head would have done the trick.

GARY
Hello, I'm Gary.

DOROTHY
Dorothy.

GARY
You look like fun.

DOROTHY
Thanks. No offence but . . . you look like a nightmare.

GARY
Oh, why do you say that?
Gary beams drunkenly, trousers still on head, plastic pint beaker of lager in hand.

DOROTHY
No reason.
Gary takes his trousers off his head, throwing them aside.

GARY
Have you got a drink?

DOROTHY
Yes, thanks. Do you want another one or are you driving?
They smile, then become nervous.

GARY
So, what do you do, Dorothy?

DOROTHY
I'm a nurse.

GARY
What does that involve?

DOROTHY
Um. Nursing.

GARY
Interesting.

DOROTHY
What about you?

GARY
I'm a sub-manager of a small security company specialising in exclusion products and industrial-fencing solutions.

DOROTHY
So, barbed wire—

GARY
Mainly barbed wire, yes.

DOROTHY
And . . . would you tend to wear trousers at work?

GARY
It depends. Fancy a dance?

DOROTHY
Don't make me conga.
He goes over to the hi-fi, takes a tape out of his shirt pocket and puts it on. 'I Should Be So Lucky' (Kylie) comes on. Dorothy looks bemused but takes Gary's hand. Led by Gary, they dance unnaturally slowly to the chirpy music.

GARY
So, do you want to go out with me?
Dorothy gives him a long look.

DOROTHY
Okay.
They dance on, romantically.

GARY
(*Referring to the music*) Always works.
Fade to the present.

20: GARY'S FLAT: LIVING ROOM

Gary is grinning nostalgically, sitting on his own again. He is toying with Dorothy's bra, variously using it as epaulettes or knee-pads.

21. BATHROOM

Meanwhile, Tony is putting on the last of his protective clothing again. He manages to open the holdall with the oven mitts on, putting his hand in and grabbing the snake. He lifts the toilet lid.

TONY
Now, don't take this personally.
He attempts to put the snake into the toilet, but part of it keeps wriggling free. He tries again, this time almost squeezing it all in. Finally he stuffs the snake in and sits on the toilet seat. Looking a bit guilty, he flushes the toilet. While he waits he idly picks up the new roll of toilet paper and tries to tease away the first square of paper. Typically, this leaves him frustrated and the paper in shreds. He puts it back. He stands up and gingerly opens the toilet lid. The snake flies out. An unseemly scramble until finally Tony manages to catch the snake and put it back in the holdall.

22. LIVING ROOM

Gary is now wearing Dorothy's bra over his clothes. Tony comes in, throws his holdall to the floor and sits down.

GARY
What's in the bag?

TONY
Snake.

GARY
Uh-huh.

TONY
Bloke in the pub said I could breed from it.

GARY
Don't you need two?
They ponder this.

TONY/GARY
No idea./Bit shaky on the old snake reproduction.

TONY
I shouldn't have bought it really, but you know what it's like – you've had a few drinks, everything looks like a great idea—

GARY
Bloke offers you a snake—

TONY
Blah blah blah . . .

GARY
'Impress your girlfriend.'

TONY
'Bags of personality. Nice and long—'

GARY
'Eats mice.'

TONY
I suppose I was lucky. He was selling a goat as well.

GARY
Oh, I could have done with a coat.

TONY
No, a goat.

GARY
Oh, no, I don't want a goat.
They sit. Gary drinks.

TONY
We'd better load it into the van.

GARY
Yeah.
They don't move.

GARY
Can you, um, leave me alone with my sofa for a moment, please, mate.

TONY
Sure.
Tony leaves the room, taking his holdall with him. Alone, Gary spreadeagles himself on the sofa, hugging it. Tony reappears moments later.

TONY
Too weird, mate.

GARY
(*Sitting up again*) Sorry, mate.

23. KITCHEN/LIVING ROOM

Later. Dusk. Dorothy and Deborah are getting food shopping out, ready to cook, pouring themselves a glass of wine.

DOROTHY
I wonder where they've gone.

DEBORAH
Probably driving around in Tony's van trying to find a big enough bin to put the sofa in.

DOROTHY
Mm.
Through the hatch we see two delivery men leaving.

DOROTHY
Thanks a lot.

DELIVERY MAN
Cheers.

DEBORAH
Bye.
We cut to the living room, where there is a (nearly) new sofa: attractive but definitely on the girly side. Deborah and Dorothy wander in.

DEBORAH
Do you think they'll like it?

DOROTHY
Probably not. Gary's suspicious of anything that hasn't turned ever so slightly brown.
They sit down on the sofa, glasses of wine in hand, sharing a bowl of crisps. They turn on the TV.

DEBORAH
So, do you reckon you and Gary will still be sitting on this sofa in twenty-five years?

DOROTHY
Oh, probably. Only the Lottery or premature death can save me now.

DEBORAH
I can't imagine my life without Tony.

DOROTHY
Oh that's sweet, Debs.

DEBORAH
No, I mean he's like having a hump, isn't he? After a while you just accept it's there.
They watch the TV.

DEBORAH
Maybe we're not so different anyway—

DOROTHY
Don't, now you're just scaring me.
Deborah reaches for the remote control.

DEBORAH
(*Referring to the TV programme*)
Oh, brilliant.

DOROTHY
So, if you could take three blokes on a desert island, who would it be?

DEBORAH
Oh, good one. Um.
Chewing moronically, they mull this over.

Sunset. From a low angle Gary and Tony are seen sitting on the sofa, in thoughtful silence.

GARY
So, do you want to, um?

TONY
Okay.
Tony puts on his oven gloves and zips open the holdall at his feet. He holds the bag open, upside down. The snake plops out.

TONY
Off you go.

GARY
Be good.
They watch the snake slither away.

TONY
Have you ever released anything into the wild?

GARY
Yeah. My tortoise, Geoff.

TONY
Why?

GARY
I think we just . . . wanted to give him a hard time.

TONY
Uh-huh.

GARY
No, he'd suffered enough. I was quite a cruel child.

TONY
Well, you mellow, don't you? One moment you're blowing up a bucket of frogs, the next you're wheeling a push chair with a little baby inside.
They ponder this.

GARY
Have you noticed, people over about forty-eight, they're not comfortable on a sofa. They always want their own chair.

TONY
It's sort of preparing for death, isn't it? They want their own vehicle.

GARY
Mm, it's like the Seven Ages of Man. There's Birth.

TONY
Childhood. Adolescence.

GARY
Sofa.
They ponder, losing interest.

TONY
Then the other three.

GARY
I suppose getting rid of this sofa will be like finally getting rid of my youth.

TONY
Mm.
We start to pull out and up, gradually revealing the location: the Giant of Cerne Abbas in all his glory . . . The sofa is to one side, e.g. as though in one of the Giant's hands.

GARY
You know one thing I'll miss

TONY
From your youth?

GARY
From my youth.

TONY
The funny haircuts?

GARY
Yeah, I'll miss that . . .

TONY
Firm flesh? It'll all be wobbly from now on, mate.

GARY
Wobbly?

TONY
Oh, yeah, all . . . smingey and wobbly.
As they disappear in the distance they get on their feet and start to bounce up and down on the sofa, like kids. Their voices dwindle:

GARY
(*Offscreen*) But what I'll really miss is – you can't be stupid when you're older, can you?

TONY
(*Offscreen*) Oh, I think you can, mate.

GARY
(*Offscreen*) Oh, good . . .

SERIES SEVEN

SERIES SEVEN: EPISODE ONE

Performance

We came back for a final trilogy of 45-minute episodes. A baby seemed the obvious but right way to bow out, although I toyed with having everyone burn to death in a barn.

In retrospect we could have saved ourselves a lot of grief by not tackling the subject of masturbation in an episode broadcast on Christmas Day. If we had known when we recorded it that it was for Christmas Day we might have snipped out Gary pumping himself up under the duvet in order to get his 'car through the garage doors', although I stand by the sticky tissues. I may have overcompensated in trying to avoid the kind of sentimentality that can ruin swan-song episodes.

The plot about Deborah being in danger of losing a leg was one of the rare occasions when producer Beryl Vertue and I disagreed. Beryl raised the spectre of our offending vast numbers of unipeds up and down the country. She was probably right – the plot didn't really work, although I think there was a kernel of a good idea there.

I shall always treasure the image of Ken the barman singing, 'I am Woman...'

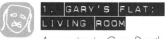

1. GARY'S FLAT: LIVING ROOM

An evening in. Gary, Dorothy and Deborah are sitting on the sofa, eyes glued to the TV.

DOROTHY
Hey, Debs, we've got some exciting news. Haven't we, Gary?

GARY
Oh, yes. Tony and me are pretty sure the woman at number 55's got three nipples.
Deborah and Dorothy stare at Gary.

GARY
Not that?

DOROTHY
No. We're definitely going to try for a baby.

GARY
Oh that. Yes.

DEBORAH
Oh, that's great. Congratulations.
Gary and Dorothy hold hands, smiling coyly.

GARY
Well, your eggs aren't as fresh as they were, are they, love?

DOROTHY
Cheers.

GARY
It's no picnic, making a good omelette out of a stale poached egg, served up in a tired old pan.

DOROTHY
Mm, and sadly the process involves having sex with Gary, but I seem to remember it's over fairly quickly.
Tony enters.

DEBORAH
Have you heard the big news?

TONY
Yeah – three nipples, in our street!

ALL
No, not that.

DEBORAH
Dorothy and Gary are going for a baby.

TONY
Yeah. Ahh. Babies. With their tiny toes and their tiny squidgy bottoms. And their tiny hands. And their tiny—

ALL
Yes, tiny, thank you. Everything tiny, mm.
Tony sits down. They watch TV for a bit.

TONY
You know what I'd like to see on TV? More programmes about how to do things more quickly. Or about how to get from one place to another.

Dorothy and Deborah look over damningly at Tony.

DOROTHY
(*To Deborah*) So, do you still want him to move in with you?

GARY
What's that?
Tony and Deborah look a little embarrassed.

TONY
Oh, we've got some news of our own. Deborah's agreed I should move in.

GARY
What's wrong with my flat?

TONY
Nothing, it's just that, you get older, and you want to have a full, grown-up relationship.
Deborah and Dorothy nod, proud of Tony.

TONY
And Deborah sometimes walks around just in her pants, and I really like to watch.

GARY
I don't know what to say. This is the end of an era. Can't you stay until the springtime?

DOROTHY
He's not emigrating to Uzbekistan. He'll be ten feet away upstairs.

TONY
(*Apologetic*) But, you see, it'll be my place.

DEBORAH
Eh?

TONY
(*Ignoring her*) I realise I've never actually created anything of my own.

GARY
You made that wooden barbecue.

TONY
Okay, I've never created anything of my own that hasn't caught fire.

GARY
Don't leave now, Tony. You've finally figured out how to work the toaster.

DOROTHY
(*Kindly*) Um, Gary, we are planning to have a baby. There'll only be room for one helpless, flatulent little bastard with a breast fixation.

GARY
I know.
Gary looks quietly upset. Belatedly understanding, Tony frowns at Dorothy.

2. GARY'S BEDROOM

The next morning. Dorothy is dozing next to Gary, who is reading a children's book. Gary pulls a lever and some penguins slide into view. He chuckles. Dorothy is starting to wake up.

GARY
They're great, kids' books. You see, you don't get sliding penguins with so-called Emily Brontë.

DOROTHY
(*Half asleep*) No, dozy bitch.

GARY
The koala bear jumps up, look. (*Demonstrating to Dorothy*) Crouching . . . jumping. Crouching . . . jumping. Crouching . . .
Dorothy snatches the book and throws it aside.

GARY
. . . hiding.

DOROTHY
Wasn't there something we were supposed to be doing?
They both ponder for a while, then realise.

GARY/DOROTHY
Oh, yes.
They kiss.

DOROTHY
Fertilise me, Gary. Fertilise me like you've never fertilised me before.
Dorothy pulls Gary on top of her. They start to make love.

GARY
Wouldn't it be weird if a woman could be made pregnant by a penguin. Imagine it: half penguin, half human. A pengman. Or a orang-utan. Half orang-utan, half human. An orangu-man.
They move around a bit more under the duvet. Nothing seems to be happening.

DOROTHY
Gary, are you all right?

GARY
Mm?
Dorothy stops moving.

DOROTHY
Um, do we have a problem?

GARY
Sorry, love?

DOROTHY
Well – how can I put this nicely – the garage doors are open, but the car doesn't want to come up the drive.

GARY
No, I'll be all right. Give me a minute.
They lie there for a while. Gary hums.

GARY
So what do you reckon, should I buy that tennis pullover I saw in Top Man?
Dorothy slides out from under Gary.

DOROTHY
We should talk about this, love. You were the same last night.

GARY
Well, I keep thinking about the sperm sitting around down there, waiting to go over the top to make a baby. All those anxious little faces.

DOROTHY
Sperm haven't got faces, Gary.

GARY
Mine have.

DOROTHY
Can't you just think of them as . . . little fish going out to play?

GARY
Fish? I've got fish inside me?

DOROTHY
Not literally fish.

GARY
I've made fish?!

DOROTHY
Well, I don't know!

GARY
That's another of the tragedies of being a man, of course. If a woman isn't into it she can just lie there and . . . plan a casserole.

DOROTHY
Yes, there is that.
Gary looks at her.

GARY
Whereas a man's got to divert blood away from all over his body, away from his . . . knees and his face, and cram it into his, you know. It's a major engineering project. And do we get any credit for it?

DOROTHY
No, I'm sorry, well done.
Dorothy puts a sympathetic arm round Gary, who goes back to his book.

GARY
Well, that's it, I'll never be able to look my mum's garage doors in the face again.

Later that day. A playground with a nearby café. Music swoops in, underscoring the romance of our two couples: Tony is pushing Deborah on a swing, Dorothy and Gary are on a seesaw.

TONY
This is great, isn't it? All coupley.

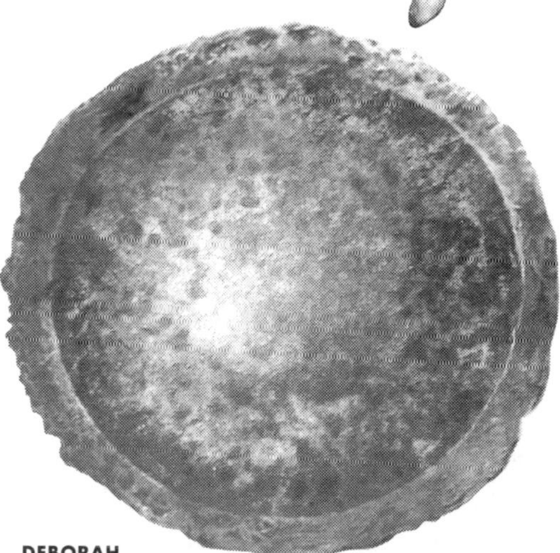

DEBORAH
Mm.
They look over at Dorothy, who is smiling indulgently as Gary gets off the seesaw and runs around after a toddler, playing.

DEBORAH
Ah, they'll make lovely parents.
Gary accidentally knocks over the toddler, then desperately tries to make amends. A young woman sits down on a swing near Deborah. Her boyfriend starts to push her. They giggle and kiss. Tony and Deborah smile, pleased to see another loving couple.

DEBORAH
Sweet.
The other boyfriend starts to push his girlfriend a little higher. She giggles, enjoying it. Tony starts to push Deborah higher.

DEBORAH
That's high enough, Tony.
The other couple go even higher, giggling. Spurred on, Tony matches them.

DEBORAH
Tony!

TONY
What, love?
The other boyfriend pushes his girlfriend even higher. Tony gives Deborah a big push. She shoots off the swing, falling hard, twisting her ankle and crying out in pain.

DEBORAH
Tony, you wanker!

TONY
Oh, God, sorry.
Deborah lies there in agony. Unsure what to do, Tony fans her with the seat of the swing, until accidentally hitting her on the nose with it.

TONY
Sorry!
Dorothy arrives, examining Deborah's ankle expertly.

DOROTHY
I think it's just a nasty sprain. I'll go to the café and get some ice.

TONY
(*Approaching*) I'll stay and—

DEBORAH
No! Keep him away! I'll go with you.
Deborah hobbles to her feet and, supported by Dorothy, heads for the nearby café. Tony and Gary sit down on a bench and wait.

TONY
So how's the old baby-making going?

GARY
Fantastic!

TONY
Fantastic?
Gary whoops.

TONY
Fantastic.

GARY
Although, can I tell you a secret? You have to swear not to tell anybody.

TONY
Sure.

GARY
To be honest I'm having a bit of trouble . . . performing.

TONY
You mean . . .?

GARY
Yes.

TONY
The fire's burning, but the log's not going on.

GARY
Yes.

TONY
Mr Toad's still curled up in Toad Hall.

GARY
Yes . . .

TONY
The Magic Bus doesn't want to go to Manchester—

GARY
Thanks. No, it doesn't. Still, it happens to every man at some time, doesn't it?

TONY
Sure, mate. You'll be all right.
He puts a hand on Gary's shoulder.

GARY
Thanks, mate.

TONY
You're no less of a man, are you? Just because . . . you're a big poof.

GARY
What—?
Tony gets up chuckling. Gary chases after him.

4. PARK CAFÉ

Ten minutes later. Outside the café, Dorothy is holding a compress of ice against Deborah's ankle. They are sucking ice creams.

DOROTHY
So, are you looking forward to Tony moving in, bringing his collection of tattered pants?

DEBORAH
I am actually. It's funny how you come to rely on someone emotionally, even if they're, well, even if they're Tony.

DOROTHY
Mm.

DEBORAH
And to be fair, he is much more grown up these days.

DOROTHY
Oh, yeah, they both are.
Unseen by Deborah and Dorothy, in the background Gary has chased Tony on to a roundabout.

DOROTHY
They're like a sweet old couple who've been going out for years, and now everything's changing.
In the background Gary is spinning Tony on the roundabout, going very fast. Tony is hanging on for dear life. Various children are watching in fear. Deborah and Dorothy, seeing nothing of this, sigh.

5. THE CROWN

That evening. Ken is standing behind the bar. Obviously making an effort, he grins cheesily at one of the few, dismal regulars in the bar. Tony is going round emptying ashtrays. He picks up one and knocks the contents into his bin. The ashtray breaks in half like an egg. Tony ponders, then puts the halves together and replaces it on the table. Ken leans forward conspiratorially to a customer.

KEN
Um, we'll probably be doing afters tonight if you fancy a drink after closing time.

CUSTOMER
I may well pop in. I'm a police officer.

KEN
Right. I don't mean here, obviously. I'll be serving in Bevvies Bar down the road.
Tony goes to another table. This time the ashtray is stuck down. He pulls hard, finally yanking it free, leaving a hole in the table and getting a face full of ash. Gary comes into the bar, in his work suit. He and Tony exchange grunts.

GARY
(*Into Tony's ear*) Tony, I was thinking, you know my little problem, you haven't told anyone about it, have you—?

KEN
Hi, Gary, I hear the boy scout's not going in the sleeping bag.
Gary reacts.

TONY
Sorry, but working together, we tend to chat about the issues of the day. (*Under his breath, to Ken*) He doesn't want to talk about it.

KEN
Oh, okay.
A pause.

KEN
So . . . you're not at home to the Big Parsnip—

GARY
Stop. Stop.

TONY
Sorry, mate.
An awkward pause. Ken serves Gary a pint.

TONY
I hear there's been a power cut in the Littlehampton area—

GARY
Right.
In annoyance Gary picks up his pint and sits down alone at a table. The four or five men in the pub all grunt sympathetically at Gary, obviously aware of his little problem. He seethes. At the bar Ken looks around at his sparsely populated pub. He waves an official-looking letter at Tony.

KEN
I've had a meemo from the brewery saying our sales figures are disappointing. In fact the phrase they use is 'Are—'

TONY
(*Reading memo*) 'Are you still open?'

KEN
So I've been thinking of some schemes to make Saturday night go with a bit more of a swing.
He gets out his notebook.

KEN
Um. 'German Night. Everyone has to bring a German'. No? 'Cabbage Night. The same, but bring a cabbage'?

TONY
Not sure.

KEN
'New Drinks Evening. Everyone has to swap drinks with the person to their left, to experience the taste of new drinks.'

TONY
No.

KEN
'Stand-up Comedy Night. Stand up in different funny ways and win a prize . . .?' (*Running out of ideas*) 'Crisp Tasting . . .' 'Saturday Night is Smoke Yourself Stupid Night . . .' 'Buy a Drink, Win a Chair . . .'
At his table Gary is quietly singing, e.g. 'My Way' as he scratches his neck with a beer mat.

TONY
I've got it. (*Pointing to Gary*) There's your answer for Saturday night.

KEN
Beer Mat Scratching Night. Yeah!

TONY
No, singing, karaoke.

KEN
That's not a bad idea. You don't think it'll lower the tone of the place?
Wide shot of the pub's desolate interior.

TONY
No.

6. GARY'S FLAT: HIS BEDROOM

Next morning. Gary is in bed with an on-edge Dorothy, who has her head in her hands. They have been trying everything.

DOROTHY
Look, honey, it doesn't matter.

GARY
I know it doesn't.

DOROTHY
(*Snapping*) Well, it does actually if we want to have a baby.

GARY
I think the problem is, sex has always been pointless, strictly speaking, and now it's for something, paradoxically—

DOROTHY
Yeah, whatever, shall I pretend to be an air hostess again?

GARY
No. Look, I know what would work.

DOROTHY
(*With strained patience*) I'm not asking my friend Sue if she'll—

GARY
No. A magazine.
Dorothy gets up and starts to get dressed into her nurse's uniform.

DOROTHY
I trust you're not referring to 'Decanter', the magazine for wine buffs.

GARY
No. Or it doesn't have to be a mag. It could be a video. Featuring ladies.

DOROTHY
No! I'm your lover, not . . . Kelly from Basildon.

GARY
I know, I know. I just need a bit of a jump-start . . . from somebody I don't know quite so well.

DOROTHY
(*Wearily*) Okay, look, why don't you buy a sex-instruction video. Would that work?

GARY
Worth a try.

DOROTHY
A proper one, though, not the latest from 'Popsy Plays Naked Volleyball After a Bit of Bogus Chitchat from Some Bloke in a Doctor's Coat' Productions.
A tentative knock on the door.

DOROTHY
It's very much safe to come in.
Deborah comes in, wincing with pain.

DEBORAH
Dorothy, will you have a look at my ankle where I sprained it?
She sits down on the bed with her back to us.

DOROTHY
My God, it's enormous.
Gary sucks in his cheeks and turns away.

DOROTHY
Look, Gary.

GARY
Yes, I know, enormous.

DOROTHY
I'll take you to the hospital.
Dorothy helps Deborah up.

DEBORAH
(*Hobbling out*) Hello, Gary. Any luck—?

GARY
No.

7. GARY'S OFFICE

Later that day. Gary and George are working. Gary starts idly singing Arthur Brown's 'Fire'.

GARY
(*Tunelessly*) Fire! Do de doo. Fire! Do de doo. Fire! Do de doo.
Gary stops to sharpen a pencil.

GEORGE
If music be the food of love, eh?

GARY
Mm. Practising for an evening of karaoke.

GEORGE
Ah, yes, it's always little swans, isn't it?

GARY
Inevitably, George, you're thinking of origami. Can you sing? Don't do it, just tell me.

GEORGE
Yes, I sang backing vocals during my folk-club days. Our combo was quite in demand in the Purley area.

GARY
Ah, yes, folk music. What instrument did you play? The hurdy-gurdy? A wooden staff banged against a sounding-diggle?

GEORGE
That's very much a clichéd view of folk music.

GARY
So what did you play, George?

GEORGE
The Dorset washboard. It's like a standard washboard except it's made of twigs.

GARY
What were you called?

GEORGE
George.

GARY
And the band?

GEORGE
Hooray, It's the Purley Kings.

GARY
I always think a good name for a folk group would be Folk Off and Die Folky.
Anthea comes in.

GEORGE
You seem rather bitter these days.

GARY
I'm sorry. Tony's moving into the flat upstairs. I'm going to miss our chats.

ANTHEA
If you love him, let him go.

GARY
Yes, always a treat to visit your mystical side, Anthea.

ANTHEA
You've got Dorothy now.

GARY
Mm, well, I'm having a small personal problem in that department.

ANTHEA
Oh, really. Can we help?
Anthea and George smile willingly.

GARY
I doubt it, to be honest. Anthea, have you ever had difficulty becoming aroused?

ANTHEA
Do you mean in the morning?

GARY
Any time.

ANTHEA
Yes, I usually find a cup of tea and five minutes with Terry Wogan does the trick.

GARY
(*On reflection*) We're not talking about the same thing, are we?

8. HOSPITAL WARD

That afternoon. Tony is at Deborah's bedside. Deborah, her foot protected under the covers, looks trapped. Out of boredom Tony has put on a rear-buttoning surgical gown. He is reading the Radio Times *out loud to Deborah and has been for some hours.*

TONY
Then at nine twenty-five on Tuesday on BBC1, *Style Challenge*. 'More makeovers'. That's in stereo. Nine-fifty on the same channel, *Kilroy*, 'Topical debate'. Also in stereo, and it's subtitled. Video plus number—

DEBORAH
Tony, you've been here for hours, you don't have to stay.

TONY
No, I want to. I feel responsible.

DEBORAH
You are. You pushed me over.

TONY
(*Reading some more*) Meanwhile on ITV, *This Morning*, video plus number 972—

DEBORAH
So are you ready to move in tonight?

TONY
Yeah. Oh, have you got room in your bathroom cabinet for my range of Toss facial products?

DEBORAH
No.

TONY
Oh, okay. Hey, it's going to be great, isn't it?

DEBORAH
Well, I think we're as ready as we'll ever be. We know each other's quirks.

TONY
I haven't got any quirks.

DEBORAH
You don't call having a lucky buttock a quirk?

TONY
Come on, everyone's got a lucky buttock, and an unlucky buttock.

DEBORAH
Name one other person with lucky buttocks.

TONY
They're not both lucky, that would be ridiculous. Anyway, you've got quirks too.

DEBORAH
What?

TONY
You wrap everything in clingfilm. An inch of sausage. Two crisps. It's like 'Coma' in your fridge.

DEBORAH
It's hygienic.

TONY
I'm scared to doze off in case I wake up with an exposed body part wrapped in clingfilm.
Tony takes off his gown and puts on the radio headphones. He starts swaying in time to the music.

TONY
(*Shouting*) We're having a karaoke night in the Crown to boost sales, otherwise it might have to shut down, which would be a bloody tragedy.
Everyone in the ward is staring at Tony. Deborah gestures for him to shush.

TONY
(*Shouting*) Oh, and Gary's still got his little problem. He asked me to score some Viagra—
Deborah yanks the headphones off him, to shut him up. She shushes him again.

TONY
(*Whispering*) Sorry. What else? Oh, bad news: we don't think the woman at number 55's got a third nipple after all. It looks like it was a button.
Dorothy enters, in uniform.

DOROTHY
Hi. How are you feeling?

TONY
Well, you feel so helpless, don't you. Oh, you don't mean me.

DEBORAH
Not great actually. Thank goodness Tony's been cheering me up for what seems like days.

DOROTHY
Tony, arse, out.

TONY
Okay.
He gives Deborah a kiss.

TONY
(*As though to a child*) Now, will you be all right?

DEBORAH
Yes.

TONY
You know where the loo is—?

DEBORAH
Bye, Tony.

DOROTHY
Ah, Tone, help me move Mr Peterson.
She takes Tony to the end of the ward. A man is lying on a trolley next to a bed, asleep after an operation.

DOROTHY
One, two, three, lift.
She and Tony lift him on to the bed, then discover that there was a small man already in that bed, and the two patients are now both lying side by side, asleep.

DOROTHY
Oh, well, I'll ask one to move later.
As she is tucking them in, she and Tony gaze back at Deborah.

TONY
Ahh . . . She's being very brave.

DOROTHY
Mm. But somehow I sense that even losing a leg would be less of a challenge than living with you.

TONY
Oh, I couldn't live with a girl with only one leg.
Dorothy gives him a peeved look. Tony gives Deborah a soppy goodbye wave. She gestures for him to leave. Tony does a stop-kidding-around gesture, then wanders off. Dorothy goes back to Deborah's bed.

DOROTHY
That had better get better – Tony says he couldn't live with you if you lost your leg.

DEBORAH
(*Panicking*) Why, am I going to—

DOROTHY
No, no, you'll be fine. They just want to keep you in for a few days.
Deborah looks relieved, then offended. Dorothy puts a thermometer into Deborah's mouth.

DEBORAH
(*Muffled*) Honestly, bloody men. They're so superficial.

DOROTHY
Mm.
They gaze at a woman visiting a patient in another bed.

DOROTHY
Nice top.

DEBORAH
Not with those shoes, though.

DOROTHY
Ooh, no.

9. GARY'S FLAT: HIS BEDROOM

Evening. Gary enters, wheeling in the TV and video. Out of his briefcase he excitedly takes a plastic bag containing a sex-instruction video, e.g. Better Sex. *He looks at it lovingly.*

GARY
'How to Enhance your Loving and Sexual Relationship, with Dr Andrew Stanway'. Nice work if you can get it, Andy.
He plugs in the TV and inserts the video.

GARY
Fast forward through that. Talking. Talking. Scary diagram. (*Pause*) More talking.
Tony wanders in, rather forlorn.

TONY
Hello.

GARY
Oh, hello.
Gary edges between Tony and the TV.

TONY
So, I'm nearly ready to move my stuff up to Debs' place.

GARY
Okay. Bye.

TONY
I've left my *Pocahontas* toothbrush and flannel set here in case I, you know, have a blazing row with Debs—

GARY
Okay, mate.

TONY
What are you doing?

GARY
Oh, you know, watching a tape.

TONY
What is it?

GARY
Oh, just some . . . *Sporting Bloomers*, you know. People banging into each other, falling over, very funny. Are you off?

TONY
(*Peering round*) There's a couple having sex on a kitchen unit, very fast.

GARY
Really? Well, they'll probably get hit by a golf ball or something in a minute . . .

TONY
Now another woman's showing a bloke she's naked under her housecoat. Ooh, looks like it's rekindled his interest in their relationship—

GARY
Okay, I bought it to spice up our sex life.

TONY
Oh, cheers . . .

GARY
My sex life, with Dorothy. We'll watch it together.

TONY
But Dorothy's working nights this week, so why are you putting it on—?

GARY
I'm testing it.

TONY
So what am I going to watch? You've taken the TV.

GARY
It's my TV. Read a book.

TONY
I haven't got any books.

GARY
Well, write one!

TONY
(*Voice cracking*) Can I watch?

GARY
No!

TONY
Please, I'd be no trouble.

GARY
No.
Tony leaves. Gary settles down to watch. Tony reappears.

TONY
I'll sit quietly.
Gary shuts the door on him. He turns on the video, watching.

SEX DOCTOR
(*On video*) '. . . really get to know your partner's private parts . . .'
Gary is dry mouthed. It is already working.

GARY
Okay.

10. GARY'S BEDROOM

The same, the next morning. The TV screen is showing snow. A haggard Gary is slumped across the bed, still wearing yesterday's clothes, trousers round his ankles. Dorothy arrives back from her shift. She picks up the sex video, reading it. Gary stirs.

DOROTHY
Hello, love.

GARY
Oh, hi.

DOROTHY
You look terrible.

GARY
Yeah, I . . . didn't get much sleep.

DOROTHY
Why?

GARY
Oh, you know. Car alarm. Then a burglar alarm. Then a . . . huge noisy ant got into the room.

DOROTHY
Shall I snuggle down with you?
She kicks off her shoes. Gary looks apprehensive.

GARY
I'd rather have some tea. How was the night shift?

DOROTHY
It's weird having Deborah there. I had to tell her off for whining. Then old sleazy Brian kept wandering in to ask her out, wheeling his squeaky drip.
Gary tuts. He sits up, finding a large empty box of tissues next to him. He discreetly throws it aside.

DOROTHY
I kept having to wheel him back to his ward. So, did the video do the trick?
She has her back to Gary, who lifts his duvet and finds a huge pile of crumpled-up tissues. He pushes them off the bed.

GARY
Not really. It's not actually very good. I'm going to have to try another one.
Dorothy scrutinises Gary.

DOROTHY
Oh, all right. You do want to have a baby, don't you, Gary?

GARY
Of course I do, love.

DOROTHY
(*Gesturing*) But maybe this . . .

GARY
Little prob—

DOROTHY
Little problem is your brain – such as it is – telling your penis – such as it is – that it doesn't want a baby.

GARY
No, absolutely not.
They exchange a loving look.

DOROTHY
It'll be good, won't it?

GARY
Yeah.
Dorothy glances at the 'loving couples' on the box of the video.

DOROTHY
That's a weird job, isn't it? Imagine writing in and volunteering yourselves.

GARY
Yeah, crazy stuff.
He quietly crumples a letter he has obviously been composing.

11. LIVING ROOM

Early evening. Gary enters, back from work, carrying a big bag. He pours out the contents onto the coffee table: half a dozen video sex guides. Tony enters from his room, to Gary's surprise and embarrassment.

GARY
I thought you'd moved in upstairs.

TONY
No, I was going to, but I've had a call from Deborah— (*Seeing the videos*) Having a night in?

GARY
Oh, these, yeah. Just trying to get a picture of the whole genre, you know.

TONY
Yeah, anyway—

GARY
You won't tell anyone I've—

TONY
Got a sex video habit, no . . .

GARY
No, I mean you really won't tell anyone this time.

TONY
No. Anyway, Dobs has just rung. Her leg's in a bad way apparently. There's a chance she'll lose it.
They sit on the sofa in silence.

GARY
Ooh. Poor old Debs, eh?

TONY
Yeah. And the thing is, I'm not sure I could live with a one-legged woman. It makes me feel a bit queasy. So I've decided not to move in upstairs yet.

GARY
Oh, right.
They are sombre, but only for a moment.

TONY
Okay!

GARY
Okay!

TONY
Hey, Ken was testing the karaoke equipment today at the Crown. (*As roadie Ken*) One-two. One-two. Rock and roll! One-TWO. It's going to be great.
They open up cans of lager.

GARY
What does that mean, 'karaoke'?

TONY
I think it's Japanese for 'drunk businessman'.

GARY
Ah. Of course, as a nation, we British are terribly inhibited.

TONY
Which is why apparently we drink more than any other nation, apart from Finland.

GARY
Hence the phrase: 'Finnish up, please!'

TONY
Mm. I always wanted to go to Lapland, home of lap-dancing.

GARY
Imagine being a reindeer, with those huge antlers.

TONY
Yeah, always having to remember when you're going under doorways—

GARY
Or getting into cars.

TONY
Mm. Or you're chatting, and you bend down to check your hooves, and you accidentally bash the reindeer you're chatting to over the head.

GARY
Nightmare.

TONY
Nightmare.
A thoughtful pause.

GARY
I'm going to miss these wide-ranging philosophical chats.

TONY
Yeah, me too.
Another thoughtful pause.

TONY
(*Brightening*) Okay, top five girl singers' arses, what've you got!?

GARY
Okay!
They rub their hands, excited.

12. HOSPITAL: TV ROOM

Morning. Deborah is in a wheelchair, blanket over her knees. Dorothy, in uniform, is sitting next to her. A few other patients are sitting around.

DEBORAH
You don't think it's a bit cruel?

DOROTHY
Pretending you might lose your leg? No, it's all part of the rough and tumble of modern relationships, isn't it?

DEBORAH
It is hurtful, though. When I think about how Tony begged me to sleep with him. Five long,

grinding years of begging. Begging in the morning. Begging in the evening. By phone.

DOROTHY
By fax.

DEBORAH
A marriage proposal in the Personal Section of *Razzle*.

DOROTHY
Oh, yes. That doesn't quite work as a romantic gesture, does it?

DEBORAH
And he always said: I may not have any professional qualifications, or a boat, but I'll never leave you.

DOROTHY
Mm. Then they sleep with you, and overnight they change from . . . Prince Edward to Freddie Starr.

DEBORAH
Mm.
Tony arrives, seeing them in a reverie.

TONY
Hello, girls.

DOROTHY
Hi, Tony.
She gets up.

DOROTHY
Well, I'll let you two lovebirds catch up on (*Looking up at TV*) Quincy.
She leaves. An awkwardness follows between Deborah and Tony.

TONY
So, how's it been?

DEBORAH
Oh, you know.

TONY
Is the leg still . . .?

DEBORAH
Touch and go, yes. So, have you moved all your stuff up into my flat?

TONY
Um. Not yet.

DEBORAH
Why?

TONY
I . . . couldn't find a good box.

DEBORAH
You're hesitating because you want to see if I'll pull through, don't you?
Tony swallows, guilty.

TONY
Yes.

DEBORAH
Thanks. Don't you love me for my personality?

TONY
Of course, love. But what I love about your personality is it comes tucked away inside a great free body. (*Romantically*) Your personality is the Bonus Ball in the Rollover Jackpot of your body.
Deborah looks at Tony in dismay.

DEBORAH
I'd still be happy to live with you if something horrible happened to you.
Tony looks guilty.

DEBORAH
Okay, well, I don't want you moving into my flat. You'd better leave.

TONY
Okay.
He gets up, looking upset.

TONY
Can I get you anything from the hospital shop?

DEBORAH
No.

TONY
They've got some very convincing rubber grapes.

DEBORAH
No, thank you.
Looking guilty, Tony leaves. He is gazing back at Deborah so walks blindly out into the corridor and is run over by a trolley.

13. SEX-VIDEO DREAM

Daytime. A parody of a sex-instruction video. Anthea and George, both looking like doctors, are talking to camera, po-faced. George drifts in and out of an American accent.

GEORGE
Never draw attention to your partner's sexual failings, however shaming they are.

ANTHEA
No, try not to do that.

GEORGE
Remember above all that making love is supposed to be fun.
'Anthea' and 'George' grin alarmingly. A cheap and cheesy graphic leads into an equally tacky sequence: a partially naked Dorothy and Tony

are having sex in front of a mock-up fireplace. Muzak fades in.

GEORGE'S VOICE-OVER
Danny and Kelsey love the sensuality of a roaring fire. And they're not afraid to try out new things.
Tony produces a feather duster out of nowhere.

ANTHEA'S VOICE-OVER
You might even contemplate safe sex involving a third person.
Gary and Deborah appear in the doorway. Gary looks timid and has his shirt or trousers off. Deborah is wearing something glamorous and skimpy.

GEORGE'S VOICE-OVER
But only if all the parties consent.
Tony interrupts his love-making and is seen inaudibly pointing at Gary and saying, 'No,' then what looks like 'Piss off.' Gary exits, looking ashamed. Deborah joins Tony and Dorothy.

DOROTHY'S VOICE-OVER
I was a bit nervous at first, but Danny was really understanding, and it all turned out all right.
Tony/Danny grins happily. An alarm clock goes off somewhere on set. The three of them look for where the sound is coming from.

14. GARY'S FLAT: HIS BEDROOM

Early morning. Gary's alarm clock is sounding. He awakes with a start, looking shagged out again after another night of sex-instruction videos. He blearily turns off the alarm clock and looks up to see the video is still on (unseen). We hear its American commentary and more muzak.

MALE SEX DOCTOR'S VOICE-OVER
Here Danny is on top, and Kelsey is rocking gently in time with him. Notice how Kelsey speeds up as she becomes more excited.

GARY
(*Joining in, off by heart*) Notice how Kelsey speeds up as she becomes more excited.

WOMAN SEX DOCTOR/GARY
(*In unison*) Cathy and Zak love this unusual position.

GARY
(*Wearily*) I've got to give this up.
The sound of the front door slamming. Gary quickly turns the video off and lies down as though asleep.

TELETUBBIES
Again! Again!
The TV has come on. Gary turns it off and lies down again. Dorothy comes in.

DOROTHY
Hi.

GARY
(*Instantly stirring*) Hi.

DOROTHY
(*Holding it up*) How's the new video?

GARY
Oh, you know. So-so.

DOROTHY
Shall we watch it?

GARY
No, let's not bother. It's hard to take them seriously. I've hardly watched them.

DOROTHY
They seem to be making some impression – yesterday you kept mumbling phrases from them in your sleep.

GARY
Oh?

DOROTHY
'Watch how Brittany goes to work on Tyler'. That seemed to be a particular favourite.

GARY
Mm.

DOROTHY
Make me some tea, love, it's your turn.

GARY
Okay.
Gary leaves the room. Dorothy goes to Gary's 'secret' drawer and finds half a dozen pseudo-educational sex videos. She opens another drawer and a dozen more videos tumble out. Dorothy sighs, annoyed. She finds a can of lager under the bed, shakes it up, and squirts it into the video player. Dorothy goes back to the bed, reclines and turns on the video player. After a moment there is a pop followed by a puff of smoke. Dorothy looks satisfied.

15. THE CROWN

Evening. The pub is busier and more festive than ever. There is a hand-written poster announcing KARAOKE NITE. The equipment is all set up on a small stage. Ken and Tony are behind the bar, wearing similar glittery tops in different colours. Ken serves Gary, having to shout above the noise.

KEN
Good turnout.

GARY
Yeah. You must be very happy.

KEN
Yeah. Hey, I hear you're into sexy videos these days, Gary?
This soars above a freak lull in the noise level. Everyone looks at Gary accusingly, then resumes their conversation. Gary glares at Tony, who has wandered over.

GARY
Yes, I am. I've got eight thousand.

KEN
I was into pornography for a while but I found that I was looking for harder and harder stuff, until eventually I was only satisfied by pictures of completely naked women.

GARY
Uh-huh.
Gary and Tony stand there marvelling at Ken.

KEN
Okay, it's time. (*To Tony*) Do you want to start?

TONY
Okay.
Tony jumps up on to the stage. Ken fiddles with the karaoke machine.

TONY
Hello, pub! You're beautiful! I'd like to start with—
The music starts up, drowning him out. He immediately goes into his rendition of something loud, The Buzzcocks' 'Ever Fallen In Love'. We fade between a succession of songs over the course of the evening. Tony singing, 'Jive Talking' on his own, doing the actions. He signals to Gary at the bar to join him. Gary refuses coyly but when eventually he does so they do impressively choreographed routines together. Ken is on a bar stool crooning something slow and MOR, e.g. 'Solitaire' by Andy Williams, complete with delicate gestures. An elderly woman sings 'Stoned Love' (the Supremes) with Gary and Tony doing doo-wops in background. Gary and Tony watch sulkily, defiantly unimpressed, as a good-looking man sings a brilliant but highly sexual version of e.g. 'It's Not Unusual' watched by admiring women. Tony and Gary sing 'Making Your Mind Up' (Bucks Fizz). At the appropriate moment they whip off Ken's apron. Ken sings along to another ballad, Helen Reddy's version of 'I am Woman'. Tony, Gary and Ken sing 'When Will I See You Again?' by the Three Degrees, with all the actions. We cut wide to reveal that the pub is completely deserted apart from a drunk asleep along the length of the bar.

16. DEBORAH'S FLAT

The next morning. The sound of the door shutting. Dorothy leads Deborah in.

DEBORAH
Thanks for looking after me, Dorothy.

DOROTHY
How does it feel?

DEBORAH
Much better, thanks.
Tony appears from the bedroom.

TONY
Hello.

DEBORAH
Oh, hi.
Tension between him and Deborah.

DOROTHY
Okay, I'll just go somewhere else.
Dorothy exits.

DEBORAH
I'm not sure I want you here.

TONY
But I've moved my stuff in.
Tony opens a cupboard, revealing various ridiculous possessions. Trying to jolly Deborah along, he puts on an Australian bush hat with lager cans dangling from strings. Deborah is not amused. Tony takes off his hat and puts on his glasses-and-flashing-red-nose set. Deborah still is not amused.

TONY
So your leg's on the mend?

DEBORAH
Yes.

TONY
I'm sorry I was a bit funny about it. I honestly don't care one way or the other about your, you know.
Deborah relents, giving him a half smile.

TONY
As long as you've still got your bum! Ha. No, seriously.

DEBORAH
To be honest I was always going to be fine. It was a bit of a test.

TONY
What?

DEBORAH
Maybe it was a bit naughty.

TONY
(*Offended*) I was worried about you! How could you do that?!

DEBORAH
I'm sorry.

TONY
Right. Well. You're not the only one with principles.
Preparing to storm out, Tony looks for something to take with him. He takes the hat, puts it on and exits. Deborah sighs, upset. Tony reappears seconds later, still wearing the hat, and gives Deborah a big kiss. The kiss goes on and on, the romance undermined by the lager cans dangling round their heads. Deborah takes it off Tony's head. They come up for air and are suddenly tense.

DEBORAH
So, this is a big step in our lives, finally living together.

TONY
Yeah. I've never lived with a woman before. At least, not with her knowing.
Tony gets emotional.

DEBORAH
Oh, Tony, you're so sweet, getting all choked up.

TONY
No, it's just, I'm going to miss my late-night chats on the sofa with Gary.

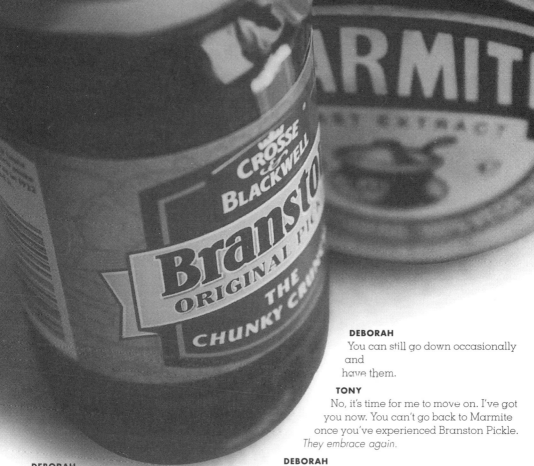

DEBORAH
You can still go down occasionally and have them.

TONY
No, it's time for me to move on. I've got you now. You can't go back to Marmite once you've experienced Branston Pickle.
They embrace again.

DEBORAH
Oh, you say the nicest things.

Meanwhile, Gary is lying in bed. Dorothy is sitting on it, clothed. She leans towards him.

DOROTHY
I've got some time off. Are you up to three days of nonstop love-making?

GARY
I am, actually.
Gary reaches for Dorothy, kissing her and lying on top of her.

GARY
I'm afraid the video player seems to have broken.

DOROTHY
Oh, no, really? I was looking forward to watching some of your tapes.

GARY
You don't need them, you've got me.
They get under the duvet and start to make love.

DOROTHY
Ooh, I say.

GARY
(*Sex-video style*) 'Why not try "talking dirty" to each other occasionally?'
They start to make love.

GARY
'Never do anything that your partner finds distasteful or unnatural.'

DOROTHY
Yes, can you stop talking like that, please, Gary?

GARY
Like what?
They resume their love-making. We pan back, voices becoming muffled under the duvet.

GARY
'Try dimming the lights, as some people are shy about revealing their bodies—'

DOROTHY
Gary, shut up.

18. DEBORAH'S FLAT

That night. Tony and Deborah are sitting on the sofa. The TV is on. They are drinking from lager cans. Deborah is making an effort but appears a little bewildered.

TONY
Okay, typical topics of conversation for blokes might include your top fives – top-five TV barmaids, top-five sexy words. Who's taller: a donkey or an ostrich. Whatever happened to Rick Astley? Which would you rather have: a huge nobbly nose or huge nobbly ears?

DEBORAH
Okay.

TONY
Right, I'll start. Hey, what do you reckon on those Spice Girls being pregnant, then?

DEBORAH
Yes, I wonder how that will affect the dynamic within the group.

TONY
No, no, you wouldn't say that, as a bloke.

DEBORAH
Wouldn't I?

TONY
No, you'd say something like: Yeah, I still think Sporty's got the best arse. Go on, try it.

DEBORAH
Okay: I still think Sporty's got the best . . . Can I say bottom instead of arse?

TONY
No.

DEBORAH
I don't like the word arse, it's common.
We start to pan back.

TONY
This isn't working.

DEBORAH
No no, give me another chance, I'll be okay.
She clears her throat.

19. OUTSIDE THE HOUSE

Meanwhile, a smooth pan back as if through the window to the outside. The camera continues to retreat. Dialogue is all voice-over.

DEBORAH
Okay. Whatever happened to Rick Astley?

TONY
He had crappy hair, didn't he?

DEBORAH
Yeah. Really crappy.

TONY
Good, good. Keep going.

DEBORAH
I think he was successful because everyone wanted to mother him, didn't they? (*Pause*) That's not right, is it?

TONY
Try again, try again . . .
We fade down on their conversation and up on Gary and Dorothy's.

GARY
So, do you reckon you're pregnant now?

DOROTHY
No, it could take years.

GARY
Oh, okay. Want to go again?

DOROTHY
All right.
The rustle of the duvet. We fade into the night.

DOROTHY
I wonder how Tony and Deborah are doing.

GARY
Shh. We're making a baby.

DOROTHY
Sorry.

GARY
(*Singing*) 'I am woman, hear me roar—'

DOROTHY
No, you're putting me off now . . .

SERIES SEVEN: EPISODE TWO

If you hang around long enough on BBC TV you get to film an episode abroad. *One Foot in the Grave* went to the Algarve, *Absolutely Fabulous* to the Alps, *Birds of a Feather* to Spain. So how amusing that we should end up in Worthing.

At one stage I planned to set an episode entirely on a cross-channel ferry, but someone painted a picture of cast and crew vomiting in force-8 gales, boom operators getting swept out to sea, fear, loathing and mutiny. As it was, Neil hurt his knee badly when he ran headlong into the water hazard on the mini-golf while escaping from Gary. If you listen carefully you can hear it crack. Now that is commitment . . .

I had always wanted to write an episode about Gary and Tony stealing something ridiculous while on a drunken bender. For a while it was going to be Simon Le Bon's porch. Then I planned to have them getting arrested, but sitcom scenes involving policemen are usually awful.

1. GARY'S FLAT: LIVING ROOM

An evening in. Gary and Dorothy are entwined lovingly on the sofa, as are Tony and Deborah. It is a tight squeeze. They are all reading.

TONY
So, are you up the duff yet, Dorothy?

DOROTHY
If it does happen, Tony, I'll be pregnant, not 'up the duff', 'sprog-farming', 'wazzed up', 'in the fat club' or any other euphemisms.

TONY
So you're not 'hanging a donut'?

DOROTHY
No.
They read on.

GARY
(*To Deborah*) What kind of birth control do you use?

DEBORAH
The 'Eugh, get-off!' method.
Tony frowns at Deborah.

DEBORAH
It can take ages to get pregnant, can't it.

TONY
Yes, everything has to be right. The womb has to be on the right cycle. The . . . placebo has to be aligned with the avery. (*Dreamy*) And the seed . . . must be freed.
They are staring at him, unnerving him.

TONY
I'll get a book out of the library.
They go back to their reading.

GARY
Well, it's that time of the year again.

DOROTHY
You're going to change your pants?

GARY
No, the International Security Equipment and Services Exhibition, ISECESEX.

DEBORAH
ISECESEX?

GARY
Yes, ISECESEX.

DOROTHY
Mm, where are you middle managers off to this year with your Easicare travel slacks and little plastic attaché cases – Acapulco? the Seychelles?

The others are smirking.

GARY
It's easy to sneer, isn't it? Okay, so maybe we are a bit earnest, but this is our one chance to let our hair down and go somewhere a bit glamorous.

DOROTHY
Where is it this year?

GARY
Worthi—

DOROTHY
Worthing, right.
Gary tries to be dignified. He shows her a leaflet.

GARY
Nice hotel and conference venue, look.

DOROTHY
Mm, in a Colditzy kind of way.

GARY
Hey, you could all come with me.
The others aren't sure.

GARY
You can stay for free in my hotel suite.

ALL
(*Variously*) Okay. Great. Sure. Let's go.

2. GROYNE VIEW HOTEL

One night a couple of weeks later. We hold a wide shot of a grand, rather faded seafront hotel: the Groyne View. A minicab pulls up containing our foursome. They struggle out with their bags.

TONY
You remember that bit in *Quadrophenia* where Sting is the bellboy at the hotel?

DEBORAH
Vaguely.

TONY
Wouldn't it be great if Sting was bellboy here? You'd be going up in the lift together, and he'd suddenly go, 'Rox-anne!'
Gary turns to pay the driver.

GARY
(*Pompous*) I'll have a receipt, please. I am an official ISECESEX delegate.

DRIVER
A what?

GARY
Just give me a receipt.

DRIVER
I've run out.

GARY
Okay, get me your chief executive on the phone.

DRIVER
Piss off.
Dorothy takes over.

DOROTHY
It's okay, I'll pay.

GARY
Listen, I'm a senior manager, and your arse is seriously on the line—

DOROTHY
Gary, get in the hotel.
Dorothy pays. The others drift towards the hotel entrance.

TONY
I love hotels, don't you. It's like having your own big house.
They enter the lobby. Hanging there are a lot of helium balloons embossed with the ISECESEX logo.

3. HOTEL ROOM

Half an hour later. A large but dowdy room with two double beds, a view of the sea and little else. Dorothy and Deborah are finishing unpacking. A few more balloons are in evidence. Gary comes in.

GARY
I've complained to the manager, and he says he'll sort it out in the morning. He knows his backside's dangerously out of whack on this one.

DOROTHY
You booked a cheaper room to save on your expenses, didn't you, Gary—

GARY
Ah, but, in fact it's all rather snazzy, isn't it? (*Looking around*) With all the lovely old . . .

DEBORAH
Mould—?

GARY
Features. Like the...
Tony stops him short as he comes out of the bathroom, wearing the shower cap, excited.

GARY
... lunatic in the bathroom.

TONY
Look, a free transparent hat! You can still see my hair underneath!
He shows them his hair, then holds up a paper ribbon.

TONY
And a paper sash round the toilet! Like on Miss World. So this is, like, Miss Toilet. And look, look, you'll never believe this.
He disappears into the bathroom for a second, then re-emerges with a loo roll.

TONY
They've folded the toilet paper into a little V, there, at the end.

DOROTHY
You don't stay in hotels very often, do you, Tony?

TONY
No.
Still excited, Tony picks up the phone and pretends to make a call.

TONY
Room service? Hello. Will you send me up someone to comb my hair nicely please.
He chuckles. The others give him pitying looks.

DEBORAH
What are we doing tomorrow?

GARY
I'll basically be attending a Q and A sesh on CCTV systems, that's in the a.m., then after a get-to-know-you ploughman's with Brian Foggit of Secu-Blast I'll be—

DOROTHY
Gary, please don't talk like that, you're making me sad.
Gary and Tony realise self-consciously that they are on the same bed, and Dorothy and Deborah are on the other bed.

GARY
You know Morecambe and Wise slept together in the same bed.

ALL
Mm.

GARY
You never felt they'd go the whole way, did you?

ALL
No.

TONY
Okay! What shall we do?

DOROTHY
I'm going to bed.

DEBORAH
Me too.

TONY
You can't go to bed this early.
They ignore him. Dorothy and Gary finish unpacking. Deborah is lying down, eyes shut. Tony notices and quietly tries to mount her.

DEBORAH
No, Tony—
Spurned, Tony gets off.

TONY
Fancy a drink, mate?

GARY
No, I need my wits about me tomorrow. In this game, if you drop your guard half an inch they have you for breakfast.

TONY
(*Disappointed*) Oh.
Tony mooches around, looking for something to do. He opens a built-in wardrobe and pretends to have been attacked by the wire coathangers.

TONY
Don't worry about me, save yourselves!

DEBORAH
(*Pleading, to Gary*) Will you take him for a walk or something?

GARY
Okay. Come on.
Tony bounds gratefully after Gary.

4. ON THE BEACH

Three in the morning. The promenade is deserted. Tony and Gary are extremely drunk and happy. They are sitting on the shoreline in a rather impressive 'car' that they have moulded out of the shingle. A bit of driftwood acts as gear lever and a hubcap for a steering wheel. They are drinking from cans of lager resting on the 'dashboard'.

GARY
You see, the thing about Dorothy is, I really love her. Well, she's very lovable. As you know . . .

TONY
Oh, I know.

GARY
And I suppose I love her because, fair do's—

TONY
Fair do's.

GARY
Fair do's.

TONY
Fair do's.

GARY
Fair do's.
That thought has petered out.

GARY
And now she is prepared to house our little baby on the inside of her body until such time as – and you know why else I love Dorothy?

TONY
She's very rude . . .?

GARY
God, yes, she's incredibly rude. But, this'll amuse you, it's not the big things I love about Dorothy—

TONY
Oh, I love the big things.

GARY
Oh, yeah, yeah I *love* the big things, but above all it's the tiny things, isn't it?

TONY
Yes. The microscopic things.

GARY
No, not that small. It's—

TONY
Is there another beer in the boot?

GARY
There is.
Gary turns round, unearths a can from the stones and gives it to Tony.

TONY
You shouldn't really be driving.

GARY
No, I'll be fine. You know, I've never said this before.

TONY
What?

A long, serious pause.

GARY
Dibble wibble wibble.
They collapse into helpless laughter, falling out of the car.

TONY
I've broken my door.

GARY
This car, it's been nothing but trouble since we got it.
They collapse into more laughter.

TONY
Shall we go for a swim?

GARY
No. That would be stupid.

TONY
Yes.

GARY
I must be getting back to my rotel hoom.

TONY
No. No! The night is still young. It's only . . . sixteen.

GARY
That is young.
They head off back to the promenade.

TONY
How did the stones get so smooth?

GARY
I think the council have got a special machine.

TONY
Oh.

5. END OF PIER

A little later. Gary is horsing around, trying to use a life-belt as a Hula-Hoop. Tony is riding a huge plastic fish bolted to a billboard inscribed: WILLIE WETFISH SAYS WELCOME TO WORTHING!

6. HOTEL ROOM

The next morning, everyone asleep. Deborah stirs, finding Tony stretched out over her, mouth open. She manages to lever him off. He groans. Deborah turns and sees a huge grinning fish propped up against a wall, obviously taken from the billboard. She shakes Tony awake. The pain of his hangover makes him cry.

DEBORAH
Tony, what's that?

TONY
Don't touch my head! Nobody touch my head!

DEBORAH
There's a huge fish in the room.
Tony reluctantly opens his eyes.

TONY
Oh, it's still there.
Dorothy and Gary are waking up.

DOROTHY
Gary.
She shakes Gary awake.

GARY
Oh, it's still there.

DEBORAH
Well, what is it?

TONY
I don't know. Cod? Haddock?

DEBORAH
No, where did you get it?

TONY
I don't know. I can't be expected to remember everything.

GARY
Oh, no, it's ten to nine.
He gets out of bed in a hurry, stopping to steady his head.

DOROTHY
How did you get it back here?
Tony and Gary ponder this.

TONY/GARY
Can't remember./No idea.

DEBORAH
It can't stay here.

TONY
Why not, you said the room needed brightening up.

DOROTHY
Not with a twelve-foot fish.
Gary, half-dressed, stands there with his sponge bag, wondering how to get past the fish into the bathroom.

GARY
(*Giving up*) Oh, never mind.

DEBORAH
This is serious, Tony, you could be done for theft and criminal damage.

TONY
Nobody will find out. We'll wait till it's quiet, then put it back, won't we, Gary?

GARY
Nothing to do with me, mate, it was your idea. I'm a respectable member of the security-equipment community.

TONY
That's not fair!

DOROTHY
(*To Gary*) You're like Batman, aren't you? By day, mild-mannered manager of a sleepy branch office, by night bat-eared

mischief-maker with your drunken Boy Wonder.

Gary gives her a look and pulls on the rest of his suit.

DOROTHY
What's that on your jacket?

GARY
Nothing.

DOROTHY
What does your little homemade badge say?

GARY
Leave me alone.

DOROTHY
Was it 'Gary Strang MA, Vice-president' by any chance?

Dorothy smiles. Gary turns away from her. He has made himself a badge with five stars, McDonald's-style.

DOROTHY
That's your MA from the University of Made-Up-Place, is it?

GARY
Ha-ha, ha-ha, ha.

DOROTHY
Five stars. Does that mean you're allowed to put the fries into the little cartons?

GARY
You can sneer. Yes, I am contributing to British industry. Your nurse's pay packet would look pretty slim if us oh-so-hilarious middle managers didn't take our jobs seriously.

DOROTHY
I'm sorry.

She tries not to smirk. Gary puts his tie on.

DOROTHY
Before you go, Gary . . .

GARY
What?

DOROTHY
Can I have a strawberry McShake, please.

GARY
Great. Don't wait up.

Looking genuinely offended, Gary leaves.

7. CONFERENCE HALL: CORRIDOR

A pegboard sign stands outside a door. The letters have been tampered with so it reads: ISECESEX SEMINAR. CCTV SYSTEMS: Q & A WITH IAN BIG TOAST OF SCURF-BLEG. The door opens and delegates in suits file out. They include Gary, who is now wearing an official delegate's badge. Gary stops to consult his conference agenda. He looks across and sees one of the few women delegates doing the same.

GARY
Hello.

WENDY
Oh, hello.
Wendy is a meeker version of Dorothy, probably with a similar hairstyle.

GARY
What did you think?

WENDY
Quite interesting.

GARY
Yes.

WENDY
I enjoyed your question about the hidden costs of failsafe wiring.

GARY
Thanks. Who do you work for?
She shows her badge.

GARY
Ah, Securimax. Hello . . . Wendy. I love your mesh.

WENDY
My what?

GARY
Your mesh, your Maximesh? Your company's fencing.

WENDY
Oh, thanks. Yes, it's a good mesh. And you . . . Gary?
She stares at his badge.

GARY
We're quite a small contracts company. I run the London sub-office. Keeps me on my toes!
They both chuckle. An awkward silence. They are obviously keen on each other.

WENDY
What are you going to now?

GARY
I've got a bit of a gap. Do you fancy a coffee?

WENDY
Mm, great.
They walk off down the corridor. Their conversation fades away.

WENDY
Have you had a chance to explore the town?

GARY
Not really. I did sit on the beach for a bit earlier this morning . . .

8. END OF PIER

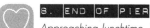

Approaching lunchtime. We pan from the billboard, now noticeably lacking its showpiece fish, to the Groyne View Hotel.

9. HOTEL ROOM

The bedside alarm clock shows ten past one. Tony has gone back to bed and is asleep, not looking his best.
A knock on the door wakes Tony up.
He groans.

TONY
(*Muffled*) Go away. I'm not very well.
He walks groggily towards the bathroom door, forgetting the big fish is there. He walks into it. A jingle of keys as someone outside tries to get in. Tony looks anxiously at the fish. He stands by the door, barring the way.

TONY
Who is it?

CHAMBERMAID
(*Offscreen*) Chambermaid.

TONY
It's okay, you don't need to do the room.

CHAMBERMAID
(*Offscreen*) All right. I'll come back later.

TONY
No, don't. I like to do all my own cleaning. I'm very fastidious.

CHAMBERMAID
(*Offscreen*) Don't you want new towels?

TONY
No, I like to wash my own towels every day, using my own special washing powder, made . . . to my own recipe.

CHAMBERMAID
(*Offscreen*) Oh. All right then.
She goes away. Tony looks at the fish. He tuts.

Lunchtime. Gary and Wendy are chatting animatedly, enjoying each other's company. More ISECESEX balloons.

GARY
Yes, I've got a sort of girlfriend, but we're not really getting along.

WENDY
Oh, why?

GARY
Funnily enough, talking to you's made me realise what's wrong: You're not embarrassed by me.

WENDY
Why's your girlfriend embarrassed by you?

GARY
I've *no idea*. Absolutely *no idea*. What about you, have you got a bloke?

WENDY
No. Mind you I am a lesbian.
Gary nods earnestly, trying to hide his disappointment. Wendy smiles.

WENDY
(*Chuckling*) Got you.
Gary joins in a bit hysterically, relieved.

WENDY
No, I never seem to meet men.
Gary does an insincere tut of sympathy.

GARY
Are you, um, doing anything this evening?

WENDY
No.

11. CRAZY-GOLF COURSE

Afternoon. A putting course, near the promenade. Dorothy knocks her golf ball into the hole. She reaches in and gets Deborah's and her ball out. Tony is further back on the same hole, spending ages lining up his putt. He finally hits the ball, failing to get it through the gate of the novelty windmill.

DOROTHY
I wonder how Gary's getting on.

DEBORAH
You don't think you were a bit hard on him this morning?

DOROTHY
I know. I'll apologise. Actually, there is a reason for it.
Dorothy looks round to check Tony can not hear. Tony, getting irritated, is starting to hit the ball wildly.

TONY
(*To the ball*) Get in, you round bastard!
Dorothy turns back to Deborah.

DEBORAH
What? What?

DOROTHY
My period's late.

DEBORAH
Hey, congratulations!
They both grin.

DEBORAH
Have you told Gary?

DOROTHY
No, I wanted to wait a bit till I was more sure. I think I'm giving him a hard time because the enormity of it's just dawning on me.
Behind them, Tony still can not get the ball through the windmill.

TONY
Bloody Dutch.

DEBORAH
Don't get ratty, Tony, it's only a game. (*To Dorothy*) Maybe Gary will guess you're pregnant.

DOROTHY
No, he still doesn't really understand periods. He thinks they're something to do with the moon.

TONY
(*Still struggling*) Get. In. The. Arsing. Windmill!

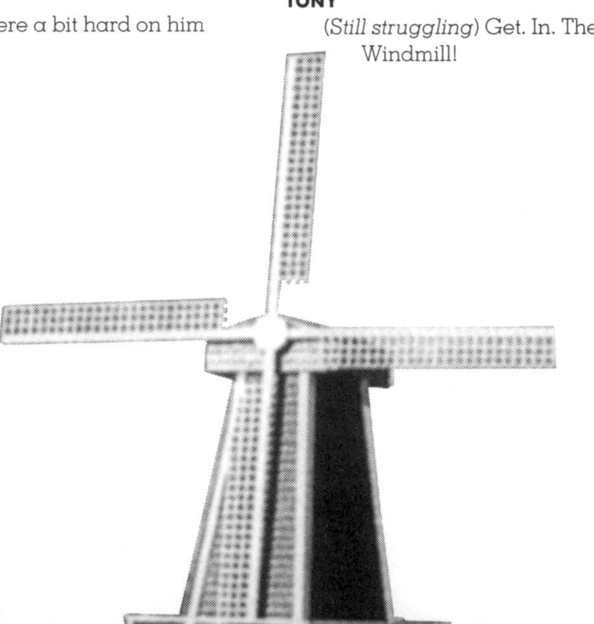

12. PROMENADE: SHELTER

That evening. Gary and Wendy are sitting, watching the sea. Gary, touchingly in love, steals a besotted glance at Wendy. He looks away. Wendy looks at him.

GARY
Are you cold?

WENDY
I am a bit actually.
Gary discreetly slips off his jacket, clearly to drape over Wendy's shoulders. But he realises how cold it is and quietly puts his jacket back on.

GARY
Shall we go back then?

WENDY
Okay.
They get up and walk back. Gary puts his hand in Wendy's.

13. HOTEL ROOM

Meanwhile, Deborah and Dorothy are sitting around, reading and listening to the radio. Tony, dressed for bed, comes out of the bathroom, brushing his teeth. He negotiates a way round the fish.

TONY
Isn't this great – a free sewing kit! I'm never ever going out again. We've got everything we need right here.

DOROTHY
(*Worried*) I thought Gary would be back by now.

DEBORAH
Don't worry, he's probably out drunkenly looking for some big plastic chips to go with old smiley here. (*To Tony*) What are you going to do with it?

TONY
I'll think of something.
Deborah drifts over to the window and gazes out.

DOROTHY
I've got a leaflet here for the Stuffed Animal Museum – anyone fancy that tomorrow?

DEBORAH
Let's play mini-golf again. It's the first sport I've been able to play without wearing two sports bras . . .
Deborah peters out, perturbed at what she can see out of the window.

DOROTHY
Or we could resume our search for the perfect winkle. Debs?

DEBORAH
Sorry?
We are looking out of the window from Deborah's perspective. Down at the pavement below Gary is kissing Wendy. He is obviously trying to be discreet, making sure they are not too much in view.

DOROTHY
What's happening out there?

DEBORAH
Very quiet.
Still from Deborah's point of view, Wendy goes off, waving goodbye. They come together again for another last kiss. Wendy ruffles Gary's hair affectionately and leaves. Deborah does a discreet wince.

14. OUTSIDE THE GROYNE VIEW HOTEL

The next morning.

15. HOTEL ROOM

Gary and Dorothy are asleep in their bed. Deborah, alone in hers, gazes across at them ruefully. She gets up and heads for the bathroom, having to bend to avoid the fish.

DEBORAH
Bloody fish.
The sound of the bath running. Dorothy stirs. She looks over at Gary with affection. One of his arms is sticking out of the bedding. She picks it up and playfully hits him round the face with it, then stuffs several of his fingers into his mouth. Gary does not stir. Dorothy lays his hand on her breast. He smiles in his sleep.

DOROTHY
Love, time to get up.
He still does not stir.

DOROTHY
Your penis has come loose.
Gary comes to immediately. Dorothy smiles at him.

DOROTHY
Hi, love. I didn't want you to miss any of your conference.

GARY
Oh, thanks.
He sits up.

DOROTHY
How did it go yesterday?

GARY
Fine. Really good, I met . . .

DOROTHY
Who?

GARY
(*Realising*) Dull people. Lots of very dull people.

DOROTHY
What did you do in the evening?

GARY
Me?

DOROTHY
Yes.

GARY
I had the *dullest dullest* time of my life. *Awful.*

DOROTHY
Maybe you should hang out with us from now on—

GARY
No, it wasn't that bad. There were some nice people. Geoff . . . Bedington. And Lance. I think there was a Wendy. And . . . Raoul.

DOROTHY
I'm sorry I was horrible to you yesterday. There was a reason.

GARY
PMT?

DOROTHY
No, the opposite in fact.

GARY
TMP?

DOROTHY
No, Gary, I think I'm pregnant.
She smiles. Gary tries to force a smile.

GARY
Oh, love, that's tremendous.
They embrace. Gary looks wan.

DOROTHY
It's still really early. I haven't even taken a test.

GARY
So what are the chances that you're pregnant?

DOROTHY
I don't know. It's impossible to say.

GARY
It must be possible, surely you can say, it can't be impossible, I mean is it very likely, or not very likely, or—

DOROTHY
Calm down, Gary. Are you all right about this?

GARY
(*Subdued*) Of course I am. I'm cock-a-hoop.

DOROTHY
Well, it may be nothing.

GARY
Uh-huh.
Tony enters, very upset.

TONY
Bad news. Read that.
He tosses the local newspaper to Gary.

DOROTHY
FIREMEN PUT OUT FIRE IN BLOCK OF FLATS. No, I'd say that was good news—

GARY
Good news, definitely.

TONY
No, underneath.

GARY
CENTREPIECE OF MUNICIPAL DISPLAY STOLEN. Ah.
The paper shows a picture of the fish in situ, with a caption: 'The missing fish mascot'.

TONY
See! Bad news, very bad.

DOROTHY
'The head of the council's Leisure Committee said angrily: 'If I get hold of the—'

TONY
Stop! Stop reading! Oh, no, I'm going to be recognised and arrested, just as I'm settling down and becoming mature. It's so ironic.
He opens the bathroom door.

TONY
(*Calling out*) Debs – I'm going to be arrested!

DOROTHY
Just own up and give it back. They'll understand.

TONY
No, there must be another way. Maybe we could . . . eat it, bit by bit. It is a fish.
Dorothy looks at Tony.

TONY
Well, I don't know. Come on, Gary, think of a plan.

GARY
(Miles away) Sorry?

16. CRAZY-GOLF COURSE

Later that day. Dorothy is playing a round with Deborah. Deborah is lining up a shot through a clown's mouth, taking it very seriously.

DEBORAH
Gary'll be fine. It's like you say, the whole thing's just a bit daunting. Remember he had that wobble after you both agreed to look after your mum's sideboard.

DOROTHY
It's not quite the same, is it. You don't have to love a sideboard and . . . pick it up from parties in scout huts when it's sixteen.
Deborah narrowly misses a putt.

DEBORAH
Bugger.
Dorothy knocks her ball casually into the hole.

DOROTHY
No, I hope you're right. I can't bear it if Gary's really changed his mind. He kept mentioning a Wendy – you know, slipping her name in in a group of names, the way he used to with Kylie when he was obsessed with her.
Deborah, her back to Dorothy, looks awkward.

DEBORAH
Um.

DOROTHY
What?
Deborah can't bring herself to say what she knows.

DEBORAH
Look, I'm sure everything will be brilliant.
Dorothy forces a smile. Deborah turns and tries to get the ball through the clown's mouth.
She misses.

DEBORAH
Oh, ha-ha, clown.

17. HOTEL CORRIDOR

An empty corridor. Tony comes out of his door, wearing dark glasses, paranoid about being recognised. He jogs to a fire cupboard, opens it and takes out a long-handled axe. Another guest comes out of their room. Tony hurriedly turns and looks the other way, out of the window, keeping the axe hidden. A moment later when the coast is clear he turns back. He has put the axe down his trousers, creating an obscene two-foot-long bulge. Another guest is standing there watching him. They exchange looks. Tony decides to brazen it out, managing with difficulty to walk past.

TONY
Hello.

18. HOTEL ROOM

Tony re-enters the room, shutting the door. He gingerly removes the axe from his trousers and approaches the fish menacingly.

TONY
Right.
With sudden force he takes a swing at the fish's grinning head. The axe bounces back, the plastic worryingly resilient.

TONY
Oh, no!
He takes another swipe, then rains blows down noisily, making hardly any impact. He pauses, exhausted.

TONY
Stop grinning!
The door opens, and the chambermaid – young, rather sulky – rushes in. She and Tony, axe in hand, exchange awkward looks.

TONY
Hi.

CHAMBERMAID
What are you doing?

TONY
What, this? Nothing.

CHAMBERMAID
That's that thing that was stolen, isn't it?

TONY
No, this is another one, we brought it with us. Inflatable. Slips inside a suitcase.

CHAMBERMAID
I'm going to have to report you.

TONY
No, don't do that. Look, let me give you something.

CHAMBERMAID
What?
He looks around, snatching up his sewing kit.

TONY
Sewing kit? Lots of different colour threads?
She just stares back.

TONY
Okay, take some of my girlfriend's clothes.
Tony opens the wardrobe door, revealing Deborah's many clothes.

TONY
The tights are rather nice – Oh, you fancy the jacket.
She has taken an expensive-looking jacket.

CHAMBERMAID
You'd better get rid of the fish.

TONY
Okay.
The chambermaid backs out of the room. Tony sighs, then does huge, childish V-signs at the door. The chambermaid catches him doing it as she returns with fresh white towels. She hands them to Tony and waits. He reluctantly hands her the axe. She leaves. Tony locks the door, wonders what to do. He gets his Swiss Army knife out of a drawer, opens the saw blade and starts to hack desperately at the fish's neck. The clock says eleven o'clock. Fade to later: half-past one. Tony is still sawing away, his shirt off, sweating, red in the face. He has only managed to cut through about six inches of the fish's neck. Deborah enters.

DEBORAH
How's it going?
Tony grunts. Deborah sits down on the bed.

DEBORAH
Tony?

TONY
What?

DEBORAH
I saw Gary kissing another woman.

TONY
A woman other than Dorothy?

DEBORAH
Yes.

TONY
Are you sure it wasn't Dorothy in disguise?

DEBORAH
Yes.

TONY
Or someone disguised as Gary?

DEBORAH
Yes!

TONY
Blimey. (*Laddish*) Weh-hey!

DEBORAH
No, Tony, no, not weh-hey!

TONY
Not weh-hey, sorry.

DEBORAH
Gary looked really keen on this girl. And Dorothy thinks she's pregnant. It's all a big mess.

TONY
Oh, yes. (Pause) Still, wey-hey!

DEBORAH
No!

TONY
No, not.

DEBORAH
Talk to Gary about it, he'll listen to you.

TONY
No, he won't. He hates doing things I tell him to do. Except his Ken Dodd impression. He doesn't mind doing that.

DEBORAH
Well, go and find this woman and warn her off Gary. We think her name's Wendy.

TONY
Why can't you do it?

DEBORAH
She'll probably think I'm just being jealous.

TONY
All right, but you must stay and saw my fish.

DEBORAH
No!
She hands him Gary's suit.

19. CONFERENCE HALL: BAR

Lunchtime. The delegates are milling. Tony, dressed in one of Gary's suits, puts his head round the corner, scanning the room.

TONY
(*To himself*) Wendy-Wendy-Wendy.
As women delegates pass him, Tony scrutinises their badges.

TONY
Cheryl . . . Angela . . . Dr Pam Popple.
Tony spots Gary on the far side of the room. He pulls back into the shadows. Gary is talking animatedly to various other men in suits, gesturing, united by the common bond of security equipment. They all go off to a seminar, Gary looking around in vain for Wendy as he is ushered out. Tony spots Wendy talking to another woman. Realising this might be her, he sidles over, 'discreetly' scrutinising her badge. The other woman

exits, leaving Wendy alone. Tony stands there. He catches her eye and smiles. She smiles back politely.

TONY
Hello.

WENDY
Hello.

TONY
How are you?

WENDY
Fine.

TONY
Do you mind talking to me, um (*Reading badge*) Wendy?

WENDY
No. You don't have a badge.

TONY
No. I'm scared of pins.

WENDY
Uh-huh.

TONY
Um, Wendy, I've got a favour to ask.

WENDY
Oh, what?
She smiles up at him charmingly. Tony loses his nerve.

TONY
Are you doing anything this evening?

20. CRAZY-GOLF COURSE

That afternoon. Deborah has a putter in her hand. Tony is with her, still wearing Gary's suit, plus some sunglasses.

DEBORAH
Why did you ask her out?

TONY
It seemed like a better way of splitting her up from Gary.

DEBORAH
Better than telling her that Gary has a long-standing girlfriend who he loves and who may be pregnant?

TONY
Yes. She might like a challenge.
Deborah goes back to concentrating on hitting her golf ball through some complicated hazard. She now looks very much the expert.

DEBORAH
So what's Wendy like?

TONY
Great. Really really nice, brilliant . . . plain, mad teeth, bottom like a huge balloon.
Deborah's jealousy calmed, she goes back to her golf shot.

DEBORAH
All right, you can go out with her once but no touching.

TONY
Thank you. So no light snogging . . .?

DEBORAH
No. Why are you wearing sunglasses?

TONY
Someone may have seen me stealing the big fish.
Deborah misses her shot. She growls and hits something with her putter. Gary turns up, seeing Tony in his suit.

GARY
Hi.

TONY
Oh, hello.

GARY
Why are you wearing my suit?

TONY
I wanted to . . . be like you. For a few hours.
Gary frowns, then shrugs. Deborah has wandered off to the next hole, lost in her golf.

TONY
So.

GARY
So.
A heavy silence.

GARY
Can I be honest with you?

TONY
Of course, mate.

GARY
I've fallen in love with someone.

TONY
Oh.

GARY
And Dorothy thinks she might be pregnant.

TONY
Ah. How do women know that?

GARY
I don't know. Something to do with . . . I don't know.

In the background Deborah is getting more and more irate as she fails to get the ball up a castle drawbridge.

TONY
Can't you just give her up?

GARY
No. I've never felt like this about another woman. I don't know what to do.
Tony looks awkward. Gary gazes out to sea. Behind them Deborah starts hitting the model castle with her putter. She is restrained by the course attendant.

21. PROMENADE: SHELTER

Meanwhile, Dorothy sits on a bench, chewing a winkle and staring out to sea. We see her in close-up. A wide shot reveals her surrounded by mainly elderly people, sitting shoulder to shoulder, all enjoying the view.

22. HOTEL ROOM

Dusk that evening. Gary enters. He sees the big plastic fish, now minus its head but still enormous. They are using it as a clothes horse with a row of knickers and tights drying on it.

GARY
Okay, you, bathroom, now.
With great difficulty he manhandles the fish into the bathroom, putting its front end in the bath. Its tail sticks out into the room. Gary sits on the bed for a while to get his breath back. He ponders, then reaches for the phone, takes a piece of paper out of his pocket and dials the number on it.

GARY
(*Into phone*) Room two nine five, please. Hi, Wendy. How are you?
As Gary listens he toys with the flex, suitably lovelorn.

GARY
(*Into phone*) Mm. Uh-huh. Mm. So can I see you tonight? (*Disappointed*) Oh, anybody I know? (*Listening*) Of course I'm jealous, I'm really keen on you. Look, I'll sort things out with my girlfriend. (*Listening*) Me? Well at the moment I'm . . . (*Gazing at the fish*) it's a bit complicated. (*Listening*) Okay, I'll speak to you later.
Gary hangs up, sadly, and goes into the bathroom.

23. HOTEL BATHROOM

A moment later. Gary gets out a small canister of lighter fluid and squirts it on to the fish. He carefully applies a match. The lighter fluid burns.

GARY
Okay. I'm taking you out of here in an ashtray.
The smoke sets off the fire alarm.

GARY
Oh, shit.
Trying to dampen down the flames, Gary grabs the shower and turns it on. Only a trickle comes out. Gary furiously shakes the drops of water at the flames. The shower powers belatedly into action, instantly dowsing the flames. The smoke alarm shuts down. Gary gratefully leaves the bathroom.

24. HOTEL ROOM

Gary re-enters, finding the chambermaid standing there.

GARY
Hello.

CHAMBERMAID
Hello.

GARY
Nothing to worry about. I've isolated the small fire.

CHAMBERMAID
What caused it?
They stare at the back end of the fish.

GARY
A naughty fish?

CHAMBERMAID
I warned your friend I'd have to report you unless you got rid of that.

GARY
Yes, he said.
Gary reluctantly goes to Deborah's wardrobe and holds open the door. The chambermaid selects another nice jacket.

CHAMBERMAID
Ta.

GARY
You're welcome.
She leaves.

25. SEAFRONT PUB

Later. Tony and Wendy are having a drink together.

WENDY
So, what's your company called?

TONY
Um, Tony's Security Company.

WENDY
What do you specialise in?

TONY
Us? At Tony's Security Company?

WENDY
M'hm?

TONY
We make . . . really scary scarecrows, for scaring away thieves.

WENDY
Oh, gosh.

TONY
So, Wendy, I'd have thought you'd have loads of guys after you.

WENDY
No, it's weird, there don't seem to be any nice men in the world, and then suddenly two come along at once.

TONY
Two?

WENDY
(*Guilty*) Yeah, I met this chap yesterday. Gary. He's really nice and funny.

TONY
Are you sure you mean Gary?

WENDY
Why, do you know him?

TONY
No, no.

WENDY
But he's still involved with his old girlfriend.

TONY
Hopeless. Don't get involved.

WENDY
So you haven't got a girlfriend?

TONY
(*Muffled*) M'hm?

WENDY
Is that a no?

TONY
Yup.
Wendy looks torn.

26. SEAFRONT RESTAURANT

Gary and Dorothy are having a tense supper. Dorothy has dressed up, made an effort. The waiter clears away their main courses, at which they have only picked. Gary selects a bread stick, twirling it in his fingers, trying to lighten the mood. They chuckle at each other.

DOROTHY
Have you met someone you like, Gary?

GARY
Do you mean Jeff Beany from—

DOROTHY
No. A woman.

GARY
(*Shifty*) No.

DOROTHY
We're not very good at being nice to each other, are we?

GARY
No.

DOROTHY
Well . . . I'm not going to start now . . .

GARY
Sure, no—

DOROTHY
. . . but this year we'll have been together for ten years, and I just wanted to say, well, thank you.

GARY
Oh, right. And . . . thank you.

DOROTHY
I think I know why we've lasted so long together.

GARY
Because we know it really annoys your parents.

DOROTHY
Partly, yes.

GARY
And because we're really alike.

DOROTHY
You're joking, aren't you?

GARY
Oh, okay.

DOROTHY
No, because we've both felt we could wander off at any time, but in the end neither of us has wanted to.

GARY
Yup.

DOROTHY
If I'm having a baby we can't wander off any more.

GARY
No.

DOROTHY
This is it.

She takes Gary's hands and pulls them to her. Gary looks touched.

DOROTHY
Sorry, I've put your sleeve in the butter.

GARY
Never mind.
They look at each other.

DOROTHY
So you'd better make your mind up.
Gary thinks for a moment.

GARY
I'm sorry, I need some air.
Dorothy watches him go.

27. PROMENADE/ CRAZY-GOLF

Meanwhile, it has started to rain. Tony and Wendy are snogging. They surface for some air. Tony looks around guiltily, afraid someone will see him. They kiss again. Gary is standing there, watching Tony and Wendy, furious. Tony sees Gary out of the corner of his eye. He interrupts the kiss.

GARY
You bastard, Tony.

WENDY
Oh, you know each other.

TONY
(*To Wendy*) Um, excuse me.
Gary bears down on him. Tony backs away.

TONY
It may not look like I'm doing this for your own good, but . . .
Gary runs after Tony, who escapes by jumping into the crazy-golf course. He hides in (e.g.) the toy windmill. They scrap inside it, smashing it down.

TONY
I thought you loved Dorothy.

GARY
I do. It's never that simple, is it.
Tony runs away, pursued by Gary. More elaborate fighting ensues. Gary and Tony stop scrapping as they realise they are being watched, by Dorothy and Wendy. Dorothy looks strained and vulnerable, Wendy rather confused. Gary looks at the two women. A tense pause, then Gary wordlessly walks towards Dorothy. Romantic music fades in as they walk back to the hotel, hand in hand. Tony is left alone with Wendy. He gestures at the broken windmill, embarrassed.

TONY
Careless. Ha. Um, look, maybe we, um—

WENDY
No, I understand.

TONY
Sorry.

WENDY
That's okay. To be honest it all seems a bit complicated.

TONY
Yeah.
Wendy wanders off. Tony tries vaguely to put the windmill back together again, holding the bits up. He lets it collapse again.

DEBORAH
Tony?
Deborah appears.

DEBORAH
How did it go?

TONY
Oh, great. No problems.
It is starting to rain quite hard. Deborah joins Tony in the crazy-golf course. She and Tony stroll along arm in arm.

DEBORAH
What's that in your hair?

TONY
Um, a bit of windmill.

DEBORAH
Ooh, look.
Deborah has found a putter and ball. She picks them up and starts to play. The camera pans away and up, leaving Tony and Deborah's conversation to fade away after a few exchanges.

DEBORAH
Just a quick go.

TONY
You can't play, it's raining.

DEBORAH
Leave me alone.

TONY
(*Heading off*) Right, I'm off.

DEBORAH
Oh, Tony, have you been in my wardrobe? Some of my clothes are missing.

TONY
Really?
She runs after Tony, catching him up. They walk off together. The camera pulls up and away, glimpsing the two couples walking

back to the hotel, arm-in-arm. Fade to the following day.

28. TRAIN: CORRIDOR

Outside the toilet. The sound of Gary and Dorothy getting hot and bothered, then sighing.

DOROTHY
(*Offscreen*) Thank God that's over.

GARY
(*Offscreen*) I just thought it would be nice to do it together, after, you know.
There is the sound of clothing being adjusted etc.

DOROTHY
(*Offscreen*) Gary, be careful. Don't wave it about like that, wipe it.

GARY
(*Offscreen*) Okay.
Someone zips up. They giggle. The door opens, and Dorothy and Gary emerge.

29. TRAIN: TOILET

We focus on the discarded box of a pregnancy-testing kit.

30. RAILWAY LINE

Rolling Sussex countryside. The train is in the distance, coming gradually nearer. The sound of Gary and Dorothy returning to the carriage, sliding the door shut. Dialogue all in voice-over.

DEBORAH
Hey, is it ready yet?

DOROTHY
Nearly.

TONY
I love trains, don't you? It's like having your own long thin bungalow.

DEBORAH
So, how did you get rid of the fish?

TONY/GARY
Sorted./Nasty business.
The fish floats into vision, supported by lots of ISECESEX helium balloons.

GARY
Okay, let's have a look.

DEBORAH
Ooh, it's exciting.
A moment while they all study the result.

DOROTHY
So two lines means pregnant, one means not?

GARY
Yes. Or is it one line? Hang on, let me read that again—

DOROTHY
Oh, give it to me.

TONY
If it's a boy or a girl, will you call it Tony?

DEBORAH
Shh!
A silence. The train runs out of shot.

DOROTHY
Oh, dear.

MATCHBOX

SERIES SEVEN: EPISODE THREE

DELIVERY

The best of the last three episodes, I think. Recording it was a happy experience, although tinged with sadness that none of us might ever work again.

Just as *Fawlty Towers* has made it impossible to write scenes about fire alarms and cars breaking down, it is difficult to top Damien being born in *Only Fools and Horses*. I was keen to proselytise on behalf of home births, although I may have spoilt it by dwelling on the risk of coming back drunk, knocking out the midwife and having to deliver the baby yourself. Huge praise for Eileen Dunwoodie, who wins the Best Bang On The Head In *Men Behaving Badly* prize, nudging out Martin Clunes being headbutted by Deborah's boyfriend in Series One, and Neil Morrissey hitting his head in his van roof in Series Two.

Neil is genuinely alarming in his moustache and glasses, suggesting a great future ahead of him playing mealy-mouthed psychopaths. I once wanted to be a postman myself, so I found it worryingly easy to share Tony's interest in the job.

So we were all set up for a new show called *Men and a Baby Behaving Badly*, with Kylie Minogue as the voice of baby Kylie, in which a fanatical postman and an out-of-work middle manager wrestle with the problems of childcare in the new millennium . . .

1. CHILDBIRTH CLASS

A weekday evening. Gary and a massively pregnant Dorothy are in a class with other expectant couples. They are sitting on the floor together. The kindly instructor has a hand-knitted version of the female birthing organs. She is easing a doll through an aperture.

INSTRUCTOR
So this is the uterus, and here is the baby with its head engaged in the birth canal.

GARY
(*Whispering*) How come yours doesn't look like that?

DOROTHY
Because I didn't knit my own groin.
They mutter over the instructor, who carries on talking in the background.

GARY
You know they shave patients before operations – are they going to shave you?
Dorothy gives Gary a weary look.

GARY
I could do that, make myself useful—

DOROTHY
We're having a home birth, nobody's going to shave me.

GARY
I could give you a quick trim, tidy you up—

DOROTHY
No, pay attention. You have to be ready to deliver this baby in an emergency. I don't want you panicking and trying to stuff the placenta back in.

GARY
I've read up. It's our little baby. I know all about it.
They smile affectionately at each other.

DOROTHY
So you don't still think test-tube babies have to smash their way out of their test tube to be born?

GARY
I was joking.

DOROTHY
Or that you have to have sex twice to have twins?
He ignores Dorothy. The instructor is pointing out more anatomical detail.

GARY
If I was redesigning the female body, I'd have—

DOROTHY
Six breasts, two-inch nipples, childbirth by a system of eggs and a choice of bottoms. Yes, I saw your drawing.

2. DEBORAH'S BEDROOM

Deborah and Tony are in bed. Tony is showing signs of early middle age, wearing glasses and reading the London A-to-Z. Deborah looks bored and restless.

DEBORAH
I'm not tired.

TONY
I think you're *too* tired. You're one over-tired lady.

DEBORAH
It's a quarter to nine, Tony, believe me, I'm not tired.
We see the four alarm clocks on Tony's bedside table. Deborah looks gloomy.

DEBORAH
Why do you always have to be up so early?

TONY
Because I'm a postman.

DEBORAH
Couldn't you just do the second post?

TONY
Oh, you're very naïve. (*Visionary*) We're the Early People, getting up before dawn. I don't mean a girl called Dawn . . .

DEBORAH
No, I understand.

TONY
It's a magical world of whistling milk people, cleaners with their cheery tins of Pledge, dogs going through bins, mad insomniacs on benches, pimps dropping off their weary prostitutes, and us postal workers. And I get the rest of the day free to potter.

DEBORAH
Oh, don't say potter.

TONY
Look, I finished my mobile for Gary and Dorothy's baby.
He produces a homemade one featuring lots of dangling postmen and post boxes.

TONY
That's me, look, with my enormous sack.

DEBORAH
Weh-hey!

TONY
What?

DEBORAH
You know, enormous sack, testicles, weh-hey.

TONY
No, this is the post bag we put the letters in. It's made out of a special material, developed by Post Office scientists at a secret location.
Deborah gives up, turning away. Tony looks at her and decides he wants sex. He lies against her, picks up the mobile and playfully drapes a miniature postman over Deborah's shoulder.

TONY
Hello, special delivery of a large sexual organ.
She ignores him. Tony drapes another postman over her shoulder.

TONY
And it's so bulky it needs two postal workers to carry it.

Still no reaction. Tony drapes a miniature post van over her shoulder.

TONY
And a van.
Deborah is still ignoring him. Tony ponders and takes off his specs. He reaches for their case, which creaks as he opens it. He cleans the glasses with the special cloth and puts them in the case, shutting it.

TONY
So can I put my letter in your box?

DEBORAH
I don't really want to, Tony, do you mind?
Tony looks disappointed. He gets his glasses out of the case again, equally fussily, and goes back to his A-to-Z. Deborah looks gloomy.

3. CHILDBIRTH CLASS

The couples are now doing an ungainly relaxation and stretching exercise.

INSTRUCTOR
Good, and now to release tension all add a grunt at the end of each stretch. Partners offer support by grunting too.
Gary rolls his eyes. The couples now let out a collective grunt every few seconds.

DOROTHY
Have you told George and Anthea the office is shutting down?

GARY
Not yet. (*Grunting*) I'm scared they'll start wailing or go into some horrifying spasm.

DOROTHY
They'll probably be delighted. Anthea will finally get a boss who doesn't lock her in the cupboard.

GARY
Sometimes it's the only language she understands.
They grunt.

GARY
George is terrified of change.

DOROTHY
Is that why you haven't changed his salary for ten years?

GARY
Money confuses him. He still pays for things by postal order. Anthea wears a nightcap in bed. She told me. They can't cope out there in the real world.
They grunt.

4. GARY'S OFFICE

The next day. Gary is at his desk, looking nervous. George is humming happily.

GARY
George, have you ever thought about getting a new job and starting again?
George chuckles. Gary joins in, then is serious.

GARY
No, have you?

GEORGE
No.

GARY
It would be good, though, wouldn't it? New people, nicer cupboards, more money.

GEORGE
Well, as you always point out, I earn a pretty hefty salary here.

GARY
No, I was lying. It's a technique I've developed.
George chuckles again, not taking Gary seriously. Gary joins in, then looks anxious.

GARY
How would you react if I were to say that Head Office has told me we have to close down in two weeks?

GEORGE
Ooh, I can't see that happening.

GARY
Well . . . it is happening.

GEORGE
No, I can't see that happening.

GARY
No, no, it is happening.

GEORGE
No, I can't see that happening.
Anthea comes in, bringing in letters.

GARY
Anthea, I've got some bad news.

ANTHEA
Is it about the new pencils?

GARY
No, worse than that. You know orders have been down this year.

ANTHEA
Yes.

GARY
Well, Derek at Head Office rang me the day before yesterday to tell me we were going to have to close.
They look at him gravely.

ANTHEA
Oh, I can't see that happening.

GEORGE
That's what I said.

ANTHEA
Security equipment's always needed. There are so many naughty people around.

GARY
Listen, Anthea, George.
Anthea and George smile amiably.

GARY
Never mind.

5. THE CROWN

Later, early evening. Ken is behind the bar, drinking with Tony, who is looking dowdy in spectacles and a postman's uniform.

KEN
So for the second-class letters, right, do you use a slower delivery van?

TONY
No.

KEN
So the letters arrive, do you throw the second-class ones on like a pile in a corner and go, 'Right, we'll deliver them when we've got time, maybe the day after tomorrow'?

TONY
No.
A pause. Tony decides it is best to ignore what he has said.

TONY
Ken, do you think women enjoy sex less than men?

KEN
General sex?

TONY
Yes.

KEN
I don't know.

TONY
Deborah's always been brilliant about humping – unless I try to put something in her ears, she's banned that – but recently I've noticed little phrases creeping in from her, like, 'Do we have to?' and 'What's in it for me?'

KEN
I had this girlfriend who only became aroused at about ten-past seven in the evening. She was like one of those geysers in Iceland that only erupts at certain times of the day.

TONY
Except people didn't, you know, gather round and take photos of her.

KEN
Not to my knowledge, no. I chucked her though because she clashed with *Emmerdale*.

TONY
That's interesting because I have a theory about Debs. I think she's more turned on after eating cheese.

KEN
General cheese?

TONY
Yeah. I was thinking back, and the last time we made love and she, you know—

KEN
Exploded like a firecracker, her body jack-knifing over and over again?

TONY
Yeah, she'd just had a fondue.

KEN
Fondue, very tasty, very underrated.

TONY
And the night she first let me sleep with her, she'd been nibbling cheese straws all day.

KEN
As you say, there's a pattern, isn't there?

TONY
And I don't like cheese, so since I've moved in with Debs she hasn't kept any in the fridge, so she's been eating less cheese so her sex drive's down.

KEN
Or is that crackers? (*Pause*) Do you get it?
Tony furrows his brow.

A little later. Deborah, Dorothy and Gary are watching TV. A muffled telephone rings, a distinctively silly sound. Without taking his eyes off the television Gary opens his brief-case. He gets out a newly bought baby's rattle and rattles it.

ALL
Ahh.
He hands it to Dorothy then gets out the mobile phone.

GARY
Hello? Oh, hi, Clive.
Dorothy rolls her eyes.

GARY
No, sorry, mate. No. No. Not really.
He hangs up.

DOROTHY
Gary, that phone's for emergencies.

GARY
It was an emergency. Clive wants us to call the baby Clive.
Tony comes in with various titbits on a large plate.

TONY
Nibbly snack?
They look at him and his plate in surprise.

DOROTHY
Are you all right, Tony?

TONY
Yeah, why?

DOROTHY
I don't associate you with finger food.

TONY
Well, I've been snacking for years on my own, and I thought it was time to make the move into communal snacking.
Dorothy reaches for a nibble, but Tony thrusts the plate under Deborah's nose.

DEBORAH
What are they?

TONY
(*Pointing*) Chunky cheese lumps. Cheese and pickle on a pole. Cheesy Bollocks – that was my own concept.

DEBORAH
Um, no, thanks.

TONY
You must, I crafted them specially for you.

DEBORAH
What's that?

TONY
Whole banana dipped in cheese.

DEBORAH
I'm not really hungry. Anyway, you hate cheese.

TONY
I suddenly realised how delicious it is.
Deborah hesitates, frowning at the food.

TONY
Mm.
Deborah's still hesitating. With trepidation Tony picks up a Cheesy Bollock and eats it.

TONY
Really nice.
He nearly retches as he tries to keep it down. The others watch with some distaste.

GARY
Tony, fancy a drink tomorrow lunchtime? I need to get drunk enough to tell George and Anthea they're being made redundant.

TONY
Yeah, we can go to our special postmen's pub near the sorting office.

GARY
Do we have to?

TONY
It's great. You hear some brilliant postal anecdotes. Go on, have a Cheesy Bollock . . .

DEBORAH
No! Hey, have you thought of a name for your baby yet?

DOROTHY
No. Gary still likes Cindy-Sue for a girl and Scamp for a boy. So I may have to kill him.

TONY
Oh, I've seen some great names on letters.
He gets out a piece of paper.

TONY
Um, Ding?

DOROTHY
No.

TONY
Abd al-Haqq, quite nice?

DOROTHY
Anything a bit less exotic?

TONY
Rimbin?

DOROTHY
No.

TONY
Bobingalooli? Actually, that might be a computer misprint. He's normally called Bob.
He gives up. Dorothy has gone into the kitchen. Deborah gets up to join her. Tony and Gary watch TV.

TONY
Cheddar Nipple?

GARY
Cheers.
Gary takes one and eats.

7. KITCHEN

Meanwhile, Deborah turns on the kettle as Dorothy lowers herself wearily into a chair.

DEBORAH
Are you all right?

DOROTHY
Yeah. I know birth is a miracle and everything, but they don't tell you by the end you feel like a horsebox.
Deborah helps her into her seat.

DOROTHY
It's okay, I'm down.

DEBORAH
I've got a bit of a problem too. Tony doesn't turn me on any more.

DOROTHY
Oh, Debs. Did he ever?

DEBORAH
Yes, in a funny sort of way.

DOROTHY
What's changed?

DEBORAH
I don't know.
They ponder this, brows furrowed.

DEBORAH
Well, he looks like a complete divvy now—

DOROTHY
... divvy, yes, that can't help. Maybe you should shave his moustache off in his sleep.

DEBORAH
I've tried, he keeps waking up. I mean, he dresses like my Dad, he bangs on about his job, he's started writing down his thoughts in a notebook.

DOROTHY
Oh, they all go through that phase.

DEBORAH
How long does it last?

DOROTHY
Until you split up.
Deborah looks bleak.

DOROTHY
Oh, it's quite a romantic idea, though, growing

old together. Sitting on park benches, feeding the ducks, leafing gently through *Saga* magazine.

DEBORAH
I suppose so.
They sigh wistfully. Dorothy drops a teaspoon. They look at it. Dorothy makes a half-hearted attempt to bend down.

DOROTHY/DEBORAH
You'd better get that./I'll get that.

8. POSTMEN'S PUB

The next day, at lunchtime. We pan round a pub full of postmen and post-women. We find a perturbed Gary, looking around, aware he is the only one not in postal uniform. Tony returns with two more pints.

TONY
(*Chuckling*) That's Geoff, he's been bitten by so many dogs they call him Costello.

GARY
Why?

TONY
Abbott and Costello. Abbott. Russ Abbott. Russ. Russell. Jack Russell. Little dog.

GARY
Right.

TONY
Bloke over there, once did his round backwards, wearing a rabbit costume.
Tony smiles, amused.

GARY
What do you call him?

TONY
Wanker.

GARY
What's your nickname?
Tony looks shifty.

TONY
They haven't given me one yet.
A couple of postmen give Tony a wave as they pass.

TONY
Magnus! Sherbet!
Gary looks jealous.

GARY
You won't . . . get a new best friend, will you, mate?

TONY
No, mate.

GARY
Thanks, mate.

TONY
It was time I settled down and got a career, though, wasn't it?

GARY
(*Genuine*) Yeah, I'm happy for you.

TONY
It's such a brilliant job—

GARY
Yep.

TONY
—stimulating, room for initiative, respect of the public, supersmart uniform—

GARY
Okay, shut it, Postie.
They gulp their lager.

TONY
So, you're going to have a little baby.

GARY
Yeah.

TONY
It's finally happened.

GARY
Yup. It puts everything into perspective.
They nod, taking in the enormity of it.

TONY
So you haven't had sex for four months?

GARY
Nope. I could do it with that bar stool right now. It wouldn't take long.

TONY
Can you not, mate. I'd lose face as a postman.

GARY
We did try to have sex a month or so ago, but it was like trying to mount a giant, pink turtle.
A postman passes by.

POSTMAN
Nobby Nofriends!
Tony does a wan little acknowledgment. Gary smirks.

GARY
Nobby No—

TONY
It's a temporary name.

9. GARY'S OFFICE

Later. George and Anthea are working quietly and happily. The door bangs open and Gary comes in, smashed out of his head but trying not to show it.

ANTHEA
Did you have a nice drink with Tony—?

GARY
Tony Postie!
He hovers in the doorway.

GARY
Yes, I did, thank you. Wait, wait, I've always wanted to do this.
Gary hangs on to the top of the door and swings round. He dismounts.

GARY
Not as much fun as I'd expected.

GEORGE
Someone's a bit squiffy.

GARY
Yes, that would be me.
Anthea tries to sneak out.

GARY
Come back, Anthea. Pull up a thing. You, too, Porgie.
Anthea and George sit down, all ears.

GARY
I've had to get squiffy to tell you this, because in a funny kind of way I care about you. That might sound a bit, I don't know, a bit stupid, a bit spooky, possibly even slightly – God, I'm getting a headache. Anyway, here we go. I have some bad news.

ANTHEA
Is it about the pen—

GARY
No, forget about the bloody pencils.
He sees Anthea and George and sobers up a little.

GARY
I'm afraid the office will be closing down in woo teeks, and we'll all be out of a job.
A stunned pause.

ANTHEA
Oh, I can't see that happening—

GEORGE
No, nor can I—

GARY
No, no, listen. Imagine this is our job.
He searches for an object on his desk, eventually finding (e.g.) a stapler.

GARY
Watch carefully. Job going out of window. Job. Window. Window. Job.
He throws the stapler out of the window, smashing the glass.

GARY
That works better if you open the window first. But do you see? There will of course be a redundy pack, a redundance. George, you've worked here for eighty-three years, so you will get three million and several hundred thousand pounds. Anthea, fifty-two years of service, so you get a small castle in Surrey. I'm very sorry about this. I, obviously, will easily find a slot with . . . Sparks and Mensa, TellyBritcom, one of those.
George and Anthea look shocked.

GARY
Shall we hug? Would that help?

ANTHEA
Right, well, I'll just carry on working.
Anthea heads for the door.

GARY
You'll find something else. You're a mad secretary. I don't mean mad. That was the talk drinking.
Anthea leaves.

GARY
Oh, blast.
Gary winces. George has gone quiet.

GARY
Say something George.

GEORGE
I can't see it happening.

GARY
Not that.

10. DEBORAH'S BEDROOM

Deborah, alone in bed, looks over at Tony's array of alarm clocks. It is about nine p.m. Tony enters with two teas and some snacks on a tray. He is wearing glasses, slippers and, over his pyjamas, his postman's jacket.
He arranges the tray on Deborah's lap and joins her in bed.

TONY
(*Casually*) As a slight change to our routine I've brought some crackers with some cheese on.

DEBORAH
No, thanks, Tony, I've brushed my teeth.

TONY
No, late-night cheesy snack, very good for the teeth. Amongst other things.

DEBORAH
I'd rather not.
Tony cups his hand to his ear.

TONY
I can hear your body crying out for cheese—

DEBORAH
(*Snapping*) No, no cheese!
Tony looks hurt. He picks up a leaflet and reads.

DEBORAH
I'm sorry, Tony.

TONY
No, that's fine.

DEBORAH
What are you reading?

TONY
The Book of Postcodes.
Depressed, Deborah sips her tea. It tastes odd.

DEBORAH
Has my tea got cheese in it?

TONY
(*Reading, lightly*) Might have a little.

DEBORAH
Tony, what's this all about?

TONY
What's what about?

DEBORAH
All the cheese!

TONY
(*Reluctantly*) I thought it turned you on.
She looks at him as though he is mad.

TONY
You haven't wanted to have sex.

DEBORAH
(*Guilty*) I know.

TONY
I mean, this has never happened before. Apart from those first five years. So what is it?
She looks over at Tony, awkwardly.

TONY
Oh, I get it. It's because I'm still only in my trial period, and I'm not a full postman yet, isn't it?

DEBORAH
No.
She looks at Tony, then at the plate.

DEBORAH
Okay, let's give it a try.
She puts all the cheese into her mouth.
Tony watches and waits.

TONY
Feel anything? I'll get some more.
He runs out for more cheese. Deborah munches disconsolately.

Day. Dorothy is on her own, vaguely tidying up but tired and uncomfortable. She drops some cutlery on her way from table to sink. She makes a half-hearted attempt to pick it up, then kicks it under the cooker. She runs the tap but finds her belly keeps her too far away from the sink to wash up. She tries to stand side-on, then gives up and lowers herself into a chair. The door-bell rings.

DOROTHY
(*Calling out*) I can't get up. Come back when I've had my baby.
The doorbell goes again. She rocks herself on to her feet and goes out.

A postman's arm is through the letter slot, stretching for a key that is on the floor. Dorothy comes in, sees Tony's arm and opens the door brusquely. Tony is in his postman's uniform.

DOROTHY
Why did you ring the bell?

TONY
I posted my key through the letter box. Force of habit. Whenever I see a letter slot these days I want to put something through it.

DOROTHY
(*Turning to go*) You want to watch that.

TONY
Oh, there's a couple of letters for you.
Dorothy puts out her hand wearily.
Tony goes out again and posts the letters.
He comes back, delighted.

TONY
Still turns me on.

DOROTHY
Will you pick them up for me, please?

TONY
(*Suddenly serious*) No, I can't. They're customer property now, I'd be breaking eight laws.
Dorothy gives him her scariest look.

TONY
So, the scary look.
He picks up the letters and hands them to Dorothy.
Then he yanks in the postal-delivery cart.

TONY
Did you see, I've allocated parking spaces. Cart. Pram.

Tony parks his cart carefully in a space on the floor marked CART. Another space is marked out for PRAM.

DOROTHY
Lovely.
Dorothy turns and goes inside.

DOROTHY
Tony, will you take away the rest of your stuff.

TONY
I'm sorry, I'm not allowed to take away stuff while wearing the Queen's postal uniform.
Dorothy has gone inside. Tony follows her.

Tony joins Dorothy, who has gone back to sponging stains off the walls. The room is half prepared. Tony gazes down at her bulging stomach.

TONY
Ah, it's amazing, isn't it?

DOROTHY
(*Genuine*) Yes, yes it is.

TONY
Can I sign it?

DOROTHY
No.
Tony wanders around, nostalgic.

TONY
I've had some top times in this room. If only these walls could speak.
We fade in snatches of odd voice-over dialogue from previous episodes.

TONY
I guarantee Deborah: sleep with me, and you'll never want another man ever again.

DOROTHY
You seemed to know exactly what you were doing actually . . .

TONY
. . . Oooh, Bananarama! . . .

GARY
So, will you be getting wipers fitted?

TONY
I was wondering what colour your bush is . . .

TONY
Debs, I've been sick!
They fade away. Tony ponders fondly.

TONY
Great.

There is a bizarre collection of childlike drawings on one wall.

TONY
Were those there when I lived here?

DOROTHY
No, it's Gary's contribution – a mural depicting key scenes from our life together.

TONY
What's happening there?
Dorothy points to a picture of two smiling, white-faced figures holding up a bottle.

DOROTHY
Our first trip to the bottle bank together.
Another picture of two very red-faced people:

DOROTHY
Our first beach holiday.
A picture of the four of them sitting on the sofa watching TV.

DOROTHY
A typical day.

TONY
(*Visibly moved*) That's me! I'm in a mural! I'm really moved.
A picture of a two grinning naked figures lying on top of each other.

DOROTHY
And Conception. That's going behind the wardrobe. Those are yours.
Tony picks up a bin-liner containing his stuff. He takes out a copy of Razzle.

TONY
There really *are* some really good articles in these, you know—

DOROTHY
Yes, can you take them away, please.
Dorothy is getting tired washing the walls. She stretches her back.

TONY
Dorothy, can I ask you something?

DOROTHY
Mm.

TONY
Am I still sexy?
Dorothy looks over at Tony, failing to look sexy in his nerdy postman's uniform.

DOROTHY
(*Unconvincing*) Yes. Um, can you help—?

TONY
I know I'm a more sensible person now, but that doesn't mean I'm not sexy, does it?

DOROTHY
No. Tony, these are your stains—

TONY
You can be sensible and sexy. Look at Michelle Pfeiffer. She'd find a welcome in the modern postal service. If she passed all the appropriate tests.
Dorothy sighs, losing her patience.

TONY
Are you feeling all right?

DOROTHY
Well, everything's twice as big as it was nine months ago, and I'm growing another head inside me, let's start there. (*Pause*) I'm sorry.
Tony looks at her for a moment but ploughs on.

TONY
I think maybe I'm still sexy but in a different way. It's like I was a Ferrari, and now I'm a really smart no-nonsense saloon—

DOROTHY
(*Snapping*) Okay, Tony, I'll tell you. You've become boring and ponderous, and Deborah actually preferred it when you were thoughtless and silly but a bit more exciting.
Dorothy stretches her back. Tony looks offended.

TONY
Well, I'm sorry, but that's the way I am now, I've matured, like a fine wine. Deborah will have to take me as I am.
He leaves, then reappears seconds later.

TONY
So I'm not sexy any more?

DOROTHY
No!
He leaves again, defiantly. A musical montage ensues, which shows the passage of two weeks.

14. LIVING ROOM

An evening in. Gary and Dorothy are watching the TV, lovingly entwined. Gary's can of lager and a bowl of nuts are resting on Dorothy's bump. The programme ends. Gary turns off the TV with the remote, gets up and leaves. He remembers seconds later and comes back to help Dorothy get up from the sofa. It takes a while.

15. DEBORAH'S BEDROOM

Early one morning. An alarm clock on Tony's bedside cabinet starts beeping. He blearily turns it off and drifts back to sleep. We take in a large plate of cheese on Deborah's bedside cabinet. An old-fashioned clockwork alarm goes off. Still with eyes shut, Deborah clambers over Tony's sleepy body and turns it off.

16. GARY'S OFFICE

A subdued Gary and George are taking things down off walls and putting files in boxes. Gary glances at the clock and goes over to the cupboard. He lets Anthea out. They exchange looks. She goes quietly back to her office.

17. DEBORAH'S BEDROOM

Four alarm clocks have already gone off and are lying around flattened. Tony is vaguely stirring. A huge, hitherto unseen alarm springs into life on the other side of the room, lights flashing, big noise. Tony falls out of bed and creeps towards it on his hands and knees.

18. LOCAL PARK

Dorothy and Gary are walking through the park, hand in hand. Dorothy stops and clutches her stomach, having a twinge. Gary goes into a panic, running around, crying out for help. Dorothy is bending over, taking deep breaths. Gary feels frantically for his mobile phone and tries to dial a number but drops the phone. He gives up on it, running around some more. Dorothy puts her hand out to stop him. False alarm. Gary calms down.

19. DEBORAH'S FLAT

Tony's post cart is laid out on newspaper. He is polishing it. Obviously still proud of his new mature self, he is wearing glasses and selected articles of uniform. Deborah enters. Tony smiles warmly. Her smile is rather forced. Tony draws her attention to a particular area of the cart that he has cleaned, talking her through the process. Deborah tries to appear impressed, then escapes. Tony watches her go, realising he has to do something. Musical montage ends.

20. GARY'S OFFICE

The last day in the office, almost everything is packed up. Anthea and George are in fact fairly chirpy, whereas Gary is already rather bereft. They are sorting through the last few things.

GARY
It's weird, isn't it? Why haven't the phones been ringing?

GEORGE
You've stolen them. They're all in your bag.

GARY
Oh, yes. Well, if you can't loot your own office, what can you do?
Anthea and George chuckle amenably.

GARY
You're both surprisingly chirpy. Are you drunk?

GEORGE
(*A bit guilty*) No, we've been headhunted by Croydon Alarms.

GARY
Oh. They know you're both a bit bonkers do they?

ANTHEA/GEORGE
Yes, they do./Yes, they like that.
Gary looks rather taken aback.

GARY
Well, that's good. Congratulations.

ANTHEA
Shall we put in a good word for you? We'll give you a reasonable reference.

GARY
Don't make me put you in the cupboard on your last day, Anthea.
Gary looks bleak. He holds up a small plastic barometer.

GARY
Complementary plywood pelican from BJB Security anyone?
Nobody's interested. Gary tosses it in a bin.

ANTHEA
Look, some old Dictaphone tapes.
She puts a tape in and plays it, smiling nostalgically.

GARY'S VOICE-OVER
(*On tape*) Thank you for your pompous letter of the whenever. Had your cretinous staff, clearly on mind-bending drugs – Anthea, you might want to tone this down – rung whatshisname – (*Calling out*) Anthea? What's the name of the fat bastard in Coventry? (*Shouting*) Anthea?!
Anthea turns off the tape.

ANTHEA/GEORGE
(*Nostalgically*) Ahh.

ANTHEA
George and I put our heads together and came up with a farewell present for you.
George hands Gary a present.

GARY
Oh, thanks. Um, I haven't bought you anything.

GEORGE
Oh. Well, perhaps we should keep this then . . .

GARY
(*Clutching his present closer to him*) No, no.
Gary unwraps a small framed picture.

GARY
Ah, it's lovely, in its own way. What is it?

ANTHEA
A picture of a yacht made out of our hair.

GEORGE
Marjorie's hairdresser friend, Joan, makes them. If you're completely bald she'll do it with toenails.

GARY
Thanks, I'm really touched.
They all smile.

GARY
Tell you what, let's go to a pub and have a farewell drink, shall we?
Anthea and George look happy. As they turn away, Gary discreetly throws their present into the bin.

21. TRENDY CLOTHES SHOP

Meanwhile. Thudding music. Tony, looking out of place in his full postman's regalia, is carrying a pile of new clothes along in his cart. He enters a changing room and emerges (as though) seconds later, dressed in desperately hip clothes. Looking in the mirror he realises these do not suit him. He goes back inside the cubicle to change.

22. CAVERNOUS PUB

Mid-afternoon. A huge empty pub, deserted apart from Gary, George and Anthea. Their table is laden with three empty champagne bottles. Gary is roaring drunk again, drinking the champagne out of a half-pint glass. He is surrounded by carrier bags with office supplies and phones sticking out the top. Anthea and George are gingerly sipping their drinks.

GARY
I'm sorry if I've ever been mean. Have I ever been mean?

ANTHEA/GEORGE
Yes.

GARY
No, you can be honest. We should be more honest. Or do I mean more sexy? Happy birthday! Or is it?
Gary drinks some more. He feels something in his pocket, yanks out his mobile phone out and tries to use it to turn on the TV.

GARY
Oh, no, it's a pheletone. Oh dear! That should have been on.
He switches it on.

GARY
Go on, you two, have a ruler.
Gary reaches into one of his many bags and hands George and Anthea both a ruler.

GARY
Well, you've been *marvellous* company over the years. I suppose there's a bit of a generation gap, but in a funny way that's the way, ah-hah-ah-hah, I like it, ah-hah-ah-hah. Although . . .
A random pause in the gibberish.

ANTHEA
It's years since I was in a public house—

GARY
Marvellous company. You, George, with your literally thousands of cardigans. And you, Anthea, with your infectious humming. Will you hum for me one last time, Anthea?
The mobile phone rings.

GARY
No, that's not it. Try again a bit lower. Oh, no, it's this.
Gary answers the phone.

GARY
Hel-lo? Right you are. Lovely. Uh-huh. Okay. See you.
He switches off the phone and has another drink.

GARY
The midwife. They've been trying to ring me for four hours. Dorothy's very much in labour.
They all show mild interest, then get up, panicking.

GARY
Oh, my God.
They all grab at Gary's many carrier bags, carrying them a few yards, things dropping out.

GARY
No, leave it, leave it. It's not important.
Gary starts to rush out, then comes back and gives Anthea a big kiss. Then, after a brief hesitation, he gives George a big kiss too and leaves.

23. STREET OUTSIDE THE PUB

Gary staggers out of the pub. A bus comes into view. Gary hails it.

GARY
Bus!
There is no bus stop, so the bus goes by.

GARY
Right, you are dead meat! You'll never work again!
A taxi comes into view. Gary wanders out into the road, holding his hand up, forcing it to stop.

GARY
Emergency! I'm having a baby!
Gary opens the taxi door and gets in.

GARY
I'm sorry. Tiny baby coming.
Go on, out you get.
An exhausted mother gets out, looking bewildered, followed by three difficult, crying children, a doddery grandparent and lots of shopping.

GARY
There'll be another one along in a minute. You'll be fine.
The taxi speeds away, abandoning the others on the pavement.

24. THE CROWN

Evening. Ken is on his own behind the bar, polishing it with a cloth. He spits on the bar but manages only to hit his arm. He wipes the spit off his arm on to the bar. Deborah comes in, looking fed up.

DEBORAH
Hi, Ken.

KEN
Hi, love. What can I get you? We've got a host of drinks on the go.

DEBORAH
Oh, anything.
She sits up at the bar.

KEN
You're looking a bit down in the dumps. Have you got the painters in?

DEBORAH
No, I'm meeting Tony here. I'm going to tell him I want him to move out of my flat.

KEN
Oh. Can I move in?

DEBORAH
No.

KEN
So what's gone wrong?

DEBORAH
Well, it's ironic. For years I've wanted Tony to be more sensible, and now he is, I realise I liked him more the way he was.

KEN
That's certainly ironic.

DEBORAH
I feel really guilty.

KEN
I think there's a lesson here for us all.
Deborah looks thoughtful.

KEN
I don't know what it is, but I sense there is one.
The door to the pub opens brusquely, and Tony stands there. He has transformed himself back to his grungey, wilder young self. He and Deborah notice each other. Deborah smiles. Tony swaggers up to the bar. Ken automatically pours him a pint.

TONY
Hi.

DEBORAH
Hello.

TONY
What have you been up to?

DEBORAH
Oh, this and that.

TONY
Great.

DEBORAH
Where are your glasses?
Tony gets his specs out of his top pocket, puts them on the bar, casually smashes them with the ashtray and then takes a swig of lager. Deborah smiles, leans over and kisses Tony. They snog romantically.

DEBORAH
Does this make me superficial?

TONY
Yup, still, not to worry. Malibu and coke for the lady, please.

DEBORAH
Okay, don't overdo it.
They stand there, smiling at each other.

DEBORAH
It's going to take quite a while to get our relationship right, isn't it.

TONY
If you say so.
Tony gulps down more lager.

TONY
Want to go back to my place and boff?

DEBORAH
No, you're still overdoing it.

TONY
Sorry.

Dusk that day. The room is now nearly finished. Dorothy has hung tasteful baby-friendly pictures over the worst of Gary's murals. Dorothy is on her knees, crouching on several pillows. She is having a horribly painful contraction. A midwife is next to her massaging her supportively.

DOROTHY
(*Very loud*) Bugger ow bugger ow ow bastard men bastard bastard men why why why help.
The pain ebbs. She breathes rhythmically.

DOROTHY
Was I shouting?

MIDWIFE
Yes. Nearly there.
Loud knocking from the communal hall.

DOROTHY
(*Calling out*) What time do you call this?!
The midwife exits.

Meanwhile Gary is feverishly looking for the right key. He finally finds it and turns it in the lock.

GARY
Hah!
Still very drunk, he drops the keys again, dropping down to pick them up.

GARY
Oh, don't be difficult, we're having a baby.

27. GARY'S FLAT: HALLWAY

The midwife rushes up to the door. As she approaches, Gary enters at speed. The door hits the midwife on the head, knocking her out. Gary rushes through, then retraces his steps, realising he has just hit someone. He sees she is out cold.

GARY
Never mind. That's probably normal.
The sound of Dorothy screaming again.
Gary runs towards her drunkenly.

Dorothy is in even greater pain. Gary rushes in as the contractions subside again.

GARY
It's okay, I'm here now, love. I'm sorry I'm late, I was drinking heavily.
He takes Dorothy in his arms.

DOROTHY
Don't ever EVER have sex with me ever again. Is that clear?

GARY
It's okay. Everything's all right.
Dorothy groans, relaxing a little.

GARY
Although I have just knocked out the midwife.
Dorothy looks up at him, gasping.

DOROTHY
What?
Gary makes a calming gesture.

DOROTHY
The baby's nearly out.

GARY
That's okay, we'll just calmly . . .
He jumps up, losing it. Dorothy starts to writhe again. Gary runs around like a headless chicken. He gets his mobile phone out of his pocket.

GARY
Ambulance, ambulance . . . What's the number?
Dorothy is doubled up with pain.

GARY
I've forgotten the number. Nine something.

DOROTHY
It's too late. Come and hold me.
Gary takes up a position near her. Dorothy grabs his hand, squeezing it hard.

GARY
Um, can you ease up a bit on the – you're breaking my finger (*Shouting now*), you're breaking my finger, it's broken, the finger's broken.
Dorothy is now in continuous pain.

GARY
Okay, now, remember what we learnt in class. I can't personally, but as I say I'm really rather pissed.
Dorothy gives him a dirty look, then winces again.

GARY
Can I get you a couple of aspirins?

DOROTHY
No!

GARY
Okay. Would you like a magazine to read, take your mind off it?

DOROTHY
Go back to work! Please, anything!

GARY
I haven't got any work. I can dedicate myself to you now.
Dorothy looks at Gary's smiling face and starts to cry. In the background, the sound of the front door opening.

GARY
It's all right, don't worry about me. You old silly.
Deborah and Tony appear. Tony is blissfully drunk. Deborah brushes past, concerned.

DEBORAH
Dorothy, what can I do?

DOROTHY
Make Gary leave.

TONY
Dorothy! How's it going?!
Deborah ushers Gary and Tony out into the kitchen.

TONY
Dorothy, Deb and me've been celebrating, we're okay again. I'm going to respond more to her needs, and she's going to . . . do something or other. Why's she squatting—?
The door shuts in Gary and Tony's faces.

TONY
Oh, I see, the baby's started!
They stand in the kitchen, both happily swaying in unison. The sound of the door being locked. Muffled shouts and groans from Dorothy continue.

TONY
Ahh.

GARY
Ahh.
Gary is rummaging in a drawer in the table.

TONY
(*Calling under the door*) Pull!

GARY
No, push—

TONY
Push!
Gary stabs the door with a carving knife, making a hole at head height. They take it in turns to peer through.

GARY
Big breaths. But you know that.

TONY
Can I get you a beer?

GARY
What was it? —imagine the pain is sand crashing on a wavy beach.

TONY
Baby coming. Stand back! Nothing to see!

GARY
I love you, Dorothy! You'll be all right. We're standing by.

TONY
Standing very by . . .
Fade to later.

29. LIVING ROOM

Later that night. Subdued lighting. Gary and Tony, now rather more sober, are sitting on the sofa, in time-honoured position, holding lager cans. They look relaxed and happy.

TONY
You could get a job . . . in a school. (*As teacher*) Oy, you, get down off that fence. I saw that.

GARY
No.

TONY
Or you could be a park keeper. With your own hut.

GARY
No, they can be very dank, those huts.

TONY
Stunt man?

GARY
Now you're talking. But nothing dangerous.

TONY
No. Only stunts involving . . .

GARY
. . . falling gently on to cushions.

TONY
Yeah. Or I could put in a good word for you down at the sorting office, with Tinyknob.

GARY
No, it's not really me.

TONY
You get to deliver your own letters.

GARY
Even so. I was never really right for my job. I always felt like a giant redwood growing in a tiny allotment. I don't mean that in an arrogant way.

TONY
No. How's Kylie?
We change angle to reveal that Gary has a new-born baby tucked away on his lap.

GARY
Still sleeping.
They both lean forward and smile lovingly at the sleeping baby.

TONY
They're always this red colour, then?

GARY
Yep.

TONY
It must be satisfying, knowing you helped to deliver your own baby.

GARY
Yeah.

TONY
Using the little-known shouting-through-a-door method.

GARY
I'll probably stay at home for a while as a house husband. That'll be nice. Bringing Dorothy tea in the mornings.

TONY
Going down the shops for those little jars of wet food.

GARY
Apparently you have to get up during the night occasionally.

TONY
Why?

GARY
I don't know. I haven't read the book yet.
Dorothy and Deborah come in. The four of them gaze adoringly at the baby.

DEBORAH
So, you don't have a name yet?

DOROTHY
No.
Tony frowns at Gary, who does an I'll-tell-her-later face.

DOROTHY
Why didn't we do this ten years ago?

GARY
We weren't grown-up enough.

DOROTHY
No.
Dorothy discreetly starts to breastfeed the baby. Tony and Gary look away, self-conscious.

TONY
Have you seen the new Peugeot 406?

GARY
Yeah, very reliable—

DEBORAH
(*Referring to the baby*) Oh, she's taking to it, look.

DOROTHY
Well, at least Gary's passed something on. As long as she doesn't—
She burps, then farts in quick succession.

DOROTHY
Oh, well, never mind.
From the perspective of the baby, we see the adult's faces one by one.

DOROTHY
(*To baby*) This is Deborah. She helped deliver you.

DEBORAH
(*Waving*) Hello!

DOROTHY
Because Daddy got drunk and knocked out the midwife.

GARY
(*To baby*) It's not actually as bad as it sounds.

DOROTHY
And this is Tony.

TONY
Hello, Kylie (*Hastily*) or whoever.

DOROTHY
He's a postman. But you might not want to get him onto that. You're having his old room, where he's had so many adventures. Many of them involving *Razzle* magazine.

GARY
So, Dorothy, any chance of, you know, tonight?
The others all look at him pointedly.

GARY
Oh, well, when you're ready. No hurry.
They sit watching the baby. We gradually pull back and fade. The baby starts to cry. Tony makes as if to give her a sip of lager.

DEBORAH
No, Tony!

TONY
I wasn't going to!

Strong Continental Lager
440 ml
Alc. 5.2% Vol

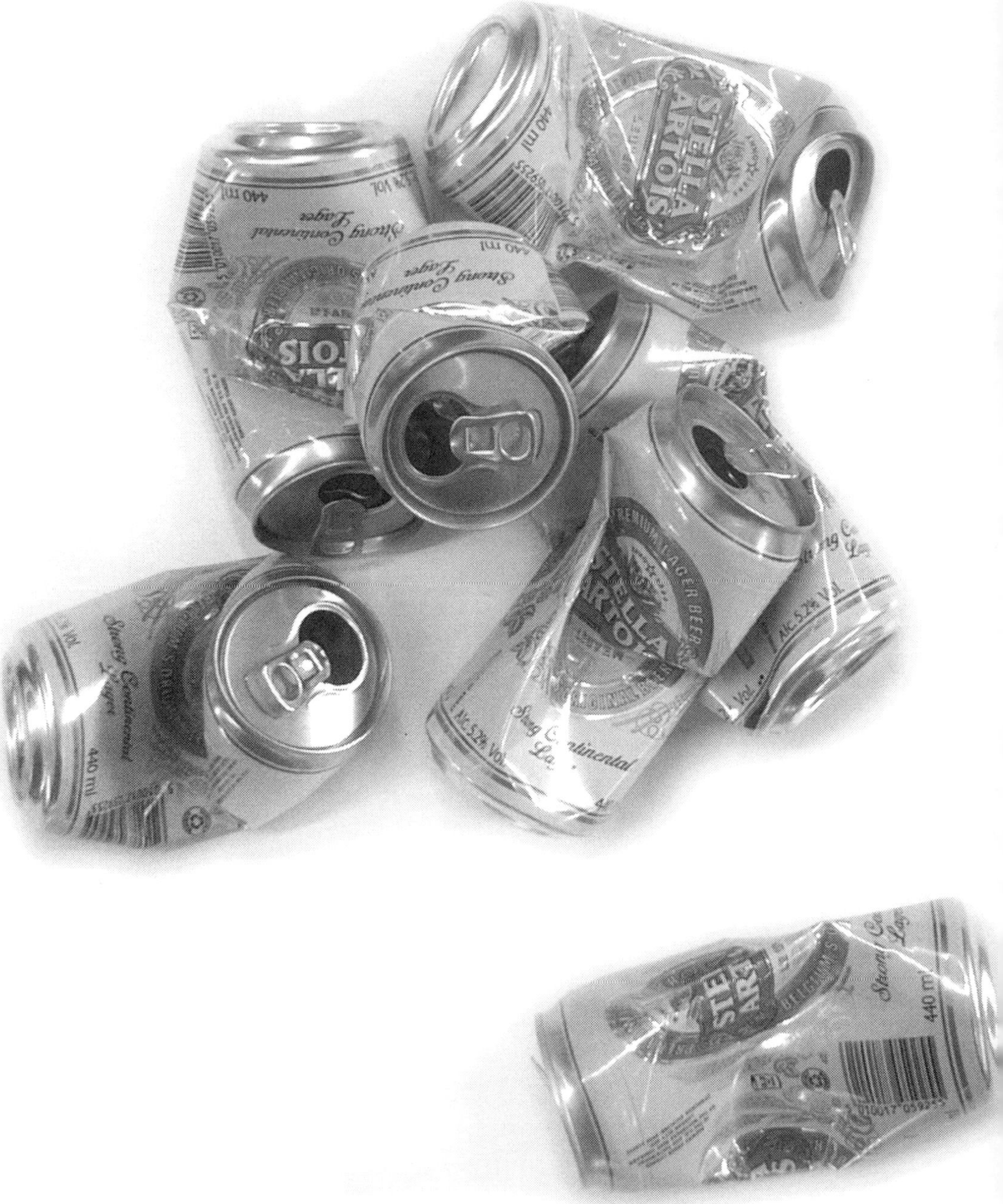

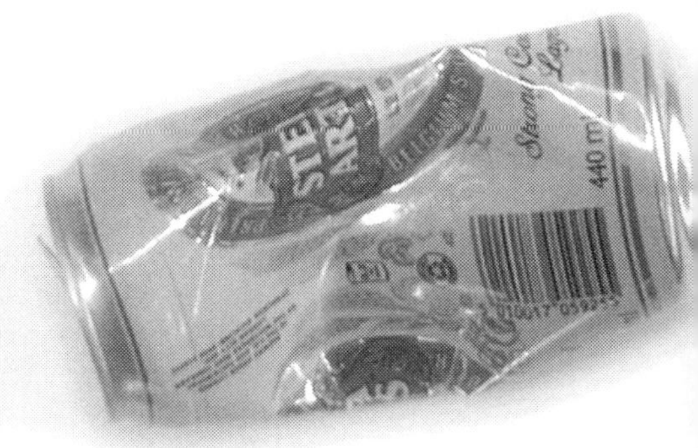

WAS BROUGHT TO YOU BY:

Writer	**Simon Nye**
Producer	**Beryl Vertue**
Director	**Martin Dennis**
Script Editor	**Elaine Cameron**
Line Producers	* **John Kay** (3 series)
	Julian Meers (2 series)
	Julian Scott (1 series)
	Debbie Vertue (1 series)
Casting Directors	**Beth Charkham** (4 series)
	Michelle Guish (3 series)
Production Designers	* **Kenneth Sharp** (5 series)
	Steve Groves
	David Buckingham
Lighting Directors	**Christopher Davies** (2 series)
	Keith Reed (5 series)
Senior Cameramen	**Roy Easton** (2 series)
	Chas Watts (5 series)
Director of Photography (location)	**John Rosenberg**
Vision Mixer	**Peter Phillips** (7 series)
Costume Designers	**Suzy Peters** (2 series)
	Christopher Marlowe (4 series)
	James Baylan (1 series)
Make-up Designers	**Carolyn Tyrer** (1 series)
	Nichola Bellamy (6 series)
Sound Supervisors	**Brian Hibbert** (1 series)
	Paul Gartrell (6 series)
Floor Managers	**Kerry Mann** (1 series)
	Patrick Vance (1 series)
	Fizz Waters (1 series)
	Tristram Shapeero (4 series)
Stage Manager	**Mary Motture** (7 series)
Production Assistants	**Rebecca Havers** (2 series)
	Angela Morgan (4 series)
	Sue Bayles (1 series)
Producer's Assistant	**Nicola Mairs**

* Sadly, John Kay and Kenneth Sharp are no longer with us but will both remain in the memory as vibrant, creative and hugely important members of the team.

MEN BEHAVING BADLY can also be seen in ...

America, Andorra, Australia, Bahrain, Barbados, Belgium, Brazil, Bulgaria, Canada, Denmark, Eire, Estonia, Finland, France, German-speaking Europe, Greece, Holland, Iceland, India, Israel, Kenya, Latvia, Lithuania, Malta, Mauritius, Middle East, Monaco, Netherlands, New Zealand, Norway, Pan European Satellite, Poland, Seychelles, Singapore, Slovenia, South Africa, Spain, Sri Lanka, Sweden, Switzerland, Thailand, Trinidad, Yugoslavia, Zimbabwe.

MEN BEHAVING BADLY

MEN BEHAVING BADLY
MEN BEHAVING BADLY
MEN BEHAVING BADLY
MEN BEHAVING BADLY
MEN BEHAVING BADLY
MEN BEHAVING BADLY
MEN BEHAVING BADLY
MEN BEHAVING BADLY
MEN BEHAVING BADLY
MEN BEHAVING BADLY
MEN BEHAVING BADLY
MEN BEHAVING BADLY
MEN BEHAVING BADLY
MEN BEHAVING BADLY
MEN BEHAVING BADLY
MEN BEHAVING BADLY
MEN BEHAVING BADLY
MEN BEHAVING BADLY
MEN BEHAVING BADLY
MEN BEHAVING BADLY
MEN BEHAVING BADLY
MEN BEHAVING BADLY
MEN BEHAVING BADLY
MEN BEHAVING BADLY
MEN BEHAVING BADLY
MEN BEHAVING BADLY
MEN BEHAVING BADLY
MEN BEHAVING BADLY
MEN BEHAVING BADLY
MEN BEHAVING BADLY
MEN BEHAVING BADLY
MEN BEHAVING BADLY
MEN BEHAVING BADLY
MEN BEHAVING BADLY
MEN BEHAVING BADLY
MEN BEHAVING BADLY
MEN BEHAVING BADLY
MEN BEHAVING BADLY
MEN BEHAVING BADLY
MEN BEHAVING BADLY
MEN BEHAVING BADLY
MEN BEHAVING BADLY
MEN BEHAVING BADLY
MEN BEHAVING BADLY